Newstrom. Reif, and Monczka: A Contingency Approach to Management: Readings
Parker: The Dynamics of Supervision
Pearce and Robinson: Readings from *Business Week*
Porter, Lawler, and Hackman: Behavior in Organizations
Prasow and Peters: Conflict Resolution in Labor Relations
Quick and Quick: Organizational Stress and Preventive Management
Reddin: Managerial Effectiveness
Rue and Holland: Strategic Management: Concepts and Experiences
Rugman, Lecraw, and Booth: International Business: Firm and Environment
Sartain and Baker: The Supervisor and the Job
Sayles: What Effective Managers Really Do . . . and How They Do It
Schlesinger, Eccles, and Gabarro: Managing Behavior in Organizations: Text, Cases and Readings
Schroeder: Operations Management: Decision Making in the Operations Function
Sharplin: Strategic Management
Shore: Operations Management
Steers and Porter: Motivation and Work Behavior
Steinhoff and Burgess: Small Business Management Fundamentals
Sutermeister: People and Productivity
Vance: Corporate Leadership: Boards, Directors, and Strategy
Walker: Human Resource Planning
Weihrich: Management Excellence: Productivity through MBO
Werther and Davis: Human Resources and Personnel Management
Wofford, Gerloff, and Cummins: Organizational Communications: The Keystone to Managerial Effectiveness

Also available from McGraw-Hill
Schaum's Outline Series In Accounting, Business & Economics

Each outline includes basic theory, definitions and hundreds of solved problems and supplementary problems with answers.

Current List Includes:

Accounting I, 3/e
Accounting II, 2/e
Advanced Accounting
Advanced Business Law
Advertising
Bookkeeping & Accounting
Introduction to Business
Business Law
Business Mathematics
Introduction to Business Organization & Management
Business Statistics, 2/e
College Business Law
Contemporary Mathematics of Finance
Cost Accounting I, 2/e
Cost Accounting II
Development Economics
Financial Accounting
Intermediate Accounting I
International Economics, 2/e
Macroeconomic Theory
Managerial Accounting
Managerial Finance
Marketing
Mathematics for Economists
Mathematics of Finance
Microeconomic Theory, 2/e
Money and Banking
Operations Management
Personal Finance & Consumer Economics
Principles of Economics
Quantitative Methods in Management
Statistics and Econometrics
Tax Accounting

AVAILABLE AT YOUR COLLEGE BOOKSTORE

ORGANIZATIONAL BEHAVIOR

Fifth Edition

Fred Luthans

George Holmes Professor of Management
University of Nebraska

McGraw-Hill Book Company

New York   St. Louis   San Francisco   Auckland   Bogotá   Caracas   Colorado Springs   Hamburg
Lisbon   London   Madrid   Mexico   Milan   Montreal   New Delhi   Oklahoma City   Panama   Paris
San Juan   São Paulo   Singapore   Sydney   Tokyo   Toronto

ORGANIZATIONAL BEHAVIOR

International Edition

`34567890 BJEFCT   943210`

This book was set in ITC Cheltenham Light by Monotype Composition Company (CCU).
The editors were Kathleen L. Loy and Cynthia L. Phelps.
The production supervisor was Denise L. Puryear.
The designer was Caliber Design Planning, Inc.
Project supervision was done by The Total Book.

Library of Congress Cataloging-in-Publication Data

Luthans, Fred.
      Organizational behavior.

      Includes indexes.
         1. Organizational behavior.   I. Title.
HD58.7.L88   1989   658.4   88-12843
ISBN 0-07-039161-0

When ordering this title use ISBN 0-07-100522-6

ABOUT THE AUTHOR

FRED LUTHANS is the George Holmes Distinguished Professor of Management at the University of Nebraska at Lincoln. He received his B.A., M.B.A., and Ph.D. from the University of Iowa and did some postdoctoral work at Columbia University. While serving in the armed forces, he taught at the U.S. Military Academy at West Point. A prolific writer, he has published fifteen books and about one hundred articles in applied and academic journals and research reports. His book *Organizational Behavior Modification,* coauthored with Robert Kreitner, won the American Society of Personnel Administration award for the outstanding contribution to human resources management, and a recent book titled *Real Managers* is the result of a four-year research study that observed managers in their natural settings. His articles are widely reprinted and have brought him the American Society of Hospital Personnel Administration award. The consulting coeditor for the McGraw-Hill Management Series, Professor Luthans also serves on a number of editorial boards. He currently is on the editorial board of the *Academy of Management Executive,* and is an associate editor for *Decision Sciences.* He has been very active in the Academy of Management over the years and was elected a Fellow in 1981. He is a former president of the Midwest Region. He was vice president, program chair of the National Academy meeting in Boston in 1984, and was president in 1986 for the celebration of the fiftieth anniversary of the Academy of Management and the Centennial of the academic field of management. Also active in the Decision Sciences Institute (DSI), he was elected a Fellow in 1987. Professor Luthans has a very extensive research program at the University of Nebraska and teaches courses in organizational behavior and management at both the graduate and undergraduate levels. He has been a visiting scholar at a number of universities and has lectured in England, Germany, Japan, Korea, Mexico, the Netherlands, Norway, National Republic of China, People's Republic of China, and Singapore. He has been on the Executive Committee of the annual Pan Pacific Conference since its beginning. This international experience and interest is reflected in his approach to the field of organizational behavior. In addition, he is an active consultant to both private- and public-sector organizations and conducts workshops on behavioral management both in this country and abroad. His most recent active involvement has been in leadership training for Wal-Mart Corporation and the National Rural Electric Cooperatives and a major Quality of Work Life project for the Omaha Public Power District.

FOR KAY, KRISTIN, BRETT, KYLE, AND PAIGE

BRIEF TABLE OF CONTENTS

CONTENTS

Contents

Contents

PART 5   THE PROCESSES AND STRUCTURE OF ORGANIZATIONAL BEHAVIOR   503

17   Communication   505

18   Decision Making and Control   531

PREFACE

Although most organizations experienced some rough times in the 1980s, they at least learned an important lesson. Managers must like and understand people. Well-known author and consultant Tom Peters says that when he taught in college, he would tell his students at the beginning that if they didn't like people they should get out now so they would not go out into the real world and screw up yet another organization.

Today's organizations need help. They may not be in the chaotic state that Peters proclaims, but few would argue that the 1980s proved at least one thing. In order to grow, and even survive, organizations of all types can no longer afford to just do business as usual. How can things get turned around and back on track as we move toward the year 2000? Technologically, most organizations are doing great. On the human side, however, most organizations need to do better. There is no question that to move ahead there is a desperate need for human as well as technologically oriented managers.

To genuinely like people and to want to work with them seems to be a basic prerequisite for effective management in the 1990s. Yet, however important and necessary it is to like people, it is not sufficient. Managers must also understand and be able to apply innovative techniques to better manage their human resources. This is where the study and application of organizational behavior becomes so important to management in the 1990s.

Like the previous editions, this latest version provides a strong conceptual framework for the study, understanding, and application of organizational behavior. However, because of the greatly accelerated rate of change facing organizations in the last few years, especially in relation to the international arena, this edition has proportionally more change than previous ones. When this book initially came out it represented the beginning of the first generation of organizational behavior texts; this fifth edition marks the beginning of a new generation. To reflect the global community in which managers now operate, this is the first text that I am aware of that has a complete chapter devoted to the international context of organizational behavior. In addition, a new chapter on organizational culture precedes the international chapter. These new chapters appear in Part One so that culture and internationalism, along with history, behavioral science, and management, provide the foundation and context for the rest of the book. Also, to reinforce the international theme throughout, examples in the text discussion, highlighted "International Application Examples" placed in subsequent chapters, and some short end-of-chapter and longer end-of-part international cases and readings are included. To attain more conceptual balance and to reflect the new generation of the study of organizational behavior, a new chapter on job attitudes and satisfaction is also included in this edition.

In addition to the three new chapters, the book has been thoroughly revised and updated to reflect emerging topics and the great number of research studies published since the last edition. Just as the actual practice side of management can no longer afford to slowly evolve, neither can the academic side of the field. With the world turned upside down for most organizations today, drastically new thinking, approaches and techniques are needed, and that also goes for the way we study and apply the field of organizational behavior.

Conceptual Framework. The book contains twenty chapters in five major parts. Part 1 provides the foundation and context for organizational behavior. The introductory chapter points out some reasons for the emerging importance of organizational behavior, defines the field, and presents an overall conceptual model to provide a framework for the rest of the book. The next chapter gives a historical and behavioral science-research methodology foundation. The last two chapters in this opening part provide a new cultural and international context for the study and application of organizational behavior.

After laying the foundation and context, the conceptual framework for the text then progresses from a micro to a macro perspective and units of analysis. Taking a very micro approach, Part 2 examines individual behavior with chapters on personality, perception, attitudes and job satisfaction, and job stress. Part 3 focuses on the important motivation and learning dimensions of organizational behavior. The chapter on the theories and processes of motivation is followed by an applied chapter on job design and goal setting, and the chapter on the theories and processes of learning is followed by an applied chapter on organizational behavior modification. Part 4 moves away from strictly micro-oriented individual concepts and applications and explores interpersonal and group behaviors, dynamics, and influence. Specific chapters are devoted to formal and informal groups, interactive behavior and conflict, power and politics, and leadership. Part 5 then moves all the way to the macro end of the continuum by focusing on the processes and structure of organizational behavior. There are chapters on communication, decision making and control, organization theory and design, and, finally, organization change, development, and the future.

The five parts and twenty chapters are fairly self-contained. Thus, a whole part, selected chapters, or even sections of chapters, could be dropped or studied in a different sequence without damaging the flow or content of the book.

New Topical Coverage. In addition to the three new chapters on "Organizational Culture," "The International Context for Organizational Behavior," and "Attitudes and Job Satisfaction," a number of new topics are added to this edition. These include the following: productivity, service sector, social learning model, genetic engineering, managerial thinking, guidelines for redesigning jobs, guidelines for providing performance feedback, pay for performance, coalitions, managerial activities, charismatic leadership, transformational leadership, managerial communication model, management information systems, listening techniques, telecommunication technology, expert systems, bureaucracy-bashing, competitiveness, and information-based organizations.

Pedagogical Features. As with the previous edition, there are several strong pedagogical features. First, each chapter opens with a contemporary (all are new for this edition) vignette drawn from the real world. These opening vignettes set a relevant applications perspective for the student and help to relate the more theoretical content of each chapter to real events, real people, and real organizations. Second, to further reflect and reinforce the applications orientation of the text, self-contained, set-off real-world application examples appear in each of the chapters. As mentioned earlier, some of these are "International Application Examples" to maintain the global perspective throughout the text. To keep these applications examples timely, all are new to this edition.

Besides the opening vignettes and the application examples, the text also features experiential exercises and cases. The end of each major part contains two or three exercises to get students involved and/or simulate solving problems or experiencing first-hand organizational behavior issues. Besides the usual end-of-chapter short discussion cases, new to this edition are "Real Cases." Again to increase the relevancy of the material to the real world, each chapter now has a case drawn from recent events relevant to the theories and research results presented in the chapter. The same is done for each of the five major parts. A long, integrative real case that is relevant to the preceding chapters is placed at the end of each part. These end-of-chapter and end-of-part real cases serve as both examples and a discussion vehicle. It is suggested that students read them, especially the longer end-of-part ones, even if they are not discussed in class. They can serve as outside readings as well as discussion cases.

New to this edition are learning objectives that start off each chapter. These objectives should help students better focus and prepare for what follows in the chapter. Finally, the chapters have the usual end-of-chapter summaries and review and discussion questions.

Intended Audience. Despite the significant changes and additions, the purpose and the intended audience of the book remain the same. Like the earlier editions, this edition is aimed at those who wish to take a totally modern, research-based approach to organizational behavior and human resources management. It does not assume the reader's prior knowledge of either management or the behavioral sciences. Thus, the book can be used effectively in the first or only course in four-year or two-year colleges. It is aimed primarily at the behavioral follow-up course to the more traditional introductory management course, or it can be used in the organizational behavior course in the M.B.A. program. I would like to acknowledge and thank my many colleagues in countries around the world who have used previous editions of the book and point out that the cultural and international additions should make this new edition even more relevant and attractive. Finally, the book should be helpful to practicing managers who want to understand and more effectively manage their most important asset—human resources.

Acknowledgments. Every author owes a great deal to others, and I am no exception. First and foremost I would like to acknowledge the help on this as well as many other writing projects that I have received from Professor Richard M. Hodgetts of Florida International University. He has been an especially valued colleague and friend over the years. Next, I would like to acknowledge the interaction I have had with my colleagues John Cullen, Daniel Ganster, and Bart Victor in the organizational behavior area at the University of Nebraska. In particular, I would like to acknowledge the total support and standards of excellence provided by my departmental chairman, Sang M. Lee. Both Cathy Jensen and Cheryl Buckridge from the Management Department staff have been very helpful. Dean Gary Schwendiman has also been very supportive. In getting started in my academic career, I never want to forget the help, encouragement, and scholarly values I received from Professors Henry H. Albers and Max. S. Wortman. Over the years, I have been very lucky to have been associated with excellent doctoral students. I would like to thank them all for teaching me as much as I have taught them. In particular, I would like to mention Professors Tim R. V. Davis of Cleveland State University, Robert Kreitner of Arizona State University, Mark Martinko of Florida State University, Kenneth Thompson of DePaul University, Diane Lockwood of Seattle University, Stuart A. Rosenkrantz of Eastern Illinois University, Nancy C. Morey of Western Illinois University, Harriette S. McCaul of North Dakota State University, James L. Nimnicht of Central Washington University, Avis L. Johnson of the University of Akron, Nancy G. Dodd of the University of Hawaii, Hilo, Dianne Welsh of Eastern Washington University, and Marilyn Fox, Barbara E. Kemmerer, Kathy Singleton, Linda Thomas, Robert Waldersee, and Steve Williams, currently of the University of Nebraska, as having had an especially important impact on my recent thinking about organizational behavior. I am also very grateful to those professors who used the previous editions of the book and gave me valuable feedback for making this revision. In particular, I would like to thank Randy L. DeSimone, Rhode Island College; Alan Hoisman, Pepperdine University; Pamela Perrewe, Florida State University; and Emery Trainham, Ashland College who read and gave their comments on the manuscript. I would also like to take this opportunity to publicly acknowledge the support and dedication I have received from my McGraw-Hill editors over the years. In particular, I feel very fortunate to have worked with Kathy Loy over the last few years. All my editors have been a great help to me, personally and professionally. Finally, as always, I am deeply appreciative and dedicate this book to my wife and children, who gave me the time and encouragement to complete this book.

Fred Luthans

Acknowledgments for Experiential Exercises

Exercises for Part 1. "Synthesis of Student and Instructor Needs" was suggested by Professor Philip Van Auken and is used with his permission; "Work-Related Organizational Behavior: Implications for the Course" is adapted from "Getting Acquainted Triads," in J. William Pfeiffer and John E. Jones (eds.), *A Handbook of Structured Experiences*, vol. I, University Associates, San Diego, Calif., 1969, and "Defining Organizational Behavior," in James B. Lau, *Behavior in Organizations*, Irwin, Homewood, Ill., 1975.

Exercises for Part 2. The exercise "Self-Perception and Development of the Self-Concept" was suggested by Philip Van Auken and is used with his permission. The "He Works, She Works" exercise is from Donald D. White and David A. Bednar, *Organizational Behavior*, Allyn and Bacon, Inc., Boston, 1987, pp. 199–200, as adapted from Natasha Josefowitz, *Pathways to Power*, Addison-Wesley, Menlo Park, California, 1980.

Exercises for Part 3. The "Motivation Questionnaire" is reprinted from "Motivation: A Feedback Exercise," in John E. Jones and J. William Pfeiffer (eds.), *The Annual Handbook for Group Facilitators*, University Associates, San Diego, Calif., 1973, pp. 43–45, and is used with permission; "Job Design Survey" is adapted from J. R. Hackman and G. R. Oldham, "Development of the Job Diagnostic Survey," *Journal of Applied Psychology*, vol. 60, 1975, pp. 159–170; "Role Playing and O.B. Mod." is adapted from Fred Luthans and Mark J. Martinko, *The Power of Positive Reinforcement*, McGraw-Hill, New York, 1978, pp. 35–38.

Exercises for Part 4. "Groups and Conflict Resolution" is from Alan Filley, *Interpersonal Conflict Resolution*, Scott, Foresman, Glenview, Ill., 1975, pp. 139–142, as adapted from William H. Haney, *Communication and Organizational Behavior*, Irwin, Homewood, Ill., 1967, pp. 319–320; "Power and Politics" is reprinted with permission from Andrew J. DuBrin, *Human Relations*, Reston, Va., 1978, pp. 122–123; "Leadership Questionnaire" is reprinted with permission from J. William Pfeiffer and John E. Jones (eds.), *A Handbook of Structured Experiences for Human Relations Training*, vol. 1, University Associates, San Diego, Calif., 1974. The questionnaire was adapted from Sergiovanni, Metzeus, and Burden's revision of the Leadership Behavior Description Questionnaire, *American Educational Research Journal*, vol. 6, 1969, pp. 62–79.

Exercises for Part 5. "Organizations" is reprinted with permission from Fremont E. Kast and Jamés E. Rosenzweig, "Our Organizational Society," in *Experiential Exercises and Cases in Management*, McGraw-Hill, New York, 1976, pp. 13–15; "Paper Plane Corporation" was contributed by Professor Louis Pothreu and is used with his permission. "Organization Development at J. P. Hunt" is reprinted with permission from Andrew D. Szilagyi and Marc Wallace, "Survey Feedback," *Organizational Behavior and Performance*, Goodyear, Santa Monica, Calif., 1980, pp. 605–606.

ORGANIZATIONAL BEHAVIOR

The Introductory Foundation and Context for Organizational Behavior

Organizational Behavior: An Exciting Field of Study and Application

What Do Effective Managers Really Do?*

Most textbooks and popular professional books in management tell managers what they *should* do to be effective. The author of your text and colleagues recently completed a massive study sponsored by the U.S. Office of Naval Research that determined, among other things, what effective practicing managers really do, as opposed to what they should do. The study first determined what managers do through freely observing them in their natural environment. The observable behaviors recorded were then categorized into traditional management activities (defined by planning, decision making, and controlling behaviors), communicating activities (defined by processing paperwork and exchanging routine information behaviors), human resource management activities (defined by training/developing, managing conflict, motivating/reinforcing, staffing, and disciplining/punishing behaviors), and networking (defined by interacting with outsiders and socializing/politicking behaviors). It was found that managers in general did these four major activities with about the same frequency.

However, the important, but difficult, question that the study then tried to answer was: What do effective real managers do? To define effectiveness that would cut across diverse organizations, a combined measure of perceived organizational unit effectiveness and subordinate satisfaction and commitment was used. Calculating the

*Source: Adapted from Fred Luthans, Richard M. Hodgetts, and Stuart A. Rosenkrantz, *Real Managers*, Ballinger, Cambridge, Mass., 1988.

correlations between the directly observed behaviors of a sample of 178 real managers' activities and the combined effectiveness measure filled out by their subordinates, the relative strengths of the contributions of the four major activities to effectiveness were, in order, as follows: (1) communication activities (45%); (2) human resource management activities (26%); (3) traditional management activities (19%); and (4) networking activities (11%). Although one could argue with the procedures and measures that were used, in this comprehensive study using systematic observation of real managers in the natural setting and multiple measures, it was found that effective managers do give relatively more attention to the *human*, rather than the conceptual or informal, dimensions of management. Effective managers in this study give more attention to communication and human resource management activities.

Learning Objectives

- PRESENT the latest productivity data on American organizations.
- ANALYZE the productivity problems facing America and some potential solutions.
- DEFINE the organizational behavior approach, explaining how it differs from other modern approaches.
- RELATE the various approaches to organizational behavior including the cognitive, behavioristic, and social learning frameworks.
- EXPLAIN the specific model for organizational behavior used in this book.

The opening study indicates, empirically, that effective managers do indeed give attention to the human side of management, which is what this book is all about. Organizational behavior is the study and application of the human side of management. This introductory chapter simply gives the perspective and approach to the field. After a discussion of the productivity problem currently facing America, the new perspective of taking an organizational behavior approach is presented. Next the definition and characteristics of organizational behavior, and how it differs from other behaviorally oriented approaches, are explained. The chapter concludes with the behavioral science perspectives and a specific model that will be used as the conceptual framework for the rest of the book.

The Emerging Importance of Organizational Behavior

Although the field of organizational behavior has been around for the past twenty years, it is the productivity problems and lack of competitiveness threatening

America's world economic leadership that have fostered an anxiety about the human side of management. This sense of alarm has led popular writer and consultant Tom Peters to declare the situation facing America today a chaotic world turned upside down. The author of *In Search of Excellence* now feels that "there are no excellent companies" and nothing short of a managerial revolution is needed to get things turned around and once again make American organizations productive and competitive in world markets.[1] Before examining and defining the new organizational behavior perspective, let us consider the facts about our problems.

Getting Your Attention

Is America really in trouble, or are the nay-saying and tales of woe just talk? How do we compare with other countries of the world, especially the highly touted Japanese? If there really is a problem, what is the major cause? What are the solutions? These questions are being increasingly asked by Americans in general and practicing managers and management students in particular.

The Productivity Picture.   The answer to whether we really have a problem has become painfully clear. The facts are that since 1973, U.S. productivity (measured by output per hour worked) has risen an average of slightly over 2 percent per year, which is considerably behind the other industrialized countries. Fortunately, the late 1980s have seen definite improvement in manufacturing productivity—an average annual increase of more than 4 percent over the past few years. This rate matches and in some cases even surpasses that of the other industrialized countries; it is nearly twice the U.S. rate of the late 1970s and matches that of the 1960s.

U.S. manufacturers made a significant comeback at the end of the 1980s because of a favorable monetary exchange rate (the dollar became cheaper in world markets) and because they were forced to become more efficient. They did so by using advanced technology such as computer-integrated and flexible manufacturing systems and by downsizing—cutting back the number of employees at all levels and getting rid of unprofitable units. For example, at the end of the 1980s, productivity of the American steel industry still trailed Germany, but drew even with Japan, and heavily restructured industries such as autos did even better. For example, Ford turned out 10 percent more autos than it did the decade before, with just about half the production workers.[2] It is important to note, however, that American manufacturers accomplished this turnaround not by managing their people more effectively but by eliminating them and implementing new technology. The further improvement in manufacturing productivity should come from more effective human resource management. The study and application of organizational behavior can help in this effort.

Problems in the Service Sector.   The situation in the labor-intensive service sector is not as good as the manufacturing sector. Since 1973 there has been no gain in average annual productivity.[3] Before stepping down as Federal Reserve Board Chairman, Paul Volcker bluntly told Congress that growth in service sector productivity had been "zilch."[4] Although it is more difficult to measure and compare, there is evidence that other countries also need to greatly improve their service sector productivity.

It is important to recognize that the service sector of the American economy is rapidly growing. The United States has moved from a preindustrial, agriculturally dominated economy, to an industrial period where manufacturing goods prevailed, to the present postindustrial era of services. In the 1950s, manufacturing accounted for about a third of employment, but today that share has dropped to below a fifth. During this same period, service jobs climbed dramatically so that today about three out of every four employees are in the service sector. While manufacturing is in the process of downsizing, services are expanding to the point where about nine out of every ten new jobs are in the service sector.

Although service sector jobs are often only associated with hamburger flippers or perhaps computer operators, this growing sector is extremely diverse. It includes industries such as food and lodging; personal and professional services; finance, insurance, and real estate; retail and wholesale trade; utilities, transportation, and communication; and not-for-profit government, health, and education. While many of the new jobs are in low-paying fast-food or health care organizations, the most rapid growth is in the relatively high paying professional, administrative, and technical service jobs.[5] Although the capital-intensive service industries such as utilities and communication are experiencing some of the same recent success as manufacturing through technical innovations,[6] the challenge facing the labor-intensive service industries is clear. They must manage their human resources more effectively to get better productivity. This is where the study and application of organizational behavior can play an especially important role.

Lack of Competitiveness in World Markets. The alarming trade deficit in recent years also indicates America is having problems. In 1985 there was a $148 billion deficit (more imports than exports). In 1987 it climbed to $171 billion, and all indications are that this level will continue in the foreseeable future. A whopping $59.8 billion of the trade deficit in 1987 was with Japan alone—up from $10.4 billion in 1980 and $1.6 billion in 1975. Although the wage differential was commonly felt to be the major explanation of the trade deficit (American workers demand and get paid much higher wages), recent data indicate that this may not be the case. Real wages of American workers have stabilized over the past fifteen years, while those of their Japanese counterparts have almost achieved parity, and developing countries such as Korea, Taiwan, and Singapore are closing the gap. In fact, depending on the value of the dollar, the Japanese per capita income has pulled up to and even surpassed Americans'. So if wage differences do not explain the trade deficit, what does? The answer to this difficult question includes many simple and complex possibilities. Often cited are the declining value of the dollar, the huge domestic and foreign debt, trade barriers, and even loss of confidence. However, another possibility that cannot and should not be overlooked is the way human resources are managed in today's organizations. The quality and cost of our goods and services make them competitive in world markets. A major, if not *the* major, competitive advantage for quality and cost comes from human resources. How these human resources are managed becomes a key to America's competitive position in the global economy, and once again, here is where the study and application of organizational behavior can make a contribution.

Tom Peters says that we had a false sense of pride in the way Americans managed their human resources and beat out foreign competition through the past thirty years. As he explains it:

> There were 20 million Russians dead, Europe was flattened, Asia was flattened. The reason we were so fantastic as exporters for 30 years was because there wasn't anybody else. It's like having the Chicago Bears play against a Brownie troop and then being proud of the score we've run up.[7]

In other words, we may have been successful in the past in spite of, rather than because of, management styles and approaches. Most everyone agrees that it is time for a new approach to management to solve our problems and get America back on track as the fastest-growing productive and competitive nation in the world. An organizational behavior perspective and approach to managing human resources can prove to be the way to move organizations ahead and solve the significant challenges facing America and, perhaps to a lesser extent, other countries of the world today.

A New Perspective for Management

Management is generally considered to have three major dimensions—technical, conceptual, and human. The technical dimension consists of the manager's expertise in computers or accounting or engineering or marketing. There seems little question that today's managers are technically competent. They know the technical requirements of their jobs inside and out. This is a major reason why this country remains the most powerful in the world. American managers have the technical know-how to get the job done. But few today would question that at least in the past, most practicing managers either ignored the conceptual and human dimensions of their job or made some overly simplistic assumptions.

Although there were certainly exceptions, most managers thought, and many still do, that their employees were basically lazy, that they were interested only in money, and that if you could make them happy, they would be productive. When such assumptions were accepted, the human problems facing management were relatively clear-cut and easy to solve. All management had to do was devise monetary incentive plans, ensure security, and provide good working conditions; morale would then be high, and maximum productivity would result. It was as simple as one, two, three. Human relations experts, industrial psychologists, and industrial engineers supported this approach, and personnel managers implemented it.

Unfortunately, this approach has not worked out in practice. Although no real harm has been done, and some good actually resulted in the early stages of organizational development, it is now evident that such a simplistic approach falls far short of providing a meaningful solution to the complex problems facing today's management. The assumptions have been questioned and for the most part have been invalidated by research and experience.

The major fault of the traditional approach is that the assumptions overlook far too many aspects of the problem. Human behavior at work is much more complicated and diverse than is suggested by the economic-security–working-conditions approach. The new organizational behavior approach assumes that employees are extremely complex and that there is a need for theoretical understanding backed by rigorous empirical research before applications can be made for managing people effectively. The transition has now been completed. The traditional human relations approach no longer has a dominant role in the behavioral approach to management. Few people would question that the organizational behavior approach, with its accompanying body of knowledge, dominates the behavioral approach to management now and will do so in the foreseeable future.

What Is Organizational Behavior?

Now that organizational behavior has become the widely accepted approach, it is beginning to develop and mature as an academic discipline. As with any other relatively new academic endeavor, however, there have been some rough spots and sidetracks in its development. Besides the healthy academic controversies over theoretical approach or research findings, perhaps the biggest problem that organizational behavior has had to face is an identity crisis. Exactly what is meant by *organizational behavior?* Is it an attempt to replace all management with behavioral science concepts and techniques? How, if at all, does it differ from good old applied or industrial psychology? Fortunately, these questions have now largely been answered to the satisfaction of most management academicians, behavioral scientists, and management practitioners.

Larry L. Cummings, the former head of the organizational behavior division of the Academy of Management and its past president, distinguished between organizational behavior and other closely related disciplines, as shown in Table 1.1. He also emphasized that organizational behavior is a way of thinking—a way of conceiving problems and articulating research and action solutions. He suggests several characteristics of organizational behavior that reflect this point of view.[8] Briefly summarized, they are the following:

1. Problems and questions are typically formulated within an independent variable–dependent variable framework. The models attempt to search for cause and effect.
2. The field is oriented toward change as a desirable outcome for organizations and persons within organizations.
3. The field has a distinctly humanistic tone, reflected in the concern for self-development, personal growth, and self-actualization. However, there is another side which emphasizes operant learning models and behavior modification and which reflects a concern with environmental determinism rather than with self-actualization.

TABLE 1.1 Distinctions between Organizational Behavior, Organizational Psychology, Organization Theory, and Personnel and Human Resources

Organizational behavior— organizational psychology (OP)	Both fields focus upon explaining human behavior within organizations. Their difference centers on the fact that OP restricts its explanatory constructs to those at the psychological level. OB draws constructs from multiple disciplines. As the domain of OP continues to expand, the difference between OB and OP is diminishing, perhaps to the point of identity between the fields.
Organizational behavior— organization theory (OT)	The distinction is based on two differences: unit of analysis and focus of dependent variables. OB is defined as the study of individual and group behavior within organizations and the application of such knowledge. OT is the study of structure, processes, and outcomes of the organization per se. The distinction is neither that OB is atheoretical and concerned only with behavior nor that OT is unique or exclusive in its attention to theory. Alternatively, the distinction can be conceived as between micro and macro perspectives on OB. This removes the awkward differentiation of behavior and theory.
Organizational behavior— personnel and human resources (P&HR)	This distinction usually depicts OB as the more basic of the two and P&HR as more applied in emphasis. OB is seen as more concept-oriented, while P&HR is viewed as emphasizing techniques or technologies. The dependent variables, behavior and affective reactions within organizations, are frequently presented as similar. P&HR can be seen as standing at the interface between the organization and the individual, focusing on developing and implementing the system for attracting, maintaining, and motivating the individual within the organization.

Source: L. L. Cummings, "Toward Organizational Behavior," *Academy of Management Review,* January 1978, p. 92.

4. The field is becoming increasingly performance-oriented. Most studies include a performance-oriented dependent variable.
5. The field is greatly influenced by norms of skepticism, caution, replication, and public exposure of knowledge based on facts. In other words, it follows the scientific method.

In summary then, organizational behavior is directly concerned with the understanding, prediction, and control of human behavior in organizations. It represents the *behavioral* approach to management, not the whole of management. Other recognized approaches to management include the process, quantitative, systems, and contingency approaches. In other words, organizational behavior does not intend to portray the whole of management. The charge that old wine (applied or industrial psychology) has merely been poured into a new bottle (organizational behavior) has also proved to be groundless. Although it is certainly true that the behavioral sciences make a significant contribution to both the theoretical and the research foundations of organizational behavior, it is equally true that applied or industrial psychology should not be equated with organizational behavior. For example, organization structure and management processes (decision making and control) play an integral, direct role in organizational behavior but have at most an indirect role in applied or industrial psychology. The same is true of many important dynamics and applications of organizational behavior. Although there will probably never be total agreement on the exact meaning or domain of organizational behavior—which is not necessarily bad, because it makes the field more exciting—there is little doubt that organizational behavior has come into its own as a field of study, research, and application.

This book on organizational behavior attempts to provide the specific, necessary background and skills to make the managers of today and tomorrow as effective with the conceptual and human dimensions of management as they have been in the past with its technical dimensions.

Approaches to Organizational Behavior

Although organizational behavior is extremely complex and includes many inputs, the cognitive, behavioristic, and social learning frameworks can be used to develop an overall model. After first examining these approaches, the last section of the chapter presents an organizational behavior model that conceptually links and structures the rest of the book.

Cognitive Framework

The cognitive approach to human behavior has many sources of input. The chapters in the next part will provide some of this background. For now, however, it can be said simply that the cognitive approach gives people much more "credit" than the other approaches. The cognitive approach emphasizes the positive and free-will aspects of human behavior and utilizes concepts such as expectancy, demand, and incentive. *Cognition*, which is the basic unit of the cognitive framework, is the act of knowing an item of information. Under this framework, cognitions precede behavior and constitute input into the person's thinking, perception, or problem-solving.

The work of Edward Tolman can be used to represent the cognitive approach. Although considered a behaviorist in the sense that he believed behavior to be the appropriate unit of analysis, Tolman felt that behavior is purposive, that it is directed toward a goal. In his laboratory experiments, he found that animals learned to expect that certain events would follow one another. For example, animals learned to behave as if they expected food when a certain cue appeared. Thus, Tolman believed that learning consists of the *expectancy* that a particular event will lead to a particular consequence. This cognitive concept of expectancy implies that the organism is thinking about, or is conscious or aware of, the goal. Thus, Tolman and others espousing the cognitive approach felt that behavior is best explained by these cognitions.

Contemporary psychologists carefully point out that a cognitive concept such as expectancy does not reflect a guess about what is going on in the mind; it is a term that describes behavior. In other words, the cognitive and behavioristic theories are not as opposite as they appear on the surface and sometimes are made out to be—for example, Tolman considered himself a behaviorist. Yet, despite some conceptual similarities, there has been a controversy throughout the years in the behavioral sciences on the relative contributions of the cognitive versus the behavioristic framework. Although the sequence is reversed (behavioristic approaches have been proposed more recently in organizational behavior because of the dissatisfaction with the cognitive approach), the controversy has carried over into the field of organizational behavior. Before discussing the input that the cognitive approach can make to a conceptual model of organizational behavior, it is necessary to have a better understanding of the behavioristic approach.

Behavioristic Framework

Chapters 11 and 12 will discuss the behavioristic school of thought in psychology. Its roots can be traced to the work of Ivan Pavlov and John B. Watson. These pioneering behaviorists stressed the importance of dealing with observable behaviors instead of the elusive mind that had preoccupied the earlier psychologists. They used classical conditioning experiments to formulate the stimulus-response (S-R) explanation of human behavior. Both Pavlov and Watson felt that behavior could be best understood in terms of S-R. A stimulus elicits a response. They concentrated mainly on the impact of the stimulus and felt that learning occurred when the S-R connection was made.

Modern behaviorism marks its beginning with the work of B. F. Skinner. Skinner is generally recognized as the most influential living psychologist. He felt that the early behaviorists helped explain respondent behaviors (those behaviors elicited by stimuli) but not the more complex operant behaviors (those behaviors which are not elicited by stimuli but which simply occur; operant behaviors are emitted by the organism). In other words, the S-R approach helped explain physical reflexes; for example, when stuck by a pin (S), the person will flinch (R), or when tapped below the kneecap (S), the person will extend the lower leg (R). On the other hand, Skinner found through his operant conditioning experiments that the consequences of a response could better explain most behaviors than eliciting stimuli could. He emphasized the importance of the response-stimulus (R-S) relationship. The organism has to operate on the environment in order to receive the desirable consequence. The preceding stimulus does not cause the behavior in operant conditioning; it serves as a cue to emit the behavior. For Skinner, behavior is a function of its consequences.

Both classical and operant conditioning are given more detailed attention in Chapter 11. For now, however, it is important to understand that the behavioristic approach is environmentally based. It implies that cognitive processes such as thinking, expectancies, and perception do not play a role in behavior. However, as in the case of the cognitive approach, which includes behavioristic concepts, some psychologists feel that there is room for cognitive variables in the behavioristic approach. In particular, a social learning approach has emerged in recent years that incorporates both cognitive and behavioristic concepts and principles.

Social Learning Framework

The cognitive approach has been accused of being mentalistic, and the behavioristic approach has been accused of being deterministic. Cognitive theorists argue that the S-R model, and to a lesser degree the R-S model, is much too mechanistic an explanation of human behavior. A strict S-R interpretation of behavior seems justifiably open to the criticism of being too mechanistic, but because of the scientific approach that has been meticulously employed by behaviorists, the operant model in particular has made a tremendous contribution to the study of human behavior. The same can be said of the cognitive approach. Much research has been done to verify its importance as an explanation of human behavior. Instead of polarization and unconstructive criticism between the two approaches, it now seems time to recognize that each can make an important contribution to the study of human behavior. The social learning approach tries to integrate the contributions of both approaches.

It must be emphasized that the social learning approach is a behavioral approach. It recognizes that behavior is the appropriate unit of analysis. Although a number of psychologists are associated with social learning, the work of Albert Bandura is probably the most representative of this approach.[9] He takes the position that behavior can best be explained in terms of a continuous reciprocal interaction between cognitive, behavioral, and environmental determinants. The person and the environmental situation do not function as independent units but, in conjunction with the behavior itself, reciprocally interact to determine behavior. Bandura explains that "it is largely through their actions that people produce the environmental conditions that affect their behavior in a reciprocal fashion. The experiences generated by behavior also partly determine what a person becomes and can do, which, in turn, affects subsequent behavior."[10] The triangular model shown in Figure 1.1 takes this work of Bandura and translates it into relevant units of analysis and variables in organizational behavior.

The specifics of social learning, such as vicarious or modeling processes, the role of cognitive mediating processes, and the importance of self-control

FIGURE 1.1 A social learning approach to organizational behavior.

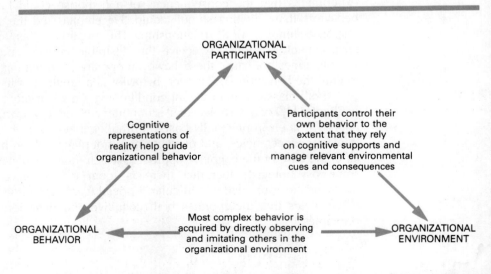

procedures, will be discussed in Chapters 11 and 12. But for now, it can be said that social learning, with its very comprehensive, interactive nature, serves as an excellent conceptual framework and point of departure for developing a meaningful model for organizational behavior.[11]

A Specific Model for Organizational Behavior

Organizational behavior has the advantage of being a relatively young and growing field of study. It can legitimately borrow, in an eclectic manner, the best from the various established frameworks for human behavior. Traditionally, most writers on organizational behavior have taken a humanistic, cognitive approach. For example, Douglas McGregor took a humanistic approach, and theorists such as Victor Vroom and Lyman Porter depended mainly on cognitive concepts in their writings on organizational behavior. In the last few years, the behavioristic model has begun to be utilized in theorizing and research on organizational behavior. In many ways, what the field of organizational behavior has been going through in recent years is a replay of the behavioristic-versus-cognitive controversy that has existed and, in many respects, still exists in psychology. Now, in organizational behavior, the time seems to have come to recognize the contributions of both approaches and to begin to synthesize and integrate both into a comprehensive model of organizational behavior. The social learning approach provides a good foundation for such an eclectic organizational behavior model.

The Goals of an Organizational Behavior Model

The reason for presenting the cognitive and behavioristic frameworks was to better understand, not evaluate, the complex phenomena collectively called *human behavior*. Understanding human behavior in organizations is also a vital goal for a model of organizational behavior. In addition, however, because organizational behavior is an applied field, two other desirable goals besides understanding are prediction and control. The field of organizational behavior serves as the basis for modern human resources management. Prediction and control of human resources are critical to the goals of a new approach to management that will help solve the problems and meet the challenges identified in the introductory comments of the chapter. Thus, the goals of a model of organizational behavior are to understand, predict, and control human behavior in organizations.

The cognitive approach seems essential to the understanding of organizational behavior. The behavioristic approach can also lead to understanding, but perhaps even more important is the contribution it can make to prediction and control. For example, on the basis of Edward Thorndike's classic law of effect, the behavioristic approach would say that organizational behavior followed by a positive or reinforcing consequence will be strengthened and will increase in subsequent frequency and that organizational behavior followed by an unpleasant or punishing consequence will be weakened and will decrease in subsequent frequency. Thus, organizational behavior can be predicted and controlled on the basis of managing the contingent environment.

If the three goals of understanding, prediction, and control are to be met by a model of organizational behavior, both the cognitive and the behavioristic approaches become vitally important. Both the internal causal factors, which are cognitively oriented, and the external environmental factors, which are behavioristically oriented, become important. In other words, the social learning approach that incorporates both cognitive and behavioristic concepts is an appropriate conceptual framework for an organizational behavior model that will help understand, predict, and control.

The S-O-B-C Model

The S-O-B-C model is used in this text to identify the major variables in organizational behavior and to show how they relate to one another. The letters stand for "stimulus," "organism," "behavior," and "consequence." Based on a social learning framework, this model recognizes the interactive nature of environmental (S and C), intrapersonal and cognitive (O), and behavioral (B) variables. In a strictly behavioristic approach, a three-variable model consisting of antecedent cues or stimuli (S), behaviors (B), and consequences (C) is typically used. However, when the human organism (O), representing cognitive mediating processes, is included, as in a social learning approach, then the four-term model results. Unlike the more limited S-B-C behavioristic model, which emphasizes the need to identify observable contingencies (S and C) for the prediction and control of behavior (B), or the O-B model, which says that internal cognitions (O) lead to behavior (B), the expanded S-O-B-C model recognizes the interactive nature of the environment (S and C), the person's cognitions (O), and the behavior itself (B) in determining behavior.

With the S-O-B-C model the antecedent cues or discriminative stimuli (S), the behavior itself (B), and the consequence (C) can be either overt (external and observable) or covert (internal and nonobservable). This, of course, represents a significant departure from more traditional behavioristic approaches that, at least implicitly, have recognized only overt variables. Once again, however, it should be remembered that the S-O-B-C model does not abandon the emphasis on behavior or the principles of the operant approach; it merely expands the group of variables to include cognitive mediating processes and covert as well as overt contingencies and behaviors. It is felt that this S-O-B-C model best identifies the relevant variables and shows how they are related in order to accomplish the goals of understanding, prediction, and control of human behavior in organizations.

Figure 1.2 graphically shows the S-O-B-C model. The variables are briefly identified, and the interactive relationship between all the variables is indicated. Obviously, this S-O-B-C model is only a "bare-bones" sketch of human behavior in organizations. It is hoped that as the remaining chapters of the book unfold, some of the fine points of the model will become clearer and that some of the

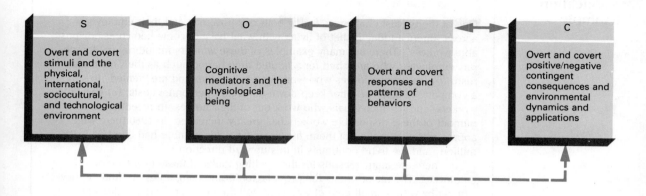

FIGURE 1.2 The S-O-B-C model.

seemingly simplistic assumptions and unsupported statements will begin to make more sense. For present purposes, this model, like any model, simply identifies the important variables and shows how they relate to one another. Particularly in the field of organizational behavior, which is still developing and has a changing theoretical base, such a model is extremely important for structuring study and further development. Figure 1.3 places the major topics of the book into the S-O-B-C model.

The Contextual Environment
for Organizational Behavior

The contextual environment for organizational behavior is placed in the S of the S-O-B-C model in Figure 1.3. Today, this context is mainly associated with the organizational culture and the international environment. Organizational culture engulfs and in many ways is the most important situational determinant of organizational behavior.

The same is true of the international context. Conceptually similar to organizational culture, the international dimensions of the situation clearly are very important to both the understanding and application of organizational behavior. For example, in Toyota City in Japan, the workers are descended from the Mikawa bushi, who were fierce warriors under the Shogun Tokugawa. Observers note that "by tradition they believe in such virtues as steadfastness, conscientiousness, frugality, and perseverance" and "when the workers finish their breaks, they run back to work."[12] Obviously, this is a much different situation for organizational behavior than in America where a manager may be faced with the so-called "disposable workers" described in the accompanying application example. The international context has become so important that a new chapter has been added and international application examples have been placed throughout this book.

**Application
Example**

Disposable Workers*

One of the biggest challenges facing both organizations and their employees across America today is that of living with what have become known as "disposable workers." There are many examples of these workers including: (a) temporary employees who are hired for a limited time period such as the Christmas rush; (b) leased employees who work for another firm and are "rented" to a company to help the latter keep down its overall personnel costs; (c) part-time workers; and (d) individuals who work out of their homes. In recent years the number of these disposable workers has greatly increased. In 1980 there were approximately 8 million of them, five years later this number had climbed to 18 million [and the trend continues in this upward direction.]

There are many reasons for the swelling ranks of these new type of employees. The major one is the profit factor. Some companies are finding they can get by with a small core of well-paid, full-time workers and supplement their ranks when they need people by hiring low-cost, disposable employees. The latter are paid less and the company does not have to provide them with costly benefit packages. There are numerous examples of firms that are using this approach. For instance, at J. C. Penney some of the telephone order takers work at home. Pacific Bell has workers ranging from budget analysts to engineers who stay at home and communicate with the office via a home computer. The Hospital Corporation of America leases workers for a psychiatric facility. IBM uses part-timers and leased workers and Apple Computer hires temporaries to staff 5 to 10 percent of its jobs. Motorola has 30 percent of its people on six-month contracts that can be terminated on 24-hours notice.

Will this growing trend result in a group of inferior workers? Will these employees feel left out? Will morale become a major problem? It is still too early to answer these questions, but one thing is certain. The trend, which is an outgrowth of cost-cutting efforts, will continue in American firms for the foreseeable future.

*****Source:** Adapted from Michael A. Pollock, "The Disposable Employee Is Becoming a Fact of Corporate Life," *Business Week*, Dec. 15, 1986, pp. 52–56.

Organization Structure and Processes

Besides organizational culture and the international context, the organization structure and processes are the other major situational input for the model shown in Figure 1.3. In viewing the organization as a system, there are two subsystems that are especially important to the study of organizational behavior. The first, structure, serves as the skeleton for the formal organization system. Structure allows the other management processes subsystem to operate. The bureaucratic model best represents the classical organization structure. Extensions and modifications of the bureaucratic model, such as centralization-decentralization, flat-tall, departmentation, and line-staff, also have an important role in classical organization structures. The modern structures of organization are based on behavioral, systems, and contingency theories and are designed to meet the challenges of growth, complexity, conflict, and change. Project, matrix, and free-form designs are examples of modern structural forms. Finally, the way jobs are designed is important to the structural situation.

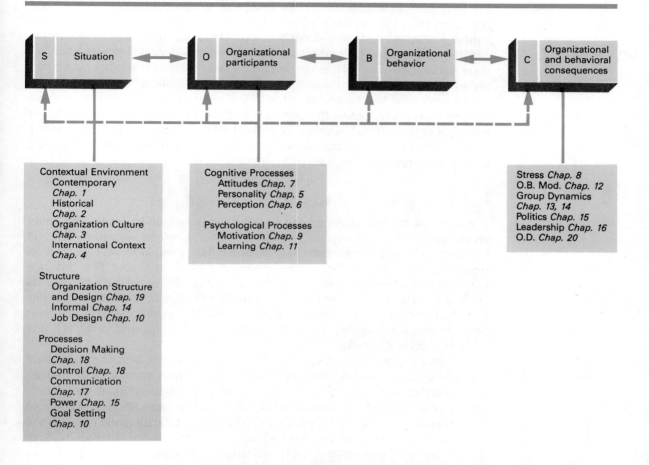

FIGURE 1.3 The conceptual framework for the study of organizational behavior.

Interacting and interdependent with the organization structure are the organization and management processes. Numerous designations are attached to the various processes, but most can be subsumed under decision making, control, communication, power, and goal setting. These organization and management processes are an integral subsystem of the formal organization system and, along with culture and structure, constitute the organizational environment in which participants operate and behave.

Organizational Participants

Organizational participants (or employees, both managers and workers) are plugged into the O portion of the model. Just as the environmental context, structure, and processes can be thought of as the situation, these participants can be thought of as consisting of the cognitive and psychological processes.

For example, analogous to the processes of decision making, control, and communication are the participants' cognitive processes of personality, perception, and attitudes and the broader-based psychological processes of motivation and learning. These processes are at the very heart of the micro study of organizational behavior. They are probably more vital than any other single part of the overall framework to the understanding of organizational behavior. However, just as separating the process from the formal organization is largely an artificial construct, so is abstracting the cognitive and psychological processes from the totality of organizational behavior. Organizational participants constantly interact with the situation (both antecedent and consequent) and the behavior itself and are not a collection of separate parts or processes.

Organizational and Behavioral Consequences

The study of the situation and the organizational participant leads to a better understanding of organizational behavior. The study of the organizational and behavioral consequences can help improve the prediction and control of organizational behavior. Again, the reader should be reminded that this is a highly simplified generalization. Cognitive and, especially, social learning theorists are beginning to provide ways to predict and control behavior, and behavioristically oriented theorists are certainly contributing to a better understanding of behavior. Nevertheless, the *emphasis* in the S-O is on understanding, and in the B-C it is on prediction and control.

Figure 1.3 indicates that certain dynamics and human resources management applications are especially relevant to the consequences portion of the model. The dynamics of groups, stress, conflict, politics, and leadership are particularly important in the study of organizational behavior. The application of managerial techniques in the areas of organizational behavior modification and organization development, or O.D., can provide feedback, leading to change—in the situation; through learning, especially in the organizational participant; and in the behavior itself. In other words, all the variables are in continuous interaction with one another and reciprocally determine one another. This interactive nature of all the variables is the essence of organizational behavior and serves as the foundation for the new behavioral approach to management.

Summary

The chapter started by pointing out the emerging importance of organizational behavior in light of the significant productivity and competitiveness problems currently facing the United States. Next, organizational behavior was precisely defined as the understanding, prediction, and control of human behavior in organizations, representing the new behavioral approach to management.

Everyone is concerned with human behavior. Yet philosophers, theologians, behavioral scientists, managers, and the person on the street have still not completely reached a true understanding of human behavior in general or of organizational behavior in particular. All people think they are experts and are defensive about their views. The difference between the behavioral science approach and the other approaches is that behavioral scientists use the methods of science and take an understanding, rather than an evaluating, approach.

The most widely recognized frameworks from the behavioral sciences are the cognitive approach, the behavioristic approach, and the newly emerging and more integrative social learning approach. The cognitive model gives the human being more "credit" and assumes that behavior is purposive and goal-oriented. Cognitive processes such as expectancy and perception help explain behavior. The behavioristic approach deals with observable behavior and the environmental contingencies of the behavior. Classical behaviorism explained behavior in terms of S-R, whereas more modern behaviorism gives increased emphasis to contingent consequences, or R-S. The social learning approach emphasizes that the person, the environment, and the behavior itself are in constant interaction with one another and reciprocally determine one another.

As defined, organizational behavior has the goals of understanding, prediction, and control. The S-O-B-C model is an eclectic model taken from both the cognitive and the behavioristic approaches, but it is based mainly on the new social learning approach. This model can perhaps best meet the goals of organizational behavior. The S-O portion deals mainly with understanding, and the B-C portion deals with prediction and control. If the environmental context (cultural and international) and organization structure and processes are thought of as the S, the organizational participant consisting of cognitive and psychological processes is thought of as the O, and the dynamics and applications are thought of as the C, the model can serve as a conceptual framework for the study of organizational behavior. The parts of this framework provide the structure for the remaining chapters of the book.

Questions for Discussion and Review

1. What are the facts on American productivity? How does it compare with that of other countries, specifically Japan?
2. What are generally considered to be the three major dimensions of management? How do they compare and contrast with one another now, and what is needed in the future?
3. How does organizational behavior relate to, or differ from, organizational psychology? Organization theory? Personnel and human resources management?
4. In your own words, identify and summarize the various frameworks for understanding organizational behavior.
5. How does the social learning approach differ from the cognitive approach? How does the social learning approach differ from the behavioristic approach?
6. Identify and explain the variables in the S-O-B-C model. How do these variables relate to one another?
7. What role do cognitive processes play in the S-O-B-C model?
8. What role does the contextual environment and organization structure and processes play in the S-O-B-C model?

References

1. Tom Peters, *Thriving on Chaos: Handbook for a Management Revolution,* Knopf, New York, 1987.
2. Sylvia Nasar, "America's Competitive Revival," *Fortune,* Jan. 4, 1988, p. 48.
3. Lindley H. Clark, Jr., "Manufacturers Grow Much More Efficient, but Employment Lags," *The Wall Street Journal,* Dec. 4, 1986, p. 1.
4. "The Service Sector's Productivity Problem," *The Wall Street Journal,* Feb. 9, 1987, p. 1.
5. Jonathan Peterson, "Much-Heralded American Service Economy Has Arrived," *Lincoln Journal,* Sept. 24, 1987, p. 28.
6. James Brian Quinn and Christopher E. Gagnon, "Will Services Follow Manufacturing into Decline?" *Harvard Business Review,* November–December 1986, pp. 95–103.
7. Jeff Gauger, "Author: U.S. Business Must Revolutionize," *Omaha World-Herald,* Feb. 14, 1986, p. 43.
8. L. L. Cummings, "Toward Organizational Behavior," *Academy of Management Review,* January 1978, pp. 93–94.
9. Albert Bandura, "Social Learning Theory," in J. T. Spence, R. C. Carson, and J. W. Thibaut (eds.), *Behavioral Approaches to Therapy,* General Learning Press, Morristown, N.J., 1976; Albert Bandura, *Social Learning Theory,* Prentice-Hall, Englewood Cliffs, N.J., 1977; and Albert Bandura, "The Self System in Reciprocal Determinism," *American Psychologist,* April 1978, pp. 344–358.
10. Bandura, *Social Learning Theory,* p. 9.
11. See Tim R. V. Davis and Fred Luthans, "A Social Learning Approach to Organizational Behavior," *Academy of Management Review,* April 1980, pp. 281–290; Robert Kreitner and Fred Luthans, "A Social Learning Approach to Behavioral Management: Radical Behaviorists Mellowing Out," *Organizational Dynamics,* Autumn 1984, pp. 61–75; and Fred Luthans and Robert Kreitner, *Organizational Behavior Modification and Beyond,* Scott, Foresman, Glenview, Ill., 1985.
12. "Toyota's Fast Lane," *Business Week,* Nov. 4, 1985, p. 43.

REAL CASE: Organizational Behavior Problems for Big Blue*

Until very recently IBM not only dominated the computer market but its competitors openly admitted that on a head-to-head basis Big Blue was almost impossible to beat. However, beginning in the mid-1980s IBM began to run into a multitude of problems.

One of the biggest headaches was the microcomputer market. Once Apple showed that there was indeed a strong demand for home computers and desktop office models, IBM introduced its now-famous IBM PC. The problem for Big Blue was that in order to sell these machines, it had to develop a retailing arm. This was unfamiliar territory for IBM, having spent most of its time and effort putting together a marketing team to sell large- and medium-size computers. The latter provide thousands of times the profit obtained from the sale of PCs. At the same time, IBM had to fight foreign competition introducing "IBM clones" that had more memory, faster computation time, and a lower price.

For the first time in history, Big Blue began to rethink its entire strategy from the ground up. Some of the major decisions and strategies that affected the behavioral side of Big Blue included the following:

1. A decision was made to reduce the workforce by 40,000 managers worldwide.
2. Many personnel were encouraged to take early retirement.
3. People who chose to stay with the firm were moved from office work to marketing jobs in the field with the focus on selling.
4. Smaller computers began to get less emphasis, and greater focus was placed on the larger models that held the highest profit.

No one could say for sure whether IBM's current approach would be successful. However, most industry analysts agreed that the changes would help make the firm more competitive in the marketplace.

1. Will changes such as those discussed in this case have any effect on the productivity of the personnel of IBM?
2. What has brought about the need for these changes? Can IBM prevent this from happening in the future? Why or why not?
3. What lesson should IBM learn from this experience to help it manage its people in the future?

Source: Some of the material in this case can be found in Marilyn A. Harris and others, "How IBM Is Fighting Back," *Business Week,* Nov. 17, 1986, pp. 152–157.

CASE: How Is This Stuff Going to Help Me?

Jane Arnold wants to be a manager. She enjoyed her accounting, finance, and marketing courses. Each of these provided her with some clear-cut answers. Now the professor in her organizational behavior course is telling her that there are really very few clear-cut answers when it comes to managing people. He has discussed some of the history of behavioral management and says that behavioral science concepts play a big role in the course. Jane is very perplexed. She came to school to get answers on how to be an effective manager, but this course surely doesn't seem to be heading in that direction.

1. How would you relieve Jane's anxiety? How is a course in organizational behavior going to make her a better manager?
2. Why did the professor start off with a brief introduction to the behavioral science framework?
3. How does a course in organizational behavior differ from courses in fields such as accounting, finance, or marketing?

**CASE:
Conceptual
Model:
Dream
or Reality?**

Hank James has been section head for the accounting group at Yake Company for fourteen years. His boss, Mary Stein, feels that Hank is about ready to be moved up to the corporate finance staff, but it is company policy to send people like Hank to the University Executive Development Program before such a promotion is made. Hank has enrolled in the program; one of the first parts deals with organizational behavior. Hank felt that after fourteen years of managing people, this would be a snap. However, during the lecture on organizational behavior the professor made some comments that really bothered Hank. The professor said:

> Most managers know their technical job but do a lousy job of managing their people. One of the problems is that just because supervisors have a lot of experience with people, they think they are experts. The fact is that behavioral scientists are just beginning to scratch the surface of understanding human behavior. In addition, to effectively manage people we also have to somehow be able to better predict and control organizational behavior. Some models are just beginning to be developed that we hope will help the manager better understand, predict, and control organizational behavior.

Hank is upset by the fact that his professor apparently discounts the value of experience in managing people, and he cannot see how a conceptual model that some professor dreamed up can help him manage people better.

1. Do you think Hank is justified in his concerns after hearing the professor? What role can experience play in managing people?
2. What is the purpose of a conceptual model such as the one presented in this chapter? How would you weigh the relative value of studying theories and research findings versus "school-of-hard-knocks" experience for the effective management of people?
3. Using the S-O-B-C model presented in the chapter, how would you explain to Hank that this could help him better manage people in his organization?

The Foundation and Background for Organizational Behavior

The Illumination Studies at the Hawthorne Works of Western Electric: A Serendipitious Discovery*

A few years ago, Western Electric phased out and shut down its Hawthorne Works outside of Chicago. However, back in 1924 the now famous illumination studies were conducted at the huge plant. The studies attempted to examine the relationship between light intensity on the shop floor of manual work sites and employee productivity. A test group and a control group were used. The test group in an early phase showed no increase or decrease in output in proportion to the increase or decrease in illumination. The control group with unchanged illumination increased output by the same amount overall as the test group. Subsequent phases brought the level of light down to moonlight intensity; the workers could barely see what they were doing, but productivity increased. The results were baffling to the researchers. Obviously, some variables in the experiment were not being held constant or under control. Something besides the level of illumination was causing the change in productivity. This something, of course, was the complex human variable.

It is fortunate that the illumination experiments did not end up in the wastebasket. Those responsible for the Hawthorne studies

*Source: The most recent and complete account of the Hawthorne studies can be found in Ronald G. Greenwood and Charles D. Wrege, "The Hawthorne Studies," in Daniel A. Wren (ed.), *Papers Dedicated to the Development of Modern Management*, Academy of Management, 1986, pp. 24–35. Also see Jeffrey A. Sonnenfeld, "Shedding Light on the Hawthorne Studies," *Journal of Occupational Behavior*, vol. 6, 1985, pp. 111–130.

had enough foresight and spirit to accept the challenge of looking beneath the surface of the apparent failure of the experiments.

In a way, the results of the illumination experiments were a serendipitous discovery, which, in research, is an accidental discovery. The classic example is the breakthrough for penicillin which occurred when Sir Alexander Fleming accidentally discovered green mold on the side of a test tube. That the green mold was not washed down the drain and that the results of the illumination experiments were not thrown into the trash basket can be credited to the researchers' not being blinded by the unusual or seemingly worthless results of their experimentation. The serendipitous results of the illumination experiments provided the impetus for the further study of human behavior at work and, most scholars would agree, mark the beginning of the field of organizational behavior.

Learning Objectives

- TRACE the early history of American management through pioneers such as William C. Durant.
- PRESENT the organizational specialists in the history of management through examples such as Henri Fayol and Alfred P. Sloan.
- DISCUSS the scientific management movement under Frederick W. Taylor.
- RELATE the early human relations movement through the Hawthorne studies.
- IDENTIFY the behavioral sciences of anthropology, sociology, psychology, and social psychology.
- EXPLAIN research methodology through theory building and the experimental, case, and survey designs.
- DEFINE reliability and the various types of validity.

Although the illumination studies at Hawthorne may be thought of as the single most important beginning of the field of organizational behavior, there are obviously other important historical and academic foundations. The purpose of this chapter is to trace through this foundation and background. The first section explores the early practice of management. Next, the emergence of the more directly relevant human relations movement is examined. The last half of the chapter is concerned with the parallel foundation for organizational behavior that comes from the behavioral sciences. After a very brief overview of anthropology, sociology, and psychology, the research methods and perspective coming from the behavioral sciences are given attention. In total, this management and behavioral science foundation serves as the point of departure for the more specialized—but more directly relevant—topics for organizational behavior in the rest of the book.

The Early Practice of Management

Although there have been managers and management as long as there have been organized civilizations, the beginning of management as we know it today is really a product of this century.

Pioneering American Managers

William C. Durant, the founder of General Motors, is an outstanding example of the initial phase of the practice of management in the twentieth century. In 1908 he laid the building blocks for the company that was to become the largest manufacturing concern in the world. Durant had the necessary entrepreneurial skills to build the giant corporation's foundation. It was essentially a one-man operation in which Durant made all major decisions, and he preferred subordinates who were yes-men. All pertinent information and records were carried in his head. His day-to-day activities and decision making were based on hunch, experience, and intuition.

Other famous pioneering managers were Henry Ford, Cornelius Vanderbilt, Andrew Carnegie, and John D. Rockefeller. All these men were brilliant but sometimes ruthless. They possessed the qualities necessary for the initial stages of industrialization. However, when the industrial revolution began to mature and become stabilized, this approach was no longer appropriate. Although Durant's style was highly effective in the early days of General Motors, after a while "chinks began to appear in the armor."[1] By 1920, General Motors was in serious financial trouble. Within a few weeks' time Durant himself had lost nearly $100 million. There were many contributing causes to the General Motors crisis. For example, insufficient use of accounting and inventory control was a big problem.[2] However, two major difficulties stood out from the rest: Durant refused to utilize staff advice, and he failed to come up with an organizational plan that could hold together the tremendous corporate structure he had created.

Some of Durant's behaviorally oriented shortcomings are exemplified by his handling of two brilliant subordinates, Walter Chrysler and Alfred P. Sloan. Chrysler, who at the time headed the Buick Division of General Motors, remembered how he pleaded with Durant to

> . . . please, now say what your policies are for General Motors. I'll work on them; whatever they are, I'll work to make them effective. Leave the operations alone; the building, the buying, the selling and the men—leave them alone, but say what your policies are.[3]

Chrysler also told of an almost unbelievable encounter he had with Durant:

> Once I had gone to New York in obedience to a call from him [Durant]; he wished to see me about some matter. For several days in succession I waited at his office, but he was so busy he could not take the time to talk with me. . . . During a lull I gained his attention for a minute. "Hadn't I better return to Flint and work? I can come back here later." "No, no. Stay right here." I waited four days before I went back to Flint; and to this day I do not know why Billy [Durant] had required my presence in New York.[4]

Because of this kind of shabby treatment, Chrysler eventually quit General Motors and founded what was to become one of that company's biggest competitors.

A similar blunder was Durant's treatment of Alfred P. Sloan. In May 1920, when General Motors was in the beginning of its decline, Sloan submitted to Durant an ingenious plan of organization. The plan reflected many insights into the company's problems and contained some logical solutions. Durant apparently ignored the plan completely. Sloan was so distraught over the outright rejection without discussion or consultation that he was about to resign from the company when the du Pont family assumed control of the corporation. In December 1920, Pierre S. du Pont resubmitted Sloan's organizational plan to the board of directors, and this time it was accepted. Sloan was made president of the company and was allowed to implement his plan. Using his new methods of management, he practically single-handedly rescued General Motors from the sure-death management methods used by Durant. The early pioneers, such as Durant, played a necessary initial role, but it was organizational specialists such as Sloan who then perpetuated and strengthened what they had founded.

Organizational Specialists

Two successful practicing managers, the French engineer and executive head Henri Fayol and General Motors' Alfred P. Sloan, best represent the "Great Organizers." Fayol's career embodied many different phases. He made his initial mark as a practicing mining engineer. Then, as a research geologist, he developed a unique theory on the formation of coal-bearing strata. This experience gave him a keen appreciation for the technical side of enterprise. However, the major portion of his career was spent practicing, and then writing about, the managerial functions and process.

In 1888, Fayol became managing director of Comambault, the well-known French combine When he assumed the top position, no dividend had been paid for three years and bankruptcy was approaching. Fayol's ingenious managerial and organizational methods soon paid off. The decline was shortly reversed, and the combine was able to make a significant contribution to the French cause during World War I. Fayol retired in 1918, but through writing and speaking engagements he succeeded in popularizing his theories and techniques of management. He maintained that the successful practicing manager should be able to handle people and should have considerable energy and courage.

Alfred P. Sloan is the other outstanding historical example of a Great Organizer. His basic organizational plan was for General Motors to maintain centralized control over highly decentralized operations. Although the du Ponts undoubtedly influenced Sloan, he is widely recognized as having made a tremendous managerial contribution.[5] His plan is largely responsible for the success story of General Motors. Dale states: "Sloan's organization study—the report on which the G.M. reorganization was based—is a remarkable document. Almost entirely original, it would be a creditable, if not a superior, organization plan for any large corporation today. It is a landmark in the history of administrative thought."[6] In the first year after the du Ponts installed Sloan as president, the company almost doubled its manufacturing capacity. The reorganization went hand in hand with increased productivity and higher profits.

Scientific Managers

The Great Organizers were concerned primarily with overall managerial organization in order for their companies to survive and prosper. The scientific management movement around the turn of the century took a narrower, operations perspective. Yet the two approaches were certainly not contradictory. The managers in both cases applied the scientific method to their problems, and they thought that effective management at all levels was the key to organizational success. The two approaches differed chiefly in that the scientific managers worked from the bottom of the hierarchy upward, whereas the organizationalists worked from the apex downward. In other words, both had essentially the same goals, but they tried to reach them from different directions.

Frederick W. Taylor is the recognized father of scientific management. Although the validity of some of Taylor's accomplishments has been questioned,[7] recent comprehensive analysis of Taylor's work concludes: "With respect to the principle of scientific decision making techniques such as time study, standardization, goal setting, money as a motivator, scientific selection, and rest pauses, Taylor's views were fundamentally correct and have been generally accepted."[8] The accompanying Application Example, From Candy to Underwear, indicates that the scientific management approach by Taylor is still alive and well in some modern applications.

Application Example

From Candy to Underwear*

The work of the scientific managers certainly did not end at the turn of the century. Their focus on efficiency and increased output is still of major interest to management, and modern technology has been of great help. Robots are an excellent example. Beginning in the 1970s some businesses began to introduce robots into the workplace. Manufacturing firms in general, and the automakers in particular, spent a great amount of money and effort to replace people with robots. Today, these machines are not limited to the auto industry. Robots can be found in many different types of business from candy making to underwear manufacturing. Because robots are now faster, lighter, stronger, and able to perform many more functions, their value and versatility to business have increased. For example, a novelties company uses a robot to stretch balloons flat so that they can be printed with slogans such as Happy Birthday; a manufacturer of school rings uses a robot to hold the rings in position while they are engraved by a laser; a custom upholstery factory uses robots to slice carpeting to fit the inside of vans. In fact, the number of uses for robots is increasing so fast that robot manufacturers are finding they no longer have to be so heavily dependent on the automakers for sales. The recognized father of scientific management, Frederick W. Taylor, was interested in increasing productivity, but it is unlikely that even he ever foresaw the day when management would be able to blend technology and the workplace so efficiently.

*Source: Adapted from Russell Mitchell and others, "Boldly Going Where No Robot Has Gone Before," *Business Week,* Dec. 22, 1986, p. 45.

Taylor dramatically contributed to increased productivity through his scientific management philosophy and principles. In Taylor's words, this approach can be summarized as (1) science, not rule of thumb; (2) harmony, not discord; (3) cooperation, not individualism; (4) maximum output, in place of restricted output; and (5) the development of each person to his or her greatest efficiency and prosperity.[9] These concepts obviously recognize and even emphasize the importance of the human element at work.

The Human Relations Movement and the Hawthorne Studies

Although the early pioneers and organizational specialists and, as pointed out above, even the scientific managers recognized the behavioral side of management, the human relations movement focused directly on the importance of human beings at work. Although there were varied and complex reasons such as the Great Depression of the 1930s and the labor union movement, the Hawthorne studies marked the beginning.

Relay Room Studies. The illumination studies (as discussed in the opening vignette of the chapter) were the first phase, but they were followed by a study in the relay room which tried to test specific variables such as length of workday, rest breaks, and method of payment. The results were basically the same as those of the illumination studies: each test period yielded higher productivity than the previous one. Even when the women were subjected to the original conditions of the experiment, productivity increased. The conclusion was that the independent variables (rest pauses and so forth) were not by themselves causing the change in the dependent variable (output). As in the illumination experiments, something was still not being controlled.

Bank Wiring Room Studies. The final phase was the bank wiring room study. As in the preceding relay room experiments, the bank wirers were placed in a separate test room. The researchers were reluctant to segregate the bank wiring group because they recognized that this would alter the realistic factory environment they were attempting to simulate. However, for practical reasons, the research team decided to use a separate room. Unlike the relay room experiments, the bank wiring room study involved no experimental changes once the study had started. Instead, an observer and an interviewer gathered objective data for study. Of particular interest was the fact that the department's regular supervisors were used in the bank wiring room. Just as in the department out on the factory floor, their main function was to maintain order and control.

The results of the bank wiring room study were essentially opposite to those of the relay room experiments. In the bank wiring room there were not the continual increases in productivity that occurred in the relay room. Rather, output was actually restricted by the bank wirers. By scientific management analysis— for example, time and motion study—the industrial engineers had arrived at a standard of 7312 terminal connections per day. This represented 2½ equipments. The workers had a different brand of rationality. They decided that 2 equipments was a "proper" day's work. Thus, 2½ equipments represented the management norm for production, but 2 equipments was the informal group norm and the actual output. The researchers determined that the informal group norm of 2 equipments represented restriction of output rather than a lack of ability to produce at the company standard of 2½ equipments.

Of particular interest from a group dynamics standpoint were the social pressures used to gain compliance to the group norms. The incentive system dictated that the more an individual produced, the more money the individual would earn. Also, the best producers would be laid off last, and thus they could be more secure by producing more. Yet, in the face of this management rationale, almost all the workers restricted output. Social ostracism, ridicule, and name-calling were the major sanctions utilized by the group to enforce this restriction. In some instances, actual physical pressure in the form of a game called "binging" was applied. In the game, a worker would be hit as hard as possible, with the privilege of returning one "bing," or hit. Forcing rate-busters to play the game became an effective sanction. These group pressures had a tremendous impact on all the workers. Social ostracism was more effective in gaining compliance to the informal group norm than money and security were in attaining the scientifically derived management norm.

Implications of the Hawthorne Studies. Despite some obvious philosophical[10] and methodological limitations by today's standards of research (which will be covered at the end of this chapter), the Hawthorne studies did provide some interesting insights that contributed to a better understanding of human behavior in organizations. For instance, one interesting aspect of the Hawthorne studies is the contrasting results obtained in the relay room and the bank wiring room. In the relay room, production continually increased throughout the test period, and the relay assemblers were very positive. The opposite was true in the bank wiring room; blatant restriction of output was practiced by disgruntled workers. Why the difference in these two phases of the studies?

One clue to the answer to this question may be traced to the results of a questionnaire administered to the women in the relay room. The original intent of the questions was to determine the health and habits of the women. Their answers were generally inconclusive except that *all* the operators indicated they felt "better" in the test room. A follow-up questionnaire then asked about specific items in the test room situation. In discussions of the Hawthorne studies, the follow-up questionnaire results, in their entirety, usually are not mentioned. Most discussions cite the women's unanimous preference for working in the test room instead of the regular department. Often overlooked, however, are the women's explanations for their choice. In order of preference, the women gave the following reasons:

1. Small group
2. Type of supervision
3. Earnings
4. Novelty of the situation

5. Interest in the experiment
6. Attention received in the test room[11]

It is important to note that novelty, interest, and attention were relegated to the fourth, fifth, and sixth positions. These last three areas usually are associated with the famous Hawthorne effect. Many social scientists imply that the increases in the relay room productivity can be attributed solely to the fact that the participants in the study were given special attention and that they were enjoying a novel, interesting experience. This is labeled the *Hawthorne effect* and is, of course, a real problem with all human experimental subjects. But to say that all the results of the relay room experiments were due to such an effect on the subjects seems to ignore the important impact of the small group, the type of supervision, and earnings. All these variables (that is, experimental design, group dynamics, styles of leadership and supervision, and rewards), and much more, separate the old human relations movement and the modern approach to the field of organizational behavior.

Behavioral Science Foundation

So far the chapter has traced the historical foundation for organizational behavior through the practice of management. This section provides the other key foundation for organizational behavior, the behavioral sciences. A working knowledge of the behavioral sciences and their research methods is a necessary prerequisite for the study of organizational behavior. A behavioral science foundation is what separates the organizational behavior approach from the older, more simplistic human relations approach. The disciplines of anthropology, sociology, and psychology and their accompanying rigorous research methods make an important contribution to a better understanding of human behavior in modern organizations.

Anthropology

A basic behavioral science foundation starts with the discipline of anthropology. *Anthropology* is literally defined as the science of man. The term combines the Greek stem *anthropo* ("man") and the noun ending *logy* ("science"). Although there are many subfields within anthropology and different units of analysis, cultural anthropology with the culture unit of analysis is most relevant to organizational behavior. The next chapter is devoted specifically to organizational culture and the accompanying International Application Example demonstrates the importance of culture to international management, which will be covered in Chapter 4. However, to serve as a foundation, especially for application to the next two chapters on organizational culture and the international context, it is important to understand how anthropologists define and use "culture."

International Application Example

> **Doing Business in the Middle East**
>
> The OPEC oil cartel awakened many people to the presence of the Middle East as a major center of world commerce. Over the last couple of years the impact of OPEC on the price of oil has been relatively small. However, industry analysts believe that by the 1990s the cartel will again be a major force with which to be reckoned. In the interim, those seeking to do business in this area of the world would do well to learn about its culture. There are a number of things that are important when dealing with Middle East clients. Here are some of their customs that will influence the way Americans should do business there.
>
> 1. Local Islamic religious custom demands that everything stop five times a day for prayers. While you are not expected to kneel or face Mecca, do not interrupt or display impatience while your host is praying.
> 2. Never refer to the "Persian Gulf." This body of water is known as the "Arabian Gulf."
> 3. While it is customary to shake hands with your host, do not be surprised if the individual welcomes you with a kiss on both cheeks. It is good manners to return the gesture at the same time.
> 4. The business week runs from Saturday to Thursday. Expect to work on Sunday.
> 5. If you are invited to the home of your host, do not be surprised if his wife is not on hand. She is probably in the kitchen preparing the meal and will not appear at the table. Do not inquire about her; this is considered impolite. Most entertaining is done with other men; wives are seldom seen.
> 6. Do not ask for an alcoholic drink. Arabs do not drink alcoholic beverages; it is a violation of their religion.
> 7. Unless your host provides you with a knife and fork, be prepared to eat with your fingers. Watch your host and let him take the lead. Also remember that eating is done with the right hand only.
> 8. During conversation, stay away from religion and politics. The growth and development of the country you are visiting is a good, safe topic.

Definition of Culture. There are numerous definitions of *culture*. After a survey of more than a hundred of them many years ago, it was concluded that the following was the most comprehensive definition: "Culture consists of patterns, explicit and implicit, of and for behavior acquired and transmitted by symbols, constituting the distinctive achievement of human groups, including their embodiments in artifacts."[12] A modern definition of "culture" would be "the acquired knowledge that people use to interpret experience and generate social behavior."[13] This latter view of culture emphasizes both *content* and *meaning* and is most applicable to organizational behavior.

Characteristics of a Culture. Although there is not complete agreement on the underlying theories, most modern anthropologists agree on certain characteristics of culture. In brief, there is general agreement that culture is:

1. *Learned.* It is not genetic or biological, but, of course, it does interact in complex ways with human biology.

2. *Shared.* People as members of groups or organizations share culture; it is not special to single individuals.
3. *Transgenerational.* It is cumulative in its development and is passed down from one generation to the next.
4. *Symbolic.* It is based on the human capacity to symbolize, to use one thing to represent another.
5. *Patterned.* It is organized and integrated; a change in one part will bring changes in another part.
6. *Adaptive.* It is based on the human capacity to adapt, as opposed to the more genetically determined adaptive process of most other animals.

Depending on the theoretical position of the anthropologist, other characteristics could be added, but for organizational behavior purposes the characteristics of learned, shared, symbolic, and patterned are especially relevant.

Significance of Culture. The important role that culture plays in human behavior may be one of the most underrated concepts in the behavioral sciences. Culture dictates what people learn and how they behave. One management theorist points out the nature and significance of culture by making an analogy with the sea: "We are immersed in a sea. It is warm, comfortable, supportive, and protecting. Most of us float below the surface; some bob about, catching glimpses of land from time to time; a few emerge from the water entirely. The sea is our culture."[14] However, it is important to recognize that when culture is applied to the field of organizational behavior, there are two distinct levels. One application of culture is as a set of general attributes of people (such as the things discussed in the previous section—learned, shared, and adaptive). In addition, culture can be used to identify the specific content of a *particular* group of people, such as blue-collar workers versus white-collar workers or high-tech employees versus customer service employees, and to treat organizations "as if" they were cultures, as the next chapter does.

Sociology

Although anthropology has made a big contribution to the understanding of organizational behavior, and in the future will undoubtedly make a bigger one, the behavioral science discipline of sociology is more widely recognized. *Sociology* is traditionally defined as the science of society. To the uninformed, its purposes and goals are often unclear. Many equate sociology with social work and the solving of social problems. Some even relate sociology to the political philosophy of socialism. In reality, sociology is at the same time narrower and broader than the areas with which it is often confused. Perhaps sociology can most accurately be described as an academic discipline that utilizes the scientific method in accumulating knowledge about social behavior. The other areas do not have this specific purpose and goal. The overall focus of sociology is on social behavior in societies, institutions, organizations, and groups.

Contemporary sociology is characterized by rigorous methodology with an empirical emphasis and conceptual consciousness. The major thrust common to all areas of sociology is toward the goal of understanding interdependent social behavior. The primary units of analysis studied by modern sociologists, going from the largest to the smallest, are the society, the institution, the organization, the group, and norms and roles. Most relevant to the study of organizational behavior are the latter three—the organization, the group, and norms and roles. In fact, whole chapters and parts of other chapters of this book are devoted to these units of analysis. Chapters 13 and 14 (on groups) and Part 5, which deals with the macro perspective of organizational behavior, as well as many of the contemporary organizational development techniques, are sociologically based.

Psychology

Whereas sociology plays a big part in the macro perspective, psychology is the most significant foundation for the micro approach to organizational behavior. As Chapter 1 indicated, the micro perspective dominates contemporary organizational behavior, so it follows that a grounding in psychology is necessary.

Modern *psychology* is almost universally defined as the science of human behavior, although psychology has many different schools of thought and units of analysis. In particular, the cognitive and behaviorist approaches discussed in the last chapter have had the most impact of late on the orientation of modern psychologists. On the whole, however, contemporary psychologists take an eclectic theoretical approach and generally divide themselves into areas such as experimental, clinical, and social. The social area is particularly relevant to organizational behavior.

There are many slight variations in the definitions of *social psychology*. One comprehensive definition is that it is the study of individual behavior in relation to the social environment. The most important part of the social environment is other persons, individually and collectively. More simply, *social psychology* is defined as the study of individual behavior within a group. This definition points out the close ties that social psychology has to psychology (individual emphasis) and sociology (group emphasis.)

The logical breakdown for analysis and study in social psychology is the individual, the group, and the interaction between the individual and the group. The last-named provides the key difference between the study of social psychology and the study of psychology and sociology. An example is the approach taken in the study of groups. Social psychology is more concerned with why an individual joins a group (affiliation) and wants to remain a member of the group (cohesion). The social psychologist focuses primarily on group structure and function only to the extent that they affect individual behavior. Besides the study of groups, topics of general interest to the social psychologist include:

1. *Attitudes,* their formation and change
2. *Communication research,* the effect that networks have on individual and group efficiency and satisfaction
3. *Problem solving,* the analysis of cooperation versus competition

4. *Social influences,* the impact of conformity and other social factors on individual behavior
5. *Leadership,* especially the identification and function of leaders and their effectiveness

More specialized theories (such as cognitive dissonance) and analysis (such as approach-avoidance conflict) are also a vital part of social psychology.

As these topics indicate, social psychology is very closely related to organizational behavior. This is evidenced by the overall orientation and table of contents of this book. Part 4, in particular, borrows heavily from the theories and research findings of social psychology. Moreover, a mutually beneficial relationship seems to exist between the disciplines of social psychology and organizational behavior. One of the major purposes of this book is to help develop and refine this relationship.

Research Methodology

All the behavioral sciences discussed so far depend upon a rigorous research methodology in order to better understand human behavior. This search for the truth of why humans behave the way they do is a very delicate and complex process. In fact, the problems are so great that many scholars, chiefly from the physical and engineering sciences, argue that there can be no precise science of behavior. They maintain that humans cannot be treated like chemical or physical elements; they cannot be effectively controlled or manipulated. For example, the critics state that, under easily controllable conditions, 2 parts hydrogen to 1 part oxygen will always result in water and that no analogous situation exists in human behavior. Human variables such as motives, learning, perception, values and even "hangovers" on the part of both subject and investigator confound the controls that are attempted. For these reasons, behavioral scientists in general and organizational behavior researchers in particular are often on the defensive and must be very careful to comply with accepted methods of science.

The Overall Scientific Perspective

Behavioral scientists in general and organizational behavior researchers in particular strive to attain the following hallmarks of any science:

1. The overall purposes are understanding/explanation, prediction, and control.
2. The definitions are precise and operational.
3. The measures are reliable and valid.
4. The methods are systematic.
5. The results are cumulative.

Figure 2.1 summarizes the relationship between the practical behavioral problems facing today's human resources managers and unanswered questions, research methodology, and the existing body of knowledge. When a question

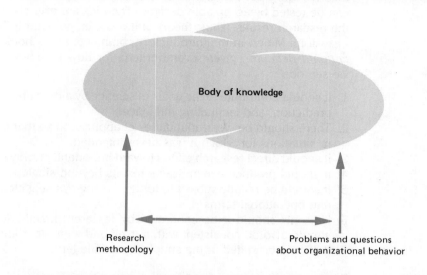

FIGURE 2.1
Simple relationships between problems, methodology, and knowledge.

arises or a problem evolves, the first place to turn for an answer is the existing body of knowledge. It is possible that the question can be immediately answered, or the problem solved, without going any further. Unfortunately, this usually is not true in the case of organizational behavior. One reason is that the amount of knowledge directly applicable to organizational behavior is relatively very small, primarily because of the newness of the field.

It must be remembered that behavioral science is relatively young and that organizational behavior is even younger—it is really a product of the 1970s. The Hawthorne studies go back over fifty years, but a behavioral science–based approach to the study and application of organizational behavior is very recent. The sobering fact is that many questions and problems in organizational behavior cannot be directly answered or solved by existing knowledge. Thus, a working knowledge of research methodology becomes especially important to future managers, both as knowledgeable and critical consumers of the rapidly expanding literature reporting the results of organizational behavior research and as sophisticated practitioners who are capable of applying appropriate research methods to solve difficult problems in the workplace.

Starting with Theory

It has often been said (usually by theoreticians) that there is nothing so practical as a good theory. Yet students of organizational behavior are usually "turned off" by all the theories that pervade the field. The reason for all the theories, of course, is the newness of the field and the fact that there are not yet many definitive answers. The purpose of any theory, including all those found in organizational behavior, is to explain and predict the phenomena in question;

theories allow the researcher to deduce logical propositions or hypotheses that can be tested by acceptable designs. Theories are ever-changing on the basis of the research results. Thus, theory and research go hand in hand.

John Miner, in the introductory comments in his book *Theories of Organizational Behavior,* gives several criteria for how to "know a good theory when we see one":

1. It should contribute to the goals of science by aiding understanding, permitting prediction, and facilitating influence.
2. There should be clear boundaries of application so that the theory is not used in situations for which it was never intended.
3. It should direct research efforts toward important, priority problems and issues.
4. It should produce generalizable results beyond single research efforts.
5. It should be readily subject to further testing by using clearly defined variables and operational terms.
6. Not only should it be confirmed by research directly derived from it, but it should also be consistent within itself and with other known facts.
7. It should be stated in the simplest possible terms.[15]

The Use of Research Designs

The research design is at the very heart of scientific methodology; it can be used to answer practical questions or to test theoretical propositions/hypotheses. The three designs most often used in organizational behavior research today are the experimental, the case, and the survey designs. All three have played important roles in the development of meaningful knowledge. The experimental design is borrowed largely from psychology, where it is used extensively, and the case and survey designs have traditionally played a bigger role in sociology. All three designs can be used effectively for researching organizational behavior.

Experimental Designs

A primary aim of any research design is to establish a cause-and-effect relationship. The experimental method offers the best possibility of accomplishing this goal. All other factors being equal, most researchers prefer this method of testing hypotheses. Simply defined, an experiment involves the manipulation of independent variables to measure their effect on, or the change in, dependent variables, while everything else is held constant or controlled. Usually, an experimental group and a control group are formed. The experimental group receives the input of the independent variables, and the control group does not. Any measured change in the dependent variable in the experimental group can be attributed to the independent variable, assuming that no change has occurred in any other variable and that no change has occurred in the control group. The controls employed are the key to the successful use of the experimental design. If all intervening variables are held constant or equal, the experimenter can conclude with a high degree of confidence that the independent variable caused the change in the dependent variable.

The Validity of Studies

The value of any research study is dependent on its validity, that is, whether the study really demonstrates what it is supposed to demonstrate. In particular, a study must have both *internal validity* and *external validity* in order to make a meaningful contribution to the body of knowledge. A study has internal validity if there are no plausible explanations of the reported results other than those reported. Some of the threats to internal validity include but are not limited to:

1. *History.* Uncontrolled intervening events that occur between the time the preexperiment measurement is taken and the time the postexperiment measurement is taken.
2. *Maturation.* Changes in the subject or subjects with the mere passing of time, irrespective of the experimental treatment.
3. *Testing.* The effect of previous testing on a subject's present performance.
4. *Instrumentation.* Changes in measures of subject performance due to changes in the instruments or observers over time.
5. *Regression.* Changes in performance due to subjects' going from extreme scores to more typical scores.
6. *Selection.* Changes due to the differences in the subjects rather than the treatment.
7. *Ambiguity about direction of causation.* Does A cause B, or does B cause A? This is a problem with correlational studies.
8. *Local history.* Changes due to the unique situation when the experimental group received the treatment.[16]

Laboratory studies usually control these threats to internal validity better than field studies do. But, as Ilgen has recently pointed out, this control afforded by the laboratory is purchased at the price of generalizability and relevance. "As a result, many behavioral scientists decry the use of any laboratory research and dismiss results obtained from such as irrelevant or, worse yet, misleading for the understanding of naturally occurring human behavior."[17]

But, in general, the threats can be minimized, even in field settings, by *pretests* (these allow the investigator to make sure that the experimental and control groups were performing at the same level before the experimental manipulations are made, and they give measurement over time); *control groups* (these permit comparison with experimental groups—they have everything the same except the experimental manipulation); and *random assignment* (this pretty well assures that the experimental and control groups will be the same, and it allows the correct use of inferential statistics to analyze the results). Thus, the threats to internal validity can be overcome with careful design of the experiment. This is not always true of external validity, which is concerned with the generalizability of the results obtained. In order for a study to have external validity, the results must be applicable to a wide range of people and situations. The field experiment tends to have better external validity than the laboratory experiment because at least the experiment takes place in a real setting.

In general, the best strategy is to use a number of different designs to answer the same question. The weaknesses of the various designs can offset one another. Normally, the research would start with a laboratory study to isolate and manipulate the variable or variables in question. This would be followed by an attempt to verify the findings in a field setting. This progression from the laboratory to the field may lead to the soundest conclusions. However, free observation in the real setting should probably even precede laboratory investigations of organizational behavior problems or questions.

Case Design

The case design makes a complete examination and analysis of one or a few behavioral entities (worker, supervisor, work group, department, organization) over an extended period. The purpose is to discover and analyze *every* aspect of the particular case under investigation. The case researcher typically uses field observation, existing records, and questionnaires and interviews to gather data. As applied to organizational behavior research, the case design should not be confused with the case-study approach used by social workers and psychotherapists or even with the "case" approach widely used in courses in business policy. The case method as used in organizational behavior research is much more rigorous and comprehensive.

The actual conduct of case research is most critical to its success. Three areas are generally recognized as being crucial for successful case research:

1. *The attitude of the investigator.* In order for the case technique to be successful, the investigator must be alertly receptive and must be seeking rather than testing. The investigator should be continuously reformulating and redirecting as new information is uncovered.
2. *The intensity of study.* An effective case analysis should obtain all information unique to the particular unit being studied and also those features which are common to other cases.
3. *The integrative ability of the investigator.* The case approach must rely on the talent of the researcher to successfully pull together many diverse findings into a unified interpretation. The final interpretation should not, however, merely reflect the investigator's predisposition.

If careful attention is given to key points such as those just outlined, the case technique can be a very effective research design. The depth of analysis attained through the technique is its major advantage. With the increasing importance of qualitative measures (techniques which try to fully describe and then interpret the meaning, not the frequency, of naturally occurring events in organizations)[18] in organizational behavior research, the case approach has taken on new respectability. This is especially true of the so-called single-case experimental designs, which can overcome the threats to internal validity, and also of the traditional control group experimental designs.[19] However, like the experimental design, single-case designs can have a problem with external validity.[20]

It is generally neither practical nor logical to generalize the results of one case analysis to other cases or to the whole. This limitation drastically reduces the external validity of the case method for building a meaningful body of knowledge. The case method does not normally provide enough evidence to prove cause and effect. On the other hand, this method does usually uncover some very meaningful insights, research questions, and hypotheses for further testing by an experimental design. In addition, its generalizability can be enhanced by replication. A case could also be made for single-case studies actually being more useful to management practitioners than large-survey studies. As Kennedy points out, large-group comparisons may not generalize to individual cases, but it is these individual, single cases that practitioners must deal with on a day-to-day basis.[21]

Survey Design

The third major design available to researchers on human behavior is the survey. This easy-to-use technique depends upon the collection of empirical data via questionnaires and interviews. It is extremely useful in dealing with some questions and problems of organizational behavior. In particular, it is useful to get at information and attitudes from a large group of subjects. The only way to get at people's feelings is to ask them in a survey or an interview.

The survey can overcome the generalizability problems facing the experimental and case designs. Whereas the case is restricted to a single unit, or to very few units of analysis, the survey has very broad coverage. Another advantage is that the survey collects original data that are adaptable to statistical analysis. Its major drawback is the lack of depth of information obtainable from the two major data collection tools: the questionnaire and the interview. Because of this limitation, some scholars within—and many outside—the behavioral sciences have totally discredited the survey as a legitimate research design. Some of this criticism, especially that relating to some of the early surveying done in the behavioral sciences, is certainly justified. Even today, some surveys concentrate only on "dust-bowl" empiricism (gathering data for data's sake) and neglect the necessary planning and design aspects. In addition, overdependence on questionnaire-generated data may be highly misleading.

An indirect measurement technique, questionnaires reflect perceptions of behavior rather than the actual behavior in the real setting. "The prospects of discovering, for example, whether leaders really do structure subordinates' paths to goals (e.g., the path-goal approach) or whether such procedures can actually be effective is more likely to be answered through real-time, in-situation observational studies, than through questionnaire investigations which are many times removed from the actual behavior."[22] For example, there is evidence that the way subordinates describe their managers' behavior on standardized questionnaires is not necessarily the same as the way the managers are observed to behave in the actual day-to-day organizational setting.[23] Observational studies are beginning to reveal managerial behavior that is quite different from what has been typically portrayed by both non-research-based management textbooks and research-based studies that have depended solely on questionnaires or interviews describing managerial behavior.[24]

There is little doubt that the field of organizational behavior has depended too much on questionnaire instruments to obtain data for all three designs—experimental, case, and survey. A multiple-measures approach that gives a degree of convergence among the various data collection techniques is needed for the future.

The key is that organizational behavior researchers need to use all the measurement techniques. In particular, more attention should be given to observational techniques that allow measurement of the interactive nature of behaviors, persons, and situations. In their rush for respectability, organizational behavior researchers may be guilty of bypassing the most widely recognized first stage of any scientific development—observation of naturally occurring events. Obviously, it is much easier to ask than to observe, and this path of least resistance is the one that has too often been followed in accumulating knowledge about organizational behavior.

Reliability and Validity of Measures

Although multiple measures can help in the search for knowledge about organizational behavior, the crux of the problem of quality of research still gets down to the reliability and validity of the measures that are used. Although reliability is not as important as validity, in order for a measure to be valid, it must also be reliable. Measurement *reliability* refers to the *accuracy* of measurement and the *consistency* of results. Reliability is not nearly as difficult to achieve as validity. Normally, all that is required for a high degree of reliability is control over the measurement conditions. However, even though the measures are reliable, it does not automatically follow that they will be valid. The measures may be accurately and consistently measuring the wrong variables. The major challenge facing organizational behavior researchers comes not from reliability but from validity.

The Validity Concept

Validity has been mentioned throughout this discussion. It is *the* key concept for determining the value of any research. Exactly what is meant by this important concept? First of all, it should be pointed out that validity is a fairly elusive concept; as Robert Guion, a recognized expert on validity, has noted, it has never enjoyed much precision of definition, and there is a lot of "loose talk" about it. This is especially true when "a bewildering number of adjectives have been attached to it, each delimiting some aspect of a broader meaning."[25] Guion feels that both practitioners and scholars need to be reminded of three important properties or characteristics of validity in general:[26]

1. Validity is an evaluation, not a fact. Validity can be expressed in broad terms (for example, "high" or "good," "moderate" or "satisfactory," and "weak" or "poor") instead of precise quantities or numbers. "To confuse an interpretation of validity with an obtained validity coefficient is probably our most mortal, or at least most mortifying, linguistic sin."[27]

2. Validity is an evaluation of the inferences about the measure drawn from scores and is not an evaluation of the measure per se. Other things (for example, the motivation of the person taking the measure) enter into the *score* besides the measure itself.
3. Validity is both derived from, and refers to, variance in a set of scores. This means that the score of an individual "may be evaluated as more or less valid only if it has been previously determined that a set of scores from a substantial number of other individuals similarly tested is a valid set."[28]

The above points put validity into its proper perspective but still do not really define the term. Very simply, validity is present when the measure is measuring what it is supposed to measure. As Guion noted, much of the confusion about validity results from the adjectives that are used with the term. For example, *face* validity, which most measures depend upon, is a pseudo type of validity and refers only to the surface appearance of the measure. In someone's subjective judgment, the measure is valid. This is a normative, as opposed to an empirical, judgment. It is now recognized that face validity is not sufficient and can be very misleading. Now attention is being focused on the different types of empirically derived validity. An examination of these different types of validity is vital to the understanding of research and to the understanding of organizational behavior in general.

Types of Validity

Traditionally it was assumed that there was one type of validity, which could be determined by a single study. Now it is recognized that there are several different types of validity and that a number of investigations are needed to assess it. Although there are variations of each, the three major categories of validity are generally recognized to be content, predictive, and construct.

Content and Predictive Validity.

In content validity the criterion is the representativeness of the measure. Obviously, this is quite subjective and can slip into being mere face validity. Predictive validity, on the other hand, calculates an objective, statistical relationship between the measure's predictors and an outside criterion. Figure 2.2 shows how this approach to predictive validity can be used.

In the bivariate scatterplot, a strong positive correlation is shown between a questionnaire score and a performance criterion. Each dot represents an employee's score on the questionnaire and his or her resulting level of performance. If a manager wanted to use this questionnaire to predict who would be successful performers if they set the score as indicated, the "hits" would far outnumber the "misses." In other words, this questionnaire would have predictive validity in this case. The hits (in quadrant 1 those who would have been selected and would have turned out to be successful and in quadrant 4 those who would not have been selected and would have turned out to be unsuccessful) show the value of such predictive measures. On the other hand, the misses, even though in the minority, are sacrificed. Especially of concern would be those in quadrant 3—they would not have been selected but would have turned out to be successful.

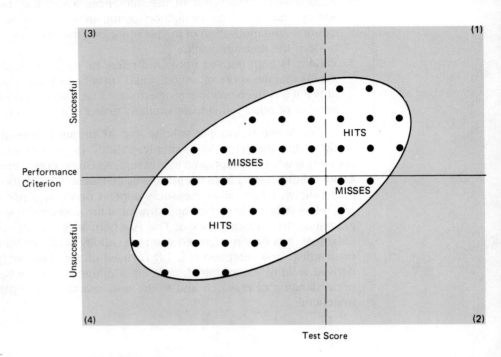

FIGURE 2.2 A predictive validity scatterplot.

Can the organization or the society as a whole afford these misses? Obviously, the answer depends on the type of job (for example, in selecting astronauts, the selection score would be set so high that there would be no misses in quadrant 2 and a lot of misses in quadrant 3) and on the social consciousness/responsibility of the organization (for example, is the organization eliminating minorities and/ or women in quadrant 3 who would have turned out to be successful?). Such a predictive validity assessment, however, is extremely valuable for many measures used in the research process.

Construct Validity. Both content and predictive (that is, criterion-related) validity have proved to be useful for determining the value of relatively simple measures used in the research process. But for measuring more complex concepts or constructs such as personality dimensions (aggressiveness or confidence), motivation (needs or expectancies), and leadership, construct validity becomes the most important issue.

In the final analysis, the other forms of validity become subsumed by construct validity; it is the crux of measurement and has significant implications for how research is done in the whole field of organizational behavior. Guion supports this view when he states: "All validity is at its base some form of construct validity. . . . The most salient of the traditionally identified aspects of validity—the only one that is salient—is construct validity. It *is* the basic meaning of validity."[29]

Unlike content or predictive validity, construct validity draws on a number of studies and sources in order to make an evaluation. Thus, it is both a logical and an empirical process.[30] The construct validation approach would involve what measurement experts call a *nomological network* (that is, a system of interrelated concepts, propositions, and laws), in which observable characteristics are related to other observables, observables are related to theoretical constructs, or one theoretical construct is related to another theoretical construct.[31] In order to have construct validity, there must be some convergence of the scores from different measurement techniques (for example, a standardized test and an observational system) that purportedly measure the same dimension of a construct. This is called *convergent validity.* In addition, there must be *discriminant validity;* that is, the test that supposedly measures the construct in question should be *unrelated* to the scores of instruments that are not supposed to measure the construct. Thus, construct validity involves both convergent and discriminant validity and can be determined by innovative experimental and statistical procedures.

Summary

This chapter first gave a historical foundation for organizational behavior from the practice of management. At the turn of the century, pioneering managers, exemplified by General Motors founder William C. Durant, dominated. Their often ruthless, one-person style then gave way to the approach used by organizational specialists (Fayol and Sloan) and scientific managers (Taylor). These latter managers recognized the human element, but the human relations approach in general and the Hawthorne studies in particular gave focal attention to the behavioral side of management.

The last half of the chapter provided a behavioral science foundation for organizational behavior. The academic discipline of anthropology, defined as the science of man, concentrates primarily on the role that culture plays in human behavior. Sociology is directly concerned with social behavior—in societies, institutions, organizations, and groups—and with roles and norms. Psychology, the science of human behavior, is vital to the micro analysis and understanding of organizational behavior. Social psychology is closest to overall behavioral science and organizational behavior.

The behavioral sciences depend upon rigorous research methodology to accumulate knowledge. This tradition has carried over to the field of organizational behavior. Experimental designs, case designs, and survey designs are used. Each of these has advantages and disadvantages, but the real issue surrounding quality research in organizational behavior is measurement reliability and validity. Reliability has to do with accuracy and consistency, and validity is present when the measure is indeed measuring what it is supposed to measure. Validity is the more important concept and can be broken down into the categories of content, predictive, and construct validity. Each is important, but construct validity is the ultimate test of most of the measures used on important constructs such as personality, motivation, and leadership in the organizational behavior field.

Questions for Discussion and Review

1. How did pioneering managers such as William Durant differ from the organizational specialists such as Henri Fayol and Alfred P. Sloan in their practice of management?
2. In the Hawthorne studies, how do you explain the fact that in the relay room experiments there were continual increases in productivity, while in the bank wiring room study there was deliberate restriction of output?
3. Why do you feel the Hawthorne studies made such an important historical contribution to the study of organizational behavior?
4. Why is the study of culture important to organizational behavior?
5. What are the major units of analysis studied by modern sociologists? Which one do you think is most relevant to organizational behavior? Why?
6. How does social psychology relate to sociology? To psychology?
7. What are the strengths and weaknesses of the three major research designs?
8. What is validity? What is its relationship to reliability? What are the differences between content, predictive, and construct validity?

References

1. Ernest Dale, *The Great Organizers*, McGraw-Hill, New York, 1960, pp. 73–74.
2. Ibid., p. 74.
3. Walter P. Chrysler, with Boyden Sparkes, *Life of an American Workman*, Dodd, Mead, New York, 1950, p. 148. (Originally published in 1937.)
4. Ibid., pp. 156–157.
5. Dale, op. cit., p. 84.
6. Ibid., p. 86.
7. Charles D. Wrege and Amedeo G. Perroni, "Taylor's Pig-Tale: A Historical Analysis of Frederick W. Taylor's Pig Iron Experiments," *Academy of Management Journal*, March 1974, pp. 6–27.
8. Edwin A. Locke, "The Ideas of Frederick W. Taylor: An Evaluation," *Academy of Management Review*, January 1982, p. 14.
9. Frederick W. Taylor, *The Principles of Scientific Management*, Harper, New York, 1911, p. 140.
10. For example, see Lyle Yorks and David Whitsett, "Hawthorne, Topeka, and the Issue of Science versus Advocacy in Organizational Behavior," *Academy of Management Review*, January 1985, pp. 21–30.
11. C. E. Turner, "Test Room Studies in Employee Effectiveness," *American Journal of Public Health*, June 1933, p. 584.
12. Alfred L. Kroeber and Clyde Kluckhohn, "Culture: A Critical Review of Concepts and Definitions," *Papers of the Peabody Museum*, vol. 47, no. 1, Harvard University, Cambridge, Mass., 1952, p. 181.

13. J. P. Spradley, *The Ethnographic Interview*, Holt, New York, 1979, p. 5.

14. Ross A. Webber, *Culture and Management*, Irwin, Homewood, Ill., 1969, p. 10.

15. John B. Miner, *Theories of Organizational Behavior*, Dryden Press, Hinsdale, Ill., 1980, pp. 7–9.

16. Thomas D. Cook and Donald T. Campbell, "The Design and Conduct of Quasi-Experiments and True Experiments in Field Settings," in M. D. Dunnette (ed.), *Handbook of Industrial and Organizational Psychology*, Rand McNally, Chicago, 1976, pp. 224–246; also see Terence R. Mitchell, "An Evaluation of the Validity of Correlational Research Conducted in Organizations," *Academy of Management Review*, April 1985, pp. 192–205.

17. Daniel R. Ilgen, "Laboratory Research: A Question of When, Not If," in Edwin A. Locke (ed.), *Generalizing from Laboratory to Field Settings*, Lexington Books, Lexington, Mass., 1986, p. 257.

18. John Van Maanen, James M. Dabbs, Jr., and Robert R. Faulkner, *Varieties of Qualitative Research*, Sage, Beverly Hills, Calif., 1982.

19. Michel Hersen and David H. Barlow, *Single Case Experimental Design*, Pergamon, New York, 1976; Judi Komaki, "Alternative Evaluation Strategies in Work Settings: Reversals and Multiple Baseline Designs," *Journal of Organizational Behavior Management*, Summer 1977, pp. 53–77; Fred Luthans and Tim R. V. Davis, "An Idiographic Approach to Organizational Behavior Research: The Use of Single Case Experimental Designs and Direct Measures," *Academy of Management Review*, July 1982, pp. 380–391; and Ronald L. Taylor and Gary L. Adams, "A Review of Single-Subject Methodologies in Applied Settings," *Journal of Applied Behavioral Science*, vol. 18, 1982, pp. 95–103.

20. Alan E. Kazdin, "Obstacles in Using Randomization Tests in Single-Case Experimentation," *Journal of Educational Statistics*, Fall 1980, pp. 253–260.

21. M. M. Kennedy, "Generalization from Single Case Studies," *Evaluation Quarterly*, November 1979, pp. 661–678.

22. Tim R. V. Davis and Fred Luthans, "Leadership Reexamined: A Behavioral Approach," *Academy of Management Review*, April 1979, p. 244.

23. Fred Luthans and Diane Lockwood, "Toward an Observation System for Measuring Leader Behavior in Natural Settings," in J. G. Hunt, D. Hosking, C. Schriesheim, and R. Stewart (eds.), *Leaders and Managers: International Perspectives of Managerial Behavior and Leadership*, Pergamon, New York, 1984, pp. 117–141.

24. Colin P. Hales, "What Do Managers Do?" *Journal of Management Studies*, January 1986, p. 22; Fred Luthans, Stuart A. Rosenkrantz and Harry Hennessey, "What Do Successful Managers Really Do?" *Journal of Applied Behavioral Science*, vol. 21, no. 3, 1986, pp. 255–270; Stephen J. Carroll and Dennis A. Gillen, "Are the Classical Management Functions Useful in Describing Managerial Work?" *The Academy of Management Review*, January 1987, pp. 38–51; and Fred Luthans, Richard M. Hodgetts, and Stuart A. Rosenkrantz, *Real Managers*, Ballinger, Cambridge, Mass., 1988.

25. Robert M. Guion, "Content Validity: Three Years of Talk—What's the Action?" *Public Personnel Management*, November–December 1977, p. 407.

26. Ibid., p. 408.

27. Ibid.

28. Ibid.

29. Ibid., p. 410.

30. Wayne Cascio, *Applied Psychology in Personnel Management*, Reston Publishing, Reston, Va., 1978, p. 95.

31. Lee J. Cronbach and Paul E. Meehl, "Construct Validity in Psychological Tests," *Psychological Bulletin*, July 1955, pp. 281–302.

REAL CASE:
Sharing the
Wealth*

One of the ways in which early managers such as Frederick Taylor got the workers to increase their output was by offering them financial incentives. The greater the amount of work employees did, the higher they were paid. This idea is certainly not lost on modern managers. A&P, the large grocery chain, is a good example. In 1974 the company had 3468 supermarkets, but by 1982 the firm was down to 1016 stores and was losing ground to the competition. In desperation, corporate management began a turnaround. One of the things it did was to work out an arrangement with the union whereby workers took a 25 percent pay cut in exchange for cash bonuses. The way the plan worked was this: if a store's employees could keep labor costs at 11 percent of sales through more efficient work methods or by boosting the amount of store traffic, they would get a cash bonus equal to ½ of 1 percent of the store's sales. If the employees could get labor costs down to 10 percent of sales, the bonus would be 1 percent of the store's sales; and at 9.5 percent of sales the bonus would go up to 1.5 percent of the store's sales.

Within four years the bonus system had spread to 281 stores, and workers were earning more money than before. Overall, the company reported that the average store had labor costs of no more than 11 percent of sales, and in some cases it was much lower. For example, in the Philadelphia store, workers were earning an average of 85 cents an hour in bonus money. In an effort to keep productivity high, workers were also beginning to suggest ways of improving efficiency. These ranged from widening the pathway between the checkout lanes and the store shelves so that checkout lines could be lengthened during peak times to adding popular ethnic foods that would attract local customers.

The results of these efforts have been commendable. The company now pays out over $7 million annually through its bonus system, costs are under control, and the company's stock has more than doubled in two years. All of this is leading some industry experts to predict that with the increasing competitiveness among food retailers the A&P profit-sharing model might well become the industry standard during the 1990s.

1. In what way does A&P use some of Frederick Taylor's scientific management principles?
2. How do the managers at A&P also make use of the behavioral lessons learned from the Hawthorne studies?
3. In what ways does this case illustrate the importance of understanding people that is a tenet of the behavioral sciences?

*__Source:__ Adapted from Christopher S. Eklund, "How A&P Fattens Profits by Sharing Them," *Business Week,* Dec. 22, 1986, p. 44.

CASE: Too Nice to People

John has just graduated from the College of Business Administration at State University and has joined his family's small business, which employs twenty-five semiskilled workers. The first week on the job his dad called him in and said, "John, I've had a chance to observe you working with the men and women for the past two days and, although I hate to, I feel I must say something. You are just too nice to people. I know they taught you that human relations stuff at the university, but it just doesn't work here. I remember when the Hawthorne studies were first reported and everybody at the university got all excited about them, but believe me, there is more to managing people than just being nice to them."

1. How would you react to your father's comments if you were John?
2. Do you think John's father understood and interpreted the Hawthorne studies correctly?
3. What phases of management do you think John's father has gone through in this family business?

CASE: Dilemma for Program Evaluation

Jane Dewy has just been assigned to the training department of a large federal agency. She is assigned to program evaluation and works directly with the training and development program for first-line supervisors. She has been charged with constructing a method of measuring the effectiveness of some of the agency's training programs. The usual evaluation procedure is to administer a reaction questionnaire, which is given to the supervisors at the end of the training program. The trainees have consistently rated the program very highly. Jane is skeptical though. She thinks that anyone who receives a week off from work to go to a training program at a vacation resort might think the program was great. She wants to find another means of evaluating the program, a means that will truly measure its results and effectiveness. She has thought of sending a questionnaire to the subordinates whom the trainees supervised, but she feels uncomfortable about sending out such questionnaires. She knows how trite and meaningless they can be. She remembers how she and most of the other trainees in training programs that she participated in over the years treated surveys—as a joke and a waste of time. Yet she has to do something to evaluate the effectiveness of the training program. She reasons that sending out another questionnaire is better than nothing.

1. Is sending out another questionnaire Jane's only alternative?
2. How could she design an experiment to evaluate the program? What would be the independent variable? What would be the dependent variable or variables?
3. Besides program evaluation, what are some other direct applications of research methodology by practicing managers?

③ Organizational Culture

Changing the Culture of the Apple*

A few years ago Apple computer suffered its first loss as a publicly held company. The firm, founded by Steve Jobs and Stephen Wozniak, had started off with a "bang" but then began to have problems. The organization had built a very successful personal computer for the home and educational market. Millions of people had bought one and were pleased with the machine. However, the company needed to come up with other products that would help it maintain and build its market share and remain profitable in an increasingly competitive business. In particular, Apple needed to get a share of the business market.

Under Jobs the company introduced its Macintosh (the "Mac") as well as a couple of other models such as the Apple III and the Lisa. None were able to compete successfully with the offerings of IBM, Hewlett-Packard, and the other business-oriented computer companies. One of the reasons was that the Apple machines were simply not designed for the business market. Many managers saw them as playthings—nothing more. The "Mac," on which Apple had staked its future, was shipping only 10,000 units a month from a plant designed to produce 80,000 units a month. Additionally, the people who had been working for Apple computer since its inception were accustomed to thinking in terms of the nonbusiness market. They did not have the right training or perspective for competing head to head with IBM. As a result, John Sculley, an

*Source: Adapted from Katherine M. Hafner and Geoff Lewis, "Apple's Comeback," *Business Week*, Jan. 19, 1987, pp. 84–89.

individual with a great deal of marketing know-how, was placed in charge of Apple.

During the first eighteen months that he was at the helm, Sculley worked to change the organization's culture and to introduce new core values that were marketing in orientation. He also began rewarding his people for focusing their attention on the business computer market, which is far more profitable than the home or educational computer markets. Within three months sales began to go up. From a quarterly low of $50 million, they reached $130 million by the end of 1986. Moreover, company revenues from commercial customers increased relative to IBM's. In 1984 Macintosh held approximately 4 percent of the personal computer market while IBM had about 34 percent. By the end of 1986, Apple's share of this market was 8 percent while IBM's was 33 percent. Even more important for the firm, its after-tax profit margin, which had fallen to 3 percent in 1985, was at 8 percent in 1986.

At the same time as its culture was changing, Apple was also investing millions into new models for the 1990s. Its "Open Mac," which uses a 32-byte chip, and its focus on larger screens, user-friendly programs, and higher-quality print machines all promised to make Apple a major force in the computer industry for years to come. Most importantly, the transformation of the work force's cultural values from a focus on computers with appeal for school and home use to more practical, business-oriented machines multi-purpose in design and need and sold by a well-trained sales force has made Apple once again a major player in the computer market.

Learning Objectives

- DEFINE organizational culture and its characteristics.
- RELATE how an organizational culture is created.
- DESCRIBE how an organizational culture is maintained.
- EXPLAIN some ways of changing organizational culture.
- PRESENT some current examples of cultures in action.

This chapter is concerned with organizational culture. The cultural concept has been a mainstay in the field of anthropology from its beginnings and even was given attention in the early development of organizational behavior.[1] However, only recently has it surfaced as a major dimension for understanding organizational behavior. Today, however, as the introductory comments of a special issue of a management journal noted, organizational culture "has acquired the status of the dominant buzz-word in the U.S. popular and academic management literature."[2] The first half of the chapter presents the overall nature of organizational culture, including its definition and characteristics and the dimensions of uniformity, strong and weak, and types of cultures. The last half is devoted to creating and maintaining a culture. Real-world examples are provided throughout and given specific attention in the last section.

The Nature of Organizational Culture

People are affected by the culture in which they live. For example, a person growing up in a middle-class family will be taught the values, beliefs, and expected behaviors common to that family. The same is true for organizational participants. An individual working for IBM, AT&T, Delta Airlines, or any other organization with a firmly established culture will be taught the values, beliefs, and expected behaviors of that organization. Society has a *social* culture; where people work has an *organizational* culture.

Definition and Characteristics

When people join an organization they bring with them the values and beliefs they have been taught. Quite often, however, these values and beliefs are insufficient for helping the individual succeed in the organization. The person needs to learn how the particular enterprise does things. A good example is the U.S. Marine Corps. During boot camp drill instructors teach recruits the "Marine way." The training attempts to psychologically strip down the new recruits and then restructure their way of thinking. They are taught to think and act like Marines. Anyone who has been in the Marines or knows someone who has will verify that the Corps generally accomplish its objective. In a less dramatic way, organizations do the same thing.

Edgar Schein, who has done considerable research and writing on the subject, has defined *organizational culture* as:

> a pattern of basic assumptions—invented, discovered, or developed by a given group as it learns to cope with its problems of external adaptation and internal integration—that has worked well enough to be considered valuable and, therefore, to be taught to new members as the correct way to perceive, think, and feel in relation to those problems.[3]

A recent review of organizational culture notes the differing perspectives and the problems associated with the conceptualization of organizational culture in the literature.[4] Most of the definitions, however, stress the importance of shared norms and values.

Organizational culture has a number of important characteristics. Some of the most readily agreed upon are the following:

1. *Observed behavioral regularities.* When organizational participants interact with one another, they use common language, terminology, and rituals related to deference and demeanor.
2. *Norms.* Standards of behavior exist including guidelines on how much work to do, which in many organizations come down to "Do not do too much; do not do too little."

3. *Dominant values.* There are major values that the organization advocates and expects the participants to share. Typical examples are high product quality, low absenteeism, and high efficiency.
4. *Philosophy.* There are policies that set forth the organization's beliefs about how employees and/or customers are to be treated.
5. *Rules.* There are strict guidelines related to getting along in the organization. Newcomers must learn these "ropes" in order to be accepted as full-fledged members of the group.
6. *Organizational climate.* This is an overall "feeling" that is conveyed by the physical layout, the way in which participants interact, and the way in which members of the organization conduct themselves with customers or other outsiders.

None of the above characteristics by themselves represent the culture of an organization. However, collectively, they can reflect the organizational culture.

Uniformity of Culture

A common misconception is that an organization has a uniform culture. However, at least as anthropology uses the concept, it is probably more accurate to treat organizations "as if" they had a uniform culture. "All organizations 'have' culture in the sense that they are embedded in specific societal cultures and are part of them."[5] According to this view an organizational culture is a common perception held by the organization's members. Everyone in the organization would have to share this perception. However, realistically, all may not do so to the same degree. As a result, there can be a dominant culture as well as subcultures throughout a typical organization.

A *dominant culture* is a set of core values shared by a majority of the organization's members. For example, most employees at Delta Airlines seem to subscribe to such values as hard work, company loyalty, and the need for customer service. At Hewlett-Packard most of the employees seem to share a concern for product innovativeness, product quality, and responsiveness to customer needs. At Wal-Mart stores, the associates—a term Wal-Mart uses for its employees that is very symptomatic of its culture—share a concern for customer service, hard work, and company loyalty. These values create a dominant culture in these organizations that helps guide the day-to-day behavior of employees.

Important, but often overlooked, are the subcultures in an organization. A *subculture* is a set of values shared by a minority, usually a small minority, of the organization's members. Subcultures typically are a result of problems or experiences that are shared by members of a department or unit. For example, each of the three major television networks—ABC, CBS, and NBC—has a number of key departments, including a news department with its own subculture. The popular movie *Broadcast News* is really about this subculture. Now, the networks strive to be as profitable as possible, and a show that does not do well will be replaced by another. However, the newspeople object to having this "bottom line" approach applied to their department. They feel the news is too important to be governed by profit criteria alone. This was brought out in *Broadcast News* when many employees in the news department were let go for budgetary reasons.

Subcultures can weaken and undermine an organization if they are in conflict with the dominant culture and/or the overall objectives. Successful firms, however, find that this is not always the case. Most subcultures are formed to help the members of a particular group deal with the specific, day-to-day problems with which they are confronted. The members may also support many, if not all, of the core values of the dominant culture.

Strong and Weak Cultures

Some organizational cultures could be labeled "strong," others "weak." There seem to be two major factors that determine the strength of an organizational culture: sharedness and intensity. *Sharedness* refers to the degree to which the organizational members have the same core values. *Intensity* is the degree of commitment of the organizational members to the core values.

The degree of sharedness is affected by two major factors: orientation and rewards. In order for people to share the same cultural values, they must know what these values are. Many organizations begin this process with an orientation program. New employees are told about the organization's philosophy and method of operating. This orientation continues on the job where their boss and

---

Application Example

The Best Companies to Work For—and Why*

Many companies have created cultures conducive to high performance. Each provides certain types of benefits or rewards that help ensure the commitment of its personnel to core cultural values. Here are some examples of what some of the best firms do.

Company	Benefit or Reward
Apple Computer, Marion Laboratories, Tandem Computer	Grant stock options to every employee.
Delta Air Lines, Digital Equipment, Exxon, Hewlett-Packard, IBM, Procter & Gamble	No layoff of personnel—ever. Lifetime employment.
Intel	After seven years with the firm an employee is eligible for eight weeks off with pay.
Northwestern Mutual Life	Free lunch for all employees every day.
Pitney Bowes	Every year the employees meet with the top officers and can ask any questions they want. Prizes are awarded for the best questions.
Reader's Digest	Four weeks of paid vacation after the first year of employment.
Time, Inc.	Any employee who works past 8 P.M. can take a taxi home and the company will pick up the tab—even if the individual lives in the next state.
Walt Disney Productions	All business air travel is first-class.

*__Source:__ Adapted from Milton Moskowitz, "Lessons from the Best Companies to Work For," *California Management Review*, Winter 1985, pp. 42–43.

coworkers share these values through both word of mouth and day-to-day work habits and example. Sharedness is also affected by rewards. When organizations give promotions, raises, recognition, and other forms of reward to those who adhere to the core values, these actions help others better understand these values. Some organizations have been labeled "the best to work for" because the rewards that they give to their people are exemplary and help reinforce commitment to core values. The accompanying Application Example, The Best Companies to Work For and Why, provides some illustrations.

The degree of intensity is a result of the reward structure. When employees realize that they will be rewarded for doing things "the organization's way," their desire to do so increases. Conversely, when they are not rewarded or they feel there is more to be gained by not doing things the organization's way, commitment to core values diminishes. Table 3.1 provides an example of how an organization can determine whether it has a strong or weak culture. Notice from the answer key that such highly successful companies as IBM, Procter & Gamble, and Morgan Guaranty all have strong cultures.

Types of Cultures

Many paradigms or models have recently been constructed to describe organizational culture. One of the most comprehensive and widely known is that by Deal and Kennedy.[6] Table 3.2 describes the four basic types of cultural profiles they uncovered. Each type is characterized by some combination of two factors: the type of risks that managers assume and the type of feedback that results from their decisions.

Most organizations are some hybrid of these cultural profiles; they do not neatly fit into any one of them. However, within the organization there are subcultures that do tend to fit into one of these four profiles. For example, according to Table 3.2, IBM's cultural profile would be that of a "work hard/play hard" company. However, because the corporation is so large and has so many different departments, this overall profile describes the enterprise in general terms only. On the other hand, people in the sales area would most certainly fit into this profile. This is in contrast to personnel in the research and development area who would be operating in a subculture best described in Table 3.2 as "bet your company."[7]

Creating and Maintaining a Culture

Some organizational cultures may be the direct, or at least indirect, result of actions taken by the founders. However, this is not always the case. Sometimes founders create weak cultures, and if the organization is to survive, a new top manager must be installed who will sow the seeds for the necessary strong culture. Thomas Watson, Sr., of IBM is a good example. When he took over the CTR Corporation, it was a small firm manufacturing computing, tabulating, and recording equipment. Through his dominant personality and the changes he made at the firm, Watson created a culture that led to the modern-day IBM

TABLE 3.1 Computing an Organizational Culture Socialization Score

Respond to the items below as they apply to the handling of professional employees. Upon completion, compute the total score. For comparison, scores for a number of strong, intermediate, and weak culture firms are to be found on the next page.

	Not True of This Company				Very True of This Company
1. Recruiters receive at least one week of intensive training.	1	2	3	4	5
2. Recruitment forms identify several key traits deemed crucial to the firm's success, traits are defined in concrete terms and interviewer records specific evidence of each trait.	1	2	3	4	5
3. Recruits are subjected to at least four in-depth interviews.	1	2	3	4	5
4. Company actively facilitates de-selection during the recruiting process by revealing minuses as well as pluses.	1	2	3	4	5
5. New hires work long hours, are exposed to intensive training of considerable difficulty and/or perform relatively menial tasks in the first months.	1	2	3	4	5
6. The intensity of entry level experience builds cohesiveness among peers in each entering class.	1	2	3	4	5
7. All professional employees in a particular discipline begin in entry level positions regardless of prior experience or advanced degrees.	1	2	3	4	5
8. Reward systems and promotion criteria require mastery of a core discipline as a precondition of advancement.	1	2	3	4	5
9. The career path for professional employees is relatively consistent over the first six to ten years with the company.	1	2	3	4	5
10. Reward systems, performance incentives, promotion criteria and other primary measures of success reflect a high degree of congruence.	1	2	3	4	5
11. Virtually all professional employees can identify and articulate the firm's shared values (i.e., the purpose or mission that ties the firm to society, the customer or its employees).	1	2	3	4	5
12. There are very few instances when actions of management appear to violate the firm's espoused values.	1	2	3	4	5
13. Employees frequently make personal sacrifices for the firm out of commitment to the firm's shared values.	1	2	3	4	5
14. When confronted with trade-offs between systems measuring short-term results and doing what's best for the company in the long term, the firm usually decides in favor of the long-term.	1	2	3	4	5
15. This organization fosters mentor-protégé relationships.	1	2	3	4	5
16. There is considerable similarity among high potential candidates in each particular discipline.	1	2	3	4	5

Compute your score: _____

TABLE 3.1 (Continued)

For comparative purposes:	Scores	
Strongly socialized firms	65–80	IBM, P&G, Morgan Guaranty
	55–64	ATT, Morgan Stanley, Delta Airlines
	45–54	United Airlines, Coca Cola
	35–44	General Foods, Pepsi Co.
	25–34	United Technologies, ITT
Weakly socialized firms	Below 25	Atari

Source: Richard Pascale, "The Paradox of 'Corporate Culture': Reconciling Ourselves to Socialization." Copyright © by the Regents of the University of California. Reprinted from the *California Management Review,* vol. 27, no. 2, Winter 1985, pp. 39, 40. By permission of the Regents.

corporation. He molded it to become the largest computer firm and one of the recognized best companies in any industry in the world.

At other times a culture must be changed because the environment changes and the previous core cultural values are not in step with those needed for survival. The opening vignette on Apple Computer is a good example. When Steve Jobs and his partner started the company, they wanted to create a culture where people could be creative, work on projects that interested them, and turn out a product that would be innovative. However, as they began broadening their horizons and trying to appeal to both the educational and the business market, the firm began to run into trouble. Its culture was not designed to compete head to head with IBM and the other computer giants. Steve Jobs was a thinker and creator, not an organizer and a manager. Apple began to lose money. A change in leadership and culture was needed. The firm turned to John Sculley, a marketing-oriented manager and organizer who began to make the necessary changes such as a strong focus on sales to business. As a result, Apple is now doing much better and appears to be bouncing back in terms of both market share and profitability.[8] The following sections take a close look at how organizational cultures get started, maintained, and changed.

How Organizational Cultures Start

While organizational cultures can develop in a number of different ways, the process usually involves some version of the following steps:

1. A single person (founder) has an idea for a new enterprise.
2. The founder brings in one or more other key people and creates a core group that shares a common vision with the founder. That is, all in this core group believe that the idea is a good one, is workable, is worth running some risks for, and is worth the investment of time, money, and energy that will be required.
3. The founding core group begins to act in concert to create an organization by raising funds, obtaining patents, incorporating, locating space, building, and so on.
4. At this point, others are brought into the organization, and a common history begins to be built.[9]

TABLE 3.2 Organizational Culture Profiles

Name of the culture	Tough-Guy, Macho	Work Hard/Play Hard
Type of risks that are assumed	High	Low
Type of feedback from decisions	Fast	Fast
Typical kinds of organizations that use this culture	Construction, cosmetics, television, radio, venture capitalism, management consulting	Real estate, computer firms, auto distributors, door-to-door sales operations, retail stores, mass consumer sales
The ways survivors and/or heroes in this culture behave	They have a tough attitude. They are individualistic. They can tolerate all-or-nothing risks. They are superstitious.	They are super salespeople. They often are friendly, hail-fellow-well-met types. They use a team approach to problem solving. They are nonsuperstitious.
Strengths of the personnel/culture	They can get things done in short order.	They are able to quickly produce a high volume of work.
Weaknesses of the personnel/culture	They do not learn from past mistakes. Everything tends to be short-term in orientation. The virtues of cooperation are ignored.	They look for quick-fix solutions. They have a short-term time perspective. They are more committed to action than to problem solving.
Habits of the survivors and/or heroes	They dress in fashion. They live in "in" places. They like one-on-one sports such as tennis. They enjoy scoring points off one another in verbal interaction.	They avoid extremes in dress. They live in tract houses. They prefer team sports such as touch football. They like to drink together.

Most of today's successful corporate giants in all industries basically followed these steps. Three well-known representative examples are IBM, McDonald's, and Wal-Mart.

- *International Business Machines.* Thomas Watson, Sr., the founder, began his business career selling office machines for the National Cash Register Company. This experience taught him both the benefits and techniques of effective salesmanship and the value of a good product. Years later when he left the company to join CTR, Watson took these concepts with him. In particular, he stressed the need for product research and development and the importance of marketing. These two ideas helped form the core cultural values of IBM's approach to business. During the 1930s and 1940s the company introduced electronic office machines, and beginning in the 1950s it complemented this line with computers. Today, Watson's core values continue to guide IBM. In

Bet Your Company High	Process Low
Slow	Slow
Oil, aerospace, capital goods manufacturers, architectural firms, investment banks, mining and smelting firms, military	Banks, insurance companies, utilities, pharmaceuticals, financial-service organizations, many agencies of the government
They can endure long-term ambiguity. They always double-check their decisions. They are technically competent. They have a strong respect for authority.	They are very cautious and protective of their own flank. They are orderly and punctual. They are good at attending to detail. They always follow established procedures.
They can generate high-quality inventions and major scientific breakthroughs.	They bring order and system to the workplace.
They are extremely slow in getting things done. Their organizations are vulnerable to short-term economic fluctuations. Their organizations often face cash-flow problems.	There is lots of red tape. Initiative is downplayed. They face long hours and boring work.
They dress according to their organizational rank. Their housing matches their hierarchical position. They like sports such as golf, in which the outcome is unclear until the end of the game. The older members serve as mentors for the younger ones.	They dress according to hierarchical rank. They live in apartments or no-frills homes. They enjoy process sports like jogging and swimming. They like discussing memos.

Source: Adapted from Terence E. Deal and Allan A. Kennedy, *Corporate Cultures: The Rites and Rituals of Corporate Life,* © 1982, Addison-Wesley, Reading, Mass. Excerpts from Chap. 6. Used with permission.

fact, at the present time, even while the corporation is cutting back its middle-level management ranks, it still continues to stress new product development and sales efforts. The culture that Watson mainly created is still alive and well at IBM.

• *McDonald's.* Ray Kroc worked for many years as a salesperson for a food supplier (Lily Tulip Cup). He learned how retail food operations were conducted. He also had an entrepreneurial streak and began a sideline business with a partner. They sold multimixers, machines that were capable of mixing up to six frozen shakes at a time. One day Kroc received a large order for multimixers from the McDonald brothers. The order intrigued Kroc, and he decided to look in on the operation the next time he was in their area. When he did, Kroc became convinced that the McDonald's fast-food concept would sweep the nation. He bought the rights to franchise McDonald's units and eventually bought out the brothers. At the same time he built the franchise on four basic concepts: quality, cleanliness, service, and price. In order to ensure that each unit offers the customer the best product at the best price, franchisees are required to attend McDonald University, where they are taught how to manage their business. Here they learn the McDonald cultural values and the proper way to run the franchise. This training ensures that franchisees all over the world are operating their units in the same way. Kroc died a few years ago, but the culture he left behind is still very much alive in McDonald's franchises across the world. In fact, new employees receive videotaped messages from the late Mr. Kroc. Some of the more interesting of his pronouncements that reflect and carry on his values are his thoughts on cleanliness: "If you've got time to lean, you've got time to clean." On the competition he says: "If they are drowning to death, I would put a hose in their mouth." And on expanding he declares: "When you're green, you grow; when you're ripe, you rot."[10] So even though he has not been involved in the business for over a decade, his legacy lives on. Even his office at corporate headquarters is preserved as a museum, his reading glasses untouched in their leather case on the desk.

- *Wal-Mart.* Sam Walton, founder of Wal-Mart Stores, Inc., opened his first Wal-Mart store in 1962. Focusing on the sale of discounted name-brand merchandise in small-town markets, he began to set up more and more stores in the Sun Belt. At the same time he began developing effective inventory control systems and marketing techniques. Today Wal-Mart has over 1000 stores and the discount retail chain is the second-largest in the country with annual sales of over $9 billion. Walton encourages his people to develop new ideas that will increase their store's efficiency. If a policy does not seem to be working, the company quickly changes it. Executives continually encourage the associates (employees) to challenge the current system and look for ways to improve it. Those who do these things are rewarded; those who do not perform up to expectations are encouraged to do better. The operating philosophy and environment at Wal-Mart is so attractive that industry analysts estimate that the company will be bigger than K mart within a decade. Walton's personal way of doing things permeates the organization. Everyone is taught this culture and is expected to operate within the core cultural values of hard work, efficiency, and customer service.[11]

Maintaining Cultures through Steps of Socialization

Once an organizational culture is started and begins to develop, there are a number of practices that can help solidify the acceptance of core values and ensure that the culture maintains itself. These practices can be described in terms of several socialization steps. Figure 3.1 illustrates the sequence of these steps.

Selection of Entry-Level Personnel. The first step is the careful selection of entry-level candidates.[12] Using standardized procedures and seeking

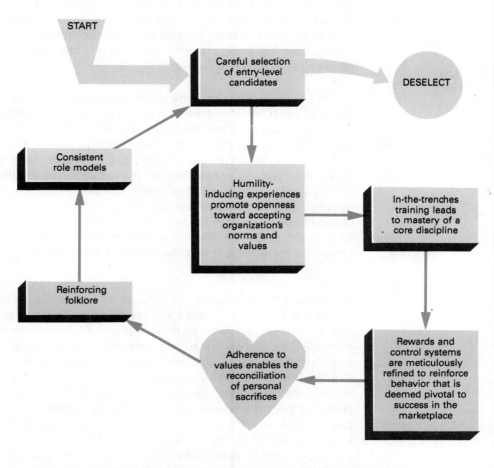

FIGURE 3.1
Steps of organization culture socialization.
(*Source*: Richard Pascale, "The Paradox of 'Corporate Culture': Reconciling Ourselves to Socialization." Copyright © by the Regents of the University of California. Reprinted from the *California Management Review*, vol. 27, no. 2, Winter 1985, p. 38. By permission of the Regents.)

specific traits that tie to effective performance, trained recruiters interview candidates and attempt to screen out those whose personal styles and values do not make a "fit" with the organization's culture.

Placement on the Job.   The second step occurs on the job itself, after the person with a fit is hired. New personnel are subjected to a carefully orchestrated series of different experiences whose purpose is to cause them to question the organization's norms and values and to decide whether or not they can accept them. For example, many organizations with strong cultures make it a point to give newly hired personnel more work than they can handle. Sometimes these assignments are beneath the individual's abilities. At Procter & Gamble, for example, new personnel may be required to color in a sales territory map. The experience is designed to convey the message, "While you're smart in some ways, you're in kindergarten as far as what you know about this organization." The objective is also to teach the new entrant into the culture the importance of humility. These experiences are designed to make newly hired personnel vulnerable and to cause them to move closer emotionally to their colleagues, thus intensifying group cohesiveness. Campus fraternities and the military have practiced this approach for years.

Job Mastery. Once the initial "cultural shock" is over, the next step is mastery of one's job. This is typically done via extensive and carefully reinforced field experience. For example, IBM puts its new employees through a program that often takes as long as six years to produce an experienced marketing representative and twelve years to turn out a full-fledged controller. As personnel move along their career path, their performance is evaluated and additional responsibilities are assigned on the basis of progress. Quite often companies establish a step-by-step approach to this career plan, which helps reduce efforts by the personnel to use political power or to take shortcuts in order to get ahead at a faster pace. As Pascale notes, "Relationships, staying power, and a constant proven track record are the inescapable requirements of advancement" during this phase.[13]

Measuring and Rewarding Performance. The next step of the socialization process consists of meticulous attention to measuring operational results and to rewarding individual performance. These systems are comprehensive, consistent, and focus on those aspects of the business that are most crucial to competitive success and to corporate values. For example, at Procter & Gamble there are three factors that are considered most important: building volume, building profit, and making changes that increase effectiveness or add satisfaction to the job. Operational measures are used to track these three factors, and performance appraisals are tied to milestones. Importantly, promotions and merit pay are determined by success in each of these critical areas. IBM personnel are taught to adhere to the core cultural values through careful monitoring of managerial performance and through continual training programs. Anyone who commits a crime against the culture such as overzealousness against the competition or harsh handling of a subordinate is sent to the "penalty box." This typically involves a lateral move to a less desirous location. For example, a branch manager in Chicago might be given a nebulous staff position at headquarters. This individual is now off-track, which can slow his or her career progress.

Adherence to Important Values. The next step involves careful adherence to the firm's most important values. Identification with these values helps employees reconcile personal sacrifices brought about by their membership in the organization. They learn to accept these values and to trust the organization not to do anything that would hurt them. As Pascale observes, "Placing one's self 'at the mercy' of an organization imposes real costs. There are long hours of work, missed weekends, bosses one has to endure, criticism that seems unfair, job assignments and rotations that are inconvenient or undesirable."[14] However, the organization attempts to overcome these costs by connecting the sacrifices to higher human values such as serving society with better products and/or services. Companies such as Delta Airlines do this very effectively.

> Prior to joining Delta airlines, candidates hear endlessly about the "Delta family feeling." Numerous anecdotes illustrate that Delta's values require sacrifices: Management takes pay cuts during lean times; senior flight attendants and pilots voluntarily work fewer hours per week in order to avoid laying off more junior employees. Candidates who accept employment with Delta tend to accept this quid pro quo, believing that the restrictions on individual action comprise a reasonable trade-off. In effect, Delta's family philosophy is deemed worthy enough to make their sacrifices worthwhile.[15]

Reinforcing the Stories and Folklore.

The next step involves reinforcing organizational folklore. This entails keeping alive stories that validate the organization's culture and way of doing things. The folklore helps explain why the organization does things a particular way. One of the most common forms of folklore is stories with morals the enterprise wants to reinforce. For example, at Procter & Gamble there is a story about the outstanding brand manager who was fired for overstating the features of a product. The moral of the story is that ethical claims are more important than making money. At AT&T there are numerous stories about field employees who made sacrifices to keep the phones working and operators who stayed on the line when a person called in and asked for emergency help because he had suffered a physical calamity. The moral of such stories is that these types of sacrifices are all in the line of duty for telephone employees, who must view their primary responsibility as that of helping the customer.

Recognition and Promotion.

The final step is the recognition and promotion of individuals who have done their jobs well and who can serve as role models to new people in the organization. By pointing out these people as winners, the organization encourages others to follow their example. Role models in strong-culture firms are regarded as the most powerful ongoing training program of all. Morgan Stanley, the financial services firm, chooses role models based on energy, aggressiveness, and team play. Procter & Gamble looks for people who exhibit extraordinary consistency in such areas as toughmindedness, motivational skills, energy, and the ability to get things done through others.[16]

Changing Organizational Culture

Sometimes an organization determines that its culture has to be changed. For example, the external environment may undergo drastic change and the organization must either adapt to these new conditions or it may not survive. This attempt to adapt can take many different forms. Simple guidelines such as developing a sense of history, creating a sense of oneness, promoting a sense of membership, and increasing exchange among members are helpful.[17] Also, organizations attempting to change their culture must be careful not to abandon their roots and blindly copy the so-called "successful" or "excellent" companies.[18]

To pragmatically change an organization culture, there will be a need for new criteria for hiring, changes in the reward structure, new criteria for promotion, or a reassignment of organizational priorities. Procter & Gamble is a good example of a firm that has successfully undergone cultural change. After this example is given, the role that Theory Z and Japanese management have played in changing organizational culture will be examined.

Changing the Culture at Procter & Gamble.

For years the culture at P&G had supported steady growth and profits. Recently, however, the company found itself under a great deal of pressure from the external competitive environment. For example, Kimberly-Clark had cut deeply into P&G's disposable-diaper market, one of the company's most lucrative market niches. At the same time, Lever Brothers was making inroads into P&G's share of the soap and detergent market. On the new product development front, things were no better. The company was having disappointing results with its Pringles potato chips and was suffering financial losses on its Coldsnap Homemade Ice Cream Mix, Wondra hand cream, and Rely Tampons. These setbacks were reflected on the company's bottom line as pretax earnings fell for the first time in over thirty years. At the same time the firm was having union problems. Its Kansas City plant voted to unionize, and the company went through a long fight with worker representatives in its effort to change work practices and improve efficiency.

These developments led P&G to make changes in its organizational culture. Some of these included:

1. The work team concept, in which production and maintenance workers—called "technicians"—are required to master and use a second skill, was extended throughout P&G's operations.
2. The lifetime-job tradition that once made P&G workers the envy of their blue-collar counterparts elsewhere gave way to layoffs.
3. The corporate paternalism of the past yielded to some hard practicalities as executives and workers alike were put on notice that plants that didn't measure up on productivity, cost, and quality would be shut down.
4. A determined management vigorously resisted attempts by organized labor to dictate how P&G's operations should be run.[19]

In addition to the above, P&G trimmed its work force by 5 percent on the plant floor and 4 percent company-wide. This was accomplished through reduced hiring, early retirement, and, in some cases, layoffs. Changing conditions had led P&G to change its culture.[20]

Changing Culture through Theory Z.

Another way in which many organizations are trying to change their culture is by becoming more "Theory Z"-oriented.[21] Drawn from the work of Ouchi,[22] and given coverage as an organization development technique in Chapter 20, Theory Z is an approach to managing that calls for more:

- Consensus decision making
- Broader participation by the workers in all phases of the operation
- Concern for the overall well-being of employees

The theory draws heavily on the Japanese approach to management. Most accurately, Theory Z is really a combination of the current American and Japanese approaches to management. The accompanying International Application Example: Theory Z in Action, contrasts the typical American and Japanese approaches and the compromising Z approach. The following description of the American subsidiary of Fujitsu Limited (the largest computer and telecommunications company in Japan) shows Theory Z in action:

> Mid-level managers work in interactive teams composed of senior managers, workers and peers. The decision-making approach is consensual, and commitment to employees is long term. Managers are individually responsible for achieving goals, but they are also expected to encourage employee participation and communication. Recreational condominiums in locations such as California's Lake Tahoe, for example, show a holistic concern for employees' family and recreational needs.[23]

International Application Example

Theory Z in Action

In the early 1980s William Ouchi's book *Theory Z: How American Business Can Meet the Japanese Challenge* pointed out the importance of organizational culture. Many American managers have studied Ouchi's book in order to gain insights regarding how the successful Japanese systems are different from their own and how their firm might successfully modify its culture by drawing on these concepts. In particular, there are seven characteristics that differentiate the approach used by the Americans (Theory A) and that of the Japanese (Theory J). Ouchi's Theory Z is a combination of these theories designed, in most cases, to modify American corporate culture and help firms compete more effectively with the Japanese. Here is how Theory Z modifies Theory A by drawing upon Theory J concepts.

Characteristics	Theory A (American)	Theory J (Japanese)	Theory Z (Modified)
Employment with a firm	Usually short-term; layoffs are quite common.	Especially in some of the large firms, it is for life. Layoffs are rare.	Fairly long term; this will help develop a loyal semipermanent work force.
Evaluation and promotion of the personnel	Very fast; individuals who are not promoted rapidly often seek employment elsewhere.	Very slow; big promotions are generally not given out for years.	Slower; more emphasis is given to training and evaluation than to promotion.
Career paths	Very specialized; people tend to stay in one area (accounting, finance, sales, etc.) for their entire career.	Very general; personnel are rotated from one area to another and become familiar with all areas of operations.	More general; emphasis is on job rotation and more broadly based training in order to give the person a better feel for the entire organization.

Characteristics	Theory A (American)	Theory J (Japanese)	Theory Z (Modified)
Decision making	Carried out by the individual manager.	Carried out via group decision making.	Carried out with more emphasis on group participation and consensus.
Control	Very explicit; people know exactly what to control and how to do it.	Very implicit and informal; people rely heavily on trust and goodwill.	More attention to informal control procedures coupled with explicit performance measures.
Responsibility	Assigned on an individual basis.	Shared collectively by the group.	Assigned on an individual basis.
Concern for the personnel	Organization is concerned primarily with the worker's work life only.	Organization is concerned with the whole life of the worker, business and social.	Organization's concern is expanded to include more aspects of the worker's whole life.

Problems with Japanese Management. In recent years an increasing number of American firms have attempted to move their culture toward a Japanese-oriented approach in the belief that the Japanese do a much better job of integrating the individual into the workplace. On the other hand, it is important to remember that not all firms believe that Japanese management techniques are the way to go. They prefer American cultural values that emphasize individualism, rapid feedback, and rewards. Additionally, some critics note that in recent years the Japanese economy has suffered setbacks that have brought changes in their organizational cultures.

It has become increasingly popular to note the "myths" of Japanese management. For instance, one myth is that the Japanese people are naturally hard-working. The facts are that foreign production data on Honda, Sony, Matsushita, and other Japanese pioneers of multinationalization show little difference in productivity among local workers in their plants in Japan, Europe, North America, or Asia.[24] Another example is that today some prominent Japanese firms do not give lifetime employment to their new people. (Most of the smaller ones never did.) Lifetime employment is reserved only for those who have been with a big firm for many years. A second change is that some Japanese firms are now putting pressure on their people to retire early so as to reduce the firms' payroll costs and remain competitive. The holistic concern for the well-being of the individual worker may be largely gone. Still another significant change is that many young people in Japan are beginning to question whether the Japanese system can function properly as societal and economic changes become more commonplace. Some of these concerns include the following:

- Decision managing by consensus, employed by many large companies, often discourages initiative and the pursuit of imaginative ideas. The basic premise of consensus decision making is homogeneity among members, not hetero-geneity.
- Personnel policies such as seniority-based wage and promotion systems cannot better compensate highly specialized employees who are fully aware of the value of their services to the company.
- Probably most important, many Japanese have started to question the notion of single-company loyalty and compensation based on seniority rather than performance. Most Japanese workers still acquire company-specific skills through in-house training and are reluctant to move. This practice is reinforced by strong social norms that make it difficult for employees to find work with other employers.[25]

Theory Z and Japanese Management Approaches in Perspective. Today, most American managers who are drawing on Theory Z and Japanese management approaches to change their organizational culture are doing so on a selective basis. They are choosing those ideas which, when appropriately modified, will result in higher productivity and efficiency. In addition, many successful American firms have really been using the so-called "Japanese" concepts for decades. IBM, Hewlett-Packard, Merck, Delta Airlines, and Johnson & Johnson, to name but a few, have long been outstanding companies because they have encouraged employee participation, rewarded teamwork, and ensured employment to their people. The "best" American firms have always been concerned with developing the right culture for their social and economic environments.

Cultures in Action: Some Current Examples

At the present time many organizations are undergoing dramatic cultural change. In most cases these changes are a result of management's deliberate attempts to adjust to changing environmental demands. Two representative examples would be what happened at General Motors when it purchased Electronic Data Systems and the aftermath of the breakup of AT&T. Following is an in-depth look at these examples of cultures in action.

The Case of General Motors/Electronic Data Systems

General Motors has maintained its position as the world's largest auto producer and is, overall, one of the biggest and most successful companies the world has ever known. Yet, despite these impressive results, the company has recently been having real trouble maintaining its lofty position. From 1980 to 1985 it lost 5 percent of its share of the auto market and has been in a constant battle with the competition to win back their customers.

An Outdated Culture. One of the reasons why GM has been falling behind is that its culture was not designed to meet the challenges of the changing auto market. Over the past five decades the company built a large bureaucracy designed to reduce risk and ensure loyalty from its managers. Many major decisions were made by committees. Although this process took a great deal of time and tended to deemphasize individual initiative, it also ensured that decisions were thought through carefully and that projects were looked at from every angle. However, when the auto market began to become more competitive because of small-sized foreign imports, GM found this culture to be unresponsive. The cultural values associated with committee decision making and the lack of risk-taking were out of step with the demands of the fast-changing auto market. As a result, GM began to look for ways of reducing its decision-making time and developing and building more competitive cars.

The Purchase of Electronic Data Systems (EDS). One of the steps GM took to improve its position in the new auto market was to purchase Electronic Data Systems (EDS), a computer-based firm founded and headed by the well-known entrepreneur Ross Perot. Starting out with $1000, Perot had created a company with sales of $600 million annually and, in the process, had become a billionaire. GM hoped to use EDS to help it develop computer systems for the production of its autos as well as to provide it with another business market. It offered Perot a large sum of money and a seat on the board of directors.

The Culture of EDS. EDS had a culture quite different from that of GM. Formulated by its founder Perot, it was built along the lines of aggressiveness, competitiveness, and the ability to change quickly to meet market conditions. The organization initially hired ex-military people who had a "gung ho" set of cultural values that became part of EDS. For example, in 1979 when the Iranian regime under Khomeini arrested two EDS executives, Perot put together a plan that resulted in a team of company executives, along with a retired military colonel, going into Iran and rescuing the men from jail. This story was told to all new recruits and served to convey the message that EDS personnel were all part of a "crack team" and that the company took care of its own. The rescue was even the subject of a TV movie.

The GM-EDS Cultural Clash. The GM culture and the EDS culture were at odds with each other from the beginning; they did not "fit." One analogy used in describing the merger was that it was like one between the Social Security Administration and the Green Berets. In any event, Perot continually complained about GM's inability to move rapidly and make changes that would help it remain competitive. GM, on the other hand, argued that Perot failed to understand that in an organization as large as GM it takes months to get things going. The tension between the chairman of the GM board and his most outspoken critic, Perot, came to an end when Perot agreed to sell his stock for $700 million and give up his seat on the board.

GM still owns EDS, but the two cultures remain very different and the automaker has been unable to get EDS to work in harmony with its bureaucracy.

Whether GM will ever get EDS to become a full-fledged member of its team and make a "fit" with its culture is debatable. For the present, however, the cultural clash is so great that the two are not working in harmony.

The Case of American Telephone and Telegraph

On January 1, 1984, the American Telephone and Telegraph Company (AT&T) monopoly on the U.S. telephone system came to an end. The local operating companies were spun off, leaving AT&T with long-distance service, the research and development facilities (Bell Labs), and the manufacturing arm (Western Electric). At the same time the breakup heralded the beginning of a highly competitive environment for the firm and the need for cultural change.

Enter the Competition. A number of long-distance competitors, including MCI, Sprint, and Allnet, were in the field, or ready to enter in the near future, thus challenging AT&T's dominance. Moreover, the government required AT&T to sell these competitors long-distance hookups that allowed them, in turn, to resell the service at a lower rate than AT&T. (This rate differential is scheduled to continue until around 1990.) If AT&T was to survive, it would have to change its culture. In the past its research and development experts and manufacturing people invented and manufactured telephone equipment at a leisurely pace. Now, new inventions would have to get to the market faster than ever or AT&T would find competitors already offering them. AT&T also had to become more marketing-oriented, able to persuade customers to buy their goods and services over those of the growing competition.

Changes in the AT&T Culture. Over the last five years AT&T has made a number of dramatic changes in its culture. First, the firm has cut back the number of employees. In 1986 alone it cut 32,000 jobs, including 11,600 management positions.[26] Gone are the days when the company guaranteed lifetime employment to its people. Second, marketing has been greatly strengthened. A massive national advertising program has been used to encourage customers to choose AT&T over the discount long-distance competitors. The company has also started offering attractive discounts to customers who do a lot of long-distance calling. Promotional efforts have also been undertaken in the form of financial incentives for those who use AT&T long-distance service. Third, the firm has diversified by entering the computer field and now offers a personal computer that is competitive with IBM, Apple, and others in this market.

The biggest challenge for AT&T has been to change its culture to a marketing-oriented one. When deregulation occurred, virtually none of the longtime employees were marketing-oriented. They had been working in a culture that put major emphasis on research and development and manufacturing. They were unprepared for the challenges that they were hit with when deregulation created a highly competitive environment. Commenting on the situation that existed when the firm was first deregulated, a *Business Week* report noted:

> . . . Some critics charge that senior management is the biggest obstacle to change. "The dilemma the company faces is having to move fast and having a group of

executives who have not grown up with the skills they need," says a consultant who has worked with AT&T since the 1970s.

For most of AT&T's 107-year history managers were modeled to excel in a regulated, monopolistic environment. The company's mission was simple: to provide the highest-quality, end-to-end universal telephone service at the lowest possible price. This gave rise to a hierarchical, functional organization dominated by engineers. And it attracted to its management ranks many who had a high sense of mission and who needed a structured environment and security.[27]

AT&T's Adjustment.   Today AT&T continues to adjust its culture. The long-distance market that was beginning to slip away to the competition is being recaptured. The company's telephone marketing efforts are in full swing and its strategy for capturing a share of the computer market continues to be implemented. Only time will tell how successful the firm will be in this latter area, but the telephone business strategy appears to be paying off as the company continues to make the transition from an R&D/production-oriented culture to a marketing-oriented culture.[28]

Summary

Organizational culture is a pattern of basic assumptions that are taught to new personnel as the correct way to perceive, think, and act on a day-to-day basis. Some of the important characteristics of organizational culture include observed behavioral regularities, norms, dominant values, philosophy, rules, and organizational climate.

While everyone in an organization will share the organization's culture, they may not do so to the same degree. There can be a dominant culture, but a number of subcultures. A dominant culture is a set of core values that is shared by a majority of the organization's members. A subculture is a set of values shared by a small percentage of the organization's members.

Some organizations have strong cultures; others have weak cultures. The strength of the culture will depend on sharedness and intensity. Sharedness is the degree to which the organizational members have the same core values. Intensity is the degree of commitment of the organizational members to the core values.

A culture typically is created by a founder or top-level manager who forms a core group that shares a common vision. This group acts in concert to create the cultural values, norms, and climate necessary to carry on this vision. In maintaining this culture, enterprises typically carry out several steps such as the following: careful selection of entry-level candidates; on-the-job experiences to familiarize the personnel with the organization's culture; mastery of one's job; meticulous attention to measuring operational results and to rewarding individual performance; careful adherence to the organization's most important values; a reinforcing of organizational stories and folklore; and, finally, recognition and promotion of individuals who have done their jobs well and who can serve as role models to new personnel in the organization.

In some cases organizations find that they must change their culture in order to remain competitive and even survive in their environment. One of the most common changes occurring in recent years is a trend toward Theory Z and Japanese management approaches. However, in some cases, including Japanese firms themselves, there is actually a trend in the other direction, with lifetime employment and decision making by consensus being eliminated or reduced. At the present time there are many examples of organizational cultures that are undergoing dramatic change. GM/EDS and AT&T are two real-world examples.

Questions for Discussion and Review

1. What is meant by the term *organizational culture*? Define it and give some examples of its characteristics.
2. There are several important characteristics of organizational culture identified in the chapter. What are these? Describe each.
3. How does a dominant culture differ from a subculture? In your answer be sure to define both terms.
4. How do strong cultures differ from weak cultures? What two factors determine the strength of the culture?
5. In what way do risk taking and feedback help create basic types of organizational culture profiles? Explain, being sure to include a discussion of these profiles in your answer.
6. How do organizational cultures develop? What four steps commonly occur?
7. How do organizations go about maintaining their cultures? What steps are involved? Describe them.
8. Why are some firms turning to a Theory Z approach to help them in modifying their organizational culture? What benefit does this approach offer? Is it best for all American firms?
9. Why is it difficult for firms like General Motors and Electronic Data Systems to merge? How can their organizational cultures prove to be a roadblock?

References

1. Nancy C. Morey and Fred Luthans, "Anthropology: The Forgotten Behavioral Science in Management History," *Best Paper Proceedings of the Academy of Management,* 1987, pp. 128–132.
2. Geert Hofstede, "Editorial: The Usefulness of the 'Organizational Culture' Concept," *Journal of Management Studies,* May 1986, p. 22.
3. Edgar H. Schein, *Organizational Culture and Leadership,* Jossey-Bass, San Francisco, 1985, p. 9.
4. Mats Alvesson, "Organizations, Culture, and Ideology," *International Studies of Management and Organization,* vol. 17, 1987, pp. 4–18.
5. Nancy C. Morey and Fred Luthans, "Refining the Displacement of Culture and the Use of Scenes and Themes in Organizational Studies," *Academy of Management Review,* April 1985, p. 221.
6. Terence E. Deal and Allan A. Kennedy, *Corporate Cultures: The Rites and Rituals of Corporate Life,* Addison-Wesley, Reading, Mass., 1982.

7. For more on this topic see Edgar H. Schein, "Coming to a New Awareness of Organizational Culture," *Sloan Management Review*, Winter 1984, pp. 3–16.
8. Katherine M. Hafner and Geoff Lewis, "Apple's Comeback," *Business Week*, Jan. 19, 1987, pp. 84–89.
9. Schein, *Organizational Culture and Leadership*, op. cit., p. 210.
10. Robert Johnson, "McDonald's Combines a Dead Man's Advice with Lively Strategy," *The Wall Street Journal*, Dec. 18, 1987, p. 1.
11. Todd Mason and Marc Frons, "Sam Walton of Wal-Mart, Just Your Basic Homespun Billionaire," *Business Week*, Oct. 14, 1985, pp. 142–147.
12. This process is described in Richard Pascale, "The Paradox of 'Corporate Culture': Reconciling Ourselves to Socialization," *California Management Review*, Winter 1985, pp. 29–38.
13. Ibid., p. 31.
14. Ibid., p. 32.
15. Ibid., p. 32.
16. For more on this process see Richard Pascale, "Fitting New Employees into the Company Culture," *Fortune*, May 18, 1984, pp. 28–43.
17. Warren Gross and Shula Shichman, "How to Grow an Organization Culture," *Personnel*, September 1987, p. 52.
18. Alan L. Wilkins and Nigel J. Bristow, "For Successful Organization Culture, Honor Your Past," *Academy of Management Executive*, August 1987, pp. 221–228.
19. Thomas M. Rohan, "P&G Fights Back," *Industry Week*, Oct. 15, 1984, pp. 65–66.
20. Jolie B. Solomon and John Bussey, "Pressed by Its Rivals, Procter & Gamble Co. Is Altering Its Ways," *The Wall Street Journal*, May 20, 1985, p. 22.
21. Charles W. Joiner, Jr., "SMR Forum: Making the 'Z' Concept Work," *Sloan Management Review*, Spring 1985, pp. 57–63.
22. William G. Ouchi, *Theory Z*, Avon, New York, 1981.
23. Richard L. Daft, *Management*, Dryden Press, Chicago, 1988, pp. 505. Also see Art Gemmell, "Fujitsu's Cross-Cultural Style," *Management Review*, June 1986, pp. 7–8.
24. Kenichi Ohmae, "Japan's Role in the World Economy," *California Management Review*, Spring 1987, p. 54.
25. S. Prakash Sethi, Nobuaki Namiki, and Carl L. Swanson, "The Decline of the Japanese System of Management," *California Management Review*, Summer 1984, p. 43.
26. "Rebuilding to Survive," *Time*, Feb. 2, 1987, p. 44.
27. "Culture Shock Is Shaking the Bell System," *Business Week*, Sept. 26, 1983, pp. 113–114.
28. For more on this topic, see Monica Langley, "AT&T Marketing Men Find Their Star Fails to Ascend as Expected," *The Wall Street Journal*, Feb. 13, 1984, pp. 1, 16.

**REAL CASE:
A Case of
Culture Shock***

For the past five years the country's major television networks—ABC, NBC, and CBS—have been undergoing a form of culture shock. The old ways of doing things are giving way to new approaches, and, in the process, those personnel who are fortunate enough to still have their jobs are being forced to accept a new set of core values or leave the organization.

*Source: Adapted from Thomas Moore, "Culture Shock Rattles the TV Networks," *Fortune*, Apr. 14, 1986, pp. 22–27.

For years the fortunes of the networks had been moving in only one direction: up. However, in the mid-1980s, revenues began to flatten out and the networks suddenly realized that the days of carefree spending were coming to an end. At the same time, two of the networks—ABC and NBC—acquired new owners. Capital Cities purchased ABC and General Electric bought RCA, the parent of NBC. CBS was not acquired by anyone, but in the process of fending off an unfriendly takeover attempt by Ted Turner, the company wound up tripling its debt.

Capital Cities, known for its careful control of finances, began to tighten expenditures at ABC. At the same time, a number of key managers voluntarily left, including the head of the network under the old management, the general counsel, the president of ABC Radio, the head of daytime programming, and the second-in-command at ABC Sports. The new management team made cuts of its own, eliminating two-thirds of the corporate communications department. New management also let it be known that the large sums that ABC was traditionally accustomed to spending to buy the rights to NFL football, the Olympic Games, and other sporting events would have to be trimmed back. The days of the open checkbook were over.

Meanwhile, over at NBC, the personnel felt they might be left alone because theirs was the most profitable of the three networks. However, given the fact that NBC represented but a small percentage of GE's overall profit, outsiders viewed this as wishful thinking. GE instructed NBC to begin sticking with new TV series that were only marginally successful, reasoning that it was cheaper to hold on than to cancel and pay the costs of getting a replacement. So there certainly was concern with improving the bottom line.

CBS began reducing its personnel. Additionally, the company president was ousted and Lawrence Tisch, the largest stockholder, was given the position. At the same time the company began sending out fewer news teams to cover stories and cutting back on its previously sky-high sports contracts. CBS also sold off its publishing division, and financial controls began to be established everywhere.

It seems that business at the networks is going to be a lot different than it was a few years ago. The new management teams are much more financially conservative and profit-oriented than were their predecessors.

1. Using Table 3-2 in this chapter, how would you describe the culture of the TV networks in 1985? How would you describe them after the changes? Explain.
2. In what way are the cultures of the networks changing under their new management teams? What is different?
3. If the current changes continue, what types of people are likely to be working at the networks in the 1990s? How would these people be different from their predecessors?

CASE: Out with the Old, In with the New

The Anderson Corporation was started in 1962 as a small consumer products company. During the first twenty years the company's research and development (R&D) staff developed a series of new products that proved to be very popular in the marketplace. Things went so well that the company had to add a second production shift just to keep up with the demand. During this time period the firm expanded its plant on three different occasions. During an interview with a national magazine, the firm's founder, Paul Anderson, said, "We don't sell our products. We allocate them." This comment was in reference to the fact that the firm had only twenty-four salespeople and was able to garner annual revenues in excess of $62 million.

Three years ago Anderson suffered its first financial setback. The company had a net operating loss of $1.2 million. Two years ago the loss was $2.8 million, and last year it was $4.7 million. The accountant estimates that this year the firm will lose approximately $10 million.

Alarmed by this information, Citizen's Bank, the company's largest creditor, insisted that the firm make some changes and start turning things around. In response to this request, Paul Anderson agreed to step aside. The board of directors replaced him with Bill Hartmann, head of the marketing division of one of the country's largest consumer products firms.

After making an analysis of the situation, Bill has come to the conclusion that there are a number of changes that must be made if the firm is to be turned around. The three most important are:

1. More attention must be given to the marketing side of the business. The most vital factor for success in the sale of the consumer goods produced by Anderson is an effective sales force.
2. There must be an improvement in product quality. Two percent of Anderson's output is defective as against ½ of 1 percent for the average firm in the industry. In the past the demand for Anderson's output was so great that quality control was not an important factor. Now it is proving to be a very costly area.
3. There must be reduction in the number of people in the operation. Anderson can get by with two-thirds of its current production personnel and only half of its administrative staff.

Bill has not shared these ideas with the board of directors, but he intends to do so. For the moment he is considering the steps that will have to be taken in making these changes and the effect that all of this might have on the employees and the overall operation.

1. What is wrong with the old organizational culture? What needs to be done to change it?
2. Why might it be difficult for Bill to change the existing culture?
3. What specific steps does Bill need to take in changing the culture? Identify and describe at least two.

**CASE:
Keeping
Things
the Same**

Metropolitan Hospital was built two years ago and currently has a work force of 235 people. The hospital is small, but because it is new, it is extremely efficient. The board has voted to increase its capacity from 60 beds to 190 beds. By this time next year the hospital will be over three times as large as it is now in terms of both beds and personnel.

The administrator, Clara Hawkins, feels that the major problem with this proposed increase is that the hospital will lose its efficiency. "I want to hire people who are just like our current team of personnel—hard-working, dedicated, talented, and able to interact well with patients. If we triple the number of employees, I don't see how it will be possible to maintain our quality patient care. We are going to lose our family atmosphere. We will be inundated with mediocrity and we'll end up being like every other institution in the local area—large and uncaring!' "

The chairman of the board is also concerned about the effect of hiring such a large number of employees. However, he believes that Clara is overreacting. "It can't be that hard to find people who are like our current staff. There must be a lot of people out there who are just as good. What you need to do is develop a plan of action that will allow you to carefully screen those who will fit into your current organizational culture and those who will not. It's not going to be as difficult as you believe. Trust me. Everything will work out just fine."

As a result of the chairman's comments, Clara has decided that the most effective way of dealing with the situation is to develop a plan of action. She intends to meet with her administrative group and determine the best way of screening incoming candidates and then helping those who are hired to become socialized in terms of the hospital's culture. Clara has called a meeting for the day after tomorrow. At that time she intends to discuss her ideas, get suggestions from her people, and then formulate a plan of action. "We've come too far to lose it all now," she told her administrative staff assistant. "If we keep our wits about us, I think we can continue to keep Metropolitan as the showcase hospital in this region."

1. What can Clara and her staff do to select the type of entry-level candidates they want? Explain.
2. How can Clara ensure that those who are hired come to accept the core cultural values of the hospital? What steps would you recommend?
3. Could Clara use this same approach if another 200 people were hired a few years from now?

[4] The International Context for Organizational Behavior

Cinderella's Castle can be seen in the background as the Dumbo the Elephant ride whirls children high above the crowd. At the same time Mickey Mouse is leading a giant parade down Main Street, and Snow White and the dwarfs are riding on one of the floats, waving at the cheering crowd. Sounds like a typical day at Disneyland. It is! However, this is not Disneyland in Anaheim, California, but Disneyland in Tokyo, Japan. The Tokyo Disneyland attracts approximately 11 million guests a year and has a gross income of more than $500 million.

How can such an American theme park like this be successful in Japan? After all, doesn't business have to cater to local tastes and culture in order to be successful? This was a question that the Japanese park's planners considered long and hard. They finally decided that the best decision was to reproduce the park just the way it is in Disneyland and Disney World in the United States. Everything from the design of the trash cans to the placement of drinking fountains is an exact replica. The only change they put in was a roof over Main Street. This was made necessary because of Tokyo's wet weather.

Over the years many nations have asked Disney to build a theme park in their country. The reason Disney chose Japan as its first

*Source: Adapted from "Disneyland Abroad: Today Tokyo, Tomorrow the World," *Business Week*, Mar. 9, 1987, pp. 68–69, and "Disneyland Goes French," *Lincoln Journal-Star*, Mar. 22, 1987.

international site was that the Japanese understand what Disney is all about. For years the company has been successfully selling its films, books, and consumer products in the Japanese market. Sometimes the emperor himself wears a Mickey Mouse watch. Quite obviously Disney was not going to have to explain Mickey Mouse or the Magic Kingdom to Japanese children. Also, Disney Enterprises did not have to put out a dime to build the park. This was done through a joint venture of two Japanese firms that spent $750 million to recreate Disneyland. Meanwhile, Disney receives royalties of 10 percent on admissions and 5 percent on sales, and advises the joint venture on how to operate efficiently.

The success of the Tokyo venture has prompted Disney to open a European version. The site will be 4500 acres near Paris and is scheduled to open in 1992 at a cost of $2 billion. Disney hopes to do as well in Paris as it has in Tokyo. Although some French people have raised objections that it will cheapen their culture, a recent poll indicated that 85 percent gave their approval. The Disneyland theme is understood by people throughout the world. It offers entertainment on an international scale. Children in Paris will love Mickey Mouse just as much as kids in Anaheim, Orlando, and Tokyo do. All over the world the name Mickey Mouse has the same meaning for them. Unlike many areas of business, Mickey transcends national boundaries and culture.

Learning Objectives

- EXAMINE the role and impact that different cultures have on organizational behavior.
- PRESENT the research on organizational behavior across cultures.
- DISCUSS the international implications of interpersonal communication.
- ANALYZE the international implications of employee motivation.
- EXPLAIN the international implications of managerial leadership.

Just as American businesses such as Disney have ignored the international context except in recent years, so has the field of organizational behavior. For example, no organizational behavior textbooks to date even include an international chapter such as this one. However, just as it is becoming increasing clear that the world is shrinking and America is part of the global economy, requiring new strategies,[1] it is becoming increasingly recognized that the international dimensions of organizational behavior are important. American employees definitely think and behave in a particular way. Many people around the world think and act similarly, but there are also some important differences. Differences even exist in the way knowledge is accumulated. For example, it has been pointed out that European behavioral scientists tend to be more cognitive and/

or psychoanalytically based while their American counterparts are more behavioristic and/or humanistically oriented.[2] In understanding and applying organizational behavior concepts in other countries around the world, it is important to be aware of these differences.

For example, in some countries managers prefer to use—and may be more effective with—an autocratic leadership style than in the typical U.S. organization. Germany is a visible example. Typical American managers who are transferred to Germany may find their leadership style to be too participative. German subordinates may expect the American to make more decisions and to consult with them less. Similarly, an American manager in Japan who decides to set up a performance-based incentive system that gives a weekly bonus to the best worker in each work group may be making a mistake. Japanese workers do not like to be singled out for individual attention and go against the group's norms and values. Perhaps this impact of differences across cultures was best stated by the cofounder of Honda Motor, T. Fujisawa, when he stated: "Japanese and American management is 95 percent the same, and differs in all important respects."[3]

This chapter examines organizational behavior from an international perspective and within an international context. It starts by using the last chapter on organizational culture as a point of departure for examining the impact that different cultures can have on organizational behavior. This gives attention both to how cultures vary and how the behaviors within these cultures can differ. The remainder of the chapter analyzes the familiar organizational behavior topics of communication, motivation, and leadership, only in an international context. Although separate chapters will be devoted to each of these areas, it is important to establish the international perspective at the very beginning of the book. The later chapters give details on these topics. Also, an international flavor is given by the International Application Examples throughout.

The Impact of Culture on International Organizational Behavior

Although the last chapter dealt specifically with *organizational* culture, which is somewhat narrower, culture per se was defined in Chapter 2 as the acquired knowledge that people use to interpret experience and generate social behavior. It is important to recognize that culture is learned and helps people in their efforts to interact and communicate with others in the society. When placed in a culture where values and beliefs are different, some people have a great deal of difficulty adjusting. This is particularly true when American businesspeople are assigned to a foreign country. They quickly learn that the values of American culture are often quite different from those of their host country. As noted by Robbins, "there is a growing body of evidence to indicate that national cultures differ widely and the result is marked differences in behavior patterns worldwide."[4]

How Do Cultures Vary?

There are several basic dimensions that differentiate cultures. The following sections examine the most important of these.

How People See Themselves.

In some countries of the world, people are viewed as basically honest and trustworthy. In others, people are regarded with suspicion and distrust. For example, a reason why the Soviet Union regards the United States with suspicion and distrust may result from the way the Russian people view themselves. They assume others are like them, that is, prepared to cut corners if they can get away with it. On the other hand, the people of many Third World countries are just the opposite. They do not lock their doors; they are very trusting and assume that no one will break in. It is forbidden to take the property of another person, and the people adhere strictly to that cultural value. In the United States, people have a mixed view of other people. Most Americans still view others as basically honest but also believe that it is important to be alert for any sign of trouble.

When people travel outside their home country, they carry their values with them just like their baggage. This sometimes results in their being surprised over the way they are treated. The following is an example:

> A young Canadian in Sweden found summer employment working in a restaurant owned by Yugoslavians. As the Canadian explained, "I arrived at the restaurant and was greeted by an effusive Yugoslavian man who set me to work at once washing dishes and preparing the restaurant for the June opening.
>
> "At the end of the first day, I was brought to the back room. The owner took an old cash box out of a large desk. The Yugoslavian owner counted out my wages for the day and was about to return the box to the desk when the phone rang in the front room. The owner hesitated: should he leave me sitting in the room with the money or take it with him? Quite simply, could he trust me?
>
> "After a moment, the man got up to answer the phone, leaving me with the open money box. I sat there in amazement; how could he trust me, someone he had known for less than a day, a person whose last name and address he didn't even know."[5]

People's Relationship to Their World.

In some societies people attempt to dominate their environment. In other societies they try to live in harmony with it or are subjugated by it. The Americans and Canadians, for example, attempt to dominate their environment. In agriculture they use fertilizers and insecticides to increase crop yields. Other societies, especially those in the Far East, work in harmony with the environment by planting crops in the right places and at the right time. In still other societies, most notably Third World countries, no action is taken regarding the subjugation of nature, so, for example, when the floods come, there are no dams or irrigation systems for dealing with the impending disaster.

Individualism versus Collectivism. Some countries of the world encourage individualism. The United States, Great Britain, and Canada are examples. In other countries collectivism, or group orientation, is important. Japan, China, and the Israeli kibbutzim emphasize group harmony, unity, commitment, and loyalty. The differences reflect themselves in many ways such as in hiring practices. In countries where individualism is important, job applicants are evaluated on the basis of personal, educational, and professional achievements. In group-oriented societies applicants are evaluated on the basis of trustworthiness, loyalty, and compatibility with coworkers.

The Time Dimension. In some societies people are oriented toward the past. In others they tend to be more focused on the present. Still others are futuristic in their orientation. Americans and Canadians are most interested in the present and the near future. Businesspeople in these countries are particularly interested in where their companies are today and where they will be in five to ten years. People who are hired and do not work out are often let go in short order. They seldom last more than one or two years. Most Europeans place more importance on the past than do North Americans. They believe in preserving history and continuing past traditions. They are concerned with the past, present, and future. Many Far Eastern countries are futuristic in their approach. The Japanese, for example, have very long-term future-oriented time horizons. When large Japanese firms hire employees, they often retain them for a long time, even for life. The firms will spend a great deal of money to train them, and there is a strong, mutual commitment on both sides. Recently, researchers have even developed ways to measure the time dimensions of organizational members.[6] Scales include those measuring punctuality, allocation, awareness, schedules and deadlines, work pace, and future orientation.

Public and Private Space. Some cultures promote the use of public space; others favor private space. For example, in Japan bosses often sit together with their employees in the same large room. The heads of some of the biggest Japanese firms may leave their chauffeur-driven limousines at home and ride the crowded public subways to work in the morning so they can be with their workers. In the Middle East there are often many people present during important meetings. These cultures have a public orientation. In contrast, North Americans prefer private space. The more restricted or confined a manager is, the more important the individual is assumed to be. Anyone coming to see the person must first go past a secretary (and sometimes more than one) before being admitted to the manager's presence.

When comparing societies in terms of the dimensions discussed above, it becomes obvious that there are major differences between the ways in which business is done in one corner of the world and another. Table 4.1, for example, provides a summary comparative analysis of U.S. and Japanese management in terms of some major business-related areas.

TABLE 4.1 Major Concepts in the Comparative Analysis of U.S. and Japanese Management

Expressions Commonly Used in Management	Principle Meanings, Interpretations, and Images	
	In United States	In Japan
Company	Team in sport	Family in village
Business goal	To win	To survive
Employees	Players in a team	Children in a family
Human relations	Functional	Emotional
Competition	Cut-throat	Cooperation or sin
Profit motivation	By all means	Means to an end
Sense of identification	Job pride	Group prestige
Work motivation	Individual income	Group atmosphere
Production	Productivity	Training and diligence
Personnel	Efficiency	Maintenance
Promotion	According to abilities	According to year of service
Pay	Service and results	Considered an award for patience and sacrifice

Source: Adapted from Motofusa Murayama, "A Comparative Analysis of U.S. and Japanese Management Systems," in Sang M. Lee and Gary Schwendiman (eds.), *Management by Japanese Systems,* Praeger, a division of Greenwood Press, Inc., New York, 1982, p. 237. Copyright © 1982 by Praeger Publishers. Used with permission.

Behavior across Cultures

Just as there are many ways that culture per se varies, there are also many ways in which behavior varies across cultures. Tables 4.2 and 4.3 provide insights into the degree to which managers agree (or disagree) regarding the value of a hierarchical structure and the necessity of bypassing that structure in getting things done. Table 4.4 shows how important management feels it is to have a precise answer to subordinate questions about work-related activities. Quite obviously, the way managers function and behave appears to be influenced by their culture.

TABLE 4.2 The Main Reason for a Hierarchical Structure Is so that Everybody Knows Who Has Authority over Whom

	Agreement Rate across Countries to the Above Statement (Least to Greatest)
United States	18%
Germany	24
Great Britain	38
Netherlands	38
France	45
Italy	50
Japan	52
Indonesia	86

Source: Adapted from Andre Laurent, "The Cultural Diversity of Western Conceptions of Management," *International Studies of Management and Organization,* Spring–Summer 1983, p. 82. Used with permission.

TABLE 4.3 In Order to Have Efficient Work Relationships, It Is Often Necessary to Bypass the Hierarchical Line

	Disagreement Rate across Countries to the Above Statement (Least to Greatest)
Sweden	22%
Great Britain	31
United States	32
Netherlands	39
France	42
Germany	46
Italy	75

Source: Adapted from Andre Laurent, "The Cultural Diversity of Western Conceptions of Management," *International Studies of Management and Organization,* Spring–Summer 1983, p. 86. Used with permission.

Dimensions of Cultural Difference

One way of examining organizational behavior across cultures and explaining the differences that exist is to look at important dimensions such as those identified by Geert Hofstede, a well-known Dutch researcher. In a huge study involving over 100,000 respondents, he found highly significant differences in the behavior and attitudes of employees and managers from different countries who worked for a major American multinational corporation.[7] Two of these differences were in individualism/collectivism and in power distance. The following sections take a close look at these and other cultural differences important to organizational behavior.

Individualism/Collectivism and Power Distance. Individualism is the tendency to take care of oneself and one's immediate family. Collectivism is characterized by a tight social framework in which people distinguish between their own group and other groups. Power distance is the extent to which less powerful members of organizations accept the unequal distribution of power,

TABLE 4.4 It Is Important for a Manager to Have At Hand Precise Answers to Most of the Questions That His Subordinates May Raise about Their Work

	Agreement Rate across Countries to the Above Statement (Least to Greatest)
Sweden	10%
Netherlands	17
United States	18
Great Britain	27
Germany	46
France	53
Italy	66
Indonesia	73
Japan	78

Source: Based on Andre Laurent, "The Cultural Diversity of Western Conceptions of Management," *International Studies of Management and Organization,* Spring–Summer 1983, p. 86. Used with permission.

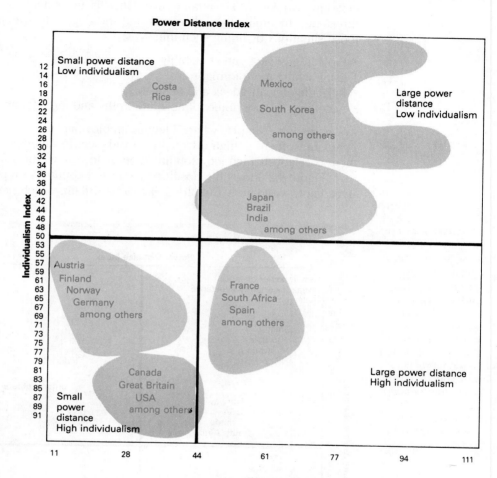

Power Distance Index

Small power distance
Low individualism

Costa
Rica

Mexico

South Korea

among others

Large power
distance
Low individualism

Japan
Brazil
India
among others

Austria
Finland
Norway
Germany
among others

France
South Africa
Spain
among others

Canada
Great Britain
USA
among others

Small
power
distance
High individualism

Large power distance
High individualism

Individualism Index

FIGURE 4.1 The position of selected countries on power distance and individualism.
(*Source:* Adapted from Geert Hofstede, "The Cultural Relativity of Organizational Practices and Theories," *Journal of International Business Studies,* Fall 1983, p. 82. Used with permission.)

i.e., the degree to which employees accept that their boss has more power than they do.

When Hofstede examined managers from fifty countries in terms of individualism and power distance, he found four basic clusters. Figure 4.1 shows that the United States has high individualism and small power distance (employees do not grant their boss much power). This is in contrast, for example, to Mexico, which has high collectivism (tight group) and large power distance (a lot of power granted to the boss). Countries that are in the same circled-in area tend to be similar in terms of individualism/collectivism and power distance. Figure 4.1 illustrates that American multinational firms doing business in Mexico would encounter much greater cultural differences than they would in France and still less if they operated in Great Britain.

Uncertainty Avoidance.

Another dimension of cultural difference is uncertainty avoidance. Uncertainty avoidance is the extent to which people feel threatened by ambiguous situations and the degree to which they try to avoid these situations by doing such things as:

- Providing greater career stability
- Establishing more formal rules
- Rejecting deviant ideas and behavior
- Accepting the possibility of absolute truths and the attainment of expertise[8]

In Japan, for example, where lifetime employment exists at least in the large companies, there is high uncertainty avoidance. In America, by contrast, where there is relatively high job mobility, there is low uncertainty avoidance.

Figure 4.2 shows the position of selected countries on power distance and uncertainty avoidance. Countries like Great Britain, which has weak uncertainty

FIGURE 4.2 The position of selected countries on power distance and uncertainty avoidance. (*Source:* Adapted from Geert Hofstede, "The Cultural Relativity of Organizational Practices and Theories," *Journal of International Business Studies,* Fall 1983, p. 84. Used with permission.)

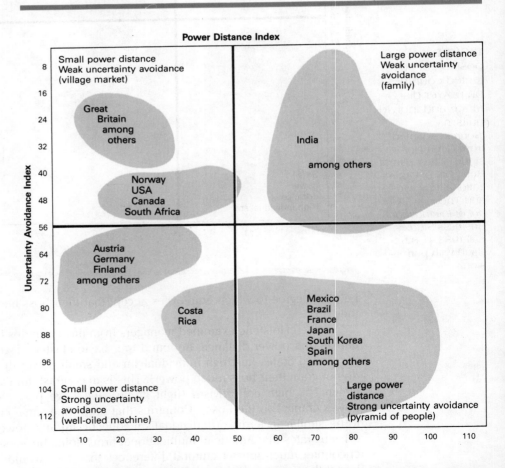

avoidance and low power distance, tend to have less hierarchy and more interaction between people. Additionally, risk taking is both expected and encouraged. Employees in high power distance and low uncertainty avoidance cultures such as India tend to think of their organizations as traditional families. Employees in countries such as Mexico and Brazil tend to think of their organizations as pyramids of people rather than as families. Employees in countries such as Austria and Finland tend to work in organizations that are highly predictable without needing a strong hierarchy. Roles and procedures are clearly defined in these cultures.

Masculinity/Femininity.   Hofstede also measured the impact of masculinity/femininity. Masculinity is the extent to which the dominant values of a society emphasize assertiveness and the acquisition of money and other material things. Femininity is the extent to which the dominant values in a society emphasize relationships among people, concern for others, and interest in quality of work life. As shown in Figure 4.3, in masculine societies such as Japan the work focus in auto factories is on efficiency. In feminine societies such as Scandinavian countries like Norway the work focus in factories is on quality of work life. This is shown in Figure 4.3.

Overall Categories for Employee Attitudes Worldwide.   Figures 4.1, 4.2, and 4.3 show how countries tend to cluster on the basis of particular cultural differences. On an overall employee attitude basis, one comprehensive analysis using eight empirical studies concluded that there are eight basic clusters in which most countries of the world can be placed. This is shown in Figure 4.4. Those which do not fit into one of these clusters include Brazil, Japan, India, and Israel. These countries appear in different clusters in different studies so, at least for the time being, more research will have to be conducted before they can be assigned to any specific cluster.[9]

As one would guess, the general attitudes of U.S. employees (work goals, values, needs, and job attitudes) are most culturally similar to those of employees in other "Anglo" countries—Canada, Australia, New Zealand, United Kingdom, Ireland, and South Africa. When American managers are dealing with employees from other clusters—Germanic, Nordic, Near Eastern, Arab, Far Eastern, Latin American, or Independent—they must recognize there will be differences. The theories and application techniques of organizational behavior discussed in the American literature will probably be relevant in the Anglo countries. It remains to be seen if the American version of organizational behavior thought is directly applicable to the other clusters.

Over time, other countries, especially Japan and Korea, may move closer to the Anglo cluster. There is already considerable evidence that this is happening. The following story told by a Japanese management expert when he recently went to a nearly empty barber shop in downtown Tokyo on a Saturday afternoon is very revealing about the changing attitudes of Japanese workers:

"Not many customers today, are there?" I said, relieved that I did not have to wait.

"That's right. Lately, business has been off Saturdays."

"When are you busiest?"

"Well, these days, around eleven, then around two or three in the afternoon on weekdays."

"But everyone around here must be working then. You mean during working hours?" I asked in disbelief.

"That's right. People these days don't want to spend their *own time* on things like haircuts."

"And in the past?"

"Well, a decade ago, we'd be busiest during the luncheon break and after five o'clock. Customers would rush to finish in less than 40 minutes."[10]

The recent widespread violent strikes in Korea, where workers are demanding their share of the economic gains, also are indicative of shifting attitudes and values in that fast-developing country.

FIGURE 4.3 The position of selected countries on uncertainty avoidance and masculinity/femininity.
(*Source:* Adapted from Geert Hofstede, "The Cultural Relativity of Organizational Practices and Theories," *Journal of International Business Studies*, Fall 1983, p. 86. Used with permission.)

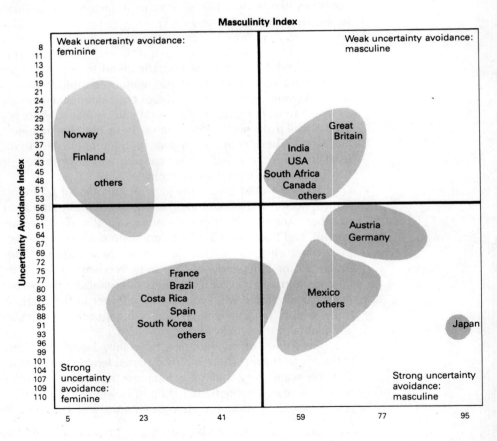

FIGURE 4.4
Country clusters based on employee attitude. (*Source:* Simcha Ronen and Oded Shenkar, "Clustering Countries on Attitudinal Dimensions: A Review and Synthesis," *Academy of Management Review,* July 1985, p. 449. Used with permission.)

The rest of the chapter will examine if the cross-cultural similarities and differences do or will have an impact on the generally recognized organizational behavior areas of communication, motivation, and leadership.

Communication in an International Environment

Although Chapter 17 discusses all dimensions of communication, it can be used here to demonstrate the impact of the international context. For example, the people at the home office of a multinational corporation (MNC) and the nationals in the foreign branch or subsidiary may not have the same meanings for the same words. An example is that Japanese managers will rarely come out with a direct "no" to another's request. A way they avoid saying "no" is to say "yes" and then follow the affirmative answer with a detailed explanation which in effect means "no".[11] The following sections examine some of the breakdowns and ways to improve communication across cultures.

Communication Breakdown across Cultures

There are a number of contributing factors leading to communication breakdown across cultures. Perhaps the best way to get at the root causes of this breakdown is through the concepts of perception, stereotyping, and ethnocentrism.

Perceptual Problems.   Chapter 6 is specifically devoted to perception. For now, however, perception can be simply defined as a person's interpretation of reality. Perceptions are learned. People are taught to "see" things in a given way. For example, when an American manager sees the wife of his Latin American host enter the door of the kitchen, he assumes that the woman is putting the finishing touches on the meal. Unknown to him perhaps is the fact that the woman is actually supervising the cooking of the food and is checking to see that everything is in order. If the American were to tell his host's wife, "You're a terrific cook," his comments probably would be greeted with a smile because the hosts would realize he did not mean to be rude. However, a fellow Latin guest would never say this to the wife for it would imply that his hosts were too poor to afford a cook.

Stereotyping Problems.   Another barrier to communication is stereotyping, also covered in Chapter 6, which is the tendency to perceive another person as belonging to a single class or category. Stereotyping is a very simple, widely used way of constructing an assumed overall profile of other people. For example, ask Americans which people try to "keep a stiff upper lip during trying times" and the most common answer is the British. Ask Americans what country of the world is famous for its auto engineering and the most common answer is Germany. Whether or not these are accurate stereotypes is immaterial. Most Americans believe them. Similarly, foreigners have their own stereotyped views of Americans. Table 4.5 provides some examples. Note from the table that Americans are regarded as energetic and industrious by most nations and none of these countries stereotype Americans as being lazy.

Ethnocentric Problems.   Ethnocentrism refers to the sense of superiority that members of a particular culture have. The Soviet Union, for example, claims that Americans believe they are the best in everything regardless of what area is under discussion. To the extent that this is true, it is an example of ethnocentrism in action. All societies promote ethnocentrism through their value structures and nationalistic spirit. People are taught the "right" way to do things, and, at least for them, it is regarded as the "best" way as well. When interacting with people on an international basis, ethnocentrism can cause communication problems. Here is an example:

> U.S. executives who consider English to be the "best" or the "most logical" language will not apply themselves to learn a foreign language which they consider "inferior"

TABLE 4.5 How Americans Are Seen by People of Other Countries

Characteristics Most Often Associated with Americans by the People of:		
France	**Japan**	**West Germany**
Industrious	Nationalistic	Energetic
Energetic	Friendly	Inventive
Inventive	Decisive	Friendly
Decisive	Rude	Sophisticated
Friendly	Self-indulgent	Intelligent

Characteristics Least Often Associated with Americans by the People of:		
France	**Japan**	**West Germany**
Lazy	Industrious	Lazy
Rude	Lazy	Sexy
Honest	Honest	Greedy
Sophisticated	Sexy	Rude

Characteristics Most Often Associated with Americans by the People of:		
Great Britain	**Brazil**	**Mexico**
Friendly	Intelligent	Industrious
Self-indulgent	Inventive	Intelligent
Energetic	Energetic	Inventive
Industrious	Industrious	Decisive
Nationalistic	Greedy	Greedy

Characteristics Least Often Associated with Americans by the People of:		
Great Britain	**Brazil**	**Mexico**
Lazy	Lazy	Lazy
Sophisticated	Self-indulgent	Honest
Sexy	Sexy	Rude
Decisive	Sophisticated	Sexy

Source: Adapted from *Newsweek,* July 11, 1983, p. 50.

or "illogical." And if they consider their nonverbal system to be the most "civilized" system, they will tend to reject other systems as "primitive." In this sense, ethnocentrism can constitute a formidable block to effective empathy and can lead not only to a complete communication breakdown but also to antagonism, or even hostility.[12]

Improving Communication Effectiveness across Cultures

How can people doing business in other countries sensitize themselves to the culture of these nations and avoid making mistakes? One of the most effective ways is by learning about the culture of that country before going there. Some firms have developed "cultural assimilator" training programs. These programmed learning approaches ask the participants to read about a particular situation and then choose one of four courses of action or type of language that they would use. After the participants have made the choice, they then immediately learn if it was right or wrong, along with an explanation. By being put through a couple

TABLE 4.6 Managing Cultural Climate

Behaviors That Help *Build* a Trust Climate	Behaviors That Help *Preclude* a Trust Climate
1. Express your doubts, concerns and feelings in an open, natural way. Encourage your subordinates to do so also.	1. Look on expressions of feelings and doubts as signs of weakness.
2. When subordinates express their doubts, concerns and feelings, accept them supportively and discuss them thoroughly.	2. Be sarcastic, but cleverly so.
3. Set honesty as one standard that will not be compromised. Demand it from yourself and from your staff.	3. Let your subordinates know that you expect them to "stretch the truth" a little if it will make the organization look good.
4. Be clear about our expectations when assigning work or eliciting opinions. Explain your reasons, wherever possible, behind requests and directions.	4. Be secretive. Never let them really be sure what's on your mind. This keeps them on their toes.
5. Encourage subordinates to look to you as a possible resource in accomplishing results, but develop and reinforce independence.	5. Discourage subordinates from coming to you for help. After all, they should be "stemwinders" and "self-starters."
6. When something goes wrong, determine what happened, not "who did it."	6. When something goes wrong, blow up, hit the ceiling, and look for the guilty party.
7. Encourage active support and participation in corrective measures from those involved.	7. Gossip about and disparage others on the staff when they are not present. Overrespond to casual comments by others about your people.
8. Share credit for successes; assume the bulk of responsibility for criticism of your unit.	8. Take credit for successes. Plan vendettas and other ploys to make other organizations look bad. Draw on subordinates for carrying these out. Always insist on plenty of documentation to protect yourself.

Source: Adapted from Philip R. Harris and Robert T. Moran, *Managing Cultural Differences*, 2d ed., Gulf Publishing, Houston, 1987, p. 50.

of hundred situations that they are likely to encounter in the foreign country, they become somewhat sensitized to the culture of that country and are able to communicate more effectively.

A second, and often complementary, approach is tó provide the trainee with educational background material on the country, including social structure, religion, values, language, and history. In particular, these training programs are designed to help managers going to a foreign assignment to create the right climate between themselves and those with whom they will be communicating. Table 4.6 provides an example of some of the behaviors American managers typically are taught to help build a climate of trust with their subordinates in a host country and those behaviors which should be avoided. Recent research indicates that both types of training methods have additive benefits in preparing managers for intercultural work assignments.[13]

Motivation of Personnel across Cultures

Besides communication, another problem in dealing with people from other countries is the tendency to assume that what motivates Americans also motivates foreign nationals. Chapters 9 and 10 are specifically devoted to motivation, but in the international context, the different meanings of work and possible differences in motivation need to be explored.

The Meaning of Work

Traditionally in the United States, work has been generally equated with economic rewards. Although Chapter 9 will point out that people have diverse needs and individual differences, Americans can still be generally characterized as working because they want to earn money with which to buy things. Thus, for many Americans, time on the job is money. This often is reflected in the way they try to get as much done in as little time as possible. Americans also like to have things spelled out so that they know what is expected of them and by when their tasks are to be accomplished. As Chapter 10 will point out, they respond to goals that help improve their performance.

The culturally determined needs help dictate the way Americans behave both at home and abroad. Unfortunately, sometimes these behaviors are not regarded in a positive light. Consider some of the following comments made by people from other countries about how Americans behave.

India. Americans seem to be in a perpetual hurry. Just watch the way they walk down the street. They never allow themselves the leisure to enjoy life; there are too many things to do.

Colombia. The tendency in the United States to think that life is only work hits you in the face. Work seems to be the one type of motivation.

Ethiopia. The American is very explicit; he wants a "yes" or "no." If someone tries to speak figuratively, the American is confused.

Turkey. Once we were out in a rural area in the middle of nowhere and saw an American come to a stop sign. Though he could see in both directions for miles and no traffic was coming, he still stopped![14]

Many Americans still believe in the work ethic. Work is a most dominant and important part of life.[15] Do people in other countries feel the same way? Table 4.7 provides a partial answer to this question. Notice that in all of the countries surveyed, work ranked first in terms of its importance in providing income. In Japan and Germany, income was relatively more important than it was to Americans. However, in countries such as Israel and the Netherlands, income was of slightly less relative importance but work that was basically interesting and satisfying was of relatively more importance. In these countries, it would be a mistake to try to motivate employees with financial incentives alone. In other words, while there are some similarities, there are also some motivational differences between employees across cultures.

Motivational Differences across Cultures

What contributes to the motivational differences across cultures? The roles of religion, the economy, uncertainty avoidance, and power distance provide some insights to this question.

TABLE 4.7 Average Number of Points Assigned to Working Functions by Country Samples

Country	Working Provides You with an Income That Is Needed	Working Is Basically Interesting and Satisfying to You	Working Permits You to Have Interesting Contacts with Other People	Working Gives You Status and Prestige
Japan	45.4	13.4	14.7	5.6
Germany	40.5	16.7	13.1	10.1
Belgium	35.5	21.3	17.3	6.9
United Kingdom	34.4	17.9	15.3	10.9
Yugoslavia	34.1	19.8	9.8	9.3
United States	33.1	16.8	15.3	11.9
Israel	31.1	26.2	11.1	8.5
Netherlands	26.2	23.5	17.9	4.9
All countries combined	35.0*	19.5	14.3	8.5

*The combined totals weigh each country equally, regardless of sample size.
Source: Adapted from MOW International Research Team, *The Meaning of Working: An International Perspective,* Academic Press, London and New York, 1985, and reported in Simcha Ronen, *Comparative and Multinational Management,* Wiley, New York, 1986, p. 144.

The Role of Religion. One answer to motivational differences across cultures may be found in religions and the accompanying values. For instance, some religious values put emphasis on allowing events to develop in their own way. Just let things happen. An example would be the Hindus in India. Most Americans, on the other hand, follow religions that teach them to try to control events. Some religions teach that people are reincarnated and will return; most Americans believe they pass this way only once and they want to get as much done here and now as they can. Some religions teach the importance of caring for others as much as oneself (collectivism); most Americans believe that the best way to help others is to ensure one's own success (individualism). These differing religious values may have an indirect and, in some cases, a direct impact on the motivation of the followers.

One international expert recently noted that the old Protestant ethic, which may no longer be dominant in North American and Western European countries, is alive and well in places such as Seoul, Soweto, and Santiago de Chile. He notes that it is operating in these formerly strong Buddhist and Catholic areas of the world much as it did in North America and Western Europe by inculcating religious values and attitudes that are conducive to success in a high-growth, capitalist economy.[16]

The Role of the Economy. Another factor that may account for motivational differences across cultures is the status of the economy in a country or region of the world and the consequent standard of living. That is, the more wealthy a country, the more likely it is that the people will have similar needs and values to those of other affluent countries. The same is true of Third World,

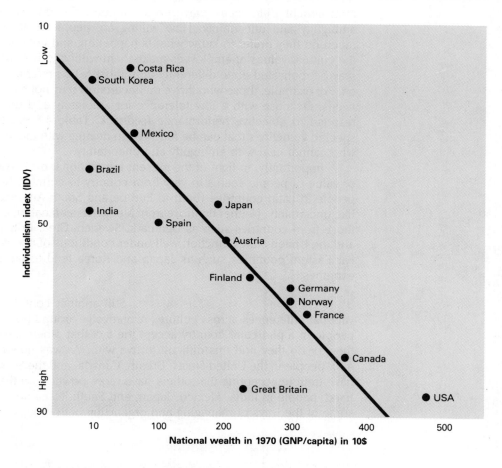

FIGURE 4.5 The relationship between GNP (per capita) and individualism for selected countries. (*Source:* Adapted from Geert Hofstede, "The Cultural Relativity of Organizational Practices and Theories," *Journal of International Business Studies,* Fall 1983, p. 80. Used with permission.)

underdeveloped countries. For example, a worker who did not have enough food for himself and his family would likely find less motivation in added responsibility or a challenging job than in money or job security. Also, countries with a high standard of living put a great deal of emphasis on individualism. Figure 4.5 illustrates this point. Notice that the United States with its high GNP per capita is also highest in individualism. Even Japan, which is in the center of the scatter diagram, is close to the trend line that runs through the figure. This indicates that as Japan's economy continues to grow, its individualism index will rise. In fact, in recent years the Japanese per capita income has approached and even surpassed the American, depending on the value of the dollar. (The wealth of Americans from past economic success remains still much greater.) So, in contrast to the Philippines, for example, Japan may be moving closer to the United States in terms of individualism because of economic reasons.

The Role of Uncertainty Avoidance. Another contributing factor to motivational differences may revolve around the cultural value of avoiding ambiguity and uncertainty. How willing are people to face uncertainty? How much do they prefer to know what is happening and not take too many risks? If the cultural values of employees make them willing to live with uncertainty, they may be motivated quite differently from those who prefer to know what is going on. For example, those who thrive on uncertainty may not have strong job security needs. Or those with a low tolerance for ambiguity and uncertainty may really respond to objective performance feedback. Table 4.8 illustrates a number of specific guidelines that can be followed in dealing with those who can and those who cannot deal with ambiguity and uncertainty.

Importantly, in light of the present international discussion, this dimension or value of people seems to vary from country to country. Research shows that people in Latin countries (both in Europe and South America) generally do not like uncertainty. Neither do those from Mediterranean nations. On the other hand, those from countries such as Denmark, Sweden, Great Britain, Ireland, Canada, and the United States function well under conditions of uncertainty or ambiguity. Far Eastern countries such as Japan and Korea tend to fall between these two extremes.[17]

The Role of Power Distance. Still another contributing factor to motivational differences across cultures may revolve around power distance. Can the people in a particular country accept the fact that others have more power than they, or do they find this difficult to live with? As was noted earlier (see Figure 4.3), people in the United States, Britain, Canada, and the Scandinavian countries have trouble accepting that others have more power than they do. On the other hand, people in India, Mexico, Japan, and South Korea do not. Table 4.9 shows some of the ways of managing and organizing both groups.

TABLE 4.8 Ways to Manage People on the Basis of Their Ability to Deal with Uncertainty or Ambiguity

Are Able to Deal with Uncertainty or Ambiguity	Do Not Like to Deal with Uncertainty or Ambiguity
Less structuring of activities	More structuring of activities
Fewer written rules	More written rules
Organizations can take many different forms	Organizations should be as uniform as possible (standardization)
Managers more involved in strategy	Managers more involved in details
Managers more interpersonally oriented and flexible in their style	Managers more task-oriented and consistent in their style
Managers more willing to make individual and risky decisions	Managers less willing to make individual and risky decisions
High labor turnover	Lower labor turnover
More ambitious employees	Less ambitious employees
Lower satisfaction scores	Higher satisfaction scores

Source: Adapted from Geert Hofstede, *Culture's Consequences: International Differences in Work Related Values,* Sage, Beverly Hills, Calif., 1980, p. 187. Copyright © 1980 by Sage Publications, Inc. Used with permission of Sage Publications, Inc.

TABLE 4.9 Ways to Manage People on the Basis of Their Acceptance or Nonacceptance of Power

Are Not Willing to Accept the Fact that Others Have More Power Than They Do	Are Willing to Accept the Fact that Others Have More Power Than They Do
Less centralization	Greater centralization
Flatter organization pyramids	Tall organization pyramids
Smaller proportion of supervisory personnel	Large proportion of supervisory personnel
Manual work same status as clerical work	White-collar jobs valued more than blue-collar jobs

Source: Adapted from Geert Hofstede, *Culture's Consequences: International Differences in Work Related Values,* Sage, Beverly Hills, Calif., 1980, p. 135. Copyright © 1980 by Sage Publications, Inc. Used with permission of Sage Publications, Inc.

Managerial Leadership across Cultures

Like communication and motivation, the important organizational behavior topic of leadership is given special treatment in a later chapter; leadership gets detailed attention in Chapter 16. For now, however, leadership can be thought of as the process of influencing others to direct their efforts toward the pursuit of specific goals. In the context of organizational behavior, leadership is mainly concerned with managerial style. The way in which this process is successfully applied, however, will vary across cultures. What is appropriate and effective managerial leadership in one country may not be in another. There are a number of possible contributing factors to the differences in effective managerial leadership across cultures. Some of the more important, and those which have been researched, include personal values, risk preference, the manager's background, interpersonal skills, and decision making.

Personal Values

Managers' personal values help shape their perception of a situation, influence their analysis of alternative solutions to a problem, and have an effect on the ultimate decision. The followers' personal values will also influence their manager. How they accept authority—their power distance—and their loyalty and commitment are examples. Such personal values on the part of both managers and subordinates will differ across cultures. For example, research by George England and his colleagues found that American and Japanese managers tend to be very pragmatic. Their personal values emphasize productivity, profitability, and achievement. Managers from India, on the other hand, tend to be less pragmatic and more moralistic. Their values emphasize equity, fairness, and the overall good of the work force.[18]

England also examined values relating to goals of business organizations. Table 4.10 reports these findings. Notice that while managers from all three countries were interested in organizational efficiency and high productivity, Americans were much higher on profit maximization and much lower on employee welfare and social welfare than were managers from India and Australia. Quite

TABLE 4.10 Values Relating to Goals of Business Organizations

Concept	Operative Score		
	India	United States	Australia
Organizational efficiency	69	65	64
High productivity	62	63	62
Organizational stability	58	41	41
Organizational growth	47	47	29
Employee welfare	44	34	45
Industry leadership	38	43	44
Profit maximization	36	58	38
Social welfare	18	8	25

Source: Adapted from George W. England, O. P. Dhingra, and Naresh C. Agarwal, *The Manager and the Man: A Cross-Cultural Study of Personal Values,* Kent State University Press, Kent, Ohio, 1974, p. 32. Used with permission.

FIGURE 4.6 Risk aversion and risk taking in selected countries of the world.
(*Source:* Adapted from L. L. Cummings, D. L. Harnett, and O. J. Stevens, "Risk, Fate, Conciliation and Trust: An International Study of Attitudinal Differences among Executives," *Academy of Management Journal,* September 1971, p. 293. Used with permission.)

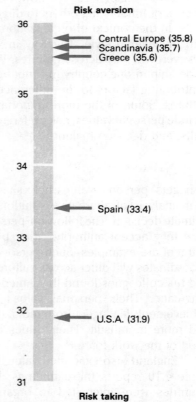

Risk aversion

36 ◄ Central Europe (35.8)
   ◄ Scandinavia (35.7)
   ◄ Greece (35.6)

35

34

         ◄ Spain (33.4)

33

32 ◄ U.S.A. (31.9)

31

Risk taking
Possible range of scores is from 16 to 48.

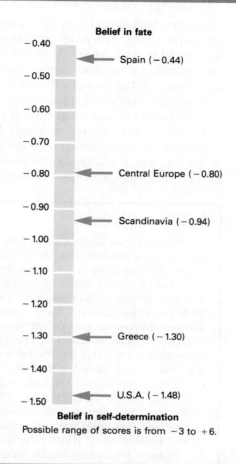

FIGURE 4.7
External versus
internal control in
selected countries
of the world.
(*Source:* Adapted
from L. L. Cum-
mings, D. L. Harnett,
and O. J. Stevens,
"Risk, Fate, Concilia-
tion and Trust: An
International Study
of Attitudinal Differ-
ences among Exec-
utives," *Academy of
Management Jour-
nal,* September 1971,
p. 294. Used with
permission.)

obviously, at least on the basis of these empirical data, the way in which American multinational corporations manage their home operations would have to be quite different from the way they would manage operations in India or Australia.

Risk Preference

Another way in which managers in other countries differ from Americans is in their risk preference. Cummings and his associates have found that American managers tend to be greater risk takers than their counterparts in Europe. Figure 4.6 shows this along a continuum. In some countries of the world, particularly those technologically advanced, managerial leaders tend to be aggressive risk takers. In other countries they tend to be either conservative or highly speculative in their risk taking.[19] Research has also found that in some countries of the world managers believe in letting things work out for themselves (fate), while in other countries the manager believes in taking charge of the situation (self-determination). Figure 4.7 shows this dimension by country.

Managers' Background

Managers' background may also influence the way their subordinates are led. Research shows that American managers come from every economic strata: lower, middle, and upper.[20] An increasingly large percentage are college-educated, but because performance is important to promotion, there is no guarantee that attending a certain school will lead to success. Although graduates of Ivy League schools and other prestigious institutions may have an advantage, many American managers from all types and sizes of colleges have made it into the upper ranks. The same pattern may not be as true in other countries. For example, in France managers often are chosen from the graduates of the *grandes écoles*. In Japan, those who gain entrance into the prestigious schools have a much better chance of becoming top managers of the large corporations. In Korea, surprisingly

Application Example

Made in the U.S.A.*

In recent years the South Koreans have begun taking advantage of the strong Japanese yen and have dramatically shifted their exports to the U.S. instead of Japan. Will this result in a backlash from the American government when they start looking for ways to correct its balance of payments problem? Will the U.S. government restrict imports from foreign countries that sell much more to America than they buy? There certainly is a possibility that this will happen, but the Koreans have an ace up their sleeve. Unlike the Japanese business leaders, most of whom are educated in Japan, the Koreans are now promoting a new generation of managers into the top spots who have one common characteristic—they have been educated in the United States.

The chairman of South Korea's largest conglomerate, Samsung, is in the process of passing the reins of power to his son, a graduate of Georgetown University. The chairman of the country's second-largest conglomerate, Hyundai, is passing power to his youngest brother, who studied at the University of Miami. Isolated cases? Hardly. The Koreans are well aware of the perception that the Japanese have created in the minds of many Americans—a country that is willing to sell to the U.S. but refuses to buy. The Koreans are determined not to allow this perception to taint its relationship with the U.S. As a result, those who speak English very well, have been educated in the States, have business associates and good friends in the U.S. and have experience dealing with the Americans are being considered for management promotion in their home country. The Koreans are convinced that the best way to avoid an American backlash is to be sensitive to the concerns of the U.S. and do nothing to create a negative image. They also believe that, whether foreign trading partners like it or not, in the long run it will be important to set up facilities in the U.S. A Korean national skilled in dealing with the Americans will be in the best position to negotiate these arrangements and ensure that the interests of the Korean firm are protected. As a result, over the next decade we are going to see the promotion into the leadership of Korean firms more and more who have been educated and socialized in the U.S.

Source: Adapted from Laxmi Nakarmi and William J. Holstein, "Korea's New Corporate Bosses: Made in America," *Business Week*, Feb. 23, 1987, pp. 58–59.

perhaps, many of the newly emerging managerial leaders have been educated in the United States. The accompanying Application Example, Made in the U.S.A., gives the details. In Russia career advancement in management is dependent on engineering or technical education and experience.

Besides educational background, class and family background also make a difference. In the United States, managers come from all classes. However, in Turkey, many of the top managers come from the upper class. In Poland, most of the business leaders come from the lower middle class. In Argentina and Peru, business leaders come from the middle class. In Chile, the landed aristocracy are the managerial leaders.

At the same time, family upbringing is important. For example, in India, it is common to accept the authority of elders. Thus, in superior-subordinate relations there is generally little delegation of authority. Instead, the head of the enterprise exercises a directive leadership style and everyone follows these orders. In the United States, on the other hand, where managers come from all classes, are relatively well educated, and have a liberal upbringing, there is more of an emphasis on participatory decision making and delegation of authority. This background will influence the way the manager exercises leadership.

Interpersonal Skills

There is research evidence that managers differ across cultures in their interpersonal skills. For example, Bass and Burger conducted a comprehensive study of managers in the United States, Belgium, Britain, France, Germany-Austria, Iberia, India, Japan, Latin America, and Scandinavia. Some of their relevant findings in relation to interpersonal styles and skills include the following:

- Spanish and Portuguese managers were most willing to be aware of other's feelings; to be concerned with their subordinates' welfare; and to accept feedback from others. The Germans, Austrians, and French were less willing to do these things. The other countries fell between these two extremely different groups.
- Managers from India were the most concerned about bureaucratic rules; the Japanese were the least concerned.
- Managers from India saw themselves as most dependent on higher authority. German and Austrian managers viewed themselves as very independent.
- Dutch managers were the most willing to cooperate with others; the French were the least willing.
- Japanese managers had a greater desire to be objective rather than intuitive than did managers from any other country.
- Japanese and Dutch managers were most locked in by group commitments and were less likely to deviate from their initial positions. Managers from the United States and Latin America showed the least commitment to their group positions, were able to reach compromises faster than the other groups, and were deadlocked much less often.
- U.S. and Latin American managers demonstrated much greater interpersonal competence than other managers.[21]

What the above once again demonstrates is that interpersonal approaches differ by culture. An American supervisor on an oil rig in Indonesia learned this the hard way. In a moment of anger, he shouted at his timekeeper to take the next boat to shore. Immediately, a mob of outraged Indonesian coworkers grabbed fire axes and went after the supervisor. He saved himself by barricading himself in his quarters. The cultural lesson this American learned: Never berate an Indonesian in public.[22]

Decision Making

Besides interpersonal skills, managerial leadership is also often expressed through decision-making skills. Chapter 18 will give specific attention to this function of management, but for now decision making can be simply thought of as the process of choosing between alternatives. However, how managers make these decisions may differ across cultures. For example, research by Heller and Yukl has found that in Argentina, Chile, and Uruguay authority is equated with rapid decision making and the emphasis on speed is more important than on generating information or carefully analyzing the data.[23]

Boards of directors in these Latin countries often hold meetings without precirculating the minutes of the last meeting or the agenda of the current one. Other researchers have found that Latin American managers also often fail to plan and rely heavily on intuition or improvisation based on emotional arguments and justifications in making their decisions.[24] Some of them also put off decisions, preferring a "wait and see" attitude that results in eventually having to use stop-gap measures to prevent the situation from getting worse.

Other research has found that managers in the United States and Sweden tend to emphasize rationality in their decision making. The Japanese, on the other hand, try to balance a concern for rationality and objectivity with the desire for group acceptance and consensus. In the Japanese system, decision making tends to flow from the bottom up. All members of the firm share the responsibility for decisions. After reaching a consensus, the originating group sends its decision to other groups for approval. The more important the decision, the higher it goes for approval within the hierarchy. This is in contrast to the American system in which decisions tend to flow from the top down and individuals, although they may be in a group or committee framework, play a more significant role.

Summary

The international context in which organizational behavior operates is becoming increasingly important as organizations expand beyond their national boundaries. Few would question that there is now a global economy and that cultural differences must be recognized in the study and understanding of organizational behavior.

The chapter started off by defining culture, which is the acquired knowledge that people use to interpret experience and generate social behavior. Whereas the last chapter focused on organizational culture per se, this chapter more directly aimed at the culture of overall societies and countries. Although it must be remembered that it is difficult to make generalizations because of so many subcultures operating in societies and countries, there are several dimensions of culture that do pretty well describe societal orientations. These dimensions were identified in the chapter as follows: how people see themselves; people's relationship to their world; individualism versus collectivism; the time dimension; and public and private space. These lead to organizational behavior differences across cultures. There are many reasons for these differences. The chapter drew heavily from the research of Hofstede who found that people tend to differ based on individualism/collectivism, power distance, uncertainty avoidance, and masculinity/femininity.

The remainder of the chapter analyzed the major organizational behavior topics of communication, motivation, and managerial leadership across cultures. Communication in an international environment often is influenced by a number of factors such as perception, stereotyping, and ethnocentrism. In helping their managers deal with these communication problems, some companies have developed cultural assimilator training programs.

Another problem facing the understanding and application of organizational behavior across cultures is exemplified by the important topic of motivation. What accounts for motivational differences across cultures? A number of factors can be cited, including religion, the state of the economy/standard of living, uncertainty avoidance, and the ways in which the society deals with power acceptance.

Managerial leadership involves influencing others to direct their efforts toward the pursuit of specific goals. There are a number of factors across cultures that influence the way in which managers lead their subordinates. Some of these factors are personal values, risk preference, the manager's background, interpersonal skills, and decision making. Each of these was discussed in the chapter. When available, research evidence was used to support the conclusions. However, a future challenge for the field of organizational behavior is to do more international research.

Questions for Discussion and Review

1. In your own words, what is meant by the term "culture"? How does it differ from "organizational culture"?
2. What are some basic dimensions that describe the cultural orientation of a society? Briefly describe each.
3. In what way do individualism/collectivism, power distance, uncertainty avoidance, and masculinity/femininity help explain cultural differences? Define and give examples of these dimensions.
4. In what way is perception a problem in dealing with employees across cultures?
5. In what way is stereotyping a problem in dealing with employees across cultures?

6. In what way is ethnocentrism a problem in dealing with employees across cultures?

7. How can multinational corporations sensitize their managers to the cultures of host countries before sending them on international assignments?

8. How does work differ in the meaning it takes on in the United States and in other countries?

9. What accounts for some of the motivational differences between employees across cultures?

10. What are some of the major factors that influence the managerial leadership process across cultures?

References

1. Christopher A. Bartlett and Sumantra Ghoshal, "Managing across Borders: New Strategic Requirements," *Sloan Management Review,* Summer 1987, p. 7.

2. Charles J. Cox and Cary L. Cooper, "The Irrelevance of American Organizational Sciences to the UK and Europe," *Journal of General Management,* Winter 1985, pp. 29–30.

3. Quoted in Nancy J. Adler, Robert Doktor, and S. Gordon Redding, "From the Atlantic to the Pacific Century: Cross-Cultural Management Reviewed," *Journal of Management,* vol. 12, no. 2, 1986, p. 295.

4. Stephen P. Robbins, *Organizational Behavior,* 3d ed., Prentice-Hall, Englewood Cliffs, N.J., 1986, pp. 494–495.

5. Nancy J. Adler, *International Dimensions of Organizational Behavior,* Kent, Boston, 1986, pp. 13, 16.

6. Jacquelyn B. Schriber and Barbara A. Gutek, "Some Time Dimensions of Work: Measurement of an Underlying Aspect of Organization Culture," *Journal of Applied Psychology,* vol. 72, 1987, pp. 642–650.

7. Geert Hofstede, *Culture's Consequences: International Differences in Work Related Values,* Sage, Beverly Hills, Calif., 1980. For a recent review and extension of Hofstede's work see Robert G. Westwood and James E. Everett, "Culture's Consequences: A Methodology for Comparative Management Studies in Southeast Asia?" *Asia Pacific Journal of Management,* May 1987, pp. 187–202.

8. Adler, op. cit., p. 41.

9. Simcha Ronen, *Comparative and Multinational Management,* Wiley, New York, 1986, pp. 266–267.

10. Kenichi Ohmae, "Japan's Role in the World Economy," *California Management Review,* Spring 1987, p. 54.

11. Don Hellriegel, John W. Slocum, and Richard W. Woodman, *Organizational Behavior,* 4th ed., West, St. Paul, Minn., 1986, p. 219.

12. Adnan Almaney, "Intercultural Communication and the MNC Executive," *Columbia Journal of World Business,* Winter 1974, p. 27.

13. P. Christopher Earley, "Intercultural Training for Managers: A Comparison of Documentary and Interpersonal Methods," *Academy of Management Journal,* December 1987, pp. 685–698.

14. Adler, op. cit., p. 63.

15. Robert A. Baron, *Behavior in Organizations,* 2d ed., Allyn & Bacon, Boston, 1986, p. 150.

16. Prof. Peter Berger, quoted in "What Is Culture's Role in Economic Policy?" *The Wall Street Journal,* Dec. 22, 1986, p. 1.
17. Ronen, op. cit., p. 170.
18. George W. England, O. P. Dhingra, and Naresh C. Agarwal, *The Manager and the Man: A Cross-Cultural Study of Personal Values,* Kent State University Press, Kent, Ohio, 1974, p. 20.
19. Ronen, op. cit., pp. 213–214.
20. David C. McClelland, *The Achieving Society,* Van Nostrand, Princeton, N.J., 1961.
21. B. M. Bass and P. C. Burger, *Assessment of Managers: An International Comparison.* Free Press, New York, 1979.
22. Richard L. Daft, *Management.* Dryden, Chicago, 1988, p. 687.
23. Frank A. Heller and Gary Yukl, "Participation, Managerial Decision-Making, and Situational Variables," *Organizational Behavior and Human Performance.* vol. 4, 1969, pp. 227–241.
24. E. C. McCann, "An Aspect of Management Philosophy in the United States and Latin America," *Academy of Management Journal.* June 1964, pp. 149–152.

**REAL CASE:
One World***

How important is it for managers to understand organizational behavior in the international context? According to the latest economic forecasts, the global economy is becoming increasingly interconnected and the United States will be exporting more services and importing more capital than ever before. As a result, American managers are going to have to learn how to deal with their foreign counterparts.

Fortune magazine recently hired Data Resources Inc. (DRI) to forecast a map of various countries' growth prospects from now to the year 2000. Here is part of what *Fortune* had to report as a result of this forecasting:

- Over the next fifteen years, DRI expects real GNP growth in the United States to average 2.6 percent a year.
- Western Europe's economies should expand at about the same pace or slightly faster.
- Japan will do better still—it will grow at a 3.5 percent annual clip.
- No country will enjoy the jackrabbit growth of the 1950s and 1960s. But newly industrialized countries (NICs) and recently awakened giants such as India and China should grow about twice as fast on average as the developed world.
- DRI expects mainland China to be the champ, with a 7.1 percent growth rate.
- Other hard-chargers include Korea (6.2 percent), Brazil (5.9 percent), and Taiwan (5.8 percent). Even troubled Mexico should average 4.7 percent.

For the United States, this time period will be one of increased exports. Merchandise sales to other countries will grow at an annual rate of about

***Source:** Adapted from Richard I. Kirkland, Jr., "We're All in This Together," *Fortune,* Feb. 2, 1987, pp. 26–69.

3 percent and the annual trade deficit is projected to stabilize. China will also become a major trading nation as it moves into first place in the area of textiles. Taiwan, South Korea, and other countries with low labor costs will begin gaining more of the world production of manufactured commodities such as basic steel and low-priced cars. South Korea will also claim around 5 percent of the global electronics market.

One of the primary developments of all this international trade will be the continued formation of international business alliances similar to those of the last five years in which AT&T joined with Olivetti to make personal computers, General Electric hooked up with Fanuc, the Japanese robot maker, and both Chrysler and General Motors entered into joint ventures with Japanese auto manufacturers. Another popular arrangement will be the use of a multinational task force to build new products. A good example is the Singer Company, which makes sewing machine shells in Cleveland, motors in Brazil, and drive shafts in Italy, and then assembles the product in Taiwan for sales throughout the world. As this trend continues, national boundaries will become increasingly irrelevant for both producers and consumers and organizations will begin thinking in terms of a world market with potential sales to 5 billion customers.

1. How important will an understanding of international organizational behavior be to a multinational manager of the 1990s?
2. How can organizations prepare their managers to better understand international organizational behavior?
3. What is the likelihood that by the year 2000 American firms with sales of $100 million or above will be earning at least a portion of this income through international sales? What significance does your answer have for the study of international organizational behavior?

CASE: I Want Out

When the Budder Mining Equipment Company decided to set up a branch office in Peru, top management felt that there were two basic avenues it could travel. One was to export its machinery and have an agent in that country be responsible for the selling. The other was to set up an on-site operation and be directly responsible for the sales effort. After giving the matter a great deal of thought, management decided to assign one of its own people to this overseas market. The person who was chosen, Frank Knight, had expressed an interest in the assignment but had no experience in South America. He was selected because of his selling skills and was given a week to clear out his desk and be on location.

When Frank arrived, he was met at the airport by Pablo Gutierrez, the local who was hired to run the office and break Frank in. Pablo had rented an apartment and car for Frank and taken care of all the chores associated with getting him settled. Frank was very impressed. Thanks to Pablo, he could devote all of his efforts to the business challenge that lay ahead.

After about six months, the vice president for marketing received a call from Frank. In a tired voice Frank indicated that even though sales were okay, he couldn't take it anymore. He wanted to come home. If nothing could be worked out within the next three months, Frank made it clear that he would resign. When his boss pressed him regarding the problems he was having, here is what Frank reported:

> Doing business over here is a nightmare. Everyone comes to work late and leaves early. They also take a two-hour rest period during the afternoon. All the offices close down during this afternoon break. So even if I wanted to conduct some business during this period, there would be no customers around anyway. Also, no one works very hard and they seem to assume no responsibility whatsoever. There seems to be no support for the work ethic among the people. Even Pablo, who looked like he was going to turn out great, has proven to be as lazy as the rest of them. Sales are 5 percent over forecast but a good 30 percent lower than they could be if everyone here would just work a little harder. If I stay here any longer, I'm afraid I'll start becoming like these people. I want out, while I still can.

1. In Frank's view, how important is the work ethic? How is this view causing him problems?
2. Why do the people not work as hard as Frank does? What is the problem?
3. What mistake is Frank making that is undoubtedly causing him problems in managing the branch office?

**CASE:
Getting
the Facts**

When California-based Dalton & Dalton (D&D) was contacted by a large conglomerate in Taiwan, the president of D&D was quite surprised. For two years D&D had been looking for an overseas conglomerate that would be interested in building and selling its high-tech medical equipment under a licensing agreement. The company had been unsuccessful because the firms with whom it had spoken were not interested in investing any of their own money. They wanted D&D to provide the financial investment while they handled the actual manufacturing and selling.

The Taiwanese conglomerate has proposed to D&D that the two companies enter into a joint venture type of licensing agreement. The way in which the business deal will work is the following:

- The Taiwanese will set up manufacturing facilities and create a marketing group to sell D&D's high-tech medical equipment.
- D&D will train twenty-five manufacturing and twenty-five salespeople from the conglomerate so that the latter understands how to make and sell this equipment. This training will take place in the States.
- D&D will have the right to send people to the manufacturing facility to ensure that the equipment is being built according to specifications and will also have the right to travel with the salespeople to ensure that the equipment is being sold properly. (Specifically, D&D would be able to monitor the technical side of the sales presentation to ensure that the equipment is being properly

represented and that the capabilities of the machinery are not being exaggerated.)

The arrangement sounds fine to the president of D&D. However, before she agrees to anything she wants to get more information on how to do business with the Taiwanese. "If we're going to enter into a business venture with a foreign company, I think we owe it to ourselves to know something about their culture and customs. I'd like to know how to interact effectively with these people and to get an idea of the types of problems we might have in communicating with them. The better we understand them, the better the chances that there will be no misunderstandings between us."

1. If you were advising the president, what types of information would you suggest be gathered?
2. What types of culturally related problems are there that could result in misunderstanding between the two parties?
3. Overall, is the president right in suggesting that they learn more about the Taiwanese before doing business with them?

Integrative Real Case for Part 1

Working for Japan Inc.*

Forget, for the moment, the droning debate about trade. Forget posturing politicians, bewildering economists, exchange rates, howls about protectionism, hollow pledges of international economic cooperation. Instead, consider that this week is Dianna Ginn's last at Hermies, a popular diner in Marysville, Ohio, a small company town in the cradle of America's rust belt. For four years the 41-year-old divorced mother of three has earned $2.40 an hour plus tips waiting on workers from the local factory—wishing all the while she had one of their high-paying jobs. On Jan. 21, three years after submitting her application, Ginn got the job she wanted. On Feb. 2 she starts working on the assembly line at the Honda Motor Corp. of America. "You talk about the American dream," said one of Ginn's customers at Hermies, "well, this is the Marysville dream: working for Honda."

Working for Honda. Or, in Norman, Okla., for Hitachi, or in LaVergne, Tenn., for Bridgestone Tire or in Perryville, Mo., for Toyoda Gosei. In communities across the United States, Japan Inc. holds out the "Help Wanted" sign and eager American workers sign on in droves. In 1986 the estimated U.S. trade deficit with Japan soared to $60 billion, but Japan's direct investment in the United States also shot up. The Japanese poured around $27 billion into plant, equipment and real estate—investment that created tens of thousands of American jobs. According to the best statistics available, nearly 250,000 Americans work for Japan Inc., making it one of the largest and fastest-growing employers in the United States. Tokyo's Ministry of International Trade and Industry predicts Japanese investment will spawn an additional 840,000 American jobs in the next decade—an estimate some analysts consider conservative.

The surging Japanese investment comes at a delicate moment in U.S.-Japanese relations. Washington's irritation with Japan's economic policy has seldom been greater, and vice versa. Last week Japan's finance minister, Kiichi Miyazawa, hurried to Washington for an emergency meeting with U.S. Treasury Secretary James A. Baker III. Miyazawa came to discuss the U.S. dollar's continuing collapse against the yen. Why was he so worried? A rising yen hurts in two ways. By making Japanese products more expensive, it could cripple the country's export-led economy. A strong yen also makes it more attractive for Japanese companies to invest here than at home. But the Baker-Miyazawa discussions resulted in no new agreements, and the dollar continued to weaken against the yen.

For the United States, that is not necessarily bad news. It means the torrent of Japanese investment won't ebb anytime soon. Japan's money represents a huge vote of confidence in the U.S. economy. And with the money comes new plants, more jobs, new technologies and, perhaps most important, a management philosophy that's arguably more equitable and efficient than any other. The

Source: Bill Powell and others, "Where the Jobs Are," *Newsweek,* Feb. 2, 1987, pp. 42–46. © 1987, Newsweek, Inc. All rights reserved. Reprinted with permission.

amount of Japanese investment here will inevitably stir controversy. "But the issue shouldn't even be debated," says the Brookings Institution's Edward Lincoln. "Their trade surplus is going to be reduced more by direct investment [abroad] than it is by change in their domestic market anyway."

The Japanese will no longer be the inscrutable, seemingly invulnerable economic rival across the ocean. They will be across the street, producing in the United States, employing American workers and managers in ever-greater numbers, operating under U.S. laws and regulations—just like American companies. A decade from now, in fact, today's debate about the U.S.-Japanese trade problem may seem strangely anachronistic. Many American workers won't be concerned with slapping tariffs on Japanese goods or with what an "appropriate" yen-dollar exchange rate is. Instead, they'll wonder if they should work for Japan Inc.—or invite their Japanese boss over for dinner.

In the eyes of many Americans, the billions of yen pouring into the United States only adds to Japan's image as an indomitable economic machine. The image and the reality, however, are now very different. The soaring yen is a boot on the neck of an economy dependent on exports, but it is hardly the only problem the Japanese confront. In fact, they face ailments that have afflicted the United States since the late 1970s: slowing domestic demand for a wide range of capital goods and stiff competition from countries with significantly lower labor costs. Throw in the threat of new protectionist barriers in the United States, says Kazuo Nukazawa of the Japan Federation of Economic Organizations, and many Japanese companies face a stark choice: "Invest overseas or perish."

No Sympathy. Don't feel too sorry for Japan, though. The nation simply has more money than it knows what to do with. The Japanese save money at an astonishing rate; of the 10 largest banks in the world, seven are in Japan. Moreover, many of the country's biggest industrial companies have so much cash "that they look like banks," as one U.S. investment banker says. The upshot: Japan may create jobs at a rapid clip in the United States for years to come. "Direct investment will be a tidal wave, but it's only starting now," says Eugene Atkinson, a managing director in Goldman Sachs & Co.'s Tokyo office.

The effects of that investment will be profound—for both the United States and Japan. Today Japan's most visible U.S. presence is in autos and consumer electronics. Conceivably, Japanese firms one day may be employers of choice in Silicon Valley and perhaps even on Wall Street, the citadel of American capitalism. And each time a major Japanese company locates a plant or an office in the United States, its major suppliers are not far behind. As a consequence, U.S. companies will face more intense competition in their own backyard. For many American businessmen, it's time to put up or shut up. Some U.S. manufacturers have pinned their economic woes on their rivals across the Pacific. U.S. companies have often accused the Japanese of pricing below cost and dumping their products into the U.S. market illegally. Now some American companies will have more than the "level playing field" they have so desired. They'll have the home-court advantage. Japan's investment in the United States "is a challenge to us," says Lincoln. "If we can't meet it, well, we deserve to work for the Japanese."

The Japanese, too, will be severely tested. They must prove they can put an American face on their vaunted consensus-management style. They will have to manage workers who believe corporate loyalty means showing up for work on time—not spending a lifetime married to a company. "Most Americans are very, very individualistic—you could almost say egotistic; they are quite different from the way we would like our people to be," concedes Asa Jonishi, senior director of Kyocera Corp., a Japanese high-tech company with U.S. operations in southern California. The president of the Building and Construction Trades Department of the AFL-CIO mocks the paternalistic style of Japanese companies: " 'We're the father and you're the children'," says Robert Georgine. " 'We'll tell you what's good for you, and you do everything you can to make us successful.' That doesn't wash here," he asserts.

Vast Differences.   Few people are so willing to dismiss the Japanese system. It may be the most productive management style in history, and an increasing number of workers and managers believe the we're-all-in-this-together attitude works just as well in the United States. Still, the cultural differences *are* vast. In some U.S. industries independent trade unions are a fact of life. So too—in every industry—are smart, assertive women. The Japanese have little experience at home with either, and that's painfully obvious to U.S. employees of Japan's biggest companies. Two weeks ago Sumitomo Corp. of America settled a sex-discrimination suit filed by a dozen former women workers. The suit alleged Sumitomo restricted women to clerical positions, never promoting them to sales and management jobs. Under the settlement—which was widely viewed as almost unconditional surrender for Sumitomo—the company promised to increase sharply the number of women in sales and management. The AFL-CIO also won a dispute recently with a major Japanese company. Toyota and its prime contractor agreed to allow union workers to build a new auto plant now under construction in Georgetown, Ky. The unions had staged a public campaign of harassment to force Toyota's Japanese contractor to hire union workers.

Bitter, publicized disputes horrify the Japanese, and they go to great lengths to avoid them. The settlement with the AFL-CIO will cost Toyota millions in additional construction costs, but the company settled to get the publicity behind it. As the Japanese presence in the United States increases, more public battles are inevitable. Even in Marysville there are people who object to Honda's presence. Some don't like what the Japanese did to Pearl Harbor; others, what they did to Detroit.

The most important task Japanese managers face is to defuse the tension. Their first step is often to minimize the Japanese presence in the company. Yuzaburo Mogi, managing director of Kikkoman Corp., a Japanese food company with a subsidiary in Wisconsin, recently wrote that "no matter how eager Americans may seem in getting Japanese investment, the failure to go local [hire Americans] may provoke a backlash and turn the welcoming mood to an anti-Japanese specter." Mogi insists that his Japanese employees working in the United States mix with local people; they must also live dispersed throughout the community and not in "Little Tokyo" ghettos.

The Japanese presence, measured by numbers, is minimal at most American subsidiaries. At Nissan Motor's Smyrna, Tenn., plant there are only 13 Japanese executives at a facility that employs 3,300. At Matsushita's huge electronics plant in Chicago, there are only a handful of Japanese executives and engineers. Numbers, however, do not equate to influence and power. Indeed, "numbers are largely irrelevant," says Thomas McCraw, a professor at the Harvard Business School and editor of a new book on the U.S.-Japan economic rivalry. McCraw believes Japan's success here will hinge on how successfully its companies delegate real responsibility to American managers and workers. Failure to do so, he argues, will cause debilitating morale problems.

Nomura Securities International, the largest Japanese stock-brokerage firm, found that out the hard way. Current and former employees say a bitter dispute at the firm a year ago resulted, in part, from simmering tension between Japanese managers and some American traders. Every Monday in Nomura's New York office senior traders met with top managers, ostensibly to discuss important management issues. "Instead," says one former Nomura trader, "the guy running the meeting would stand up and say so-and-so has a birthday this week and so-and-so is going out to Los Angeles to meet with someone from another firm— totally irrelevant stuff." Then, former employees say, after that meeting broke up each week, the top Japanese officials trooped off into another room and held *another* meeting. "It was consensus management all right," adds a current Nomura insider, "a consensus of the Japanese." Nomura brought in new management after several traders left the firm, and insiders say the atmosphere, though still less than ideal, has improved significantly.

Wielding Power. What happened at Nomura is relatively rare. But the perception that Americans can never attain positions of power hurts Japanese companies trying to do business here. It prevents them from hiring top-level management talent in the United States. A more realistic concern for title-conscious American executives is that upward mobility in a Japanese firm will be limited. The president in most cases is going to be Japanese. Still, Americans can wield power. Consensus management often strips much of the meaning from titles. Says Pat Park, assistant general manager of Haseko, the Los Angeles subsidiary of a Japanese real-estate development company: "There are many times when I'm the janitor here, picking up rubbish. But there are also many times when major decisions are made because I say so. There's more equity in Japanese companies."

Americans hold key positions at several of the biggest Japanese companies in the world. At Daiwa Securities in New York, vice chairman Paul Aron's authority is undisputed. He is a respected Wall Street veteran, and Daiwa's Tokyo office seeks his opinion on a wide range of management issues. At Nissan Motors in Smyrna, Americans are also in control. President Marvin Runyon and director of product quality Joe Desarla spent 37 and 14 years, respectively, at Ford. "We're not a Japanese company," insists Runyon; "we're an American company." Desarla says Nissan in America retains what Detroit did well, dumps what it did poorly and adopts some of the Japanese philosophy on the shop floor. The plant, operating since 1983, is nearly as productive as its sister plants in Japan.

In manufacturing industries, the shop floor is where the competitive battles are won or lost. In the United States, they have mostly been lost. But as one

American executive working for a Japanese company in Tokyo says, "Where the Japanese go for hearts and minds is not in the boardroom, but on the shop floor." Their ability to manage a manufacturing operation transcends national borders. At New United Motors in Fremont, Calif., Toyota and GM together successfully revamped an auto plant in the shell of a strife-torn GM factory closed in 1982. And unlike Nissan in Smyrna, Fremont is a union shop—though one with remarkably few work rules and hierarchy.

Not every Japanese company that builds or buys a plant here will operate flawlessly. The United States is still a tough environment in which to manufacture efficiently. For that reason, argues Tokyo-based McKinsey & Co. consultant Kenichi Ohmae, some Japanese companies will fail.

Bottom Lines. The best companies—the Sonys and the Toyotas—won't. They can make quality goods at competitive prices anywhere. More Japan-in-America success stories are inevitable. For Americans the question is, whose success is it: theirs, or ours? The correct answer—in a world in which capital crosses borders at the touch of a computer key—is that the *question* is becoming irrelevant. Nissan worker J. R. McGowan understands that better than most. "When I was hired," he says, "I wore my Nissan uniform everywhere, and some people stopped me and asked if I was working for those 'blank, blank' Japanese." In time, though, the hostility diminished. "The bottom line," says McGowan, "is that I'm building a truck somebody's going to be riding in. I might be driving this truck, so I'm going to do it right."

In the late 1960s the United States dominated the world economically. In a book called "The American Challenge," French journalist Jean-Jacques Servan-Schreiber foresaw dire consequences for a Europe overwhelmed by American investment and ingenuity. Sitting by helplessly, he wrote, the Europeans would see "American investment skim gently across the earth . . . and watch what it takes away." Japan today is a great economic power with a vast amount of money to invest around the globe. But Europe today is hardly an American economic colony; companies such as Ford and IBM are simply part of the economic landscape, like Renault or Siemens. Americans probably don't need to worry about what Japanese investment "will take away." It won't take away much—and people like Dianna Ginn will be too busy making money to notice anyway.

Questions

1. What implications does this case have for the field of organizational behavior in general? For understanding organizational culture? For recognizing the international context? Give specific examples from the case to support your statements.
2. One statement in the case is that Japan Inc. has "a management philosophy that's arguably more equitable and efficient than any other." Which way would you argue? Why?
3. What are some of the biggest organizational behavior problems that the Japanese face in doing business in America? Give specific examples from the case.

Experiential Exercises for Part 1

EXERCISE: Synthesis of Student and Instructor Needs

Goals:
1. To "break the ice" in using experiential exercises
2. To initiate open communication between the students and the instructor regarding mutual learning goals and needs
3. To stimulate the students to clarify their learning goals and instructional needs and to commit themselves to these
4. To serve as the first exercise in the "experiential" approach to management education

Implementation:
1. The class is divided into groups of four to six students each.
2. Each group openly discusses what members would like from the course and drafts a set of learning objectives and instructional aims. The group also makes up a list of learning/course objectives which they feel the instructor wants to pursue. (About twenty minutes.)
3. After each group has "caucused," a group spokesperson is appointed to meet with the instructor in an open dialogue in front of the class about course objectives.
4. The instructor meets with each group representative at the front of the classroom to initiate an open dialogue about the semester of learning. (About thirty minutes.) Several activities are carried out:
   a. Open discussion of the learning objectives of both the students and the instructor
   b. Recognition of the constraints faced by each party in accommodating these goals
   c. Identification of areas of goal agreement and disagreement, and feasible compromises
   d. Drafting a set of guidelines for cooperation between the parties, designed to better bring about mutual goal attainment

EXERCISE: Work-Related Organizational Behavior: Implications for the Course

Goals:
1. To identify course topic areas from the participant's own work experience
2. To introduce experiential learning

Implementation

Task 1: Each class member does the following:

1. Describes an experience in a past work situation that illustrates something about organizational behavior. (Some students have had only part-time work experience or summer jobs, but even the humblest job is relevant here.)
2. Explains what it illustrates about organizational behavior. (Time: five minutes for individuals to think about and jot down notes covering these two points.)

Task 2: The class forms into triads and each triad does the following:

1. Member A tells his or her experience to member B. Member B listens carefully,

110

paraphrases the story back to A, and tells what it illustrates about organizational behavior. Member B must do this to A's satisfaction that B has understood fully what A was trying to communicate. Member C is the observer and remains silent during the process.

2. Member B tells his or her story to C, and A is the observer.
3. Member C tells his or her story to A, and B is the observer. (Each member has about five minutes to tell his or her story and have it paraphrased back by the listener. The instructor will call out the time at the end of each five-minute interval for equal apportionment of "airtime" among participants. Total time: fifteen minutes.)

Task 3: Each triad selects one of its members to relate his or her incident to the class. The instructor briefly analyzes for the class how the related story fits in with some topic to be studied in the course, such as perception, motivation, communication, conflict, or leadership. The topic areas are listed in the table of contents of this book.

PART 2

Basic Understanding of Individual Behavior

⑤ Personality

Do successful managers have any common personality traits? Is there anything that distinguishes them from their less successful counterparts? In an effort to identify personality similarities among the most coveted managers, *Fortune* magazine recently asked a dozen executive search firms to give their top picks for chief executive officer (CEO) in ten different industries: aerospace and defense, communications, diversified manufacturing, energy equipment manufacturing, financial services, food and drugs, high technology, retailing and fashion, and travel. From the list of 150 names, further pruning was conducted until there were but three individuals for each industry. Finally, from each threesome one was chosen over the others. What were the major characteristics and personality traits of the winners? Here is the profile:

1. All were in their forties and considered ripe for plucking by other firms that were looking for chief executive officers.
2. They were action-oriented, able to institute and carry out change.
3. They had the ability to build a sense of shared values regarding where the enterprise should be heading.
4. They were self-confident and had the ability to take risks without undue worry.
5. They had excellent communication skills.
6. They had high integrity.

Source: Adapted from Roy Rowan, "America's Most Wanted Managers," *Fortune,* Feb. 3, 1986, pp. 18–19.

7. They had achieved a pattern of accomplishment in whatever jobs they undertook.
8. They had a commitment to what they were doing and were willing to pay the price to get there.
9. They had a vision that could be imparted to others.
10. They liked competitive sports.

These particular characteristics and personality traits were evident in the brief description that the executive recruiters gave of the ten winners. Some of these descriptions included the following:

- A driver, a strong, abilitious leader, grounded in all aspects of the industry.
- Bright, aggressive, goal-oriented. Leads by example. A workaholic who wins loyalty and results.
- Good strategic thinker. Personable, sensitive to people. Versatile.
- Charismatic, creative, gutsy. Has unbelievable energy and Boy Scout ethics.
- Keen mind, intuitive, but also strong numbers man. Inspirational leader.

Learning Objectives

- DEFINE the overall meaning of personality.
- DESCRIBE personality development by use of the stage theories.
- DISCUSS the major input that biological, cultural, and family determinants make to personality development.
- EXPLAIN the important role that socialization plays in personality development.

This chapter discusses the cognitive processes that are important to the understanding of organizational behavior. It takes a micro perspective from the *whole person*, personality standpoint. Organizational participants operate as a whole, not as a series of distinct parts. To make a very simple analogy, the various psychological processes may be thought of as the pieces of a jigsaw puzzle, and personality as the completed puzzle picture. As was recently noted, "events in the external environment (including the presence and behavior of others) strongly influence the way people behave at any particular point in time; yet people always bring something of themselves to the situation. We often refer to this 'something,' which represents the unique qualities of the individual, as *personality*."[1]

The discussion of personality in this chapter is aimed at improving the understanding of the complexities of today's employees. Such understanding is vital to the study and analysis of organizational behavior, but it offers only a few *direct* applications of its content to the management of human resources. It attempts to be more education- than applications-oriented, and it serves as the natural conceptual introduction to the second part of the book, which examines organizational behavior from an individual, micro perspective.

The first section of the chapter defines and clarifies the concept of personality. The next section is devoted to personality development and includes discussions of some well-known theories on stages of development formulated by Freud, Erikson, Piaget, and Argyris. The third section breaks down the determinants of personality development into biological, cultural, family, social, and situational categories. Some of the more important research findings on these determinants of personality are included, and the socialization process is given detailed attention because it is especially relevant to organizational behavior.

The Meaning of Personality

Through the years there has not been universal agreement on the exact meaning of personality. Much of the controversy can be attributed to the fact that people in general and behavioral scientists define *personality* from different perspectives. Most people tend to equate personality with social success (good, popular, or "a lot of personality") and to describe personality by a single dominant characteristic (strong, weak, shy, or polite). When it is realized that more than 4000 words can be used to describe personality this way, the definitional problem becomes staggering. Psychologists, on the other hand, take a different perspective. For example, the descriptive-adjective approach commonly used by most people plays only a small part. However, scholars cannot agree on a definition of personality because they operate from different theoretical bases. As long as there is disagreement on the theory of personality, there will be disagreement on its definition.

The word "personality" has an interesting derivation. It can be traced to the Latin words *per sona,* which translate as "to speak through." The Latin term was used to denote the masks worn by actors in ancient Greece and Rome. This Latin meaning is particularly relevant to the contemporary analysis of personality. Common usage of the word emphasizes the role which the person (actor) displays to the public. The academic definitions are concerned more directly with the person (actor) than with the role played. Probably the most meaningful approach would be to include both the person and the role.

In addition, some personality theorists emphasize the need to recognize the person-situation *interaction,* that is, the social learning aspects of personality. Such a social learning interpretation may be the most comprehensive and meaningful to the overall study of human/organizational behavior. Thus, a comprehensive discussion of personality should include the uniqueness of each situation (rather than the commonality assumed by the more traditional approaches to personality), and any measure of personality must attempt to assess the person-situation interaction. In summary, in this book "personality" will mean how people affect others and how they understand and view themselves, as well as their pattern of inner and outer measurable traits, and the person-situation interaction.

How people affect others depends primarily upon their external appearance (height, weight, facial features, color, and other physical aspects) and behavior (vulgar, friendly, courteous, and so on). The role concept is closely tied to these aspects of personality. A very large, friendly worker will have a different impact on other people from that of a very small, courteous manager. Obviously, all the ramifications of perception enter into these aspects of personality.

People's attempts to understand themselves are called the *self-concept* in personality theory. The self is a unique product of many interacting parts and may be thought of as the personality viewed from within.

The pattern of measurable traits such as external appearance and behavior adds an important dimension to the understanding of the human personality. The person-situation interaction dimension of personality extends this trait approach. Each situation, of course, is different. The differences may seem to be very small on the surface, but when filtered by the person's cognitive mediating processes, they can lead to quite large, subjective differences and diverse behavioral outcomes. Thus, this last dimension suggests that people are not static, acting the same in all situations, but instead are ever-changing and flexible. For example, employees can change depending on the particular situation they are in interaction with. Even everyday work experience can change people. The sections in this chapter dealing with the socialization process and the situation are relevant to this important person-situation interaction.

In summary, the personality is a very diverse and complex psychological concept. It incorporates almost everything covered in this book, and more. As defined above, personality is concerned with external appearance and behavior, self, measurable traits, and situational interactions. Probably the best statement on personality was made many years ago by Kluckhohn and Murray, who said that, to some extent, a person's personality is like all other people's, like some other people's, and like no other people's.[2]

The Development of Personality

Study of, and research on, the development of personality has traditionally been an important area for understanding human behavior. The developmental approach is actually a form of personality theory, but, in contrast to most personality theories, it is highly research-oriented. Modern developmental psychology does not get into the argument of heredity versus environment or of maturation versus learning. The human being consists of both physiological *and* psychological interacting parts. Therefore, heredity, environment, maturation, and learning *all* contribute to the human personality.

The study of personality development can be divided into two separate but closely allied approaches. One approach has attempted to identify specific physiological and psychological stages that occur in the development of the human personality. The other approach has tried to identify the important determinants of personality. The "stage" approach has been theoretical in nature, whereas the search for major determinants has been more empirically based.

There are many well-known stage theories of personality development. Most deal with psychosocial development rather than directly with personality development. As with most aspects of personality, there is little agreement among psychologists about the exact stages. In fact, a growing number of today's psychologists contend that there are *no* identifiable stages. Their argument is that personality development consists of a continuous process, and the sequence is based solely upon the learning opportunities available. The opposing view supports stages in personality development. The following sections summarize the major stage theories of personality development.

Freudian Stages

Sigmund Freud was a pioneering stage theorist. Although the analysis of stages of development can be traced as far back as the ancient Greeks, it was Freud who first formulated a meaningful stage theory. He felt that a child progresses through four identifiable stages of psychosexual development: oral; anal; phallic, or oedipal; and genital. Freud believed these stages to be the main driving forces behind the personality.

Today, the Freudian stages often seem silly or even bizarre. Modern psychologists are generally not in agreement with Freud's theory of stages. However, they do give Freud credit for providing some valuable insights and for initiating the meaningful study of personality development. The major disagreement centers on Freud's terminology and the degree to which he carried the stages, rather than on the possibility that he was totally wrong. For example, with regard to Freud's choice of words, one modern personality theorist notes: "Without having at hand a suitable set of learning concepts and terms for personality development, Freud relied on his own preference for a 'body language': he preferred to say 'oral' rather than 'dependent,' 'anal' rather than 'compulsive,' 'genital' rather than 'mature.' "[3] Unfortunately, when one assesses Freud's contribution to the understanding of personality development, the sexually oriented terms seem to overshadow the underlying concepts.

Neo-Freudian Stages

Besides the controversy over terminology, the major disagreement with Freud has to do with the heavy emphasis he placed on the sexual and biological factors in the developing personality. This criticism seems to be more legitimate. Among others, Erik Erikson felt that relatively more attention should be given to the social rather than the sexual adaptations of the individual. He identified the eight psychosocial stages shown in Table 5.1.[4]

Erikson asserted that a psychosocial crisis occurs within each of the stages listed in the table and that in order for the person to have a normal, fulfilling personality, each crisis should be optimally resolved. Probably the most widely known crisis identified by Erikson is the identity experience of adolescents. He believed that the optimum outcome of this teenage crisis is the reintegration of past goals with present goals. For purposes of the study of organizational behavior, the most relevant stage is that of the young and middle-aged adult. Typical organizational participants in the midst of their productive years are in this stage.

TABLE 5.1 Erikson's Psychosocial Stages

Stage of Development	Age
1. Mouth and senses	0–1
2. Eliminative organs and musculature	1–2
3. Locomotion and the genitals	3–5
4. Latency	6–puberty
5. Puberty and adolescence	
6. Early adulthood	
7. Young and middle adulthood	
8. Mature adulthood	

In Erikson's thinking, the crisis that the person faces at this time is one of generativity versus stagnation. The best outcome for personality fulfillment would be an attitude of *production* and concern with the world and future generations. Put another way, according to Erikson, young and middle-aged adults who solve their psychosocial crises by being productive will develop the healthiest personalities. The employing organization should permit and take advantage of this productivity. More recently, specific attention has been given to adult life stages and their impact on career development and planning.

Adult Life Stages

The work of Daniel Levinson on adult life stages has received considerable attention. He believes that "the life structure evolves through a relatively orderly sequence throughout the adult years,"[5] and, unlike other stage theories that are event-oriented (for example, marriage, parenthood, or retirement), his is age-based. In particular, he believes there is little variability (a maximum of two or three years) in four identifiable stable periods:

1. Entering the adult world (ages twenty-two to twenty-eight)
2. Settling down (ages thirty-three to forty)
3. Entering middle adulthood (ages forty-five to fifty)
4. Culmination of middle adulthood (ages fifty-five to sixty)

He identifies four transitional periods:

1. Age-thirty transition (ages twenty-eight to thirty-three)
2. Mid-life transition (ages forty to forty-five)
3. Age-fifty transition (ages fifty to fifty-five)
4. Late adult transition (ages sixty to sixty-five)

Like previous stage theories of personality, Levinson's theory of adult life stages has a lot of intuitive and popular appeal, but, as is also the case with previous stage theories, the research is quite mixed. For example, one study utilizing longitudinal data found no support for Levinson's hypothesis that there should be greater variability in work attitudes during transitional as compared with stable developmental periods or that the greatest variability occurs during the mid-life transition.[6] In other words, there may be such large individual differences among people that the stage theories don't really hold up. However, there is some empirical support for Levinson's framework as it pertains to occupational experience, such as the reasons for changing jobs during the establishment period of adulthood and the mid-life transition period.[7] Thus, as a general guideline, and always recognizing that there will be individual differences, these stage theories can be useful for individual career planning and development.

Hall has synthesized Levinson's theory and other adult stage theories (in particular the work of Erikson and Super) into an overall model for career stages. Figure 5.1 shows that there are four major career stages. During the first stage there is considerable *exploration.* The young employee is searching for an identity and undergoes considerable self-examination and role tryouts. This stage usually results in taking a number of different jobs and is, in general, a very unstable and relatively unproductive period in the person's career. In the second stage, *establishment,* the employee begins to settle down and indicates a need for intimacy. This is usually a growing, productive period in the employee's career. The third stage of *maintenance* occurs when the person levels off into a highly productive plateau and has a need for generativity (the concern to leave something to the next generation). This need often leads the person to assume a paternalistic or perhaps a mentor role with younger subordinates. As shown in Figure 5.1, the person may either have a growth spurt or become stagnant and decline during

FIGURE 5.1 A career-stage model. (*Source:* Adapted from Douglas T. Hall, *Careers in Organizations,* Goodyear, Santa Monica, Calif., 1976, p. 57.)

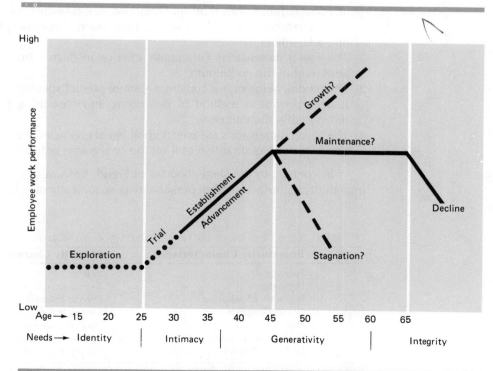

this third career stage. The final stage, *decline,* is self-explanatory. The person indicates a need for integrity (that is, the person needs to feel satisfied with his or her life choices and overall career). With the recent changes in mandatory retirement laws, better medical treatment, and the expectations of society concerning "gray power," this last stage may undergo drastic changes in the years ahead. Older employees may overcome the heretofore assumed decline in this stage of their careers.

Such a career-stage model has received some empirical support.[8] It should be able to help individuals gain a better understanding of their future and assist them in their successful career planning and development process.

Immaturity to Maturity

In a departure from the strict stage approach, organizational behavior theorist Chris Argyris has identified specific dimensions of the human personality as it develops. Argyris proposes that the human personality, rather than going through precise stages, progresses along a continuum from immaturity as an infant to maturity as an adult. However, at any age, people can have their degree of development plotted according to the seven dimensions shown in Table 5.2.

Argyris carefully points out that this model does not imply that all persons reach or strive for all dimensions on the mature end of the continuum. He further explains:

1. The seven dimensions represent only one aspect of the total personality. Much also depends upon the individual's perception, self-concept, and adaptation and adjustment.
2. The seven dimensions continually change in degree from the infant to the adult end of the continuum.
3. The model, being only a construct, cannot predict specific behavior. However, it does provide a method of describing and measuring the growth of any individual in the culture.
4. The seven dimensions are based upon latent characteristics of the personality, which may be quite different from the observable behavior.[9]

In contrast to the stage theories of Freud, Erikson, and Levinson, Argyris's immaturity-maturity model of personality is specifically directed to the study and

TABLE 5.2 The Immaturity-Maturity Continuum

Immaturity Characteristics	Maturity Characteristics
Passivity	Activity
Dependence	Independence
Few ways of behaving	Diverse behavior
Shallow interests	Deep interests
Short-time perspective	Long-time perspective
Subordinate position	Superordinate position
Lack of self-awareness	Self-awareness and control

Source: Adapted from Chris Argyris, *Personality and Organization,* Harper, New York, 1957, p. 50.

analysis of organizational behavior. Argyris assumes that the personalities of organizational employees can be generally described by the mature end of the continuum. This being the case, in order to obtain full expression of employees' personalities, the formal organization should allow for activity rather than passivity, independence rather than dependence, long-time rather than short-time perspective, occupation of a position higher than that of peers, and expression of deep, important abilities.[10] Argyris argues that too often the exact opposite occurs. The mature organizational participant becomes frustrated and anxious and is in conflict with the modern formal organization. In other words, Argyris sees a *basic incongruity* between the needs of the mature personality and the nature of the formal organization. This incongruity premise is an important cornerstone for the entire conceptualization of person-organization structure interaction, which was discussed in relation to the organizational behavior model presented in this book. It is also particularly relevant to the analysis of stress in Chapter 8.

Major Determinants of Personality

What determines personality? Of all the complexities and unanswered questions in the study of human behavior, this question may be the most difficult. The problem lies in the fact that the cognitive and psychological processes, plus many other variables, *all* contribute to personality. However, for ease of study and analysis, the determinants of personality can perhaps best be grouped in five broad categories: biological, cultural, familial, social, and situational.

Biological Contributions

The study of the biological contributions to personality can be divided into several major approaches: heredity, managerial thinking, biofeedback, and physical characteristics.

The Role of Heredity.
The impact of heredity on personality is a very active but still unsettled area of understanding. One problem is that geneticists face a major obstacle in gathering information scientifically on the human being. Animal scientists can conduct highly controlled breeding experiments, but geneticists studying human heredity cannot. Through research on animals, it has been clearly shown that both physical and psychological characteristics can be transmitted through heredity. However, in the case of humans, who cannot be subjected to the necessary controls, the evidence is much less conclusive. Studies of twins, which permit some control over the critical variables, have proved to be newsworthy. For example, the now famous "Jim twins," who were identical twins separated at birth, were both named Jim by their adoptive parents. When they were reunited for the first time at age thirty-nine, there were eerie similarities:

> Both of their first wives were named Linda, their second wives Betty. One named his son James Alan, the other James Allan and both had dogs named Toy. They both chain-smoked Salems, had served as sheriff's deputies, and both drove their Chevro-

lets from Ohio to the same three-block beach on Florida's Gulf Coast. Both chewed their fingernails to the nub, disliked baseball, were mediocre students, enjoyed stock car racing and had basement workshops. They had both built circular benches around a tree in their respective yards. They had both inexplicably gained 10 pounds at about the same time in their lives and then lost it. They both felt they had suffered heart attacks but had not and they both started getting migraine headaches of about the same duration in the same period of their lives.[11]

There are other such publicized cases of similarities of twins raised apart which would support the position that heredity plays the major role in personality and behavior (that is, identical twins have the same genetic endowment, but if they are raised apart they have different environments, and thus similarities support the heredity position, while differences support the environment position). The recent highly publicized results of a long-term study of more than 350 pairs of twins conducted by psychologists at the University of Minnesota give unprecedented support to the influence of heredity.[12] Of particular relevance to the study of organizational behavior was the finding that the traits relating to leadership, traditionalism, and obedience to authority were most strongly determined by heredity. Other relevant traits that seemed to be mostly determined by heredity in this study were alienation, vulnerability or resistance to stress, and risk seeking. The study is not automatically accepted because of measurement problems and controls it used. In other words, the heredity-versus-environment debate is still alive, and no definitive conclusions are yet possible.

Genetic Engineering and Intelligence. Despite the continuing debate on heredity versus environment, recent breakthroughs in genetics (for example, the discovery of the double-helix model of DNA) have opened up potential ways of altering and controlling behavior. This is called *genetic engineering.* Genetics experts feel that some aspects of the human personality are at least partly affected by heredity. In particular, the impact of heredity on intelligence has created much controversy. Geneticists have been joined by some educational psychologists, such as Arthur Jensen, in claiming that intelligence is largely inherited. This, of course, has implications for racial differences, which adds emotional fuel to the fire. For example, the Prime Minister of Japan recently created considerable controversy both here and abroad when he publicly stated:

> So high is the level of education in our country that Japan's is an intelligent society. Our average score is much higher than those of countries like the U.S. There are many blacks, Puerto Ricans and Mexicans in America. In consequence the average score over there is exceedingly low.[13]

Naturally, American minority members were incensed by this statement and demanded an apology. However, statistically the Japanese may have a higher average IQ score than Americans. For example, a study published by British psychologist Robert Lynn reported that Japan's mean national IQ is 111, compared with the American norm of 100.[14] The major issue of the controversy is how intelligence is measured. Until this is fully resolved, the controversy and emotional debates will continue. In the meantime, there seems little doubt that the role of heredity in behavior will receive increased attention in the coming years.

Managerial Thinking. After much research, some behavioral scientists are concluding that managers think differently from the general population. For example, England's Elliott Jaques concludes that unlike most people, executives can see a long way into the future, identify the steps necessary for some move that will take years to complete, envision the consequences of each step, and then take the measures to set everything in motion.[15] He notes that Japan's Konosuke Matsushita has laid down a 250-year plan for his giant company.[16] Other researchers conclude that senior managers have a greater capacity for differentiation (looking at things in different ways) and integration (pulling things together), and are flexible.[17]

Split-Brain Thinking. Split-brain (right versus left) psychology is closely related to managerial thinking, but it has less research backup. The split-brain fad was carried over to the management field when Henry Mintzberg wrote a widely read article entitled "Planning on the Left Side and Managing on the Right." He went so far as to declare, "Which hemisphere of one's brain is better developed may determine whether a person ought to be a planner or a manager."[18] This article and others in the popular management and psychology literature have generated considerable interest among industrial training and development personnel. Some workshops and training sessions are based on split-brain psychology.

Split-brain psychology is the subject of a controversy that can be traced back to the classic mind-body dualism debate in psychology: Are the mind and the body separate entities, or is the mind simply a function of the physical being? Work done on ESB (electrical stimulation of the brain) suggests that there are clearly identifiable portions of the physical brain that control "mind" functions such as emotion and aggression. There is also evidence to indicate that the right hemisphere of the brain may have functions such as those listed in the right-hand column of Table 5.3 and that the left hemisphere may have the functions listed in the left-hand column of the table. But these areas are still open for further research.

As the discussion of the split brain indicates, there are more questions raised than answers provided.[19] Yet few would disagree with the idea that the brain certainly holds many unlocked secrets for the future, and some training experts, such as General Electric's Ned Herrmann, suggest that the future is already here. He feels that enough is known about the brain to design and deliver new learning and training systems.[20]

Biofeedback. Similar to the results of work on the brain have been some of the widely publicized and spectacular results of biofeedback training (BFT). Until recently, physiologists and psychologists felt that certain biological functions such as brain-wave patterns, gastric secretions, and fluctuations in blood pressure and skin temperature were beyond conscious control. Now a growing number of scientists believe that these involuntary functions can be consciously controlled through biofeedback. In BFT the individual learns the internal rhythms of a particular body process through electronic signals fed back from equipment that is wired to the body area (for example, skin, brain, or heart). From this biofeedback

TABLE 5.3 Summary of Characteristics and Dimensions Attributed to the Left and Right Hemispheres of the Brain

Left Hemisphere (Right Side of Body)	Right Hemisphere (Left Side of Body)
Speech/verbal	Spatial/musical
Logical, mathematical	Holistic
Linear, detailed	Artistic, symbolic
Sequential	Simultaneous
Controlled	Emotional
Intellectual	Intuitive, creative
Dominant	Minor (quiet)
Worldly	Spiritual
Active	Receptive
Analytic	Synthetic, gestalt-oriented
Reading, writing, naming	Facial recognition
Sequential ordering	Simultaneous comprehension
Perception of significant order	Perception of abstract patterns
Complex motor sequences	Recognition of complex figures

Source: Adapted from Robert J. Trotter, "The Other Hemispheres," *Science News,* Apr. 3, 1976, p. 219.

the person can learn to control the body process in question. A very simple example of biofeedback involves holding a thermometer between the index finger and the thumb. If the person watches the thermometer and concentrates and thinks very hard about the finger and the thumb getting warmer, the temperature may begin to rise.

It is now generally recognized that BFT has several medical applications. For example, it may be used to alleviate migraine headaches by diverting blood from the throbbing region to other parts of the body; cerebral palsy patients have learned to control muscle spasms by listening to clicks from a feedback machine wired to the body; people with dangerously irregular heart rhythms have learned to modify them by watching blinking lights that tell them when the heart is functioning properly; and, on the lighter side, a person can control an electric train through brain waves.[21] Such applications of biofeedback are now widely used by therapists and in clinics and hospitals across the United States.[22]

Physical Characteristics and Rate of Maturing. A third biologically based approach to the study of personality is to analyze the effects of physical characteristics and rate of maturing. Despite the tremendous potential offered by the study of genetics, the brain, and biofeedback, this approach has already proved to be a significant contributor to the study of personality. An individual's physical appearance, which is said to be a vital ingredient of the personality, is biologically determined. The fact that a person is tall or short, fat or skinny, handsome or ugly, or black or white will influence the person's effect on others, and this in turn will affect the self-concept.

There are entire theories of personality based upon body build. Sheldon's classic theory, which correlates certain body builds (endomorphic, mesomorphic, and ectomorphic) with specific personality traits, is an example. However, most modern psychologists do not go so far as Sheldon in emphasizing the importance of physical attributes. There are too many exceptions for such a theory to be meaningful. On the other hand, practically all would agree that physical characteristics have at least some influence on the personality.

This same reasoning is applied to the rate of maturation. A rapidly maturing boy or girl is exposed to different physical and social situations and activities from those to which a slowly maturing child is exposed. This differing rate of maturation will be reflected in the personality.

Cultural Contributions

Traditionally, cultural factors are usually considered to make a more significant contribution to personality than biological factors. The learning process plays an important role in personality development. Often, however, in discussions that stress either the cognitive or the reinforcement aspects of this process, nothing is mentioned about what is learned—the *content*. Yet, in terms of personality development, the content is probably as important as the process. Culture is the key concept in analyzing the content of learning because what a person learns has content. The prevailing culture dictates *what* a person will learn. It is the context in which everything else takes place. The accompanying International Application Example, Gift Giving in Western Europe, provides an example of such a cultural context.

As indicated in the introductory comments of this book, culture has become a major concept in the study of organizational behavior. Chapters 3 and 4 were specifically devoted to it. Culture can also be used to better understand personality development. For example, the methods by which an infant is fed and is toilet-trained and the ways in which the person later makes the transition from adolescence to adulthood are all culturally determined. As indicated by the discussion of the stage theories, such cultural events contribute significantly to the personality. The culture largely determines attributes such as independence, aggression, competition, and cooperation.

For example, Western cultures generally reward a person for being independent and competitive, while Oriental cultures do not. It follows that a person reared in a Western culture has a different personality from that of a person reared in an Oriental culture. A person who is biologically of Western descent but is brought up in an Oriental culture will have an Oriental type of personality, and vice versa.

Despite the importance of the cultural contribution to personality, a linear relationship cannot be established between personality and a given culture. One problem in complex societies stems from the existence of numerous subcultures within a given culture. For example, the Protestant ethic may be a dominant value of Western culture. However, there are extreme value differences among socioeconomic classes, ages, and geographic regions. The point is that it is wrong to assume that all workers or managers in Western societies possess the Protestant ethic. On the other hand, this does not rule out the fact that culture affects personality. The difficulty comes when broad generalizations are made. When analyzing organizational behavior, the *relevant* cultural impact must be recognized.

Gift Giving in Western Europe

Culture is important in understanding not only Americans' personalities but those of other countries as well. Western Europe is a good example. The United States does considerable business there, so it is very helpful for American businesspeople to know how to act in this corner of the globe. For example, when doing business with Europeans, when is it acceptable to give a gift and how should it be done? The following are some useful guidelines for gift giving in Western Europe:

1. Do not give a business gift at the first meeting. This is considered bad manners.
2. If you are going to send flowers to your dinner hostess, send them ahead rather than handing them to her upon your arrival. This gives her time to arrange and place them as she wants. It also prevents any embarrassment among the other guests who may show up at the same time you do and be empty-handed.
3. When sending flowers, be sure of your choice. In France, chrysanthemums are associated with mourning. In France and Germany, red roses are a gift only between lovers.
4. Good chocolates and liqueurs are excellent house gifts. If the occasion demands something more elaborate, small porcelain and silver gifts such as candlesticks or table lighters are good choices.
5. Never give perfume or men's cologne as a gift. This is considered too personal for a business gift to or from either sex.
6. Do not enclose your business card with the gift. This is considered crass. Instead write a note on a blank card.

Contributions from the Family

Whereas the culture generally prescribes and limits what a person can be taught, it is the family, and later the social group, which selects, interprets, and dispenses the culture. Thus, the family probably has the most significant impact on early personality development; later, the socialization process takes over.

The parents play an especially important part in the identification process, which is important to the person's early development. Usually, the parent of the same sex as the child will serve as the model for the child's development. Also, a substantial amount of empirical evidence indicates that the overall home environment created by the parents, in addition to their direct influence, is critical to personality development. For example, children with a markedly institutional upbringing (orphans) and children reared in a cold, unstimulating home are much more likely to be socially and emotionally maladjusted than children raised by parents in a warm, loving, and stimulating environment. The key variable here does not seem to be the parents per se, but rather the type of atmosphere that is generated for the child.

Research Study on Parental Influence. A classic study by James Abegglen effectively points up the impact of the parents on the personalities of very successful executives.[23] He conducted a detailed case study of twenty executives who had risen from a lower-class childhood to hold top-ranking positions with business firms. Data were accumulated from interviews which at first focused on personal and job histories and then on the use of eight thematic apperception cards (pictures about which subjects tell a story or report what they see). It was found that fifteen of the twenty executives, while children, had had what Abegglen calls a "separation trauma" with their fathers. Two fathers had died during the childhood of the subjects, two subjects had lived with their mothers following a divorce, six of the fathers had been in severe business and financial difficulties, and in five cases the fathers had been seriously ill. The fathers were blamed by the sons for the hardships suffered by the family. They were described as inept, sometimes hostile, and usually inadequate. The mother, on the other hand, was generally viewed as being economically and morally stable but not "motherly" in the sense of being affectionate.

The results obtained by Abegglen indicate that a classic Freudian reaction formation had taken place. The normal positive identification process between father and son had been blocked. Instead, the son negatively identified with his father and strove to be the opposite from him. This negative identification seemed to be a major motivating force throughout the son's life. The high needs for achievement and the low needs for affiliation exhibited by the subjects can be traced back to the negative identification in childhood. Thus, the father and mother (who transmitted values that were conducive to upward striving) seemed to have had a great deal of influence on the personalities of this group of business executives.

The Abegglen study has potentially significant implications for the study of organizational behavior. For instance, the case histories of organizational participants might provide much insight into their behavior. Yet, as with most studies of this nature in the behavioral sciences, broad generalizations or grandiose conclusions are unwarranted. One organizational behavior expert, in evaluating the Abegglen study, cautions:

> Intriguing as Abegglen's findings are, it must be remembered that they were drawn from a small and highly select group. He has demonstrated that an early reaction-formation can lead to a lifelong pattern of achievement striving and upward mobility; but so can other kinds of psychological relationships. Sons who are disappointed in their fathers are not destined to corner the market in successful careers![24]

Birth-Order Data. Siblings (brothers and sisters) also contribute to personality. So far, studies of birth order have produced some very interesting but inconclusive results. Studies by social psychologists have found that firstborn and only children have a stronger need to affiliate than children born later. The conclusion drawn from one such research study is that "firstborn children, at least in our society, are probably more anxious, more dependent on others, especially in anxious situations, and more inclined to go along with the group than are other children."[25] Other research evidence, although it is far from being conclusive, indicates that firstborns may be more serious, less carefree, and more likely to be a problem than later-borns.[26]

Staunch advocates of birth-order data claim it is possible to describe major personality characteristics solely on the basis of position in the family constellation. For example, one psychologist gives specific personality sketches for the oldest and youngest brothers of one or more brothers (OBB and YBB, respectively) and for the oldest and youngest brothers of sisters (OBS and YBS, respectively). These four types have equivalent female counterparts making a total of eight combinations. This approach even makes suggestions, based upon empirical data, as to the kind of worker each type will be. For example, the OBB is a good worker and independent; the YBB fakes independence and tends to be an irregular worker; the OBS, who is also said to be a "true ladies' man" who adores women, is a responsible worker; and the YBS, who is greatly loved by women, is not a very regular or systematic worker but is capable of great accomplishments.[27] On the surface, there seems to be a great deal of truth to these descriptions and possible implications for management. For example, if found to correlate with employment variables, birth order may take on added significance in the selection process. At the present time, however, birth-order data, like astrology charts, make a lot of surface sense but need much more scientific research before any definitive conclusions can be drawn.

The Socialization Process

Besides the biological, cultural, and family influences on personality, there is increasing recognition given to the role of other relevant persons, groups, and especially organizations, which greatly influence an individual's personality. This is commonly called the *socialization process*. It is especially relevant to organizational behavior because the process is not confined to early childhood; rather, it takes place throughout one's life. In particular, evidence is accumulating that socialization may be one of the best explanations for why employees behave the way they do in today's organizations. For example, Edgar Schein notes: "It is high time that some of our managerial knowledge and skill be focused on those forces in the organization environment which derive from the fact that organizations are social systems which do socialize their new members. If we do not learn to analyze and control the forces of organizational socialization, we are abdicating one of our primary managerial responsibilities."[28] A recent study found that the socialization tactics that organizations employ (e.g., providing information to newcomers, new recruits going through common learning experiences, and so forth) does have the intended impact. It was found that different patterns of socialization lead to different forms of newcomer adjustment to organizations.[29]

Socialization starts with the initial contact between a mother and her new infant. After infancy, other members of the immediate family (father, brothers, and sisters), close relatives and family friends, and then the social group (peers, school friends, and members of the work group) play influential roles. Of particular interest is Schein's idea that the organization itself also contributes to socialization.[30] He points out that the process includes only the learning of those values, norms, and behavior patterns which, from the organization's and the work group's points of view, are necessary for any new organization member to learn. The following are widely accepted characteristics of such organizational socialization of employees:

1. Change of attitudes, values, and behaviors
2. Continuity of socialization over time
3. Adjustment to new jobs, work groups, and organizational practices
4. Mutual influence between new recruits and their managers
5. Criticality of the early socialization period[31]

Accordingly, organization members must learn things like not to drive a Ford if they are working for Chevrolet, not to criticize the company in public, and not to wear the wrong kind of clothes or be seen in the wrong kind of place.[32] They must understand "who holds power and who does not, which informal networks of communication are reliable and which are unreliable, and what political maneuvers they are likely to encounter in their department or unit. In short, if they wish to survive and prosper in their new work home, they must soon come to 'know the ropes.' "[33]

The example of the GM purchase of EDS discussed in Chapter 3 and given further attention in the accompanying Application Example, Personality Clash in Corporate America, indicates the type of conflict that may result from two very different socialized managers and companies trying to work together. With the increasing number of mergers and acquisitions occurring in corporate America, this can be a real problem.

Application Example:

Personality Clash in Corporate America*

As General Motors began to lose ground in the auto industry, it started searching for acquisitions that would diversify the company and help it recapture its position. For example, GM Chairman Roger B. Smith felt that the purchase of the Electronic Data Systems Corporation (EDS) would help accomplish this new strategy. EDS had been founded by Ross Perot, the billionaire well known for such exploits as sponsoring a rescue in the Middle East. EDS and Perot, Smith believed, would both be welcome additions to GM. However, this did not turn out to be the case.

Perot's personality was much different from Smith's. Perot was an entrepreneur used to getting things done quickly. He "shot from the hip" and expected to "call all the shots." Smith, on the other hand, had a more methodical style. A professional manager, he was accustomed to doing things more slowly. The huge GM bureaucratic machine could not move rapidly and Smith understood this.

Unfortunately, the two men were unable to get along. Perot soon became convinced that GM had to undertake many changes if it was to be more competitive, and these had to be undertaken as soon as possible. Smith felt that Perot failed to understand how GM worked. Something had to be done—and it was. GM bought back Perot's stock for $700 million, and Perot agreed to give up his seat on the GM board of directors. Industry analysts were quick to point out that the company's board of director meetings were now likely to be more quiet ones, but they wondered if GM would be better off for having lost the services of one of the most astute and intelligent managers in the country.

*Source: Adapted from William J. Hampton and Todd Mason, "GM Hasn't Bought Much Peace," *Business Week*, Dec. 15, 1986, pp. 24–26.

Studies have indicated that socialization is important not only to new organization members but also in the superior-subordinate relationship and when people switch jobs (for example, when they move from a line to a staff position) or are promoted.[34] Van Maanen also suggests specific socialization strategies, such as formal or informal, individual or collective, sequential or nonsequential, and fixed or variable.[35] For example, a company may use a sequential socialization strategy to groom people for top management positions by first rotating them through a series of relevant functional specialties. Another organization, say, a government agency, may take someone with political power from the rank and file and make that person the head of the agency. This nonsequential strategy will result in different personal (that is, the personality will be affected) and organizational outcomes. Recently, there has been increasing agreement concerning the specific strategies that will lead to successful organizational socialization. These can be summarized as follows:

1. Provide a challenging first job.
2. Provide relevant training.
3. Provide timely and consistent feedback.
4. Select a good first supervisor to be in charge of socialization.
5. Design a relaxed orientation program.
6. Place new recruits in work groups with high morale.[36]

Such deliberate socialization strategies have tremendous potential impact on human resources management and organizational effectiveness.

More Immediate Situational Considerations

The socialization process is obviously concerned with the situational impact on personality and thus falls in line with a social learning perspective. The cultural and family impact is more concerned with the historical nature of personality development. Both the cultural/family and the socialization processes are important to personality, but it should also be recognized that the immediate situation may in the final analysis predominate. As the S-O-B-C model in Chapter 1 showed, it is the situation interacting with the human being, including the individual's personality, that is the vital antecedent to behavior. An example is the worker whose developmental history has shaped a personality which incorporates a high need for power and achievement. When placed in a highly bureaucratized work situation, this individual may become frustrated and behave apathetically and/or aggressively. Thus, on the surface this worker appears to be lazy and/or a troublemaker. Yet the developmental history would predict that the individual would be a very hard worker, striving to get ahead.

The countless potential combinations of the situation and the human being make it virtually impossible always to predict accurately, from the developmental history alone, the ways in which the personality will be behaviorally expressed. The interaction is too complex, and when the role of consequences is included, it becomes obvious that the developmental aspects of personality by themselves do not provide the answer of understanding, predicting, and controlling human behavior.

Research on the Immediate Situational Impact.

The very dramatic, classic study by Stanley Milgram gives support to the important role that the immediate situation plays in the human personality. He conducted a series of tightly controlled experimental studies that used almost 1000 adult subjects.[37] These subjects were not students, ranged from twenty to fifty years of age, and came from a wide variety of occupations (unskilled, skilled, white-collar, sales, business, and professional). Each experimental session consisted of a naive subject, an accomplice, and the experimenter. The experimenter explained that the subject would be part of a learning experiment to test the effect of punishment on memory. After a rigged drawing on roles to be played, the naive subject always became the "teacher" and the accomplice became the "learner" in the experiment. The learner (the experimenter's accomplice) was then taken to the next room and strapped into a sinister-looking "electric chair," which the subject could see through a glass partition. The experimenter carefully explained that the teacher (the naive subject) would administer increasing levels of shock to the learner whenever a mistake was made. The shock generator had clearly marked voltage levels that ran from 15 to 450 volts and printed descriptions that ranged from "Slight Shock" to "Danger: Severe Shock." To convince the naive subjects of the authenticity of the shock device, they were given a real shock from the 45-volt switch.

For control purposes, the accomplices' responses to the shocks were broadcast from a premade tape, and of course they did not actually receive any shocks. Starting with what the subject believed to be a 75-volt shock, the learner began to grunt and moan. As the succeeding shocks increased in voltage, the cries became louder and more desperate. The learner pleaded with the teacher to have mercy and stop the experiment. Whenever the teacher (subject) would hesitate to administer more shock, the experimenter would prod the teacher on by saying, "You have no other choice; you must go on!" Finally, the learner could give no more answers, and the naive subject was told by the experimenter to give the maximum-voltage shock. Contrary to common or expert opinion, almost two-thirds of the subjects went ahead and administered what they thought was a very dangerous, severe shock that might even lead to death. Milgram, who was obviously disturbed by his findings, stated:

> With numbing regularity good people were seen to knuckle under the demands of
> authority and perform actions that were callous and severe. Men who are in everyday
> life responsible and decent were seduced by the trappings of authority, by the
> control of their perceptions, and by the uncritical acceptance of the experimenter's
> definition of the situation, into performing harsh acts.[38]

Implications of the Milgram Study.

Compared with the developmental aspects of personality, relatively little attention has been given to the situational impact. Yet Milgram's research suggests the very powerful role that the immediate situation can play in the human personality. In fact, he calls for a theory that would provide a definition and typology of situations. He believes that if such guidance were available, certain definable properties of situations could be transformed into psychological forces in the individual.[39] In other words, studying the situational determinants may be of as much value as studying case histories. To prove the point, Milgram put leading advocates of the case-history approach to the test. Forty psychiatrists from a prestigious medical school were asked to predict the behavior of the subjects in the shock experiment. The highly trained experts did a very poor job. They estimated that only about one-tenth of 1 percent of the subjects would administer the maximum-voltage shock, when in fact almost 63 percent did so.

The Milgram research certainly does not completely rule out the importance of the developmental aspects of personality. Rather, it demonstrates that the immediate situation may potentially have a very big impact on the behavioral expression of the personality, even to the point where it seems to override what one would predict on the basis of the developmental history. The experimenter in the Yale psychological laboratory where the studies were conducted produced a situation in which people violated their moral codes. They were obedient to scientific authority. When the setting was moved to a run-down commercial building under the guise of Research Associates of Bridgeport, the percentage of those who obeyed to the end dropped to 48 percent.

The results of Milgram's studies produced a strong emotional reaction from both academicians and the public. Critics claim that Milgram was unethical, and they doubt that the subjects really believed that they were administering such a severe shock. Milgram answers the first charge by saying that every precaution was taken and that all subjects were carefully debriefed. He supported those who disobeyed and assured those who obeyed that their behavior was perfectly normal and that other subjects had shared their conflicts. Follow-up questionnaires found that almost everyone thought the experiment had been worthwhile and that only 1 percent of the subjects were sorry they had participated. As for the charge concerning the validity of the study, Milgram has data from direct observation, interviews, and questionnaires to support his claim that the subjects accepted the experiment at face value. He feels that not one subject suspected the deception.

In his book *Obedience to Authority* Milgram expounds on some of his original findings and discusses the follow-up on the modifications and variations. The following summarizes some of the finer points of, and variations in, obedience to authority:

1. Obedience decreases when the learner is in the same room as the teacher and decreases further when the teacher must touch the learner directly to administer the shock. The modern state, of course, is designed for impersonality; people can pull switches and drop bombs without ever seeing the victims.
2. Obedience drops sharply when the experimenter is absent. To commit acts they would otherwise consider immoral, people must have authority behind them.
3. Obedience drops when the subject is in a group of rebellious peers. Rebels awaken the subject to the possibility of disobedience and, in this case, to its benign results. The group offers social support for the decision to disobey.
4. By contrast, obedience increases when the subject is merely an accessory to

the crime and does not actually have to pull the shock lever. In such a case, thirty-seven subjects out of forty stay in the experiment to the end.[40]

The findings of Milgram's study have implications for explaining the behavior during some of the highly publicized war atrocities (for example, at Auschwitz in World War II and My Lai in the Vietnam war). In fact, the studies are sometimes called the "Eichmann experiments," after the Nazi war criminal Adolf Eichmann. Some of the anxieties of Milgram and the implications of the study have also been captured in a fictionalized television drama, *The Tenth Level*. Besides the emotional impact the studies have on people, Milgram's work does have significant implications for understanding organizational behavior. Although this chapter has been concerned primarily with the impact of the situation on personality, in the broader sense the Milgram study reinforces the importance that the situation also has on overall human behavior. As stated by Milgram: "A situation exerts an important press on the individual. It exercises constraints and may provide push. In certain circumstances it is not so much the kind of person a man is, as the kind of situation in which he is placed, that determines his actions."[41] Once again, the person-situation interaction surfaces as an important, but often overlooked, dynamic in the understanding of human behavior.

Summary

Personality represents the "whole person" concept. It includes perception, learning, motivation, and more. Definitionally, people's external appearance and behavior, their inner awareness of self, their pattern of measurable traits, and the person-situation interaction make up their personalities. Freud's and Erikson's classic stage theories of personality development have made significant contributions to areas such as career development, but Argyris's seven-dimension continuum of immaturity-maturity is of more relevance to the study of organizational behavior. Determining the inputs into personality may be the most complex and difficult task in the study of human behavior, but a comprehensive approach would have to include biological, cultural, family, socialization, and immediate situational factors.

Questions for Discussion and Review

1. Critically analyze the statement that "the various psychological processes can be thought of as pieces of a jigsaw puzzle, and personality as the completed puzzle picture."
2. What is the comprehensive definition of "personality"? Give brief examples of each of the major elements.
3. What are the various factors in the biological contributions to personality? The cultural contributions? The family contributions? The socialization contributions? The immediate situational contributions?
4. How does the study of personality help an understanding of organizational behavior?

References

1. Don Hellriegel, John W. Slocum, and Richard W. Woodman, *Organizational Behavior,* 4th ed., West, St. Paul, Minn., 1986, p. 63.
2. Clyde Kluckhohn and H. A. Murray, "Personality Formation: The Determinants," in C. Kluckhohn and H. A. Murray (eds.), *Personality,* Knopf, New York, 1948, p. 35.
3. Walter Mischel, *Introduction to Personality,* Holt, New York, 1971, p. 43.
4. Erik Erikson, *Childhood and Society,* 2d ed., Norton, New York, 1963. Also see Mischel, op. cit., pp. 39–41.
5. Daniel J. Levinson, *The Seasons of a Man's Life,* Knopf, New York, 1978, p. 49.
6. Richard E. Kopelman and Michael Glass, "Test of Daniel Levinson's Theory of Adult Male Life States," *National Academy of Management Proceedings,* 1979, pp. 79–83.
7. Raymond Hill and Edwin L. Miller, "Job Change and the Middle Seasons of a Man's Life," *Academy of Management Journal,* March 1981, pp. 114–127.
8. Stephen A. Stumpf, "Career Roles, Psychological Success and Job Attitudes," *Journal of Vocational Behavior,* August 1981, pp. 98–112.
9. Chris Argyris, *Personality and Organization,* Harper, New York, 1957, pp. 51–53.
10. Ibid., p. 53.
11. Kay Bartlett, "Twin Study: Influence of Genes Surprises Some," *Lincoln Journal and Star,* Oct. 4, 1981, p. 3F.
12. "Genes, Not Child-Rearing, Dictate Personality More," *Omaha World-Herald,* Dec. 3, 1986, p. 54.
13. "Nakasone's World-Class Blunder," *Time,* Oct. 6, 1986, p. 66.
14. Ibid.
15. Walter Kiechel, "How Executives Think," *Fortune,* Feb. 4, 1985, p. 127.
16. Ibid.
17. Ibid., p. 128.
18. Henry Mintzberg, "Planning on the Left Side and Managing on the Right," *Harvard Business Review,* July–August 1976, p. 49.
19. For a recent critical review, see Terence Hines, "Left Brain/Right Brain Mythology and Implications for Management and Training," *Academy of Management Review,* October 1987, pp. 600–606.
20. Ned Herrmann, "The Creative Brain," *Training and Development Journal,* October 1981, pp. 10–16.
21. *Newsweek,* Oct. 14, 1974, pp. 76–77.
22. "Stress: Can We Cope?" *Time,* June 6, 1983, p. 53.
23. James C. Abegglen, "Personality Factors in Social Mobility: A Study of Occupationally Mobile Businessmen," *Genetic Psychology Monographs,* August 1958, pp. 101–159.
24. Saul W. Gellerman, *Motivation and Productivity,* American Management Association, New York, 1963, p. 147.
25. Bernard Berelson and Gary A. Steiner, *Human Behavior,* Harcourt, Brace & World, New York, 1964, p. 74.
26. Ibid., p. 73.
27. Walter Toman, "Birth Order Rules All," *Psychology Today,* December 1970, pp. 46–49.
28. Edgar H. Schein, "Organizational Socialization and the Profession of Management," in David Kolb, Irwin Rubin, and James McIntyre (eds.), *Organizational Psychology: A Book of Readings,* Prentice-Hall, Englewood Cliffs, N.J., 1971, pp. 14–15.
29. Gareth R. Jones, "Socialization Tactics, Self-Efficiency, and Newcomers' Adjustments to Organizations," *Academy of Management Journal,* June 1986, pp. 262–279.

30. Schein, op. cit., p. 3.
31. Daniel C. Feldman and Hugh J. Arnold, *Managing Individual and Group Behavior in Organizations*, McGraw-Hill, New York, 1983, pp. 79–80.
32. Schein, op. cit.
33. Robert A. Baron, *Behavior in Organizations*, 2d ed., Allyn and Bacon, Boston, 1986, p. 65.
34. John Gabarro, "Socialization at the Top: How CEOs and Subordinates Evolve Interpersonal Contracts," *Organizational Dynamics*, Winter 1979, pp. 3–23.
35. John Van Maanen, "People Processing: Strategies of Organizational Socialization," *Organizational Dynamics*, Summer 1978, pp. 19–36.
36. Feldman and Arnold, op. cit., pp. 83–86.
37. Stanley Milgram, "Some Conditions of Obedience and Disobedience to Authority," *Human Relations*, February 1965, pp. 57–76.
38. Ibid., p. 75.
39. Ibid.
40. See *Psychology Today*, June 1974, p. 77.
41. Milgram, op. cit., p. 72.

REAL CASE: Entrepreneurial Women*

According to the Small Business Administration, from 1977 to 1983 women have started their own businesses at twice the rate that men have. Today, female entrepreneurs own over 25 percent of all small businesses in the country and, in most cases, these enterprises are less than five years old. At this rate, women will own half of all the businesses in the country by the turn of the century.

What types of personalities do entrepreneurial women have? Recent research shows that many of them fit the classic entrepreneurial mold. They are risk takers; they want to provide new goods and services in a wide variety of fields; they are seeking job satisfaction and a chance to run an operation of their own; and they want to make a great deal of money. Researchers have also found the following to be true of the typical female entrepreneur: (a) she is the first-born child of middle-class parents; (b) her father tended to be self-employed while her mother was a homemaker; (c) she has an undergraduate degree in the liberal arts; (d) she is married with children; and (e) she is between the ages of thirty-five and forty-five when beginning her first business venture.

Despite their success, things have not been easy for female entrepreneurs. Many of them have found that they must overcome their early training. Notes one business consultant: "What girls are taught as acceptable behavior is in sharp contrast to what you do in business." Kindness, nurturing, and supportive behaviors are often viewed as signs of weakness by competitive male entrepreneurs. Many women also tend to be conservative, unwilling to borrow money and expand as rapidly as they should. Additionally, they

*Source: Adapted from Lois Therrien and others, "What Do Women Want? A Company They Can Call Their Own," *Business Week*, Dec. 22, 1986, pp. 60–62.

tend to have less experience in supervising people, negotiating deals, and handling finances. On the other hand, the president of a management group which advises new ventures reports that women entrepreneurs are hard-working, more creative than men, and better decision makers because they follow their instincts. And a researcher in the field reports that entrepreneurial women tend to use a more egalitarian management style than do men and this results in a more relaxed, creative environment. As a result, many women are finding greater satisfaction and success in running their own enterprise than in working for someone else.

1. Does the profile of the female entrepreneur provided in this case lend credence to the importance of birth-order rank? Explain.
2. How does the socialization process reduce the possibilities of some women ever becoming successful entrepreneurs?
3. Given your answer to number 2, how do you explain the increase in the number of female entrepreneurs?

CASE: Cheerleader versus Activist

Liz Schmit grew up in a Midwestern town of 25,000 people. She was the third generation of the Schmit family in this town. Her grandparents, who had come from Germany, were retired, but they took care of her and her younger brother whenever her mother and dad had to go someplace—like a wedding or a funeral. Neither of Liz's parents had attended college, but once her father took an IQ test and scored almost in the genius category. Her parents always encouraged her to do well in school and saved their money so that she could go to State University. Liz also worked during the summer to save money for college. She did very well academically in high school and was a varsity cheerleader. She went on to State University, joined a sorority, majored in English, graduated with honors, and took a job with Landis and Smith Advertising Agency. Liz, now thirty-seven years old, has been with L&S for fifteen years and has a good work record.

One of Liz's coworkers is Todd Long. Todd grew up in a suburb of Los Angeles. Both his parents had attended UCLA, and he saw his grandparents, who were retired military people, only a few times. While Todd was growing up, his parents were gone a lot. His mother arranged for baby-sitters while she got her degree at UCLA. It was always assumed that when Todd graduated from high school he too would go to UCLA. Todd did not participate in many extracurricular activities, but he graduated in the top 10 percent of his high school class. At UCLA he majored in journalism and was very active in the student movement in the late 1960s. Upon graduation, he cut his hair and went to work for L&S. Todd, now thirty-nine, has been employed by L&S for twelve years and has a very good work record.

The job of copy editor is now open, and Liz and Todd are the two top candidates. The head of L&S, Stacy McAdams, made it clear that "this job requires a good personality. The person will be in contact with all the people in the office, and we need someone who can get along well with others and still be able to coordinate the work and meet our critical deadlines."

1. On the basis of the brief sketches of these two people, what do you think their personalities are like? Use the determinants of personality and give an example of each determinant that can be found in the description of this situation.
2. Who do you think will get the job? You can discuss the male/female implications; however, solely on the basis of the personalities that you outlined in question 1, who do you think *would* get the job? Who do you think *should* get the job?
3. What did the boss mean when she said that a "good personality" is required? Is there such a thing? Do you feel that personality has much of an input into this type of staffing decision? Should it have an input? Why?
4. Do you think the socialization processes at L&S have completely overcome Liz's and Todd's biological, cultural, and family influences? Why or why not?

6 Perception

Everyone is now familiar with the famous cola wars. In order to spur on sales, and defeat its rival Pepsi-Cola, Coca-Cola decided to employ the tried-and-true marketing strategy of coming out with a "new and improved" product. Procter & Gamble had perfected this strategy in selling its laundry detergents and huge line of packaged goods. The strategy is based on the contention that if consumers perceive a "new and improved" product, they will buy it. Coca-Cola did extensive market research to perfect a new, sweeter cola formula. This research indicated that soft-drink consumers preferred this new taste and would buy the product. Coke launched its new Coke product on the basis of this information. The public reaction is now history. The marketers failed to anticipate the loyalty to the "old" or "classic" Coke. Many soft-drink consumers, fueled by the media, perceived new Coke as an infringement on their habits and ties to the past. They openly rebelled, and it appeared that Coca-Cola had made a serious blunder. However, the company quickly countered with another tried-and-true strategy—if you can't lick 'em, join 'em—and put old Coke back on the market. The result was that with both new Coke and Classic Coke, Coca-Cola was able to increase its overall market share, its ultimate objective. Its management learned some important lessons about the complexities of consumer perceptions.

Learning Objectives

- DEFINE the overall nature of perception, explaining how it differs from sensation.
- DISCUSS perceptual selectivity, including the external attention factors and internal set factors.
- EXPLAIN perceptual organization, including figure-ground, grouping, constancy, context, and defense principles.
- IDENTIFY the dimensions of social perception, including attribution, stereotyping, and halo.

The last chapter dealt with the whole person, personality concept. This chapter isolates out one of the human cognitive processes—perception. As indicated earlier, cognitions are basically bits of information, and the cognitive processes involve the ways in which people process that information. In other words, the cognitive processes suggest that, like computers, humans are information processors. However, today's complex computers are very simple information-processing units when compared with *human information processing.*

Like the soft-drink consumers in the opening example, people's individual differences and uniqueness are largely the result of the cognitive processes. The S-O-B-C model presented in Chapter 1 indicated that the cognitive processes play an important mediational role (O) between the stimulus situation (S) and the behavior (B). Although there are a number of cognitive processes (imagination, perception, and even thinking), it is generally recognized that the perceptual process is a very important one that takes place between the situation and the behavior and is most relevant to the study of organizational behavior. For example, the observation that a department head and a subordinate may react quite differently to the same top management directive can be better understood and explained by the perceptual process. Also, recent research indicates that things such as age perceptions can affect promotion and performance. One such study found that a recent merger largely failed because one company's forty-year-old executives and the other company's sixty-five-year-old executives differed over which group was better able to make decisions.[1] It was a matter of differing age perceptions.

In this book, perception is presented as an important cognitive variable to be considered in understanding organizational behavior. The environment (both antecedent and consequent), plus other psychological processes such as learning and motivation and the whole of personality, is also important. However, for the most part, although much of the material on perception is basic knowledge in the behavioral sciences, it has been largely overlooked or not translated for use by those in the organizational behavior field. All the topics covered in this chapter are concerned with understanding organizational behavior, and they have many direct applications to organization and management practice.

The first major section presents a theoretical discussion of the general nature and significance of the perceptual process. The relationship between sensation and perception is clarified, and some of the important perceptual subprocesses are discussed. The second section covers the various aspects of perceptual selectivity. Both external factors (intensity, size, contrast, repetition, motion, and novelty and familiarity) and internal ones (motivation, personality, and learning) are included. The third section discusses the role that the perceptual set plays in the workplace. The next section is concerned with perceptual organization. The principles of figure-ground, grouping, constancy, and context are given primary emphasis. The last section focuses on social perception—the phenomena of attribution, stereotypes, and the halo effect.

The Nature and Importance of Perception

The key to understanding perception is to recognize that it is a unique *interpretation* of the situation, not an exact recording of it. In short, perception is a very complex cognitive process that yields a unique picture of the world that may be quite different from reality.

Recognition of the difference between the perceptual world and the real world is vital to the understanding of organizational behavior. A specific example would be the universal assumption made by managers that subordinates always want promotions, when, in fact, many subordinates really feel psychologically *forced* to accept a promotion. Managers seldom attempt to find out, and sometimes subordinates themselves do not know, whether the promotion should be offered. In other words, the perceptual world of the manager is quite different from the perceptual world of the subordinate, and both may be very different from reality. If this is the case, what can be done about it from a management standpoint? The best answer seems to be that a better understanding of the concepts involved should be developed. Direct applications and techniques should logically follow complete understanding. The rest of the chapter is devoted to providing a better understanding of the cognitive process of perception.

Sensation versus Perception

There is usually a great deal of misunderstanding about the relationship between sensation and perception. Behavioral scientists generally agree that people's "reality" (the world around them) depends on their senses. However, the raw sensory input is not enough. They must also process these sensory data and make sense out of them in order to understand the world around them. Thus, the starting point in the study of perception should clarify the relationship between perception and sensation.

The Senses

There is not full agreement as to the differences and similarities between sensation and perception. The physical senses are considered to be vision, hearing, touch, smell, and taste. There are many other so-called "sixth senses." However, none of these sixth senses is fully accepted. The five senses are constantly bombarded by numerous stimuli that are both outside and inside the body. Examples of outside stimuli include light waves, sound waves, mechanical energy of pressure, and chemical energy from objects that one can smell and taste. Inside stimuli include energy generated by muscles, food passing through the digestive system, and glands secreting behavior-influencing hormones. These examples indicate that sensation deals chiefly with very elementary behavior that is determined largely by physiological functioning. In this way, the human being uses the senses to experience color, brightness, shape, loudness, pitch, heat, odor, and taste.

Definition of Perception

Perception is much more complex and much broader than sensation. The perceptual process can be defined as a complicated interaction of selection, organization, and interpretation. Although perception depends largely upon the senses for raw data, the cognitive process may filter, modify, or completely change these data. A simple illustration may be seen by looking at one side of a stationary object, for example, a statue or a tree. By slowly turning the eyes to the other side of the object, the person probably *senses* that the object is moving. Yet the person *perceives* the object as stationary. The perceptual process overcomes the sensual process and the person "sees" the object as stationary. In other words, the perceptual process adds to, and subtracts from, the "real" sensory world. The following are some organizational examples which point out the difference between sensation and perception:

1. The purchasing agent buys a part that she thinks is best, not the part that the engineer says is the best.
2. A subordinate's answer to a question is based on what he heard the boss say, not on what the boss actually said.
3. The same worker may be viewed by one supervisor as a very good worker and by another supervisor as a very poor worker.
4. The same widget may be viewed by the inspector to be of high quality and by a customer to be of low quality.

Subprocesses of Perception

The existence of several subprocesses gives evidence of the complexity and the interactive nature of perception. Figure 6.1 shows how these subprocesses relate to one another. The first important subprocess is the *stimulus* or *situation* that is present. Perception begins when a person is confronted with a stimulus or a situation. This confrontation may be with the immediate sensual stimulation or with the total physical and sociocultural environment. An example is the employee who is confronted with his or her supervisor or with the total formal organizational environment. Either one or both may initiate the workings of the employee's perceptual process. In other words, this represents the S↔O in the model of Chapter 1.

In addition to the S↔O interaction there are the internal cognitive processes

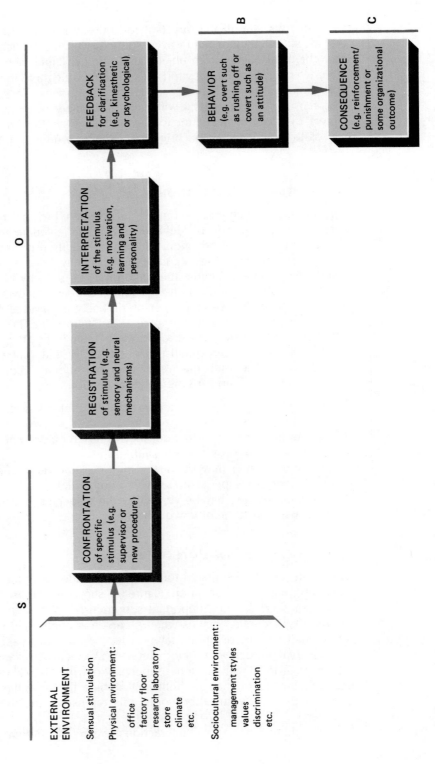

FIGURE 6.1 The subprocesses of perception.

144

of *registration*, *interpretation*, and *feedback*. During the registration phenomenon, the physiological (sensory and neural) mechanisms are affected; the physiological ability to hear and see will affect perception. Interpretation is the most significant cognitive aspect of perception. The other psychological processes will affect the interpretation of a situation. For example, in an organization, employees' interpretations of a situation are largely dependent upon their learning and motivation and their personality. An example would be the kinesthetic feedback (sensory impressions from muscles) that helps assembly line workers perceive the speed of materials moving by them on the line. An example of psychological feedback that may influence an employee's perception is the supervisor's raised eyebrow or a change in voice inflection. The behavioral termination of perception is the reaction or behavior, either overt or covert, which is necessary if perception is to be considered a behavioral event and thus an important part of organizational behavior. As a result of perception, an employee may move rapidly or slowly (overt behavior) or make a self-evaluation (covert behavior).

As shown in Figure 6.1, all these perceptual subprocesses are compatible with the S-O-B-C model presented in Chapter 1. The stimulus or environmental situation is part of the S; registration, interpretation, and feedback occur within the complex O; the resulting behavior is the B; and the consequences of this behavior make up the C. The subprocesses of registration, interpretation, and feedback are internal cognitive processes that are unobservable, but the situation, behavior, and consequences indicate that perception is indeed related to behavior. Perceptual selectivity and organization, which are discussed next, play a key role in the internal cognitive aspects of perception.

Perceptual Selectivity

Numerous stimuli are constantly confronting everyone all the time. The noise of the air conditioner or furnace, the sound of other people talking and moving, and outside noises from cars, planes, or street repair work are a few of the stimuli affecting the other senses—plus the impact of the total environmental situation. Sometimes the stimuli are below the person's conscious threshold. The accompanying Application Example, Subliminal Perception in the Workplace, gives some examples of this subliminal perception.

With all this stimulation impinging upon people, how and why do they select out only a very few stimuli at a given time? Part of the answer can be found in the principles of perceptual selectivity.

External Attention Factors

Various external and internal attention factors affect perceptual selectivity. The external factors consist of outside environmental influences such as intensity, size, contrast, repetition, motion, and novelty and familiarity.

Intensity. The intensity principle of attention states that the more intense the external stimulus, the more likely it is to be perceived. A loud noise, strong odor,

Subliminal Perception in the Workplace*

Subliminal perception involves giving a message below the person's level of consciousness. This device has been banned in uses such as advertising to get people to buy a product without their awareness. For example, flashing on a movie theater screen, "Go get a cola, you are thirsty" so fast that the person is unaware of the message but stimulated to obey it is not permitted. Recently, however, some business organizations have begun to use this approach to cut employee and customer theft, reduce employee accidents and injuries, and even increase productivity. For example, Proactive Systems Inc., a company that specializes in this approach (although it is careful to point out that what it is doing is really not subliminal and does not violate any constitutional rights) has been successful in conveying messages such as "Stay honest, don't steal, obey the law" to discourage shoplifting in retail stores such as Jay Jacobs, a Seattle-based chain with 102 stores. To cut down accidents, Proactive Systems puts out messages, in places such as warehouses, that whisper, "Slouch is ouch, life straight is great." One large company is using the approach to increase productivity by repeatedly subjecting employees to the phrases, "I feel good about my job," "I like myself," and "My job is important." A spokesperson for the company states that since the system was installed, "turnover has dropped, productivity has gone up and morale seems to have improved."

***Source:** Adapted from "Whispering Computers Aim to Cut Thefts," Omaha World-Herald, May 18, 1985, p. 30.

or bright light will be noticed more than a soft sound, weak odor, or dim light. Advertisers use intensity to gain the consumer's attention. Examples include bright packaging and television commercials that are slightly louder than the regular program. Supervisors may yell at their subordinates to gain attention. This last example also shows that other, more complex psychological variables may overcome the simple external variable. By speaking loudly, the supervisor may actually be turning the subordinates off instead of gaining their attention. These types of complications enter into all aspects of the perceptual process. As with the other psychological concepts, a given perceptual principle cannot stand alone in explaining complex human behavior. The intensity principle is only one small factor in the perceptual process, which is only a part of the cognitive processes, which are only a part of what goes into human behavior. Yet, for convenience of presentation and for the development of basic understanding, these small parts can be effectively isolated for study and analysis.

Size.   Closely related to intensity is the principle of size. It says that the larger the object, the more likely it will be perceived. The largest machine "sticks out" when personnel view a factory floor. The maintenance engineering staff may pay more attention to a big machine than to a smaller one, even though the smaller one costs as much and is as important to the operation. A 6-foot 4-inch, 250-pound supervisor may receive more attention from his subordinates than a 5-foot 10-inch, 160-pound supervisor. In advertising, a full-page spread is more attention-getting than a few lines in the classified section.

Contrast. The contrast principle states that external stimuli which stand out against the background or which are not what people are expecting will receive their attention. Figure 6.2 demonstrates this perceptual principle. The black circle on the right appears much larger than the one on the left because of the contrast with the background circles. Both black circles are exactly the same size. In a similar manner, plant safety signs which have black lettering on a yellow background or white lettering on a red background are attention-getting; and when the 6-foot 4-inch, 250-pound supervisor mentioned above is placed next to a 5-foot 4-inch, 130-pound supervisor, the smaller one will probably receive as much notice as the bigger one. A worker with many years of experience hardly notices the deafening noise on the factory floor of a typical manufacturing operation. However, if one or more of the machines should come suddenly to a halt, the person would immediately notice the difference in noise level.

The contrast principle can be demonstrated by the experience of some companies with training disadvantaged, unskilled workers. In designing these training programs, some firms have found that they have more success when they conduct the initial sessions in the disadvantaged person's own environment. The familiar location relieves some of the tension and creates a more favorable learning atmosphere. However, at some point the disadvantaged person must make the transition to the organizational environment. A regular, quiet classroom in the organization does not seem to be enough. One company learned that when the entire training of the disadvantaged trainees was conducted in a clean, quiet factory classroom, their subsequent performance was very poor. Fortunately, the company did not jump to the conclusion that the workers were "no good" or untrainable. Instead, through rational behavior analysis, the company discovered that the poor performance was due to the extremely loud noises that occurred on the assembly line. The workers were not accustomed to the noise because their training had taken place under nice, clean, quiet conditions. When the workers were placed on the noisy factory floor, the contrasting din drew all their attention and adversely affected their performance. To solve this problem,

FIGURE 6.2 The contrast principle of perception: Which black circle is larger?

the company conducted the training sessions right next to the noisy factory floor. By the end of the training sessions, the workers were used to the noise, and they performed very well when subsequently placed on the job.

Repetition. The repetition principle states that a repeated external stimulus is more attention-getting than a single one. Thus, a worker will generally "hear" better when directions for a dull task are given more than once. This principle partially explains why supervisors have to give directions over and over again for even the simplest of tasks. Workers' attention for a boring task may be waning and the only way they hear directions for the task is when the supervisors repeat themselves several times. Advertisers trying to create a unique image for a product which is undifferentiated from its competitors—such as aspirin, soap, and deodorant—rely heavily on repetitious advertising.

Motion. The motion principle says that people will pay more attention to moving objects in their field of vision than they will to stationary objects. Workers will notice materials moving by them on a conveyor belt but they may fail to give proper attention to the maintenance needs of the stationary machine next to them. In addition, the assembly line workers may devote their entire attention to the line of slowly moving materials they are working on and fail to notice the relatively nice working conditions (pastel-colored walls, music, and air conditioning). Advertisers capitalize on this principle by creating signs which incorporate moving parts. Las Vegas at night is an example of advertisement in motion.

Novelty and Familiarity. The novelty and familiarity principle states that either a novel or a familiar external situation can serve as an attention getter. New objects or events in a familiar setting or familiar objects or events in a new setting will draw the attention of the perceiver. Job rotation is an example of this principle. Changing workers' jobs from time to time will tend to increase the attention they give to the task. Switching from a typewriter to a word processor may not motivate the clerical staff, but it will increase their attention until they become accustomed to the new job. The same is true for the previously mentioned disadvantaged people newly trained for their first job assignments. The work environment is a completely novel experience for them. If supervisors use familiar street jargon in communicating with the employees, they may receive more attention from them. However, once again, this approach could backfire unless properly handled. The same is true in a foreign context. The accompanying International Application Example shows some of the blunders U.S. advertising language has made in foreign countries.

Internal Set Factors

The concept of *set* is an important cognition in selectivity. It can be thought of as an internal form of attention getting and is based largely on the individual's complex psychological makeup. People will select out stimuli or situations from the environment that appeal to, and are compatible with, their learning and

**International
Application
Example**

Sometimes It Doesn't Translate

While marketing people in the United States have produced some outstanding advertisements, it is not always possible to take these same ads and use them in other countries. Why not? Because the perceptions are not the same. Here are some classic examples.

1. "Schweppes Tonic Water" was initially translated to the Italian as "il water." However, the copywriters quickly corrected their mistake and changed the translation to "Schweppes Tonica." In Italian "il water" means water in the bathroom commode.
2. When Pepsi-Cola ran an ad slogan of "Come Alive with Pepsi," it did very well in the United States. However, the company had to change its slogan in some foreign countries because it did not translate correctly. In German the translation of "Come alive" is "Come out of the grave." In Asia the phrase is translated, "Bring your ancestors back from the grave."
3. When General Mills attempted to capture the British market with its breakfast cereal, it ran a picture of a freckled, red-haired, crew-cut grinning kid saying, "See kids, it's great!" The company failed to realize that the typical British family, not so child-centered as the U.S. family, would not be able to identify with the kid on the carton. Result: sales were dismally low.
4. General Motors initially had trouble selling its Chevrolet Nova in Puerto Rico. It failed to realize that while the name "Nova" in English means "star," in Spanish the word sounds like "no va," which means "it doesn't go."
5. Rolls-Royce attempted to market one of its models in Germany under the name "Silver Mist." It soon discovered that the word "mist" in German means "excrement."

motivation and with their personality. Although these aspects are given specific attention in Part 3, a very brief discussion here will help in the understanding of perception.

Learning and Perception

Although interrelated with motivation and personality, learning may play the single biggest role in developing perceptual set. Read the sentence in the triangle below:

TURN
OFF THE
THE ENGINE

It may take several seconds to realize there is something wrong. Because of familiarity with the sentence from prior learning, the person is perceptually set to read "Turn off the engine." This illustration shows that learning affects set by creating an *expectancy* to perceive in a certain manner. As pointed out in Chapter 1, such expectancies are a vital element in the cognitive explanations of behavior. This view states simply that people see and hear what they expect to see and hear. This can be further demonstrated by pronouncing the following words very slowly:

M-A-C-T-A-V-I-S-H

M-A-C-D-O-N-A-L-D

M-A-C-B-E-T-H

M-A-C-H-I-N-E-R-Y

If the last word was pronounced "Mac-Hinery" instead of "machinery," the reader was caught in a verbal response set.

There are many other illustrations that are commonly used to demonstrate the impact of learning on the development of perceptual set. Figure 6.3 is found in many introductory psychology textbooks. What is perceived in this picture? If one sees an attractive, apparently wealthy young woman, the perceiver is in agreement with about 60 percent of the people who see the picture for the first time. On the other hand, if an ugly, poor old woman is seen, the viewer is in agreement with about 40 percent of first viewers. Obviously, two completely distinct women can be perceived in Figure 6.3. Which woman is seen supposedly depends on whether the person is set to perceive young, beautiful women or old, ugly women. How did you come out?

How Figure 6.3 is perceived can be radically influenced by a simple learned experience. When first shown a clear, unambiguous picture of a beautiful young woman (Figure 6.4) and then shown Figure 6.3, the person will almost always report seeing the young woman in Figure 6.3. If the clear picture of the old

FIGURE 6.3
Ambiguous picture of a young woman and an old woman. (*Source*: Edwin G. Boring, "A New Ambiguous Figure," *American Journal of Psychology,* July 1930, p. 444. Also see Robert Leeper, "A Study of a Neglected Portion of the Field of Learning—The Development of Sensory Organization," *Journal of Genetic Psychology,* March 1935, p. 62. Originally drawn by cartoonist W. E. Hill and published in *Puck,* Nov. 6, 1915.)

Old woman   Young woman

FIGURE 6.4
Clear picture of
the young and old
woman.
(*Source*: Robert
Leeper, "A Study of
a Neglected
Portion of the Field
of Learning—The
Development
of Sensory Or-
ganization," *Journal
of Genetic Psychol-
ogy*, March 1935,
p. 62.)

woman is seen first (Figure 6.4), the viewer will subsequently report seeing the old woman in Figure 6.3.

In addition to the young woman–old woman example, there is a wide variety of commonly used illusions that effectively demonstrate the impact of learned set on perception. An illusion may be thought of as a form of perception that badly distorts reality. Figures 6.5 and 6.6 show some of the most frequently used forms of perceptual illusion. The two three-pronged objects in Figure 6.5 are drawn contrary to common perceptions of such objects. In Figure 6.6*a*, the length of the nose (from the tip to the X) is exactly equal to the vertical length of the face. In Figure 6.6*b*, the height of the hat is exactly equal to the width of the brim. Both shapes in Figure 6.6*c* are exactly the same size, and in Figure 6.6*d* the lines *AX, CX, CB,* and *XD* are of equal length.

Figure 6.7 brings out the role that learned set plays in perception even more strongly than Figure 6.6. The three men in Figure 6.7 are drawn exactly equal in height. Yet they are perceived to be of different heights because the viewer has learned that the cues found in the picture normally imply depth and distance. A lot of what a person "sees" in the world is a result of past experience and learning. Even though the past experience may not be relevant to the present situation, it is nevertheless used by the perceiver.

FIGURE 6.5
Common illu-
sions.

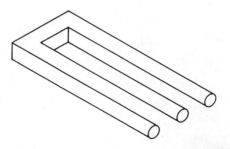
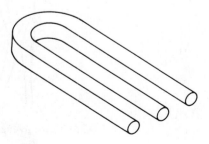

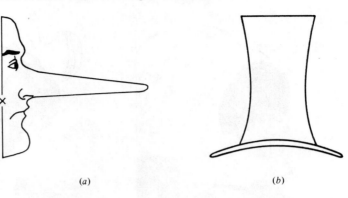

FIGURE 6.6
Common perceptual illusions.
(*Sources*: These illusions are found in almost all introductory psychology textbooks. For example, see Gregory A. Kimble and Norman Garmezy, *General Psychology*, 2d ed., Ronald, New York, 1963, pp. 324–325.)

(a)   *(b)*

(c)   *(d)*

FIGURE 6.7 The role that learning plays in perception.

Perceptual Set in the Workplace

Perceptual set has many direct implications for organizational behavior. In organizational life, some employees have learned to perceive the world around them in the same way. For example, the single sentence "I cannot recommend this young man too highly" was reproduced and distributed to several managers in the same organization. Although this statement is ambiguous and unclear, without exception all the managers interpreted this to be a positive recommendation.[2] They had all learned to perceive this statement the same way—positive and favorable.

In most cases, however, learning leads to extreme individual differences. For example, the young woman–old woman illustration demonstrates that the same stimulus may be perceived two completely different ways (young and beautiful or old and ugly) because of the way the individual is set to perceive. Numerous instances of this situation occur in a modern organization. Participants may perceive the same stimulus or situation in entirely different ways. A specific organizational example might be a poor output record in the production department of a manufacturing plant. The engineer perceives the solution to this problem as one of improved machine design. The personnel manager perceives the solution as one of more training and better wage incentives. The department head perceives the solution to be more effective organizing, planning, and controlling. On the other hand, the workers may perceive the low output with pleasure because it is a way of "getting back" at their supervisor, whom they dislike. For the purpose of this discussion, it is not important who is right or wrong in this example; rather, the point is that all the relevant personnel perceive the *same* situation in completely *different* ways.

Another common example is the differences in perception that occur between the union and management. Some industrial relations researchers believe that perceptual differences are a major explanation for industrial disputes. The same "facts" in a dispute are perceived quite differently by union members and by management. For example, union members may perceive that they are underpaid, whereas management perceives that they are overpaid for the amount of work they do. In reality, pay may have nothing to do with the ensuing dispute. Maybe it is a matter of the workers not having control over their own jobs and getting any recognition and they are reacting by perceiving that they are underpaid.

Motivation and Perception

Besides the learned aspects of perceptual set, motivation also has a vital impact on perceptual selectivity. The primary motives of sex and hunger could be used to demonstrate the role that motivation plays in perception.

In traditional American culture, the sex drive has been largely suppressed, with the result being an unfulfilled need for sex. Accordingly, any mention of sex or a visual stimulus dealing with sex is very attention-getting to the average American. The picture of a scantily clad or naked male or female is readily perceived. On the other hand, as nudity becomes increasingly commonplace in magazines, motion pictures, live entertainment, and fashions, the human anatomy slowly begins to lose its appeal as an attention getter. Analogously, however, if there is a great need for food in the culture, the mention, sight, or smell of food is given a great deal of attention.

The secondary motives also play an important role in developing perceptual set. A person who has a relatively high need for power, affiliation, or achievement will be more attentive to the relevant situational variables. An example is the worker who has a strong need for affiliation. When such a worker walks into the lunchroom, the table where several coworkers are sitting tends to be perceived, and the empty table or the one where a single person is sitting tends to get no attention. Although very simple, the lunchroom example points out that perception may have an important impact on motivation, and vice versa. This demonstrates once again the interrelatedness of these concepts.

Personality and Perception

Closely related to learning and motivation is the personality of the perceiving person, which affects what is attended to in the confronting situation. For example, senior-level executives often complain that the new young "hot shots" have trouble making the "tough" personnel decisions concerning terminating or reassigning people and paying attention to details and paperwork. The young managers, in turn, complain about the "old guard" resisting change and using rules and paperwork as ends in themselves. The senior- and junior-level executives' personalities largely explain these perceptions.

The growing generation gap recognized in recent years definitely contributes to differing perceptions. An example can be found in the perceptions of modern movies. Older people tend either to be disgusted by or do not understand some of the popular movies of recent years. Those in the thirty-five to forty-five age group tend to perceive these movies as "naughty but neat." Young, college-age people tend to perceive them as "where it's at." They tend to get neither uptight nor titillated. Of course, there are individual differences in all age categories, and the above example tends to stereotype (this is discussed later in the chapter) people by age. Yet it does show how personalities, values, and even age may affect the way people perceive the world around them.

Perceptual Organization

The discussion of perceptual selectivity was concerned with the external and internal variables that gain an individual's attention. This section focuses on what takes place in the perceptual process once the information from the situation is received. This aspect of perception is commonly referred to as *perceptual organization*. An individual seldom perceives patches of color or light or sound. Instead, the person will perceive organized patterns of stimuli and identifiable whole objects. For example, when a college student is shown a football, the student does not normally perceive it as the color brown or as grain-leather in texture or as the odor of leather. Rather, the student perceives a football which has, in addition to the characteristics named, a potential for giving the perceiver fun and excitement as either a participant or a spectator. In other words, the person's perceptual process organizes the incoming information into a meaningful whole.

Figure-Ground

Figure-ground is usually considered to be the most basic form of perceptual organization. The figure-ground principle means simply that perceived objects stand out as separable from their general background. It can be effectively demonstrated as one is reading this paragraph. In terms of light-wave stimuli, the reader is receiving patches of irregularly shaped blacks and whites. Yet the reader does not perceive it this way. The reader perceives black shapes—letters, words, and sentences—printed against a white background. To say it another way, the reader perceptually organizes incoming stimuli into recognizable figures (words) that are seen against a ground (white page).

Another interesting figure-ground illustration is shown in Figure 6.8. At first glance, one probably perceives a jumble of black, irregular shapes against a white background. Only when the white letters are perceptually organized against a black background will the words FLY and TIE literally jump out with clarity. This illustration shows that perceptual selectivity will influence perceptual organization. The viewer is set to perceive black on white because of the black words (figures) throughout the book. However, in Figure 6.8 the reverse is true. White is the figure and black is the ground.

Perceptual Grouping

The grouping principle of perceptual organiz   cy to group several stimuli together into a rec   is very basic and seems to be largely inborn. Ther   s

566 - 568

FIGURE 6.8
Illustrations of figure-ground. (*Sources*: (*a*) Warner Brown and Howard Gilhousen, *College Psychology*, Prentice-Hall, Englewood Cliffs, N.J., 1949, p. 330; (*b*) Jerome Kagan and Ernest Havemann, *Psychology: An Introduction*, Harcourt, Brace & World, New York, 1968, p. 166.)

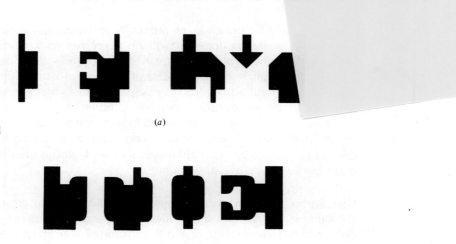

(*a*)

(*b*)

in grouping. When simple constellations of stimuli are presented to people, they will tend to group them together by closure, continuity, proximity, or similarity.

Closure. The closure principle of grouping is closely related to the gestalt school of psychology. A basic gestalt principle is that a person will sometimes perceive a whole when one does not actually exist. The person's perceptual process will close the gaps which are unfilled from sensory input. In the formal organization, participants may either see a whole where none exists or not be able to put the pieces together into a whole that does exist. An example of the first case is the department head who perceived complete agreement among the members of her department on a given project when, in fact, there was opposition from several members. The department head in this situation closed the existing gaps and perceived complete agreement when, in fact, it did not exist. An example of the other side of the coin is the adage of not being able to see the forest (whole) because of the trees (parts). High degrees of specialization have often resulted in functionally oriented managers' losing sight of the whole organization's objectives. Specialists may get so caught up in their own little area of interest and responsibility that they may lose sight of the overall goal. They cannot close their part together with the other parts to perceive the whole.

Continuity. Continuity is closely related to closure. Some psychologists do not even bother to make a distinction between the two grouping principles. However, there is a slight difference. Closure supplies *missing* stimuli, and the continuity principle says that a person will tend to perceive *continuous* lines or patterns. This type of continuity may lead to inflexible, or noncreative, thinking on the part of organizational participants. Only the obvious, continuous patterns or relationships will be perceived. For example, a new design for some productive process or product may be limited to obvious flows or continuous lines. New, innovative ideas or designs may not be perceived. Continuity can greatly influence the systems design of an organizational structure.

Proximity. The principle of proximity, or nearness, states that a group of stimuli that are close together will be perceived as a whole pattern of parts belonging together. For example, several employees in an organization may be identified as a single group because of physical proximity. Several workers who work on a particular machine may be perceived as a single whole. If the output is low and the supervisor reports a number of grievances from the group, management may perceive all the workers on the machine as one troublemaking group when, in fact, some of the workers are loyal, dedicated employees. Yet, the fact remains that often departmental or work groups are perceived as a single entity because of physical proximity.

Similarity. The principle of similarity states that the greater the similarity of the stimuli, the greater the tendency to perceive them as a common group. Similarity is conceptually related to proximity but in most cases is stronger than proximity. In an organization, all employees who wear white collars may be perceived as a common group, when, in reality, each worker is a unique individual. Similarity also applies to minorities and women. There is a tendency to perceive minority and women employees as a single group, the famous "they."

Perceptual Constancy

Constancy is one of the more sophisticated forms of perceptual organization. It gives a person a sense of stability in a changing world. Constancy permits the individual to have some constancy in a tremendously variable and highly complex world. Learning plays a much bigger role in the constancy phenomenon than in figure-ground or grouping phenomena.

The size, shape, color, brightness, and location of an object are fairly constant regardless of the information received by the senses. It should be pointed out that perceptual constancy results from *patterns* of cues. These patterns are for the most part learned, but each situation is different and there are interactions between the inborn and learned tendencies within the entire perceptual process.

If constancy were not at work, the world would be very chaotic and disorganized for the individual. An organizational example would be the worker who must select a piece of material or a tool of the correct size from a wide variety of materials and tools at varying distances from a work station. Without perceptual constancy, the sizes, shapes, and colors of objects would change as the worker moved about and would make the job almost impossible.

Perceptual Context

The highest, most sophisticated form of perceptual organization is context. It gives meaning and value to simple stimuli, objects, events, situations, and other persons in the environment. The principle of context can be simply demonstrated by the well-known doodles shown in Figure 6.9 (answers are given in refer-

FIGURE 6.9
Doodles: Illustration of the role that context plays in perception.

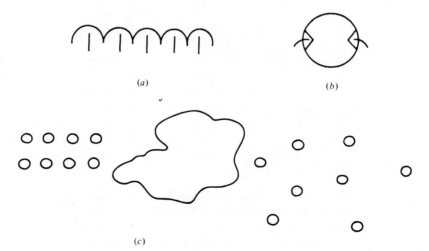

(a)

(b)

(c)

ence [3]). The visual stimuli by themselves are meaningless. Only when the doodles are placed in a verbal context do they take on meaning and value to the perceiver.

The organizational culture and structure provide the primary context in which workers and managers do their perceiving. Thus, a verbal order, a memo, a new policy, a suggestion, a raised eyebrow, or a pat on the back takes on special meaning and value when placed in the context of the work organization. Chapters 3 and 4 on culture and the international context and those in Part 5 on structure and processes form the major context in which organizational participants perceive.

Perceptual Defense

Closely related to context is perceptual defense. A person may build a defense (a block or a refusal to recognize) against stimuli or situational events in the context that are personally or culturally unacceptable or threatening. Accordingly, perceptual defense may play an influential role in understanding union-management or supervisor-subordinate relationships.

Although there is some conflicting evidence, most studies verify the existence of a perceptual defense mechanism. Two examples are classic studies which found barriers to perceiving personality-threatening words[4] and identification thresholds for critical, emotionally toned words.[5] In another study more directly relevant to organizational behavior, the researchers describe how people may react with a perceptual defense that is activated in them when they are confronted with a fact that is inconsistent with a preconceived notion.[6] In this study, college students were presented with the word "intelligent" as a characteristic of a factory worker. This was counter to their perception of factory workers, and they built defenses in the following ways:

1. *Denial.* A few of the subjects denied the existence of intelligence in factory workers.
2. *Modification and distortion.* This was one of the most frequent forms of defense. The pattern was to explain away the perceptual conflict by joining intelligence with some other characteristic, for example, "He is intelligent, but doesn't possess the initiative to rise above his group."
3. *Change in perception.* Many of the students changed their perception of the worker because of the intelligence characteristic. The change, however, was usually very subtle; for example, "He cracks jokes" became "He's witty."
4. *Recognition, but refusal to change.* Very few subjects explicitly recognized the conflict between their perception of the worker and the characteristic of intelligence that was confronting them. For example, one subject stated, "the traits seem to be conflicting . . . most factory workers I have heard about aren't too intelligent."[7]

The general conclusion to be drawn from this classic study is that people may learn to avoid perceiving certain conflicting, threatening, or unacceptable aspects of the context.

These and other relevant experiments have been summarized into three general explanations of perceptual defense:

1. Emotionally disturbing information has a higher threshold for recognition (that is, we do not perceive it readily) than neutral or nondisturbing information. This is why a chain of events may be seen differently by those who are not personally involved and by those who are involved; thus, warning signs of trouble are often not seen by those who will be most affected by the trouble.

2. Disturbing information and stimuli are likely to bring about substitute perceptions which are distorted to prevent recognition of the disturbing elements. In this way a manager can perceive that workers are happy, when actually they are disgruntled. Then when a grievance committee is formed or a strike takes place, the manager cannot perceive that these "happy" workers are participating willingly and concludes that it is because they have fallen victim to some agitator and that things in the shop are still basically fine.

3. Emotionally arousing information actually does arouse emotion, even though the emotion is distorted and directed elsewhere. Kicking the cat, snarling at the kids, cutting someone off for trying to pass you on the right while driving home, and browbeating an underling all offer a sense of relief and are good substitutes for perceiving that people "upstairs" think you are an idiot.[8]

Such findings as the above help explain why some people, especially supervisors and subordinates in an organization, have a "blind spot." They do not "see" or they consistently misinterpret certain events or situations. As the accompanying Application Example, Police Perceptions, indicates, certain groups such as the police must be very careful not to make such misinterpretations.

Application Example	**Police Perceptions**
	Training police to handle or quell a riot normally includes a session or two on the importance of accurately perceiving what is happening within an unruly crowd. This need for accurate perception has resulted from several incidents in which instigators of riots deliberately attempted to provoke police into acting in a violent manner. It has been shown in several riots that what the police perceived as a threat to their lives was really nothing more than a deliberate attempt to provoke them with harmless acts or objects. For example, crumpled paper has been mistaken for a rock in the fist of an angry rioter. The sound of a thrown light bulb breaking has been confused with a gun discharging. A protruding stick being carried by a protester has been confused from a distance with the barrel of a rifle. All these possible misperceptions could lead, and in some cases have led, to violence and death. Training the police in accurate perception can be a life-or-death matter.

Social Perception

Although context and perceptual defense are closely related to social perception, this section gives recognition to social perception per se. The social aspects of perception are given detailed coverage because they play such an important role in organizational behavior. Social perception is directly concerned with how one individual perceives other individuals.

Characteristics of Perceiver and Perceived

A summary of research findings on some specific characteristics of the perceiver and the perceived reveals a profile of the perceiver as follows:

1. Knowing oneself makes it easier to see others accurately.
2. One's own characteristics affect the characteristics one is likely to see in others.
3. People who accept themselves are more likely to be able to see favorable aspects of other people.
4. Accuracy in perceiving others is not a single skill.[9]

These four characteristics greatly influence how a person perceives others in the environmental situation.

There are also certain characteristics of the person being perceived which influence social perception. Research has shown that:

1. The status of the person perceived will greatly influence others' perception of the person.
2. The person being perceived is usually placed into categories to simplify the viewer's perceptual activities. Two common categories are status and role.
3. The visible traits of the person perceived will greatly influence others' perception of the person.[10]

These characteristics of the perceiver and the perceived suggest the extreme complexity of social perception. Organizational participants must realize that their perceptions of another person are greatly influenced by their own characteristics and of the characteristics of the other person. For example, if a manager has high self-esteem and the other person is physically attractive and pleasant and comes from the home office, then the manager will likely perceive this other person in a positive, favorable manner. On the other hand, if the manager has low self-esteem and the other person is an arrogant, unattractive salesperson, the manager will likely perceive this other person in a negative, unfavorable manner. Such attributions that people make of others play a vital role in their social perceptions and resulting behavior.

Participants in formal organizations are constantly perceiving one another. Managers are perceiving workers, workers are perceiving managers, line personnel are perceiving staff personnel, staff personnel are perceiving line personnel, superiors are perceiving subordinates, subordinates are perceiving superiors, and on and on. There are numerous complex factors which enter into such social perception, but the primary factors are found in the psychological processes and personality.

Attribution

Attribution refers simply to how a person explains the cause of another's or of his or her own behavior. The perceiver categorizes these causes or attributions into three major source dimensions: person, entity, and context.[11] In recent years attribution theories have been playing an increasingly important role in work motivation, performance appraisal, and leadership.[12]

For example, attributions have been found to strongly affect evaluations of others' performance, to determine the manner in which supervisors behave toward subordinates, and to influence personal satisfaction with one's work.[13] These attribution theories of motivation will be covered in Chapter 9. Applied to social perception, attribution is the search for causes (attributes) in making interpretations of other persons or of oneself. For example, what the manager attributes the cause of a subordinate's behavior to be will affect the manager's perception of, and resulting behavior toward, the subordinate. If the subordinate's outstanding performance is attributed to a new machine or engineering procedure, the perception and resulting treatment will be different from the perception and resulting treatment if the performance is attributed to ability and drive. The same is true of attributions made of one's own behavior. Perceptions and thus behaviors will vary depending on whether internal, personal attributions or external, situational attributions are made. In other words, the type of causal attributions one makes greatly affects perception, and, as the later discussions of motivation and leadership will indicate, there is growing evidence that this attributional process and the form it takes seem to greatly affect the resulting organizational behavior.

Stereotyping

In addition to attribution, there are two other important areas of social perception that are especially relevant to the understanding of organizational behavior. These are the common errors or problems that creep into social perception called *stereotyping* and the *halo effect.*

The term *stereotype* refers to the tendency to perceive another person (hence social perception) as belonging to a *single* class or category. From attribution theory, a stereotype also involves general agreement on the attributed traits and the existence of a discrepancy between attributed traits and actual traits.

The word stereotype is derived from the typographer's word for a printing plate made from previously composed type. In 1922, Walter Lippmann applied the word to perception. Since then, stereotyping has become a frequently used term to describe perceptual errors. In particular, it is employed in analyzing prejudice. Not commonly acknowledged is the fact that stereotyping may attribute favorable or unfavorable traits to the person being perceived. Most often a person is put into a stereotype because the perceived knows only the overall category to which the person belongs. However, because each individual is unique, the real traits of the person will generally be quite different from those the stereotype would suggest.

Stereotyping greatly influences social perception in today's organizations. Common stereotyped groups include managers, supervisors, union members, minorities, women, white- and blue-collar workers, and all the various functional and staff specialists, for example, accountants, salespeople, computer programmers, and engineers. There is a consensus about the traits possessed by the members of these categories. Yet in reality there is often a discrepancy between the agreed-upon traits of each category and the actual traits of the members. In other words, not all engineers carry calculators and are coldly rational, nor are all personnel managers do-gooders who are trying to keep workers happy. On the contrary, there are individual differences and a great deal of variability among members of these groups. In spite of this, other organization members commonly make blanket perceptions and behave accordingly. For example, in one classic research study it was found that individuals will both perceive and be perceived according to whether they are identified with a union or a management group. "Thus, 74 percent of the subjects in the managerial group chose the word 'honest' as a description of Mr. A, *when he was identified as a manager.* The same managerial subjects, however, chose the word 'honest' to describe Mr. A only 50 percent of the time when he was identified as a representative of the union."[14] There are numerous other research studies and common, everyday examples which point out the stereotyping that occurs in organizational life.

The Halo Effect

The *halo effect* in social perception is very similar to stereotyping. Whereas in stereotyping the person is perceived according to a single category, under the halo effect the person is perceived on the basis of one trait. Halo is often discussed in performance appraisal when a rater makes an error in judging a person's total personality and/or performance on the basis of a single trait such as intelligence, appearance, dependability, or cooperativeness. Whatever the single trait is, it may override all other traits in forming the perception of the person.

A recent comprehensive review of the performance appraisal literature found that the halo effect was the dependent variable in over a third of the studies and was found to be a major problem affecting appraisal accuracy.[15] Examples of the halo effect are the extremely attractive woman secretary who is perceived by her male boss as being an intelligent, good performer, when, in fact, she is a poor typist and quite dense, and the good typist who is also very bright but who is perceived by her male boss as a "secretary," not as a potential manager with the ability to cope with important responsibilities. One classic research study noted three conditions under which the halo effect is most marked: (1) when the traits to be perceived are unclear in behavioral expressions, (2) when the traits are not frequently encountered by the perceiver, and (3) when the traits have moral implications.[16]

Many other research studies have pointed out how the halo effect can influence perception. For example, one study found that when two persons were described as having identical personalities except for one trait—the character qualities in one list included the trait *warm* and, in the other list, the trait *cold*—two completely different perceptions resulted.[17] In other words, one trait blinded the perceiver to all other traits in the perceptual process. Another study also documented the impact of the halo effect on employee perceptions in a company that was in receivership. Although the company paid relatively high wages and provided excellent working conditions and at least average supervision, the employees did not perceive these favorable factors. The insecurity produced an inverse halo effect so that insecurity dominated over the pay and positive conditions of the job.[18] The results of this study make the point that "when there's one important 'rotten' attitude, it can spoil the 'barrel' of attitudes."[19]

Like all the other aspects of the psychological process of perception discussed in this chapter, the halo effect has important implications for the study and eventual understanding of organizational behavior. Unfortunately, even though halo error is one of the longest recognized and most pervasive problems associated with applications such as performance appraisal in the field of organizational behavior, attempts at solving it have not yet been very successful.[20] The "perceptual and cognitive differences among raters may affect their ratings as much as or more than the nature of the rating scale itself."[21]

Summary

Perception is an important mediating cognitive process. Through this complex process, persons make interpretations of stimulus situations they are faced with. Both selectivity and organization go into perceptual interpretations. Externally, selectivity is affected by intensity, size, contrast, repetition, motion, novelty, and familiarity. Internally, perceptual selectivity is influenced by the individual's motivation, learning, and personality. After the stimulus situation is filtered by the selective process, the incoming information is organized into a meaningful whole. Figure-ground is the most basic form of perceptual organization. Another basic form is the grouping of constellations of incoming stimuli by closure, continuity, proximity, and similarity. The constancy, context, and defensive aspects of perceptual organization are more complex. The social context in particular plays an important role in understanding human behavior in organizations.

Questions for Discussion and Review

1. Do you agree with the opening observation that people are human information processors? Why?
2. How does sensation differ from perception?
3. Give some examples of the external factors that affect perceptual selectivity.
4. Explain how perceptual constancy works.
5. What does "stereotyping" mean? Why is it considered to be a perceptual problem?
6. What effect can the perceptual process have on organizational behavior?

REFERENCES

1. *The Wall Street Journal*, Dec. 2, 1986, p. 1.
2. John Swanda, *Organizational Behavior*, Alfred, Sherman Oaks, Calif., 1979, p. 91.
3. The answers to the doodles in Fig. 6.9 are: (*a*) the start of a "rat race"; (*b*) two mice in a beer can; (*c*) a column of ants marching through spilled whiskey.

4. Jerome S. Bruner and Leo Postman, "Emotional Selectivity in Perception and Reaction," *Journal of Personality*, September 1947, pp. 69–77.
5. Elliott McGinnies, "Emotionality and Perceptual Defense," *Psychological Review*, September 1949, pp. 244–251.
6. Mason Haire and Willa Freeman Grunes, "Perceptual Defenses: Processes Protecting an Organized Perception of Another Personality," *Human Relations*, November 1950, pp. 403–412.
7. Ibid., pp. 407–411.
8. David J. Lawless, *Organizational Behavior*, Prentice-Hall, Englewood Cliffs, N.J., 1979, p. 85.
9. Sheldon S. Zalkind and Timothy W. Costello, "Perception: Some Recent Research and Implications for Administration," *Administrative Science Quarterly*, September 1962, pp. 227–229.
10. Ibid., p. 230.
11. Daniel R. Ilgen and Janet Favero, "Limits in Generalization from Psychological Research to Performance Appraisal Processes," *Academy of Management Review*, April 1985, p. 314.
12. For summaries of this literature, see James C. McElroy, "A Typology of Attribution Leadership Research," *Academy of Management Review*, July 1982, pp. 413–417; James C. McElroy and Charles B. Shrader, "Attribution Theories of Leadership and Network Analysis," *Journal of Management*, vol. 12, no. 3, 1986, pp. 351–362; and Christy L. DeVader, Allan G. Bateson, and Robert G. Lord, "Attribution Theory: A Meta-Analysis of Attributional Hypotheses," in Edwin A. Locke (ed.), *Generalizing from Laboratory to Field Settings*, Lexington (Heath), Lexington, Mass., 1986, pp. 63–81.
13. See Robert A. Baron, *Behavior in Organizations*, Allyn and Bacon, Boston, 1986, pp. 131–132, 190; and Joseph F. Porac, Gail Nottenburg, and James Eggert, "On Extending Weiner's Attributional Model to Organizational Contexts," *Journal of Applied Psychology*, February 1981, pp. 124–126.
14. Mason Haire, "Role-Perception in Labor-Management Relations: An Experimental Approach," *Industrial and Labor Relations Review*, January 1955, p. 208.
15. H. John Bernardin and Peter Villanova, "Performance Appraisal," in Locke, op. cit., pp. 45 and 53.
16. Jerome S. Bruner and Renato Tagiuri, "The Perception of People," in Gardner Lindzey (ed.), *Handbook of Social Psychology*, Addison-Wesley, Reading, Mass., 1954, p. 641.
17. S. E. Asch, "Forming Impressions of Personalities," *Journal of Abnormal and Social Psychology*, July 1946, pp. 258–290.
18. Byron A. Grove and Willard A. Kerr, "Specific Evidence on Origin of Halo Effect in Measurement of Employee Morale," *Journal of Social Psychology*, August 1951, pp. 165–170.
19. Timothy W. Costello and Sheldon S. Zalkind, *Psychology in Administration*, Prentice-Hall, Englewood Cliffs, N.J., 1963, p. 35.
20. Rick Jacobs and Steve W. J. Kozlowski, "A Closer Look at Halo Error in Performance Ratings," *Academy of Management Journal*, March 1985, pp. 201–212.
21. Berkeley Rice, "Rating People: Performance Review," *Current*, December 1985, p. 12.

**REAL CASE:
A New
Perception
of Work***

Today's young workers are fed up with the way they are being treated and believe that their best hope for the future rests with unions, right? Wrong! Recent research shows that over half of the U.S. labor force is under 35 years of age and these workers believe that their future depends heavily on helping their employers succeed. Moreover, these young workers are willing to sacrifice a lot for their job and are eager to upgrade their skills.

Many young workers in the 1970s were not happy with their working conditions and spent a lot of their time and energy fighting with management. One of the classic cases was the General Motors assembly line at Lordstown, Ohio. The antimanagement attitude was so strong that workers sabotaged the assembly line and deliberately produced defective products. On some days there were so many cars in the repair lot that it was jammed to capacity. As a result, management would have to send some of the workers home until it could fix the defective cars and make room in the repair lot. No matter. The next day the workers would again foul up the production schedule and be sent home.

Today things are a lot different. Employee perceptions are that through hard work they can improve their job situation. Instead of looking for ways to fight with management and destroy the company, young people are now looking for ways to cooperate. Additionally, many of them are seeking additional training, often at their own expense, so that they can qualify for higher-level jobs. Technical skills are particularly important since many blue-collar jobs are being automated and those who know how to work with computers and high-tech machinery stand the best chance of avoiding a layoff. At the same time, money is proving to be a major motivator. *Fortune* magazine reports that most young workers between the ages of 18 to 35 are making anywhere from $14,000 to $40,000 a year as skilled machinists, medical technicians, repairpersons, and computer operators. In addition, many people have outside jobs that pay them "off the books" so that the cash is never reported to the government.

What has led to this apparently new perception of work? It appears to be a result of young people's view of economic reality. Aware of the fact that Japan constitutes a major threat to the United States and that a number of blue-collar industries are now in decline, workers are showing a willingness to adapt to new conditions. Reports *Fortune*, "Across the U.S. companies moving to make old plants competitive are getting little but praise from workers who have grown up with the idea that the Japanese are invading U.S. markets, that Japanese employees work for less, and that Japanese plants are newer and cleaner and more efficient."

At the same time, these workers are showing less interest in unionizing than did their predecessors. Many of them openly admit that union rules

***Source:** Adapted from Michael Brody, "Meet Today's Young American Worker," *Fortune*, Nov. 11, 1985, pp. 91–98.

and regulations often stymie progress and result in higher production costs which, in the long-run, may threaten their very own economic survival. They believe that their best chance for success rests with the growth of the company and their own abilities to move up the hierarchy to better-paying jobs. They appear determined to learn whatever new skills are needed to ensure their continued employment.

1. How does the perception of today's young workers toward their work differ from that of employees of the 1970s? Explain.
2. What motivates today's young people to improve their technical skills and seek upward mobility?
3. Why are today's young people different from earlier generations of workers in their perception of unions?

CASE: Space Utilization

Sherman Adder, assistant plant manager for Frame Manufacturing Company, is chairperson of the ad hoc committee for space utilization. The committee is made up of the various department heads in the company. The plant manager of Frame has given Sherman the responsibility for seeing whether the various office, operations, and warehouse facilities of the company are being optimally utilized. The company is beset by rising costs and the need for more space. However, before okaying an expensive addition to the plant, the plant manager wants to be sure that the currently available space is being utilized properly.

Sherman opened up the first committee meeting by reiterating the charge of the committee. Then Sherman asked the members if they had any initial observations to make. The first to speak was the office manager. He stated, "Well, I know we are using every possible inch of room that we have available to us. But when I walk out into the plant I see a lot of open spaces. We have people piled on top of one another, but out in the plant there seems to be plenty of room." The production manager quickly replied, "We do not have a lot of space. You office people have the luxury facilities. My supervisors don't even have room for a desk and a file cabinet. I have repeatedly told the plant manager we need more space. After all, our operation determines whether this plant succeeds or fails, not you people in the front office pushing paper around." Sherman interrupted at this point and said, "Obviously we have different interpretations of the space utilization around here. Before further discussion I think it would be best if we have some objective facts to work with. I am going to ask the industrial engineer to provide us with some statistics on plant and office layouts before our next meeting. Today's meeting is adjourned."

1. What perceptual principles are evident in this case?
2. What concept was brought out when the production manager labeled the office personnel a bunch of "paper pushers"? Can you give other organizational examples of this concept?

3. Do you think that Sherman's approach to getting "objective facts" from statistics on plant and office layout will affect the perceptions of the office and production managers? How does such information affect perception in general?

CASE: Same Accident: Different Perceptions

According to the police report, on July 9 at 1:27 p.m., bus number 3763 was involved in a minor noninjury accident. Upon arriving at the scene of the accident, police were unable to locate the driver of the bus. Since the bus was barely drivable, the passengers were transferred to a backup bus, and the damaged bus was returned to the city bus garage for repair.

The newly hired general manager, Aaron Moore, has been going over the police report and two additional reports. One of the additional reports was submitted by Jennifer Tye, the transportation director for the City Transit Authority (CTA), and the other came directly from the driver in the accident, Michael Meyer. According to Tye, although Mike has been an above-average driver for almost eight years, his performance has taken a drastic nosedive during the past fifteen months. Always one to join the other drivers for an after-work drink or two, Mike recently has been suspected of drinking on the job. Furthermore, according to Tye's report, Mike was seen having a beer in a tavern located less than two blocks from the CTA terminal at around 3 p.m. on the day of the accident. Tye's report concludes by citing two sections of the CTA Transportation Agreement. Section 18a specifically forbids the drinking of alcoholic beverages by any CTA employee while on duty. Section 26f prohibits drivers from leaving their bus unattended for any reason. Violation of either of the two sections results in automatic dismissal of the employee involved. Tye recommends immediate dismissal.

According to the driver, Michael Meyer, however, the facts are quite different. Mike claims that in attempting to miss a bicycle rider he swerved and struck a tree, causing minor damage to the bus. Mike had been talking with the dispatcher when he was forced to drop his phone receiver in order to miss the bicycle. Since the receiver broke open upon impact, Mike was forced to walk four blocks to the nearest phone to report the accident. As soon as he reported the accident to the company, Mike also called the union to tell them about it. Mike reports that when he returned to the scene of the accident, his bus was gone. Uncertain of what to do and a little frightened, he decided to return to the CTA terminal. Since it was over a 5-mile walk and because his shift had already ended at 3 p.m., Mike stopped in for a quick beer just before getting back to the terminal.

1. Why are the two reports submitted by Jennifer and Mike so different? Did Jennifer and Mike have different perceptions of the same incident?
2. What additional information would you need if you were in Aaron Moore's position? How can he clarify his own perception of the incident?
3. Given the information presented above, how would you recommend resolving this problem?

7 Attitudes and Job Satisfaction

"Sorry, but we're going to have to let you go!" This is a statement that many managers have been hearing lately as an increasing number of organizations have begun cutting back. This development has not been confined to just small firms or those with financial problems. Many large, successful firms have also been letting managers go, especially those in the middle ranks. Retrenchment and downsizing have become facts of business life in the effort to trim costs and improve competitive position and bottom-line profits.

The large firms that have been cutting back their management staffs read like a *Who's Who of American Business.* Some of those on the list include Apple Computer, Bank of America, CBS, Combustion Engineering, Dow Chemical, Du Pont, Eastman Kodak, Ford, Greyhound, IBM, Merck, Monsanto, Polaroid, and Time. What is particularly unusual is that the people who are being let go or forced into early retirement are not always those who have been doing a poor job. Many have been with the company for years and have always performed well. However, companies are now coming to the conclusion that it costs too much to keep these people on the payroll.

An example, and one of the biggest shockers, has been the drastic reduction at CBS News. The company has long been known for

*Source: Adapted from Bruce Nussbaum and others, "The End of Corporate Loyalty," *Business Week*, Aug. 4, 1986, pp. 42–49; and Peter J. Boyer, "For Many Who Remain, Sadness Turns to Anger over CBS Dismissals," *New York Times*, Mar. 9, 1987, p. 16.

its outstanding news coverage, and opinion polls have consistently shown Dan Rather to be the best known and most trusted news anchor in the country. Yet his department was given a sharp axe soon after Larry Tisch became president of CBS. Many of the staff were very bitter about the development, referring to it as a "disaster." Not only were 215 news people let go but some of them, like Ike Pappas, the well-known reporter who had covered the world for CBS News for twenty-two years, were considered mainstays of the news department. Upon hearing about Pappas, Andy Rooney, the *60 Minutes* commentator, remarked, "This guy Tisch put his money in the company; but I put my life into the company, and so did Ike Pappas and a lot of other people. I own that company, Tisch does not own that company. That's the way I feel. It's Ike's company more than it is Tisch's company."

The attitudes of other CBS personnel were similar. One staff member at *60 Minutes* suggested that their crew be sent out with Mike Wallace to CBS headquarters to interview Mr. Tisch for a future program. Others noted that Mr. Tisch had said that no further cuts would be made after the ones that had occurred the previous year. Still others said nothing, but it was obvious that they were dissatisfied with the turn of events. While the attitude of CBS News personnel was highly negative, CBS corporate management was upbeat. Corporate headquarters pointed to the fact that the news department's budget had increased dramatically over the past nine years and the current cuts would reduce that budget by only 10 percent. Mr. Tisch summed up his personal feeling by saying, "It's painful for everybody, but in the long run, it's better for everybody. They all know it's overstaffed." Many CBS insiders felt that Mr. Tisch was speaking only for himself.

Learning Objectives

- EXAMINE the emotional, informational, and behavioral components of attitudes.
- EXPLAIN how attitudes are formed, the functions they perform, and how they are changed.
- DISCUSS the meaning of job satisfaction of American employees.
- IDENTIFY the major sources and outcomes of job satisfaction.

This chapter deals with the attitudes and job satisfaction expressed by personnel at companies such as CBS and other contemporary organizations. The chapter begins by exploring the nature of attitudes from all dimensions. Next, the focus is on employee attitudes and satisfaction and how they are measured. The last section discusses the sources and consequences of job satisfaction in the modern workplace.

The Nature and Dimensions of Attitudes

The term "attitude" frequently is used in describing people and explaining their behavior. Examples include: "He has a poor attitude." "I like her attitude." "Our workers turn out poor-quality products because they have poor attitudes." More precisely, an *attitude* can be defined as a persistent tendency to feel and behave in a particular way toward some object. For example, George does not like working the night shift. He has a negative attitude toward this work assignment.

Attitudes are a complex cognitive process, but can be characterized three ways. First, they tend to persist unless something is done to change them. For example, if George is transferred to the day shift, his attitude may become positive. Second, attitudes can fall anywhere along a continuum from very favorable to very unfavorable. At the present time, George's attitude may be moderately unfavorable. If he is transferred to the day shift, his attitude may change to highly favorable. Third, attitudes are directed toward some object about which a person has feelings and beliefs. In George's case this is the work shift. The following sections discuss the various dimensions of attitudes, including the basic components, formation, functions, and, finally, how they can be changed.

Components of Attitudes

Attitudes can be broken down into three basic components: emotional, informational, and behavioral. The emotional component includes the person's feelings about an object, i.e., positive, neutral, or negative. Thus, emotion is given the greatest attention in the organizational behavior literature in relation to job satisfaction.[1] In addition, the expression of emotions—either positive, like a customer service representative; negative, like a bill collector or police officer; or neutral, like an academic administrator or public servant—is also important to work behavior.

The informational component consists of the beliefs and information the individual has about the object. It makes no difference whether or not this information is empirically real or correct. A supervisor may believe that two weeks of training is necessary before a worker can operate a particular piece of equipment. In reality, the average worker may be able to operate the machine successfully after only four days of training. Yet, the information the supervisor is using (that two weeks is necessary) is the key to his attitude about training.

The behavioral component consists of a person's tendencies to behave in a particular way toward an object. For example, the supervisor in the above paragraph may assign two weeks of machine training to all his new people.

It is important to remember that of the three components of attitudes, only the behavioral component can be directly observed. One cannot see another person's feelings (the emotional component) or the beliefs and informational component. These two components can only be inferred. For example, when the supervisor assigns a new employee to two weeks of training on the equipment, it is only inferred that (1) the supervisor has strong feelings about the length of training required; and (2) the individual believes that this length of training is

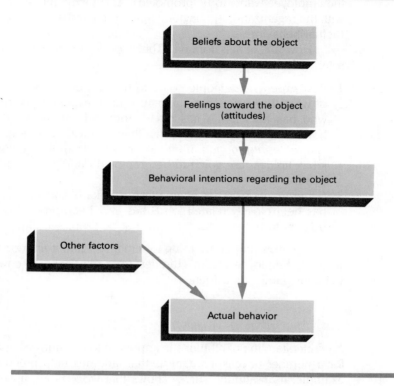

FIGURE 7.1 A model of job attitudes.
(*Source*: Adapted from Martin Fishbein and I. Ajzen, *Beliefs, Attitudes, Intentions and Behavior: An Introduction to Theory and Research*, Addison-Wesley, Reading, Mass., 1975.)

necessary. In the study of organizational behavior, although these inferences are important to recognize and understand, the relationship that attitudes have to behavior are especially important.

In gaining a clearer understanding of the relationship between attitudes and behavior, it is helpful to examine both the causes and effects of attitudes. Fishbein and Ajzen, for example, have done this by taking the three components of attitudes and relating them to one another.[2] Figure 7.1 illustrates this. The informational component that contains the beliefs about the object provides the basis for attitude. One's feeling toward the object (the emotional component) is the attitude itself. The behavioral intentions (the behavioral component) describe what the person is inclined to do toward the object. The supervisor in our earlier example may be inclined to favor two weeks of training for new machine operators. The actual behavior is a function of beliefs, attitudes, behavioral intentions, and a host of other factors.

Attitude Formation

As seen in Figure 7.1, attitudes are a result of beliefs. If employees believe that their current job will provide them with the experience and training necessary to be promoted, the resulting job attitude will be positive (assuming, of course, that the employee wants to be promoted). As a result, the employee will want to stay with the organization (behavioral intentions) and will be as productive as possible (actual behavior).

How are beliefs formed? There are four processes that play an important role:

1. *Past experience.* People come to believe, or not believe, things on the basis of what they have seen happen or have experienced in the past. If everyone who has held job A has been promoted within six months, current job A holders are likely to believe that they also will be promoted within six months.
2. *Available information.* If employees hear from the personnel department that job A holders are going to be promoted rapidly, this will influence what they believe.
3. *Generalizations.* These come from similar events or situations. If no one who has held closely related job B has ever been promoted, this may lead job A holders to believe that they will not be promoted either.

The most important thing to remember about attitude formation is that it is learned. Employees learn attitudes from experiences, coworkers, group memberships, family, and friends.

Functions of Attitudes

An understanding of attitudes is important to the study of organizational behavior for a number of reasons. One is that attitudes help predict work behavior. For example, if an attitude survey shows that workers are upset by a change in the work rules and the next week absenteeism begins to increase sharply, management may conclude that a negative attitude toward work rules led to an increase in worker absenteeism. Another reason why an understanding of attitudes is important is that attitudes help people adapt to their work environment. Katz has noted that attitudes serve four important functions in this process.[3]

The Adjustment Function.
Attitudes often help people adjust to their work environment. When employees are well treated by the boss, they are likely to develop a positive attitude toward supervision and the organization. When employees are berated and given minimal salary increases, they are likely to develop a negative attitude toward supervision and the organization. These attitudes help employees adjust to their environment and are a basis for future behaviors. For example, if employees who are well treated are asked about supervision or the organization, they are likely to say good things. Just the reverse would probably be true for those berated and given minimal salary increases.

The Ego-Defensive Function.
Besides helping employees adjust, attitudes also help them defend their self-images. For example, an older manager whose decisions are continually challenged by a younger subordinate manager may feel that the latter is brash, cocky, immature, and inexperienced. In truth, the younger subordinate may be right in challenging the decisions. The older

manager may not be a very effective leader and may constantly make poor decisions. On the other hand, the older manager is not going to admit this, but will try to protect his ego by putting the blame on the other party. As a result, the older manager will have a negative attitude toward the younger one. The same is undoubtedly true for the younger manager, who will feel that the boss is not doing a good job. This attitude helps the younger person protect her ego. If the subordinate were to change this perception and believe that the boss was doing a good job, she would also have to stop criticizing the boss. Quite obviously this is something that the younger person does not want to do. So the attitude serves to justify the action and to defend the ego.

The Value-Expressive Function.

Attitudes provide people with a basis for expressing their values. For example, a manager who believes strongly in the work ethic will tend to voice attitudes toward specific individuals or work practices as a means of reflecting this value. A supervisor who wants a subordinate to work harder might put it this way, "You've got to work harder. That's been the tradition of the company since it was founded. It helped get us where we are today, and everyone is expected to subscribe to this ethic." A company president who believes strongly in the need to support the United Way campaign might tell the top management, "Everyone in this firm from top to bottom ought to support United Way. It's a wonderful organization and it does a great deal of good for our community. I don't know where we'd be without it." In both these cases, attitudes serve as a basis for expressing one's central values.

The Knowledge Function.

Attitudes help supply standards and frames of reference that allow people to organize and explain the world around them. For example, a union organizer may have a negative attitude toward management. This attitude may not be based in fact, but it does help the individual relate to management. As a result, everything that management says is regarded by the union organizer as nothing more than a pack of lies, a deliberate distortion of the truth, or an attempt to manipulate the workers. Regardless of how accurate a person's view of reality is, attitudes toward people, events, and objects help the individual make sense out of what is going on. Table 7.1 provides a further explanation and summarizes the functions of attitudes.

Changing Attitudes

Employee attitudes can be changed, and sometimes it is in the best interests of management to try to do so. For example, if employees believe that their employer does not take care of them, management would like to change this attitude. Sometimes attitude change is difficult to accomplish because of certain barriers. After these barriers are examined, some ways of overcoming them and effectively changing attitudes will be examined.

Barriers to Changing Attitudes.

There are two basic barriers that can prevent people from changing their attitude. One is called prior commitments.

TABLE 7.1 Determinants of Attitude Formation, Arousal, and Change in Relation to Type of Function

Function	Origin and Dynamics	Arousal Condition	Change Condition
Adjustment	Utility of attitudinal object in need satisfaction; maximizing external rewards and minimizing punishments	1. Activation of needs 2. Salience of cues associated with need satisfaction	1. Need deprivation 2. Creation of new needs and new levels of aspiration 3. Shifting rewards and punishments 4. Emphasis on new and better paths for need satisfaction
Ego defense	Protection against internal conflicts and external changes	1. Posing of threats 2. Appeal to hatred and repressed impulses 3. Rise in frustrations 4. Use of authoritarian suggestion	1. Removal of threats 2. Catharsis 3. Development of self-insight
Value expression	Maintenance of self-identity; enhancing favorable self-image; self-expression and self-determination	1. Salience of cues associated with values 2. Appeal to individual to reassert self-image 3. Ambiguities that threaten self-concept	1. Some degree of dissatisfaction with self 2. Greater appropriateness of new attitude for the self 3. Control of all environmental supports to undermine old values
Knowledge	Need for understanding, meaningful cognitive organization, consistency, and clarity	Reinstatement of cues associated with old problems or of old problems themselves	1. Ambiguity created by new information or by change in environment 2. More-meaningful information about problems

Source: Adapted from T. W. Costello and S. S. Zalkind, *Psychology in Administration*, Prentice-Hall, Englewood Cliffs, N.J., 1963, p. 274.

This occurs when people feel a commitment to a particular course of action and are unwilling to change. For example, the president of the company graduated from an Ivy League school and was personally instrumental in hiring the new head of the personnel department, who had graduated from the same school. Unfortunately, things are not working out well. The personnel manager is not very good. However, because the president played such a major role in hiring the personnel manager, the chief executive is unwilling to admit the mistake. Using the ego-defensive function of attitudes, the president distorts all negative information received about the personnel manager and continues to believe that everything is going well and the right selection decision was made.

A second barrier is a result of insufficient information. Sometimes people do not see any reason to change their attitude. The boss may not like a subordinate's negative attitude, but the latter may be quite pleased with his or her own behavior. Unless the boss can show the individual why a negative attitude is detrimental to career progress or salary raises or some other desirable personal objective, the subordinate may continue to have a negative attitude. This is particularly true when the attitude is a result of poor treatment by management. The worker will use the negative attitude to serve an adjustment function, i.e., "I can't respect a manager that treats me the way this one does."

Providing New Information.
Fortunately, there are ways in which the barriers can be overcome and attitudes can be changed. One of these is by providing new information. Sometimes this information will change a person's beliefs and, in the process, his or her attitudes. In one classic study it was found that union workers had an antimanagement attitude. However, when some of the workers were promoted into the management ranks, their attitudes changed.[4] They became aware of what the company was doing to help the workers, and, over time, this new information resulted in a change in their beliefs about management and their attitude toward both the company and the union. They became more procompany and less prounion.

Use of Fear.
A second way of changing attitudes is through the use of fear. Some researchers have found that fear can cause some people to change their attitudes. However, the degree of fear seems to be important to the final outcome. For example, if low levels of fear arousal are used, people often ignore them. The warnings are not strong enough to warrant attention. If moderate levels of fear arousal are used, people often become aware of the situation and will change their attitudes. However, if high degrees of fear arousal are used, people often reject the message because it is too threatening and thus not believable. They essentially dig in their heels and refuse to be persuaded. A good example is provided in the case of anti–cigarette smoking commercials. The Department of Health and Human Services found that when it ran ads using patients who were dying of cancer, the message was so threatening to smokers that they shut it out; they refused to listen. As a result, the commercials did not have the desired impact. Health officials found that moderate fear arousal commercials were the most effective ones.

Resolving Discrepancies.
Another way in which attitudes can be changed is by resolving discrepancies between attitudes and behavior. For example, research shows that when job applicants have more than one offer of employment and are forced to choose, they often feel that their final choice may have been a mistake. However, this mild conflict or dissonance does not usually last very long. The theory of cognitive dissonance says that people will try to actively reduce the dissonance by attitude and behavior change.[5] Thus, when people take new jobs and begin working, they also start to have negative feeling toward the firms that were not chosen and positive ones toward the company that was chosen. The result may be that the new employees conclude they did indeed make the right choice.

Influence of Friends or Peers.
Still another way in which attitude changes can come about is through persuasion from friends or peers. For example, if Joe

Smith has been padding his expense account and finds out that his other friends in sales have not, he is likely to change his own attitude. This assumes that Joe likes his coworkers and they have some persuasive control over him. On the other hand, if Joe believes that the other salespeople are all lazy and would pad their accounts if they only knew how, he is unlikely to change his attitude toward doing so.

Additionally, it is important to remember that when a particular matter is of personal interest to people, they are likely to reject extreme discrepancies between their current behavior and that of others. For example, if the other salespeople tell Joe that they never pad their expenses while he is padding his by several thousand dollars annually, Joe is unlikely to let them influence him. There are too many benefits to be achieved if he just keeps on doing what he has been doing.

The Coopting Approach.   A final way in which attitude changes often take place is by coopting. This means taking people who are dissatisfied with a situation and getting them involved in improving things. For example, Nancy Jones feels that more needs to be done in improving employee benefits. As a result, the company appoints Nancy as a member of the employee benefits committee. By giving her the opportunity to participate in employee benefits decision making, the company increases the chances that Nancy's attitude will change. Once she begins realizing how these benefits are determined and how long and hard the committee works to ensure that the personnel are given the best benefits possible, she is likely to change her attitude.

The Importance of Employee Attitudes and Job Satisfaction

Employee attitudes are important to management because they affect organizational behavior. In particular, attitudes relating to job satisfaction are of major interest to the field of organizational behavior and the practice of human resource management.

What Is Meant by Job Satisfaction?

Locke gives a comprehensive definition of job satisfaction as "a pleasurable or positive emotional state resulting from the appraisal of one's job or job experience."[6] Job satisfaction is a result of employees' perception of how well their job provides those things which are viewed as important. It is generally recognized in the organizational behavior field that job satisfaction is the most important and frequently studied attitude.[7]

There are three important dimensions to job satisfaction. First, job satisfaction is an emotional response to a job situation. As such, it cannot be seen; it can only be inferred. Second, job satisfaction is often determined by how well outcomes meet or exceed expectations. For example, if organizational participants feel that they are working much harder than others in the department but are receiving fewer rewards, they will probably have a negative attitude toward the work, the boss, and/or coworkers. They will be dissatisfied. On the other hand, if they feel they are being treated very well and are being paid equitably, they are likely to have a positive attitude toward the job. They will be job-satisfied. Third, job satisfaction represents several related attitudes. Smith, Kendall, and Hulin have suggested that there are five job dimensions that represent the most important characteristics of a job about which people have affective responses. These are:

1. *Work itself*—the extent to which the job provides the individual with interesting tasks, opportunities for learning, and the chance to accept responsibility
2. *Pay*—the amount of financial remuneration that is received and the degree to which this is viewed as equitable vis-à-vis others in the organization
3. *Promotion opportunities*—the chances for advancement in the hierarchy
4. *Supervision*—the abilities of the superior to provide technical assistance and behavioral support
5. *Co-workers*—the degree to which fellow workers are technically proficient and socially supportive[8]

Measuring Job Satisfaction

There are a number of ways of measuring job satisfaction. Some of the most common include rating scales, critical incidents, interviews, and action tendencies.

Rating Scales. The most common approach for measuring job satisfaction is the use of rating scales. One of the most popular is the Minnesota Satisfaction Questionnaire (MSQ). Figure 7.2 illustrates a short form of the MSQ. This instrument provides a detailed picture of the specific satisfactions and dissatisfactions of employees.

Another popular rating scale is the Job Descriptive Index (JDI). This scale measures the dimensions identified by Smith, Kendall, and Hulin in the five points cited in the previous section. Figure 7.3 provides an example of the index. It has been widely used by organizational behavior researchers over the years and provides a broad picture of employee attitudes toward the major components of jobs.

Still another popular instrument is the Porter Need Satisfaction Questionnaire (NSQ), shown in Figure 7.4. It is typically used for management personnel only. The questions focus on particular problems and challenges faced by managers.

Rating scales offer a number of important advantages in measuring job satisfaction. One is that they are usually short and can be filled out quickly and easily. Another is that they tend to be worded in general language so that they can be used with employees in many different types of organizations. A third is that because they have been so widely used in research, there is usually normative data available so that the responses can be compared with those of employees in other organizations who have taken the test in previous years.

Ask Yourself: How satisfied am I with this aspect of my job?

Very Sat. means I am very satisfied with this aspect of my job.
Sat. means I am satisfied with this aspect of my job.
N means I can't decide whether I am satisfied or not with this aspect of my job.
Dissat. means I am dissatisfied with this aspect of my job.
Very Dissat. means I am very dissatisfied with this aspect of my job.

On my present job, this is how I feel about . . .	Very Dissat.	Dissat.	N	Sat.	Very Sat.
1. Being able to keep busy all the time	☐	☐	☐	☐	☐
2. The chance to work alone on the job	☐	☐	☐	☐	☐
3. The chance to do different things from time to time	☐	☐	☐	☐	☐
4. The chance to be "somebody" in the community	☐	☐	☐	☐	☐
5. The way my boss handles the staff	☐	☐	☐	☐	☐
6. The competence of my supervisor in making decisions	☐	☐	☐	☐	☐
7. Being able to do things that don't go against my conscience	☐	☐	☐	☐	☐
8. The way my job provides for steady employment	☐	☐	☐	☐	☐
9. The chance to do things for other people	☐	☐	☐	☐	☐
10. The chance to tell people what to do	☐	☐	☐	☐	☐
11. The chance to do something that makes use of my abilities	☐	☐	☐	☐	☐
12. The way company policies are put into practice	☐	☐	☐	☐	☐
13. My pay and the amount of work I do	☐	☐	☐	☐	☐
14. The chances for advancement on this job	☐	☐	☐	☐	☐
15. The freedom to use my own judgment	☐	☐	☐	☐	☐
16. The chance to try my own methods of doing the job	☐	☐	☐	☐	☐
17. The working conditions	☐	☐	☐	☐	☐
18. The way my coworkers get along with each other	☐	☐	☐	☐	☐
19. The praise I get for doing a good job	☐	☐	☐	☐	☐
20. The feeling of accomplishment I get from the job	☐	☐	☐	☐	☐
	Very Dissat.	Dissat.	N	Sat.	Very Sat.

FIGURE 7.2 The Minnesota Satisfaction Questionnaire.
(*Source:* D. J. Weiss, R. V. Dawis, G. W. England, and L. H. Lofquist, *Manual for the Minnesota Satisfaction Questionnaire.* Minnesota Studies in Vocational Rehabilitation, vol. 22. University of Minnesota Industrial Relations Center, Minneapolis, 1967. Reprinted by permission.)

On the negative side, these instruments are based on the assumption that the personnel are willing to respond honestly and that they are able to describe their feelings accurately. Another problem is the underlying assumption that the questionnaire items are valid (they measure what they are supposed to measure) and reliable (they accurately and consistently measure). Validity and reliability were discussed in Chapter 2.

Critical Incidents. The critical incidents approach to the measurement of job satisfaction was popularized by Frederick Herzberg. He and his colleagues used this technique in their research on the two-factor theory of motivation.[9] Employees were asked to describe incidents on their job when they were particularly satisfied and dissatisfied. These incidents were then content-analyzed in determining which aspects were most closely related to positive and negative attitudes. Chapter 9, on motivation, will consider these research results as part of a detailed discussion of the two-factor theory.

FIGURE 7.3
Sample of the Job Descriptive Index. (*Source*: Reprinted by permission of Dr. P. C. Smith. Copyright 1975, 1985, Bowling Green University, Department of Psychology, Bowling Green, Ohio.)

Think of your present work. What is it like most of the time? In the blank beside each word given below, write

Y for "Yes" if it describes your work
N for "No" if it does NOT describe it
? if you cannot decide

Think of the pay you get now. How well does each of the following words or phrases describe your present pay? In the blank beside each word, put

Y if it describes your pay
N if it does NOT describe it
? if you cannot decide

Think of the opportunities for promotion that you have now. How well does each of the following words or phrases describe this? In the blank beside each word, put

Y for "Yes" if it describes your opportunities for promotion
N for "No" if it does NOT describe them
? if you cannot decide

WORK ON PRESENT JOB	PRESENT PAY	OPPORTUNITIES FOR PROMOTION
___ Routine	___ Income adequate for normal expenses	___ Promotion on ability
___ Satisfying	___ Insecure	___ Dead-end job
___ Good	___ Less than I deserve	___ Unfair promotion policy
___ Tiring	___ Well paid	___ Regular promotions

Think of the kind of supervision that you get on your job. How well does each of the following words or phrases describe this? In the blank beside each word below, put

Y if it describes the supervision you get on your job
N if it does NOT describe it
? if you cannot decide

Think of the majority of the people that you work with now or the people you meet in connection with your work. How well does each of the following words or phrases describe these people? In the blank beside each word below, put

Y if it describes the people you work with
N if it does NOT describe them
? if you cannot decide

SUPERVISION	PEOPLE ON YOUR PRESENT JOB
___ Impolite	___ Boring
___ Praises good work	___ Responsible
___ Influential	___ Intelligent
___ Doesn't supervise enough	___ Talk too much

Part 2: Basic Understanding of Individual Behavior

FIGURE 7.4
Sample items
from the Porter
Need Satisfaction
Questionnaire.
(*Source*: L. W. Por-
ter, "A Study of Per-
ceived Need Satis-
faction in Bottom
and Middle Manage-
ment Jobs," *Journal
of Applied Psychol-
ogy*, vol. 45, 1961, p.
3. Copyright 1961 by
The American Psy-
chological Associa-
tion. Reprinted by
permission of the
publisher and au-
thor.)

Instructions: Circle the number on the scale that represents the amount of the characteristic being rated. Low numbers represent low or minimum amounts, and high numbers represent high or maximum amounts.

1. The opportunity for personal growth and development in my management position.
   a. HOW MUCH IS THERE NOW?
      (Minimum) 1   2   3   4   5   6   7   (Maximum)
   b. HOW MUCH SHOULD THERE BE?
      (Minimum) 1   2   3   4   5   6   7   (Maximum)

2. The feeling of security in my management position.
   a. HOW MUCH IS THERE NOW?
      (Minimum) 1   2   3   4   5   6   7   (Maximum)
   b. HOW MUCH SHOULD THERE BE?
      (Minimum) 1   2   3   4   5   6   7   (Maximum)

One of the major benefits of the critical incidents approach is that it allows the respondents to say whatever they want. The individuals are not restricted by predetermined categories or events as on a structured questionnaire. On the other hand, the approach is time-consuming and there is the chance that both the responses and the interpretations will be biased. The respondents might tell the interviewer what they think the interviewer wants to hear or something that makes them look good such as, "I like it best when my supervisor gets out of my hair and lets me do the job my way. No one knows how to do this work better than I do."

Interviews. Another method of assessing job satisfaction is through the use of personal interviews. This approach allows for an in-depth exploration of job attitudes. If the respondent says something that the interviewer does not understand or would like to learn more about, the interviewer can follow up with additional questions. On the negative side, responses can be misinterpreted and thus lead to erroneous conclusions. A second problem is the possibility of interviewer bias. The way in which the individual asks the questions or the types of information the person chooses to record can affect the outcome. Finally, there is the cost factor. Interviews are a relatively time-consuming and thus expensive way of gathering information.

Action Tendencies. Action tendencies are the inclinations people have to approach or to avoid certain things. By gathering information about how they feel like acting with respect to their jobs, the job satisfaction can be measured. Figure 7.5 provides some examples of action tendencies.

There are a number of advantages associated with this approach to measuring attitudes. One is that less self-insight is required by the respondent. Thus, the chance of self-bias is reduced. A second is that the approach provides greater

FIGURE 7.5
Sample items for
an action ten-
dency schedule
for job satisfac-
tion.
(*Source*: Edwin A.
Locke, "Nature
and Causes of Job
Satisfaction," in M. D.
Dunnette (ed.),
*Handbook of Indus-
trial and Organiza-
tional Behavior*,
Rand McNally, Chi-
cago, 1976, p.
1336. © John Wiley
& Sons Inc. Used
with permission.)

1. When you wake up in the morning, do you feel reluctant to go to work?
2. Do you ever feel reluctant to go home from work at night because of the enjoyment you are getting from the job?
3. Do you often feel like going to lunch at work sooner than you do?
4. Do you feel like taking a coffee break more often than you should?
5. Do you ever wish you could work at your job on evenings or weekends?
6. Are you sometimes reluctant to leave your job to go on a vacation?
7. When you are on vacation, do you ever look forward to getting back to work?
8. Do you ever wake up at night with the urge to go to work right then and there?
9. Do you ever wish holidays or weekends would get over with so that you could go back to work?
10. If you were starting over in your working career, would you lean toward taking the same type of job you have now?
11. Would you be tempted to recommend your present job to a friend with the same interests and education as yours?

opportunity for people to express their in-depth feelings than do many other, more surface job satisfaction instruments.

Job Satisfaction of American Employees

Are most workers dissatisfied with their jobs? Job attitude surveys generally reveal that they are not, although job satisfaction continues to be a major concern. Although surveys are reported all the time, the University of Michigan's Survey Research Center and the National Opinion Research Center have found that workers in a wide range of jobs across a diverse set of organizations consistently report that they are generally satisfied with their jobs.

There are, however, some differences that can be discerned. For example, professional and white-collar occupations report higher levels of satisfaction than do blue-collar types of occupations over the years. The important special case of female managers as reported in the accompanying Application Example, It's All Up to Management, indicates considerable dissatisfaction among this small but growing segment of the work force. In addition to females, job satisfaction can be examined in other groups such as young workers, blue-collar workers, and middle managers.

Young Workers. Young workers seem to be less satisfied with their jobs than their older counterparts. There are a number of reasons for this. One is that young workers come into the workplace with high expectations that may not be fulfilled, as jobs prove insufficiently challenging or meaningful. Another reason for dissatisfaction is that many young graduates of colleges and even high schools may be overqualified for their jobs. For example, the Bureau of Labor Statistics estimates that the number of college graduates exceeds job openings that require college degrees by about 1 million a year. As a result, some college graduates

Application Example

It's All Up to Management*

A recent survey by *Working Woman* reveals that there are a lot of female managers who are not satisfied with their jobs. The survey addressed many of the most commonly cited "female issues," including sexual harassment, low salaries, and ceilings on advancement, but none of these were the greatest problem. The major mistake, according to the respondents (many of whom are managers and professional, college-educated, and making a good salary) was that top management is no longer running companies that are good places to work. In particular, they faulted management for not doing a good job with goal-setting, crisis management, elimination of red tape, assigning reasonable work loads, and providing feedback on job performance. Some of the responses from the 7800 individuals who participated in the study were the following:

Management Does a Poor Job with . . .	Total Respondents	Those "Very Satisfied" with Job	Those Thinking of Looking for Another Job
Goal-setting	58%	18%	63%
Crisis management	64	21	19
Keeping procedures free of red tape	61	22	59
Making employees feel like important individuals	55	14	67
Assigning reasonable work loads	53	19	62
Providing feedback on job performance	48	15	69

Even more interesting, perhaps, is the fact that few other factors made a significant difference in how satisfied the respondents felt at work. The impact of the woman's age, educational level, job title, family and marital status, number of jobs held or job changes, or number of years in the workplace had no effect on the person's respect for management. Even major upheavals did not have a critical long-term effect on job satisfaction. Approximately half the group of respondents had had a radical career change, a third had taken a year or more off work, a fourth had changed jobs in order to follow their husband, and a fifth had been fired from a job. None of these factors had any effect on their job satisfaction. In short, the problem seems not to be with the respondents, but with the management. The latter are not making today's organization a good, satisfying place in which to work.

The results are clear. If management wants to improve work attitudes among female employees, it will be necessary to change the way things are currently being done. If organizations can do such things as create a good climate, make people feel important, and provide feedback on job performance, work attitudes may improve. It's all up to management.

Source: Adapted from Jane Ciabattari, "The Biggest Mistake Top Managers Make," *Working Woman*, October 1986, p. 54.

are taking lower-income, lower-status jobs, and this is leading to frustration and lack of job satisfaction on their part. One young person put it this way:

> I didn't go to school for four years to type. I'm bored; continuously humiliated. They sent me to Xerox school for three hours. . . . I realize that I sound cocky, but after you've been in the academic world, after you've had your own class [as a student teacher] and made your own plans, and someone tries to teach you to push a button—you get pretty mad. They even gave me a gold plated plaque to show I've learned how to use the machine.[10]

Another reason why young employees are dissatisfied with their jobs is that they do not have any authority or control over their work. They find that their bosses are in charge and they must respond to their directives. This situation is quite different from what they encountered at home and school, where they had some influence on events.

Blue-Collar Workers.   Many blue-collar workers do not believe that there is much opportunity for either themselves or their children. In fact, for the first time in decades, the children of many blue-collar workers are becoming blue-collar workers themselves. Today, about 50 percent of all blue-collar workers have high school diplomas; in 1960 this was but 25 percent. These workers are becoming better educated, but their opportunities are not improving.

Many blue-collar workers are particularly frustrated by the lack of respect accorded them. The popular press often portrays them in negative terms. For example, newspaper stories that report cases in which plumbers or electricians earn $50 an hour while the average person earns far less continue to appear and give the impression that many blue-collar people are overpaid for doing menial work.

Another problem is the increasing feeling among blue-collar workers that there are not enough of the good things of life to go around and they are failing to receive their fair share. In truth, many blue-collar workers are barely able to keep up with the cost of living because of low wages and inflation.

Middle Managers.   Many middle managers feel that their organizations are not doing enough for them. One of their major complaints in recent years has been the decline in organizational loyalty to the personnel. Years ago middle managers used to believe that if they did a good job, they could expect the company to take care of them. This is no longer true. As the opening vignette pointed out, the cutbacks in recent years have gutted the middle ranks of many organizations. For example, big, prestigious companies such as IBM, USX, United Airlines, and AT&T have for the first time begun to cut deeply into their middle management ranks. In 1986 alone, AT&T eliminated 11,600 management positions.[11] Here are some representative examples of the trumatic effect such cuts have on the middle managers affected:

- I was hurt. After 34 years with the company, I was surprised that it came down to an economic relationship between the two of us. I thought I was in a family kind of thing.

   —Married man, 57, nudged into early retirement by a big drug company.

- It was pretty traumatic. My self-worth was nil. It was the worst period of my life. Today you can't count on working for a company for 20 to 30 years. It's important to stay flexible.
  —Married man, 43, victim of cutbacks at a large minerals company.
- It was like some unseen hand that came down from on high. People are freaked out and anxious. I've never seen anything like it.
  —Single woman, 30, who survived white-collar cutbacks at a major oil company.[12]

Even middle managers who have survived these cutbacks feel that they do not have much influence in the organization or control over their careers. They are paid to do their work and not to ask a lot of questions. Middle managers continue to share the goals of top management, but they are more concerned, anxious, and dissatisfied than ever about their own careers.

Sources and Consequences of Job Satisfaction

Organizational behavior researchers have long been interested in the major influences on job satisfaction as well as the outcomes that can be expected from such satisfaction. The following examines both of these areas.

Influences on Job Satisfaction

There are a number of factors that influence job satisfaction. The major ones can be summarized by recalling the dimensions identified earlier: pay, the work itself, promotions, supervision, the work group, and working conditions.

Pay. Wages are a significant factor in job satisfaction. Money not only helps people attain their basic needs but is instrumental in providing upper-level need satisfaction. Employees often see pay as a reflection of how management views their contribution to the organization. Fringe benefits are also important, but they are not as influential. One reason undoubtedly is that most employees do not even know how much they are receiving in benefits. Moreover, most tend to undervalue these benefits because they cannot see their practical value.[13] Chapters in the next part of the book will examine pay as a reinforcer.

The Work Itself. The content of the work itself is another major source of satisfaction. For example, research related to the job characteristics approach to job design, covered in Chapter 10, shows that feedback from the job itself and autonomy are two of the major job-related motivational factors. The survey reported in the Application Example echoes these findings. Some of the most important ingredients of a satisfying job uncovered by this survey included interesting and challenging work, work that is not boring, and a job that provides status.[14]

Promotions. Promotional opportunities seem to have a varying effect on job satisfaction. This is because promotions take a number of different forms and have a variety of accompanying rewards. For example, individuals who are promoted on the basis of seniority often experience job satisfaction but not as much as those who are promoted on the basis of performance. Additionally, a promotion with a 10 percent salary raise is typically not as satisfying as one with a 20 percent salary raise. This helps explain why executive promotions may be more satisfying than promotions that occur at the lower levels of organizations.

Supervision. Supervision is another moderately important source of job satisfaction. Chapter 16 discusses the impact of leadership style. For now, however, it can be said that there seem to be two dimensions of supervisory style that affect job satisfaction. One is employee-centeredness. This is measured by the degree to which a supervisor takes a personal interest in the employee's welfare. It commonly is manifested in ways such as checking to see how well the subordinate is doing, providing advice and assistance to the individual, and communicating with the worker on a personal as well as an official level. American employees generally complain that their supervisors don't do a very good job on these dimensions. For example, a recent large survey found that less than half of the respondents felt their bosses provided them regular feedback or tried to solve their problems.[15]

The other dimension is participation or influence, as illustrated by managers who allow their people to participate in decisions that affect their own jobs. In most cases this approach leads to higher job satisfaction. For example, a recent comprehensive meta-analysis concluded that participation does have a positive effect on job satisfaction. A participative climate created by the supervisor has a more substantial effect on workers' satisfaction than does participation in a specific decision.[16]

Work Group. The nature of the work group will have an effect on job satisfaction. Friendly, cooperative coworkers are a modest source of job satisfaction to individual employees. The work group serves as a source of support, comfort, advice, and assistance to the individual worker. A "good" work group makes the job more enjoyable. However, this factor is not essential to job satisfaction. On the other hand, if the reverse conditions exist—the people are difficult to get along with—this may have a negative effect on job satisfaction. For example, many women have low job satisfaction because they feel they are subject to male stereotyping that hinders their chances for promotion. This stereotyping seems to exist even among well-educated managers.[17]

Working Conditions. Working conditions are another factor that have a modest effect on job satisfaction. If the working conditions are good (clean, attractive surroundings, for instance), the personnel will find it easier to carry out their jobs. If the working conditions are poor (hot, noisy surroundings, for example), personnel will find it more difficult to get things done. In other words, the effect of working conditions on job satisfaction is similar to that of the work group. If things are good, there will not be a job satisfaction problem; if things are poor, there will be.

Most people do not give working conditions a great deal of thought unless they are extremely bad. Additionally, when there are complaints about working conditions, these sometimes are really nothing more than manifestations of other problems. For example, a manager may complain that his office has not been properly cleaned by the night crew, but his anger is actually a result of a meeting he had with the boss earlier in the day in which he was given a poor performance evaluation.

Outcomes of Job Satisfaction

If job satisfaction is high, will the employees perform better and the organization be more effective? If job satisfaction is low, will there be performance problems and ineffectiveness? This question has been asked by both researchers and practitioners through the years. There are no simple answers. In examining the outcomes of job satisfaction, it is important to break down the analysis into a series of specific subtopics. The following examines the most important of these.

Satisfaction and Productivity. Are satisfied workers more productive than their less-satisfied counterparts? This "satisfaction-performance controversy" has raged over the years. Although most people assume a positive relationship, the preponderance of research evidence indicates that there is no strong linkage between satisfaction and productivity. For example, a recent comprehensive meta-analysis of the research literature found only a .17 average correlation between job satisfaction and productivity.[18] Satisfied workers will not necessarily be the highest producers. There are many possible mediating variables, the most important of which seems to be rewards. If people receive rewards they feel are equitable, they will be satisfied and this is likely to result in greater performance effort. Also, there is considerable debate whether satisfaction leads to performance or performance leads to satisfaction. The chapters in the next part of the book will examine in detail these and other possible dimensions of the relationship.

Satisfaction and Turnover. Does high employee job satisfaction result in low turnover? Unlike that between satisfaction and productivity, research has uncovered a moderate relationship between satisfaction and turnover.[19] High job satisfaction will not, in and of itself, keep turnover low, but it does seem to help. On the other hand, if there is considerable job dissatisfaction, there is likely to be high turnover. One group of researchers found that for women eighteen to twenty-five, satisfaction was an excellent predictor of whether or not they changed jobs. On the other hand, as job tenure (length of time on the job) increased, there was less likelihood of their leaving.[20] Tenure has also been found to lessen the effects of dissatisfaction among male employees.[21]

There are other factors, such as commitment to the organization, that play a role in this relationship between satisfaction and turnover. Some people cannot see themselves working anywhere else, so they remain regardless of how dissatisfied they feel. Another factor is the general economy. When things in the economy are going well and there is little unemployment, typically there will be an increase in turnover because people will begin looking for better opportunities with other organizations. Even if they are satisfied, many people are willing to leave if the opportunities elsewhere promise to be better. On the other hand, if jobs are tough to get, dissatisfied employees will stay where they are. On an overall basis, however, it is accurate to say that job satisfaction is important in employee turnover. Although absolutely no turnover is not necessarily beneficial to the organization, a low turnover rate is usually desirable because of training costs and the drawbacks of inexperience.

Satisfaction and Absenteeism. Research has pretty well demonstrated an inverse relationship between satisfaction and absenteeism.[22] When satisfaction is high, absenteeism tends to be low; when satisfaction is low, absenteeism tends to be high. However, similar to the other relationships with satisfaction, there are moderating variables such as the degree to which people feel that their jobs are important. For example, research among state government employees has found that those who believed that their work was important had lower absenteeism than did those who did not feel this way. Additionally, it is important to remember that while high job satisfaction will not necessarily result in low absenteeism, low job satisfaction is likely to bring about high absenteeism.[23]

Other Effects of Job Satisfaction. In addition to the above, there are a number of other effects brought about by high job satisfaction. Research reports that highly satisfied employees tend to have better mental and physical health, learn new job-related tasks more quickly, have fewer on-the-job accidents, and file fewer grievances. From an overall standpoint, then, most organizational behavior researchers as well as practicing managers would argue that job satisfaction is important to an organization. Some critics have argued, however, that this is pure conjecture because there is so much we do not know about the positive effects of satisfaction. On the other hand, when job satisfaction is low, there seem to be negative effects on the organization that have been documented. So if only from the standpoint of viewing job satisfaction as a minimum requirement or point of departure, it is of value to the organization's overall health and effectiveness and is deserving of study and application in the field of organizational behavior.

Summary

Attitude is a persistent tendency to feel and behave in a particular way toward some object. Attitudes are a complex cognitive process but have three basic characteristics: they persist unless changed in some way; they range along a continuum; and they are directed toward an object about which a person has feelings and beliefs. Attitudes also have three components: emotional, informational, and behavioral. They are a result of beliefs formed through past experience, available information, generalizations from past events or situations, and/or the influence of people whom one trusts.

Attitudes often help employees to adapt to their work environment. There are four functions that attitudes play in this process: (1) they help people adjust to their environment; (2) they help people defend their self-image; (3) they provide people with a basis for expressing their values; and (4) they help supply standards and frames of reference that allow people to organize and explain the world around them.

It is sometimes difficult to change attitudes. One reason is prior commitments. A second is insufficient information on the part of the person. Research shows that some of the ways of bringing about attitude changes include providing new information, use of fear, resolving discrepancies between behavior and attitude, persuasion from friends or peers, and coopting.

Job satisfaction is a pleasurable or positive emotional state resulting from the appraisal of one's job or job experience. There are a number of ways of measuring job satisfaction. Some of these include rating scales, critical incidents, interviews, and action tendencies. Each was explained in the chapter.

Research generally shows over the years that most workers are satisfied with their jobs. However, there are some groups that are less satisfied than others. For example, a substantial percentage of young workers, women, blue-collar workers, and middle managers are not very satisfied. A number of factors influence job satisfaction. Some of the major ones include pay, the work itself, promotions, supervision, the work group, and working conditions. There are a number of outcomes of job satisfaction. For example, although the relationship with productivity is not clear, low job satisfaction tends to lead to both turnover and absenteeism, while high job satisfaction often results in fewer on-the-job accidents and work grievances and less time needed to learn new job-related tasks. Quite obviously, positive job satisfaction has real and potential benefits for the organization.

Questions for Discussion and Review

1. In your own words, what is an attitude? What are three characteristics of attitudes?
2. What are the three components of attitudes?
3. How are beliefs formed? In what way do beliefs affect attitudes? In your answer, use an example.
4. Attitudes serve four important functions for individuals. What are these four functions?
5. What types of barriers prevent people from changing their attitudes? How can attitudes be changed?
6. What is meant by the term "job satisfaction"? How does it relate to attitudes?
7. Describe each of the following measures of job satisfaction: rating scales, critical incidents, interviews, action tendencies.
8. In general, how satisfied are young people with their jobs? Blue-collar workers? Middle managers? Women? Explain.
9. What are some of the major factors that influence job satisfaction?
10. What are some of the important outcomes of job satisfaction?

References

1. Anat Rafaeli and Robert I. Sutton, "Expression of Emotion as Part of the Work Role," *Academy of Management Review*, January 1987, p. 23.
2. Martin Fishbein and I. Ajzen, *Belief, Attitude, Intention, and Behavior: An Introduction to Theory and Research*, Addison-Wesley, Reading, Mass., 1975.
3. D. Katz, "The Functional Approach to the Study of Attitudes," *Journal of Opinion Quarterly*, Summer 1960, pp. 163–204.
4. S. Lieberman, "The Effect of Changes in Roles on the Attitudes of Role Occupants," *Human Relations*, November 1956, pp. 385–402.
5. Leon Festinger, *A Theory of Cognitive Dissonance*, Stanford University, Stanford, Calif., 1957.
6. E. A. Locke, "The Nature and Cause of Job Satisfaction," in M. D. Dunnette (ed.), *Handbook of Industrial and Organizational Psychology*, Rand McNally, Chicago, 1976, p. 1300.
7. Terence R. Mitchell and James R. Larson, Jr., *People in Organizations*, 3d ed., McGraw-Hill, New York, 1987, p. 146.
8. P. C. Smith, L. M. Kendall, and C. L. Hulin, *The Measure of Satisfaction in Work and Retirement*, Rand McNally, Chicago, 1969.
9. Frederick Herzberg, Bernard Mausner, and Barbara Bloch Snyderman, *The Motivation to Work*, 2d ed., Wiley, New York, 1959.
10. *Work in America*, Report of the Secretary of Health, Education and Welfare, MIT Press, Cambridge, 1973, p. 45.
11. "Rebuilding to Survive," *Time*, Feb. 16, 1987, p. 44.
12. Bruce Nussbaum and others, "The End of Corporate Loyalty," *Business Week*, Aug. 4, 1986, p. 42.
13. Brenda Major and Ellen Konar, "An Investigation of Sex Differences in Pay Expectations and Their Possible Causes," *Academy of Management Journal*, December 1984, pp. 777–792.
14. Jane Ciabattari, "The Biggest Mistake Top Managers Make," *Working Woman*, October 1986, p. 48.
15. "Labor Letter," *The Wall Street Journal*, Dec. 22, 1987, p. 1.
16. Katharine I. Miller and Peter R. Monge, "Participation, Satisfaction, and Productivity: A Meta-Analytic Review," *Academy of Management Journal*, December 1986, p. 748.
17. Peter Dubno, "Attitudes toward Women Executives: A Longitudinal Approach," *Academy of Management Journal*, March 1985, pp. 235–239.
18. M. T. Iffaldano and P. M. Muchinsky, "Job Satisfaction and Job Performance: A Meta-Analysis," *Psychological Bulletin*, vol. 97, 1985, pp. 251–273.
19. For an example of a recent study that verifies the relationship between satisfaction and turnover see Thomas W. Lee and Richard T. Mowday, "Voluntarily Leaving an Organization: An Empirical Investigation of Steers and Mowday's Model of Turnover," *Academy of Management Journal*, December 1987, pp. 721–743.
20. Sookom Kim, Roger Roderick, and John Shea, *Dual Careers: A Longitudinal Study of the Labor Market Experience of Women*, vol. 2, U.S. Government Printing Office, Washington, D.C., 1973, pp. 55–56.
21. Herbert Parnes, Gilbert Nestel, and Paul Andrisani, *The Pre-Retirement Years: A Longitudinal Study of the Labor Market Experience of Men*, vol. 3, U.S. Government Printing Office, Washington, D.C., 1973, p. 37.
22. K. Dow Scott and G. Stephen Taylor, "An Examination of Conflicting Findings on the Relationship between Job Satisfaction and Absenteeism: A Meta-Analysis," *Academy of Management Journal*, September 1985, pp. 599–612.

23. C. W. Clegg, "Psychology of Employee Lateness, Absenteeism, and Turnover: A Methodological Critique and an Empirical Study," *Journal of Applied Psychology*, February 1983, pp. 88–101.

**REAL CASE:
Goodbye at 45***

When Joseph Rockom began working at American Microsystems, a semiconductor manufacturer in California's Silicon Valley, in 1968, he looked forward to a long and fulfilling career. Through hard work, diligence, and loyalty he rose to the rank of vice president and chief financial officer. Then a major slump hit the high-tech industry. Cost cutting began in earnest and American Microsystems started laying off some of its managers. One morning Rockom came to work and found that his name was on the latest list of those being laid off. After seventeen years of hard work and devotion, he was out on the street.

The above story is not an isolated case. In recent years, thousands of executives have been laid off. At AT&T, Exxon, General Electric, and other firms that were once regarded as havens of career stability, the managerial ranks are beginning to be thinned by layoffs. A *Fortune* survey found that of 250 managers who were let go, it usually takes four to six months before new employment is found and, in more cases than not, the individual goes to work for a smaller company and at the same or lower salary. Moreover, in over half the cases, the individual ends up supervising fewer employees than previously.

How do executives feel about being let go? Many of them say they have a negative attitude toward their old company, especially in those cases where the individual worked for ten or more years. There is the feeling that the company did not hold up its end of the bargain. This negative attitude is becoming more and more widespread. For example, a survey conducted by *Business Week* found that most middle managers felt that salaried employees are less loyal to their company than previously. Only 5 percent felt that salaried employees are more loyal. Additionally, 44 percent of the managers reported that they felt that even if they did a good job, they might not be able to stay with their current employer for as long as they would like. Moreover, of those who stay, attitudes often are not very positive. The reason is not hard to understand. The *Business Week* report provided some background with the following description:

But not all survivors are winners. After downsizing there often is a sense of loss of control—by both managers and employees. This is most demoralizing in companies where survivors discover that they are working for managers who have been demoted one, two, or even three grades. At Exxon, "so many managers have been demoted, there is a layer on top of me—

*Source: Adapted from Peter Nulty, "Pushed Out at 45—Now What?" *Fortune*, Mar. 2, 1987, pp. 26–30; and Bruce Nussbaum, "The End of Corporate Loyalty," *Business Week*, Aug. 4, 1986, pp. 42–49.

people in their 40s and 50s—that I will never get through," says one 30-year-old employee. "For the survivors, there are no opportunities. Moving up is a thing of the past." For this employee and others like her, Exxon has become a way station to a better job.

Those who get demoted don't take a salary cut, but they don't expect to be getting any increases either—not for a long time, anyway. "Some people were demoted four levels," says one employee. "They'll have to wait years. Some people in their 50s never expect to get a raise again."

1. Before the layoffs, what type of attitude would you think most of the managers in these firms had toward their company?
2. After the layoffs, what would you expect to happen to the attitudes of those who still had their jobs? Why?
3. In what way might job satisfaction be a problem for companies that have trimmed back their staff?

CASE: Doing His Share

When Ralph Morgan joined the Beacher Corporation, he started out as an assembler on the line. Ralph remained in this position for five years. During this time there were two major strikes. The first lasted five weeks; the second went on for eighteen weeks. As a member of the union, Ralph was out of work during both of these periods, and in each case the strike fund ran out of money before a labor agreement was reached.

Last year Ralph was asked if he would like to apply for a supervisory job. The position paid $2500 more than he was making, and the chance for promotion up the line made it an attractive offer. Ralph accepted.

During the orientation period, Ralph found himself getting angry at the management representative. This guy seemed to believe that the union was too powerful and management personnel had to hold the line against any further loss of authority. Ralph did not say anything, but he felt the speaker was very ill informed and biased. Two developments have occurred over the last six months, however, that have led Ralph to change his attitude toward union-management relations at the company.

One was a run-in he had with a shop steward who accused Ralph of deliberately harassing one of the workers. Ralph could not believe his ears. "Harassing a worker? Get serious. All I did was tell him to get back to work," he explained to the steward. Nevertheless, a grievance was filed and withdrawn only after Ralph apologized to the individual whom he supposedly harassed. The other incident was a result of disciplinary action. One of the workers in his unit came late for the third day in a row and, as required by the labor contract, Ralph sent him home without pay. The union protested, claiming that the worker had really been late only twice. When Ralph went to the personnel office to get the worker's clock-in sheets, the one for the first day of tardiness was missing. The clerks in that office, who were union members, claimed that they did not know where it was.

In both of these cases, Ralph felt the union went out of its way to embarrass him. Earlier this week the manager from the orientation session called Ralph. "I've been thinking about bringing line supervisors into the orientation meetings to discuss the union's attitude toward management. Having been on the other side, would you be interested in giving them your opinion of what they should be prepared for and how they should respond?" Ralph said he would be delighted. "I think it's important to get these guys ready to take on the union and I'd like to do my share," he explained.

1. What was Ralph's attitude toward the union when he first became a supervisor? What barriers were there that initially prevented him from changing his attitude regarding the union?
2. Why did Ralph's attitude change? What factors accounted for this?
3. Are workers who are recruited for supervisory positions likely to go through the same attitude changes as Ralph?

CASE: Measuring Job Satisfaction In a Hospital

Trudy Willworth is the training and development director of a large metropolitan hospital. She has been in her current position only two weeks, but she is already putting together a long-range plan of action designed to improve employee performance throughout the hospital.

One of the things that Trudy feels is important is job satisfaction. She is convinced that happy workers are productive workers. She also believes that the best way to determine whether people are satisfied in their jobs is to systematically measure their job satisfaction. Unfortunately, she is not sure how to go about doing this. She has talked to a number of colleagues inside the hospital and other personnel managers she met through the City Personnel Association. She has received a variety of suggestions. The two most common are (1) to have a job satisfaction questionnaire filled out by everyone and (2) to conduct interviews with a large portion of the hospital work force. Trudy is not sure which of these two approaches, if either, would be best.

Trudy is also thinking about how the results can be interpreted. If she finds that job satisfaction is low, what will this mean? Can it be used to explain absenteeism, tardiness, or low productivity. She is not sure. This is why she has been thinking about holding off on gathering this information and, instead, devoting herself to other important training issues. Unfortunately, earlier this morning Trudy received a memo from the head administrator. "I am looking forward to the results of your job satisfaction survey," he wrote. "Please send me a copy as soon as it is available. If possible, I would like to report the findings to the board of trustees at next month's meeting." Trudy is not sure what to do but is certain about one thing: there is no turning back now. She has to measure job satisfaction and write up the results for the administrator.

1. Is Trudy right in thinking that satisfied workers are productive workers?
2. Should she use a rating scale approach or interviews to measure satisfaction? Why?
3. If the results show that job satisfaction is low, would this help explain the tardiness and absenteeism that is higher than normal? Why or why not?

8 Job Stress

Several years ago, the then forty-eight-year-old head of the huge
Tenneco Corporation, James L. Ketelsen, underwent double bypass
surgery. His doctors mainly attributed his heart problem to a lack
of exercise and the wrong food. Ketelsen's reaction was to build
one of the most complete and elaborate food and fitness centers in
corporate America. Open to all Tenneco employees, the two-story,
100,000 square-foot facility in Houston cost $11 million. It includes
indoor gardens drip-watered from above to simulate rainfall, employee and executive dining and training areas, four racquetball
courts, dressing rooms, Nautilus exercise equipment, a sauna and
whirlpool bath, and a jogging track. The staff includes a doctor,
nurse, physiologist, eight fitness trainers, and an executive chef.
Upon entering the facility, participants insert a metal card into
a computer. When a workout is completed, the card is reinserted
and a description of what was done is punched in. The computer
then feeds back a "fitness profile" that indicates the number of
calories burned off in the exercise and how close the employee is
to the goals established. William Baun, the head of health and
fitness at Tenneco, states that these programs pay off in reduced
health care costs and absenteeism and in higher morale and productivity. His research at Tenneco shows "a positive association
exists between above-average job performance and exercise adherence." His research further indicates the average health care claim
for nonexercising females at Tenneco to be $1,535.83, to only

*Source: Adapted from Bob Gatty, "How Fitness Works Out," Nation's Business, July
1985, pp. 18–20.

$639.07 for those who exercise. For males it was $1,003.87 for nonexercisers, compared with $561.68 for exercisers. Baun states that this program at Tenneco is proof that "an organization of healthy people creates a positive work environment in which the major company goals may be achieved."

Learning Objectives

- DEFINE stress by giving attention to what it is not.
- IDENTIFY the extraorganizational, organizational, group, and individual stressors.
- DISCUSS the effects of stress, including physical, psychological, and behavioral problems.
- PRESENT both individual and organizational strategies for coping with stress.

The opening example shows the impact that stress can have on today's managers and what some enlightened corporations are doing to help their employees cope with it. A leading expert on stress, cardiologist Robert Eliot, gives the following prescription for dealing with stress: "Rule No. 1 is, don't sweat the small stuff. Rule No. 2 is it's all small stuff. And if you can't fight and you can't flee, flow."[1] What is happening in today's organizations, however, is that the "small stuff" is getting to employees, and they are not going with the "flow." Job stress or "burnout" is a major buzzword and concern of the times. One estimate is that stress-related illness is costing the American economy $100 billion a year, which is ten times more than all labor strikes combined.[2]

This chapter first explores the meaning of stress and why it has emerged as a major topic for the study of organizational behavior and the practice of human resources management. Next the major causes of stress in jobs today (extraorganizational, organizational, group, and individual stressors) are examined. This is followed by an analysis of the effects that job stress has on both the individual and the organization. The last part of the chapter is devoted to the coping strategies that can be used at the individual and organizational levels to manage stress effectively.

The Meaning of Stress

Stress is usually thought of in negative terms. It is thought to be caused by something bad (for example, a college student is placed on scholastic probation, a loved one is seriously ill, or the boss gives a formal reprimand for poor performance). This is a form of distress. But there is also a positive, pleasant side of stress caused by good things (for example, a college student makes the dean's list; an attractive, respected acquaintance asks for a date; an employee is offered a job promotion at another location). This is a form of *eustress*. This latter term was coined by the pioneers of stress research from the Greek *eu,* which means "good." In other words, stress can be viewed in a number of different ways and has been described as the most imprecise word in the scientific dictionary. The word "stress" has also been compared with the word "sin": "both are short, emotionally charged words used to refer to something that otherwise would take many words to say."[3]

Although there are numerous definitions and much debate about the meaning of job stress,[4] Ivancevich and Matteson define *stress* simply as "the interaction of the individual with the environment," but then they go on to give a more detailed working definition, as follows: "an adaptive response, mediated by individual differences and/or psychological processes, that is a consequence of any external (environmental) action, situation, or event that places excessive psychological and/or physical demands upon a person."[5] Beehr and Newman define *job stress* as "a condition arising from the interaction of people and their jobs and characterized by changes within people that force them to deviate from their normal functioning."[6] Taking these two definitions and simplifying them for the purposes of this chapter, "stress" is defined as an adaptive response to an external situation that results in physical, psychological, and/or behavioral deviations for organizational participants.

It is also important to point out what stress is *not:*

1. *Stress is not simply anxiety.* Anxiety operates solely in the emotional and psychological sphere, whereas stress operates there and also in the physiological sphere. Thus, stress may be accompanied by anxiety, but the two should not be equated.
2. *Stress is not simply nervous tension.* Like anxiety, nervous tension may result from stress, but the two are not the same. Unconscious people have exhibited stress, and some people may keep it "bottled up" and not reveal it through nervous tension.
3. *Stress is not necessarily something damaging, bad, or to be avoided.* Eustress is not damaging or bad and is something people should seek out rather than avoid. The key, of course, is how the person handles the stress. Stress is inevitable; distress may be prevented or can be effectively controlled.[7]

The Background on Stress

Concern about the impact of stress on people has its roots in medicine and specifically in the pioneering work of Hans Selye, the recognized father of stress. In his search for a new sex hormone, he serendipitously (see Chapter 1 for a discussion of serendipity, or accidental discovery) discovered that tissue damage is a nonspecific response to virtually all noxious stimuli. He called this phenomenon the *general adaptation syndrome* (GAS), and about a decade later he introduced the term "stress" in his writings.

The GAS has three stages: alarm, resistance, and exhaustion. In the alarm stage an outside stressor mobilizes the internal stress system of the body. There are a number of physiological and chemical reactions such as increased pituitary and adrenaline secretions; noticeable increases in respiration, heart rate, and blood pressure; and a heightening of the senses. If the stressor continues, then the GAS moves into the resistance stage, during which the body calls upon the needed organ or system to deal with the stressor. However, while there may be a great deal of resistance to one stressor during this second stage, there may be little, if any, resistance to other, unrelated stressors. This helps explain why a person going through an emotional strain may be particularly vulnerable to other illness or disease. Finally, if the stressor persists over a long period of time, the reserves of the adaptive mechanisms during the second stage may become drained, and exhaustion sets in. When this happens, there may be a return to the alarm stage, and the cycle starts again with another organ or system, or the "automatic shutoff valve" of death occurs. This GAS process, of course, can be very hard on the person and takes its toll on the human body.

Besides the physiologically oriented approach to stress represented by the classic GAS model, which remains a vital dimension of modern stress research and stress management, attention is also being given to the psychological (for example, mood changes, negative emotions, and feelings of helplessness) and the behavioral (for example, directly confronting the stressors or attempting to obtain information about the stressors) dimensions of stress. All three dimensions (physiological, psychological, and behavioral) are important to the understanding of job stress and coping strategies in modern organizations.

The Causes of Stress

The antecedents of stress, or the so-called "stressors," affecting today's employees are summarized in Figure 8.1. As shown, these causes come from both outside and inside the organization and from the groups that employees are influenced by and from employees themselves.

Extraorganizational Stressors

Although most analyses of job stress ignore the importance of outside forces and events, it is becoming increasingly clear that these have a tremendous impact. Taking an open-systems perspective of an organization (that is, the organization is greatly affected by the external environment), it is clear that job stress is not just limited to things that happen inside the organization, during working hours. Extraorganizational stressors include things such as societal/technological change, the family, relocation, economic and financial conditions, race and class, and residential or community conditions.[8]

The phenomenal rate of social and technical change, which is given detailed attention in Chapter 20, has had a great effect on people's lifestyles, and this of course is carried over into their jobs. Although medical science has increased the life spans of people and has eradicated or reduced the threat of many diseases, the pace of modern living has increased stress and decreased personal *wellness*. This latter concept of wellness has been defined as "a harmonious and

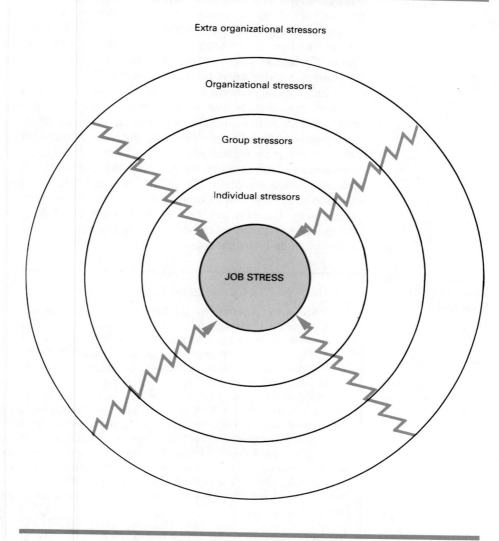

FIGURE 8-1
Categories of
stressors affecting
job stress.

productive balance of physical, mental, and social well being brought about by the acceptance of one's personal responsibility for developing and adhering to a health promotion program."[9] Because people tend to get caught up in the rush-rush, mobile, urbanized, crowded, on-the-go lifestyle of today, their wellness in general has deteriorated, and the potential for stress on the job has increased.

As Chapter 5 indicated, a person's family has a big impact on personality development. A family situation—either a brief crisis, such as a squabble or the illness of a family member, or long-term strained relations with the spouse or children—can act as a significant stressor for employees. So can relocating the family because of a transfer or a promotion. For most people in the 1980s, their financial situation, as a result of the recessionary economy, has proved to be a stressor. Many people have been forced to take a second job ("moonlight"), or the spouse has had to enter the work force in order to make ends meet. This reduces time for recreational and family activities. The overall effect on the employees is more stress on their primary jobs.

Sociological variables such as race, sex, and class can also become stressors. Sociologists have noted over the years that minorities may have more stressors than whites. More recently, research has found that women experience more psychological distress than men, but men are more prone to severe physical illness.[10] For professional women, the particular sources of stress have been identified as discrimination, stereotyping, the marriage/work interface, and social isolation.[11] Also, people in the middle and upper classes may have particular or common stressors. The same is true of the local community or region that one comes from. For example, one researcher identified the condition of housing, convenience of services and shopping, neighborliness, and degree of noise and air pollution as likely stressors.[12]

Application Example

> ### Middle-, Not Top-Level, Managers Most Stressed?*
>
> Although it is commonly thought that top-level management in modern organizations are in the most stressful positions, there is some evidence that middle-level managers really are under more stress. Rita Numerof, a stress researcher, concludes that top executives have the ability and authority to both make the decisions and make things happen. On the other hand, middle-level managers "who have limited authority and are not properly rewarded are more at risk. Often the middle manager doesn't have enough authority to fulfill many of the things he is responsible for fulfilling." This means that there are more people affected by stress in organizations than just the top executives. Numerof points out that this is not all bad because stress is a source of motivation and is healthy as long as it's not overwhelming. She notes, "A world without stress would be a boring, boring place." The key is to develop a personal plan to manage stress. "If you enjoy playing racquetball, fine. I tell people to do whatever makes them relax. However, for some people, losing at a game of racquetball is more stressful than work."
>
> *Source:* Adapted from "Middle Jobs Most Stressed," *Lincoln Journal*, Oct. 14, 1985, p. 5.

Organizational Stressors

Besides the potential stressors that occur outside the organization, there are also those associated with the organization itself. Although the organization is made up of groups and individuals, there are also more macro-level dimensions, unique to the organization, that contain potential stressors. Figure 8.2 shows that these macro-level stressors can be categorized into organizational policies, structures, physical conditions, and processes. Although these areas are given specific attention in Parts 4 and 5 of this book, it should be noted that as organizations

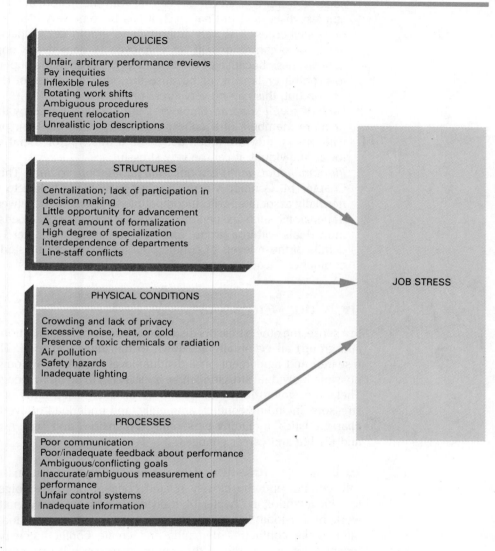

FIGURE 8-2
Macro-level organizational stressors.
(*Source*: Adapted from Arthur P. Brief, Randall S. Schuler, and Mary Van Sell, *Managing Job Stress*, Little, Brown, Boston, 1981, p. 66.)

become larger and more complex, there are more and more accompanying stressors for individual employees in their jobs. Most of the stressors shown in Figure 8.2 are the direct result of very large, highly complex organizations.

Group Stressors

Chapters 13 and 14 indicate the tremendous influence that the group has on behavior. The group can also be a potential source of stress. These group stressors can be categorized into three areas:

1. *Lack of group cohesiveness.* Starting with the historically famous Hawthorne studies, discussed in Chapter 2, it has become very clear that cohesiveness, or "togetherness," is very important to employees, especially at the lower levels of organizations. If an employee is denied the opportunity for this cohesiveness because of the task design, because the supervisor does things to prohibit or limit it, or because the other members of the group shut the person out, this can be very stress-producing.

2. *Lack of social support.* Employees are greatly affected by the support of one or more members of a cohesive group. By sharing their problems and joys with others, they are much better off. If this type of social support is lacking for an individual, it can be very stressful.

3. *Intraindividual, interpersonal, and intergroup conflict.* This is the topic of Chapter 14. Conflict is very closely conceptually linked to stress. Conflict is normally associated with incompatible or hostile acts between intraindividual dimensions such as personal goals or motivational needs/values, between individuals within a group, and between groups. Chapter 14 will go into the details of these levels of conflict, but for now it can be said simply that such conflict can lead to considerable stress for individuals.[13]

Individual Stressors

In a sense, the other stressors discussed so far (extraorganizational, organizational, and group) all eventually get down to the individual level. There is also more research and agreement on individual-level stressors. Although there are many possible individual stressors, three areas seem to be more recognized than others. These are, going from very narrow to broader-based units of analysis, (1) role stressors, including conflict, ambiguity, and underload or overload; (2) personal characteristics, including personality dimensions and Type A behavior patterns; and (3) life and career changes.

Role Characteristics. Like the conflict at organizational and group levels, role conflict and the closely related concept of role ambiguity will be given specific attention in Chapter 14. Individual employees have multiple roles (family, work, professional, recreational, church, club, community, and so on), and these often make conflicting demands and create conflicting expectations. After a recent extensive search of the empirical research it was concluded that "work schedule, work orientation, marriage, children, and spouse employment patterns may all produce pressures to participate extensively in the work role or the family role."[14] Stress results when the time demands for the work role is incompatible with the time pressures of the family role or vice versa.

Role ambiguity results from inadequate information or knowledge to do a job. This ambiguity may be due to inadequate training, poor communication, or the deliberate withholding or distortion of information by a coworker or supervisor. In any event, the result of role conflict and ambiguity is stress for the individual, and there is a substantial body of research indicating undesirable outcomes for the individual and the organization.[15] Role overload and/or underload (being asked to do too much or too little), which has not received as much attention as role conflict and ambiguity, may be just as stress-provoking.

Type A Characteristics. The discussion of personality in Chapter 5 pointed out the complexity of, and individual differences in, personality characteristics and traits. Personality traits such as authoritarianism, rigidity, masculinity, femininity, extroversion, supportiveness, spontaneity, emotionality, tolerance for ambiguity, locus of control, anxiety, and the need for achievement have been uncovered by research as being particularly relevant to individual stress.[16] Most recent attention, however, has centered on the so-called "Type A personality."

Although heart researchers have been working on the use of personality types and the resulting behavior patterns in order to predict heart attacks since the 1950s, in the late 1960s Friedman and Rosenman popularized the use of Type A and opposing Type B personalities in the study of stress.[17] These were portrayed as relatively stable characteristics, and in Friedman and Rosenman's extensive studies they found the Type A profile correlated highly with experienced stress and dangerous physical consequences.

Table 8.1 gives the reader a chance to see whether he or she tends to be a Type A or a Type B personality. A majority of Americans are Type A, and an even higher percentage of managers are Type A; one study found that 60 percent of the managers sampled were clearly Type A and that only 12 percent were Type B.[18]

TABLE 8.1 Type A–Type B Self-Test*

To determine your Type A or Type B profile, circle the number on the continuums (the verbal descriptions represent endpoints) that best represents your behavior for each dimension.

Am casual about appointments	1 2 3 4 5 6 7 8	Am never late
Am not competitive	1 2 3 4 5 6 7 8	Am very competitive
Never feel rushed, even under pressure	1 2 3 4 5 6 7 8	Always feel rushed
Take things one at a time	1 2 3 4 5 6 7 8	Try to do many things at once; think about what I am going to do next
Do things slowly	1 2 3 4 5 6 7 8	Do things fast (eating, walking, etc.)
Express feelings	1 2 3 4 5 6 7 8	"Sit" on feelings
Have many interests	1 2 3 4 5 6 7 8	Have few interests outside work

Total your score: _____ Multiply it by 3: _____ . The interpretation of your score is as follows:

Number of points	Type of personality
Less than 90	B
90 to 99	B+
100 to 105	A−
106 to 119	A
120 or more	A+

Source: Adapted from R. W. Bortner, "A Short Rating Scale as a Potential Measure of Pattern A Behavior," *Journal of Chronic Diseases,* vol. 22, 1966, pp. 87–91.

TABLE 8.2 Profiles of Type A and Type B Personalities

Type A Profile	Type B Profile
Is always moving	Is not concerned about time
Walks rapidly	Is patient
Eats rapidly	Doesn't brag
Talks rapidly	Plays for fun, not to win
Is impatient	Relaxes without guilt
Does two things at once	Has no pressing deadlines
Can't cope with leisure time	Is mild-mannered
Is obsessed with numbers	Is never in a hurry
Measures success by quantity	
Is aggressive	
Is competitive	
Constantly feels under time pressure	

Friedman and Rosenman define the Type A personality as "an action-emotion complex that can be observed in any person who is aggressively involved in a chronic, incessant struggle to achieve more and more in less and less time, and if required to do so, against the opposing efforts of other things or other persons."[19] Table 8.2 briefly summarizes the Type A and Type B profiles. Obviously, Type A employees (managers, salespersons, staff specialists, secretaries, or rank-and-file operating employees) experience considerable stress. They are the ones who:

1. Work long, hard hours under constant deadline pressures and conditions for overload
2. Often take work home at night or on weekends and are unable to relax
3. Constantly compete with themselves, setting high standards of productivity that they seem driven to maintain
4. Tend to become frustrated by the work situation, to be irritated with the work efforts of others, and to be misunderstood by superiors[20]

At first, because of Rosenman and Friedman's studies, it was generally thought that Type A's were much more prone to the worst outcome of stress: heart attacks.[21] More recently, however, a number of studies have been unable to confirm their findings.[22] For example, Type A's may release and better cope with their stress than do Type B's. The controversy surrounding the conflicting conclusions are discussed in the accompanying Application Example: Is Being a Type A Dangerous?

Besides the debate surrounding the impact of Type A personality on health is the question of the success of Type A's versus Type B's. It is pretty clear that Type A's are typically on a "fast track" to the top. They are more successful than Type B's. However, at the *very* top they do not tend to be as successful as Type B's, who are more patient and take a broader view of things.[23] The key may be to shift from Type A to Type B behavior, but, of course, most Type A's are unable and *unwilling* to make the shift and/or to cope with their Type A characteristics.

Application Example:

Is Being a Type A Dangerous?*

The complexities involved in studying behavior are exemplified by the recent controversy surrounding the link between the Type A personality and heart disease. Most people have heard of the Type A personality—competitive, driven, and impatient—and its association with heart disease. Decades of research have supported the link.

Meyer Friedman and Ray Rosenman, California cardiologists, are noted for discovering the link. Their findings were replicated by several larger studies. The most compelling evidence came from the Western Collaborative Group Study (WCGS), an eight-year study ending in 1969. The study showed that Type A men had twice as many heart attacks or other forms of heart disease than anyone else.

However, a seven-year study ending in 1982 found contradictory results. The Multiple Risk Factor Intervention Trial (MRFIT) was sponsored by the National Heart, Lung, and Blood Institute to single out the deadliest risks of heart disease. Their results failed to show that Type A men were more likely to develop heart disease than anyone else.

How do researchers explain such conflicting findings? One test is to compare measurement techniques. Both the WCGS and the MRFIT used structured interviews to identify Type A's. The structured interview is considered to be the most accurate assessment technique for identifying Type A's since it not only evaluates the content of answers but also accounts for tone of voice, facial expressions, and gestures—important indicators of the impatience characteristic of Type A's.

Not only is the technique important but also how it is used. For example, Larry Scherwitz, a psychologist at the University of California, San Francisco, listened to the interview tapes of both the WCGS and the MRFIT. He noticed that the MRFIT interviewers asked the questions faster than the WCGS interviewers. He believes this could have skewed the MRFIT results.

According to Scherwitz, the fast-paced interviewers come across as cold and uninterested. He believes that the hostile Type A's responded by hiding their hostile feelings—making them appear to be Type B's. The more sensitive Type B's, on the other hand, may have reacted more curtly—responding like Type A's. Such responses may have led to mislabeling which could have easily confounded the results.

Rosenman also points out an important flaw with the MRFIT. "Type A's are not going to sign up for studies like this, with once-a-week follow-ups and lots of paperwork. You don't get impatient, hostile people volunteering to do this." Rosenman emphasizes the importance of how subjects are selected. However, he does not indicate how subjects were contacted for the WCGS. Although other areas of the studies' designs need to be considered, these two areas show why rigorous methodology is necessary for conclusive findings.

Whether the Type A personality is dangerous is still a subject for debate. Further research with attention to methodology is needed before any conclusions can be made.

*__Source:__ Adapted from Joshua Fischman, "Type A on Trial," *Psychology Today*, February 1987, pp. 42–50.

TABLE 8.3 Relative Weights of Life Changes

Life Change	Relative Weight
Death of spouse	100
Divorce	73
Jail term	63
Death of close family member	63
Major personal injury or illness	53
Marriage	50
Fired from work	47
Retirement	45
Sex difficulties	39
Business readjustment	39
Change to a different line of work	36
Change in responsibilities at work	29
Trouble with boss	23
Change in work hours or conditions	20
Vacation	13
Christmas	12
Minor violations of the law	11

Source: Adapted from L. O. Ruch and T. H. Holmes, "Scaling of Life Changes: Comparison of Direct and Indirect Methods," *Journal of Psychosomatic Research*, vol. 15, 1971.

Life and Career Changes.   Like technological and social change, life and/or career changes can be stress-producing. Life's changes may be slow (getting older) or sudden (the death of a spouse). These changes have been portrayed in novels and movies as having a dramatic effect on people (for example, the heroine who pines for a dead lover until she herself dies).

Medical researchers have verified that especially sudden life changes do in fact have a very stressful impact on people.[24] They found a definite relationship between the degree of life changes and the subsequent health of the person. Table 8.3 shows the relative standings of certain life changes. The more change, the poorer the subsequent health. These life changes can also directly influence job performance. One psychologist, Faye Crosby, reports that divorce interferes with work more than any other trauma in a person's life. She says, "During the first three months after a spouse walks out, the other spouse—male or female—usually is incapable of focusing on work."[25]

The same can be said for career changes. Being suddenly thrust into a new job with new responsibilities can be very stressful. Underpromotion (being stuck in a dead-end job that is way below the person's capabilities) and overpromotion (being placed in a job that the person is unqualified for) can also be stress-provoking. Career planning can prevent such stress-producing situations for employees. Such coping strategies are given attention in the last part of the chapter.

The Effects of Job Stress

As was pointed out in the introductory comments, stress is not automatically bad for individual employees or their organizational performance. In fact, it is generally recognized that at least low levels of stress can even enhance job performance. For example, one recent study found that mild stress, such as getting a new supervisor or being involuntarily transferred, may result in an increased search for information in the job.[26] This may lead employees to new and better ways of doing their jobs. Also, mild stress may get employees' "juices" flowing and lead to increased activity, change, and overall better performance. People in certain jobs, such as in sales or creative fields (for example, newspaper journalists and television announcers who work under time pressures), would seem to benefit from a mild level of stress. People in other jobs, such as police officers or physicians, may not benefit from constant mild stress.

Research is also emerging that indicates that the level of difficulty and nature of the task being performed and personal situational variables may affect the relationship between stress and performance.[27] However, it is still safe to conclude that:

1. The performance of many tasks is in fact strongly affected by stress.
2. Performance usually drops off sharply when stress rises to high levels.[28]

It is the dysfunctional effects of high levels of stress that should be and are a major concern for contemporary society in general and for effective human resources management in particular. The problems due to high levels of stress can be exhibited physically, psychologically, or behaviorally by the individual.

Physical Problems Due to Stress

Most of the attention and the basic research over the years have been devoted to the impact that stress has on physical health. A high level of stress is accompanied by high blood pressure and high levels of cholesterol and can result in heart disease,[29] ulcers, and arthritis. There may even be a link between stress and cancer.[30]

Obviously, such serious physical ailments have a drastic effect on the individual; not always so obvious, but just as serious, are the effects that physical problems such as heart disease can have on the organization. Ivancevich and Matteson have provided the following worksheet for computing the costs of replacing employees lost to heart disease in a company employing 4000 people:[31]

1. Number of employees	4000
2. Men in age range forty-five to sixty-five (0.25 × line 1)	1000
3. Estimated deaths due to heart disease per year (0.006 × line 2)	6
4. Estimated premature retirement due to heart problems per year (0.003 × line 2)	3
5. Company's annual personnel losses due to heart disorders (sum of lines 3 and 4)	9
6. Annual replacement cost: the average cost of hiring and training replacements for experienced employees (line 5 × $4300)	$38,700
7. Number of employees who will eventually die of heart disease if present rate continues (0.5 × line 1)	2000

These figures are just estimates, but they dramatically illustrate how heart disease alone can affect costs and sheer numbers of employees in a typical organization. Not all heart disease can be directly linked to stress; environmental conditions and the person's general state of health, heredity, and medical history can also contribute. However, stress can and does contribute to this dreaded disease and to other physical problems as well.

Psychological Problems Due to Stress

While considerable attention has been given to the relationship between stress and physical health, especially within the medical community, not as much has been given to the impact of stress on mental health. Yet, at least indirectly if not directly, the psychological problems resulting from stress may be just as important to day-to-day job performance than the physical problems, if not more important.

High levels of stress may be accompanied by anger, anxiety, depression, nervousness, irritability, tension, and boredom. The effects of this on individual employees are changes in mood and other emotional states and, especially relevant to job performance, lowered self-esteem,[32] resentment of supervision, inability to concentrate and make decisions, and job dissatisfaction.[33] These outcomes of stress can have a direct cost effect on the organization. For example, the National Centers for Disease Control recently reported that psychological stress is the source of numerous job-related insurance claims.[34]

Of even greater significance, the outcomes of stress can have a subtle, but very real, affect on the styles and effectiveness of managers in key positions. For example, managers who are under constant stress may become very moody, and their subordinates soon learn not to disturb them, even with important information, because they will just "bite your head off." Such managers may also realize, at times, that they are acting this way; they may feel that they are not living up to the expectations of their important position and suffer a loss of self-esteem. In this state they may also procrastinate and continue to put things off and not make needed decisions. And, finally, they may resent their boss for trying to get them back on the track and begin to hate the job in general. Coworkers, subordinates, and superiors may become very disgusted with such a manager and explain the behavior away as being the result of a "rotten personality," when in fact the problems are the result of stress. If the manager had a heart attack, everyone would feel sorry and say that he or she was under too much stress, but moodiness, low self-esteem, inability to make a decision, and dissatisfaction with the boss and the job cause people to get angry and say that the manager is "no darned good" or "can't get along with anyone." Both a heart attack and a psychological problem may have the same cause (too much stress), and although people may react to them differently, the negative effect on performance is the same in the case of a psychological problem, or perhaps even worse.

Behavioral Problems Due to Stress

As has been the case with other topics covered in this book, the *behavioral* unit of analysis may be most helpful in analyzing the effects of job stress. Direct behaviors that may accompany high levels of stress include undereating or overeating, sleeplessness, increased smoking and drinking, and drug abuse.

When it is realized that 6 percent of the population are alcoholics, that another estimated 10 percent are problem drinkers, and that 6 billion doses of amphetamines and barbiturates are consumed annually,[35] the potential problems for employee behavior caused by alcohol and drug abuse become dramatically clear.

Although problems with alcohol have been recognized for a number of years, severe problems stemming from drug abuse have emerged more recently. For example, Kidder, Peabody, the New York-based investment bank, spent $100,000 on a drug program in 1986 and many other firms such as Lockheed and Southern California Rapid Transit have drug-testing programs for their employees.[36]

One company had such a problem with on-the-job drinking that it bought a breath-alcohol meter to test its employees. The president of the union in this firm stated: "there were a couple of people who came to work drunk every day."[37] Although the meter has not been used as yet, one worker was overheard to say, "I guess I'll have to stop going to the bar at lunchtime."[38] Besides being dangerous, as in this company, which used a lot of saws and punches, these problems may be manifested by tardiness, absenteeism, and turnover.

There is some research evidence indicating the relationship between stress and especially absenteeism and turnover.[39] For example, workers may experience stress and react by getting drunk and staying home from work the next day with a hangover. They then feel bad about this drinking. They may feel that they are letting everyone down "the morning after" and eventually quit or be fired from the job. In the meantime the absenteeism rate climbs, and subsequently the turnover rates increase, both of which are very costly to the organization in terms of filling in for absent workers and replacing those who have left. Staying away from a job that is causing stress or quitting the job is a "flight" reaction to the situation. Actually, this may be a healthier reaction than a "fight" reaction, in which the person may stay on the stress-producing job and become angry and/ or aggressive.

Like the psychological problems resulting from stress, the behavioral problems are often not attributed to stress by coworkers or supervisors and generate little sympathy. But, also like the psychological and the physical symptoms of stress, the behavioral problems can be controlled, more effectively managed, and even prevented by the individual and the organization. These coping strategies are discussed next.

Coping Strategies for Stress

Much of the discussion so far in this chapter and, at least indirectly, a lot of the material in subsequent chapters (for example, discussions of job design, goal setting, organizational behavior modification, group dynamics, management of conflict, communication skills, political strategies, leadership styles, organization processes and design, decision-making skills, control techniques, management of change, and organization development techniques) suggest ways to manage and more effectively cope with stress. The accompanying Application Example,

Taking Time to Manage Time, suggests some simple techniques such as time management that can be used to cope with stress. Generally speaking, however, there are two major approaches to dealing with job stress.

**Application
Example:**

Taking Time to Manage Time*

One of the major causes of stress for managers comes from time pressures. No matter how fast some managers work and how much time they put in, they are still unable to get all their work done. One of the most effective ways of dealing with this problem is the use of time management techniques. Today many organizations from Chase Manhattan to Exxon to Xerox are training their managers how to get more done in less time. Some of the most helpful guidelines for effective time management are the following:

1. Make out a "to do" list that identifies everything that must be done during the day. This helps keep track of work progress.
2. Delegate as much minor work as possible to subordinates.
3. Determine when you do the best work—morning or afternoon—and schedule the most difficult assignments for this time period.
4. Set aside time, preferably at least one hour, during the day when visitors or other interruptions are not permitted.
5. Have the secretary screen all incoming calls in order to turn away those that are minor or do not require your personal attention.
6. Eat lunch in the office one or two days a week in order to save time and give yourself the opportunity to catch up on paperwork.
7. Discourage drop-in visitors by turning your desk so you do not have eye contact with the door or hallway.
8. Read standing up. The average person reads faster and more accurately when in a slightly uncomfortable position.
9. Make telephone calls between 4:30 and 5:00 P.M. People tend to keep these conversations brief so that they can go home.
10. Do not feel guilty about those things that have not been accomplished today. Put them on the top of the "to do" list for tomorrow.

***Source:** Some of this example is adapted from "Ten Tricks to Keep Time Eaters Away!" Working Woman, August 1986, p. 71.

First are the individual strategies, which tend to be more reactive in nature. That is, they tend to be ways of coping with stress that has already occurred. Some individual strategies, such as physical exercise, can be both reactive and proactive, but most are geared toward helping the person who is already suffering from stress. The second general approach is to develop a more proactive set of strategies at the organizational level. The idea behind these organizational strategies is to remove existing or potential stressors and thus, like preventive medicine, prevent the onset of stress for individual jobholders.

Individual Coping Strategies

Today, when self-help remedies, do-it-yourself approaches, weight-loss clinics and diets, health food, and physical exercise are being given so much attention in the mass media and when people are actually taking responsibility, or know they *should* be taking responsibility, for their own wellness, individual coping strategies for dealing with stress make sense. In other words, most people don't have to be convinced of the value of taking charge and actually making a change in their lives.

Some specific techniques that individuals can use to eliminate or more effectively manage inevitable, prolonged stress include the following:

1. *Exercise.* Today, it is not whether you win or lose, but whether you get some good exercise that counts. People of all ages are walking, jogging, swimming, riding bicycles, or playing softball, tennis, or racquetball in order to get some exercise to combat stress. Although this seems to make a great deal of sense and many laypeople and physicians swear by it, there still is no conclusive evidence that exercise will directly reduce the chances of heart disease or stroke. But there seems little doubt that it can help people better cope with stress, even if only as a result of the side effects, such as relaxation, enhanced self-esteem, and simply getting one's mind off work for a while.

2. *Relaxation.* Whether a person simply takes it easy once in a while or uses specific relaxation techniques such as biofeedback or meditation, the intent is to eliminate the immediately stressful situation or manage a prolonged stressful situation more effectively. Taking it easy may mean curling up with a good book in front of a fireplace or watching something "light" (not a violent program or a sports program) on television. Biofeedback was discussed in Chapter 5. Meditation involves muscle and mental relaxation; the person slowly repeats a peaceful phrase or word or concentrates on a mental picture in a quiet location. There is some research evidence that such meditation can have a desirable physical[40] and mental[41] impact on people. Whether it can have a practical impact on job stress is yet to be determined. However, a number of firms are using it. For example, a stockbroker who regularly uses meditation recently stated, "It's widely known that this industry has a lot of stress. So where a lot of people drink alcohol, we mediate. It's not that we don't feel stress. It just doesn't hit us as much."[42]

3. *Behavioral self-control.* Chapter 12 gives specific attention to behavioral self-control. By deliberately managing the antecedents and the consequences of their own behavior, people can achieve self-control. For example, sales managers who have a steady stream of customer complaints all day could change the antecedent by having an assistant screen all complaints and allow only exceptions to reach them. They could also manage the consequences by rewarding themselves with an extra break when they remain calm and collected after interacting with a particularly angry customer. Besides managing their own behavior to reduce stress, people can also become more aware of their limits and of "red flags" that signal trouble ahead. They can avoid people or situations that they know will put them under stress. In other words, this strategy involves individuals' controlling the situation instead of letting the situation control them.

4. *Cognitive therapy.* Besides behavioral self-control techniques, a number of clinical psychologists have entered the stress field in recent years with cognitive

therapy techniques. Techniques such as Ellis's rational emotive model[43] and Meichenbaum's cognitive behavior modification have been successfully used to reduce test anxiety[44] and have recently been used as an individual strategy for reducing job stress. One study described the approach as follows:

> Participants were taught that much of their experienced strain (anxiety, tension, etc.) is caused by their cognitions ("self-talks"). This part of the treatment program, then, consisted of off-line lectures and interactive discussions designed to help participants (a) recognize events at work and what cognitions they elicit; (b) become aware of the effects of such cognitions on their physiological and emotional responses; (c) systematically evaluate the objective consequences of events at work; and (d) replace self-defeating cognitions that unnecessarily arouse strain (e.g., "I'm an incompetent worker who cannot handle the workload") with more adaptive appraisals (e.g., "I handle this workload as well as anyone else," or "the workload is too high and I should approach my supervisor").[45]

When this coping strategy (combined with some simple relaxation techniques) was systematically evaluated by a field experimental design in a social service agency, it was found to have a positive impact on some of both the physiological (epinephrine, a hormone produced by the adrenal glands) and the psychological (depression) variables measured.[46] However, there were no significant effects on some of the other variables measured, and the treatment effects were not replicated in a subsequent intervention on the original control group. Another study evaluated a similar cognitive therapy approach applied to police academy trainees. This study found that in simulated exercises, those who used the cognitive strategy performed more effectively and exhibited greater self-control and less strain than those who did not use the approach.[47] However, there were methodological flaws[48] that probably prevent definitive conclusions at this point on the value of the cognitive approach to managing stress. Yet, as is true of the other strategies discussed so far, there is enough promise to continue its use in trying to cope with stress.

5. *Networking.* One clear finding that has come out of social psychology research over the years is that people need and will benefit from social support. Applied as a strategy to reduce job stress, this would entail forming close associations with trusted, empathetic coworkers and colleagues who are good listeners and confidence builders. These friends are there when needed and provide support to get the person through stressful situations. Today, such alliances, especially if deliberately sought out and developed, are called *networks.* Although the relationship between social support and stress reduction appears complicated,[49] there is some research evidence that a networking strategy may be able to help people cope better with job stress[50] and be more effective[51] and successful managers.[52]

Organizational Coping Strategies

Organizational coping strategies are designed by management to eliminate or control organizational-level stressors in order to prevent or reduce job stress for individual employees. Earlier in the chapter, the organizational stressors were categorized in terms of overall policies, structures, physical conditions, and processes/functions (see Figure 8.2). It logically follows that these areas would be the focus of attention in developing organizational coping strategies. In other words, each of the specific stressors would be worked on in order to eliminate or reduce job stress. For example, in the policy area, attention would be given to making performance reviews and pay plans as equitable and as fair as possible. In the structural area, steps would be taken to back away from high degrees of formalization and specialization. The same would be done in the areas of physical conditions (for example, safety hazards would be removed, and lighting, noise, and temperature would be improved) and processes/functions (for example, communication and information would be improved, and ambiguous or conflicting goals would be clarified or resolved). In addition, the Association for Fitness in Business estimates that 12,000 companies today offer stress-coping programs ranging from counseling services, lunchtime stress management seminars, and wellness publications to elaborate company-run fitness centers where employees can sweat out the tension.[53]

In addition to working on each specific organizational stressor identified in Figure 8.2, more generalized strategies might include the following:

1. *Create a supportive organizational climate.* Most large organizations today tend to be highly formalized bureaucratic structures with accompanying inflexible, impersonal climates. This can lead to considerable job stress. A coping strategy would be to make the structure more decentralized and organic, with participative decision making and upward communication flows. In theory, these structural and process changes would create a more supportive climate for employees and would prevent or reduce their job stress. The chapters in Part 5 of the book will analyze the details of organization structure and processes and the ramifications that they can have for the effective management of stress; however, as a number of reviews of literature on stress have pointed out, "the evidence bearing on relationships between climate factors and stress is speculative and needs to be empirically tested."[54]

2. *Enrich the design of tasks.* Chapter 10 is specifically devoted to job design. As will be brought out there, enriching jobs either by improving job content factors (such as responsibility, recognition, and opportunities for achievement, advancement, and growth[55]) or by improving core job characteristics (such as skill variety, task identity, task significance, autonomy, and feedback[56]) may lead to motivational states or experienced meaningfulness, responsibility, and knowledge of results. Presumably, these enriched tasks will eliminate the stressors found in more routine, structured jobs. However, as Chapter 10 will point out, not all people respond favorably to enriched job designs, and therefore, at least with some people some of the time, the enriched job may actually lead to increased job stress. For example, an individual with low growth needs and/or fear of failure may experience increased stress in an enriched job. Overall, however, careful managing of task design may be an effective way to cope with job stress.

3. *Reduce conflict and clarify organizational roles.* Role conflict and ambiguity was identified earlier as a major individual stressor. It is up to management to reduce the conflict and clarify *organizational* roles so that this cause of

stress can be eliminated or reduced. Each job should have clear expectations and the necessary information and support so that the jobholder is not left with conflicting demands or an ambiguous understanding of what he or she is to do. A specific role clarification strategy might be to have the person occupying a role obtain a list of expectations from each role sender. This list would then be compared with the focal person's expectations, and any differences would be openly discussed to clarify ambiguities and negotiated to resolve conflict.[57]

4. *Plan and develop career paths and provide counseling.* Traditionally, organizations have shown only passing interest in the career planning and development of their employees. Individuals are left to decide career moves and strategies on their own and, at most, get paternalistic advice once in a while from a supervisor. This situation is analogous to that of students at a large university who are simply names on an adviser's computer printout sheet, which contains the names of hundreds of advisees. This obviously can be a source of considerable uncertainty and stress for both the students and the professor. The same is true for members of any large organization; the stress is created by not knowing what their next move is or how they are going to make it.

The Use of Career Planning Techniques

An organizational coping strategy to alleviate this type of stress would be to set up a career planning and development process. This could range all the way from a total, comprehensive, organizational entry-to-exit approach at one extreme, to a self-guided workbook or one-shot annual workshop, at the other. The following are some examples of programs and techniques, all or some of which could be used by any organization to help combat stress:

1. Devices designed to aid the individual in self-assessment and increased self-understanding. These are normally workbooks, workshops, and one-on-one career counseling sessions.
2. Devices designed to communicate opportunities. These range from the *Dictionary of Occupational Titles* to listings or postings of job openings to descriptions of careers and jobs transmitted through individuals.
3. Career counseling through interviews. Counseling sessions may be conducted by managers, counseling professionals, personnel and educational specialists, and people outside the organization.
4. Workshops and educational activities designed to assist the individual in goal setting and establishing action plans for change.
5. Educational and experimental programs which prepare the individual with skills and knowledge for new activities and new careers or which enhance capability for the current job.
6. Organizational development and job design and development programs aimed at restructuring work for improved personal growth and enhanced job satisfaction.
7. Programs that enhance the individual's opportunities to make job and career changes. These may be rotational programs, employee-transfer request systems,

opportunity search systems external to the organization, and general how-to books on job and career change.[58]

Although a recent review found very little systematic evaluation of organizational-level stress management programs,[59] some successful career programs in industry are described below:

1. *General Electric.* GE has developed a set of four workbooks/manuals that (*a*) cover the employee's initial exploration of life issues that affect career decisions, (*b*) include a career planning guide for the employee and a guide to facilitate effective career interviews with employees, and (*c*) give suggestions on how to design and conduct career planning workshops and seminars. These materials are available throughout the company to assist employees in career planning and development efforts.

2. *Minnesota Mining and Manufacturing.* The 3M program consists of the following dimensions: (*a*) a concerted effort (for example, meetings and referrals) to communicate an awareness of program services for careers and to encourage use of the programs; (*b*) a career information center, with a career counseling staff, which provides information on career paths (not openings) in the company, aids for career planning, and self-development programs; (*c*) management training on career counseling; (*d*) career growth workshops (four sessions over four weeks that help individuals assess themselves and their current jobs, make action plans, and hold discussions with the boss); and (*e*) transition workshops, which provide intensive help to those identified as available for transfer.

3. *IBM.* IBM has a general, corporation-wide program that involves primarily managerial training in career counseling and provides printed and cassette materials to support career planning and development. The key element is a voluntary annual supervisor-subordinate career counseling session. A one-page action plan results from this session. In addition, many IBM facilities give more extensive support in terms of workbooks and workshops.[60]

As is true of the other coping strategies discussed in this last part of the chapter, there are no guarantees that an organizational career process will prevent employee stress. But, also like the other strategies, it *may* help, and because job stress is such a big problem and is getting worse, something needs to be done. The individual and organizational coping strategies outlined here are certainly a step in the right direction, if not the final answer.

Summary

This chapter examined job stress. Although not always bad for the person (for example, the father of stress, Hans Selye, feels that complete freedom from stress is death[61]) or the organization (low levels of stress may lead to performance improvement), stress is still one of the most important and serious problems facing the field of organizational behavior. Defined as an adaptive response to an external situation that results in physical, psychological, and/or behavioral deviations for organizational participants, stress was first studied in terms of

Selye's general adaptation syndrome. The three stages of GAS are alarm, resistance, and exhaustion. Since this beginning, which concentrated mainly on the physiological dimensions of stress, attention has also shifted to the psychological and behavioral dimensions.

The causes of stress can be categorized into extraorganizational, organizational, group, and individual stressors. In combination or singly, they represent a tremendous amount of potential stress impinging upon today's jobholder—at every level and in every type of organization. The effects of such stress can create physical problems (heart disease, ulcers, arthritis, and maybe even cancer), psychological problems (mood changes, lowered self-esteem, resentment of supervision, inability to make decisions, and job dissatisfaction), and/or behavioral problems (tardiness, absenteeism, turnover, and accidents). A number of individual and organizational strategies have been developed to cope with these stress-induced problems. Exercise, relaxation, behavioral self-control techniques, cognitive therapy techniques, and networking are some potentially useful coping strategies that individuals can apply to help combat existing stress. Taking a more proactive approach, management of organizations could create a more supportive climate, enrich tasks, reduce conflict and clarify roles, and set up a systematic career planning and development program. Whether on an individual or an organizational level, steps need to be taken to prevent or reduce job stress.

Questions for Discussion and Review

1. How is stress defined? Is it always bad for the individual? Explain.
2. What is the general adaptation syndrome? What are the stages?
3. What are the general categories of antecedents or stressors that can affect job stress? Give some examples of each.
4. Job stress can have physiological, psychological, and behavioral effects. Give an example of each and cite some research findings on the relationship between job stress and these outcomes.
5. Coping strategies for job stress were given for both the individual and the organizational levels. Summarize and evaluate these various strategies for preventing and/or more effectively managing stress.
6. What would be some examples of career planning programs and techniques? How could these be used to manage stress?

References

1. "Stress: Can We Cope?" *Time,* June 6, 1983, p. 48.
2. "Unraveling Stress, *The Economist,* Apr. 13, 1985, p. 82.
3. John M. Ivancevich and Michael T. Matteson, *Organizational Behavior and Management,* Business Publications, Plano, Tex., 1987, p. 211.
4. See Terry A. Beehr, "The Current Debate about the Meaning of Job Stress," *Journal of Organizational Behavior Management,* Fall/Winter 1986. pp. 5–18.
5. Ivancevich and Matteson, *Organizational Behavior and Management,* pp. 6, 8–9.

6. T. A. Beehr and J. E. Newman, "Job Stress, Employee Health, and Organizational Effectiveness: A Facet Analysis, Model, and Literature Review," *Personnel Psychology,* Winter 1978, pp. 665–699.

7. This is based on Hans Selye, *Stress without Distress,* Lippincott, Philadelphia, 1974; and James C. Quick and Jonathan D. Quick, *Organizational Stress and Preventative Management,* McGraw-Hill, New York, 1984, pp. 8–9.

8. John M. Ivancevich and Michael T. Matteson, *Stress and Work,* Scott, Foresman, Glenview, Ill., 1980, p. 145.

9. Robert Kreitner, "Personal Wellness: It's Just Good Business," *Business Horizons,* May–June 1982, p. 28.

10. Todd D. Jick and Linda F. Mitz, "Sex Differences in Work Stress," *Academy of Management Review,* July 1985, pp. 408–420.

11. Debra L. Nelson and James C. Quick, "Professional Women: Are Distress and Disease Inevitable?" *Academy of Management Review,* April 1985, pp. 206–218.

12. R. Marens, "The Residential Environment," in A. Campbell, P. E. Converse, and W. L. Rodgers (eds.), *The Quality of American Life,* Russell Sage, New York, 1976.

13. Ivancevich and Matteson, *Stress and Work,* pp. 125–129.

14. Jeffrey H. Greenhaus and Nicholas J. Beutell, "Sources of Conflict between Work and Family Roles," *Academy of Management Review,* January 1985, p. 80.

15. For example, see R. L. Kahn, D. M. Wolfe, R. P. Quinn, J. D. Snoeck, and R. A. Rosenthal, *Organizational Stress: Studies in Role Conflict and Ambiguity,* Wiley, New York, 1964; Robert H. Miles, "An Empirical Test of Causal Inference between Role Perceptions of Conflict and Ambiguity and Various Personal Outcomes," *Journal of Applied Psychology,* June 1975, pp. 334–339; Robert H. Miles, "Role Requirements as Sources of Organizational Stress," *Journal of Applied Psychology,* April 1976, pp. 172–179; Andrew D. Szilagyi, Henry P. Sims, and Robert T. Keller, "Role Dynamics, Locus of Control and Employee Attitudes and Behavior," *Academy of Management Journal,* June 1976, pp. 259–276; and Arthur G. Bedeian and Achilles A. Armenakis, "A Path-Analytic Study of the Consequences of Role Conflict and Ambiguity," *Academy of Management Journal,* June 1981, pp. 417–424.

16. Arthur P. Brief, Randall S. Schuler, and Mary Van Sell, *Managing Job Stress,* Little, Brown, Boston, 1981, p. 94.

17. Meyer Friedman and Ray H. Rosenman, *Type A Behavior and Your Heart,* Knopf, New York, 1974.

18. John H. Howard, David A. Cunningham, and Peter A. Rechnitzer, "Health Patterns Associated with Type A Behavior: A Managerial Population," *Journal of Human Stress,* March 1976, pp. 24–31.

19. Friedman and Rosenman, op. cit.

20. Brief, Schuler, and Van Sell, op. cit., pp. 11–12.

21. R. Rosenman and M. Friedman, "The Central Nervous System and Coronary Heart Disease," *Hospital Practice,* vol. 6, 1971, pp. 87–97.

22. "Unraveling Stress," *The Economist,* Apr. 13, 1985, p. 82 and Jerry E. Bishop, "Prognosis for the 'Type A' Personality Improves in a New Heart Disease Study," *The Wall Street Journal,* Jan. 14, 1988, p. 29.

23. Richard M. Steers, *Introduction to Organizational Behavior,* 2d ed., Scott, Foresman, Glenview, Ill., 1984, p. 518.

24. T. H. Holmes and R. H. Rahe, "Social Readjustment Rating Scale," *Journal of Psychosomatic Research,* vol. 11, 1967, pp. 213–218.

25. *The Wall Street Journal,* Dec. 23, 1986, p. 1.

26. Howard M. Weiss, Daniel R. Ilgen, and Michael E. Sharbaugh, "Effects of Life and Job Stress on Information Search Behaviors of Organization Members," *Journal of Applied Psychology,* February 1982, pp. 60–62.

27. Beehr and Newman, op. cit.; David C. McClelland and John B. Jemmott, "Power Motivation, Stress and Physical Illness," *Journal of Human Stress,* December 1980, pp. 6–15; John M. Ivancevich, Michael T. Matteson, and Cynthia Preston, "Occupational Stress, Type A Behavior, and Physical Well Being," *Academy of Management Journal,* June 1982, pp. 373–391; and Ahmed A. Abdel-Halim, "Effects of Role Stress–Job Design–Technology Interaction on Employee Work Satisfaction," *Academy of Management Journal,* June 1981, pp. 260–273.

28. Robert A. Baron, *Behavior in Organizations,* 2d ed., Allyn and Bacon, Boston, 1986, p. 223.

29. Thomas G. Cummings and Cary L. Cooper, "A Cybernetic Framework for Studying Occupational Stress," *Human Relations,* May 1979, pp. 395–418.

30. K. Bammer and B. H. Newberry (eds.), *Stress and Cancer,* Hogrefe, Toronto, 1982.

31. Ivancevich and Matteson, *Stress and Work,* p. 92.

32. J. E. McGrath, "Stress and Behavior in Organizations," in M. D. Dunnette (ed.), *Handbook of Industrial and Organizational Psychology,* Rand McNally, Chicago, 1976.

33. Beehr and Newman, op. cit.; A. A. McLean, *Work Stress,* Addison-Wesley, Reading, Mass., 1980; and Cary L. Cooper and Judi Marshall, "Occupational Sources of Stress," *Journal of Occupational Psychology,* March 1976, pp. 11–28.

34. "Job Stress Said a 'Substantial Health Problem,'" *Lincoln Journal,* Oct. 6, 1986, p. 15.

35. Ivancevich and Matteson, *Stress and Work,* p. 96.

36. *The Wall Street Journal,* Oct. 14, 1986, p. 1, and *The Wall Street Journal,* Nov. 11, 1986, p. 35.

37. "Firm Hopes Breath Meter Curbs Workers' Drinking," *Lincoln Journal,* June 11, 1983, p. 13.

38. Ibid.

39. For example, see Lyman W. Porter and Richard M. Steers, "Organizational, Work, and Personal Factors in Employee Turnover and Absenteeism," *Psychological Bulletin,* August 1973, pp. 151–176; Richard M. Steers and Susan R. Rhodes, "Major Influences on Employee Attendance: A Process Model," *Journal of Applied Psychology,* August 1978, pp. 391–407; and W. H. Mobley, R. W. Griffeth, H. H. Hand, and B. M. Meglino, "Review and Conceptual Analysis of the Employee Turnover Process," *Psychological Bulletin,* May 1979, pp. 493–522.

40. Robert K. Wallace and Herbert Benson, "The Physiology of Meditation," *Scientific American,* February 1972, pp. 84–90.

41. Terri Schultz, "What Science Is Discovering about the Potential Benefits of Meditation," *Today's Health,* April 1972, pp. 34–37.

42. "Executives Meditating to Success," *Omaha World-Herald,* Feb. 11, 1986, p. 9.

43. A. Ellis, *Reason and Emotion in Psychotherapy,* Lyle Stuart, New York, 1962.

44. D. H. Meichenbaum, "Cognitive Modification of Test-Anxious College Students," *Journal of Consulting and Clinical Psychology,* vol. 39, 1972, pp. 370–378.

45. Daniel C. Ganster, Bronston T. Mayes, Wesley E. Sime, and Gerald D. Tharp, "Managing Organizational Stress: A Field Experiment," *Journal of Applied Psychology,* October 1982, p. 536.

46. Ibid., pp. 533–542.

47. I. G. Sarson, J. H. Johnson, J. P. Berberich, and J. S. Siegel, "Helping Police Officers to Cope with Stress: A Cognitive Behavioral Approach," *American Journal of Community Psychology,* vol. 7, 1979, pp. 593–603.

48. Ganster, Mayes, Sime, and Tharp, op. cit., p. 534.

49. Anson Seers, Gail W. McGee, Timothy T. Serey, and George B. Graen, "The Interaction of Job Stress and Social Support: A Strong Inference Investigation," *Academy of Management Journal,* June 1983, pp. 273–284.

50. McLean, op. cit.

51. John Kotter, *The General Manager,* Free Press, New York, 1982.

52. Fred Luthans, Stuart A. Rosenkrantz, and Harry W. Hennessey, "What Do Successful Managers Really Do? An Observation Study of Managerial Activities," *Journal of Applied Behavioral Science,* vol. 21, no. 3, 1985, pp. 255–270.

53. Laurie Hays, "But Some Firms Try to Help," *The Wall Street Journal,* Apr. 24, 1987, p. 16D.

54. Ivancevich and Matteson, *Stress and Work,* p. 212. Also see Newman and Beehr, op. cit.

55. F. Herzberg, B. Mausner, and B. Snyderman, *The Motivation to Work,* Wiley, New York, 1959.

56. J. Richard Hackman and Greg R. Oldham, "Motivation through the Design of Work: Test of a Theory," *Organizational Behavior and Human Performance,* August 1976, pp. 250–279.

57. J. R. P. French and R. D. Caplan, "Psychosocial Factors in Coronary Heart Disease," *Industrial Medicine,* vol. 39, 1970, pp. 383–397.

58. Donald B. Miller, "Career Planning and Management in Organizations," *S.A.M. Advanced Management Journal,* Spring 1978. [Reprinted in Mariann Jelinek (ed.), *Career Management,* St. Clair Press, Chicago, 1979, pp. 357–358.]

59. John M. Ivancevich and Michael T. Matteson, "Organizational Level Stress Management Interventions: A Review and Recommendations," *Journal of Organizational Behavior Management,* Fall/Winter 1986, pp. 229–248.

60. Miller, op. cit., pp. 355–356.

61. Selye, *Stress without Distress.*

REAL CASE:
Getting Along
without
The Boss*

When Everett Suters started his own business, he never realized that his personality and disposition had not prepared him for the rigors of the task he was undertaking. Suters is a high achiever and, like most of these people, he believed strongly in the old maxim, "If you want something done right, do it yourself." The problem, however, was that within a short period of time his health began to be affected.

Suters started out working in the sales area of a large corporation. He was very successful at this job because he quickly realized that the most important thing in selling is hard work. If he called on a customer and the individual was not interested in buying his product, he would go on to another location and call on another customer. The more people he called on, the higher his sales volume. His success was determined by how long and how hard he worked.

However, when he started his own business, Suters soon realized that his previous success strategy would not work. As his computer-service business increased its customer base, more and more work fell on Suters' shoulders. He found himself scurrying from one project to the next. There never was any time for planning for the future. The entire day was spent handling rush projects. His appointment calendar was so filled with things

Source: Adapted from Everett T. Suters, "Overdoing It," *Inc.,* November 1986, pp. 115–116.

to do that he even found himself having trouble handling emergency situations. At the same time he began getting angry at his personnel, whom he saw as not working as hard as he nor as concerned with the success of the operation as he was.

Exhausted and burned out after two years, Suters decided to take a month's vacation. It was the only way of ensuring that his health did not totally break down. When he returned, refreshed and ready to start again, Suters found that things were running smoothly. With him out of the way, the staff was able to plan more projects, get things organized, and not have to wait until they got an okay from the boss on everything. Quite obviously, Suters had been burning himself out with overwork and proving to be ineffective in the process.

Now aware that his stress was caused by inefficient management practices and an overcommitment to working harder rather than smarter, Suters began changing his operational methods. He began delegating more authority to his staff and refusing to handle busywork projects that could easily be managed by someone else. He stopped agreeing to help customers with all of their problems and began to face the fact that many of his clients were making unreasonable demands on the company. This freed up a great deal of personal time for more important projects. He also began setting and reviewing organizational priorities so that he knew where the company was going and how it would get there. In summarizing his new approach, Suters points to three important steps: (a) plan to do more than you can do; (b) prioritize what you plan to do by importance and urgency; and (c) commit yourself to *less* than you can do and *only* to those projects that are the most important or urgent. In summing up what he has learned as president of his company, Suters says:

> This is not to suggest that it's easy to maintain this management style. As with most addicts, reformed overachievers have to be on the alert constantly to keep from backsliding. Over the course of any year, my company hires new people, and the old syndrome starts to creep back. Even experienced people begin to depend too much on me. So every year I take the cure: three weeks away to prove to myself and to the members of my staff that they can get along without me.

1. What caused Suters' job stress? (Use Figure 8.2 in formulating your answer.)
2. What were some of the individual coping strategies Suters employed to help him deal with his stress problem.
3. What lessons can be learned by managers from Suters' personal experience? Identify and describe three of them.

**CASE:
Sorry,
No Seats
Are Left;
Have a
Nice Flight**

Jim Miller has been a ticket agent for Friendly Airlines for the past three years. This job is really getting to be a hassle. In order to try to reduce the mounting losses that Friendly has suffered in recent months, management have decided to do two things: (1) overbook their flights so that every seat possible will be filled and (2) increase their service to their customers and live up to their name. Jim, of course, is at the point of application of this new policy. When checking in passengers, he is supposed to be very courteous and friendly, and he has been instructed to end every transaction with the statement, "Have a nice flight." The problem, of course, is that sometimes there are more passengers holding confirmed reservations checking in than there are seats on the plane. Rightfully, these people become extremely upset with Jim and sometimes scream at him and even threaten him. During these confrontations Jim becomes "unglued." He breaks into a sweat, and his face turns bright red. The company guidelines on what to do in these situations are very vague. When Jim called his supervisor for advice, he was simply told to try to book passengers on another flight, but be friendly.

1. Is Jim headed for trouble? What would be some physical, psychological, and behavioral outcomes of this type of job stress?
2. What could the company do to help reduce the stress in Jim's job?
3. What individual coping strategies could Jim try in this situation?

**CASE:
A Gnawing
Stomachache**

Sandy Celeste was thirty years old when her divorce became final. She was forced to go to work to support her two children. Sandy got married right after graduating from college and had never really held a full-time job outside the home. Nevertheless, because of her enthusiasm, education, and maturity, she impressed the personnel manager at Devon's Department Store and was immediately hired. The position involves supervising three different departments of women's clothing. Sandy's training consisted of approximately two months at another store in the Devon chain. She spent this training period both selling merchandise and learning the supervisor's responsibilities. On the first day of her supervisory job, Sandy learned that, because of size constraints at the store, eight different women's clothing departments are all located in the same area. In addition to Sandy, there are two other supervisors in the other departments. These three supervisors share the service of twenty-eight full- and part-time salespeople. Since the various departments are so jammed together, all the salespeople are expected to know each department's merchandise. Devon's merchandising philosophy is that it will not finish one department or storewide sale without starting another. Both the clerks and the supervisors, who work on a commission and salary basis, are kept busy marking and remarking the merchandise as one sale stops and another starts. To make matters worse, Devon's expects the employees to remark each item just prior to closing time the night after a big sale. The pressure is intense, and customers are often neglected. However, all the salespeople realize that when the customer suffers, so do their commissions. As a supervisor, Sandy is expected to enforce the company's policy rigidly. Soon after taking the position as supervisor, Sandy began to experience severe headaches and a gnawing stomachache. She would like to quit her job, but realistically she can't because the pay is good and she needs to support her children.

1. To what do you attribute Sandy's health problems? What are some possible extraorganizational, organizational, group, and individual stressors?
2. Is there anything that this company could do to alleviate stress for its supervisors? What individual coping strategies could Sandy try?

Integrative Real Case for Part 2:

Pressure, Pressure Everywhere*

Blame what you will—jobs, spouses, bills, kids, the complexities of life—stress has become one of America's most common health problems.

Some researchers still are debating who is at greatest risk from stress. Meanwhile, sufferers who want relief are embracing a number of treatments for the problem, some helpful, some doubtful and some downright loony.

All the fuss is warranted. Chronic, unrelenting psychological stress has been linked to a long list of ailments, including drug and alcohol abuse, heart disease, hypertension, obesity, sleep disorders, depression and immune-system malfunctions. Each in turn could prompt other illnesses.

When it comes to dealing with stress, "There is no one coping strategy that is best for all people," says Marianne McManus, a psychiatry professor at the University of Southern California. So therapists, consultants and physicians try to analyze a person's life style and the causes of stress before suggesting one or more stress-reduction techniques.

For Harvey Schoenfeld, exercise tops the list. The 49-year-old service manager at a New York pharmaceutical concern puts on a pair of boxing gloves three times a week at Gleason's Gym in Brooklyn and goes at it. "You pray you don't get killed," he says, but people "need something to relieve the tension of a day's work."

Researchers studied athletes to determine how exercise helps reduce stress. Trained athletes, they found, have a lower level of stress hormones in their blood and a higher level of natural tranquilizing hormones. So, they figure, exercise either slows the production of stress hormones or burns them up, while also decreasing the body's sensitivity to discomfort.

After a particularly hectic day at Guild Investment Management, Malibu, Calif., executives gather in a conference room for transcendental meditation. "We just loosen our ties and go for it," explains Allen Teague, a 45-year-old vice president there. After 20 minutes, "You feel like you've had a five- or six-hour nap," he says. Meditation, scientists have learned, reduces stress by slowing down the body's involuntary nervous system, reducing the skin's sensitivity and changing electrical activity of the brain to patterns associated with relaxation.

Biofeedback helped Ralph Herrera, a 43-year-old California Highway Patrol officer, with his stress problems. He had thought he was having a heart attack three years ago when he suddenly had a hard time breathing and a crushing feeling in his chest. But a trip to the hospital told him he was wrong.

Nine months and several episodes later, he got the diagnosis from the Drake Institute of Behavioral Medicine in Santa Monica. "The vessels in my heart would go into spasms whenever I got under any kind of stress, and that was causing shortness of breath and dizziness," he says. At first he didn't have a lot of faith in the biofeedback that was prescribed. But after about three weeks of training, he learned to control his involuntary response to stress.

*Source: Meg Sullivan, "Pressure, Pressure, Everywhere," The Wall Street Journal, Apr. 24, 1987, pp. 16D, 18D. Used with permission of The Wall Street Journal, © Dow Jones & Company Inc. (1987). All rights reserved.

Mark Rothschild also suffers from stress, the most bothersome symptom of which is grinding his teeth in his sleep. But he has decided to grin and bear it with the help of a $300 oral splint. He wears the splint at night for relief from stress-induced facial pain. "I was getting neck, jaw and head aches so severe they would make me nauseous," remembers Mr. Rothschild, a Chicago manufacturing executive. But the splint ended the pain.

Jacob Bernstein, a Los Angeles internist and cardiologist, says physicians prescribe a wide range of braces for muscle tension related to emotional stress, including wrist braces, knee braces, neck braces and corsets for the back. "If it's very severe," he says about the back pain, "we even use steel stays."

But William Solberg, a researcher at a University of California, Los Angeles, clinic, says braces and splints are the easy way out. He estimates that 60% to 80% of the folks who come to his clinic for mouth guards fail to also use the clinic's stress therapy. "It's a lot easier to use a mouth guard than to get into repeated classes or therapy," he says. "Even though a mouth guard has to be adjusted three or four times, wearing one doesn't involve probing your personality."

Some people find relief by removing themselves from the source of stress. "I think probably 25% to 50% of the patients I see might find relief by a change in environment," says Dennis Munjack, director of the Anxiety Disorder Clinic at Los Angeles County–USC Medical Center. Children, who might benefit by being removed from an abusive parent or a difficult or dangerous school, account for most of those cases.

But Dr. Munjack doesn't advise such avoidance for adults. "Relieving stress involves more than a change in setting," he says. Patients should ask themselves why "other people invariably are able to control the same situation a lot better than they do."

Prescription drugs have their place in managing stress, although physicians caution against overuse that might lead to dependency. Even the much-maligned Valium is useful in treating short-term traumatic situations such as an illness, a death or the loss of a job, researchers say. Other drugs help stress patients through such specific ordeals as public performances, flying and severe depression.

Researchers still are debating the role diet plays in handling stress. Most say there is no magic diet for reducing stress and suggest to their patients only the sensible approach of eating well-balanced meals.

But Judith Wurtman, a Massachusetts Institute of Technology research scientist who has written a book called "Managing Your Mind and Mood Through Food," believes a high-protein, low-carbohydrate diet can lead to stress by blocking production of the brain's natural calming chemicals and boosting production of the chemicals that prompt alertness. Eating carbohydrates, on the other hand, can help a person feel relaxed or calm, she says. "The tranquilizer of the '80s is going to be candy."

At the other end of the spectrum from the studied advice of the experts are the stress-relief methods of the desperate and the adventurous. At "float centers," billed by their owners as "60-minute vacations," staff members submerge tense clients in body-temperature water laced with salts. A California stress fighter holds "healing concerts" with German gongs and Tibetan cymbals, which supposedly realign the body's natural energy. And a New Mexico medicine woman has her followers gather regularly in the mountains to perspire amid heated stones in a teepee-like "sweat lodge."

But San Francisco stress guru Meyer Friedman says that in the whole world of stress management, "The wackiest thing is telling people they can go to a two- or three-day seminar and change belief systems that have been with them for 40 years." He worries that such courses encourage stress sufferers to only fight the symptoms rather than to confront the cause of their stress.

Dr. Friedman, along with Ray Rosenman, started pioneering stress research in the late 1950s that determined that Type A personalities—impatient, competitive, aggressive people—were three times more likely to get heart disease than their mild-mannered Type B counterparts. Now, a 10-year-long National Heart, Lung and Blood Institute study says Type A's are at no higher risk for heart disease than anyone else.

But critics of the institute's research point out that the study was voluntary and that Type A's, who are hard-driven and intensely impatient, wouldn't volunteer for a study. So, the critics conclude, the folks the institute called Type A's probably weren't.

Dr. Friedman's research has continued to turn up a strong correlation between the personality type and the incidence of heart disease. The 76-year-old physician's latest study, published in the October 1986 issue of the *American Heart Journal,* found that heart-attack victims cut their risk for a second attack in half by completing training he has devised.

The two-year program at the Meyer Friedman Institute in San Francisco includes patience-building drills such as driving in the slow lane of traffic or standing in long lines at banks. Jack Morrison, a 59-year-old executive recruiter who had a heart attack in 1977, finished the program. He credits the program with helping him to avoid a second heart attack.

Before the program, Mr. Morrison recalls, "When I was out driving, it was always a competition between me and every car and light." After months of intensive coaching, Mr. Morrison says he's figured out how to "smell the flowers and appreciate life."

Questions

1. What implications does this case have for the study and understanding of personality? For perception? For attitudes and job satisfaction? For job stress? Give specific examples from the case to support your statements.
2. Asking oneself the question "Why are other people invariably able to control the same situation a lot better than I do?" is suggested as a way to relieve stress. From the principles of perception and from the dimensions of personality studied in this part of the book, would this make sense?
3. Of all the programs discussed for coping with stress, which one do you feel has the most potential for today's manager?

Experiential Exercises for Part 2

EXERCISE: Self-Perception and Development of the Self-Concept

Goals:
1. To enable the students to consider their own self-concepts and to compare this with how they feel they are perceived by others
2. To explore how the self-concept in personality is formed largely on the basis of feedback received from others (the reality that we "mirror ourselves in others")
3. To stimulate student thinking about how management of human resources may involve perception and personality

Implementation:
1. The students take out a sheet of paper and fold it in half from top to bottom.
2. The students write "How I See Myself" and "How I Think Others See Me."
3. The students write down five one-word descriptions (adjectives) under each designation which, in their opinion, best describe how they perceive themselves and how others perceive them.
4. The students then share their two lists with their classmates (in dyads and triads, or the whole class) and discuss briefly. Each person may communicate what he or she is most proud of.
5. The instructor may participate in the exercise by sharing his or her list of adjectives.

EXERCISE: He Works, She Works

Objective:
To increase your awareness of common stereotypes that exist in many organizations about male and female characteristics.

Instructions:
1. Complete the "He Works, She Works" worksheet. In the appropriate spaces, write what you think the stereotyped responses would be. Do not spend too much time considering any one item. Rather, respond quickly and let your first impression or thought guide your answer.
2. Compare your individual responses with those on the "He Works, She Works" answer sheet provided by your instructor.
3. Compare your individual responses with those of other class members or participants. It is interesting to identify and discuss the most frequently used stereotypes.

He Works, She Works (Worksheet)

The family picture is on *his* desk: *(e.g., He's a solid, responsible family man.)*	The family picture is on *her* desk: *(e.g., Her family will come before her career.)*
His desk is cluttered:	*Her* desk is cluttered:
He's talking with coworkers:	*She's* talking with coworkers:
He's not at his desk:	*She's* not at her desk:
He's not in the office:	*She's* not in the office:
He's having lunch with the boss:	*She's* having lunch with the boss:
The boss criticized *him:*	The boss criticized *her:*
He got an unfair deal:	*She* got an unfair deal:
He's getting married:	*She's* getting married:
He's going on a business trip:	*She's* going on a business trip:
He's leaving for a better job:	*She's* leaving for a better job:

PART 3

Motivation and Learning: The Focus of Organizational Behavior

⑨ Motivation: Needs and Processes

Radical But Successful Approaches to Motivating Employees*

What do North American Tool and Die, Data Design, Fel-Pro, Odetics, JBM Electronics, AST Research, Telecalc, J. P. Industries, Intertec Components, Action Instruments, and Diversified Systems have in common? Hardly household names, these firms use very extreme—some would say radical—approaches to motivating their employees. For example, at Data Design, employees are given stock in the company and memberships in health clubs, which is not too unusual. However, to boost esprit de corps, the managers also get together to jump out of airplanes, plunge over waterfalls, scale mountains, and sleep in the snow. This is unusual! Not all these firms are high-tech, way-out California operations. For example, Fel-Pro is a very old, family-held company in Skokie, Illinois, that manufactures gaskets and sealants for engines. It owns a converted horse farm where employees can garden on weekends, send their children to summer camp, or get married. It also has a day-care center and a gym. No holiday goes by without a gift for each worker such as a box of candy on Valentine's Day and a turkey on Christmas. In addition, every important event in an employee's life receives a cash gift: $100 for a birth, $500 for an adoption, and up to $5000 for a child's college tuition. If this isn't enough, try this: Fel-Pro also employs a part-time sculptor to create gasket art to lift employees' esthetic spirits.

*****Source:** Adapted from Gene Stone and Bo Burlingham, "Workstyle," *Inc.*, January 1986, pp. 45–54.

Like these two firms, the others take radical approaches to motivating their employees. Most important, these approaches work. Indeed, in terms of profitability, growth, productivity, customer satisfaction, or any other measure of success, these firms are among the best in their industries. For example, Data Systems made $2 million on $11 million in revenues and Fel-Pro is highly profitable, with $170 million in sales.

Learning Objectives

- DEFINE the motivation process
- IDENTIFY the primary, general, and secondary motives
- DISCUSS the Maslow, Herzberg, and Alderfer content theories of work motivation
- EXPLAIN the Vroom, Porter-Lawler, equity, and attribution process theories of work motivation

Motivation is a basic psychological process. Few would deny that it is the most important focus in the micro approach to organizational behavior. Many people equate the causes of behavior with motivation. Chapter 1 and the four preceding chapters emphasized that the causes of behavior are much broader and more complex than can be explained by motivation alone. However, motivation should never be underrated. Along with perception, personality, attitudes, and learning, it is presented here as a very important process in understanding behavior. Nevertheless, it must be remembered that motivation should not be thought of as the only explanation of behavior. It interacts with and acts in conjunction with other mediating processes and the environment. It must also be remembered that, like the other mediating processes, motivation cannot be seen. All that can be seen is behavior. Motivation is a hypothetical construct that is used to help explain behavior; it should not be equated with behavior. In fact, while recognizing the "central role of motivation," many of today's organizational behavior theorists "think it is important for the field to reemphasize behavior."[1]

This chapter presents motivation as a basic psychological process. The more applied aspects of motivation, as demonstrated in the opening vignette, are covered in the next chapter on job design and goal setting. The first section of this chapter clarifies the meaning of motivation by defining the relationship between its various parts. The need-drive-goal cycle is defined and analyzed. The next section is devoted to an overview of the various types of needs or motives: primary, general, and secondary. The motives within the general and secondary categories are given major attention, and a summary of supporting research findings on these motives is included. The last half of the chapter presents the content and process theories of, and approaches to, work motivation.

The Meaning of Motivation

Today, virtually all people—laypeople and scholars—have their own definition of motivation. Usually one or more of the following words are included in the definition: "desires," "wants," "wishes," "aims," "goals," "needs," "drives," "motives," and "incentives." Technically, the term *motivation* can be traced to the Latin word *movere,* which means "to move." This meaning is evident in the following comprehensive definition: Motivation is a process that starts with a physiological or psychological deficiency or need that activates behavior or a drive that is aimed at a goal or incentive. Thus, the key to understanding the process of motivation lies in the meaning of, and relationship between, needs, drives, and incentives.

Figure 9.1 graphically depicts the motivation process. Needs set up drives aimed at incentives; this is what the basic process of motivation is all about. In a systems sense, motivation consists of these three interacting and interdependent elements:

1. *Needs.* The best one-word definition of a need is *deficiency.* Needs are created whenever there is a physiological or psychological imbalance. For example, a need exists when cells in the body are deprived of food and water or when the personality is deprived of other people who serve as friends or companions.
2. *Drives.* With a few exceptions,[2] drives or motives (the two terms are often used interchangeably) are set up to alleviate needs. A drive can be simply defined as a deficiency with direction. Drives are action-oriented and provide an energizing thrust toward goal accomplishment. They are at the very heart of the motivational process. The examples of the needs for food and water are translated into the hunger and thirst drives, and the need for friends becomes a drive for affiliation.
3. *Incentives.* At the end of the motivation cycle is the incentive defined as anything that will alleviate a need and reduce a drive. Thus, attaining an incentive will tend to restore physiological or psychological balance and will reduce or cut off the drive. Eating food, drinking water, and obtaining friends will tend to restore the balance and reduce the corresponding drives. Food, water, and friends are the incentives in these examples.

FIGURE 9.1 The basic motivation process.

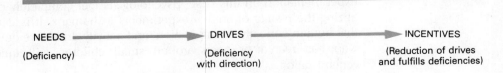

NEEDS	DRIVES	INCENTIVES
(Deficiency)	(Deficiency with direction)	(Reduction of drives and fulfills deficiencies)

Primary Motives

Psychologists do not totally agree on how to classify the various human motives, but they would acknowledge that some motives are unlearned and physiologically based. Such motives are variously called *physiological, biological, unlearned,* or *primary.* The last term is used here because it is more comprehensive than the others. The use of the term *primary* does not imply that this group of motives always takes precedence over the general and secondary motives. Although the precedence of primary motives is implied in some motivation theories, there are many situations in which general and secondary motives predominate over primary motives. Common examples include celibacy among priests and fasting for a religious, social, or political cause. In both cases, learned secondary motives are stronger than unlearned primary motives.

Two criteria must be met in order for a motive to be included in the primary classification: It must be *unlearned,* and it must be *physiologically based.* Thus defined, the most commonly recognized primary motives include hunger, thirst, sleep, avoidance of pain, sex, and maternal concern.

General Motives

A separate classification for general motives is not always given. Yet such a category seems necessary because there are a number of motives which lie in the gray area between the primary and secondary classifications. To be included in the general category, a motive must be unlearned but not physiologically based. Although not all psychologists would agree, the motives of curiosity, manipulation, activity, and affection seem best to meet the criteria for this classification. An understanding of these general motives is important to the study of human behavior—especially in organizations. They are more relevant to organizational behavior than the primary motives.

The Curiosity, Manipulation, and Activity Motives

Early psychologists noted that the animals used in their experiments seemed to have an unlearned drive to explore, to manipulate objects, or just to be active. This was especially true of monkeys that were placed in an unfamiliar or novel situation. These observations and speculations about the existence of curiosity, manipulation, and activity motives in monkeys were later substantiated through experimentation. In this case, psychologists feel completely confident in generalizing the results of animal experiments to humans. It is generally recognized that human curiosity, manipulation, and activity drives are quite intense; anyone who has reared or been around small children will quickly support this generalization.

Although these drives often get the small child into trouble, curiosity, manipulation, and activity, when carried forward to adulthood, can be very beneficial. If these motives were stifled or inhibited, the total society might become very stagnant. The same is true on an organizational level. If employees are not allowed to express their curiosity, manipulation, and activity motives, they may not be motivated. For example, sticking an employee behind a machine or a desk for eight hours a day may stifle these general motives.

The Affection Motive

Love or affection is a very complex form of general drive. Part of the complexity stems from the fact that in many ways love resembles the primary drives and in other ways it is similar to the secondary drives. In particular, the affection motive is closely associated with the primary sex motive, on the one hand, and with the secondary affiliation motive, on the other. For this reason, affection is sometimes placed in all three categories of motives, and some psychologists do not even recognize it as a separate motive.

Affection merits specific attention because of its growing importance to the modern world. There seems to be a great deal of truth to the adages, "Love makes the world go round" and "Love conquers all." In a world where we suffer from interpersonal, intraindividual, and national conflict and where quality of life and human rights are becoming increasingly important to modern society, the affection motive takes on added importance in the study of human behavior.

Secondary Motives

Whereas the general drives seem relatively more important than the primary ones to the study of human behavior in organizations, the secondary drives are unquestionably the most important. As a human society develops economically and becomes more complex, the primary drives, and to a lesser degree the general drives, give way to the learned secondary drives in motivating behavior. With some glaring exceptions that have yet to be eradicated, the motives of hunger and thirst are not dominant among people living in the economically developed Western world. This situation is obviously subject to change; for example, the "population bomb" or the "energy crisis" may alter certain human needs. But for now, the learned secondary motives dominate.

Secondary motives are closely tied to the learning concepts that will be discussed in Chapter 11. In particular, the learning principle of reinforcement is conceptually and practically related to motivation. The relationship is obvious when reinforcement is divided into primary and secondary categories and is portrayed as incentives. Although some discussions regard reinforcement and motivation as equivalent, they are treated separately in this book. Once again, however, it should be emphasized that although the various behavioral concepts can be separated for study and analysis, in reality concepts like reinforcement and motivation do not operate as separate entities in producing human behavior. The interactive effects are always present.

A motive must be learned in order to be included in the *secondary* classification. Numerous important human motives meet this criterion. Some of the more important ones are power, achievement, and affiliation, or, as they are commonly referred to today, *n Pow, n Ach,* and *n Aff.* In addition, especially in reference to organizational behavior, security and status are also important secondary motives.

The Power Motive

The power motive is discussed first because it has been formally recognized and studied for a relatively long time. The leading advocate of the power motive was the pioneering behavioral scientist Alfred Adler. Adler officially broke his close ties with Sigmund Freud and proposed an opposing theoretical position. Whereas Freud stressed the impact of the past and of sexual, unconscious motivation, Adler substituted the future and a person's overwhelming drive for superiority or power.

To explain the power need—the need to manipulate others or the drive for superiority over others—Adler developed the concepts of *inferiority complex* and *compensation.* He felt that every small child experiences a sense of inferiority. When this feeling of inferiority is combined with what he sensed as an innate need for superiority, the two rule all behavior. The person's lifestyle is characterized by striving to compensate for feelings of inferiority, which are combined with the innate drive for power.

Although modern psychologists do not generally accept the tenet that the power drive is inborn and so dominant, in recent years it has prompted renewed interest. The quest for power is readily observable in modern American society. The politician is probably the best example, and political scandals make a fascinating study of the striving for, and use of, power in government and politics. However, in addition to politicians, anyone in a responsible position in business, government, unions, education, or the military may also exhibit a considerable need for power. The power motive has significant implications for organizational leadership and for the informal, political aspects of organizations. Chapter 15 will examine in detail the dynamics of power. It has emerged as one of the most important dynamics in the study of organizational behavior.

The Achievement Motive

Whereas the power motive has been recognized and discussed for a long time, only very recently has there been any research activity. The opposite is true of the achievement motive. Although it does not have as long a history as the other motives, more is known about achievement than about any other motive because of the tremendous amount of research that has been devoted to it. The Thematic Apperception Test (TAT) has proved to be a very effective tool in researching achievement. The TAT can effectively identify and measure the achievement motive. The test works in the following manner: One picture in the TAT shows a young man plowing a field; the sun is about to sink in the west. The person taking the test is supposed to tell a story about what he or she sees in the picture. The story will project the person's major motives. For example, the test taker may say that the man in the picture is sorry the sun is going down because he still has more land to plow and he wants to get the crops planted before it rains. Such a response indicates high achievement. A low achiever might say that the man is happy the sun is finally going down so that he can go into the house, relax, and have a cool drink. The research approach to achievement has become so effective that it is often cited by psychologists as a prototype of how knowledge and understanding can be gained in the behavioral sciences.

David C. McClelland, a Harvard psychologist, is most closely associated with study of the achievement motive, and, as Chapter 15 will indicate, he is now doing considerable research on power as well. McClelland thoroughly investigated and wrote about all aspects of *n Ach* (achievement). Out of this extensive research has emerged a clear profile of the characteristics of the high achiever. Very simply, the achievement motive can be expressed as a desire to perform in terms of a standard of excellence or to be successful in competitive situations. The specific characteristics of a high achiever can be summarized in the following sections.

Moderate Risk Taking. Taking moderate risks is probably the single most descriptive characteristic of the person possessing high *n Ach*. On the surface it would seem that a high achiever would take high risks. However, once again research gives a different answer from the commonsense one. The ring-toss game can be used to demonstrate risk-taking behavior. It has been shown that when ring tossers are told that they may stand anywhere they want to when they toss the rings at the peg, low and high achievers behave quite differently. Low achievers tend either to stand very close and just drop the rings over the peg or to stand very far away and wildly throw the rings at the peg. In contrast, high achievers almost always carefully calculate the exact distance from the peg that will challenge their own abilities. People with high *n Ach* will not stand too close because it would be no test of their ability simply to drop the rings over the peg. By the same token, they will not stand ridiculously far away because luck and not skill would then determine whether the rings landed on the peg. In other words, low achievers take either a high or low risk, and high achievers take a moderate risk. This seems to hold true both for the simple children's game and for important adult decisions and activities.

Need for Immediate Feedback. Closely connected to high achievers' taking moderate risks is their desire for immediate feedback. People with high *n Ach* prefer activities which provide immediate and precise feedback information on how they are progressing toward a goal. Some hobbies and vocations offer such feedback, and others do not. High achievers generally prefer hobbies such as woodworking or mechanics, which provide prompt, exact feedback, and they shy away from the coin-collecting type of hobby, which takes years to develop. Likewise, high achievers tend to gravitate toward, or at least to be more satisfied in, jobs or careers, such as sales or certain management positions, in which they are frequently evaluated by specific performance criteria. On the other end of the scale, high *n Ach* persons are generally not to be found, or tend to be frustrated, in research and development or teaching vocations, where feedback on performance is very imprecise, vague, and long-range.

Satisfaction with Accomplishment.

High achievers find accomplishing a task intrinsically satisfying in and of itself, or they do not expect or necessarily want the accompanying material rewards. A good illustration of this characteristic involves money, but not for the usual reasons of wanting money for its own sake or for the material benefits that it can buy. Rather, high *n Ach* people look at money as a form of feedback or measurement of how they are doing. Given the choice between a simple task with a good payoff for accomplishment, and a more difficult task with a lesser payoff, other things being equal, high achievers generally choose the latter.

Preoccupation with the Task.

Once high achievers select a goal, they tend to be totally preoccupied with the task until it is successfully completed. They cannot stand to leave a job half finished and are not satisfied with themselves until they have given their maximum effort. This type of dedicated commitment is often reflected in their outward personalities, which frequently have a negative effect on those who come into contact with them. High achievers often strike others as being unfriendly and as "loners." They may be very quiet and may seldom brag about their accomplishments. They tend to be very realistic about their abilities and do not allow other people to get in the way of their goal accomplishments. Obviously, with this type of approach, high achievers do not always get along well with other people. Typically, high achievers make excellent salespersons but seldom good sales managers.

The accompanying Application Example, High Achievers in Action, gives the strategies entrepreneurs use to start new businesses. Almost all such entrepreneurs have a relatively high need for achievement.

The Affiliation Motive

Affiliation plays a very complex but vital role in human behavior. Sometimes affiliation is equated with social motives and/or group dynamics. As presented here, the affiliation motive is neither as broad as is implied by the definition of social motives nor as comprehensive or complex as is implied by the definition of group dynamics. The study of affiliation is further complicated by the fact that some behavioral scientists believe that it is an unlearned motive. Going as far back as the Hawthorne studies, the importance of the affiliation motive in the behavior of organizational participants has been very clear. Employees, especially rank-and-file employees, have a very intense need to belong to, and be accepted by, the group. This affiliation motive is an important part of group dynamics, which is the subject of Chapter 13.

The Security Motive

Security is a very intense motive in a fast-paced, highly technological society such as is found in modern America. The typical American can be insecure in a

Application Example

High Achievers in Action*

One of the best examples of high achievers are entrepreneurs who start and manage their own businesses. While many of these owner-managers do not stay in business more than five years, a large percentage are very successful and manage to keep their enterprises afloat for an indefinite period. How do successful entrepreneurs operate? By sidestepping the potential pitfalls and problems before they even open the doors of their new venture. Prior to starting, they take steps to ensure that the enterprise is able to survive the first two years—the most critical period for most small business ventures. Some of the strategic steps they take include the following:

1. Draw up a five-year plan. This ensures entrepreneurs that they will have yardsticks to aim for during the first sixty months of operation. The plan often has both annual and quarterly forecasts.
2. Raise more money than is needed. One of the biggest problems is running out of capital. To ensure that this does not happen, successful entrepreneurs allow for a margin of error by starting out with more money than they estimate will be needed. Then, if sales are not generated as quickly as forecasted, the new company has enough capital to tide it over.
3. Test the market. Successful entrepreneurs look over their market and ensure that there is sufficient demand for their goods or services. If the demand is weak, they look for different geographic locales. If the demand is strong, they look for specific target markets they can further exploit.
4. Don't take no for an answer. If the bank turns down an application for a loan, successful entrepreneurs find out why. If there is something wrong with their financial plan, they fix it. If their projected costs of operations are too high, they figure out ways of reducing them. They then return to the bank and get the loan—or find another financial institution that is willing to give them the loan.

*__Source:__ Adapted from "Expert Advice: How to Reduce Your Risk as an Entrepreneur," *Working Woman,* January 1987, p. 62.

---

number of areas of everyday living—for example, being liable for payments on a car or house, keeping a lover's or a spouse's affections, staying in school, getting into graduate school, or obtaining and/or keeping a good job. Job insecurity, in particular, has a great effect on organizational behavior. For example, a recent Opinion Research Corporation study found that managers are worrying more about job security.[3] On the surface, security appears to be much simpler than other secondary motives, for it is based largely on fear and is avoidance-oriented. Very briefly, it can be said that people have a learned security motive to protect themselves from the contingencies of life and actively try to avoid situations which would prevent them from satisfying their primary, general, and secondary motives.

In reality, security is much more complex than it appears on the surface. There is the simple, conscious security motive described above, but there also seems to be another type of security motive that is much more complicated and difficult to identify. This latter form of security is largely unconscious but may greatly influence the behavior of many people. The simple, conscious security motive is typically taken care of by insurance programs, personal savings plans, and other fringe benefits at the place of employment. An innovative company such as the Washington, D.C.–based insurance company Consumers United Group never lays off its employees and has a minimum annual salary of $18,000 designed to give a family a secure, decent living.[4] On the other hand, the more complex, unconscious security motive is not so easily fulfilled but may have a greater and more intense impact on human behavior. Although much attention has been given to the simple security motive, much more understanding is needed concerning the role of the unconscious, complex security motive.

The Status Motive

Along with security, the status or prestige motive is especially relevant to a dynamic society. The modern affluent person is often pictured as a status seeker. Such a person is accused of being more concerned with the material symbols of status—the right clothes, the right car, the right address, and a swimming pool or the latest personal computer—than with the more basic, human-oriented values in life. Although the symbols of status are considered a unique by-product of modern society, the fact is that status has been in existence since there have been two or more persons on the earth.

Status can be simply defined as the *relative* ranking that a person holds in a group, organization, or society. Under this definition, any time two or more persons are together, a status hierarchy will evolve, even if both have equal status. The symbols of status attempt to represent only the relative ranking of the person in the status hierarchy. The definition also corrects the common misconception that "status" means "high status." Everyone has status, but it may be high or low, depending on how the relative positions are ranked.

How are status positions determined? Why is one person ranked higher or lower than another? In the final analysis, status determination depends upon the prevailing cultural values and societal roles. Status-determining factors generally have quite different meanings, depending on the values of the particular culture. An example of the impact of cultural values on status is the personal qualities of people. In some cultures, the older persons are, the higher their status. However, in other cultures, once a person reaches a certain age, the status goes downhill. It must be remembered that such cultural values are highly volatile and change with the times and circumstances. There are also many subcultures in a given society which may have values different from the prevailing values of society at large and correspondingly different statuses.

Work-Motivation Approaches

So far, motivation has been presented as a basic psychological process consisting of primary, general, and secondary motives and drives such as the *n Pow, n Aff,* and *n Ach* motives. In order to understand organizational behavior, these basic motives must be recognized and studied. However, these serve as only background and foundation for the more directly relevant work-motivation approaches.

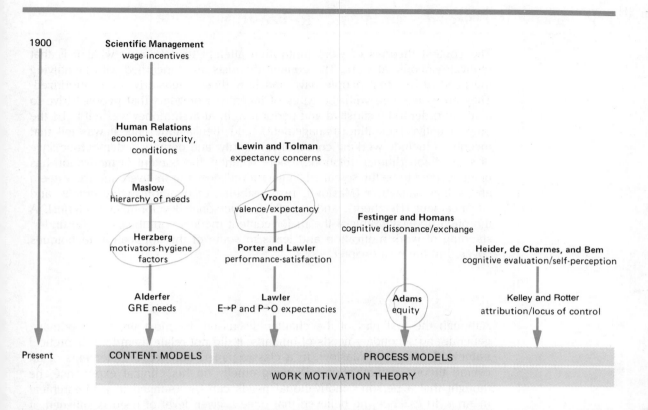

FIGURE 9.2 The theoretical development of work motivation.

Figure 9.2 graphically summarizes the various theoretical streams for work motivation. In particular, the figure shows four major approaches. The content models go as far back as the turn of the century, when pioneering scientific managers such as Frederick W. Taylor, Frank Gilbreth, and Henry L. Gantt proposed sophisticated wage incentive models to motivate workers. Next came the human relations movement, and then the content models of Maslow, Herzberg, and Alderfer. More recent developments have come from process models. Most work has been done on expectancy-based process models, but recently, equity and attribution theories have received attention. These process models are cognitively based; other cognitive models exist in psychology, but equity and attribution are the ones that have had the greatest influence on work motivation so far. Figure 9.2 purposely shows that at present there is a lack of integration or synthesis of the various models. In addition to this need for integration, a comprehensive assessment of the status of work-motivation theory also noted the need for contingency models and group/social processes.[5] At present, however, a group of content models can be identified and a group of process models can be identified, but an overall theory of work motivation does not exist.

The Content Theories of Work Motivation

The content theories of work motivation attempt to determine what it is that motivates people at work. The content theorists are concerned with identifying the needs/drives that people have and how these needs/drives are prioritized. They are concerned with the types of incentives or goals that people strive to attain in order to be satisfied and perform well. At first, money was felt to be the only incentive (scientific management), and then a little later it was felt that incentives include working conditions, security, and perhaps a democratic style of supervision (human relations). More recently, the content of motivation has been deemed to be the so-called "higher-level" needs or motives, such as esteem and self-actualization (Maslow); responsibility, recognition, achievement, and advancement (Herzberg); and growth and personal development (Alderfer). A thorough understanding of the major content models contributes to the understanding of work motivation and leads to some of the application techniques covered in the next chapter.

Maslow's Hierarchy of Needs

Although the first part of the chapter discussed the most important primary, general, and secondary needs of humans, it did not relate them to a theoretical framework. Abraham Maslow, in a classic paper, outlined the elements of an overall theory of motivation.[6] Drawing chiefly on his clinical experience, he thought that a person's motivational needs can be arranged in a hierarchical manner. In essence, he believed that once a given level of need is satisfied, it no longer serves to motivate. The next higher level of need has to be activated in order to motivate the individual.

Maslow identified five levels in his need hierarchy (see Figure 9.3). They are, in brief, the following:

1. *Physiological needs.* The most basic level in the hierarchy, the physiological needs, generally corresponds to the unlearned primary needs discussed earlier. The needs of hunger, thirst, sleep, and sex are some examples. According to the theory, once these basic needs are satisfied, they no longer motivate. For example, a starving person will strive to obtain a carrot that is within reach. However, after eating his or her fill of carrots, the person will not strive to obtain another one and will be motivated only by the next higher level of needs.
2. *Safety needs.* This second level of needs is roughly equivalent to the security need. Maslow stressed emotional as well as physical safety. The whole organism may become a safety-seeking mechanism. Yet, as is true of the physiological needs, once these safety needs are satisfied, they no longer motivate.
3. *Love needs.* This third, or intermediate, level of needs loosely corresponds to the affection and affiliation needs. Like Freud, Maslow seems guilty of poor choice of wording to identify his levels. His use of the word "love" has many misleading connotations, such as sex, which is actually a physiological need.

FIGURE 9.3
Maslow's hierarchy of needs.

Perhaps a more appropriate word describing this level would be "belongingness" or "social."

4. *Esteem needs.* The esteem level represents the higher needs of humans. The needs for power, achievement, and status can be considered to be part of this level. Maslow carefully pointed out that the esteem level contains both self-esteem and esteem from others.

5. *Needs for self-actualization.* This level represents the culmination of all the lower, intermediate, and higher needs of humans. People who have become self-actualized are self-fulfilled and have realized all their potential. Self-actualization is closely related to the self-concept discussed in Chapter 5. In effect, self-actualization is the person's motivation to transform perception of self into reality.

Maslow did not intend that his need hierarchy be directly applied to work motivation. In fact, he did not delve into the motivating aspects of humans in organizations until about twenty years after he originally proposed his theory. Despite this lack of intent on Maslow's part, others, such as Douglas McGregor, in his widely read book *The Human Side of Enterprise*, popularized the Maslow theory in management literature. The need hierarchy has had a tremendous impact on the modern management approach to motivation.

In a very rough manner, Maslow's need hierarchy theory can be converted into the content model of work motivation shown in Figure 9.4. If Maslow's estimates are applied to an organization example, the lower-level needs of personnel would be generally satisfied (85 percent of the basic needs and 70 percent of the security needs), but only 50 percent of the belongingness needs, 40 percent of the esteem needs, and a mere 10 percent of the self-actualization needs would be met.

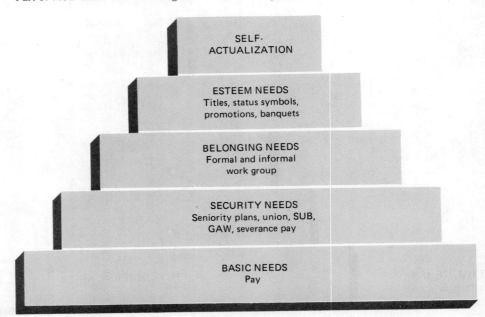

FIGURE 9.4
A hierarchy of
work motivation.

On the surface, the content model shown in Figure 9.4 and the estimated percentages given by Maslow seem logical and applicable to the motivation of humans in today's organizations. Maslow's need hierarchy has often been uncritically accepted by writers of management textbooks and by practitioners. Unfortunately, the limited research that has been conducted lends little empirical support to the theory. About a decade after publishing his original paper, Maslow did attempt to clarify his position by saying that gratifying the self-actualizing need of growth-motivated individuals can actually increase rather than decrease this need. He also hedged on some of his other original ideas, for example, that higher needs may emerge after lower needs that have been unfulfilled or suppressed for a long period are satisfied. He stressed that human behavior is multidetermined and multimotivated.

Most research findings indicate that Maslow's is not the final answer in work motivation. Yet the model does make a significant contribution in terms of making management aware of the diverse needs of humans at work. As one recent comprehensive analysis concluded, "indeed, the general ideas behind Maslow's theory seem to be supported, such as the distinction between deficiency needs and growth needs."[7] However, the number and names of the levels are not so important, nor, as the studies show, is the hierarchical concept. What is important is the fact that humans in the workplace have diverse motives, some of which are "high-level." In other words, such needs as esteem and self-actualization are important to the content of work motivation. The exact nature of these needs and how they relate to motivation are not clear. To try to overcome some of the problems of the Maslow hierarchy, Alderfer has recently proposed the ERG model, which contains three groups of needs. This model will be covered after the discussion of Herzberg's two-factor theory.

Herzberg's Two-Factor Theory of Motivation

Herzberg extended the work of Maslow and developed a specific content theory of work motivation. He conducted a widely reported motivational study on about 200 accountants and engineers employed by firms in and around Pittsburgh, Pennsylvania. He used the critical incident method of obtaining data for analysis. The professional subjects in the study were essentially asked two questions: (1) When did you feel particularly good about your job—what turned you on; and (2) when did you feel exceptionally bad about your job—what turned you off?

Responses obtained from this critical incident method were interesting and fairly consistent. Reported good feelings were generally associated with job experiences and job content. An example was the accounting supervisor who felt good about being given the job of installing new computer equipment. He took pride in his work and was gratified to know that the new equipment made a big difference in the overall functioning of his department. Reported bad feelings, on the other hand, were generally associated with the surrounding or peripheral aspects of the job—the job context. An example of these feelings was related by an engineer whose first job was to keep tabulation sheets and manage the office when the boss was gone. It turned out that his boss was always too busy to train him and became annoyed when he tried to ask questions. The engineer said that he was frustrated in this job context and that he felt like a flunky in a dead-end job. Tabulating these reported good and bad feelings, Herzberg concluded that job satisfiers are related to job content and that job dissatisfiers are allied to job context. Herzberg labeled satisfiers *motivators*, and he called the dissatisfiers *hygiene factors*. Taken together, they became known as Herzberg's *two-factor theory of motivation*.

* **Relation to Maslow.** Herzberg's theory is closely related to Maslow's need hierarchy. The hygiene factors are preventive and environmental in nature, and they are roughly equivalent to Maslow's lower-level needs (see Table 9.1). These hygiene factors prevent dissatisfaction, but they do not lead to satisfaction. In effect, they bring motivation up to a theoretical zero level and are a necessary "floor" to prevent dissatisfaction, and they serve as a takeoff point for motivation. By themselves, the hygiene factors do not motivate. Only the motivators (see Table 9.1) motivate humans on the job. They are roughly equivalent to Maslow's higher-level needs. According to the Herzberg theory, an individual must have a job with a challenging content in order to be truly motivated.

TABLE 9.1 Herzberg's Two-Factor Theory

Hygiene Factors	Motivators
Company policy and administration	Achievement
Supervision, technical	Recognition
Salary	Work itself
Interpersonal relations, supervisor	Responsibility
Working conditions	Advancement

Contribution to Work Motivation. Herzberg's two-factor theory cast a new light on the content of work motivation. Up to this point, management had generally concentrated on the hygiene factors. When faced with a morale problem, the typical solution was higher pay, more fringe benefits, and better working conditions. However, as has been pointed out, this simplistic solution did not really work. Management are often perplexed because they are paying high wages and salaries, have an excellent fringe-benefit package, and provide great working conditions, but their employees are still not motivated. Herzberg's theory offers an explanation for this problem. By concentrating only on the hygiene factors, management are not motivating their personnel.

There are probably very few workers or managers who do not feel that they deserved the raise they received. On the other hand, there are many dissatisfied workers and managers who feel they did not get a large-enough raise. This simple observation points out that the hygiene factors seem to be important in preventing dissatisfaction but do not lead to satisfaction. Herzberg would be the first to say that the hygiene factors are absolutely necessary to maintain the human resources of an organization. However, as in the Maslow sense, once "the belly is full" of hygiene factors, which is the case in most modern organizations, dangling any more in front of employees will not motivate them. According to Herzberg's theory, only a challenging job which has the opportunities for achievement, recognition, responsibility, advancement, and growth will motivate personnel.

Critical Analysis of Herzberg's Theory. Although Herzberg's two-factor theory became very popular as a textbook explanation of work motivation and was widely accepted by practitioners, it also is true that from an academic perspective the theory oversimplifies the complexities of work motivation. When researchers deviate from the critical incident methodology used by Herzberg, they do not get the two factors. There seem to be job factors that lead to both satisfaction and dissatisfaction. These findings indicate that a strict interpretation of the two-factor theory is not warranted.

In spite of the obvious limitations, few would question that Herzberg contributed substantially to the study of work motivation. He extended Maslow's need hierarchy concept and made it more applicable to work motivation. Herzberg also drew attention to the importance of job content factors in work motivation, which previously had been badly neglected and often totally overlooked. The job design technique of job enrichment is also one of Herzberg's contributions. Job enrichment is covered in detail in the next chapter. Overall, Herzberg added much to the better understanding of job content factors and satisfaction, but, like his predecessors, he fell short of a comprehensive theory of work motivation. His model describes only some of the content of work motivation; it does not adequately describe the complex motivational process of organizational participants.

Alderfer's ERG Theory

An extension of the Herzberg and, especially, the Maslow content theories of work motivation comes from the work of Clayton Alderfer. He formulated a need category model that was more in line with the existing empirical evidence. Similar to Maslow and Herzberg, he does feel that there is value in categorizing needs and that there is a basic distinction between lower-order needs and higher-order needs.

Alderfer identified three groups of core needs: existence, relatedness, and growth (hence ERG theory). The *existence needs* are concerned with survival (physiological well-being). The *relatedness needs* stress the importance of interpersonal, social relationships. The *growth needs* are concerned with the individual's intrinsic desire for personal development. Figure 9.5 shows how these groups of needs are related to the Maslow and Herzberg categories. Obviously, they are very close, but the ERG needs do not have strict lines of demarcation.

Alderfer is suggesting more of a continuum of needs than hierarchical levels or two factors of prepotency needs. Unlike Maslow and Herzberg, he does not contend that a lower-level need has to be fulfilled before a higher-level need is motivating or that deprivation is the only way to activate a need. For example, under ERG theory the person's background or cultural environment may dictate that the relatedness needs will take precedence over unfulfilled existence needs and that the more the growth needs are satisfied, the more they will increase in intensity.

There has not been a great deal of research on ERG theory. Although there is some evidence to counter the theory's predictive value, most contemporary analyses of work motivation tend to support Alderfer's theory over Maslow's and Herzberg's. Overall, the ERG theory seems to take some of the strong points of the earlier content theories but is less restrictive and limiting. The fact remains, however, that the content theories in general lack explanatory power over the complexities of work motivation and, with the possible exception of the implications for job design of Herzberg's work, do not readily translate to the actual practice of human resources management.

FIGURE 9.5
The relationship between Alderfer's ERG needs, Maslow's five-level hierarchy, and Herzberg's two-factor theory.

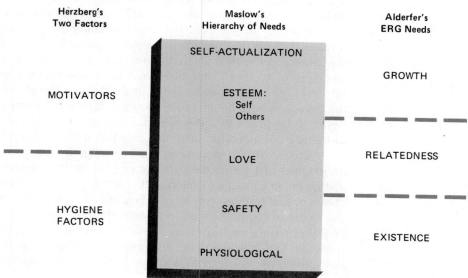

Herzberg's Two Factors	Maslow's Hierarchy of Needs	Alderfer's ERG Needs
MOTIVATORS	SELF-ACTUALIZATION	GROWTH
	ESTEEM: Self Others	
	LOVE	RELATEDNESS
HYGIENE FACTORS	SAFETY	
	PHYSIOLOGICAL	EXISTENCE

The Process Theories of Work Motivation

The content models attempted to identify what motivates people at work (for example, self-actualization, responsibility, and growth); they tried to specify correlates of motivated behavior. The process theories, on the other hand, are more concerned with the cognitive antecedents that go into motivation or effort and, more important, with the way they relate to one another. As Figure 9.2 shows, the expectancy models make the most significant contribution to understanding the complex processes involved in work motivation. After these are examined, equity and attribution theories will also be presented and analyzed as major process models of work motivation.

Vroom's Expectancy Theory of Motivation

As shown in Figure 9.2, the expectancy theory of work motivation has its roots in the cognitive concepts of pioneering psychologists Kurt Lewin and Edward Tolman and in the choice behavior and utility concepts from classical economic theory. However, the first to formulate an expectancy theory directly aimed at work motivation was Victor Vroom. Contrary to most critics, Vroom proposed his expectancy theory as an alternative to the content models, which he felt were inadequate explanations of the complex process of work motivation. At least in academic circles, his theory has become a popular explanation for work motivation and has generated considerable research.

Figure 9.6 briefly summarizes the Vroom model. As shown, the model is built around the concepts of valence, instrumentality, and expectancy and is commonly called the *VIE theory*.

Meaning of the Variables.
By *valence*, Vroom means the strength of an individual's preference for a particular outcome. Other terms that might be used include *value*, *incentive*, *attitude*, and *expected utility*. In order for the valence to be positive, the person must prefer attaining the outcome to not attaining it. A valence of zero occurs when the individual is indifferent toward the outcome; the valence is negative when the individual prefers not attaining the outcome to attaining it. Another major input into the valence is the *instrumentality* of the first-level outcome in obtaining a desired second-level outcome. For example, the person would be motivated toward superior performance because of the desire to be promoted. The superior performance (first-level outcome) is seen as being instrumental in obtaining promotion (second-level outcome).

Another major variable in the Vroom motivational process is *expectancy*. Although at first glance the expectancy concept may seem to be the same as the instrumentality input into valence, it is actually quite different. Expectancy relates efforts to first-level outcomes (see Figure 9.6), while instrumentality relates first-level outcomes and second-level outcomes. In other words, expectancy is the probability (ranging from 0 to 1) that a particular action or effort will lead to a particular *first-level* outcome. *Instrumentality* refers to the degree to which a first-level outcome will lead to a desired *second-level* outcome. In summary, the

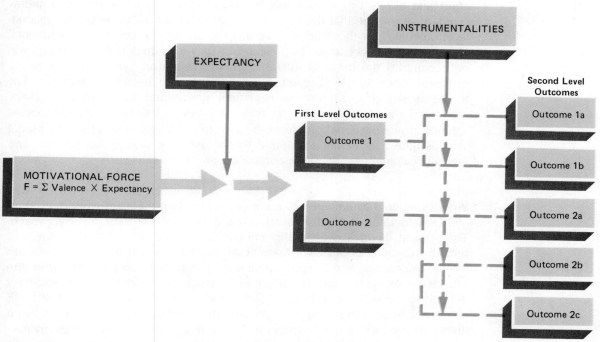

FIGURE 9.6 The Vroom expectancy, or VIE, theory of work motivation.

strength of the motivation to perform a certain act will depend on the algebraic sum of the products of the valences for the outcomes (which include instrumentality) times the expectancies.

Implications of the Vroom Model for Organizational Behavior. Vroom's theory departs from the content theories in that it depicts a process of cognitive variables that reflects individual differences in work motivation. It does not attempt to describe what the content is or what the individual differences are. Everyone has a unique combination of valences, instrumentalities, and expectancies. Thus, the Vroom theory indicates only the conceptual determinants of motivation and how they are related. It does not provide specific suggestions on what motivates organizational members, as the Maslow, Herzberg, and Alderfer models do.

Although the Vroom model does not directly contribute much to the techniques of motivating personnel in an organization, it is of value in understanding organizational behavior. It can clarify the relationship between individual and organizational goals. For example, suppose workers are given a certain standard for production. By measuring the workers' output, management can determine how important their various personal goals (second-level outcomes such as money, security, and recognition) are; the instrumentality of the organizational goal (the first-level outcome, such as the production standard) for the attainment of the personal goals; and the workers' expectancies that their effort and ability will accomplish the organizational goal. If output is below standard, it may be that the workers do not place a high value on the second-level outcomes; or they may not see that the first-level outcome is instrumental in obtaining the second-level outcomes; or they may think that their efforts will not accomplish the first-level outcome. Vroom feels that any one, or a combination, of these possibilities will result in a low level of motivation to produce. The model is designed to help management understand and analyze workers' motivation and identify some of the relevant variables; it does not provide specific solutions to motivational problems. Besides the application problem, the model also assumes, as earlier economic theory did, that people are rational and logically calculating. Such an assumption may be unrealistic.

Importance of the Vroom Model. Probably the major reason why Vroom's model has emerged as an important modern theory of work motivation and has generated so much research is that it does not take a simplistic approach. The content theories oversimplify human motivation. Yet the content theories remain extremely popular with practicing managers because the concepts are easy to understand and to apply to their own situations. On the other hand, the VIE theory recognizes the complexities of work motivation, but it is relatively difficult to understand and apply. Thus, from a theoretical standpoint, the VIE model seems to help managers appreciate the complexities of motivation, but it does not give them much practical help in solving their motivational problems.

In some ways Vroom's expectancy model is like marginal analysis in economics. Businesspeople do not actually calculate the point where marginal cost equals marginal revenue, but it is still a useful concept for a theory of the firm. The expectancy model attempts only to mirror the complex motivational process; it does not attempt to describe how motivational decisions are actually made or to solve actual motivational problems facing a manager.

The Porter-Lawler Model

Comments throughout the chapter have referred to the controversy over the relationship between satisfaction and performance that has existed since the human relations movement. The content theories implicitly assume that satisfaction leads to improved performance and that dissatisfaction detracts from performance. The Herzberg model is really a theory of job satisfaction, but still it does not deal with the relationship between satisfaction and performance. The Vroom model also largely avoids the relationship between satisfaction and performance. Although satisfactions make an input into Vroom's concept of valence and although the outcomes have performance implications, it was not until Porter and Lawler refined and extended Vroom's model (for example, the relationships are expressed diagrammatically rather than mathematically, there are more variables, and the cognitive process of perception plays a central role) that the relationship between satisfaction and performance was dealt with directly by a motivation model.

Porter and Lawler start with the premise that motivation (effort or force) does not equal satisfaction and/or performance. Motivation, satisfaction, and performance are all separate variables and relate in ways different from what was traditionally assumed. Figure 9.7 depicts the multivariable model used to explain the complex relationship that exists between motivation, performance, and satisfaction. As shown in the model, boxes 1, 2, and 3 are basically the same as the Vroom equation. It is important, however, that Porter and Lawler point out that effort (force or motivation) does not directly lead to performance. It is mediated by abilities/traits and role perceptions. More important in the Porter-Lawler model is what happens after the performance. The rewards that follow and how these are perceived will determine satisfaction. In other words, the Porter-Lawler model suggests—and this is a significant turn of events from traditional thinking—that performance leads to satisfaction.

A recent comprehensive review of research verifies the importance of rewards in the relationship between performance and satisfaction. Specifically it was concluded that performance and satisfaction will be more strongly related when rewards are made contingent upon performance than when they are not.[8]

Implications for Practice. Although the Porter-Lawler model is more applications-oriented than the Vroom model, it is still quite complex and has proved to be a difficult way to bridge the gap to actual management practice. To Porter and Lawler's credit, they have been very conscious of putting their theory and research into practice. They recommend that practicing managers go beyond traditional attitude measurement and attempt to measure variables such as the

FIGURE 9.7 The Porter-Lawler motivation model.
(*Source*: Lyman W. Porter and Edward E. Lawler III, *Managerial Attitudes and Performance*, Irwin, Homewood, Ill., 1968, p. 165. Used with permission.)

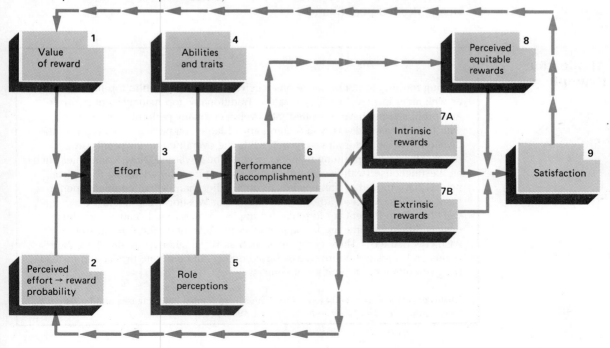

values of possible rewards, the perceptions of effort-reward probabilities, and role perceptions. These variables, of course, can help managers better understand what goes into employee effort and performance. Giving attention to the consequences of performance, Porter and Lawler also recommend that organizations critically reevaluate their current reward policies. They stress that management should make a concentrated effort to measure how closely levels of satisfaction are related to levels of performance. These types of recommendations have been verified by research.

Contributions to Work Motivation. The Porter and Lawler model has definitely made a significant contribution to the better understanding of work motivation and the relationship between performance and satisfaction, but, to date, it has not had much impact on the actual practice of human resources management. Yet the expectancy models provide certain guidelines that can be followed by human resources management. For example, on the front end (the relationship between motivation and performance), it has recently been suggested that the following barriers must be overcome:

1. Doubts about ability, skill, or knowledge
2. The physical or practical possibility of the job
3. The interdependence of the job with other people or activities
4. Ambiguity surrounding the job requirements[9]

In addition, on the back end (the relationship between performance and satisfaction), guidelines such as the following have been suggested:

1. Determine what rewards each employee values
2. Define desired performance

Application Example

Linking Manager's Rewards with Unit Performance*

Linking rewards to performance has received recent attention in top management, as well as in low-level employee ranks. Traditionally, top management bonuses and profit sharing have been tied into overall company performance. However, with the increased diversity and autonomy of large companies, a manager in one division may be performing very well while the overall company profits are down. This high-performing manager may not be rewarded. Now, companies such as Westinghouse (with twenty-three units ranging from broadcasting to nuclear power) have moved to link rewards to unit, rather than overall company, performance results. As the head of compensation for Westinghouse noted, "we can't have one [incentive] formula that applies to everyone because each business is different. Some are in tough growth markets, and others are in stable, cash-cow markets." Thus, companies such as Westinghouse are dropping their bonus and stock-option incentives based on overall corporate profits and instead tying rewards more to unit profit centers.

***Source:** Adapted from Larry Reibstein, "Firms Trim Annual Pay Increases and Focus on Long Term," *The Wall Street Journal*, Apr. 10, 1987; p. 21.

3. Make desired performance attainable
4. Link valued rewards to performance[10]

The last point above is getting recognition in the management compensation plans of many big companies, as indicated by the accompanying Application Example.

In addition to these guidelines, by recognizing the reward implications in the Porter-Lawler model, especially the intrinsic-extrinsic distinction, there has been a move away from a strictly cognitive view of work motivation and toward more of an operant, environmentally based view of motivation. Chapters 11 and 12 will discuss this view in detail.

Equity Theory of Work Motivation

Equity theory has been around just as long as the expectancy theories of work motivation. However, only recently has equity as a process of motivation received widespread attention in the organizational behavior field. As Figure 9.2 indicates, its roots can be traced back to cognitive dissonance theory and exchange theory. As a theory of work motivation, credit for equity theory is usually given to J. Stacy Adams. Simply put, the theory argues that a major input into job performance and satisfaction is the degree of equity (or inequity) that people perceive in their work situation. In other words, it is another cognitively based motivation theory, and Adams depicts a specific process of how this motivation occurs.

Inequity occurs when a person perceives that the ratio of his or her outcomes to inputs and the ratio of a relevant other's outcomes to inputs are unequal. Schematically this is represented as follows:

$$\frac{\text{Person's outcomes}}{\text{Person's inputs}} < \frac{\text{other's outcomes}}{\text{other's inputs}}$$

$$\frac{\text{Person's outcomes}}{\text{Person's inputs}} > \frac{\text{other's outcomes}}{\text{other's inputs}}$$

Equity occurs when

$$\frac{\text{Person's outcomes}}{\text{Person's inputs}} = \frac{\text{other's outcomes}}{\text{other's inputs}}$$

Both the inputs and the outputs of person and other are based upon the person's perceptions. Age, sex, education, social status, organizational position, qualifications, and how hard the person works are examples of perceived input variables. Outcomes consist primarily of rewards such as pay, status, promotion, and intrinsic interest in the job. In essence, the ratio is based upon the person's *perception* of what the person is giving (inputs) and receiving (outcomes) versus the ratio of what the relevant other is giving and receiving. This cognition may or may not be the same as someone else's observation of the ratios or the same as the actual, realistic situation.

If the person's perceived ratio is not equal to the other's, he or she will strive to restore the ratio to equity. This "striving" to restore equity is used as the explanation of work motivation. The strength of this motivation is in direct proportion to the perceived inequity that exists. Adams suggests that such motivation may be expressed in several forms. To restore equity, the person may alter the inputs or outcomes, cognitively distort the inputs or outcomes, leave the field, act on the other, or change the other.

It is important to note that inequity does not come about only when the person feels cheated. For example, Adams has studied the impact that perceived overpayment has on inequity. His findings suggest that workers prefer equitable payment to overpayment. Workers on a piece-rate incentive system who feel overpaid will reduce their productivity in order to restore equity. More likely, however, is the case of people who feel underpaid (outcome) or overworked (input) in relation to others in the workplace. In the latter case, there would be motivation to restore equity in a way that may be dysfunctional from an organizational standpoint. For example, the owner of an appliance store in Oakland, California, allowed his employees to set their own wages. Interestingly, none of the employees took an increase in pay, and one serviceman actually settled on lower pay because he did not want to work as hard as the others.[11]

To date, research that has specifically tested the validity of Adam's equity theory has been fairly supportive. A comprehensive review found considerable laboratory research support for the "equity norm" (persons review the inputs and outcomes of themselves and others, and if inequity is perceived, they strive to restore equity) but only limited support from more relevant field studies.[12] One line of recent field research on equity theory uses baseball players. One study of players who played out their option year, and thus felt they were inequitably paid, performed as the theory would predict.[13] Their performance decreased in three of four categories (not batting average) during the option year, and when they were signed to a new contract, the performance was restored. However, a more recent study using the same type of sample, only larger, found the opposite to what equity theory would predict.[14] Mainly, performance improved during the option year. The reason, of course, was that the players wanted to look especially good, even though they felt they were inequitably paid, in order to be in a stronger bargaining position for a new contract. In other words, there are no easy answers or 100 percent predictive power when applying a cognitive process theory such as equity. Another critique suggests that the time lag effects of inequity have also been overlooked.[15]

The work on equity theory goes beyond expectancy theory as a cognitive explanation of work motivation and serves as a point of departure for attribution theory and locus of control explanations.

Attribution Theory and Locus of Control

Chapter 6, on perception, discussed the important role of attributions in the cognitive processes of individuals. Recently, the attributions that people make and the locus of control that they perceive have emerged as important explanations of work motivation. Unlike the other motivation theories, attribution theory is more a theory of the relationship between personal perception and interpersonal behavior than a theory of individual motivation. Kelley stresses that it is concerned mainly with the cognitive processes by which an individual interprets behavior as being caused by (or attributed to) certain parts of the relevant environment. It is concerned with the "why" questions of motivation and behavior. Since most causes, attributes, and "whys" are not directly observable, the theory says that people must depend upon cognitions, particularly perception. The attribution theorist assumes that humans are rational and are motivated to identify and understand the causal structure of their relevant environment. It is this search for attributes that characterizes attribution theory.

Although attribution theory has its roots in all the pioneering cognitive theorists' work (for example, that of Lewin and Festinger), in de Charms's ideas on cognitive evaluation, and in Bem's notion of "self-perception," the theory's initiator is generally recognized to be Fritz Heider. Heider believed that both internal forces (personal attributes such as ability, effort, and fatigue) and external forces (environmental attributes such as rules and the weather) combine additively to determine behavior. He stressed that it is the *perceived*, not the actual, determinants that are important to behavior. People will behave differently if they perceive internal attributes from the way they will behave if they perceive external attributes. It is this concept of differential ascriptions that has very important implications for work motivation.

Types of Attributions. Using *locus of control*, work behavior may be explained by whether employees perceive their outcomes as controlled internally or externally. Employees who perceive internal control feel that they personally can influence their outcomes through their own ability, skills, or effort. Employees who perceive external control feel that their outcomes are beyond their own control; they feel that external forces control their outcomes. What is important is that this perceived locus of control may have a differential impact on their performance and satisfaction. For example, studies by Rotter and his colleagues suggest that skill versus chance environments differentially affect behavior.[16] In addition, a number of studies have been conducted in recent years to test the attribution-theory–locus-of-control model in work settings. One study found that internally controlled employees are generally more satisfied with their jobs, are more likely to be in managerial positions, and are more satisfied with a participatory management style than employees who perceive external control.[17] Other studies have found that internally controlled managers are better performers,[18] are more considerate of subordinates,[19] tend not to burn out,[20] and follow a more strategic style of executive action.[21] In addition, the attribution process has been shown to play a role in coalition formulation in the political process of organizations. In particular, coalition members made stronger internal attributions, such as ability and desire, and nonmembers made stronger external attributions, such as luck.[22]

Implications of the Attribution Process. The implication of these studies is that internally controlled managers are better than externally controlled managers. However, such generalizations are not yet warranted because there is some contradictory evidence. For example, one study concluded that the ideal manager may have an external orientation because the results indicated that externally controlled managers were perceived as initiating more structure and consideration than internally controlled managers.[23] In addition to the implications for managerial behavior and performance, attribution theory has been shown to have relevance in explaining goal-setting behavior,[24] leadership behavior,[25] and poor employee performance.[26] A review article concludes that locus of control is related to the performance and satisfaction of organization members and may moderate the relationship between motivation and incentives.[27]

In addition, attributions are related to *organizational symbolism,* which in effect says that in order to understand organizations one must recognize their symbolic nature.[28] Much of organization is based on attributions rather than physical or observed realities under this view. For example, research has found that symbols are a salient source of information used by people in forming their impressions of psychological climate.[29]

Attribution theory seems to hold a great deal of promise for the better understanding of organizational behavior. However, for the future, other dimensions besides the internal and external locus of control will have to be accounted for and studied. One social psychologist, for example, suggests that a stability (fixed or variable) dimension must also be recognized.[30] Experienced employees will probably have a stable internal attribution about their abilities, but an unstable internal attribution concerning effort. By the same token, these employees may have a stable external attribution about task difficulty but an unstable external attribution about luck.

Besides the stability dimension, other researchers suggest that dimensions such as consensus (do others act this way in a situation?), consistency (does this person act this way in this situation at other times?), and distinctiveness (does this person act differently in other situations?) will affect the type of attributions that are made.[31] For example, if there is high consensus, consistency, and distinctiveness, then attributions to external causes are made, but if there is low consensus and distinctiveness and high consistency, then attributions to internal causes are made. Thus, in trying to understand the poor performance of a subordinate, if there seems to be high consensus (others are also performing poorly on this task), high consistency (this poor performer does not do well on this task at any time or in any place), and high distinctiveness (this subordinate has done well on other tasks), then the supervisor would make an external attribution, that is, that this subordinate is having bad luck or something is wrong that is beyond the control of the subordinate. By the same token, if in analyzing this same poor performer it is determined that there is low consensus (others are performing well on this task), low distinctiveness (this subordinate does poorly on other tasks as well), and high consistency (this poor performer does not do well on this task at any time or in any place), then the supervisor would make an internal attribution, that is, that the subordinate just doesn't have the ability or necessary motivation to perform well. There is some empirical evidence from research on the attributions made by nursing supervisors that supports these theoretical propositions.[32]

In other words, attribution theory recognizes the complexity of human behavior, and this must be part of a theory that attempts to *explain* and *understand* organizational behavior. As has recently been pointed out, it should not be restrictive. Theoretical, information processing, and situational factors all affect the attribution models of organizational behavior.[33] Despite this complexity, and unlike some of its predecessors in the cognitive approaches to motivation discussed earlier, it does seem to have more potential for application and relevance, instead of being a purely academic exercise in theory building.

Summary

Motivation is a basic psychological process. The comprehensive understanding of motivation lies in the need-drive-incentive sequence, or cycle. The basic process involves needs (deficiencies), which set drives in motion (deficiencies with direction) to accomplish incentives (anything which alleviates a need and reduces a drive). The drives or motives may be classified into *primary, general,* and *secondary* categories. The primary motives are unlearned and physiologically based. Common primary motives include hunger, thirst, sleep, avoidance of pain, sex, and maternal concern. The general motives are also unlearned but are not physiologically based. Curiosity, manipulation, activity, and affection are examples of general motives. Secondary motives are learned and are most relevant to the study of organizational behavior. The needs for power, achievement, affiliation, security, and status are major motivating forces in the behavior of organizational participants.

When the theories of motivation are specifically focused on work motivation, there are several popular approaches. The Maslow, Herzberg, and Alderfer models attempt to identify specific content factors in the individual (in the case of Maslow and Alderfer) or in the job environment (in the case of Herzberg) that motivate employees. Although such a content approach has surface logic, is easy to understand, and can be readily translated into practice, the research evidence points out some definite limitations. There is very little research support for these models' theoretical basis and predictability. The trade-off for simplicity sacrifices true understanding of the complexity of work motivation. On the positive side, however, the content models have given emphasis to important content factors that were largely ignored by the human relationists. In addition, the Alderfer model allows more flexibility, and the Herzberg model is useful as an explanation for job satisfaction and as a point of departure for job design covered in the next chapter.

The process theories provide a much sounder theoretical explanation of work-motivation. The expectancy model of Vroom and the extensions and refinements provided by Porter and Lawler help explain the important cognitive variables and how they relate to one another in the complex process of work motivation. The Porter-Lawler model also gives specific attention to the important relationship between performance and satisfaction. Porter and Lawler propose that performance leads to satisfaction, instead of the human relations assumption of the reverse. A growing research literature is somewhat supportive of these expectancy models, but conceptual and methodological problems remain. Unlike the content models, these expectancy models are relatively complex and difficult to translate into actual practice, and consequently they have generally failed to meet the goals of prediction and control of organizational behavior. More recently, in academic circles, equity theory and especially attribution theory and locus of control have received increased attention. These were presented, in the additive sense, for the better understanding of work motivation. Both process theories—the equity model, which is based upon perceived input-outcome ratios, and attribution theory, which ascribes internal or external causes to behavior—lend increased understanding to the complex cognitive process of work motivation but have the same limitation as the expectancy models for prediction and control in the practice of human resources management. Attribution theory and locus of control, as potentially important contributions to the cognitive development of work-motivation theory, may be able to overcome some of the application limitations of the process theories of work motivation and bring us closer to the goals of prediction and control.

Questions for Discussion and Review

1. Briefly define the three classifications of motives. What are some examples of each?
2. What are the characteristics of high achievers?
3. How is status defined? What are some determinants of status?
4. What implications does the security motive have for modern human resources management?
5. In your own words, briefly explain Maslow's theory of motivation. Relate it to work motivation and Alderfer's ERG model.
6. What is the major criticism of Herzberg's two-factor theory of motivation? Do you think it has made a contribution to the better understanding of motivation in the workplace? Defend your answer.
7. In Vroom's model, what are valence, expectancy, and force? How do these variables relate to one another and to work motivation? Give realistic examples.
8. In your own words, briefly explain the Porter-Lawler model of motivation. How do performance and satisfaction relate to each other?
9. Briefly give an example of an inequity that a manager of a small business might experience. How would the manager strive to attain equity in the situation you describe?
10. What is attribution theory? How can analysis of locus of control be applied to workers and managers?

References

1. Martin G. Evans, "Organizational Behavior: The Central Role of Motivation," *Journal of Management*, vol. 12, no. 2, 1986, p. 203.
2. The most frequently cited exception is the need for oxygen. A deficiency of oxygen in the body does not automatically set up a corresponding drive. This is a fear of

high-altitude pilots. Unless their gauges show an oxygen leak or the increased intake of carbon dioxide sets up a drive, they may die of oxygen deficiency without a drive ever being set up to correct the situation. The same is true of the relatively frequent deaths of teenagers parked in "lovers' lanes." Carbon monoxide leaks into the parked automobile, and they die from oxygen deficiency without its ever setting up a drive (to open the car door).

3. "Labor Letter," *The Wall Street Journal,* Nov. 11, 1986, p. 1.
4. "Labor Letter," *The Wall Street Journal,* Mar. 31, 1987, p. 1.
5. Terrence R. Mitchell, "Motivation: New Directions for Theory, Research, and Practice," *Academy of Management Review,* January 1982, p. 86.
6. A. H. Maslow, "A Theory of Human Motivation," *Psychological Review,* July 1943, pp. 370–396.
7. Robert A. Baron, *Behavior in Organizations,* 2d ed., Allyn and Bacon, Boston, 1986, p. 78.
8. Philip M. Podsakoff and Larry Williams, "The Relationship between Job Performance and Job Satisfaction," in Edwin Locke (ed.), *Generalizing from Laboratory to Field Settings,* Lexington Books, Lexington, Mass., 1986, p. 244.
9. James M. McFillen and Philip M. Podsakoff, "A Coordinated Approach to Motivation Can Increase Productivity," *Personnel Administrator,* July 1983, p. 46.
10. Robert A. Baron, *Behavior in Organizations,* Allyn and Bacon, Boston, 1983, p. 137.
11. Robert E. Callahan, C. Patrick Fleenor, and Harry R. Knudson, *Understanding Organizational Behavior,* Merrill, Columbus, Ohio, 1986, pp. 108–109.
12. Michael R. Carrell and John E. Dittrich, "Equity Theory: The Recent Literature, Methodological Considerations, and New Directions," *Academy of Management Review,* April 1978, pp. 202–210.
13. Robert G. Lord and Jeffrey A. Hohenfeld, "Longitudinal Field Assessment of Equity Effects on the Performance of Major League Baseball Players," *Journal of Applied Psychology,* February 1979, pp. 19–26.
14. Dennis Duchon and Arthur G. Jago, "Equity and Performance of Major League Baseball Players: An Extension of Lord and Hohenfeld," *Journal of Applied Psychology,* December 1981, pp. 728–732.
15. Richard A. Cosier and Dan R. Dalton, "Equity Theory and Time: A Reformulation," *Academy of Management Review,* April 1983, pp. 311–319.
16. Julian B. Rotter, Shephard Liverant, and Douglas P. Crowne, "The Growth and Extinction of Expectancies in Chance-Controlled and Skilled Tasks," *The Journal of Psychology,* July 1961, pp. 161–177.
17. Terence R. Mitchell, Charles M. Smyser, and Stan E. Weed, "Locus of Control: Supervision and Work Satisfaction," *Academy of Management Journal,* September 1975, pp. 623–631.
18. Carl R. Anderson, Don Hellriegel, and John W. Slocum, Jr., "Managerial Response to Environmentally Induced Stress," *Academy of Management Journal,* June 1977, pp. 260–272. The higher performance of internally-controlled managers was verified by the use of student subjects in a study by Carl R. Anderson and Craig Eric Schneier, "Locus of Control, Leader Behavior and Leader Performance among Management Students," *Academy of Management Journal,* December 1978, pp. 690–698.
19. Margaret W. Pryer and M. K. Distenfano, "Perceptions of Leadership, Job Statisfaction, and Internal-External Control across Three Nursing Levels," *Nursing Research,* November–December 1971, pp. 534–537.
20. Eli Glogow, "Research Note: Burnout and Locus of Control," *Public Personnel Management,* Spring 1986, p. 79.
21. Danny Miller, Manfred F. R. Kets DeVries, and Jean-Marie Toulouse, "Top Executive

Locus of Control and Its Relationship to Strategy-Making, Structure, and Environment,” *Academy of Management Journal*, June 1982, pp. 237–253.

22. John A. Pearce and Angelo S. DeNisi, “Attribution Theory and Strategic Decision Making: An Application to Coalition Formation,” *Academy of Management Journal*, March 1983, pp. 119–128.
23. Douglas E. Durand and Walter R. Nord, “Perceived Leader Behavior as a Function of Personality Characteristics of Supervisors and Subordinates,” *Academy of Management Journal*, September 1976, pp. 427–438.
24. Dennis L. Dossett and Carl I. Greenberg, “Goal Setting and Performance Evaluation: An Attributional Analysis,” *Academy of Management Journal*, December 1981, pp. 767–779.
25. Bobby J. Calder, “An Attribution Theory of Leadership,” in Barry Staw and Gerald Salancik (eds.), *New Directions in Organizational Behavior*, St. Clare Press, Chicago, 1977, pp. 179–204; and James C. McElroy, “A Typology of Attribution Leadership Research,” *Academy of Management Review*, July 1982, pp. 413–417; and Gregory Dobbins, “Effects of Gender on Leaders’ Responses to Poor Performers: An Attributional Interpretation,” *Academy of Management Journal*, September 1985, pp. 587–598; James C. McElroy and Charles B. Shrader, “Attribution Theories of Leadership and Network Analysis,” *Journal of Management*, vol. 12, no. 3, 1986, pp. 351–362.
26. Terence R. Mitchell and Robert E. Wood, “Supervisors’ Responses to Subordinate Poor Performance: A Test of an Attribution Model,” *Organizational Behavior and Human Performance*, February 1980, pp. 123–138.
27. Paul E. Spector, “Behavior in Organizations as a Function of Employees’ Locus of Control,” *Psychological Bulletin*, May 1982, pp. 482–497.
28. Peter J. Frost, “Special Issue on Organizational Symbolism,” *Journal of Management*, vol. 11, no. 2, 1985, pp. 5–9.
29. Suzyn Ornstein, “Organizational Symbols: A Study of Their Meanings and Influences on Perceived Psychological Climate,” *Organizational Behavior and Human Decision Processes*, October 1986, pp. 207–229.
30. Bernard Weiner, *Theories of Motivation,* Rand McNally, Chicago, 1972, Chap. 5.
31. Harold H. Kelley, “The Process of Causal Attribution,” *American Psychologist*, February 1973, pp. 107–128.
32. Mitchell and Wood, op. cit.
33. Robert G. Lord and Jonathan E. Smith, “Theoretical, Information Processing, and Situational Factors Affecting Attribution Theory Models of Organizational Behavior,” *Academy of Management Review*, January 1983, pp. 50–60.

REAL CASE: Motivation in the Name of Greed*

When the common stock in a company goes up dramatically, investors who have bought in before the rise stand to make a great deal of profit. A few years ago *Business Week* made an analysis of the stocks of companies that were about to be acquired by other firms and surprisingly found that, in many cases, the stock rose very quickly *before* the takeover was

*Source: Some of the information in this case can be found in William B. Glaberson, “Who’ll Be the Next to Fall?” *Business Week*, Dec. 1, 1986, pp. 31–33; and Chris Welles and Gary Weiss, “A Man Who Made a Career of Tempting Fate,” *Business Week*, Dec. 1, 1986, pp. 34–35.

announced. What conclusion did the reporters reach? There were a number of people who had inside information and were using it to buy into the stocks of firms before they went up.

The Securities and Exchange Commission (SEC) began to investigate and soon found that there were stock traders who, indeed, did have insider information. One of these was David Levine, who used the information to make millions of dollars. Another was Ivan Boesky, who allegedly received information from Levine and used it to buy stocks in advance of takeovers. For example, Boesky bought 337,000 shares of Nabisco and 301,800 of HNB in advance of public announcements. As a result, he made a profit of $8.1 million in a matter of weeks. In another case, Levine told Boesky about FMC's plans to recapitalize. Boesky made $1 million on the basis of this inside information.

Aware of the fact that Levine was an important source of inside information, Boesky struck a deal with him. He agreed to pay Levine 5 percent of all profits he made as a result of stocks he bought on the basis of tips from Levine and 1 percent of all profits based on inside information that helped him decide how to play a stock in which he already held a position.

Eventually, the SEC caught up with Levine and then Boesky. Levine was forced to return his gains and was barred for life from working in the brokerage industry. Boesky was fined over $100 million, and he allowed the authorities to tap his phone and listen to inside information being provided to him by others.

Why did Levine and Boesky get caught up in this type of illegal scheme? People who knew them said that the two felt that they were doing what many people on Wall Street had been doing for years. Additionally, these individuals felt that the two investors were more interested in making money in order to prove how clever they were than in amassing a fortune for the purpose of providing for their families.

1. How would you describe the motivation behind what Levine and Boesky did? Use Maslow's need hierarchy to explain your answer.
2. How could Alderfer's ERG theory be used to describe Levine's and Boesky's behavior?
3. How could the Porter-Lawler model be used to explain their behavior?

CASE: Star Salesperson

While growing up, Jerry Slate was always rewarded by his parents for showing independence. When he started school, he was successful both inside and outside the classroom. He was always striving to be things like traffic patroller and lunchroom monitor in grade school. Yet his mother worried about him because he never got along well with other children his own age. When confronted with this, Jerry would reply, "Well, I don't need them. Besides, they can't do things as well as I can. I don't have time to help them; I'm too busy improving myself." Jerry went on to do very well in both high school and college. He was always at or near the top of his class academically and was a very good long-distance runner for the track teams in high school and college. In college he shied away from joining a fraternity and lived in an apartment by himself. Upon graduation he went to work for a large insurance company and soon became one of the top salespersons. Jerry is very proud of the fact that he was one of the top five salespersons in six out of the eight years he has been with the company.

At the home office of the insurance company, the executive committee in charge of making major personnel appointments was discussing the upcoming vacancy of the sales manager's job for the Midwestern region. The personnel manager gave the following report: "As you know, the Midwestern region is lagging far behind our other regions as far as sales go. We need a highly motivated person to take that situation over and turn it around. After an extensive screening process, I am recommending that Jerry Slate be offered this position. As you know, Jerry has an outstanding record with the company and is highly motivated. I think he is the person for the job."

1. Do you agree with the personnel manager? Why or why not?
2. Considering Jerry's background, what motives discussed in the chapter would appear to be very intense in Jerry? What motives would appear to be very low? Give specific evidence from the case for each motive.
3. What type of motivation is desirable for people in sales positions? What type of motivation is desirable for people in managerial positions?

CASE: What Do They Want?

Mike Riverer is vice president of manufacturing and operations of a medium-size pharmaceutical firm in the Midwest. Mike has a Ph.D. in chemistry but has not been directly involved in research and new-product development for twenty years. He is from the "school of hard knocks" when it comes to managing operations, and he runs a "tight ship." The company does not have a turnover problem, but it is obvious to Mike and other key management personnel that the hourly people are only putting in their eight hours a day. They are not working anywhere near their full potential. Mike is very upset with the situation because, with rising costs, the only way that the company can continue to prosper is to increase the productivity of its hourly people.

Mike called in his personnel manager and laid it on the line. "What is it with our people, anyway? Your wage surveys show that we pay near the top in this region, our conditions are tremendous, and our fringes choke a horse. Yet these people still are not motivated. What in the world do they want?" The personnel manager replied, "I have told you and the president time after time that money, conditions, and benefits are not enough. Employees also need other things to motivate them. Also, I have been conducting some random confidential interviews with some of our hourly people, and they tell me that they are very discouraged because, no matter how hard they work, they get the same pay and opportunities for advancement as their coworkers who are just scraping by." Mike then replied, "Okay, you are the motivation expert; what do we do about it? We *have* to increase their performance."

1. Explain the "motivation problem" in this organization in terms of the content models of Maslow, Alderfer, and Herzberg. What are the "other things" that the personnel manager is referring to in speaking of things besides money, conditions, and fringe benefits that are needed to motivate employees?
2. Explain the motivation of the employees in this company in terms of one or more of the process models. On the basis of the responses during the confidential interviews, what would you guess are some of the expectancies, valences, inequities, and attributions of the employees in this company? How about Mike? Do you think he is internally or externally controlled?
3. How would you respond to Mike's last question and statement if you were the personnel manager in this company?

CASE: Tom, Dick, and Harry

You are in charge of a small department and have three subordinates—Tom, Dick, and Harry. The key to the success of your department is to keep these employees as motivated as possible. Here is a brief summary profile on each of these subordinates.

Tom is the type of employee who is hard to figure out. His absenteeism record is much higher than average. He greatly enjoys his family (a wife and three small children) and thinks they should be central to his life. The best way to describe Tom is to say that he is kind of a throwback to the hippie generation and believes deeply in the values of that culture. As a result, the things that the company can offer him really inspire him very little. He feels that the job is simply a means of financing his family's basic needs and little else. Overall, Tom does an adequate job and is very conscientious, but all attempts to get him to do more have failed. He has charm and is friendly, but he is just not "gung-ho" for the company. He is pretty much allowed to "do his own thing" as long as he meets the minimal standards of performance.

Dick is in many respects opposite from Tom. Like Tom, he is a likable guy, but unlike Tom, Dick responds well to the company's rules and compensation schemes and has a high degree of personal loyalty to the company. The problem with Dick is that he will not do very much independently. He does well with what is assigned to him, but he is not very creative or even dependable when he is on his own. He also is a relatively shy person who is not very assertive when dealing with people outside the department. This hurts his performance to some degree because he cannot immediately sell himself or the department to other departments in the company or to top management.

Harry, on the other hand, is a very assertive person. He will work for money and would readily change jobs for more money. He really works hard for the company but expects the company also to work for him. In his present job, he feels no qualms about working a sixty-hour week, if the money is there. Even though he has a family and is supporting his mother, he once quit a job cold when his employer didn't give him a raise on the premise that he was already making too much. He is quite a driver. A manager at his last place of employment indicated that, while Harry did do an excellent job for the company, his personality was so strong that they were glad to get rid of him. His former boss noted that Harry just seemed to be pushing all the time. If it wasn't for more money, it was for better fringe benefits; he never seemed satisfied.

1. Can you explain Tom's, Dick's, and Harry's motivation by one or more of the work-motivation models discussed in this chapter?
2. Using Alderfer's ERG theory, what group of core needs seems to dominate each of these three subordinates?
3. Using the attribution-theory approach, what type of locus of control do you feel guides each of these three employees in his present job?

10 Motivation Applied: Job Design and Goal Setting

In the football special issue of *Sports Illustrated*, Oklahoma's All-American linebacker Brian Bosworth was quoted as saying that at a summer job at General Motors's Oklahoma City plant, coworkers taught him how to be creative in assembly work. He explained that they showed him how to insert bolts in hard-to-reach places so they would rattle when the proud new car owner would turn a corner or hit a bump. The flashy—some would say nasty—"Boz" (6 feet 2 inches, 240 pounds of dynamite on the football field) proudly announced that "if you own a Celebrity or Century made in 1985 in Oklahoma City, that car is [messed up] if I had anything to do with it." He declared that each bolt carried a note that said: "Aha! You found me!" and glibly added, "I love the thought of people going absolutely crazy, saying, 'Where is that . . . rattle coming from?'"

Obviously, the General Motors Corporation and the state of Oklahoma were embarrassed by Bosworth's creativity. As a spokeswoman for General Motors pointed out, "plant employees were upset by the comments, especially someone saying something like that in this age of competitiveness." Boz received so much heat that he later denied putting the loose bolts in the cars. He has since moved on to the National Football League as a starting linebacker for the Seattle Seahawks.

Source: Adapted from "Boz Retreats," *Lincoln Journal*, Oct. 14, 1986, p. 12.

Learning Objectives

- DISCUSS the background of job design as an applied area of work motivation.
- DEFINE the job enrichment and job characteristics approach to job design.
- PRESENT the quality of work life (QWL) and sociotechnical approach to job design.
- EXPLAIN goal setting theory and guidelines from research.
- DESCRIBE management by objectives (MBO).

The preceding chapter was devoted to the basic motivational process and the various theoretical approaches to work motivation. In this chapter the more applied areas of motivation are examined: job design and goal setting. In recent years, relatively more research has been generated in these two areas than elsewhere in the field of organizational behavior. It is becoming increasingly clear that appropriately designing jobs can have a positive impact on both employee satisfaction and quality of performance. The same is true of goal setting, which has been held up as a prototypical model for how theory should or can lead to application. The purpose of this chapter is to give some of the background, review the related research, and spell out some of the specific applications for these important areas of the field of organizational behavior.

Job Design

Job design has emerged as an important application area for work motivation and the study of organizational behavior. In particular, job design is based on an extensive and still-growing theoretical base, it has had considerable research attention in recent years, and it is being widely applied to the actual practice of management.

Initially, the field of organizational behavior paid attention only to job enrichment approaches to job design. Now, with *quality of work life* (QWL) becoming a major societal issue in this country and throughout the world, job design has taken a broader perspective. Figure 10.1 summarizes the various dimensions of a comprehensive look at job design. Job enrichment still dominates the job design literature on organizational behavior, but from the perspective of job characteristics rather than Herzberg's motivators. Goal setting is beginning to be linked to the design of jobs, and the sociotechnical approach to job design is most closely associated with QWL. Job engineering, job enlargement, and job rotation are considered to have historical significance for job design, but they are not in the current mainstream of job design research or application.

Background on Job Design

Job design concerns and approaches are usually considered to have begun with the scientific management movement at the turn of the century. Pioneering

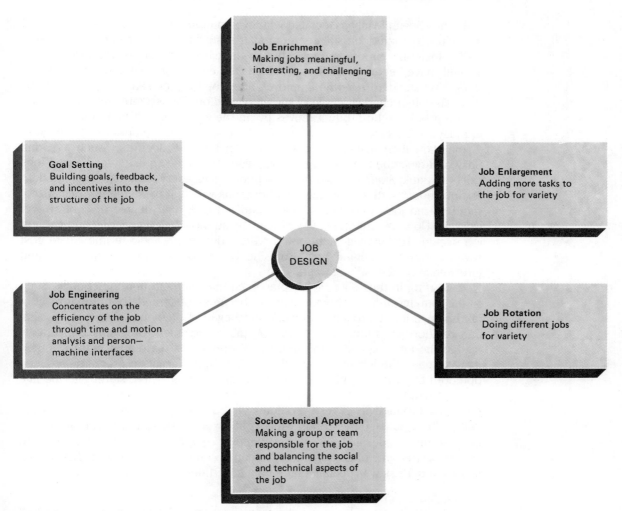

FIGURE 10.1 Various approaches to job design.
(*Source*: Adapted from Don Hellriegel, John W. Slocum, and Richard W. Woodman, *Organizational Behavior*, 4th ed., West, St. Paul, Minn., 1986, p. 363.)

scientific managers such as Frederick W. Taylor and Frank Gilbreth systematically examined jobs with techniques such as time and motion analysis. Their goal was to maximize human efficiency in jobs. Taylor suggested that task design might be the most prominent single element in scientific management.

The scientific management approach evolved into what is now generally called *job engineering*. This industrial engineering approach is concerned with product, process, and tool design; plant layout; standard operating procedures; work measurement and standards; worker methods; and human-machine interactions. It has been the dominant form of job design analysis since the turn of the century; it went hand in hand with automation in the previous generation, and it has been closely associated with cybernation (automatic feedback control mechanisms) and sophisticated computer systems in more recent times. Especially blue-collar production jobs, but an increasing number of white-collar jobs as well, have become highly specialized (the employee does one or a very few tasks) and standardized (the employee does the task the same way every time).

The often cited example of the employee on the assembly line who puts a nut on a bolt as the product moves by on the conveyor belt is all too common in today's manufacturing plants across the country. And, unfortunately, in order to maintain their sanity, some of those on the line do things such as Brian Bosworth described in the opening vignette. The same types of specialized jobs exist in banks, offices, hospitals, schools, and every other kind of modern organizational setting. The general consensus was that these highly specialized, standardized jobs were very efficient and led to a high degree of control over workers. Up to recent times, few people questioned the engineering approach to job design. Top management could readily determine and see immediate cost savings from job engineering. But side effects on quality, absenteeism, and turnover were generally ignored.

Starting in the 1950s, some practicing managers around the country, such as the founder of IBM, Thomas Watson, became concerned about the impact of job engineering approaches to work and began implementing job enlargement and rotation programs. Essentially, the job enlargement programs horizontally loaded the job (expanded the number of operations performed by the worker, that is, made the job less specialized), and the job rotation programs reduced boredom by switching people around to various jobs. Then, starting in the late 1960s, there began to be increasing concern with employee dissatisfaction and declining productivity. These problems were felt to be largely the result of so-called "blue-collar blues" and "white-collar woes." There is now an awakened interest in job design, and it has become the focus of attention for both academicians and practitioners of human resources management. Newspaper stories and TV news specials commonly have titles such as the following:

"Is the American Worker Alienated?"
"Today's Worker: Idealism's Gone"
"Is the Work Ethic Going out of Style?"
"Boredom Spells Trouble"
"If Japan Can, Why Can't We?"

A new look at job design seemed to provide a ready answer to the problems of stagnated productivity and deteriorating human resources of organizations. In particular, the reported successes of the early job enlargement programs, plus the increasingly popular motivation theories of Maslow and Herzberg (discussed in the last chapter), led first to the job enrichment movement in job design.

Job Enrichment

Job enrichment represents an extension of the earlier, more simplified job rotation and job enlargement techniques of job design. Since it is a direct outgrowth of

TABLE 10.1 Examples of Job Enrichment

Old Situation	Situation after Job Enrichment
Each employee was rotated among all machines.	Each employee is assigned to only two machines.
When machine failure occurred, operator called on maintenance group.	Each operator is given training in maintenance; each conducts preventive and corrective maintenance on the two machines for which he or she is responsible.
Operator changed the slicing blade (the most important component of the machine) following a rigid rule contained in a manual.	Operator is given authority to decide when to replace the blade, based on his or her own judgment.
Supervisor monitored operator and corrected unsatisfactory performance.	A performance feedback system has been developed that provides daily information on operators' work quality directly to them.
Individuals performed a specialized task on units passing by them.	Three- to five-person teams build an entire unit.
Supervisor decided who should do what.	The team decides who should do what.
Inspectors and supervisor tested output and corrected performance.	The team conducts its own quality audits.

Source: Adapted from Ross A. Webber, *Management,* rev. ed., Irwin, Homewood, Ill., 1979, p. 82. These examples were provided to Webber by Davis R. Sirota, Wharton School, University of Pennsylvania.

Herzberg's two-factor theory of motivation, the assumption is that in order to motivate personnel, the job must be designed to provide opportunities for achievement, recognition, responsibility, advancement, and growth. The technique entails "enriching" the job so that these factors are included. In particular, *job enrichment* is concerned with designing jobs that include a greater variety of work content; require a higher level of knowledge and skill; give workers more autonomy and responsibility in terms of planning, directing, and controlling their own performance; and provide the opportunity for personal growth and a meaningful work experience. As opposed to job enlargement, which horizontally loads the job, job enrichment *vertically* loads the job; for example, there are not necessarily more tasks to perform, but more responsibility and autonomy. Table 10.1 gives some specific examples of job enrichment.

Similar to the other application techniques discussed in this book, job enrichment is not a panacea for all job design problems facing modern management. Job enrichment is a valuable motivational technique, but management must use it selectively and give proper recognition to the complex human and situational variables. The newer job characteristics models of job enrichment are beginning to do this.

The Job Characteristics Approach to Task Design

To meet some of the limitations of the Herzberg approach to job enrichment (which he prefers to call *orthodox job enrichment,* or OJE), a group of researchers has begun to concentrate on the relationship between certain job characteristics or the job scope and employee motivation. J. Richard Hackman and Greg Oldham

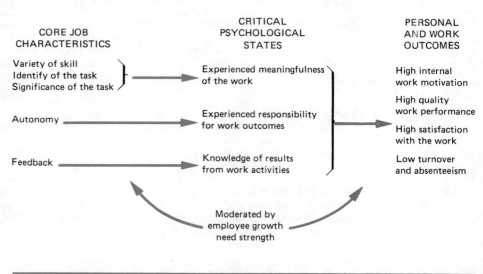

FIGURE 10.2 The Hackman-Oldham job characteristics model of work motivation. (*Source*: Adapted from J. Richard Hackman and Greg R. Oldham, "Motivation through the Design of Work: Test of a Theory." *Organizational Behavior and Human Performance*, vol. 16, 1976, pp. 250–279.)

developed the most widely recognized model of job characteristics shown in Figure 10.2. This model recognizes that certain job characteristics contribute to certain psychological states and that the strength of employees' need for growth has an important moderating effect. Table 10.2 summarizes what is meant by each of the job characteristics and psychological states.

TABLE 10.2 The Dimensions in the Hackman-Oldham Model

Core Job Dimensions

1. Variety of *skill*. This refers to the degree to which the job requires the person to do different things and involves the use of a number of different skills, abilities, and talents.
2. *Identity of the task*. This involves a complete module of work; the person can do the job from beginning to end with a visible outcome.
3. *Significance of the task*. This is concerned with the importance of the job. Does it have a significant impact on others—both internal and external to the organization?
4. *Autonomy*. This refers to the amount of freedom, independence, and discretion the person has in areas such as scheduling the work, making decisions, and determining how to do the job.
5. *Feedback*. This involves the degree to which the job provides the person with clear and direct information about job outcomes and performance.

Critical Psychological States

1. *Experienced meaningfulness*. This is concerned with the extent to which the person experiences the work as important, valuable, and worthwhile.
2. *Experienced responsibility*. This is concerned with the degree to which the individual feels personally responsible or accountable for the results of the work.
3. *Knowledge of results*. This involves the degree to which the person understands on a regular basis how effectively he or she is performing in the job.

Source: Adapted from David A. Nadler, J. Richard Hackman, and Edward E. Lawler, *Managing Organizational Behavior*, Little, Brown, Boston, 1979, pp. 81–82.

In essence, the model says that certain job characteristics lead to critical psychological states. That is, skill variety, task identity, and task significance lead to experienced meaningfulness; autonomy leads to the feeling of responsibility; and feedback leads to knowledge of results. The more these three psychological states are present, the more employees will feel good about themselves when they perform well. Hackman states: "The model postulates that internal rewards are obtained by an individual when he *learns* (knowledge of results) that he *personally* (experienced responsibility) has performed well on a task that he *cares* about (experienced meaningfulness)."[1] Hackman then goes on to point out that these internal rewards are reinforcing to employees, causing them to perform well. If they don't perform well, they will try harder in order to get the internal rewards that good performance brings. He concludes: "The net result is a self-perpetuating cycle of positive work motivation powered by self-generated rewards. This cycle is predicted to continue until one or more of the three psychological states is no longer present, or until the individual no longer values the internal rewards that derive from good performance."[2]

An example of an enriched job according to the Hackman-Oldham job characteristics model would be that of a surgeon. Surgeons must draw on a wide variety of skills and abilities; usually surgeons can readily identify the task because they handle patients from beginning to end (that is, they play a role in the diagnosis, perform the operation, and are responsible for postoperative care and follow-up); the job has life-and-death significance; there is a great deal of autonomy, since surgeons have the final word on all decisions concerning patients; and there is clear, direct feedback on whether the operation was successful. At the other extreme would be assembly line workers in blue-collar jobs or clerk-typists in white-collar jobs. All five core job dimensions would be low or nonexistent in the latter jobs.

There are several ways that the Hackman-Oldham model can be used to diagnose the degree of task scope that a job possesses. For instance, a manager could simply assess a particular job by clinically analyzing it according to the five core dimensions, as was done in the example of the surgeon's job, discussed above. Others have suggested a specific checklist, which would include such items as the use of inspectors or checkers, labor pools, or narrow spans of control, to help pinpoint deficiencies in the core dimensions.[3] More systematically, Hackman and Oldham have developed a questionnaire, the Job Diagnostic Survey (JDS), to analyze jobs. The questions on this survey yield a quantitative score that can be used to calculate an overall measure of job enrichment, or what is increasingly called *job scope*—to differentiate it from Herzberg-type job enrichment. The formula for this motivating potential score (MPS) is the following:

$$\text{MPS} = \left[\frac{\text{skill variety} + \text{task identity} + \text{task significance}}{3} \right] \times \text{autonomy} \times \text{feedback}$$

Notice that the job characteristics of skill variety, task identity, and task significance are combined and divided by 3, while the characteristics of autonomy and feedback stand alone. Also, since skill variety, task identity, and task significance are additive, any one or even two of these characteristics could be completely missing and the person could still experience meaningfulness, but if either autonomy or feedback were missing, the job would offer no motivating potential (MPS = 0) because of the multiplicative relationships.

The JDS is a widely used instrument to measure task characteristics or task scope, but the research on the impact that the motivating potential of a job has on job satisfaction and performance is not that clear. Most of the support for the model comes from Hackman and his colleagues, who claim that people on enriched jobs (according to their characteristics as measured by the JDS) are definitely more motivated and satisfied and, although the evidence is not as strong, may have better attendance and performance effectiveness records.[4]

Emerging Approaches to Task Design

The Hackman-Oldham model and the JDS measurement tool still constitute the dominant task characteristics approach to job design, but there are also some other models and measurement techniques that offer variations. The need for alternatives to the traditional task characteristics approach is becoming increasingly clear to those who study the relationship between job scope and satisfaction or other outcomes. Of particular importance are employees' *perceptions* of the task characteristics and the role of *moderating variables.* For example, studies have shown that perceptual assessments of task characteristics vary with the individual's frame of reference and job attitudes.[5] Thus, the effect of the task design may have nothing to do with the objective characteristics of the job but, rather, be associated with the individual's perception of the job design.

This concern with the impact of employee perceptions of task scope is closely related to the importance that contemporary researchers are also placing on moderating variables in the analysis of job design. The original work on job characteristics models and the more recent studies have begun to identify a number of important moderating effects on the job scope–job satisfaction relationship.[6] It is generally recognized, for example, that the need strength of the employee will have an important moderating effect on the relationships between job scope and employee outcomes.[7] However, a comprehensive analysis is critical of the theoretical statements of the job characteristics model in general and of the hypothesized moderator variables in particular.[8]

Guidelines for Redesigning Jobs

To redesign jobs, specific guidelines such as those found in Figure 10.3 are offered. Such easily implementable guidelines make the job design area popular and practical for more effective human resource management. An example would be the recent application in a large department store.[9] In a training session format, the sales employees' jobs were redesigned in the following manner:

1. *Skill variety:* The salespeople were asked to try to think of and use
   a. different selling approaches
   b. new merchandise displays
   c. better ways of recording sales and keeping records

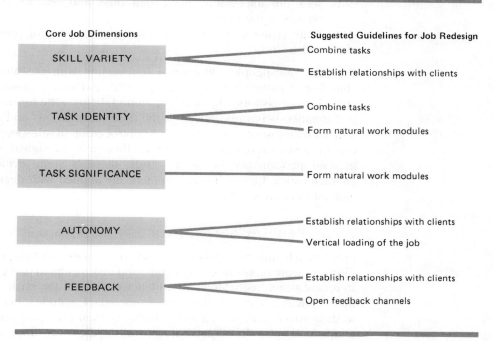

FIGURE 10.3
Specific guidelines for redesigning jobs for the more effective practice of human resources management.
(*Source*: Adapted from J. Richard Hackman, Greg R. Oldham, Robert Janson, and Kenneth A. Purdy, "A New Strategy for Job Enrichment," *California Management Review*, Summer 1975, pp. 57–71.)

2. *Task identity:* The salespeople were asked to
   a. keep a personal record of daily sales volume in dollars
   b. keep a record of number of sales/customers
   c. mark off a display area that you consider yours—keep it complete and orderly
3. *Task significance:* The salespeople were reminded that
   a. selling a product was the basic overall objective of the store
   b. the appearance of the display area was important to selling
   c. to customers, they are "the store;" they were told that courtesy and pleasantness help to build the store's reputation and set the stage for future sales
4. *Autonomy:* The salespeople were
   a. encouraged to develop and use their own unique approach and sales pitch
   b. allowed freedom to select their own break and lunch times
   c. encouraged to make suggestions for changes in all phases of the policy and operations
5. *Feedback from the job itself:* Salespeople were
   a. encouraged to keep personal records of their own sales volume
   b. encouraged to keep a sales/customer ratio
   c. reminded that establishing a good rapport with customers is also a success; they were told that if the potential customer leaves with a good feeling about the store and its employees, the salesperson has been successful
6. *Feedback from agents:* Salespeople were encouraged to
   a. observe and help each other with techniques of selling

   b. seek out information from their boss and relevant departments on all phases of their jobs
   c. invite customer reactions and thoughts concerning merchandise, service, and so forth

Both the salespeoples' functional (conversing with customers, showing merchandise, handling returns, and so forth) and dysfunctional (socializing with coworkers or visitors, idly standing around, being gone for no legitimate reason) performance behaviors moved in the desired directions and a subanalysis also indicated they were more satisfied. A control group of salespeople, with everything else the same except they did not have their jobs redesigned, showed no change in their performance behaviors. Thus, there is some evidence that the job characteristics approach can be practically applied with desirable performance and satisfaction results.

A Social Information Processing Approach

In addition to the contingency approach, a social information processing approach (SIPA) to work motivation in general[10] and task design in particular[11] has emerged in recent years. As Salancik and Pfeffer explain it, the basic premise of SIPA is that "individuals, as adaptive organisms, adapt attitudes, behaviors, and beliefs to their social context and to the reality of their own past and present behavior and situation."[12] Thus, according to SIPA, there are three major causes of a jobholder's perceptions, attitudes, and actual behavior:

1. The jobholder's cognitive evaluation of the real task environment
2. The jobholder's past actions, including reinforcement history and learning
3. The information that the immediate social context provides

Salancik and Pfeffer give the third point above the most weight. They suggest that social information or social cues are much more dominant in how jobholders view their tasks than the real task environment or past actions are. This approach to task design has generated considerable research in recent years.[13] The results to date have generally been quite supportive of the notion that social cues, such as negative versus positive coworker comments, may be more important to the way employees perceive their tasks than characteristics such as whether the job is enriched or unenriched. In other words, as in other areas of organizational behavior, the importance of the social environment is becoming recognized in the job design area. Most recently, research suggests that an integrated approach to job design that includes both objective job characteristics and social information may be the most effective.[14]

Quality of Work Life and Sociotechnical Design

So far, the discussion of job design has revolved mainly around the job enrichment approach and a micro perspective of the relationships between job characteristics or scope and employee satisfaction. The concern for quality of work life (QWL) and the accompanying sociotechnical approach to job design take a more macro perspective.

Unlike the job enrichment approach, QWL is not based on a particular theory, nor does it advocate a particular technique for application. Instead, QWL is more concerned with the overall climate of work. One recent analysis of QWL described it as "(1) a concern about the impact of work on people as well as on organization effectiveness, and (2) the idea of participation in organizational problem solving and decision making."[15] The recognized purpose is to change the climate at work so that the human-technological-organizational interface leads to a better quality of work life. Although how this is actually accomplished and exactly what is meant by a better *quality* of work life are still unclear, there are a number of analyses and applications of the closely associated sociotechnical approach to job design.

Unlike the more general concept of QWL, the sociotechnical approach to job design (which is sometimes even equated with QWL) has a systems theoretical base. In particular, the sociotechnical approach to job design is concerned with the interface between the technological system and the social system. In application, this translates into the redesign of technological work processes and the formation of autonomous, self-regulating work groups or teams. A few widely publicized projects have used this approach.

The Volvo Project

The sociotechnical approach to job design has an international flavor, and although the Swedish automaker Saab pioneered the use of autonomous work groups to work on automobile subassembly, the more widely publicized example is that of a Volvo automobile plant in Sweden. When Pehr Gyllenhammar took over as the head of Volvo, Sweden's largest employer, he was convinced that the very serious turnover and absenteeism problems were symptomatic of the values of the employees. Hand in hand with the emerging values of society as a whole, the Volvo employees were demanding more meaningful work—better pay and security, but also participation in the decision-making process and self-regulation. But the technological work process for making automobiles (that is, the assembly line) did not allow such values to be expressed, and the results were turnover, absenteeism, and low-quality performance.

Under Gyllenhammar's leadership, which took a sociotechnical approach, technological changes were made to reflect more of a natural module of work rather than a continuous work flow, and autonomous work groups were formed. These groups consisted of five to twelve workers who elected their own supervisors and scheduled, assigned, and inspected their own work. Group rather than individual piece rates were used, and all group members made the same amount, except the elected supervisor.

This sociotechnical approach (changing the technological process and utilizing autonomous, self-regulating work groups) was at first applied on a piecemeal basis around the company. Then the new Kalmar assembly plant was completely redesigned along the lines of a sociotechnical approach. On the technological side, the conventional continuous assembly line was changed so that the work remains stationary. A special carrier was developed to transport the car to the various work groups. On the social side, about twenty-five groups made up of about twenty members each perform work on the various modules of an automobile (electrical system, instrumentation, steering and controls, interior, and so forth). These work teams organize any way they want, and they contract with management to deliver a certain number of products per day, for example, brake systems installed or interiors finished. The workers have almost complete control over their own work, scheduling the pace of work and break times. Also important, these teams inspect their own work, and feedback is given to each group via a TV screen at the work station.

In line with more general quality of work-life objectives, a more humane work climate was designed for this Volvo plant. The plant layout is set up to be very light and airy and have a low noise level. There are carpeted "coffee corners," where the groups take their breaks, and there are well-equipped changing rooms.

After this approach to job design was installed at Volvo, turnover and absenteeism were reduced, and quality of work life was reportedly improved. To date, however, no systematic analysis has demonstrated that causal inferences can be made. However, the Volvo top management feel that their new approach to job design has been successful. The latest update from those at the scene is that there have been "false starts, errors, outright failures and, periodically, brilliant breakthroughs."[16] Objectively, the fact is that Kalmar, where QWL is used, has the lowest assembly costs of all Volvo plants.

Other Sociotechnical Projects

Although the Volvo project is the most famous, a few companies in the United States have also tried a sociotechnical approach to job design. Probably the most widely reported example is that of the General Foods plant in Topeka, Kansas, which produces Gaines pet food. Similar to the Kalmar Volvo plant, this Topeka plant was technologically designed to be compatible with autonomous work groups. The groups were set up in basically the same way as those at the Volvo plant. They had shared responsibility and worked for a coach rather than a supervisor. Status symbols such as parking privileges were abolished.

Initially, the reports on this General Foods project were very favorable. The employees themselves expressed very positive attitudes toward this new approach to work, and management reported that after implementing the project, 35 percent fewer employees were needed to run the plant, quality rejects dipped 92 percent below the industry norm, annual savings of $600,000 resulted from the reduction of variable manufacturing costs, and turnover dropped below the company average.[17] However, more recent reports do not paint such a rosy picture.[18] Some former employees at the Topeka plant indicate that the approach has steadily eroded. Apparently, some managers at the plant are openly hostile to the project because it has undermined their power, authority, and decision-making flexibility. The project became a media event, and some of the results need tempering.

Besides the General Foods project, General Motors, Weyerhaeuser, TRW, North American Tool & Die, Double Rainbow Gourmet Ice Creams, Rushton

Mining, Harman International, Heinz, and Nabisco have reportedly initiated sociotechnical programs similar to the General Foods project. According to mainly testimonial evidence, these programs have supposedly resulted in savings due to lower turnover, absenteeism, and accident rates; reduced supervision; better product and service quality; and more efficient working methods.[19] One comprehensive assessment carried out over a period of several years at the Harman International QWL project at Bolivar, Tennessee, concluded that

> . . . jobs objectively became more secure; productivity and product quality rose; accidents decreased at a faster rate than their industry average; minor accidents declined while minor illnesses rose; short-term absences due to sickness declined; manufacturing supplies and machine downtime increased; and employee earnings held steady. Also, grievances decreased 51 percent and absences due to lack of work decreased 94 percent.[20]

There is also some evidence that the larger the company in terms of number of employees, the more QWL-type programs there will be.[21] The accompanying Application Example gives the reasons why one CEO is sold on QWL for his company. There have also been reportedly successful applications in public-sector organizations such as the Tennessee Valley Authority and the city government of Jamestown, New York,[22] and to office systems.[23] Obviously, with the conflicting reports coming out of the Topeka plant serving as a reminder and the beginning of research indicating that QWL efforts may have little impact on economic performance,[24] more systematic evaluations are needed before any broad conclusions on the effectiveness of these sociotechnical programs can be drawn. But with the gathering societal support for the improvement of QWL,

---

Application Example

Why Quality of Work Life at JBM Electronics*

The head of St. Louis–based JBM Electronics, 61-year-old Irwin Mintz, was recently asked why his company was so deeply involved with quality of work life for its employees. He candidly gave, in reverse order, the following three reasons:

1. "I like to be liked. I'll admit it. And the better environment you create for your employees, the more they're going to think of you as one heck of a guy."
2. Besides the purely selfish reason, Mintz also notes that JBM, with sixty employees and 2.5 million in sales, has to compete for the best people with bigger companies in the area such as McDonnell Douglas. He states, "If salary were all we could offer, we'd never be able to attract and keep really first-rate people. There's got to be something else, something more important than money."
3. Most important to Mintz, however, is the impact that QWL has on performance and profits. In his words: "If this is a good place to work, a place where someone can do really good work and have fun doing it, feel full of excitement instead of full of fear, then we're going to get employees who will stay here longer and be more productive—we're going to be able to put out a superior product on a consistent basis, in a more efficient manner."

Source: Adapted from Gene Stone and Bo Burlingham, "Workstyle," *Inc.*, January 1986, pp. 47–48.

there is no question but that the sociotechnical approach should and will play an increasingly important role in job design in particular and in the field of organizational behavior in general.

Goal Setting

Goal setting is often given as an example of how the field of organizational behavior should progress from a sound theoretical foundation to sophisticated research to the actual application of more effective management practice. There has been considerable theoretical development of goal setting, coming mainly from the cognitively based work of Edwin Locke and his colleagues. To test the theory, there has been considerable research in both laboratory and field settings on the various facets of goal setting. Finally, and important to an applied field such as organizational behavior, goal setting has become an effective tool for the practice of human resources management and an overall performance system approach in the form of management by objectives, or MBO.

Theoretical Background of Goal Setting

A 1968 paper by Locke is usually considered to be the seminal work on a theory of goal setting.[25] He gives considerable credit to Ryan[26] for stimulating his thinking on the role that intention plays in human behavior, and he also suggests that goal-setting theory really goes back to scientific management at the turn of the century. He credits its first exponent, Frederick W. Taylor, with being the "father of employee motivation theory,"[27] and he says that Taylor's use "of tasks was a forerunner of modern day goal setting."[28]

Although Locke argues that expectancy theories of work motivation originally ignored goal setting and were nothing more than "cognitive hedonism,"[29] his theoretical formulation for goal setting is very similar. He basically accepts the purposefulness of behavior, which comes out of Tolman's cognitive theorizing (see Chapter 1), and the importance of values or valence and consequences. Thus, as in the expectancy theories of work motivation (see Chapter 9), *values and value judgments,* which he defines as the things the individual acts upon to gain and/or to keep, are important cognitive determinants of behavior. He then goes on to say that emotions or desires are the way the person experiences these values. In addition to values, *intentions* or *goals* play an important role as cognitive determinants of behavior. It is here, of course, where Locke's theory of goal setting goes beyond expectancy theories of work motivation. He feels that people strive to attain goals in order to satisfy their emotions and desires. Goals provide a directional nature to people's behavior and guide their thoughts and actions to one outcome rather than another. The individual then responds and performs according to these intentions or goals, even if the goals are not attained. Consequences, feedback, or reinforcement are the result of these responses. Figure 10.4 summarizes the goal-setting theory. Reviews of the literature generally provide considerable support for the theory.[30]

As previously noted, except for the concept of intentions or goals, Locke's theory is very similar to the other process theories (most notably the Porter-

FIGURE 10.4
Locke's goal-setting theory of work motivation.

Lawler expectancy model) of work motivation and more recently has been explained in terms of attribution theory, discussed in the last chapter.[31] To Locke's credit, he does carefully point out that goal setting is not the only, or necessarily the most important, concept of work motivation. He notes that the concepts of need and value are the more fundamental concepts of work motivation and are, along with the person's knowledge and premises, what determine goals.

Unlike many other theorists, Locke is continually refining and developing his theory. Recently he has given attention to the role that commitment plays in the theory. He recognized from the beginning that if there is no commitment to goals, goal setting will not work. However, to clarify some of the confusion surrounding its use, Locke and his colleagues define commitment as "one's attachment to or determination to reach a goal, regardless of the goal's origin" and developed a cognitive model to explain the process.[32]

Locke is an ardent supporter of the cognitive interpretation of behavior and is an outspoken critic of the environmentally based operant theory of behavior and its applications through organizational behavior modification.[33] Despite his plea for a complex cognitive interpretation of behavior, he maintains: "Goal setting is simply the most directly useful motivational approach in a *managerial* context, since goals are the most immediate regulators of human action and are more easily modified than values of subconcious premises."[34] It is this practical utility of goal-setting theory that has made it an important contribution to the study and application of organizational behavior.

Research on the Impact of Goal Setting

Locke's theory has generated considerable research. In particular, a series of laboratory studies by Locke and his colleagues and a series of field studies by Gary Latham and his colleagues have been carried out to test the linkage between goal setting and performance:[35]

1. *Specific goals* are better than vague or general goals such as "do your best." In other words, giving a salesperson a specific quota or a worker an exact number of units to produce should be preferable to setting a goal such as "try as hard as you can" or "try to do better than last year."
2. *Difficult, challenging goals* are better than relatively easy, mundane goals. However, these goals must be reachable and not so hard to attain that they would be frustrating.
3. *"Owned" and accepted goals* arrived at through participation, seem preferable to assigned goals. Although the research is not as clear here as in the first two guidelines[36] there is evidence that people who set their goals through a participative process, and who thus own their goals, will perform better than

those who are told what their goals are going to be. As the accompanying Application Example demonstrates, personal goals can lead individuals to career success.

4. *Objective, timely feedback about progress toward goals* is preferable to no feedback. Although researchers are still trying to understand the exact effect of feedback (discussed further in Chapter 11), it is probably fair to say that feedback is a necessary but not sufficient condition for successful application of goal setting.

Application Example

Making Personal Goal Setting Pay Off*

Can personal goal setting really help get things done? The answer seems to be yes. Goals not only help people perform better, but can also be an important means of improving career opportunities and getting top dollar. For example, some goals that seem to have particular value to those interested in building a reputation as an expert in their career include the following:

1. *Get something published in your area of expertise.* Examples include writing an article or, even better, a book. Publications help one's expertise and are a good credential to have. The best publisher to use is one that currently markets to those in related career fields. Hence, the publication is likely to be read by relevant others, and the author's reputation will spread. Another good outlet is the local newspaper, which often publishes business-related articles. Many papers have a business section that caters specifically to those interested in picking up the latest information and tips.

2. *Be a lecturer or panelist.* This is another good way to get publicity, and there are many opportunities. Three common ones include guest teaching at a local university, being a luncheon speaker at a local club or professional group, and serving as a panelist for a job seminar at a local college.

3. *Get media coverage.* Work to get on radio or TV programs. Quite often local programmers are looking for people to interview or to discuss some recent topic of interest. If you can become known as a local expert in some area that is continually in the news such as productivity problems or how to manage people more effectively, you will be asked back time and again.

4. *Use professional associations.* The best way to become known as an expert in your area is by receiving recognition from your peers in professional associations. By joining these associations and becoming active first at the local- and then national-level meetings, you ensure that others in your field get to know who you are and what you stand for. As a result, your visibility in the marketplace increases and so do your chances of being tapped for more important, higher-paying jobs either in your company or with the competition.

Source: Adapted from "How to Boost Your Career Visibility—For Top Dollar," *Working Woman,* January 1987, p. 55.

Although the above practical guidelines are as sound as any in the entire field of organizational behavior, it must be remembered that, as with any complex phenomenon, there still appear to be many important moderating variables in the relationship between goal setting and performance, and there are some contradictory findings.[37] For example, a study by Latham and Saari found that a supportive management style had an important moderating effect and that, contrary to the results of previous studies, specific goals did not lead to better performance than a generalized goal such as "do your best."[38] However, another study did find a highly significant relationship between goal level and performance.[39] Another recent analysis indicates there are also some unexplored areas, such as the distinction between quantity and quality goals,[40] and task complexity,[41] that limit the application of goal setting. Despite some of the contrary findings, on balance there has been impressive support for the positive impact of setting specific, difficult goals that are accepted and of providing feedback on progress toward goals.

MBO: The Application of Goal Setting to System Performance

A logical extension of goal setting is the very popular, widely used management-by-objectives, or MBO, approach to planning, control, personnel appraisal, and overall system performance. MBO has been around for almost thirty years and thus preceded the theory and research on goal setting per se. MBO is usually attributed to Peter Drucker, who coined the term and suggested that a systematic approach to setting of objectives and appraising by results would lead to improved organizational performance and employee satisfaction. Today, practically every large business firm and a growing number of nonbusiness organizations have implemented some form of MBO.

Not surprisingly, universal agreement does not exist among scholars and practitioners on exactly what is meant by MBO. Despite the variations, there is general agreement that MBO involves a series of systematic steps that follow a process similar to the one shown in Figure 10.5. A review of these steps will clarify the MBO approach.

Setting Overall Objectives.
MBO takes a from-the-top-down approach. If MBO is implemented on an organization-wide basis, the top management team gets together to formulate overall objectives. The usual procedure is first to identify key-results areas in the organization. A key-results area is one that has the greatest impact on the overall performance of the organization. It may be sales volume or market share, production output, or quality of service. After the key-results areas are identified, measures of performance are determined. Objectives are always stated so that they can be objectively measured. Finally, the actual objectives are agreed upon (usually with input from all members of the top management staff but with final authority vested in the chief operating executive). These objectives are results-oriented and are stated in objective, measurable terms with target dates and accompanying action plans that propose how the objectives will be accomplished.

Developing the Organization for an MBO System.
After the overall objectives have been formulated, it is vital that the organization be prepared to

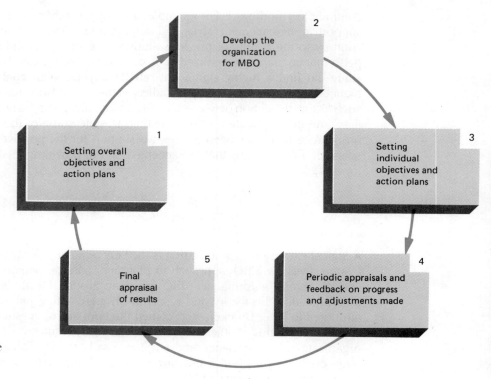

FIGURE 10.5 The MBO process.

implement the system downward. What too often happens is that the chief executive, or someone who is close to the executive, gets sold on the idea of MBO. A memo is sent out to all personnel saying that the organization will go onto an MBO system next Monday morning. This type of approach to implementing MBO is a good way of ensuring that the program will not work. The people and the organization itself must be developed so that MBO can be successfully implemented. Such an organization development effort often involves using the techniques that will be discussed in Chapter 20, on organization development. There may also be a need for a reorganization to accommodate the MBO system. The needed development may take anywhere from a few weeks to several years, depending on the current stage of development of the human resources of the organization.

Setting Individual Objectives. Once the overall objectives have been set and the organization is developed to the point of accommodating an MBO system, individual objectives are set. These individual objectives are determined by each superior-subordinate pair, starting at the top and going down as far as the system is to be implemented. The scenario for this process would be something like the following: The boss would contact each of his or her subordinates and say:

> As you know, we have completed our MBO orientation and development program, and it is now time to set individual objectives. I would like you to develop by next Tuesday a proposed set of objectives for your area of responsibility. Remember that your set of objectives should be in line with the organization's overall objectives, which you have a copy of, and they should be able to contribute to the objectives that you interact with, namely, my objectives, the other units' objectives on your same level, and your subordinates' objectives. Your objectives should be stated in quantifiable, measurable terms and should have a target date. I will also have some suggestions that I think should be given top priority for your area of responsibility. We will sit down and have an open give-and-take session until we reach a *mutually* agreeable set of objectives for your area of responsibility.

In line with the goal-setting research, these objectives should be specific, difficult, and accepted. Like the overall objectives, this set of individual objectives should also be accompanied by action plans developed to spell out how the objectives are to be accomplished.

Appraisal by Results. So far, only the setting-of-objectives part of MBO has been discussed. However, these objectives play a vital role in the feedback and appraisal part of MBO. Individuals will be given feedback and will be appraised on the basis of how they perform in accordance with the objectives that are set. This feedback and appraisal process takes place on both a periodic (at least every quarter in most MBO systems) and an annual basis. The appraisal sessions attempt to be diagnostic rather than purely evaluative. This means simply that the subordinate's superior assesses the reasons why objectives were either attained or not attained, rather than giving punishments or rewards for failure or success in meeting objectives.

   Periodic reviews are conducted in order to provide feedback and evaluate progress toward the attainment of objectives. They give the opportunity to make the necessary changes in objectives. Every organization is operating in such a dynamic environment that objectives set at the beginning of the period (usually the fiscal year) may be rendered obsolete in a few months because of changing conditions. Priorities and conditions are constantly changing; these must be monitored in the periodic review sessions, and the needed changes must be made. Constant revision of the individual objectives and, to a lesser degree, of the overall objectives makes MBO a living system that is adaptable to change. At the annual review session, an overall diagnosis and evaluation is made according to results attained, and the system starts over again.

Critical Analysis of MBO

Table 10.3 summarizes some of the generally recognized strengths and weaknesses of MBO systems. Such a list can serve as a beneficial guideline to more effective implementation. However, despite its widespread use and the relatively great amount of research conducted on goal setting per se, there has been relatively little systematic research on the impact of MBO.

Although there are numerous descriptive articles on MBO[42] (that is, they define the approach, suggest the steps for implementation, and analyze the advantages and disadvantages), to date only a couple of studies have used a control group design and hard performance data to analyze the impact of MBO on performance. One comprehensive study in an industrial setting did find that MBO had a favorable impact on several measures of qualitative and quantitative performance.[43] But a later study that evaluated MBO in a bank found no statistically significant differences between the experimental (those under MBO) and the control group (those not under MBO) on several performance measures.[44] Another study which examined the impact that MBO had on performance and satisfaction in a state government human services agency had somewhat, but not completely, supportive findings.[45] Two of the five measures of the quantity of performance showed statistically significant improvement, and a combined measure was also significant. A matched control group (those not on the MBO system) showed no improvement in these measures over the same time period. Although a control group was not available for comparison, the MBO group did show significant improvement on all three measures of quality of performance. The MBO group also indicated a significant improvement in satisfaction with supervision, but there was a nonsignificant change in job satisfaction.

With the few exceptions reported above, which have yielded mixed results, the other reported studies on the impact of MBO do not use control group designs and depend on questionnaires that attempt to tap the perceptions of performance improvement and managerial attitudes. Most of the subjective criticism relates mainly to how managers actually use the MBO process rather than how it is supposed to be used.[46]

TABLE 10.3 Potential Advantages of, and Problems with, MBO

Potential Advantages	Potential Problems
There can be improved short- and long-range planning.	MBO may be used as a whip, especially when it is closely tied to wage and salary programs.
MBO can provide a procedure for controlling work progress and results.	MBO may fail to receive continual top management commitment and support and may not reach the lower managerial levels.
There can be improved commitment to the organization because of increased motivation, loyalty, and participation of employees.	There may be an overemphasis on production and productivity.
MBO can lead to improved clarity of the manager's role and priorities.	Managers may not be adequately trained in the MBO process or in effective ways to coach and counsel subordinates.
There can be improved communication— especially upward and horizontal.	MBO may fail to provide adequate personal incentives to improve performance. The emphasis is only on the benefits to the organization and not on the development of the participating managers.

Source: Adapted from John M. Ivancevich et al., "Goal Setting: The Tenneco Approach to Personnel Development and Managerial Effectiveness," *Organizational Dynamics,* Winter 1978, pp. 60–61.

Thus, once again there is not enough research on overall MBO systems to draw any sound conclusions. But, as the earlier discussion of goal setting pointed out and as the relatively great amount of research on participation and feedback has demonstrated (this will be covered in Chapter 11), research on the various subelements can be used to support MBO. There seems little question that MBO holds enough promise to continue its widespread applications. It is readily adaptable and can be used in conjunction with other modern human resources management techniques such as job enrichment and organizational behavior modification, which is examined in Chapter 12. MBO's greatest advantage is that it combines good, sound management techniques for decision making, communication, and control with basic behavioral requirements. Goal setting, feedback about performance, participative decision making, open two-way communication, and self-control are some of the very positive characteristics of MBO. This unique combination makes MBO worthy of careful consideration. Although there can be problems and although more research is needed, MBO, if carefully implemented and developed, seems to hold a great deal of promise for management in the future.

Summary

This chapter dealt with two of the most important application areas that have emerged in the field of organizational behavior and human resources management. The first part examined job design. Although the concern for designing jobs goes back to the scientific management movement at the turn of the century, the recent concern for the quality of work life (QWL) has led to renewed interest in, and research on, job design. The older job engineering and job enlargement and rotation approaches have given way to a job enrichment approach. Based primarily on the work of Herzberg, job enrichment has been popular (at least in the literature) but may be overly simplistic.

The newest approach to job design tries to determine the important job characteristics that relate to psychological or motivational states that in turn relate to employee satisfaction and performance. Characteristics such as skill variety, task identity, task significance, autonomy, and feedback do seem to be related to employee satisfaction and quality of work. But the way employees perceive these characteristics and the importance of moderating variables such as growth-need strength are being shown to have an important impact on the relationship between job scope and job satisfaction and employee performance. Alternative models are beginning to account for these effects and also to recognize the impact of more macrooriented variables such as organization structure and technology. More in line with this macro perspective and incorporating QWL concerns is the sociotechnical approach to job design. Sociotechnical projects at Volvo in Sweden and at General Foods and other companies in this country have reportedly been quite successful. Yet, as is true of the other techniques discussed in this book, more systematic research is needed for the future.

The last half of the chapter dealt with the applications-oriented areas of goal setting in general and of management by objectives (MBO) in particular. Basing his approach on a cognitive perspective, Locke has developed a goal-setting theory of motivation. This theory emphasizes the important relationship between goals and performance. Laboratory and field studies have generally verified this relationship. In particular, the most effective performance seems to result when specific, difficult goals are accepted and when feedback on progress and results is provided. An extension and systematic application of the goal-setting approach is MBO. A total performance system, MBO is widely used, and although more research is needed, this use seems justified.

Questions for Discussion and Review

1. Compare and contrast the engineering versus the enrichment approach to job design.
2. What are the core job characteristics in the Hackman-Oldham model? How do you calculate the motivating potential of a job? How would a professor's job and a janitor's job measure up on these characteristics? Be specific in your answer.
3. Describe the sociotechnical project at Volvo. Would you rather work there or at the typical automobile plant in this country? Why?
4. Considering that former employees at the General Foods plant indicate there may be some problems with sociotechnical design, what do you think the future holds for this type of approach? Do you think QWL will and should be legislated? Why?
5. In your own words, describe the theory behind goal setting. What has the research generally found in testing this theory?
6. Summarize the five basic steps of MBO. What have been the research findings on MBO?

References

1. J. Richard Hackman, "Work Design," in J. Richard Hackman and J. Lloyd Suttle (eds.), *Improving Life at Work*, Goodyear, Santa Monica, Calif., 1977, p. 129.
2. Ibid., p. 130.
3. David Whitsett, "Where Are Your Enriched Jobs?" *Harvard Business Review*, January–February 1975, pp. 74–80.
4. J. Richard Hackman, Greg R. Oldham, Robert Janson, and Kenneth Purdy, "A New Strategy for Job Enrichment," *California Management Review*, Summer 1975, pp. 55–71.
5. Charles A. O'Reilly, G. Nicholas Parlette, and Joan R. Bloom, "Perceptual Measures

of Task Characteristics: The Biasing Effects of Differing Frames of Reference and Job Attitudes," *Academy of Management Proceedings,* 1979, pp. 64–68.

6. Eugene F. Stone, "The Moderating Effect of Work Related Values on the Job Scope–Job Satisfaction Relationship," *Organizational Behavior and Human Performance,* April 1976, pp. 147–168; Daniel Ganster, "Individual Differences and Task Design: A Laboratory Experiment," *Organizational Behavior and Human Performance,* August 1980, pp. 131–146; and Cathy J. Rudolf, Lawrence Peters, and Thomas Reynolds, "The Moderating Effect of Job Adaptation on the Job Scope Affective Response Relationship," *Academy of Management Proceedings,* 1979, pp. 69–73.

7. Paul E. Spector, "Higher-Order Need Strength as a Moderator of the Job Scope–Employee Outcome Relationship: A Meta Analysis," *Journal of Occupational Psychology,* vol. 58, no. 2, 1985, pp. 119–127.

8. Karlene Roberts and William Glick, "The Job Characteristics Approach to Task Design: A Critical Review," *Journal of Applied Psychology,* April 1981, pp. 193–217.

9. Fred Luthans, Barbara Kemmerer, Robert Paul, and Lew Taylor, "The Impact of a Job Redesign Intervention on Sales-persons' Observed Performance Behaviors," *Group and Organization Studies,* March 1987, pp. 55–72.

10. Terence R. Mitchell, "Motivation: New Directions for Theory, Research and Practice," *Academy of Management Review,* January 1982, p. 80.

11. Gerald Salancik and Jeffrey Pfeffer, "A Social Information Processing Approach to Job Attitudes and Task Design," *Administrative Science Quarterly,* June 1978, pp. 224–253.

12. Ibid., p. 226.

13. See Gary J. Blau and Ralph Katerberg, "Toward Enhancing Research with the Social Information Processing Approach to Job Design," *Academy of Management Review,* October 1982, pp. 543–550; William H. Glick, G. Douglas Jenkins, and Nina Gupta, "Method versus Substance: How Strong Are Underlying Relationships between Job Characteristics and Attitudinal Outcomes?" *Academy of Management Journal,* September 1986, pp. 441–464; and Joe G. Thomas, "Sources of Social Information," *Human Relations,* vol. 39, no. 9, 1986, pp. 855–870.

14. Ricky W. Griffin, Thomas S. Bateman, Sandy J. Wayne, and Thomas C. Head, "Objective and Social Factors as Determinants of Task Perceptions and Responses: An Integrated Perspective and Empirical Investigation," *Academy of Management Journal,* September 1987, pp. 501–523.

15. David A. Nadler and Edward E. Lawler III, "Quality of Work Life: Perspectives and Directions," *Organizational Dynamics,* Winter 1983, p. 26.

16. Berth Jönsson and Alden G. Lank, "Volvo: A Report on the Workshop on Production Technology and Quality of Working Life," *Human Resources Management,* Winter 1985, p. 463.

17. Richard E. Walton, "How to Counter Alienation in the Plant," *Harvard Business Review,* November–December 1972, p. 77.

18. "Stonewalling Plant Democracy," *Business Week,* Mar. 28, 1977, pp. 78–81, and Lyle Yorks and David Whitsett, "Hawthorne, Topeka, and the Issue of Science versus Advocacy in Organizational Behavior," *Academy of Management Review,* January 1985, pp. 24–26.

19. Deborah Shaw Cohen, "The Quality of Work Life Movement," *Training HRD,* January 1979, p. 24; Gene Stone and Bo Burlingham, "Workstyle," *Inc.,* January 1986, pp. 45–54.

20. Barry A. Macy, "The Quality-of-Worklife Project at Bolivar, *Monthly Labor Review,* July 1980, p. 42.

21. Gerald D. Klein, "Employee-Centered Productivity and QWL Programs: Findings from an Area Study," *National Productivity Review*, Autumn 1986, p. 350.
22. Cohen, op. cit.
23. Joyce M. Ranney, "Bringing Sociotechnical Systems from the Factory to the Office," *National Productivity Review*, Spring 1986, pp. 124–133.
24. Harry C. Katz, Thomas A. Kochan, and Mark R. Weber, "Assessing the Effects of Industrial Relations Systems and Efforts to Improve the Quality of Working Life on Organizational Effectiveness," *Academy of Management Journal*, September 1985, pp. 509–526.
25. Edwin A. Locke, "Toward a Theory of Task Motivation and Incentives," *Organizational Behavior and Human Performance*, May 1968, pp. 157–189.
26. T. A. Ryan and P. C. Smith, *Principles of Industrial Psychology*, Ronald, New York, 1954; and T. A. Ryan, *International Behavior*, Ronald, New York, 1970.
27. Edwin A. Locke, "The Ubiquity of the Technique of Goal Setting in Theories of and Approaches to Employee Motivation," *Academy of Management Review*, July 1978, p. 600.
28. Edwin A. Locke, "The Ideas of Frederick W. Taylor: An Evaluation," *Academy of Management Review*, January 1982, p. 16.
29. Edwin A. Locke, "Personnel Attitudes and Motivation," *Annual Review of Psychology*, vol. 26, 1975, pp. 457–480, 596–598.
30. A. J. Mento, R. P. Steele, and R. J. Karren, "A Meta-Analytic Study of the Effects of Goal Setting on Task Performance: 1966–1984," *Organizational Behavior and Human Decision Processes*, vol. 39, 1987, pp. 52–83.
31. Edwin A. Locke, "Personnel Attitudes and Motivation," pp. 457–480, 596–598.
32. Edwin A. Locke, Gary P. Latham, and Miriam Erez, "The Determinants of Goal Commitment," *Academy of Management Review*, January 1988, p. 24.
33. See Edwin A. Locke, "The Myths of Behavior Mod in Organizations," *Academy of Management Review*, October 1977, pp. 543–553; and Edwin A. Locke, "Resolved: Attitudes and Cognitive Processes Are Necessary Elements in Motivational Models," in Barbara Karmel (ed.), *Point and Counterpoint in Organizational Behavior*, Dryden Press, Hinsdale, Ill., 1980, pp. 19–42.
34. Locke, "The Ubiquity of the Technique of Goal Setting," p. 599.
35. Locke, "Toward a Theory of Task Motivation and Incentives," summarizes the laboratory studies; and Gary P. Latham and Gary A. Yukl, "A Review of the Research on the Application of Goal Setting in Organizations," *Academy of Management Journal*, December 1975, pp. 824–845, summarizes the field studies. The most recent comprehensive summaries of this expanding research can be found in Edwin A. Locke, Karylle A. Shaw, Lise M. Saari, and Gary P. Latham, "Goal Setting and Task Performance: 1969–1980," *Psychological Bulletin*, July 1981, pp. 125–152; Gary P. Latham and Thomas W. Lee, "Goal Setting," in Edwin A. Locke (ed.), *Generalizing from Laboratory to Field Settings*, Lexington Books, Lexington, Mass., 1986, pp. 101–117; and Mark E. Tubbs, "Goal Setting: A Meta-Analytic Examination of the Empirical Evidence," *Journal of Applied Psychology*, vol. 71, no. 3, 1986, pp. 474–483.
36. For example, see Gary P. Latham and Gary A. Yukl, "The Effects of Assigned and Participative Goal Setting on Performance and Job Satisfaction," *Journal of Applied Psychology*, April 1976, pp. 166–171; Katherine I. Miller and Peter Monge, "Participation, Satisfaction, and Productivity: A Meta-Analytic Review," *Academy of Management Journal*, December 1986, pp. 727–753.
37. See Richard D. Arvey, H. Dudley Dewhirst, and Edward M. Brown, "A Longitudinal Study of the Impact of Changes in Goal Setting on Employee Satisfaction," *Personnel Psychology*, Autumn 1978, pp. 595–608; John R. Hollenbeck and Arthur P. Brief, "The

Effects of Individual Differences and Goal Origin on Goal Setting and Performance," *Organizational Behavior and Human Decision Processes*, vol. 40, 1987, pp. 392–414.

38. Gary P. Latham and Lise M. Saari, "Importance of Supportive Relationships in Goal Setting," *Journal of Applied Psychology*, April 1979, pp. 151–156.

39. Howard Garland, "Goal Level and Task Performance: A Compelling Replication of Some Compelling Results," *Journal of Applied Psychology*, April 1982, pp. 245–248.

40. James T. Austin and Philip Bobko, "Goal Setting Theory: Unexplored Areas and Future Research Needs," *Journal of Occupational Psychology*, vol. 58, no. 4, 1985, pp. 289–308.

41. Donald J. Campbell, "Task Complexity: A Review and Analysis," *Academy of Management Review*, January 1988, pp. 40–52.

42. For example, McConkie has made a comprehensive summary of thirty-nine experts' descriptions of MBO. See Mark L. McConkie, "A Clarification of the Goal Setting and Appraisal Processes in MBO," *Academy of Management Review*, January 1979, pp. 29–40.

43. J. M. Ivancevich, "Changes in Performance in a Management by Objectives Program," *Administrative Science Quarterly*, vol. 19, 1974, pp. 563–574.

44. Jan P. Muczyk, "A Controlled Field Experiment Measuring the Impact of MBO on Performance Data," *Journal of Management Studies*, October 1978, pp. 318–329.

45. Kenneth R. Thompson, Fred Luthans, and Will Terpening, "The Effects of MBO on Performance and Satisfaction in a Public Sector Organization," *Journal of Management*, Spring 1981, pp. 53–69.

46. Don Hellriegel, John W. Slocum, and Richard W. Woodman, *Organizational Behavior*, 4th ed., West, St. Paul, Minn., 1986, pp. 448–449.

**REAL CASE:
AT&T's Goals***

American Telephone & Telegraph (AT&T) has always carefully developed a strategic plan for getting things done. In recent years, however, deregulation has caused a major change in the way the company does business. AT&T now realizes that careful goal setting is the key to success in besting the competition—and the firm has put together a series of important goals that are crucial to its long-term strategy. Three of these goals are the following:

1. In the short run, costs are to be cut by 20 percent. This will enable the firm to reduce about $32 billion in annual expenses. A large portion of this will come from elimination of approximately 33,000 jobs over the next year, bringing to about 80,000 the number of positions that have been cut since deregulation went into effect.

2. The firm intends to strengthen its long-distance business by modernizing its network and by lobbying for higher rates of return. The company also intends to bring together its sales and service forces for computer and telephone equipment into one group that will push long-distance service as well.

3. The company plans on bolstering future growth through a process called

Source: Adapted from John J. Keller, "Can Jim Olson's Grand Design Get AT&T Going?" *Business Week*, Dec. 22, 1986, pp. 48–49.

"data networking." The essence of this approach is that the firm intends to push complete computer and communications systems, including long-distance network services, to U.S. and international customers.

Will these goals be attained? Top management certainly thinks so. Pointing to the fact that the company has tremendous untapped potential in the communications business, management believes that a better-designed, goal-oriented approach can help unleash this potential. The market for AT&T's products and services is $135 billion and growing at an annual rate of 15 percent. If the firm can formulate specific goals and then break these down into action-oriented plans, it is convinced that it can capture a larger share of the communications market while keeping the competition at bay.

1. What are the four criteria that goals should have in order for them to improve performance? In your answer be sure to use Latham and Locke's research to guide you.
2. Could the three major goals set forth in this case be used as a basis for overall organizational strategy? Why or why not?
3. How could AT&T use MBO?

CASE: The Rubber Chicken Award

Kelly Sellers is really fed up with his department's performance. He knows that his people have a very boring job, and the way the technological process is set up leaves little latitude for what he has learned about vertically loading the job through job enrichment. Yet he is convinced that there must be some way to make it more interesting to do a dull job. "At least I want to find out for my people and improve their performance," he thinks.

The employees in Kelly's department are involved in the assembly of small hair dryer motors. There are twenty-five to thirty steps in the assembly process, depending upon the motor that is being assembled. The process is very simple, and currently each worker completes only one or two steps of the operation. Each employee has his or her own assigned workstation and stays at that particular place for the entire day. Kelly has decided to try a couple of things to improve performance. First, he has decided to organize the department into work groups. The members of each group would be able to move the workstations around as they desired. He has decided to allow each group to divide the tasks up as they see fit. Next, Kelly has decided to post each group's performance on a daily basis and to reward the group with the highest performance by giving them a "rubber chicken" award that they can display at their workbenches. The production manager, after checking with engineering, has reluctantly agreed to Kelly's proposal on a trial basis.

1. Do you think Kelly's approach to job redesign will work? Rate the core job dimensions from the Hackman-Oldham model of Kelly's employees before

and after he redesigned their jobs. What could he do to improve these dimensions even more?

2. How do you explain the fact that Kelly feels he is restricted by the technological process but has still redesigned the work? Is this an example of sociotechnical job redesign?

3. What will happen if this experiment does not work out and the production manager forces Kelly to return to the former task design?

CASE: Specific Goals for Human Service

Jackie Jordan is the regional manager of a state human services agency that provides job training and rehabilitation programs for deaf persons. Her duties include supervising counselors as well as developing special programs. One of the difficulties that Jackie has had was with a project supervisor, Kathleen O'Shean. Kathleen is the coordinator of a three-year federal grant for a special project for the deaf. Kathleen has direct responsibility for the funds and the goals of the project. The federal agency that made the grant made continuance of the three-year grant conditional upon some "demonstrative progress" toward fulfilling the purpose of the grant. Jackie's problem with Kathleen was directly related to this proviso. She repeatedly requested that Kathleen develop some concrete goals for the grant project. Jackie wanted these goals written in a specific, observable, and measurable fashion. Kathleen continually gave Jackie very vague, nonmeasurable platitudes. Jackie, in turn, kept requesting greater clarification, but Kathleen's response was that the work that was being done was meaningful enough and took all her time. To take away from the work itself by writing these specific goals would only defeat the purpose of the grant. Jackie finally gave up and didn't push the issue further. One year later the grant was not renewed by the federal government because the program lacked "demonstrated progress."

1. Do you think Jackie was right in requesting more specific goals from Kathleen? Why or why not?

2. Do you think the federal government would have been satisfied with the goal-setting approach that Jackie was pushing as a way to demonstrate progress?

3. Would you have handled the situation differently if you were Jackie? How?

11 Learning: Concepts and Principles

Positive Discipline: Punishing Workers with a Day Off*

Disciplining employees has been a continuing problem. Traditionally, companies have relied on progressive discipline, giving an oral reprimand, then a written reprimand, then a suspension and/or docking pay, and then termination. This approach treats problem employees worse and worse and expects them to get better and better. It just has not been working very well. Today, a growing number of firms such as AT&T, General Electric, Tampa Electric, New York Air, Martin Marietta, and Union Carbide have gone 180 degrees and have tried what has become known as positive discipline. Here's how it works:

1. When employees break a rule or do poor-quality work or are chronically absent or tardy, they first get an oral "reminder" of the deficiency and how to correct it instead of the traditional reprimand.
2. The second infraction draws a written reminder pointing out the problem and how to correct it.
3. Next comes a paid day off. Often called a "decision making leave day," this represents a radical departure from traditional discipline. At this point disciplined employees are usually required to agree in writing (or orally in some union shops) to be on their best behavior for the following year.
4. If employees still do not shape up after the paid day off, then they are terminated.

*Source: Adapted from Laurie Baum, "Punishing Workers with a Day Off," *Business Week*, June 16, 1986, p. 80.

This radical approach seems to work. One manager at Tampa Electric initially thought it was ridiculous, until he tried it. He said, "It sounded like a reward for bad behavior, like a gimmick from some consultant." Then he tried it on a lazy mechanic. "We gave him a day off to decide if he wanted his job, and we sure got his attention. He turned around on his own." As a young construction worker with Martin Marietta who was positively disciplined commented: "It got me to change my attitude. I was embarrassed in front of everyone when they told me I had the day off. I didn't want that to happen again." Since his "day off" this worker received two promotions and a 50 percent raise in pay.

Learning Objectives

- DEFINE the types and theories of learning with special attention given to classical and operant approaches.
- EXPLAIN social learning theory with special attention given to modeling processes and applications.
- DISCUSS reinforcement and the law of effect.
- ANALYZE organizational reward systems with special attention given to feedback and money.
- RELATE the techniques of administering reinforcement.
- PRESENT the meaning of punishment and the ways to administer it.

Along with motivation, learning has occupied a central role in the micro perspective of organizational behavior. Whereas motivation has been a more popular construct over the years in the field of organizational behavior, learning has been more dominant in the field of psychology. Learning has been given secondary attention in the study of organizational behavior. However, few organization behavior theorists and researchers would challenge the statement that learning is involved in almost everything that everyone does. Learning definitely affects human behavior in organizations. There is little organizational behavior that is not either directly or indirectly affected by learning. For example, a worker's skill, a manager's attitude, a supervisor's motivation, and a secretary's mode of dress are all learned.

Learning, of course, is also involved in the consequences of organizational behavior. The S-O-B-C model of Chapter 1 has feedback loops to and from all the variables. These feedback loops represent interactions, but they also could be thought of as learning. The purpose of this chapter is to present an overview of the learning process and some of the basic principles which will contribute to the better understanding, prediction, and control of organizational behavior and which will serve as a foundation for the application techniques discussed in the next chapter.

The first section distinguishes between the various types of learning and summarizes the major theoretical approaches. The next section is concerned with the reinforcement principle and its application. Included are discussions of the law of effect, types of reinforcement, and organizational reward systems. The third section deals with techniques of administering reinforcement. The last section is devoted to the effect of punishment on learning and behavior.

Types and Theories of Learning

Learning is a term frequently used by a great number of people in a wide variety of contexts. Yet, despite its diverse use, academicians have generally recognized one, or at most two, ways in which behavior can be acquired or changed. Starting with the early behaviorists (for example, John B. Watson and later B. F. Skinner), the most common explanation of learning has been *direct*, noncognitively mediated, classical and operant conditioning. Most of the learning principles that have been developed over the years and the discussion in this chapter and the next are greatly influenced by this approach to learning. However, recognition of the interactive nature of human behavior and the role of cognitive contingencies that fall under the social learning theory described in Chapter 1 implies other explanations of learning. In particular, learning can also be explained by cognitively or noncognitively mediated vicarious or *modeling* processes and/or by cognitively or noncognitively mediated *self-control* processes.[1] These three types of learning—direct, modeling, and self-control—suggest that there are different theoretical bases for learning, and these will be drawn upon in the following sections.

The most basic purpose of any theory is to better explain the phenomenon in question. When theories become perfected, they have universal application and should enable prediction and control. Thus, a perfected theory of learning would have to be able to explain all aspects of learning (how, when, and why), have universal application (for example, to children, college students, managers, and workers), and predict and control learning situations. To date, no such theory of learning exists. Although there is general agreement on some principles of learning, there is still disagreement on the theory behind it. This does not mean that no attempts have been made to develop a theory of learning. In fact, the opposite is true. The most widely recognized theoretical approaches follow the behavioristic and cognitive models discussed in Chapter 1 and the newly emerging social learning theory. An understanding of these three learning theories is important to the study of organizational behavior.

Connectionist, Behavioristic Theories of Learning

The dominant and best-researched theory comes out of the behavioristic school of thought in psychology. Most of the principles of learning discussed in this chapter and the applications discussed in the next chapter are based on operant, or Skinnerian, behaviorism.

The classical behaviorists, such as Pavlov and Watson, attributed learning to the association or connection between stimulus and response. The operant behaviorists, in particular Skinner, give more attention to the role that consequences play in learning, or the R-S (response-stimulus) connection. The emphasis on the connection (S-R or R-S) has led some to label these the *connectionist* theories of learning. The S-R deals with classical or respondent conditioning, and the R-S deals with instrumental or operant conditioning. An understanding of these conditioning processes is vital to the study of learning and serves as a point of departure for understanding and modifying organizational behavior.

Classical Conditioning. Pavlov's classical conditioning experiment using dogs as subjects is undoubtedly the single most famous study ever conducted in the behavioral sciences. A simple surgical procedure permitted Pavlov to measure accurately the amount of saliva secreted by a dog. When he presented meat powder (unconditioned stimulus) to the dog in the experiment, Pavlov noticed a great deal of salivation (unconditioned response). On the other hand, when he merely rang a bell (neutral stimulus), the dog had no salivation. The next step taken by Pavlov was to accompany the meat with the ringing of the bell. After doing this several times, Pavlov rang the bell without presenting the meat. This time, the dog salivated to the bell alone. The dog had become classically conditioned to salivate (conditioned response) to the sound of the bell (conditioned stimulus). The classical experiment was a major breakthrough and has had a lasting impact on the understanding of learning.

Pavlov went beyond the simple conditioning of his dogs to salivate to the sound of the bell. He next paired a black square with the bell. After a number of trials with this pairing, the dogs salivated to the black square alone. The original conditioned stimulus (bell) had become a reinforcing unconditioned stimulus for the new conditioned stimulus (black square). When the dogs responded to the black square, they became what is known as *second-order-conditioned.* Pavlov was able to obtain no higher than third-order conditioning with his dogs.

Most behavioral scientists agree that humans are capable of being conditioned higher than the third order. The exact number is not important, but the potential implications of higher-order conditioning for human learning and behavior should be recognized. For example, higher-order conditioning can explain how learning can be transferred to stimuli other than those used in the original conditioning. The existence of higher-order conditioning shows the difficulty of tracing the exact cause of a certain behavior. Another important implication concerns the principle of reinforcement. Higher-order conditioning implies that reinforcement can be acquired. A conditioned stimulus becomes reinforcing under higher-order conditioning. It substantiates, and perhaps offers a plausible explanation for, the secondary rewards which play such an important role in organizational behavior.

Despite the theoretical possibility of the widespread applicability of classical conditioning, most modern theorists agree that it represents only a very small part of total human learning. Skinner in particular felt that classical conditioning explains only respondent (reflexive) behaviors. These are the involuntary responses that are elicited by a stimulus. Skinner felt that the more complex, but common, human behaviors cannot be explained by classical conditioning alone. He felt that most human behavior affects, or operates on, the environment. The latter type of behavior is learned through operant conditioning.

Operant Conditioning. Operant conditioning is concerned primarily with learning that occurs as a *consequence* of behavior. It is not concerned with the eliciting causes of behavior, as classical or respondent conditioning is. The specific differences between classical and operant conditioning may be summarized as follows:

1. In classical conditioning, a change in the stimulus (unconditioned stimulus to conditioned stimulus) will elicit a particular response. In operant conditioning, one particular response out of many possible ones occurs in a given stimulus situation. The stimulus situation serves as a cue in operant conditioning. It does not elicit the response but serves as a cue for a person to emit the response. The critical aspect of operant conditioning is what happens as a consequence of the response. The strength and frequency of classically conditioned behaviors are determined mainly by the frequency of the eliciting stimulus (the environmental event that precedes the behavior). The strength and frequency of operantly conditioned behaviors are determined mainly by the consequences (the environmental event that follows the behavior).
2. During the classical conditioning process, the unconditioned stimulus, serving as a reward, is presented every time. In operant conditioning, the reward is presented only if the organism gives the correct response. The organism must operate on the environment in order to receive a reward. The response is instrumental in obtaining the reward. Table 11.1 gives some examples of classical (S-R) and operant (R-S) conditioning.

Operant conditioning has a much greater impact on human learning than classical conditioning. Operant conditioning also explains, at least in a very simple sense, much of organizational behavior. For example, it might be said

TABLE 11.1 Examples of Classical and Operant Conditioning

Classical Connection		
	(S) Stimulus ⟶	(R) →Response
The individual:	is stuck by a pin	flinches
	is tapped below the kneecap	flexes lower leg
	is shocked by an electric current	jumps/screams
	is surprised by a loud sound	jumps/screams

Operant Connection		
	(R) Response ⟶	(S) →Stimulus
The individual:	works	is paid
	talks to others	meets more people
	enters a restaurant	obtains food
	enters a library	finds a book
	works hard	receives praise and a promotion

that employees work eight hours a day, five days a week, in order to feed, clothe, and shelter themselves and their families. Working (conditioned response) is instrumental only in obtaining the food, clothing, and shelter. Some significant insights can be directly gained from this kind of analysis. The consequences of organizational behavior can change the environmental situation and largely affect subsequent employee behaviors. Although some organizations are concerned with trying to unlearn their managers' behaviors, as indicated in the accompanying Application Example, most are concerned with the analysis of the consequences

Application Example

Unlearning*

While reinforcement is the key to learning, there are a number of firms that are now providing their managers with training programs that try to get them to "unlearn" or undo previous learning. In particular, these companies want to teach their managers that sometimes the old cliché "If at first you don't succeed, try, try again" may not be a good one. Sometimes it is important to know when to quit trying and move on to something else. This is particularly true when a manager faces a "no win" situation in which managers end up wasting their time. For example, many managers fail to realize that some projects will not come to fruition and it is best to terminate them early. Once it becomes obvious that the undertaking is going to take a lot more time or money than the firm can or should wisely invest, it is time to drop this project and go on to another one. Managers who fail to realize this often endanger their own careers in the process. They are viewed as "win at all costs" types and are soon tabbed as too hard-headed for further promotion.

   What kinds of guidelines should managers follow in learning when to push forward and when to back off? Some of the most important are these:

1. *Set realistic, but not perfectionistic, work standards.* If too much time is exhausted on one project, other more lucrative ones may suffer as a result.
2. *It is often better to perform consistently well than to have a perfect score.* Managers who strive for perfect scores often contribute less to the organization than do those who consistently do a better-than-average job.
3. *Remember that planning is important.* Managers who figure out what needs to be done in their department and then match the tasks with personnel abilities often achieve outstanding results. It is not necessary to spend countless hours in the planning process; a few hours a week is often more than enough.
4. *Sometimes it is impossible to prevent things from going wrong.* All managers have problems with their projects. These are to be expected. The important thing is to accept problems as inevitable and learn from them so that they are not repeated in the future.
5. *Keep the door open for improvement.* Many companies provide advice and assistance in the form of coaching, counseling, mentoring, and outside consulting. Successful managers learn to accept this help and profit from it. Those who do not often find their career opportunities stymied or end up leaving the firm because they are unable to be team players. They put their ego ahead of the company's welfare.

Source: Adapted from Jack Falvey, "How to Know When to Cut Your Losses," *Working Woman*, December 1986, pp. 27–28.

of organizational behavior to help accomplish the goals of prediction and control. Some organizational behavior researchers are currently using the operant framework to analyze the effectiveness of managers at work.[2] In addition, the next chapter will discuss in detail most of these aspects of operant conditioning and the applications of operant conditioning to organizational behavior.

Cognitive Theories of Learning

Edward Tolman was portrayed in the introductory chapter as a pioneering cognitive theorist. He felt that learning consists of a *relationship between cognitive environmental cues and expectation.* He developed and tested this theory through controlled experimentation. He was one of the first to use the now famous white rat in psychological experiments. He found that a rat could learn to run through an intricate maze, with purpose and direction, toward a goal (food). Tolman observed that at each choice point in the maze, expectations were established. In other words, the rat learned to *expect* that certain cognitive cues associated with the choice point might eventually lead to food. If the rat actually received the food, the association between the cue and the expectancy was strengthened, and learning occurred. In contrast to the S-R and R-S learning in the classical and operant approaches, Tolman's approach could be depicted as S-S (stimulus-stimulus).

Tolman's experiments proved to be embarrassing to the operant learning theorists. For example, in his famous place-learning experiments he trained a rat to turn right in a "T" maze in order to obtain food. Then he started the rat from the opposite part of the maze; according to operant theory, the rat should have turned right because of past conditioning. But in Tolman's experiments the rat instead turned toward where the food had been placed. Tolman concluded that the rat's behavior was purposive, that is, that the rat formed a cognitive map to figure out how to get to the food. In other words, Tolman said that reinforcement is not a precondition for learning to take place. One stimulus leads to another stimulus, or S-S, rather than the classical S-R or the operant R-S explanation.

Tolman also conducted latent learning and transposition experiments to demonstrate that reinforcement is not needed for learning to occur. However, in time the behavioristic theorists were able to negate Tolman's results. By using more controlled experimental procedures, they were able to verify their predictions. For example, when there were perfectly sterile conditions in the place-learning experiments (for example, when a bubble was placed over the maze and the runways were carefully scrubbed), the rat turned right as conditioned instead of purposively going toward the food.

Even though most of Tolman's experiments have been discredited, he made a significant contribution to the development of learning theory. He forced behaviorists to develop more complex explanations of behavior, and he pinpointed the need to consider cognitions as having at least a possible mediating role between the stimulus environment and the behavior. The theory building has served as a transition and an integrating mechanism leading toward social learning theory, which will be covered in the next section.

Besides being the forerunner of modern social learning theory, Tolman's S-S cognitive theory also had a great impact on the early human relations movement. Industrial training programs in the 1940s and 1950s drew heavily on Tolman's ideas. Programs were designed to strengthen the relationship between cognitive cues (supervisory, organizational, and job procedures) and worker expectations (incentive payments for good performance). The theory was that the worker would learn to be more productive by building an association between taking orders or following directions and expectancies of monetary reward for this effort.

Today, the cognitive theories are very much alive and well. The discussions of motivation theories and techniques in the preceding two chapters are based largely on the cognitive approach. Expectations, attributions and locus of control, and goal setting (which are in the forefront of modern work motivation) are all cognitive concepts and represent the purposefulness of organizational behavior. Many researchers are currently concerned about the relationship or connection between cognitions and organizational behavior.[3]

Social Learning Theory

Chapter 1 introduced social learning theory. It was said that social learning theory combines and integrates both behavioristic and cognitive concepts and emphasizes the interactive nature of cognitive, behavioral, and environmental determinants. This social learning approach was used as the basis for developing the S-O-B-C conceptual framework for this book.

It is important to recognize that social learning theory is a *behavioral* theory and draws heavily from the principles of classical and operant conditioning. But equally important is the fact that social learning theory goes beyond classical and operant theory by recognizing that there is more to learning than direct learning via antecedent stimuli and contingent consequences. Social learning theory posits that learning can also take place via vicarious or modeling and self-control processes. Thus, social learning theory agrees with classical and operant conditioning processes but says they are too limiting.

Modeling Processes. The vicarious or modeling processes essentially involve observational learning. "Modeling in accordance with social learning theory can account for certain behavior acquisition phenomena that cannot be easily fitted into either operant or respondent conditioning."[4]

Many years ago, Miller and Dollard suggested that learning need not result from discrete stimulus-response or response-consequence connections. Instead, learning can take place through imitating others. Albert Bandura is most closely associated with the modern view of modeling as an explanation of learning. He states:

> Although behavior can be shaped into new patterns to some extent by rewarding and punishing consequences learning would be exceedingly laborious and hazardous if it proceeded solely on this basis. . . . [I]t is difficult to imagine a socialization process in which the language, mores, vocational activities, familial customs and educa-

tional, religious and political practices of a culture are taught to each new member by selective reinforcement of fortuitous behaviors, without benefit of models who exemplify the cultural patterns in their own behavior. Most of the behaviors that people display are learned either deliberately or inadvertently, through the influence of example.[5]

Bandura has done considerable research that demonstrates that people can learn from others.[6] This learning takes place in two steps. First, the person observes how others act and then acquires a mental picture of the act and its consequences (rewards and punishers). Second, the person acts out the acquired image and if the consequences are positive, he or she will tend to do it again. If the consequences are negative, the person will tend not to do it again. This, of course, is where there is a tie-in with operant theory. But because there is cognitive, symbolic representation of the modeled activities instead of discrete response-consequence connections in the acquisition of new behavior, modeling goes beyond the operant explanation. In particular, Bandura concludes that modeling involves interrelated subprocesses such as *attention, retention,* and *motoric reproduction,* as well as reinforcement. Others emphasize that a primary basis of vicarious learning is a cognitively held "script" on the part of the observer of a model.[7] This script is a procedural knowledge or cognitive structure or framework for understanding and doing behaviors.

Modeling Applications. There is a growing literature that suggests that modeling can be effectively applied to the field of organizational behavior.[8] A specific modeling strategy could be used to improve human performance in today's organizations.[9] Such a strategy might include the following steps:

1. Precisely identify the goal or target behavior that will lead to performance improvement.
2. Select the appropriate model and modeling medium (for example, a live demonstration, a training film, or a videotape).
3. Make sure the employee is capable of meeting the technical skill requirements of the target behavior.
4. Structure a favorable learning environment which increases the probability of attention and reproduction and which enhances motivation to learn and improve.
5. Model the target behavior and carry out supporting activities, such as role playing. Clearly demonstrate the positive consequences of the modeled target behavior.
6. Positively reinforce reproduction of the target behavior both in training and back on the job.
7. Once it is reproduced, maintain and strengthen the target behavior, first with a continuous schedule of reinforcement and later with an intermittent schedule.[10]

A number of studies show that such modeling procedures have had a very favorable impact on industrial training programs.[11] For example, in one study, forty first-line supervisors who received modeling training in nine interpersonal skill areas (for example, orienting a new employee, reducing absenteeism, and overcoming resistance to change) were judged to be significantly more effective than a group of matched supervisors who did not receive the training.[12]

Reinforcement: The Key to Learning

Reinforcement plays a central role in the learning process. Most learning experts agree that reinforcement is the single most important principle of learning. Yet there is much controversy over its theoretical explanation. The first major theoretical treatment given to reinforcement in learning and the theory that still dominates today is Thorndike's classic law of effect.

The Law of Effect

In Thorndike's own words, the law of effect is simply stated thus: "Of several responses made to the same situation, those which are accompanied or closely followed by satisfaction (reinforcement) . . . will be more likely to recur; those which are accompanied or closely followed by discomfort (punishment) . . . will be less likely to occur."[13] From a strictly empirical standpoint, most behavioral scientists, even those with a cognitive orientation, generally accept the validity of this law. It has been demonstrated time after time in highly controlled learning experiments and is directly observable in everyday learning experiences. Desirable or reinforcing consequences will increase the strength of a response and increase its probability of being repeated in the future. Undesirable or punishing consequences will decrease the strength of a response and decrease its probability of being repeated in the future. Despite the wide acceptance of this law, there is disagreement when it is carried a step further and used as an overall theory or an absolute requirement for learning.

As the discussion of cognitive learning theory indicated, Tolman and other critics of the requirement of reinforcement use such concepts as that of latent learning to make their point. For example, in latent learning experiments it was shown that rats that were reinforced after successful trials in running a maze showed fewer errors than rats that were not reinforced. However, once the rat was reinforced after a number of nonreinforced trials, there were very few errors. In other words, even though the nonreinforced rats were not as efficient, when they finally were reinforced, they were more efficient. The explanation offered was that learning indeed takes place during the nonreinforcement trials and that the reinforcement only makes it worthwhile. Like the researchers who conducted the place-learning experiments, the behaviorists were eventually able to show that, under highly controlled experimental conditions, such latent, nonreinforced learning did not occur.

Despite the theoretical controversy, few would argue against the importance of reinforcement to the learning process. Theoretical attempts besides the law of effect have generally failed to explain reinforcement fully. However, as with the failure to develop a generally accepted overall theory of learning, the lack of an accepted theory of reinforcement does not detract from its extreme importance.

Definition of Reinforcement

The term *reinforcement* is conceptually related to the psychological process of motivation, which was covered in the preceding chapters. There is a temptation to equate reinforcement with motivation. Although this is sometimes deliberately or nondeliberately done, this book treats them separately. Motivation is a basic psychological process and is broader and more complex than is implied by the learning principle of reinforcement as used here. In addition, the need states that are so central to motivation are cognitive in nature; they are unobservable inner states. Reinforcement, on the other hand, is environmentally based. Reinforcers under a behavioristic perspective are external, environmental events that follow a response. In general terms, motivation is an internal explanation of behavior, and reinforcement is an external explanation of behavior. Thus, the perspectives and explanation of behavior as being due to motivation and reinforcement are quite different.

An often cited circular definition of reinforcement says that it is anything the person finds rewarding. This definition is of little value because the words "reinforcing" and "rewarding" are used interchangeably, but neither one is operationally defined. A more operational definition can be arrived at by reverting back to the law of effect. Under this law, reinforcement can be defined as anything that both increases the strength of response and tends to induce repetitions of the behavior that preceded the reinforcement.

A reward, on the other hand, is simply something that the person who presents it deems to be desirable. A reward is given by a person who thinks it is desirable. Reinforcement is functionally defined. Something is reinforcing only if it strengthens the response preceding it and induces repetitions of the response. For example, a manager may ostensibly reward an employee who found an error in a report by publicly praising the employee. Yet, upon examination it is found that the employee is embarrassed and harassed by coworkers, and error-finding behavior decreases in the future. In this example, the "reward" is *not* reinforcing. Even though there is this technical difference between a reward and a reinforcer, the terms are often used interchangeably and will be in this book.

To better understand reinforcers it is necessary, besides clearing up the differences between reinforcers and rewards, to make the distinctions between positive and negative reinforcers.

Positive and Negative Reinforcers

There is much confusion surrounding the terms *positive reinforcement* and *negative reinforcement* and the terms *negative reinforcement* and *punishment.* First of all, it must be understood that reinforcement, positive or negative, strengthens the response and increases the probability of repetition. But the positive and negative reinforcers accomplish this impact on behavior in completely different ways. Positive reinforcement strengthens and increases behavior by the *presentation* of a desirable consequence. Negative reinforcement strengthens and increases behavior by the *termination* or *withdrawal* of an undesirable consequence. Figure 11.1 briefly summarizes the differences between positive and

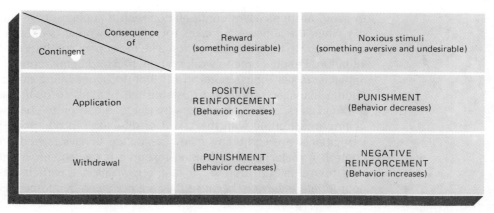

Contingent / Consequence of	Reward (something desirable)	Noxious stimuli (something aversive and undesirable)
Application	POSITIVE REINFORCEMENT (Behavior increases)	PUNISHMENT (Behavior decreases)
Withdrawal	PUNISHMENT (Behavior decreases)	NEGATIVE REINFORCEMENT (Behavior increases)

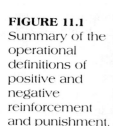

FIGURE 11.1
Summary of the operational definitions of positive and negative reinforcement and punishment.

negative reinforcement and punishment. Giving praise to an employee for the successful completion of a task could be an example of *positive* reinforcement (if this does in fact strengthen and subsequently increase this task behavior). On the other hand, a worker is *negatively* reinforced for getting busy when the supervisor walks through the area. Getting busy terminates being "chewed out" by the supervisor.

Negative reinforcement is more complex than positive reinforcement, but it should not be equated with punishment. In fact, they have an opposite effect on behavior. Negative reinforcement strengthens and increases behavior, while punishment weakens and decreases behavior. However, both are considered to be forms of negative control of behavior. Negative reinforcement is really a form of social blackmail because the person will behave in a certain way or be punished. A discussion of escape and avoidance learning will help clarify this aspect of negative reinforcement.

Escape-Avoidance Learning: A Special Case of Negative Reinforcement

A learning phenomenon which demonstrates the impact of negative reinforcement is escape-avoidance learning. It goes a step beyond simple conditioning by using negative reinforcement. A simple escape learning experiment involves shocking a rat in a Skinner box. Only pressing the bar will terminate the shock. The rat must learn to press the bar to escape the pain from the shock. Once escape is learned, avoidance can also be learned. In the Skinner box, a light may be timed to go on a few seconds before the shock is administered. The rat can learn to avoid the shock altogether by running over to press the bar whenever the bulb lights up.

Humans learn escape-avoidance in much the same way. For example, workers may learn to escape a boring job with no challenge by organizing into informal groups or by playing games during working hours. When the quitting whistle blows, the aversive situation stops, and the employees return to being very active, serious-minded individuals. In another situation a worker may learn to avoid an unpleasant confrontation with a supervisor by knowing the time of day when the supervisor makes rounds. The worker is either conveniently gone or too busy to have any interaction with the supervisor, thus avoiding a punishing situation. People come to work on time to *avoid* being reprimanded by the boss. Supervisors get their reports in on time to *avoid* being punished by the boss. Middle managers conform to established policies to *avoid* being punished by top managers, and top managers try to look good on the balance sheet to *avoid* getting into trouble with the board of directors. In other words, organizational participants are exhibiting many avoidance behaviors and are under negative control. A major goal for human resource management would be somehow to turn this situation around so that organizational participants would perform appropriate behaviors because they are *positively* reinforced for doing so.

Ways to Identify Positive Reinforcers

Since some of the commonly used organizational rewards are not necessarily positive reinforcers, it is vitally important that objective measures be used whenever possible to tell whether a reward is in fact a positive reinforcer. Several techniques are available to help determine potential positive reinforcers. The most accurate method of identifying positive reinforcers, but often the most difficult to implement, is to empirically analyze each individual's history of reinforcement. Knowledge of what a particular person likes and dislikes, gained through experience, can help in this regard. However, in cases where there is little or no experience with the individual, several self-reporting techniques can be used.

The most straightforward technique is simply to ask what the person finds to be rewarding. Although the person may not always tell the truth, it is nonetheless a logical point of departure for identifying potential reinforcers. Table 11.2 gives examples of questions that employees could be asked to help identify potential

TABLE 11.2. Questions That Could Be Asked in an Employee Reinforcer Survey

Employee Reinforcer Survey
1. In my free time my favorite activity is _____
2. I would like to visit _____
3. My favorite sports activity is _____
4. My favorite hobby is _____
5. Something that I really want to buy is _____
6. If I had $50 to spend on myself right now, I would _____
7. My job would be more rewarding if _____
8. If my manager would _____ I would enjoy working here.
9. I would work harder if _____
10. The place that I most like to shop is _____

Source: Adapted from Lawrence M. Miller, *Behavior Management*, Wiley, New York, 1978, p. 149.

TABLE 11.3 Classifications of On-the-Job Rewards

Contrived On-the-Job Rewards				Natural Rewards	
Consumables	**Manipulatables**	**Visual and Auditory**	**Tokens**	**Social**	**Premack**
Coffee-break treats	Deck accessories	Office with a window	Money	Friendly greetings	Job with more responsibility
Free lunches	Wall plaques	Piped-in-music	Stocks	Informal recognition	Job rotation
Food baskets	Company car	Redecoration of work environment	Stock options	Formal acknowledgment of achievement	Early time off with pay
Easter hams	Watches		Movie passes		Work on personal project on company time
Christmas turkeys	Trophies	Company literature	Trading stamps (green stamps)	Feedback about performance	
Dinners for the family on the company	Commendations	Private office	Paid-up insurance policies	Solicitations of suggestions	Use of company machinery or facilities for personal projects
Company picnics	Rings/tie pins	Popular speakers or lecturers	Dinner and theater tickets	Solicitations of advice	
After-work wine and cheese parties	Appliances and furniture for the home	Book club discussions	Vacation trips	Compliment on work progress	Use of company recreation facilities
	Home shop tools		Coupons redeemable at local stores	Recognition in house organ	Special assignments
	Garden tools		Profit sharing	Pat on the back	
	Clothing			Smile	
	Club privileges			Verbal or nonverbal recognition or praise	

Source: Fred Luthans and Robert Kreitner, *Organizational Behavior Modification and Beyond,* Scott, Foresman, Glenview, Ill., 1985, p. 127.

reinforcers. Employees could fill out such a form when they are hired, or every year or so, to help the manager find specific rewards for each employee.

Organizational Reward Systems

The technique discussed above can be used to help identify organizational rewards. Although reinforcers are highly individualized, research and experience have shown that there are several rewards that most organizational participants find positively reinforcing. These can be classified as *contrived* and *natural* rewards. Contrived rewards are brought in from outside the work environment and generally involve costs for the organization over and above the existing situation. Examples would include the consumables, manipulatables, visual and auditory reinforcers, and tokens listed in Table 11.3. The two most widely used and effective contrived rewards are feedback about performance and money. Natural rewards, as Table 11.3 shows, are already part of the work environment.

Feedback as a Reinforcer. The literature on the impact that feedback has on organizational participants was discussed in Chapter 10. There is little question that despite the tremendous amount of data being generated by computerized information systems in modern organizations, individuals still receive very little, if any, feedback about their performance. People generally have an intense desire to know *how* they are doing, especially if they have some degree of achievement motivation (see Chapter 9). It is generally accepted that feedback enhances individual performance.[14] A recent comprehensive review (thirty laboratory and forty-two field experiments) concluded that objective feedback had a positive effect.[15] In general, feedback should be as *p*ositive, *i*mmediate, *g*raphic, and *s*pecific—i.e., the acronym PIGS—as possible to be effective.[16]

Despite the recognized importance, there is some disagreement as to whether feedback per se is automatically reinforcing or simplistic.[17] For example, after reviewing the existing research literature on feedback, one researcher concluded that its impact is contingent upon factors such as the nature of the feedback information, the process of using feedback, individual differences among the recipients of the feedback, and the nature of the task.[18] One study, for instance, found that self-generated feedback with goal setting had a much more powerful effect on technical/engineering employees than externally gener-ated feedback with goal setting.[19] Also a recent study found subjects rated specific feedback more positively than they rated nonspecific feedback, and preferred feedback that suggested an external cause of poor performance to feedback that suggested an internal cause.[20] And the source of the feedback seems important as well. Not only are the amount and the frequency of feedback generated by a source important, but also the consistency and usefulness of the information generated, as a recent study found. Individuals viewed feedback from formal organizations least positively, from coworkers next, then from supervisors and tasks, and the best was self-generated feedback.[21]

Despite these qualifications and contingencies, a general guideline regarding feedback about performance is that it can be an effective positive reinforcer. For example, a supervisor faced with the problem of people taking unscheduled breaks successfully used feedback to reinforce them for staying on the job. Specifically, the supervisor calculated the exact cost for each worker in the unit (in terms of lost group piece-rate pay) every time any one of them took an unscheduled break. This information regarding the relatively significant amount of lost pay when any one of them took an unscheduled break was fed back to the employees of the unit. After this feedback, staying on the job increased in frequency, and taking unscheduled breaks dramatically decreased. The feedback pointed out the contingency that staying on the job meant more money. At least in this case, money proved to be a more reinforcing consequence than the competing contingencies of enjoying social rewards with friends in the rest room and withdrawing from the boring job. The feedback in this case clarified the monetary contingency.

Money as a Reinforcer.

Despite the tendency in recent years to downgrade the importance of money as an organizational reward, there is ample evidence that money can be positively reinforcing for most people. The downgrading of money is partly the result of the motivation theories of Maslow and Herzberg, plus the publicity given to surveys which consistently place wages and salaries near the middle of the list of employment factors that are important to workers and managers.

There are also recent studies indicating that a salary increase, no matter how large, merely intensifies the belief that the employee deserves more.[22] The idea here is that once the money covers the basic needs, people use it to get ahead, which is always just out of reach. Although money was probably overemphasized in classical management theory and motivation techniques, the pendulum now seems to have swung too far in the opposite direction. Money remains a very important but admittedly complex potential reinforcer.

In terms of Maslow's hierarchy, money is often equated only with the most basic level of needs. It is viewed in the material sense of buying food, clothing, and shelter. Yet money has a symbolic as well as an economic material meaning. It can provide power and status and can be a means to measure achievement. In the latter sense, money can be used as an effective positive reinforcement intervention strategy.

Accepting the importance of money as a possible reinforcer does not mean that the traditional techniques for dispensing it are adequate. Starting with the scientific management movement at the turn of the century, numerous monetary incentive techniques have been developed.

The standard base-pay technique provides for minimum compensation for a particular job. Pay by the hour for workers and the base salary for managers are examples. The technique does not reward above-average performance or penalize below-average performance, and it is controlled largely by the job rather than by the person performing the job. A variable-pay technique, however, attempts to reward according to individual or group differences and is thus more human- than job-controlled. Seniority variable-pay plans recognize age and length-of-service differentials, and merit-pay and individual- or group-incentive plans attempt to reward contingently on the basis of performance. The accompanying Application Example shows how this could be used even with members of Congress. In addition, Cleveland's Parker Hannifin Corporation gives quarterly bonuses to its best-performing divisions; Pacific Gas and Electric has an award program for 8000 managers, and 2500 of these managers vie for bonuses under a "Superior Pay for Superior Performance" program; Bank of America increased by 29 percent the number of managers whose salary depends on performance; and Hewlett-Packard and Bechtel have had longstanding salary programs based on merit.[23]

Incentive plans involve piece rates, bonuses, or profit sharing. A third technique, supplementary pay, has nothing to do with the job or performance per se. The extensive fringe-benefit package received by employees in most modern organizations is an example. These supplements can be very costly to organizations. The U.S. Chamber of Commerce reported that employee benefits in the mid-1980s cost companies over $8000 per employee.[24]

Analyses of the role of money are usually couched in cognitive terms. However, from these cognitive explanations it is very clear that the real key in assessing the use of money as a reinforcer is not necessarily whether it satisfies inner needs but rather how it is administered. In order for money to be effective

Application Example

Contingent Pay for Congressional Performance*

Each year elected members of Congress and the Senate resolve to reduce government spending. Yet each year the deficit grows larger. Economists Dwight R. Lee and Richard B. McKenzie offer an interesting solution to this problem in their book *Regulating Government*. They suggest that action is not taken on government spending because "members of Congress receive the same annual pay no matter whether the deficit is $50 billion, $100 billion, or $200 billion." They believe the system of pay needs to be modified. According to their proposal, members of Congress would receive a base pay of $75,000 per year (based on the current level of pay). However, incentives would be offered for reducing the deficit. In other words, the smaller the deficit, the larger their pay. With such incentives, members of Congress could earn up to $300,000 per year.

Although they base their proposal on the "public choice" school of economics, the same solution could have come out of the operant school of learning. Operant principles state that in order to increase desired behavior (reducing the deficit), one must reinforce such behavior (offer money for budget reductions). Industrial organizations, of course, have used such practices for years. For example, production workers receive piece rate incentive pay. Managers receive bonuses for department and overall organization performance. Salespersons receive commissions for sales. Given the popularity and effectiveness of such contingent reward plans, tying rewards to lawmakers' performance may make sense.

***Source:** Adapted from David R. Henderson, "In Defense of 'Public Choice,' " *Fortune*, Jan. 19, 1987, pp. 141–146.

---

in the organizational reward system, it must be administered contingently on the employee's exhibiting critical performance behavior.

Unfortunately, about the only reinforcing function that pay currently has in organizations is to reinforce employees for walking up to the pay window or for opening an envelope every two weeks or every month. With the exception of some piece-rate incentive systems and commissions paid to salespersons, pay is generally not contingent on the performance of critical behaviors. One experimental study clearly demonstrated that money contingently administered can have a positive effect on employee behavior. A contingently administered monetary bonus plan significantly improved the punctuality of workers in a Mexican division of a large U.S. corporation.[25] It should be pointed out, however, that the mere fact that money was valued by the Mexican workers in this study does not mean that it would have the same impact on all workers. For example, in a study of managers in the Social Security Administration, merit pay seemingly had no effect on organizational performance.[26]

In a society with an inflationary economy and nonmaterialistic social values, money may be much less likely to be a potential reinforcer for critical job behaviors. Money certainly cannot be automatically dismissed as a positive reinforcer, but, because of its complexity, it may also turn out to be a reward but not a reinforcer. Only objective measurement will determine whether in fact money is an effective positive reinforcer for the critical behavior in question.

Natural Reinforcers. Besides contrived rewards, which most organizations tend to depend upon, a host of overlooked natural reinforcers are available. Potentially very powerful, these are the rewards that exist in the natural occurrence of events.[27] Table 11.3 categorizes natural reinforcers.

Social rewards such as recognition, attention, and praise tend to be very reinforcing for most people. In addition, few people become satiated with social rewards. However, similar to contrived rewards, social rewards must be administered on a contingent basis. For example, a pat on the back or verbal praise that is randomly given (as under the old human relations approach) may have more of a punishing, "boomerang" effect than a positive reinforcement effect. But genuine social rewards, contingently administered for performance of the target behavior, can be a very effective positive reinforcer for most employees. The added benefit of such a strategy, in contrast to the use of contrived rewards, is that the cost of social rewards to the organization is absolutely nothing.

In Table 11.3, Premack rewards refer to the work of psychologist David Premack.[28] Simply stated, the Premack principle is that high-probability behaviors can be used to reinforce low-probability behaviors. For example, if there are two tasks, A and B, and the person prefers task A to task B, the Premack principle says that the person should perform task B first and then task A. In this sequence, completing task A serves as a contingent reinforcer for completing task B, and the person will perform better on both tasks than if the sequence were reversed. In common practice, people often tend to do the task they like best first and to put off the less pleasant task. This common sequence of doing things is in direct violation of the Premack principle and can contribute to ineffective performance.

Applied to organizational reward systems, the Premack principle would suggest that a natural reinforcer could always be found. Certain job activities could always be used to reinforce other job activities. No matter how much employees dislike their jobs, there are going to be some things they like to do better than others. Premack sequencing would allow the more-desired activities to reinforce the less-desired activities. The Premack rewards listed in Table 11.3 can be used to reinforce the less desirable activities on a job.

Techniques of Administering Reinforcement

The preceding discussion was concerned primarily with the theoretical basis, categories, and content of reinforcement. The importance of the role of reinforcement in the study of organizational behavior cannot be overemphasized. It plays a central role in human resources management areas such as training, appraisal, adaptation to change, and performance. Modification of certain specific aspects of organizational behavior, such as tardiness or participation, and overall organization development also depend upon reinforcement. Reinforcement will increase the strength of desired organizational behavior and the probability of its being repeated. How reinforcement is administered is also important. For example, during the acquisition phase of classical conditioning experiments, every conditioned response is reinforced. This seldom occurs in reality. Human behavior in organizations or everyday life is generally reinforced on an intermittent or random basis. The exact pattern and timing of the reinforcement have a tremendous impact on the resulting behavior. In other words, how the reward is administered can greatly influence the specific organizational behavior that takes place. The four major techniques of administering rewards are fixed ratio, fixed interval, variable ratio, and variable interval schedules.

Fixed Ratio Schedules

If a schedule is administered on a ratio basis, reinforcement is given after a certain *number* of responses. If the schedule is a fixed ratio, the exact number of responses is specified. A fixed ratio that reinforces after every response is designated as 1:1. The 1:1 fixed ratio is generally used in basic conditioning experiments, and almost every type of learning situation must begin with this schedule. However, as learning progresses, it is more effective to shift to a fixed ratio of 2:1, 4:1, 8:1, and even 20:1.

Administering rewards under a fixed ratio schedule tends to produce a high rate of response that is characterized as vigorous and steady. The person soon determines that reinforcement is based on the number of responses and performs the responses as quickly as possible in order to receive the reward. A common example of how the fixed ratio schedule is applied to industrial organizations is the piece-rate incentive system. Production workers are paid on the basis of how many pieces they produce (number of responses). Other things being equal, the worker's performance responses should be energetic and steady. In reality, of course, other things are not always equal, and a piece-rate incentive system may not lead to this type of behavior. Nevertheless, knowledge of the effects of the various methods of administering rewards would be extremely valuable in analyzing employee-incentive systems.

Fixed Interval Schedules

A second common way to administer rewards is on a fixed interval basis. Under this schedule, reinforcement is given after a specified period of *time*, which is measured from the last reinforced response. The length of time that can be used by this schedule varies a great deal. In the beginning of practically any learning situation, a very short interval is required. However, as learning progresses, the interval can be stretched out.

Behavior resulting from a fixed interval method of reinforcing is quite different from that exhibited as a result of a fixed ratio schedule. Whereas under a fixed ratio schedule there is a steady, vigorous response pattern, under a fixed interval schedule there is an uneven pattern that varies from a very slow, unenergetic response immediately following reinforcement to a very fast, vigorous response immediately preceding reinforcement. This type of behavior pattern can be explained by the fact that the person figures out that another reward will not immediately follow the last one. Therefore, the person may as well relax a little until it is time to be rewarded again. A common example of administering rewards on a fixed interval schedule is the payment of employees by the hour, week, or month. Monetary reinforcement comes at the end of a period of time. In practice, however, even though people are paid by the hour, they receive their reward only weekly, biweekly, or monthly. This time interval is generally too long to be an effective form of reinforcement for the work-related behavior.

Variable or Intermittent Schedules

Both ratio and interval schedules can be administered on a variable or intermittent basis. This means that the reinforcement is given in an irregular or unsystematic manner. In variable ratio, the reward is given after a number of responses, but the exact number is randomly varied. When the variable ratio is expressed as some number—say, 1:50—this means that on the *average* the organism is reinforced after fifty responses. However, in reality the ratio may randomly vary from 1:1 to 1:100. In other words, each response has a chance of being reinforced regardless of the number of reinforced or nonreinforced responses that have preceded it.

The variable interval schedule works basically the same as the variable ratio schedule except that a reward is given after a randomly distributed length of time rather than after a number of responses. A fifty-minute variable interval schedule means that on the *average,* the individual is reinforced after fifty minutes, but the actual reinforcement may be given anywhere from every few seconds to every two or three hours.

Behavior under Variable Schedules. Both variable ratio and variable interval schedules tend to produce stable, vigorous behavior. The behavior under variable schedules is similar to that produced by a fixed ratio schedule. Under a variable schedule, the person has no idea when the reward is coming, and so the behavior tends to be steady and strong. It logically follows that variable schedules are very resistant to extinction.

Variable schedules are not very effective in highly controlled learning experiments and are seldom used. On the other hand, they are the way in which many real-life, everyday learning situations are reinforced. Although primary reinforcers for humans are administered on a relatively fixed basis (for example, food is given three times a day at mealtimes, and organization compensation plans are on either a fixed ratio or a fixed interval basis), most of the other human behavior that takes place is reinforced in a highly variable manner. For example, practically all social rewards are administered on a variable basis. Attention, approval, and affection are generally given as rewards in a very random fashion.

Administration of Reinforcement in Human Resources Management

The fixed ratio and fixed interval schedules and the variable ratio and variable interval schedules are not the only methods of administering rewards. Many other possible combinations exist. However, these four schedules are the way most employees in today's organizations are reinforced. Much of the learning and resulting behavior of every worker, supervisor, salesperson, engineer, and executive is determined by when and how they are reinforced. Even the automobile industry learned, the hard way, that customers' buying behavior in the 1980s was greatly affected by schedules of reinforcement.

The automobile companies depended on cash rebates and cut-rate financing to stimulate the sales of their new cars. These programs were *randomly* offered; that is, there was a variable interval schedule of reinforcement. Under such a schedule, behavior is very resistant to extinction. Thus, what happened was that long-run sales were not stimulated by a one-shot rebate program; instead, customers did not buy after the rebate expired, and sales declined. As explained by one industry analyst: "The auto industry's on-again, off-again pattern of rebates over the past two years has conditioned the customer to wait—almost indefinitely—for some giveaway."[29] Under this variable schedule of reinforcement, when the expensive giveaways stopped coming, it took a long time to convince car buyers, as it did Skinner's pigeons, that there wasn't any point in continuing to wait.

Besides this real example of consumer behavior, there is a growing research literature on the impact that continuous versus variable schedules have on employee behavior. The problem is, however, that job simulation studies conducted with student subjects in laboratory settings have different results from those of studies using actual workers in a field setting. The laboratory studies found that variable schedules led to better performance.[30] This verified what the operant learning theorists had been saying over the years. However, a couple of studies conducted on tree-planting crews found that continuous schedules of reinforcement actually led to better performance.[31] Both the laboratory and, especially, the field studies had definite methodological problems that prevent any definitive conclusions. A follow-up study of the tree-planting crews did try to eliminate some of the problems and still found that the employees as a whole performed better on a continuous schedule of reinforcement.[32] Yet, despite this overall finding, the researchers recognize that some limitations still remain and that there are individual differences. For example, inexperienced subjects worked better on a variable schedule.

Although the research results on the application of schedules are not yet very clear and cannot be generalized for monetary schedules,[33] there are still some guidelines that can be given for effective human resources management. For example, rewards should be given as soon after the desired response as possible, not two weeks or a month later, as in the case of most of today's employees' paychecks. In addition, ratio schedules are generally more desirable than interval schedules because they tend to produce steady, strong responses, but as the discussion of the research indicated, specific guidance on the use of continuous versus variable schedules cannot yet be given. Although some types of employees may work better under continuous schedules, variable schedules may be better for other types of employees and certainly are more resistant to extinction. Understanding and then applying what is known about the administration of reinforcement can be of great assistance to modern human resources managers. In fact, one of the most important functions of all managers may well be the way they administer reinforcement to their people. The next chapter carries this discussion further by giving specific attention to behavioral-change strategies for modern human resources management.

The Effect of Punishment

Punishment is one of the most used but least understood and badly administered aspects of learning. Whether in rearing children or dealing with subordinates in a complex organization, parents and supervisors often revert to punishment instead of positive reinforcement in order to modify or control behavior. Punishment is commonly thought to be the reverse of reinforcement but equally effective in altering behavior. However, this simple analogy with reinforcement may not be warranted. The reason is that punishment is a very complex phenomenon and must be carefully defined and used.

The Definition of Punishment

The meaning of *punishment* was mentioned earlier. To reiterate, punishment is anything which weakens behavior and tends to decrease its subsequent frequency. The punishment process is very close to extinction—both have the effect of decreasing the behavioral frequency—but technically there is a difference. Punishment usually consists of the *application* of an undesirable or noxious consequence, but it can also be defined as the *withdrawal* of a desirable consequence that is normally in the person's environment *before* the undesirable behavior occurs. Extinction, on the other hand, is the *withdrawal* of a desirable consequence that is contingent upon the person's behavior. The withdrawal of the desirable consequence under extinction occurs *after* the behavior is emitted. Thus, taking away certain organizational privileges from a manager who has a poor performance record could be thought of as punishment, and moving a very friendly, talkative typist to another part of the office could be thought of as an extinction strategy for the typist's socializing behavior.

Regardless of the distinction between extinction and punishment, in order for punishment to occur, there must be a weakening of, and a decrease in, the behavior which preceded it. Just because a supervisor gives a "tongue-lashing" to a subordinate and thinks this is punishment, it is not necessarily that unless the behavior that preceded the tongue-lashing weakens and decreases. In many cases when supervisors think they are punishing employees, they are in fact reinforcing them because they are giving attention, and attention tends to be very reinforcing. This explains the common complaint that supervisors often make: "I call Joe in, give him heck for goofing up, and he goes right back out and goofs up again." What is happening is that the supervisor thinks Joe is being punished, when operationally what is obviously happening is that the supervisor is reinforcing Joe's undesirable behavior by giving him attention and recognition.

Administering Punishment

Opinions on administering punishment range all the way from the one extreme of dire warnings never to use it to the other extreme that it is the only effective way to modify behavior. As yet, research has not been able to support either view completely. However, there is little doubt that the use of punishment tends to cause many undesirable side effects. Neither children nor adults like to be punished. The punished behavior tends to be only temporarily suppressed rather than permanently changed, and the punished person tends to get anxious or "uptight" and resentful of the punisher. Thus, the use of punishment as a strategy to control behavior is a "lose-lose" approach. Unless the punishment is severe, the behavior will reappear very quickly, but the more severe the punishment, the bigger the side effects such as "hate" and "revenge."

To minimize the problems with using punishment, the person administering it must always provide an acceptable alternative to the behavior that is being punished. If they do not, the undesirable behavior will tend to reappear and will cause fear and anxiety in the person being punished. The punishment must always be administered as close in time to the undesirable behavior as possible. Calling subordinates into the office to give them a reprimand for breaking a rule the week before is not effective. All the reprimand tends to do at this time is to punish them for getting caught. It has little effect on the rule-breaking behavior.

Attention must also be exercised so that what is intended as punishment does not in fact act as a reward for the recipient. A supervisor who shouts at a worker may be rewarding this individual's position as the informal leader of a work-restricting group. The same is true of the example, given in the last section, of punishment turning into rewarding attention. It is very easy for supervisors or managers to use punishment, but it is very difficult for them to effectively administer punishment so as to modify or change undesirable behavior. There is also recent evidence that, like reinforcement, vicarious punishment can be effectively used in a work setting.[34]

A rule of thumb for managers should be: Always attempt to reinforce instead of punish in order to change behavior. Furthermore, the use of an extinction strategy (nonreinforcement) is usually more effective in decelerating undesirable behaviors than the use of punishment because no bad side effects accompany extinction. As one comprehensive analysis of punishment concluded, "in order to succeed, (punishment) must be used in an orderly, rational manner—not, as is too often the case, as a handy outlet for a manager's anger or frustration. If used with skill, and concern for human dignity, it can be useful."[35] The next chapter will get into these behavioral-change strategies in more depth and will apply them more directly to human resources management.

Summary

Learning is a major psychological process that has been largely neglected in the study of organizational behavior. It has not been generally recognized that there are different types of learning and different theoretical explanations of learning (operant, cognitive, and social). Despite the controversy surrounding learning theory, there are many accepted principles of learning that are derived largely from experimentation and the analysis of operant conditioning. Reinforcement is the single most important concept in the learning process and is most relevant to the study of organizational behavior. On the basis of the classic law of effect, *reinforcement* can be operationally defined as anything which increases the strength of response and which tends to induce repetitions of the behavior that preceded the reinforcement. Within the organizational reward system, both contrived and natural rewards are important to employee behavior and performance. Rewards may be positive or negative. They may be administered on a fixed ratio or fixed interval basis or on a variable ratio or variable interval basis. The effective administration of reinforcement and punishment may be one of the most critical challenges facing modern human resources management.

Questions for Discussion and Review

1. Do you agree with the statement that learning is involved in almost everything that everyone does? Explain.
2. What are the major dimensions of operant, cognitive, and social learning theories?
3. What is the difference between classical and operant conditioning?
4. What is the difference between positive and negative reinforcement? What is the difference between negative reinforcement and punishment?
5. What is the difference between contrived and natural rewards? What role does money play in the organizational reward system? What could be done to make it more effective?
6. Why is the administration of reinforcement so vitally important to learning and management practice?
7. Make arguments for and against punishment.

References

1. Tim R. V. Davis and Fred Luthans, "A Social Learning Approach to Organizational Behavior," *Academy of Management Review,* April 1980, pp. 281–290.
2. For example, see Judith L. Komaki, "Toward Effective Supervision: An Operant Analysis and Comparison of Managers at Work," *Journal of Applied Psychology,* vol. 71, no. 2, 1986, pp. 270–279.
3. For example, see Dennis A. Gioia and Henry P. Sims, Jr., "Cognition-Behavior Connections: Attribution and Verbal Behavior in Leader-Subordinate Interactions," *Organizational Behavior and Human Decision Processes,* vol. 37, 1986, pp. 197–229.
4. Thomas C. Mawhinney, "Learning," in Dennis W. Organ and Thomas Bateman, *Organizational Behavior,* 3d ed., Business Publications, Plano, Tex., 1986, pp. 90–91.
5. Albert Bandura, "Social Learning Theory," in J. T. Spence, R. C. Carson, and J. W. Thibaut (eds.), *Behavioral Approaches to Therapy,* General Learning, Morristown, N.J., 1976, p. 5.

6. See Albert Bandura, *Social Learning Theory,* Prentice-Hall, Englewood Cliffs, N.J., 1977, for a summary of this research.

7. Dennis A. Gioia and Charles C. Manz, "Linking Cognition and Behavior: A Script Processing Interpretation of Vicarious Learning," *Academy of Management Review,* July 1985, pp. 527–539.

8. Charles C. Manz and Henry P. Sims, Jr., "Vicarious Learning: The Influence of Modeling on Organizational Behavior," *Academy of Management Review,* January 1981, pp. 105–113; and Henry P. Sims and Charles C. Manz, "Modeling Influences on Employee Behavior," *Personnel Journal,* January 1982, pp. 58–65.

9. Kenneth E. Hultman, "Behavior Modeling for Results," *Training and Development Journal,* December 1986, p. 60.

10. Fred Luthans and Robert Kreitner, *Organizational Behavior Modification and Beyond,* Scott, Foresman, Glenview, Ill., 1985, p. 157.

11. Robert F. Burnaska, "The Effects of Behavior Modeling Training upon Managers' Behaviors and Employees' Perceptions," *Personnel Psychology,* Autumn 1976, pp. 329–335; Allen I. Kraut, "Developing Managerial Skills via Modelling Techniques: Some Positive Research Findings—A Symposium," *Personnel Psychology,* vol. 29, 1976, pp. 325–328; Gary P. Latham and Lise M. Saari, "Application of Social-Learning Theory to Training Supervisors through Behavioral Modeling," *Journal of Applied Psychology,* June 1979, pp. 239–246; and Phillip J. Decker, "The Enhancement of Behavior Modeling Training of Supervisory Skills by the Inclusion of Retention Processes," *Personnel Psychology,* Summer 1982, pp. 323–332.

12. Latham and Saari, op. cit.

13. Edward L. Thorndike, *Animal Intelligence,* Macmillan, New York, 1911, p. 244.

14. D. M. Prue and J. A. Fairbank, "Performance Feedback in Organizational Behavior Management: A Review," *Journal of Organizational Behavior Management,* Spring 1981, pp. 1–16.

15. Richard E. Kopelman, "Objective Feedback," in Edwin A. Locke (ed.), *Generalizing from Laboratory to Field Settings,* Lexington Books, Lexington, Mass., 1986, pp. 119–145.

16. Fred Luthans, Richard M. Hodgetts, and Stuart A. Rosenkrantz, *Real Managers,* Ballinger, Cambridge, Mass., 1988, pp. 141–142.

17. Daniel R. Ilgen, Cynthia D. Fisher, and M. Susan Taylor, "Consequences of Individual Feedback on Behavior in Organizations," *Journal of Applied Psychology,* August 1979, pp. 349–371.

18. David A. Nadler, "The Effects of Feedback on Task Group Behavior: A Review of the Experimental Research," *Organizational Behavior and Human Performance,* June 1979, pp. 309–338.

19. John M. Ivancevich and J. Timothy McMahon, "The Effects of Goal Setting, External Feedback, and Self-Generated Feedback on Outcome Variables: A Field Experiment," *Academy of Management Journal,* June 1982, pp. 359–372.

20. Robert C. Linden and Terence R. Mitchell, "Reactions to Feedback: The Role of Attributions," *Academy of Management Journal,* June 1985, pp. 291–308.

21. David M. Herold, Robert C. Linden, and Marya L. Leatherwood, "Using Multiple Attributes to Assess Sources of Performance Feedback," *Academy of Management Journal,* December 1987, pp. 826–835.

22. "Labor Letter," *The Wall Street Journal,* Jan. 20, 1987, p. 1.

23. "Labor Letter," *The Wall Street Journal,* Mar. 31, 1987, p. 1.

24. "Labor Letter," *The Wall Street Journal,* Dec. 16, 1986, p. 1.

25. Jaime A. Hermann, Ana I. deMontes, Benjamin Dominguez, Francisco deMontes, and

B. L. Hopkins, "Effects of Bonuses for Punctuality on the Tardiness of Industrial Workers," *Journal of Applied Behavioral Analysis,* Winter 1973, pp. 563–570.

26. Jone L. Pearce, William B. Stevenson, and James L. Perry, "Managerial Compensation Based on Organizational Performance: A Time Series Analysis of the Effects of Merit Pay," *Academy of Management Journal,* June 1985, pp. 261–278.
27. Luthans and Kreitner, op. cit.
28. David Premack, "Reinforcement Theory," in David Levine (ed.), *Nebraska Symposium on Motivation,* University of Nebraska Press, Lincoln, 1965, pp. 123–180.
29. Robert L. Simison, "Why Are Auto Sales Strictly for the Birds? Just Ask Any Pigeon," *The Wall Street Journal,* Dec. 15, 1982, p. 1.
30. Gary A. Yukl, Kenneth N. Wexley, and J. D. Seymore, "Effectiveness of Pay Incentives under Variable Ratio and Continuous Schedules of Reinforcement," *Organizational Behavior and Human Performance,* October 1975, pp. 227–243.
31. Gary A. Yukl and Gary P. Latham, "Consequences of Reinforcement Schedules and Incentive Magnitudes for Employee Performance: Problems Encountered in an Industrial Setting," *Journal of Applied Psychology,* June 1975, pp. 294–298; and G. A. Yukl, G. P. Latham, and E. D. Pursell, "The Effectiveness of Performance Incentives under Continuous and Variable Ratio Schedules of Reinforcement," *Personnel Psychology,* vol. 29, 1976, pp. 221–231.
32. Gary P. Latham and Dennis L. Dossett, "Designing Incentive Plans for Unionized Employees: A Comparison of Continuous and Variable Ratio Reinforcement Schedules," *Personnel Psychology,* Spring 1978, pp. 47–61.
33. Thomas C. Mawhinney, "Reinforcement Schedule Stretching Effects," in Edwin A. Locke (ed.), *Generalizing from Laboratory to Field Settings,* Lexington Books, Lexington, Mass., 1986, pp. 181–186.
34. Mel E. Schnake, "Vicarious Punishment in a Work Setting," *Journal of Applied Psychology,* vol. 71, no. 2, 1986, pp. 343–345.
35. Robert A. Baron, *Behavior in Organizations,* Allyn and Bacon, Boston, 1986, p. 51.

REAL CASE: Where Money Is the Name of the Game*

Ivan Boesky used to tell his dinner guests, his colleagues, students in business schools where he was asked to speak, and anyone else who would listen that he made his money in the stock market by always conducting a highly thorough, detailed analysis of a company before he bought its stock. While this sounds logical, in truth Boesky was making millions because of the inside tips that were being provided to him by investment bankers who knew which companies were about to be purchased by other firms and whose stocks were likely to be driven up. If anything, Boesky focused less on hard work than he did on unethical, illegal business practices. He was not alone. In other financially related cases, E. F. Hutton, the prestigious brokerage was found to be involved in a check-kiting scheme, and the Bank of Boston was discovered to be laundering money.

These developments are leading many people to ask what has

***Source:** Adapted from Myron Magnet, "The Decline and Fall of Business Ethics," *Fortune,* Dec. 8, 1986, pp. 65–72.

happened to business ethics. Especially in the financial field, it appears that money has become more than just an immediate reinforcer for performance behaviors. Those who make a great deal of money are admired; those who make very little are ignored. Unfortunately, how they make it may be losing all significance. Consider some of the following tactics that have been used in recent years by investment bankers to garner high profits from their firms and high bonuses for themselves.

- A company president went to an investment bank to seek help in financing a major expansion. The investment banker lied to the president, telling him that his company was a target for a takeover by a large firm and the only way to prevent it was to fight back. The banker offered the services of his company to help in the fight. The president agreed, thankful that he had found out the news in advance. The investment banker, meanwhile, scurried about and found a company that was interested in making a play for the president's firm, thus proving that the warnings were justified. When all was said and done, the investment bank made a great deal of money for its services.
- A company engaged an investment banking firm to help it buy another company. Unknown to the buyer, the investment banker had another client whom he then talked into also bidding for the firm. Both companies continued to raise their price until one won. Since the investment bank received a percentage of the selling price, it profited from this bidding war.
- A company went to an investment banker and showed the latter all of its analysis on a firm it wanted to buy. The analysis described why the firm was a good buy and helped justify to the banker why his firm should get involved in helping put together the deal. The banker, in turn, showed the materials to another client firm that was willing to pay an even higher price for this company and did so. The investment bank made a small fortune on the deal.

Why does there seem to be such a sudden rash of these illegal or questionable business tactics? Many people feel it is a result of learning. Many young executives have learned to respect money and in the investment banking arena, there is a lot of money to be earned. In the 1960s an investment banker would start at around $9,000 a year. Today the figure is close to $100,000 annually and can run up into the millions if the individual puts together a couple of lucrative deals for the investment bank. As was recently noted:

> They have their own ethic, and it centers on money, as is increasingly true for the ethic of the culture at large. "Where we saw in the Sixties the notion of public service, in the Eighties money is the thing," says a Harvard professor. For the get-rich-quick mergers and acquisitions generation, it sometimes seems that money is the only value. "The people with the most money are admired regardless of how they achieved it," says James Schrei-

ber, a New York lawyer who specializes in cases involving securities fraud. The investment banking boom gives these people their chance to be rich, and they are taking it. "For them, it's money *now*," says one of their elders in the business. "It's Las Vegas."

1. Is money a reinforcer to the investment bankers described in this case?
2. In what way do you think the investment banking houses have encouraged their people to engage in unethical practices?
3. If the investment banking houses wanted to stop this type of behavior, what would you suggest they do?

**CASE:
Contrasting
Styles**

Henry Adams has been a production supervisor for eight years. He came up through the ranks and is known as a tough but hardworking supervisor. Jerry Wake has been a production supervisor for about the same length of time and also came up through the ranks. Jerry is known as a nice, hardworking guy. Over the past several years these two supervisors' sections have been head and shoulders above the other six sections on hard measures of performance (number of units produced). This is true despite the almost opposite approaches the two have taken in handling their workers. Henry explained his approach as follows:

The only way to handle workers is to come down hard on them whenever they make a mistake. In fact, I call them together every once in a while and give them heck whether they deserve it or not, just to keep them on their toes. If they are doing a good job, I tell them that's what they're getting paid for. By taking this approach, all I have to do is walk through my area, and people start working like mad.

Jerry explained his approach as follows:

I don't believe in that human relations stuff of being nice to workers. But I do believe that a worker deserves some recognition and attention from me if he or she does a good job. If people make a mistake, I don't jump on them. I feel that we are all entitled to make some errors. On the other hand, I always do point out what the mistake was and what they should have done, and as soon as they do it right I let them know it. Obviously, I don't have time to give attention to everyone doing things right, but I deliberately try to get around to people doing a good job every once in a while.

Although Henry's section is still right at the top along with Jerry's section in units produced, personnel records show that there has been 3 times as much turnover in Henry's section than in Jerry's section, and the quality-control records show that Henry's section has met quality standards only twice in the last six years, while Jerry's has missed attaining quality standards only once in the last six years.

1. Both these supervisors have similar backgrounds. On the basis of learning, how can you explain their opposite approaches to handling people?

2. What are some of the examples of punishment, positive reinforcement, and negative reinforcement found in this case? What schedule of reinforcement is Jerry using? If Jerry is using a reinforcement approach, how do you explain this statement: "I don't believe in that human relations stuff of being nice to workers"?
3. How do you explain the performance, turnover, and quality results in these two sections of the production department?

CASE: Volunteers Can't Be Punished

Ann-Marie Jackson is the head of a volunteer agency in a large city. She is in charge of a volunteer staff of over twenty-five people. Weekly she holds a meeting with this group in order to keep them informed and teach them the specifics of any new laws or changes in state and federal policies and procedures that might affect their work, and she discusses priorities and assignments for the group. This meeting is also a time when members can share some of the problems and concerns for what they are personally doing and what the agency as a whole is doing. The meeting is scheduled to begin at 9 A.M. sharp every Monday. Lately, the volunteers have been filtering in every five minutes or so until almost 10 A.M. Ann-Marie has felt she has to delay the start of the meetings until all the people arrive. The last few weeks the meetings haven't started until 10 A.M. in fact, at 9 A.M. nobody has shown up. Ann-Marie cannot understand what has happened. She feels it is important to start the meetings at 9 A.M. so that they can be over before the whole morning is gone. On the other hand, she feels that her hands are tied because, after all, the people are volunteers and she can't punish them or make them get to the meetings on time.

1. What advice would you give Ann-Marie? In terms of reinforcement theory, explain what is happening here and what Ann-Marie needs to do to get the meetings started on time.
2. What learning theories (operant, cognitive, and/or social) could be applied to Ann-Marie's efforts to teach her volunteers the impact of new laws and changes in state and federal policies and procedures?
3. How could someone like Ann-Marie use modeling to train her staff to do a more effective job?

12 Organizational Behavior Modification

In terms of growth and influence, the service sector in America is booming. For example, since the last recession in 1982, 85 percent of the 12.6 million new jobs are in the service industries. However, the problem is that there is little service in these service industries. Tom Peters, the best-selling coauthor of *In Search of Excellence*, is on record as stating that "in general, service in America stinks!" Popular comedian Jay Leno loves to relate the story of when he chided a supermarket clerk for failing to say thank you. She snapped, "It's printed on your receipt!" Unfortunately, this statement reflects the status of personal service in the American service sector. This state of affairs is not true in other parts of the world. Although there are always exceptions, most world travelers would argue that they get better service abroad.

Obviously, there are many contributing factors to the service problem—low pay, understaffing, new marketing schemes, changing values, and computerization are just a few. However, there are some organizations that are offering quality service by simply following some of the principles of organizational behavior modification (O.B. Mod.). Here are just two such success stories:

1. Seattle-based Nordstrom's department stores drills its staff with the dogma that the customer is always right. They pay their

Source: Adapted from Stephen Koepp, "Pul-eeze! Will Somebody Help Me?" *Time*, Feb. 2, 1987, pp. 56–57.

people 20 percent more than competitors and deliberately con-gratulate and encourage them for good work. As far as conse-quences of customer complaints, employees are instructed to replace anything on demand, no matter how expensive, no questions asked.
2. In the Minneapolis area, Byerly's supermarkets are known for their customer service. In good O.B. Mod. terms, the head, Don Byerly, explains the success of his stores this way: "The only reason people will come back to our store is because of what happened to them the last time they were here." For example, Byerly's employees will put customers' groceries in their cars as many supermarkets do, but on the rare times when the bags are put in the wrong car, Byerly's, unlike other stores, will deliver the right goods to the customer's door, along with a free cake or other goodie by way of apology.

Some would say these are just commonsense approaches to good, old-fashioned customer service. Yet, by following the principles of O.B. Mod., organizations can put service back into the service industry and rob Jay Leno of material for his jokes.

Learning Objectives

- IDENTIFY the five steps of O.B. Mod.: identify, measure, analyze, intervene, and evaluate.
- DISCUSS the experience of using O.B. Mod. in manufacturing and nonmanufacturing applications.
- EXPLAIN behavioral self-management.
- PRESENT the applications of behavioral self-management.
- ANALYZE O.B. Mod. as a method of improving human performance in today's organizations.

Chapter 1 introduced the environment-based behavioristic approach to organizational behavior. This approach emphasizes the important role that the environment plays in organizational behavior. In particular, the B-C (behavior-consequence) part of the S-O-B-C model of organizational behavior recognizes the importance of environmental consequences in the prediction and control of organizational behavior. Chapter 11 added some depth of understanding to this approach by explaining behavioral learning concepts, especially reinforcement. With the exception of Chapter 11, the motivation chapters in this part are presented mainly from an internal, cognitive perspective.

This chapter is devoted specifically to an applied, behavioral approach to the practice of human resources management. Employee behaviors and their direct impact on performance effectiveness are the focus of attention. The concepts and techniques presented in this chapter are not proposed as an alternative to the more traditional and widely accepted methods of human resources management presented in the other chapters. Instead, the suggested behavioral approach in this chapter is meant to supplement and to be used in combination with the other approaches.

O.B. Mod. has its roots in modern behaviorism. Modern behaviorism stems from the significant distinction that B. F. Skinner made between respondent or reflexive behaviors, which are the result of classical conditioning, and operant behaviors, which are the result of operant conditioning (see Chapter 11 for a detailed discussion of the difference). In today's complex organizations, very few of the behaviors of participants are the result of classical conditioning; the mechanistic S-R type of behaviorism is of little value for analyzing or changing organizational behaviors. Operant conditioning is a much better basis for the pragmatic analysis and change of organizational behavior. Most recently a social learning approach as outlined in Chapters 1 and 11 has been suggested as the most comprehensive theoretical base for the understanding of organizational behavior in general and for application areas such as O.B. Mod.

This chapter builds on and applies the material given in Chapters 1 and 11. The chapter is devoted to a fairly detailed explanation and analysis of this approach to human resources management. All the steps of O.B. Mod. (identification, measurement, analysis, intervention, and evaluation) are given attention, but relatively more attention is given to the intervention strategies that can be used to change employee behaviors. The last part of the chapter reports in detail on some actual experiences with, and research findings on, the application of O.B. Mod. in practicing organizations.

The Steps of O.B. Mod.

As a specific approach to human resources management, O.B. Mod. can be portrayed as a five-step problem-solving model. Figure 12.1 shows this model. O.B. Mod. can be used in a step-by-step process to actually change performance-related employee behaviors in today's organizations. Again, the reader should remember that O.B. Mod. is only one technique; there are others, such as job design and goal setting, discussed in Chapter 10, and the techniques discussed in other chapters of the book. The following sections discuss the various steps of O.B. Mod.

Step 1: Identification of Critical Behaviors

In this first step the critical behaviors that make a significant impact on performance (making or selling widgets or providing a service to clients or customers) are identified. In every organization, regardless of type or level, numerous behaviors are occurring all the time. Some of these behaviors have a significant impact on performance, and some do not. The goal of the first step of O.B. Mod. is to identify the critical behaviors—the 5 to 10 percent of the behaviors that may account for up to 70 or 80 percent of the performance in the area in question.

Methods of Identifying Critical Behaviors.   The process of identifying critical behaviors can be carried out in a couple of ways. One approach is to

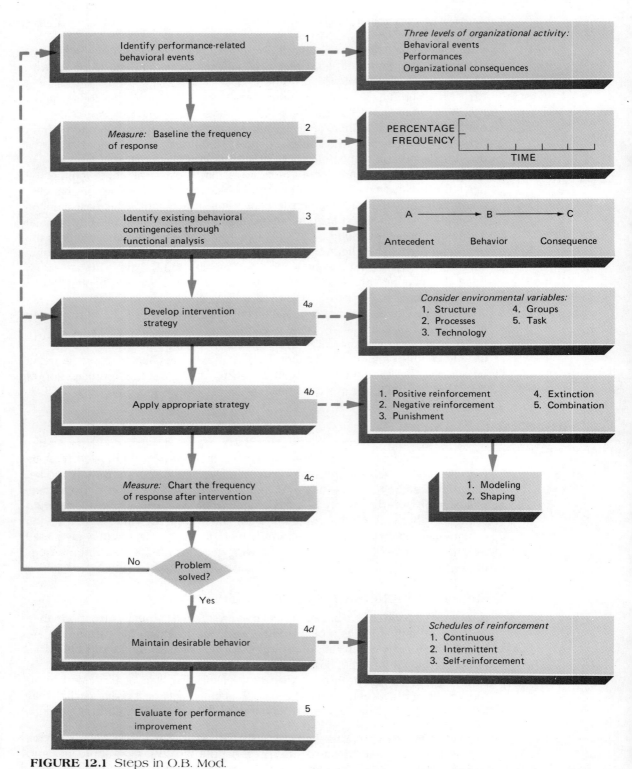

FIGURE 12.1 Steps in O.B. Mod.
(*Source:* Fred Luthans and Robert Kreitner, "The Management of Behavioral Contingencies," *Personnel,* July–August 1974, p. 13.)

have the person closest to the job in question—the immediate supervisor or the actual jobholder—determine the critical behaviors. This goes hand in hand with using O.B. Mod. as a problem-solving approach for the individual manager. Its advantages are that the person who knows the job best can most accurately identify the critical behaviors, and, because that person is participating, he or she may be more committed to carrying the O.B. Mod. process to its successful completion.

Another approach to identifying critical behaviors would be to conduct a systematic *behavioral audit.* The audit would use internal staff specialists and/or outside consultants. The audit would systematically analyze each job in question, in the manner that jobs are analyzed using job analysis techniques commonly employed in personnel administration. The advantages of the personal approach (where the jobholder and/or the immediate supervisor makes a vital input into the audit) can be realized by the audit. In addition, the advantages of staff expertise and consistency can be gained.

Guidelines for Identifying Critical Behaviors. Regardless of the method used, there are certain guidelines that can be helpful in identifying critical behaviors. First, only direct performance behaviors are included. An employee's "bad attitude" and someone's "goofing off" all the time are unacceptable. Only direct performance behaviors such as absenteeism or attendance, tardiness or promptness, complaints or constructive comments, and doing or not doing a particular task or procedure that leads to quantity and/or quality outcomes play a role in O.B. Mod. Something like goofing off is not acceptable because it is not operationally measurable. It could be broken down into measurable behaviors such as not being at the work station, being tardy when returning from breaks, spending time at the water cooler, disrupting coworkers, and even flirting with employees of the opposite sex. However, for a behavior to be identified as a critical behavior appropriate for O.B. Mod., there must be a positive answer to the questions (1) can it be measured? and (2) does it have a direct impact on a performance outcome?

Another helpful guideline for identifying such behaviors is to work backward from an obvious performance deficiency. Just as not all behaviors contribute to performance (for example, complaining behavior may have nothing to do with performance), not all performance problems can be traced to behaviors. For example, the cause of poor performance of a production unit in a manufacturing organization may be faulty machinery, poorly trained workers (they do not know the proper procedures), or unrealistically high production standards. Each of these possible causes is not, at least directly, a behavioral problem. The same is true of the person who does not have the ability to produce at an acceptable level. This is a selection problem, not a behavioral problem. However, after noting the possibility of performance problems that are not behaviorally related, it should be emphasized that in general such problems are the exception rather than the rule. Most organizations do not have problems with their technology or the ability or training of their people, but they have many behaviorally related performance problems. Desirable behaviors (those which contribute to performance goals) need to be strengthened and accelerated in frequency, and undesirable behaviors (those which detract from, or are dysfunctional to, performance goals) need to be weakened and decelerated in frequency. As in the initial step of any problem-solving process, these behaviors must be properly identified, or the subsequent steps of O.B. Mod. become meaningless for attaining the overall goal of performance improvement.

Step 2: Measurement of the Behaviors

After the behaviors have been identified in step 1, they are measured. A baseline frequency is obtained by determining (either by observing and counting or by extracting from existing records) the number of times that the identified behavior is occurring under present conditions. Often this baseline frequency is in and of itself very revealing. Sometimes it is discovered that the behavior identified in step 1 is occurring much less or much more frequently than anticipated. The baseline measure may indicate that the problem is much smaller or much bigger than was thought to be the case. In some instances the baseline measure may cause the "problem" to be dropped because its low (or high) frequency is now deemed not to need change. For example, attendance may have been identified in step 1 as a critical behavior that needed to be changed. The supervisor reports that the people "never seem to be here." The baseline measure, however, reveals that there is 96 percent attendance, which is deemed to be acceptable. In this example, the baseline measure rules out attendance as being a problem. The reverse, of course, could also have occurred. Attendance may have been a much bigger problem than anticipated.

The purpose of the baseline measure is to provide objective frequency data on the critical behavior. A baseline frequency count is an operational definition of the strength of the behavior under existing conditions. Such precise measurement is the hallmark of any scientific endeavor, and it separates O.B. Mod. from more subjective human resources management approaches, such as participation. Although the baseline is established before the intervention to see what happens to the behavior as a result of the intervention, it is important to realize that measures are taken after the intervention as well. Busy managers may feel that they do not have time to record behavioral frequencies objectively, but, at least initially, they must record them in order to use the O.B. Mod. approach effectively. The following discussion of tally sheets and charting points out how to minimize the problems associated with this second step of O.B. Mod.

Tally Sheets. A tailor-made tally sheet should be designed for each behavior. A piece of notebook paper usually is sufficient. Figure 12.2 shows a typical tally sheet. As shown, the tallies usually record behavioral frequencies in relation to time. The frequencies are usually broken down in a "yes"-"no" type of format, which greatly simplifies the job of the recorder. However, such an approach requires precise definitions of what constitutes a frequency. For example, say that the identified behavior is tardiness in returning from breaks. A decision must be made on what is considered tardy. Say that it is decided (and this may be different from situation to situation) that five minutes or over is tardy. The recorder then has a definite guideline for checking "yes" or "no" for frequency of tardiness behavior.

	Monday		Tuesday		Wendesday		Thursday		Friday	
Times	Yes	No	Yes	No	Yes	No	Yes	No	Yes	No

Employee:_____ Behavior:_____
Position:_____ Supervisor:_____

FIGURE 12.2 A typical tally sheet.

The time dimension on the tally sheet can also follow some specific guidelines to simplify the recorder's job. With some behaviors, such as attendance or complaints, it may be feasible to record every occurrence. However, with many other behaviors recording every frequency would be so time-consuming that it would be practically impossible. With behaviors of the latter type, time-sampling techniques have been used successfully by industrial engineers for years. An example of a time-sampling approach would be to randomly select a time during each working hour to observe the behavior. As in any sampling procedure, if the times are in fact random, confident generalizations can be made to the whole day.

Charting the Behaviors. The data collected on the tally sheets are transferred to a chart or graph like the one shown in Figure 12.3. As shown, the frequencies of behaviors are along the vertical axis, and time is on the horizontal axis. Percentage rather than raw frequency is usually used. This also simplifies the recorder's job because it permits the recorder to miss a time or two during the day, or even entire days, without badly distorting the data. Charting critical behaviors is important to O.B. Mod. because it permits quick, accurate visual inspection of the frequency data.

The Role of the Recorder. The role assumed by the recorder can be important not only to the measurement step but also to the credibility and ethics of the entire approach. As Chapter 2 pointed out, there is a real need for accurate, observational measures of organizational behavior. This is true not only when

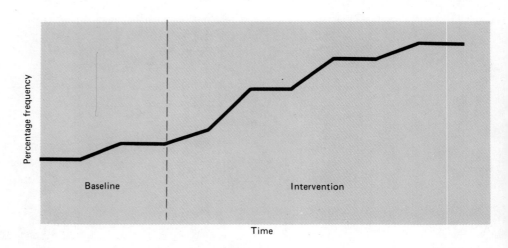

FIGURE 12.3
Charting critical
behaviors.

using the O.B. Mod. approach but also for gathering data for any research purpose in organizational behavior. Questionnaire and interview data were criticized in Chapter 2 as being highly reactive. However, the mere presence of an observer (recorder) may also badly distort the behaviors being measured. For this reason, it is important that observational data be gathered as unobtrusively as possible.

Advocating the use of unobtrusive, unnoticed observational measures does not mean that hidden observers or hidden audio and/or video equipment should be used. Obviously, such practice gets into ethical and legal problems. With possibly a few exceptions (for example, security), such hidden or deceptive approaches cannot be justified. On the other hand, straightforward observational techniques that use common sense can minimize the reactive effects on those being measured. The recorder should be completely open to any questions that the person being observed may have. Most employees in modern organizations are not sensitive to being measured because industrial engineers and personnel specialists have been doing it for years. There have certainly been abuses of this in the past, but lessons have been learned and the abuses can be eliminated.

Many data on typical behaviors (for example, absenteeism and quantity and quality of output) are already being gathered by other techniques. All that recorders have to do is retrieve these data; they do not have to intrusively intervene. Finally, self-reporting procedures can be employed to gather data. Having people reinforced for honestly and accurately keeping records on their own targeted behaviors will eliminate the need for a recorder.

Step 3: Functional Analysis of the Behavior

Once the performance behavior has been identified and a baseline measure has been obtained, a functional analysis is performed. As Chapters 1 and 11 brought out, both the antecedent (the S in the S-O-B-C model) and the consequent (the C in the model) environments are vital to the understanding, prediction, and control of human behavior in organizations. In Table 12.1 a simple operant-based A-B-C functional analysis is shown. Remember that in an operant approach, cognitive mediating processes (represented by the O) do not play a role. Such an omission may detract from the comprehensive understanding of organizational behavior and the analysis of modeling and self-control processes, but for pragmatic application, an A-B-C functional analysis is sufficient.[1] A four-term S-O-B-C functional analysis, which accounts for cognitive mediating processes (the O) and covert (unobservable) as well as overt contingencies, is more appropriate for the broader-based social learning approach and is more applicable to a behavioral self-management approach.[2] In the A-B-C functional analysis, A is the antecedent cue, B is the performance behavior identified in step 1, and C is the contingent consequence. Table 12.1 identifies some of the A's, B's, and C's for attendance and absenteeism. A recent review of absenteeism found work unit size, worker responsibility, and organizational scheduling three potential ante-

TABLE 12.1 An Example of Functional Analysis

Functional Analysis of Attendance Behaviors

A — Antecedent cues	B — Behaviors	C — Consequences
Awareness of any consequence	Going to bed on time	Reward programs
Advertising	Setting the alarm	Contingent time-off
Meetings	Waking up	Gifts and prizes
Memorandums	Getting dressed	Preferred jobs
Orientation	Getting children off to school	Social
Bulletin board	Leaving home	Attention
Observation of any consequence	Getting a baby-sitter	Recognition
Social status and pressure	Driving to work	Praise
Temporal cues	Reporting to work	Feedback
Special events		Data on attendance
Weather		

Functional Analysis of Absenteeism Behaviors

A — Antecedent cues	B — Behaviors	C — Consequences
Illness/accident	Getting up late	Discipline programs
Hangover	Sleeping in	Verbal reprimands
Lack of transportation	Staying home	Written reprimands
Traffic	Drinking	Pay docks
No day-care facilities	Fishing/hunting	Layoffs
Family problems	Working at home	Dismissals
Company policies	Visiting	Social consequences from coworkers
Group/personal norms	Caring for sick child	Escape from, and avoidance of working
Seniority/age		Nothing
Awareness/observation of any consequence		

Source: Fred Luthans and Mark Martinko, "An Organizational Behavior Modification Analysis of Absenteeism," *Human Resources Management,* Fall 1976, p. 15.

cedent influences that could be used to improve employee attendance and feedback, rewards, and punishers as effective attendance control procedures.[3]

This functional analysis step of O.B. Mod. brings out the problem-solving nature of the technique. Both the antecedent cues that emit the behavior, and sometimes control it, and the consequences that are currently maintaining the behavior must be identified and understood before an effective intervention strategy can be developed. The accompanying Application Example gives the functional analysis of a production supervisor's problem of his workers taking unscheduled breaks.

Application Example

Functional Analysis in Action

In an actual case of an O.B. Mod. application, a production supervisor in a large manufacturing firm identified unscheduled breaks as a critical behavior affecting the performance of his department. It seemed that workers were frequently wandering off the job, and when they were not tending their machines, time was lost—and irrecoverable production. When a baseline measure of this critical behavior was obtained, the supervisor was proved to be right. The data indicated that unscheduled breaks (defined as leaving the job for reasons other than to take a scheduled break or to obtain materials) were occurring in the department on a relatively frequent basis. The functional analysis was performed to determine the antecedent(s) and consequence(s) of the unscheduled-break behavior.

It was found that the clock served as the antecedent cue for the critical behavior. The workers in this department started work at 8 A.M., they had their first scheduled break at 10 A.M., and they had lunch at noon. They started again at 1 P.M., had a break at 3 P.M., and quit at 5 P.M. The functional analysis revealed that almost precisely at 9 A.M., 11 A.M., 2 P.M., and 4 P.M. the workers were leaving their jobs and going to the rest room. In other words, the clock served as a cue for them to take an unscheduled break midway between starting time and the first scheduled break, between the first scheduled break and lunch, between lunch and the scheduled afternoon break, and between the afternoon break and quitting time. The clock did not *cause* the behavior; it served only as a cue to emit the behavior. On the other hand, the behavior was under stimulus control of the clock because the clock dictated when the behavior would occur. The consequence, however, was what was maintaining the behavior. The critical behavior was a function of its consequences. The functional analysis revealed that the consequence of the unscheduled-break behavior was escaping from a dull, boring task (that is, the unscheduled-break behavior was being negatively reinforced) and/or meeting with coworkers and friends to socialize and have a cigarette (that is, the unscheduled-break behavior was being positively reinforced). Through such a functional analysis the antecedents and consequences are identified so that an effective intervention strategy can be developed.

The functional analysis pinpoints one of the most significant practical problems of using an O.B. Mod. approach to change critical performance behaviors. Only the *contingent* consequences have an impact on subsequent behavior. The functional analysis often reveals that there are many competing contingencies for every organizational behavior. For example, a supervisor may be administering what he or she believes to be contingent punishment for an undesirable behavior. In many cases the persons who are supposedly being punished will allow their coworkers' rewards to be the contingent consequence, and their undesirable behavior will increase in subsequent frequency. In other words, the supervisor's punishment is not contingent; it has no impact on the subordinates' subsequent behavior. The functional analysis must make sure that the *contingent* consequences are identified, and the analyst must not be deluded by the consequences that on the surface appear to be affecting the critical behavior.

Step 4: Development of an Intervention Strategy

The first three steps in an O.B. Mod. approach are preliminary to the action step, the intervention. The goal of the intervention is to strengthen and accelerate desirable performance behaviors and/or weaken and decelerate undesirable behaviors. There are several strategies that can be used, but the main ones are positive reinforcement, punishment–positive reinforcement, and extinction–positive reinforcement strategies.

A Positive Reinforcement Strategy. The last chapter devoted considerable attention to the concept of reinforcement. A *positive reinforcer* was defined as a consequence which strengthens the behavior and increases its subsequent frequency. It was also brought out that negative reinforcement (the termination or withdrawal of an undesirable consequence) has the same impact on behavior; that is, it strengthens and increases subsequent frequency. Yet positive and not negative reinforcement is recommended as an effective intervention strategy for O.B. Mod. The reason is that positive reinforcement represents a form of positive control of behavior, while negative reinforcement and punishment represent forms of negative control of behavior. As Chapter 11 pointed out, negative reinforcement is actually a type of "blackmail" control of behavior; the person behaves in a certain way in order not to be punished. Most organizations today control participants in this manner. People come to work in order not to be fired, and they look busy when the supervisor walks by in order not to be punished. Under positive control, the person behaves in a certain way in order to receive the desired consequence. Under positive control, people come to work in order to be recognized for making a contribution to their department's goal of perfect attendance, or they keep busy whether the supervisor is around or not in order to receive incentive pay or because they get self-reinforcement from doing a good job. Positive control through a positive reinforcement intervention strategy is much more effective and long-lasting than negative control. It creates a much healthier and more productive organizational climate.

A Punishment–Positive Reinforcement Strategy. There is no debate that a positive reinforcement strategy is the most effective intervention for O.B. Mod. Yet realistically it is recognized that in some cases the use of punishment to weaken and decelerate undesirable behaviors cannot be avoided.

This would be true in the case of something like unsafe behaviors that need to be immediately decreased. However, as was pointed out in Chapter 11, so many negative side effects accompany the use of punishment that it should be avoided if at all possible. Punished behavior tends to be only temporarily suppressed; for example, if a supervisor reprimands a subordinate for some undesirable behavior, the behavior will decrease in the presence of the supervisor but will surface again when the supervisor is absent. In addition, a punished person becomes very anxious and uptight; reliance on punishment may have a disastrous impact on employee satisfaction and create unnecessary stress.

Perhaps the biggest problem with the use of punishment, however, is that it is very difficult for a supervisor to switch roles from punisher to positive reinforcer. Some supervisors and managers rely on punishment so much in dealing with their subordinates that it is almost impossible for them to administer positive reinforcement effectively. This is a bad situation for the management of human resources because the use of positive reinforcement is a much more effective way of changing employee behavior. If punishment is deemed to be necessary, the desirable alternative behavior (for example, safe behavior) should be positively reinforced at the first opportunity. Use of this combination strategy will cause the alternative desirable behavior to begin to replace the undesirable behavior in the person's behavioral repertoire. Punishment should never be used alone as an O.B. Mod. intervention. If punishment is absolutely necessary, it should always be used in combination with positive reinforcement.

An Extinction–Positive Reinforcement Strategy.

An extinction strategy is a much more effective way to decrease undesirable behavior than punishment. As the previous chapter pointed out, extinction has the same impact on behavior as punishment (although it does not act as fast), but extinction does not have the negative side effects of punishment. Punishment can be thought of as the application of a noxious or aversive consequence or the *deliberate withdrawal* of a positively reinforcing consequence that is already a part of the person's environment. Extinction involves the *withdrawal* of a desirable consequence that is contingent upon the person's behavior; this happens after the behavior is emitted. More simply, however, extinction can be defined as providing *no* consequence. Obviously, there is a fine line between extinction and the withdrawal of a positive reinforcement type of punishment. In fact, there is such a fine distinction between the two that some behaviorists do not even deal with extinction. They simply operationally define anything which decreases behavior as punishment. But the important point for human resources management is that undesirable behavior can be decreased without the accompanying negative side effects of punishment. This can be done by making sure that there is no consequence for the undesirable behavior, that is, by putting it on extinction.

In the functional analysis performed in step 3 of O.B. Mod., the consequences of maintaining the critical behavior were identified. The extinction strategy would eliminate those consequences of the critical behaviors that were to be decelerated. For example, if complaining was the targeted behavior and the functional analysis revealed that the supervisor's attention to the complaining behavior was maintaining it, the extinction strategy would be to have the supervisor ignore the complaints—not give them any attention. The supervisor might be able to avoid the complainer. Walking away from the person when he or she started to complain might be punishing, but if handled properly, that is, in a nonobvious manner, it could be an extinction strategy without the negative side effects. Again, as with any intervention strategy, whether it was effective in reducing the behavior can be known only by what happens to the frequency measures after the intervention. Also, similar to the punishment strategy, extinction should be used only in combination with positive reinforcement. The desirable alternative behavior would be positively reinforced at the first opportunity. The positively reinforced behavior would begin to replace the undesirable behavior. In the example of the complaining behavior, when the person did not complain, the supervisor would notice this and give attention to the person for making constructive comments and not complaining.

Because most organizational behaviors are being reinforced on intermittent schedules, which Chapter 11 pointed out are very resistant to extinction, the use of the extinction strategy may take time and patience. But as a long-range strategy for weakening undesirable behaviors and decelerating the frequency of their occurrence, extinction can be effective. In general, the very simple rule of thumb to follow in employing an O.B. Mod. intervention strategy is to positively reinforce desirable behaviors and make sure that undesirable behaviors are not reinforced. This simple guideline may have as big an impact on effective human resources management as any single other thing the supervisor or manager can do. But once again it should be pointed out that understanding and using the other concepts and techniques discussed in the previous and the following chapters are also necessary for the complex, challenging job of effective human resources management.

Step 5: Evaluation to Ensure Performance Improvement

A glaring weakness of most human resources management techniques is the absence of any systematic, built-in evaluation. A comprehensive analysis of the evaluation of human resources programs concluded that the typical approach is "to review a program with one or two vice presidents at the corporate office, various managers in the field, and perhaps a group of prospective trainees. It continues to be used until someone in a position of authority decides that the program has outlived its usefulness. All of this is done on the basis of opinion and judgment."[4] Such haphazard evaluations have resulted in the termination of some effective programs and the perpetuation of some ineffective ones. In either case, there are severe credibility problems, and today all programs dealing with people, whether they are government welfare programs or human resources management programs, are under the pressure of accountability. Human resources managers no longer have the luxury of just trying something new and different and hoping they can improve performance. Today there is pressure for everything that is tried to be *proved* to have value. As in the case of the validity of selection and appraisal techniques, which are currently under scrutiny, systematic evaluations of human resources management techniques should have been done all along.

O.B. Mod. attempts to meet the credibility and accountability problems head-on by including evaluation as an actual part of the process. In this last step of the model, the need for four levels of evaluation (reaction, learning, behavioral change, and performance improvement) is stressed. The *reaction level* refers simply to whether the people using the approach and those having it used on them like it. If O.B. Mod. is well received and there is a positive reaction to it, there is a better chance of its being used effectively. In addition, reaction evaluations are helpful because (1) positive reactions help ensure organizational support, (2) they can provide information for planning future programs, (3) favorable reactions can enhance the other levels of evaluation (learning, behavioral change, and performance improvement), and (4) they can provide useful comparative data between units and across time.[5]

The second level of evaluation is learning. This is especially important when first implementing an O.B. Mod. approach. Do the people using the approach understand the theoretical background and underlying assumptions and the meaning of, and reasons for, the steps in the model? If they do not, the model will again tend to be used ineffectively. The third level is aimed at *behavioral change.* Are behaviors actually being changed? The charting of behaviors gives objective data for this level of evaluation. The fourth and final level, *performance improvement,* is the most important. The major purpose of O.B. Mod. is not just to receive a favorable reaction, learn the concepts, and change behaviors. These dimensions are important mainly because they contribute to the overriding purpose, which is to improve performance. "Hard" measures (for example, data on quantity and quality, turnover, absenteeism, customer complaints, employee grievances, length of patient stay, number of clients served, and rate of return on investment) and scientific methodology as discussed in Chapter 2 are used whenever possible to evaluate systematically the impact of O.B. Mod. on performance.

Experience with the Application of O.B. Mod.

There is a growing body of research that evaluates the effectiveness of O.B. Mod. when applied in manufacturing as well as in nonprofit and service-oriented organizations. In addition to the direct application of O.B. Mod. as described in this chapter, considerable basic research has been conducted on operant and social learning variables in experimental psychology. For many years and in very recent times, a number of studies have assessed the application of closely related behavioral management techniques. The *Handbook of Organizational Behavior Management* summarizes these findings as follows:[6]

1. *Employee productivity.* By far most applications have focused on this area. The considerable number of research studies clearly indicate that employee productivity or task completion is positively affected by behavioral management techniques. After reviewing a number of field studies, it was concluded that

the improvement of either quantity or quality of employee output cuts across virtually all organizational settings and all intervention techniques.[7]

2. *Absenteeism and tardiness.* This is probably the second biggest area of application. Studies that have examined this area have used some combination of rewards (for example, small monetary bonuses or lottery incentive systems) for attendance or promptness and/or punishers for absenteeism or tardiness. One extensive search of this literature found very positive results.[8] The six most sound methodological studies reported an 18 to 50 percent reduction in the absence rate and a 90 percent reduction in the frequency of tardiness. One study found a positive, causal impact that an O.B. Mod. program had on the attendance of employees in a bank.[9]

3. *Safety and accident prevention.* Most organizations, especially manufacturing firms and others in which dangerous equipment is used, are very concerned about safety. However, since accidents occur at such a relatively low frequency, most studies have focused on reducing identifiable safety hazards or increasing safe behaviors (for example, wearing earplugs, the utilization of which went from 35 to 95 percent, according to one study;[10] wearing hard hats; or keeping the safety guard in place on dangerous equipment). A review article indicates the considerable success that behavioral management techniques have had in these areas.[11] Some actual company examples include Boston Gas where employees without accidents are eligible for lottery drawings; Virginia Electric & Power Co. where employees can win from $50 to $1000 for safe work habits; Southern New England Telecommunications which gives gift coupons to employees without accidents; and Turner Corp., a New York–based engineering and construction firm, where employees can earn company stock if they meet safety goals. All of these companies report improved accident rates.[12]

4. *Sales performance.* Sales managers and trainers have traditionally relied on internal motivation techniques to get their salespeople to improve their performance. For example, one behavioral management consultant tells about a company that gave its sales personnel a typical high-powered, multimedia training program which supposedly taught them effective selling skills. However, when the enthusiastic trainees finished the program and actually tried the things presented to them in the program, they received little if any feedback or reinforcement. Within a few weeks the enthusiasm began to wane, and, most important, actual sales performance began to decline.[13] In other words, even though these salespeople had probably acquired effective selling skills during their training, the environment did not support the use of these skills. An O.B. Mod. approach, in which important selling behaviors such as customer approach, suggestive statements, and closing statements are identified, measured, analyzed, intervened, and evaluated, would be an alternative to the motivation-skill-teaching approach. A recent comprehensive review of the behavioral approach to sales in restaurants, retail stores, wholesale establishments, and telephone operations found considerable success.[14] By using a combination of antecedent and consequence intervention strategies, dramatic improvements were shown in areas such as wine and dessert sales, average customer transactions, customer assistance, sales forecasting, sales-call frequency, sales of telephone services, and airline reservations. The successful

application of O.B. Mod. to the selling, absent-from-the-work-station, and idle-time behaviors of clerks in a large retail store is reported in detail later in the chapter.

Although the above results are not exhaustive and do not always reflect the exact O.B. Mod. model outlined in this chapter, they are representative of the growing application of this behavioral approach to human resources management. In addition, a comprehensive review generally supports the above findings.[15] The following sections summarize the research on direct applications of O.B. Mod. as conducted by the author of this text and his colleagues.

Manufacturing Applications of O.B. Mod.

To date, most of the direct applications of O.B. Mod. have been in manufacturing firms of all sizes.

The First Application. The initial study was conducted over fifteen years ago in a medium-size light manufacturing firm located in a large city. Two groups (experimental and control) of nine production-type supervisors were used in the study. The experimental group received training, essentially on the five steps, discussed earlier in this chapter, of the O.B. Mod. approach. The results showed that O.B. Mod. had a definite positive impact on reaction, behavioral change, and performance. Learning was not evaluated in this study. Questionnaires administered to the trained supervisors indicated that they liked the O.B. Mod. approach, and the supervisors indicated that their subordinates seemed to react positively. On the charts kept by each trainee (step 2) it was clearly shown that in all cases they were able to change critical behaviors. Examples of behavioral changes accomplished by the supervisors included decreasing the number of complaints, reducing the group scrap rate, decreasing the number of overlooked defective pieces, and reducing the assembly reject rate.[16] The most important result of the study, however, was the significant impact that the O.B. Mod. approach had on the performance of the supervisors' departments. By use of a pretest-posttest control group experimental design, it was found that the experimental group's departments (those in which the supervisors used O.B. Mod.) outperformed the control group's departments. Figure 12.4 shows the results. Statistical analysis revealed that the department production rates of supervisors who used O.B. Mod. increased significantly more than the department production rates of the control supervisors (those who were not using O.B. Mod.).[17]

The Second Study. A replication in a larger plant obtained almost identical results to those of the original study on all levels of evaluation (including learning). The following summarizes some typical cases of behavioral change that occurred in the production area of the larger manufacturing firm:

1. *Use of idle time.* One supervisor had a worker with a lot of idle time. Instead of using this time productively by helping others, the worker would pretend to look busy and stretch out the day. After getting a baseline measure and doing a functional analysis, the supervisor intervened by giving the worker

FIGURE 12.4
Performance results of experimental (those who used the O.B. Mod. approach) and control groups.
(*Source:* Robert Ottemann and Fred Luthans, "An Experimental Analysis of the Effectiveness of an Organizational Behavior Modification Program in Industry," *Academy of Management Proceedings,* 1975, p. 141.)

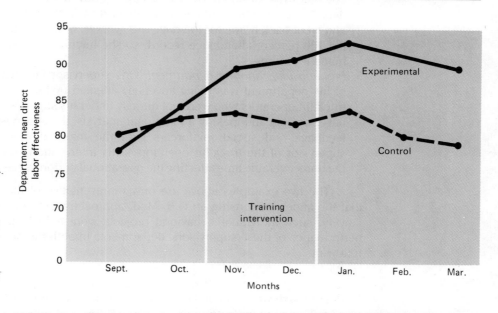

social reinforcers (attention, praise, and recognition) contingent upon the worker's helping out at other jobs during idle time. Eventually the supervisor also reinforced the worker through assigning more responsibility. This approach dramatically increased the worker's productive use of idle time.

2. *Low performer.* A production worker in one of the supervisor's departments was producing way below standard (80.3 percent of standard on a six-month baseline). The low performance was not deemed to be an ability, technical, training, or standards problem. After the functional analysis, the supervisor used an intervention of feedback and social reinforcers to increase the types of behaviors that would lead to higher output. This intervention resulted in a 93 percent of standard performance level, with no decrease in quality.

3. *Group quality.* One supervisor had a problem with the quality of work in his department. The baseline measure verified this problem. After the functional analysis, the supervisor used feedback and social reinforcers on the group as a whole. Shortly after the use of this intervention strategy, the group attained the quality standard for the first time in three years.

4. *Group attendance.* Another supervisor felt that he had an attendance problem in his department. The baseline measure revealed 92 percent attendance, which was not as big a problem as he had thought. However, he established the goal of 100 percent. After he used daily feedback and social reinforcers on the group, 100 percent attendance was attained very rapidly. An interesting anecdote told by the supervisor was that one of his workers was riding to work from a small town in a car pool early one morning when they hit a deer.

The car was disabled by the accident. Coworkers who worked in other departments in the plant and were also riding in the car pool called relatives and went back home for the day. This worker, however, did not want to spoil the 100 percent attendance record, so she hitchhiked to work by herself and made it on time.

5. *Problem with another department.* One supervisor felt that the performance of his department was being adversely affected by the unrecoverable time of truck-lift operators who were not directly under his supervision. After obtaining baseline data and making a functional analysis, the supervisor decided to use feedback and social reinforcers with the informal group leader and the supervisor of the truck-lift operators. This intervention substantially reduced the unrecoverable time affecting the operational performance of his department.

The five examples above are only representative of the types of behavior that the supervisors using an O.B. Mod. approach were able to change. Cumulatively, such individual behavioral projects were able to improve the overall performance of these supervisors' departments in both the original study and the follow-up.

Application to an Entire Small Manufacturing Plant. Next, the O.B. Mod. approach was extended beyond the first-line supervisory level of application to a total small manufacturing plant with all levels of management and to a very large multiplant manufacturing firm. In the small manufacturing plant, O.B. Mod. was implemented in three major phases.[18] The first phase was primarily educational and consisted of training all three levels of management (first the owner/ manager, then the four department heads, and finally the eight supervisors) in the O.B. Mod. approach, basically following the five-step model discussed in this chapter. The second stage involved simulation/experiential exercises. At first, the participants analyzed case studies and developed intervention strategies. Then, once both the participants and the researchers/trainers had developed confidence in the participants' skills, the participants applied the O.B. Mod. approach to their own work areas in a manner similar to that already described in the first study. The third and final phase involved the development of a total organizational performance management system. In this phase, all levels of management collaborated to identify key behaviors and performance indices. An organization-wide feedback system was then developed on the basis of key behaviors and performance measures. In addition, programs for specific problem areas were developed.

The results of this comprehensive, *total organization* application indicated that there were significant improvements in both quantity and quality of performance. In fact, *record* performance was attained. Statistical analyses demonstrated the significance of these changes, and simple inspection of the graphic representation of the data shown in Figure 12.5 shows the impact that the O.B. Mod. approach had in this company. The left-hand portion of the graph depicts the average levels and variability of both quantity and quality prior to the intervention. The next segment of the graph displays the effects of a type of contingent time-off (Friday afternoon was given off for reaching a stated level of performance

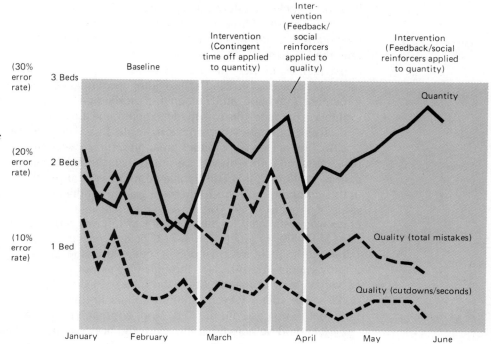

FIGURE 12.5 The impact of O.B. Mod. on the total performance improvement of a small factory. (*Source:* Fred Luthans and Jason Schweizer, "How Behavior Modification Techniques Can Improve Total Organizational Performance," *Management Review.* September 1979, p. 49.)

during the week) intervention strategy on quantity when no consequences were being applied to quality. As evidenced by the changes illustrated, quantity improved with the application of the contingent time-off consequences, while the quality level, for which consequences were not changed, remained about the same. The third segment demonstrates that the contingent application of social reinforcers had a positive impact on quality, while the quantity levels remained about the same. Finally, the last segment demonstrates improved levels of both quality and quantity under the control of the feedback system and contingent social reinforcement.

Whereas the first study used a control group design, the multiple-baseline design was deemed to be more appropriate for the evaluation where the total organization was being impacted by the O.B. Mod. approach. Such designs give considerable weight to the conclusion that the O.B. Mod. approach did indeed cause the total performance of this organization to improve.

Application to a Very Large Multiplant Firm. Still another study of the application of O.B. Mod. was conducted in eleven major product areas in two plants of a very large labor-intensive firm.[19] One hundred and thirty-five production supervisors were trained in and then implemented an O.B. Mod. approach. Specifically, these supervisors first made a detailed analysis/audit that identified objective, measurable employee behaviors in their respective departments that contributed to quality and/or quantity performance. These included behaviors such as performing a particular operation more efficiently or delivering a certain piece of material in a more timely manner. The supervisors then quantitatively measured and charted the frequency of occurrence of these identified behaviors. This was followed by an analysis of the antecedents and consequences of the critical behavior (that is, an A-B-C functional analysis). The intervention step consisted of providing performance feedback and social reinforcement (attention and recognition) for progress and attainment. Finally, an evaluation of the results was made to determine the exact impact on performance.

The results are summarized in Table 12.2. The O.B. Mod. approach had a positive impact on all product areas in which it was applied. The impact had wide variation, but it should be noted that although there was only a 2 percent gain in product 2, this still translated to an annualized value of nearly $900,000 in this company, and the 1.4 percent gain in product 6 equated to an annualized value of about $750,000. The projected annual values of the gains in other product areas were estimated for this company as follows: product 1, +$259,000; product 3, +$510,000; product 4, +$371,000; and product 5, an impressive +$2.276 million. Although information for computing the actual dollar values of the improvements in products 7 through 11 was not available, they were judged to be very similar in magnitude to the others. Besides this tremendous impact on dollar value added (several million dollars in this company), it is important to note that in no case did the O.B. Mod. approach have a negative impact.

It should be noted that this study did not contain the rigorous methodology of the other manufacturing applications. Thus, the results in this case cannot lead to the same causal conclusions concerning the impact of O.B. Mod. Yet there is still considerable evidence that O.B. Mod. did lead to the improved performance. For instance, when examined closely, the performance changes

TABLE 12.2 The Impact of O.B. Mod. on the Quantity and Quality of Performance in a Large Production Operation

Product	Group	Quality Improvement, Percent	Quantity Improvement, Percent
1	B	50	
2	A		2
3	A	15	
4	A	23	
	C	64	
5	A	35	
	C	51	
6	A		1.4
7	B		16
8	B		16
9	B	42	
10	B	39	
11	B		52

Source: Adapted from Fred Luthans, Walter S. Maciag, and Stuart A. Rosenkrantz, "O.B. Mod.: Meeting the Productivity Challenge with Human Resource Management," *Personnel,* March–April 1983, p. 31. Groups A and B are two shifts in one plant, and group C is at another plant in the same company.

following the staggered starting dates of the program support the conclusion that the effects were indeed caused by the O.B. Mod. approach rather than some other factor. This is a simplified version of the multiple-baseline design from which causal conclusions can be drawn. In every product area tracked in this part of the analysis, the start of the O.B. Mod. program was followed almost immediately by a clear improvement in the quality or quantity of performance.

Contingent Time Off in a Manufacturing Plant. A contingent time-off (CTO) program was tried in a unit of a fairly large high-technology firm.[20] Most organizations in recent times have not had the luxury of using monetary reward systems to increase the performance of their employees. A potentially powerful, but largely overlooked, alternative is the use of contingent time off. This usually involves employees' attaining "earned time" (that is, leisure time or time off from the job) once both quantity and quality performance standards are met. In other words, CTO focuses on performance results, not hours worked. Time off, not just the pay, becomes the reward. Labor costs do not decrease under a CTO program, but performance may substantially increase at no additional cost to the employer.

Using an O.B. Mod. approach, it was determined by a combined team of in-house staff members and researchers that quantity and quality of performance were a problem in this high-technology manufacturing plant, which consisted of noninterdependent work groups that assembled different products. Measurement revealed that one representative group was producing an average of 160 units per day with about 10 percent rejects. Functional analysis revealed that this group could probably produce more than this with better quality, if there were reinforcing consequences for doing so. Since this firm did not have funds available for monetary incentives, a CTO intervention was applied. The contingency contract was: *If* the group produced 200 units with three additional good units for every defective unit, *then* they could leave work for the rest of that day. Within a week of the time the CTO intervention was implemented, the group was producing more than 200 units with an average of 1.5 percent rejects. These employees, who had formerly *put in* an eight-hour day, were now *working* an average of 6 hours per day, and, more important, they increased their performance by 25 percent with better quality at no additional cost to the company.

Except for some minor problems with parts availability, the employees obviously reacted very favorably to the CTO plan, and, of course, management was very happy with record performance with no additional labor costs. It was a "win-win" strategy. However, there is an interesting but disturbing postscript to this success story. After things had been going along very well (for example, there were plans to implement CTO in all independent work units in the plant), there was an unanticipated changeover in top management. Unfortunately, the new general manager reviewed the CTO plan and concluded: "If employees can produce 200 units in six hours, then they were goldbricking before. Given that we pay them for an eight-hour day, they should be able to produce at least 240 units." The manager then proceeded to terminate the CTO plan and told the group to "get with it." As would be predicted from a behavioral perspective, production immediately dropped in this group to 140 units, 20 units below the original productivity rate. The contingency contract was broken, and the employees were punished for being productive. The lesson to be learned here, of course, is that there must be a strong commitment on the part of management to carry through and support contingency contracts, such as the CTO plan, if the desired results are to be achieved and then maintained. Behavior is a function of its consequences: if reinforced, it will increase; if punished, it will decrease. Not living up to contingency contracts can have disastrous results.

Nonmanufacturing Applications: Health and Service Industries

The studies discussed above do provide considerable evidence that an O.B. Mod. approach can have a positive impact on employee performance, at least in relatively structured environments such as are found in most manufacturing plants. But what about less-structured, nonmanufacturing organizations? Research indicates that similar results are possible in these organizations as well.

In a large hospital application, eleven supervisors from medical service, business, and operations units were given O.B. Mod. training in eight sessions over a two-month period.[21] During the O.B. Mod. training these hospital supervisors learned the principles of O.B. Mod. and used the five-step approach; that is, they identified, measured, functionally analyzed, and intervened to change key performance behaviors of their subordinates, and then they evaluated the results in their respective areas of responsibility. The results of this program are shown in Table 12.3. Although the researchers were unable to employ an experimental design in this study (and therefore cause-and-effect conclusions are not warranted), the simple before-and-after analysis provides a rather convincing argument that the O.B. Mod. approach was effective in modifying a broad range of performance-related behaviors in a hospital setting. The O.B. Mod. approach seemed to affect both the quality and the quantity performance measures. Moreover, the data indicate that each of the O.B. Mod.–trained supervisors was successful in applying the intervention, despite the wide variety of situations encountered.

In another nonmanufacturing organization, a somewhat different type of O.B. Mod. application was tried.[22] Instead of training supervisors to use an O.B. Mod. approach, the researchers themselves carried out the steps normally handled by the supervisors. An experiment (an A-B-A compared with a control group, that is, a true experimental design) was conducted in a major metropolitan department store. Critical performance behaviors of eighty-two retail clerks from sixteen randomly selected departments were identified. These behaviors included selling, stock work, idle behaviors, absenteeism from the workstation, and miscellaneous. Next, the baseline measure of these behaviors was obtained by observational and work-sampling techniques. A detailed analysis was then conducted to determine the appropriate performance goals for these behaviors. For example, on the basis of job descriptions, organizational goals and policies, direct observations, and role playing, it was determined that (1) salespersons, except

TABLE 12.3 Performance Measures before and after an O.B. Mod. Training Program in a Large Hospital

Unit	Measure	Pre-intervention	Post-intervention	Percent Change
Emergency room clerks	Registration errors (per day)	19.16	4.58	76.1
Hardware engineer group, HIS	Average time to repair (minutes)	92.53	33.25	61.4
Medical records file clerks	Errors in filing (per person per audit)	2.87	0.078	97.3
Medical records	Complaints	8.0	1.0	875.0
Transcriptionists	Average errors	2.07	1.4	33.0
	Average output	2258.0	2303.33	2.0
Heart station	EKG procedures accomplished (average)	1263.0	1398.97	11.0
	Overdue procedures	7.0*	4.0	42.8
Eye clinic	Daily patient throughput	19.0	23.0	21.0
	Daily patient teaching documentation	1.0	2.8	180.0
	Protocols produced	0.0	2.0	200.0
Pharmacy technicians	Drug output (doses)	348.8	422.1	21.0
	Posting errors	3.67	1.48	59.7
	Product waste (percent)	5.8	4.35	25.0
Radiology technicians	Average patient throughput (procedural)	3849.5	4049.0	5.0
	Retake rate (percent)	11.2	9.95	11.2
Patient accounting	Average monthly billings	2561.0	3424.5	33.7
Admitting office	Time to admit (minutes)	43.73	13.57	68.97
	Average cost	$15.05	$11.73	22.0
Data center operations	Systems log-on (time)	1.54	1.43	13.4

*Estimate. All averages are arithmetic means.
Source: Adapted from Charles A. Snyder and Fred Luthans, "Using O.B. Mod. to Increase Hospital Productivity," *Personnel Administrator,* August 1982, p. 72.

when they had an excused absence, should be present in the department, within 3 feet of displayed merchandise, during assigned working hours; (2) when customers came to the department, they should be offered assistance or acknowledged and promised immediate aid within five seconds; and (3) the display shelf should be filled to at least 70 percent capacity.

The intervention consisted of contingently applying time off with pay or equivalent cash and an opportunity to compete for a free vacation for two for attaining the performance goals. Observationally gathered behavioral data were collected during and after this intervention. For computational and graphic presentation, the selling, stock work, and miscellaneous behaviors were collapsed into a single category, called *aggregate retailing behavior,* and absence from the workstation and idle time were also combined for this purpose. Figure 12.6 shows the results. The baseline frequencies of these behaviors were not significantly different, but immediately on the first day of the intervention the aggregate retailing behavior of the experimental group dramatically increased, and there was a huge decline in the average incidence of absence from the workstation and idleness. As shown, this frequency maintained itself even after the intervention

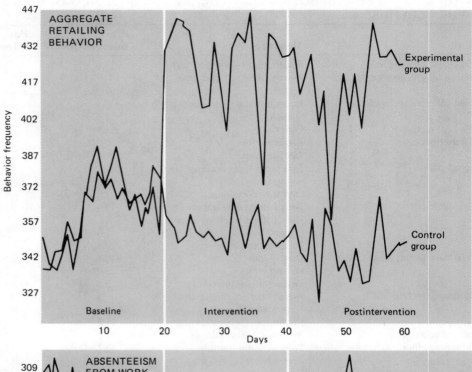

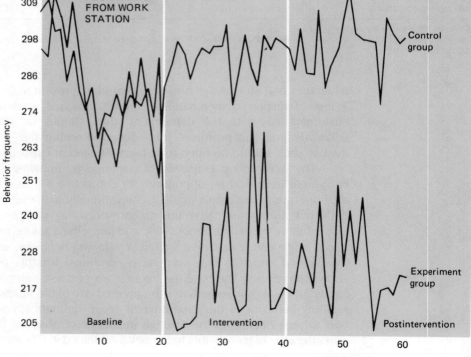

FIGURE 12.6
Results of a positive reinforcement intervention on salespersons' performance behaviors.
(*Source*: Adapted from Fred Luthans, Robert Paul, and Douglas Baker, "An Experimental Analysis of the Impact of Contingent Reinforcement on Salespersons' Performance Behaviors," *Journal of Applied Psychology*, June 1981, pp. 318–319.)

was withdrawn. This suggests that other, more natural reinforcers in the environment and perhaps self-reinforcement had taken over.

A recent systematic replication using tighter controls in the field setting found generally similar results during the intervention, but also a reversal (there was a return to preintervention levels of performance behaviors) during the postintervention phase.[23] This type of replication and more research in more settings is needed before any definitive conclusions and broad generalizations about O.B. Mod. can be drawn. But at least for now, O.B. Mod. does seem to hold considerable potential for the effective management of human resources.

Behavioral Self-Management

So far the discussion of O.B. Mod. has been oriented toward how people can manage others' behavior more effectively. Now, in this section, attention is shifted toward how people can better manage their own behavior. How to manage oneself more effectively has been almost completely ignored, except for some accolades concerning positive thinking and the popular time-management guidelines. But, in the final analysis, self-management may be the basic prerequisite for the effective management of organizations, groups, and individual subordinates; in fact, it has been suggested that behavioral self-management may be the important missing link, or at least the overlooked first step in the inductive chain, in managerial effectiveness.[24] In fact, as the accompanying Application Example demonstrates, self-management may even have societal implications. The first part of this section discusses the meaning and background of self-management. Next, specific strategies for application are presented, and finally the application experience on this self-approach to management is summarized.

The Meaning and Background of Self-Management

In the past, whenever discussions of self-management took place, the importance of positive thinking, willpower, and perhaps self-motivation was brought out. This approach to self-management certainly didn't do any harm, and it may have done some people some good. However, an O.B. Mod. approach to self-management can be used as a systematic approach to more effective management.

A formal definition of *behavioral self-control* is as follows: "The manager's deliberate regulation of stimulus cues, covert processes, and response consequences to achieve personally identified behavioral outcomes."[25] In addition to this definition, there are three conditions that need to be met in an O.B. Mod. approach to self-management:

1. The individual manager must be the proactive agent of change.
2. Relevant stimulus cues, cognitive processes, and response consequences must be brought under control by the manager.
3. The manager must be consciously aware of how a personally identified target outcome is being achieved.[26]

The above definitions and criteria make a clear distinction between an O.B. Mod. approach and traditional positive-thinking approaches to self-management,

**Application
Example**

Making It in America*

Self-management can have societal as well as individual implications for managers. For example, many immigrants to this country have been able to succeed thanks to their ability to manage their behavioral contingencies. One of the best recent examples is provided by Russians who have come to the United States in the last two decades. Although they were raised in Communist Russia, they already had the basic ingredients for success in a capitalistic system. By applying for visas to leave the Soviet Union, they automatically lost their jobs. This forced them to manage behavioral contingencies to even survive. They became particularly adept at black market activities and other under-the-table dealings. Many of them learned how to trade in such desired commodities as tickets to the opera, caviar, and reconditioned cars. With the money they earned, they kept themselves and their families alive until they could get to the United States.

Today Russian émigrés live in a number of different areas around the country. One is Brighton Beach in Brooklyn where some of them have become millionaires in less than a decade. Through self-management and an economic system that rewards efficiency and the ability to cater to customer demand, these émigrés have found that hard work and a willingness to take risks have resulted in greater payoffs than they ever dreamed imaginable. Consider the following examples:

- Abram Gin started out driving a taxi. He saved his money and then moved into the limousine business. With his profits, he expanded the operation. He also went into real estate. Today he and his partners are worth over $25 million.
- Zindel Selmanovitch came to the United States in 1972. An engineer by training, he spoke no English. Four years later he had a real estate license and had put himself through graduate business school, while working at a variety of different jobs from plumbing to pumping gas. Today he manages a $30 million portfolio of loans to 150 companies.
- Eduard Nakhamkin was a professor of mathematics and aviation in the Soviet Union. He came to New York in 1975 and raised $2000 by selling some artwork he brought with him. He used the money to open a small art gallery. The early years were difficult, but he persevered. Today he has three galleries in New York City and two more in San Francisco. He also owns two restaurants and maintains an apartment in Manhattan, a home on Long Island, and a residence in Spain.

Quite obviously these are examples of successful self-management.

Source: Adapted from Alex Taylor III, "Russia's Newest Export: Capitalism," *Fortune*, Dec. 8, 1986, pp. 119–126.

or even time-management approaches. In the case of time management, prescriptive guidelines are offered (for example, delegate more, reduce paperwork, and establish goals), but no suggestions as to exactly *how* to accomplish these objectives or how to deal with other-imposed or self-imposed environmental antecedents and consequences are given. There is considerable theoretical and research backup for an O.B. Mod. approach to self-management.

The last chapter indicated that behavioral self-control is a vital part of social learning theory, along with modeling and cognitive mediating processes. As was pointed out, it is important to recognize that the social learning approach is a behavioral theory and depends heavily upon classical and operant principles. Thus, behavioral self-management fits into the O.B. Mod. framework.

To B. F. Skinner, the notion of self-control is no different from other forms of operant behavioral control. In the strict (Skinnerian) operant interpretation, behavior is deemed to be under the control of the stimulus environment (that is, the antecedent, discriminant stimulus) and of the contingent consequences, irrespective of whether these are manipulated by individuals themselves or by others in the environment. In other words, under the operant view, behavioral self-control depends on the individual's ability to manage the stimulus environment and the contingent consequences. However, just as social learning theory accepts the operant principles but goes beyond them, so does the approach to self-management suggested here.

To review again, the social learning approach encompasses the operant premise of the importance of the antecedent and consequent environment; in addition, however, it recognizes and gives attention to the role of cognitive mediating processes—thoughts, feelings, and self-evaluative behavior—and it recognizes that the antecedents and consequences can be covert (inner and unobservable) as well as overt (external and observable). This extension from the operant to the social learning view is also represented by a move from the three-term antecedent-behavior-consequence functional analysis (A-B-C) to the four-term stimulus-organism-behavior-consequence functional analysis (S-O-B-C). In other words, behavioral self-management falls within an expanded O.B. Mod. framework and depends on the S-O-B-C functional analysis.

Strategies for Behavioral Self-Management

Besides the S-O-B-C functional analysis, which is used to help identify and more effectively manage the environmental contingencies and the cognitive mediating processes, there are two other major strategies for effective behavioral self-management; these are discussed below.

Stimulus Management. This strategy is concerned with the antecedent or stimulus side and can be either covert or overt. Stimulus management involves the gradual removal of, or only selective exposure to, stimuli that evoke behaviors whose frequency the manager is trying to decrease or wants to eliminate altogether. At the same time, or alternatively, the manager would deliberately introduce new cuing stimuli or rearrange existing stimuli in order to evoke behavior that he or she wants to create or whose frequency is to be increased.

For example, managers who want to decrease the amount of time spent in idle chitchat with subordinates could have their secretaries screen all visits and apply certain criteria before a subordinate is allowed into the office. This method of stimulus management—the removal or selective exposure of the stimulus (visiting subordinates)—will decrease the amount of unproductive time spent chatting with subordinates. This same strategy could also be used by managers who want to increase informal interactions with subordinates. They could schedule weekly appointments with each subordinate or have their coffee breaks and those of their subordinates scheduled together. The introduction of the new stimulus (having subordinates come up to the office) or the rearrangement of the existing stimuli (scheduling the coffee breaks to coincide) would evoke more informal interactions with subordinates.

Consequence Management. This second major strategy concentrates on the consequence side of the self-behavior. It involves the contingent application of new reinforcers or the rearrangement of existing ones to increase the behavior in subsequent frequency, or the application of punishers to decrease it. This strategy is basically the same as the intervention strategies for O.B. Mod. discussed so far, except that the self-reinforcers and punishers can be covert as well as overt.

An example of a self-reinforcement strategy would be that of managers who want to limit their weekly staff meetings to an hour. When they are able to do this, they could reinforce themselves by having a cup of coffee (overt) or by simply congratulating themselves and feeling good about it (covert). If they do not keep the meeting time to an hour, they could punish themselves by staying after work for the amount of time over an hour (overt) or simply by admonishing themselves and feeling bad about it (covert).

Analogous to the point made in this chapter and the last one, that positive reinforcers tend to be more effective than punishers, it is also generally found, at least in clinical applications, that self-reinforcement is a more effective strategy than self-punishment. The problem with self-punishment, besides people's tendency only to suppress rather than change the behavior, is that if a punishment is too aversive, the person just won't use it. Thus, the dilemma for a self-punishment strategy is to find a punisher that will in fact decrease the behavior but, at the same time, will not be so aversive that the person will avoid using it.

Other Strategies. There are slight variations in the two main strategies discussed above, in addition to several other possibilities. A variation of stimulus management—or, more accurately, a part of stimulus management—is the goal-setting procedure discussed in Chapter 10. Self-goal setting can serve as both a cuing stimulus and feedback, and accomplishment of progress and attainment of self-goals can be the reinforcers. The same is true of a self-recording strategy. In a feedforward-feedback sense, self-recording can serve both as a reminder and as a cue for the behavior ("I have to record every hour" or "I have to record every occurrence," for example) and also reinforce it ("I can see the progress I am making from the records I am keeping"). Some psychologists believe that self-observation is a necessary first step in any program of self-change. Finally, the rehearsal and modeling techniques that were discussed in Chapter 11 could be used in self-control. This can be found in the following example: "A salesperson could rehearse a sales presentation both covertly and overtly and thereby refine it. Then through intentionally imagining the desirable consequences of a successful sale, feelings of confidence could be reinforced".[27]

Applications of Self-Management

Although the research on and application of behavioral self-management are just getting under way, a number of line and staff managers in a wide variety of positions such as advertising, retailing, manufacturing, and public service have applied it in the hope of increasing their effectiveness.[28] For example, one assistant manager in a retail store determined that one of the major problems detracting from her effectiveness was her overdependence on her boss. With the help of the researcher, she systematically applied self-management to try to reduce this behavior.

She first used the S-O-B-C model to functionally analyze and identify the relevant environmental and cognitive variables. She then set up a combination stimulus and consequence management strategy to decrease her visits with (that is, her dependence on) her boss. This strategy consisted mainly of self-recording. She maintained a record of the number of times she resisted going to see her boss when she normally would have, and she also kept track of the number of times she did visit with her boss and what was discussed. The index card she carried and the notebook record she kept served to cue the appropriate behavior—to resist visiting her boss and take her own action—and the feedback served to reinforce the appropriate behavior and punish the inappropriate behavior.

Using a reversal design to evaluate the intervention, it was concluded that this approach did indeed have its intended effect on the targeted behavior. Figure 12.7 shows the results. Both the boss and this assistant manager were pleased with the results. Once the study was over, the assistant manager reported that she would go back to using self-management to control this behavior and would try to use the approach with other dysfunctional behaviors as well.

Another example is that of an advertising manager who systematically applied self-management to three critical behaviors that were targeted for analysis and change: not processing enough paperwork, leaving the office without telling anyone, and failing to fill out a daily expense form. In other words, the more important-sounding but highly unrealistic, and in some cases nonexistent, management activities such as strategic planning or matrix management were not the problems facing this manager. He had problems with too much paperwork, keeping his staff informed of his whereabouts, and meeting bureaucratic requirements such as filling out his expense vouchers. Behavioral self-management is especially adaptable to these mundane, yet cumulatively very important, activities that contribute to managerial effectiveness.

After carefully analyzing the paperwork process in S-O-B-C terms, the manager, in conjunction with the researcher, set up a combination stimulus and consequence strategy to reduce the number of unprocessed paperwork items at the end of each day. In particular, the inflows of paperwork items were categorized, and the behaviors to be performed by both the manager and his secretary were cognitively clarified. For example, the secretary now screened out some of the items according to certain criteria and presented other items in consolidated form. The manager, instead of vacillating over each item and then putting it on ever-higher piles on his desk, now acted immediately, noted an action step, or put the item in his out box. He also employed a self-monitoring strategy whereby

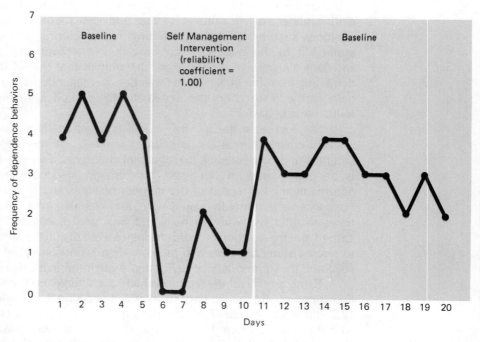

FIGURE 12.7 A reversal design to analyze the effects of self-management on a manager's dependence behaviors.
(*Source:* Fred Luthans and Tim R. V. Davis, "Behavioral Self-Management: The Missing Link in Managerial Effectiveness," *Organizational Dynamics,* Summer 1979, p. 53.)

he recorded each item by category, noted what action was taken, and transferred these data in summary form to a wall-chart display. This self-monitoring provided both feedforward (cuing stimulus) and feedback (reinforcement from progress). Figure 12.8 shows the significant results. The numbers along the upper graph represent the total number of incoming paperwork items. Obviously, the number of unprocessed items on the desk during the baseline period (an average of 9.4) was greatly reduced when self-management was applied (an average of only 0.22).

The same type of approach (that is, S-O-B-C functional analysis and stimulus and consequence management strategies to change the targeted behavior in the desired direction) was applied to the problem of leaving the office without informing the staff and to the problem of filling out expense vouchers. Figure 12.8 shows that these dysfunctional behaviors also dramatically improved after the self-management approach. The use of the multiple-baseline design lends considerable support to the conclusion that the self-management was responsible for the improvement in the dysfunctional behaviors. The manager was able to exercise self-control over his dysfunctional behaviors, and the result was that he was a more effective manager.

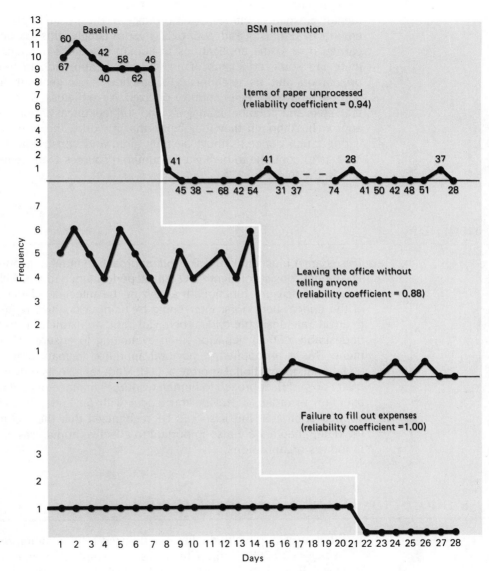

FIGURE 12.8 A multiple-baseline design to analyze the effects of self-management of dysfunctional behaviors. (*Source:* Fred Luthans and Tim R. V. Davis, "Behavioral Self-Management: The Missing Link in Managerial Effectiveness," *Organizational Dynamics*, Summer 1979, p. 56.)

O.B. Mod. in Perspective

The analysis of the manufacturing and nonmanufacturing applications and behavioral self-management indicates that O.B. Mod. can and does work to improve performance in today's organizations. Yet some of the theories that O.B. Mod. is based upon and specific behavior modification applications made in mental hospitals, clinics, classrooms, and especially prisons still generate emotional criticism and controversy. Surprisingly, this concern has not really carried over to the applications in human resources management. To be sure, there are some criticisms of an O.B. Mod. approach in terms of theoretical orientation and its usefulness to practice,[29] but generally the ethics of the approach have not been unduly criticized. Nevertheless, there are probably many managers and potential managers who still feel uneasy about using an O.B. Mod. approach. Although they may agree that it works, they still feel it is somehow wrong. Such concerns must be fully aired and constructively analyzed if O.B. Mod. is to continue to be a viable human resources management approach now and in the future.

Summary

This chapter presented an O.B. Mod. approach to human resources management. The model consists of identifying critical performance-related behaviors, obtaining a baseline measure, functionally analyzing the antecedents and the consequences of the critical behaviors, intervening by using a positive reinforcement strategy to accelerate desirable critical behaviors and an extinction strategy to decelerate undesirable critical behaviors, and evaluating to ensure performance improvement. This is an applied, behavioral approach to management rather than just an internal, motivational approach. O.B. Mod. represents only one, but potentially a very powerful, approach to human resources management. It was given detailed attention in order to provide the reader with an in-depth understanding of an applied approach, but it should be recognized that the techniques covered in the other chapters are also important to effective human resources management in today's organizations.

Questions for Discussion and Review

1. What are some methods that can be used to identify important performance behaviors in O.B. Mod.? What are some simple guidelines that can be used?
2. One O.B. Mod. theorist once said, "In effect, behavior charts are minibehavioral experiments." Explain.
3. Why is positive reinforcement a more effective intervention strategy than punishment? What, if anything, is the difference between a punishment strategy and an extinction strategy?
4. Briefly summarize the procedures and results of at least one manufacturing and one nonmanufacturing study reported in the chapter. How would you go about implementing and evaluating an O.B. Mod. approach in an organization you are familiar with? Be specific in your answer.

5. What are the definition and criteria of behavioral self-management? How does it differ from traditional positive-thinking approaches to self-control? How does it differ from time management?
6. Identify and give an example of stimulus and consequence management in self-management.

References

1. See Fred Luthans, "Resolved: Functional Analysis Is the Best Technique for Diagnostic Evaluation of Organizational Behavior," in Barbara Karmel (ed.), *Point and Counterpoint in Organizational Behavior,* Dryden, Hinsdale, Ill., 1980, pp. 48–60.
2. See Tim R. V. Davis and Fred Luthans, "Leadership Reexamined: A Behavioral Approach," *Academy of Management Review,* April 1979, pp. 237–248; Fred Luthans and Tim R. V. Davis, "Operationalizing a Behavioral Approach to Leadership," in E. G. Miller (ed.), *Proceedings of the Midwest Academy of Management,* 1979, University of Michigan Press, Ann Arbor, pp. 144–155; and Tim R. V. Davis and Fred Luthans, "A Social Learning Approach to Organizational Behavior," *Academy of Management Review,* April 1980, pp. 281–290.
3. V. Mark Durand, "Employee Absenteeism: A Selective Review of Antecedents and Consequences," *Journal of Organizational Behavior Management,* Spring/Summer 1985, p. 157.
4. Kenneth N. Wexley and Gary P. Latham, *Developing and Training Human Resources,* Scott, Foresman, Glenview, Ill., 1981, p. 78.
5. Ibid., pp. 81–84.
6. See Lee W. Frederiksen (ed.), *Handbook of Organizational Behavior Management,* Interscience-Wiley, New York, 1982, pp. 12–14; these findings are summarized in Fred Luthans and Robert Kreitner, *Organizational Behavior Modification and Beyond,* Scott, Foresman, Glenview, Ill., 1985, chap. 8.
7. Frederiksen, op. cit., p. 14.
8. R. W. Kempen, "Absenteeism and Tardiness," in Frederiksen, op. cit., p. 372.
9. Fred Luthans and Terry L. Maris, "Evaluating Personnel Programs through the Reversal Technique," *Personnel Journal,* October 1979, pp. 692–697.
10. Dov Zohar and Nahum Fussfeld, "A Systems Approach to Organizational Behavior Modification: Theoretical Considerations and Empirical Evidence," *International Review of Applied Psychology,* October 1981, pp. 491–505.
11. Beth Sulzer-Azaroff, "Behavioral Approaches to Occupational Health and Safety," in Frederiksen, op. cit., pp. 505–538.
12. "Labor Letter," *The Wall Street Journal,* Jan. 27, 1987, p. 1.
13. Thomas K. Connellan, *How to Improve Human Performance,* Harper & Row, New York, 1978, pp. 170–174.
14. Robert Mirman, "Performance Management in Sales Organizations," in Frederiksen, op. cit., pp. 427–475.
15. Kirk O'Hara, C. Merle Johnson, and Terry A. Beehr, "Organizational Behavior Management in the Private Sector: A Review of Empirical Research and Recommendations for Further Investigation," *Academy of Management Review,* October 1985, pp. 848–864.
16. These examples are reported in detail, including the charts, in Luthans and Kreitner, op. cit.
17. Robert Ottemann and Fred Luthans, "An Experimental Analysis of the Effectiveness of

an Organizational Behavior Modification Program in Industry," *Academy of Management Proceedings*, 1975, pp. 140–142.

18. Fred Luthans and Jason Schweizer, "How Behavior Modification Techniques Can Improve Total Organizational Performance," *Management Review*, September 1979, pp. 43–50.

19. Fred Luthans, Walter S. Maciag, and Stuart A. Rosenkrantz, "O.B. Mod.: Meeting the Productivity Challenge with Human Resource Management," *Personnel*, March–April 1983, pp. 28–36.

20. Diane L. Lockwood and Fred Luthans, "Contingent Time Off: A Nonfinancial Incentive for Improving Productivity," *Management Review*, July 1984, pp. 48–52.

21. Charles A. Snyder and Fred Luthans, "Using O.B. Mod. to Increase Hospital Productivity," *Personnel Administrator*, August 1982, pp. 67–73.

22. Fred Luthans, Robert Paul, and Douglas Baker, "An Experimental Analysis of the Impact of Contingent Reinforcement on Salespersons' Performance Behaviors," *Journal of Applied Psychology*, June 1981, pp. 314–323.

23. Fred Luthans, Robert Paul, and Lew Taylor, "The Impact of Contingent Reinforcement on Retail Salespersons' Performance Behaviors: A Replicated Field Experiment," *Journal of Organizational Behavior Management*, Spring/Summer 1985, pp. 25–35.

24. Luthans and Davis, "Behavioral Self-Management," pp. 42–60. Also see Charles C. Manz, *The Art of Self-Leadership*, Prentice-Hall, Englewood Cliffs, N.J., 1983; and Charles C. Manz, "Self-Leadership: Toward an Expanded Theory of Self-Influence Processes in Organizations," *Academy of Management Review*, July 1986, pp. 585–608.

25. Luthans and Davis, "Behavioral Self-Management," p. 43.

26. Ibid.

27. Charles C. Manz and Henry P. Sims, "Self-Management as a Substitute for Leadership: A Social Learning Perspective," *Academy of Management Review*, July 1980, pp. 364–365.

28. The examples and discussion in this section are drawn from Luthans and Davis, "Behavioral Self-Management," pp. 51–59.

29. For example, see M. Hammer, "The Application of Behavior Conditioning Procedures to the Problems of Quality Control: Comment," *Academy of Management Journal*, December 1971, pp. 529–532; Fred Fry, "Operant Conditioning and O.B. Mod.: Of Mice and Men," *Personnel*, July–August 1974, pp. 17–24; W. F. Whyte, "Skinnerian Theory in Organizations" *Psychology Today*, April 1972, pp. 66–68; Edwin A. Locke, "The Myths of Behavior Mod in Organizations," *Academy of Management Review*, October 1977, pp. 543–553; Patricia Cain Smith, "Resolved: Functional Analysis Is the Best Technique for Diagnostic Evaluation of Organizational Behavior," in Karmel, op. cit., pp. 60–81; Don Hellriegel, John Slocum, and Richard W. Woodman, *Organizational Behavior*, 4th ed., West, St. Paul, Minn., 1986, pp. 163–164.

REAL CASE: Forget the Raise, How about a Nice Bonus?*

Most white-collar workers get an annual raise. However, there is a current trend in some firms toward eliminating the annual raise and in its place giving people one-time bonuses. For example, a person making $30,000 could expect to get a $1500 raise if the company gave an across-the-board 5 percent salary increase. Under a one-time bonus approach, however, the

***Source:** Adapted from Aaron Bernstein, "How'd You Like a Big Fat Bonus—And No Raise?" *Business Week*, Nov. 3, 1986, pp. 30–31.

individual would get $1500, but this would leave the base pay at $30,000. General Electric has used this approach with some of its salaried personnel. So has Bell Atlantic.

What are reasons for substituting a bonus system for an annual raise? One reason is that the company can now establish a clear contingency between performance and pay. If the manager performs well, the firm can give a bonus. If the manager does not perform well, no bonus is given. A second, less-talked-about reason is that many insurance and retirement benefit programs are tied directly to the individual's base pay. If the base pay remains steady, so do the accompanying expenses.

Most industry analysts believe that employees will fight attempts to substitute bonuses for annual raises. However, from the standpoint of modifying organizational behavior and getting people to conform to company performance goals, there may be merit in a bonus system. In fact, one consulting group recently reported that currently only about 7 percent of the firms they surveyed were using the bonus system, but another 20 to 30 percent of these firms were considering the idea.

1. What type of O.B. Mod. intervention strategy is a bonus system?
2. Why would personnel prefer an annual raise rather than a bonus?
3. How could a company evaluate the usefulness of the two approaches in deciding which was more effective?

CASE:
Up the
Piece Rate

Larry Ames has successfully completed a company training program in O.B. Mod. He likes the approach and has started using it on the workers in his department. Following the O.B. Mod. model, he has identified several performance behaviors, measured and analyzed them, and used a positive reinforcement–extinction intervention strategy. His evaluation has showed a significant improvement in the performance of his department. Over coffee one day he commented to one of the other supervisors, "This contingent reinforcement approach really works. Before, the goody-goody people up in personnel were always telling us to try to understand and be nice to our workers. Frankly, I couldn't buy that. In the first place, I don't think there is anybody who can really *understand* my people—I certainly can't. More important, though, is that under this approach I am only nice *contingently*—contingent upon good performance. That makes a lot more sense, and my evaluation proves that it works." The other supervisor commented, "You are being reinforced for using the reinforcement technique on your people." Larry said, "Sure I am. Just like the trainer said: 'Behavior that is reinforced will strengthen and repeat itself.' I'm so reinforced that I am starting to use it on my wife and kids at home, and you know what? It works there, too."

The next week Larry was called into the department head's office and was told, "Larry, as you know, your department has shown a substantial increase in performance since you completed the O.B. Mod. program. I have sent our industrial engineer down there to analyze your standards. I have received her report, and it looks like we will have to adjust your rates upward by 10 percent. Otherwise, we are going to have to pay too much incentive pay. I'm sure you can use some of the things you learned in that O.B. Mod. program to break the news to your people. Good luck, and keep up the good work."

1. Do you think Larry's boss, the department head, attended the O.B. Mod. program? Analyze the department head's action in terms of O.B. Mod.
2. What do you think will be Larry's reaction now and in the future? How do you think Larry's people will react?
3. Given the 10 percent increase in standards, is there any way that Larry could still use the O.B. Mod. approach with his people? With his boss? How?

CASE: A Tardiness Problem

You have been getting a lot of complaints recently from your boss about the consistent tardiness of your work group. The time-sheet records indicate that your people's average start-up time is about ten minutes late. While you have never been concerned about the tardiness problem, your boss is really getting upset. He points out that the tardiness reduces the amount of production time and delays the start-up of the assembly line. You realize that the tardiness is a type of avoidance behavior—it delays the start of a very boring job. Your work group is very cohesive, and each of the members will follow what the group wants to do. One of the leaders of the group seems to spend a lot of time getting the group into trouble. You want the group to come in on time, but you don't really want a confrontation on the issue because, frankly, you don't think it is important enough to risk getting everyone upset with you. You decide to use an O.B. Mod. approach.

1. Trace through the five steps in the O.B. Mod. model to show how it could be applied to this tardiness problem. Make sure you are specific in identifying the critical performance behaviors and the antecedents and consequences of the functional analysis.
2. Do you think the approach you have suggested in your answer to question 1 will really work? Why or why not?

Integrative Real Case for Part 3

More Bang for the Buck*

One of America's oldest social pacts—that a day's work is worth a day's pay—is undergoing radical change.

After decades of letting labor unions, management and the market set the price for a job well done, an increasing number of companies are using pay incentives and participatory management techniques to get more bang for their payroll bucks.

These arrangements—often called "pay for performance"—are meant to tie the employee's compensation to the success of the company.

Advocates say the plans improve corporations' competitiveness by giving workers a stake in the enterprise and its future.

Detractors say the arrangements shift onto workers risks that traditionally have been borne by management and stockholders and, at worst, can return production employees to little more than piece workers.

There is no dispute, however, over the fundamental impact that pay for performance is having in the workplace.

Union National Bank in Little Rock, Ark., has 70 percent of its 500 employees, from entry-level clerks to senior vice presidents, on some sort of incentive-pay program.

If they work hard enough, employees can double their base pay. Most earn about 25 percent of what they take home from performance bonuses.

For the bank, the incentive program, based on behavioral principles set out by William Abernathy, a Memphis consultant, has allowed it to hold the line on hiring and base-pay increases, improve productivity and almost double the net profit per employee compared with its Little Rock competitors.

"Many of the ones who are on it love it," said Wayne Dierks, senior vice president and personnel director at Union National. "The poor performers aren't as wild about it."

Teresa Lee, 22, one of Union National's star tellers, is not a poor performer. Because she is a pro at balancing her accounts at the end of the day, drumming up extra sales for the bank and handling up to 500 transactions on a busy day, she has managed to add up to $130 a week to her paycheck.

Miss Lee acknowledges it would be "nice" to have the $130 guaranteed in her salary, but she points out that people who sit and do nothing don't deserve to make as much as she does.

Nucor Corp. in Charlotte, N.C., which owns a network of highly profitable small steel mills, has all of its 4,400 workers on an incentive-pay plan, based on production for hourly workers and profitability for salaried people.

Nucor's steelworkers make about half of the base wage of workers at bigger mills—about $7.50 an hour—but bonuses boost that amount to an average of $30,000 a year, with some workers getting as much as $40,000. The average for the industry is about $27,000.

On jobs such as steel straightening, where the industry average might be

---

***Source:** Cindy Skrzychi, "Pay for Performance Is Changing U.S. Workplace," *The Washington Post,* reprinted in *Omaha World-Herald,* May 28, 1987, pp. 43–44. Used with permission.

10 tons an hour, Nucor workers have been known to turn out 40 tons. Quality is not sacrificed, said Nucor personnel manager Jim Coblin, because quality is part of what the bonus is based on.

Tardiness or absences cut bonus pay, the vacation plan is modest, and the benefits package is slightly less than what major steel companies offer.

The company has a no-layoff policy and goes to a shorter work week in difficult times, thus reducing bonus pay for everyone.

McDonnell Douglas Electronics Co. has decided to spur productivity with quarterly bonuses based on the company's return on investment. The union plant chairman now sits in on business decisions.

Some pay-for-performance programs peg pay to individual and group performance or to the short- or long-term profitability of the company.

In most cases, the underlying assumption is that if the company makes money, so do the workers. If the company does not, the workers go without a portion of pay or bonuses.

Other arrangements allow workers to earn extra money beyond their base salaries, much as executives or sales personnel traditionally have earned bonuses.

Unlike traditional profit-sharing plans, which often defer income, many of the new incentive plans offer immediate payment and can mean a freeze or reduction in base wages.

Use of such non-traditional plans, according to a survey by the American Productivity Center in Houston, has grown strikingly in the last five years. Of 1,600 respondents to a survey covering 40 industries, 75 percent had implemented at least one new pay or incentive system. Seventy percent of the remaining respondents indicated they might revamp their pay plans to include some non-traditional system.

What companies are sacrificing are more traditional pay and perquisites. The survey showed that 36 percent of the companies responding have significantly reduced or eliminated across-the-board pay increases for their workers, while 27.6 percent have done away with cost-of-living raises and 25.2 percent have dropped merit increases.

Among executives, status symbols such as company cars, reserved parking and separate dining rooms are declining in number.

Among the more popular programs that are changing the contours of the American paycheck in both the salaried and hourly ranks are:

- *Gain sharing.* An estimated 2,000 companies have adopted gain sharing, which rewards large units of workers, from managers to laborers, with bonuses for improved performance. A variety of targets and formulas are used to determine gains that are shared weekly, monthly or annually. It is the fastest-growing form of incentive.
- *Small-group incentives.* These go to small groups of workers and are based on group performance. Use of the plans is growing, primarily among managerial and professional workers. Bonus payments usually constitute a higher percentage of base pay than in gain-sharing plans.
- *Individual incentives.* These are used primarily among managers and professionals but are becoming more common in gauging wages for those in

information-related industries where computers often can tally the amount of work done.

- *Pay for knowledge.* Pay is based not on job classification but on how much an employee knows or on a repertoire of skills that has been learned. A Department of Labor report shows the system is most commonly used among production workers. It cited one General Motors plant where workers could earn 72 cents more an hour for acquiring new skills.

Workers are being put on notice that parts of their paychecks are up for grabs because of changes in the American workplace as well as elsewhere in the world.

Pressure on the United States to narrow its trade deficit and regain its competitive muscle probably is playing the biggest role in the move to variable pay.

"Workers increasingly understand that we live in a competitive world, and they can no longer assume their industry will be around forever," said Democratic presidential candidate and former Arizona Gov. Bruce Babbitt. "It will mean some risks on both sides and require a more cooperative approach. The purpose of this is not to impoverish the work force, but a recognition that we will all be better off if we can structure pay to productivity."

Along with Babbitt, many of the Democratic presidential contenders have expressed interest in structuring pay to performance as part of an antidote to America's economic ills.

Economists such as Pat Choate of TRW Inc. and Lester Thurow of the Massachusetts Institute of Technology have their own ideas about how tax incentives might encourage companies and workers to share the wealth through incentive programs. Sen. Dale Bumpers, D-Ark., has proposed legislation that would exclude 25 percent of profit-sharing distributions from taxation.

The idea of structuring pay as part base wage, part bonus is advocated by MIT economist Martin Weitzman, who believes giving employers more wage flexibility will encourage them to hire more workers in good economic times and fire fewer workers in downturns—sort of like a shock absorber.

Proponents of dramatic pay-for-performance plans point to the success Japan has had in keeping unemployment low, partly because it pegs about one-quarter of an average worker's compensation to a twice-yearly bonus that depends on the movement of certain business indicators.

British lawmakers also are considering abandoning automatic wage increases in some cases and linking pay to profits, with a portion exempt from taxes.

The history of collective bargaining is rich with examples of unorthodox pay schemes, including the current profit-sharing plans that Ford and General Motors offer hourly workers.

But some organized-labor experts caution that they see little evidence of increased employment security for workers who are cut into profits. "It protects management against their own mistakes and gets workers to carry some of the costs," said AFL-CIO economist John Zalusky.

Zalusky added that workers don't mind being paid for their own performance, but it's something else entirely to be paid for the firm's performance.

Nevertheless, compensation consultants say business is brisk with companies exploring whether now may be the time to wean workers off a guaranteed wage, often linked more in theory than practice to the employee's performance.

A study done for the Public Agenda Foundation found that almost 75 percent of workers in 845 companies said the quality and effort they put into their jobs had little to do with pay. The same number cited the lack of connection between pay and performance as the reason why they weren't trying very hard at work.

Meanwhile, raises have been steadily shrinking for many groups of employees as inflationary pressure on wages has abated and competitive pressure has intensified. Hewitt Associates reports that salaried employees can expect raises of about 5 percent this year, compared with 10 percent in 1981.

Similarly, hourly workers, when their pay is adjusted for inflation, also have seen their wages eroding in the last decade.

In unionized industries, such as aerospace, steel and health care, approximately 1.7 million workers covered by 236 agreements now receive a percentage of their earnings in lump-sum payments. Though many workers like the quick infusion of cash they get from a lump-sum payment, the bonus does not compound in their basic pay or benefits.

For the short term, at least, many companies that have instituted programs such as gain sharing, pay for knowledge or even lump-sum bonuses say they are happy with the results.

What is less easy to assess is how work relationships change. How do employees get along at work when they are asked to compete with themselves and others? How does the boss really feel when one of his subordinates makes more than he does? Are the performance standards set by a company or manager fair and reasonable? Can an employee be motivated by the long-term, impersonal goal of profits for the company?

Questions

1. How does pay for performance as discussed in this case relate to motivation and reinforcement as discussed in this part of the book? Relate specific examples from the case to specific theories in the text.
2. How, if at all, do the techniques discussed in the text relate to white-collar service or professional/managerial performance?
3. The case ends with a series of questions for the future. How would you answer these questions on the basis of your knowledge gained from the chapters in this part of the book? Take any two questions and give a specific answer.

Experiential Exercises for Part 3

EXERCISE: Motivation questionnaire

Goals:
    1. To experience firsthand the concepts of one of the work-motivation theories—in this case, the popular Maslow hierarchy of needs
    2. To get personal feedback on your opinions of the use of motivational techniques in human resources management

Implementation:
    The following questions have seven possible responses:

    1. Please mark one of the seven responses by circling the number that corresponds to the response that fits your opinion. For example, if you "strongly agree," circle the number "+3."
    2. Complete every item. You have about ten minutes to do so.

	Strongly Agree	Agree	Slightly Agree	Don't Know	Slightly Disagree	Disagree	Strongly Disagree
	+3	+2	+1	0	−1	−2	−3
1. Special wage increases should be given to employees who do their jobs very well.	+3	+2	+1	0	−1	−2	−3
2. Better job descriptions would be helpful so that employees will know exactly what is expected of them.	+3	+2	+1	0	−1	−2	−3
3. Employees need to be reminded that their jobs are dependent on the company's ability to compete effectively.	+3	+2	+1	0	−1	−2	−3
4. Supervisors should give a good deal of attention to the physical working conditions of their employees.	+3	+2	+1	0	−1	−2	−3
5. Supervisors ought to work hard to develop a friendly working atmosphere among their people.	+3	+2	+1	0	−1	−2	−3
6. Individual recognition for above-standard performance means a lot to employees.	+3	+2	+1	0	−1	−2	−3
7. Indifferent supervision can often bruise feelings.	+3	+2	+1	0	−1	−2	−3
8. Employees want to feel that their real skills and capacities are put to use on their jobs.	+3	+2	+1	0	−1	−2	−3
9. The company retirement benefits and stock programs are important factors in keeping employees on their jobs.	+3	+2	+1	0	−1	−2	−3

(continued)

	Strongly Agree	Agree	Slightly Agree	Don't Know	Slightly Disagree	Disagree	Strongly Disagree
	+3	+2	+1	0	-1	-2	-3
10. Almost every job can be made more stimulating and challenging.	+3	+2	+1	0	-1	-2	-3
11. Many employees want to give their best in everything they do.	+3	+2	+1	0	-1	-2	-3
12. Management could show more interest in the employees by sponsoring social events after hours.	+3	+2	+1	0	-1	-2	-3
13. Pride in one's work is actually an important reward.	+3	+2	+1	0	-1	-2	-3
14. Employees want to be able to think of themselves as "the best" at their own jobs.	+3	+2	+1	0	-1	-2	-3
15. The quality of the relationships in the informal work group is quite important.	+3	+2	+1	0	-1	-2	-3
16. Individual incentive bonuses would improve the performance of employees.	+3	+2	+1	0	-1	-2	-3
17. Visibility with upper management is important to employees.	+3	+2	+1	0	-1	-2	-3
18. Employees generally like to schedule their own work and to make job-related decisions with a minimum of supervision.	+3	+2	+1	0	-1	-2	-3
19. Job security is important to employees.	+3	+2	+1	0	-1	-2	-3
20. Having good equipment to work with is important to employees.	+3	+2	+1	0	-1	-2	-3

Scoring:

1. Transfer the numbers you circled in the questionnaire to the appropriate places in the spaces below.

Statement no.	Score	Statement No.	Score
10	____	2	____
11	____	3	____
13	____	9	____
18	____	19	____
Total	____	Total	____
(Self-actualization needs)		(Safety needs)	

Statement no.	Score	Statement No.	Score
6	___	1	___
8	___	4	___
14	___	16	___
17	___	20	___
Total	___	Total	___
(Esteem needs)		(Basic needs)	

Statement no.	Score
5	___
7	___
12	___
15	___
Total	___
(Belongingness needs)	

2. Record your total scores in the following chart by marking an "X" in each row next to the number of your total score for that area of needs motivation.

	−12	−10	−8	−6	−4	−2	0	+2	+4	+6	+8	+10	+12
Self-actualization													
Esteem													
Belongingness													
Safety													
Basic													

Low use — High use

By examining the chart you can see the relative strength you attach to each of the needs in Maslow's hierarchy. There are no right answers here, but most work-motivation theorists imply that most people are concerned mainly with the upper-level needs (that is, belongingness, esteem, and self-actualization).

EXERCISE: Job design survey

Goals:

1. To experience firsthand the job characteristics approach to job design, in this case through the Hackman-Oldham Job Diagnostic Survey (JDS)

2. To get personal feedback on the motivating potential of your present or past job and to identify and compare its critical characteristics

Implementation:

1. Please describe your present job (or a job you have held in the past) as objectively as you can. Circle the number that best reflects the job.

a. How much *variety* is there in your job? That is, to what extent does the job require you to do many different things at work, using a variety of your skills and talents?

1 ---------- 2 ---------- 3 ---------- 4 ---------- 5 ---------- 6 ---------- 7

Very little; the job requires me to do the same routine things over and over again.	Moderate variety.	Very much; the job requires me to do many different things, using a number of different skills and talents.

b. To what extent does your job involve doing a *"whole"* and *identifiable piece of work?* That is, is the job a complete piece of work that has an obvious beginning and end, or is it only a small part of the overall piece of work, which is finished by other people or by machines?

1 ---------- 2 ---------- 3 ---------- 4 ---------- 5 ---------- 6 ---------- 7

My job is only a tiny part of the overall piece of work; the results of my activities cannot be seen in the final product or service.	My job is a moderate-sized "chunk" of the overall piece of work; my own contribution can be seen in the final outcome.	My job involves doing the whole piece of work, from start to finish; the results of my activities are easily seen in the final product or service.

c. In general, *how significant or important* is your job? That is, are the results of your work likely to significantly affect the lives or well-being of other people?

1 ---------- 2 ---------- 3 ---------- 4 ---------- 5 ---------- 6 ---------- 7

Not very significant; the outcomes of my work are *not* likely to have important effects on other people.	Moderately significant.	Highly significant; the outcomes of my work can affect other people in very important ways.

d. How much *autonomy* is there in your job? That is, to what extent does your job permit you to decide on *your own* how to go about doing the work?

1 ---------- 2 ---------- 3 ---------- 4 ---------- 5 ---------- 6 ---------- 7

Very little; the job gives me almost no personal "say" about how and when the work is done.	Moderate autonomy; many things are standardized and not under my control, but I can make some decisions about the work.	Very much; the job gives me almost complete responsibility for deciding how and when the work is done.

e. To what exent does doing the *job itself* provide you with information about your work performance? That is, does the actual *work itself* provide clues about how well you are doing—aside from any feedback coworkers or supervisors may provide?

1 ---------- 2 ---------- 3 ---------- 4 ---------- 5 ---------- 6 ---------- 7

Very little; the job itself is set up so that I could work forever without finding out how well I am doing.

Moderately; sometimes doing the job provides feedback to me; sometimes it does not.

Very much; the job is set up so that I get almost constant feedback as I work about how well I am doing.

2. The five questions above measure your perceived skill variety, task identity, task significance, autonomy, and feedback in your job. The complete JDS uses several questions to measure these dimensions. But to get some idea of the motivating potential, use your scores (1 to 7) for each job dimension and calculate as follows:

$$MPS = \frac{\text{skill variety} + \text{task identity} + \text{task significance}}{3} \times \text{autonomy} \times \text{feedback}$$

Next, plot your job design profile and MPS score on the graphs below. These show the national averages for all jobs. Analyze how you compare and suggest ways to redesign your job.

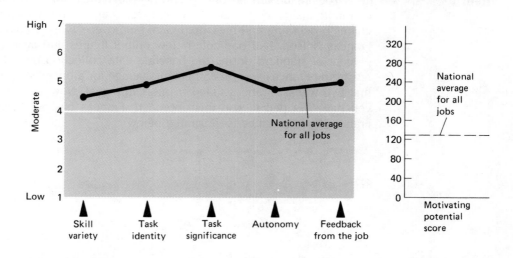

EXERCISE: **Role playing and O.B. Mod.**

Goal: To experience the application of the O.B. Mod. approach to human resources management

Implementation: This role-playing situation involves two people: Allen, the supervisor of claims processing in a large insurance firm, and Frances, an employee in the department. One person will be selected to play the role of Allen, and another will play Frances. The information on, and background for, each of the participants follow.

When the participants have carefully read their roles, the supervisor, Allen, will be asked to conduct a performance-related discussion with Frances. Those who are not playing one of the roles should carefully observe the conversation between Allen and Frances and provide the information requested below. The observers should not necessarily read the roles of Allen and Frances.

1. List those words, phrases, or sentences that Allen used that seemed particularly reinforcing.
2. List any words, phrases, or sentences used by Allen that may have been punishing.
3. List any suggestions that you have for improving Allen's future conversations with employees.
4. Using the steps of O.B. Mod. (identify, measure, analyze, intervene, and evaluate), how would you (or your group) improve the human performance in this claims department? Be as specific as you can for each step. You may have to fabricate some of the examples.

Role-playing situation for Allen:

After reading the information below, you are to conduct a performance-related discussion with Frances in order to reward increased productivity.

You are the supervisor of twenty people in the claims processing department of a large insurance company. Several weeks ago, you established standards for claims processing and measured each employee's work output. One employee, Frances Nelson, had particularly low output figures and averaged less than 80 percent of standard during the baseline data collection period. Your target for rewarding Frances was an 85 percent average for a one-week period. During the first two weeks, Frances failed to meet this goal. Now, in the third week after you have decided to use this approach, Frances has achieved the new goal. Frances's performance is illustrated below.

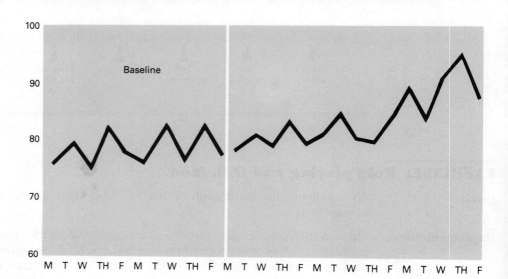

Role-playing situation for Frances:

After reading the information below, you are to be interviewed by your supervisor concerning your performance.

You are Frances Nelson, an employee in the claims processing division of a large insurance company. Recently, your supervisor, Allen Parks, insituted a new system of measuring performance in the department. Most of the other employees have already discussed their performance with him, but for some reason Allen has not yet talked with you. Now this morning, Allen said he wanted to have a talk about your performance. You are somewhat anxious about what he will have to say. You know that you are not the best employee in the department, but you do make your best effort. You hope that Allen will recognize this and not be too hard on you.

Interpersonal and Group Behaviors, Dynamics and Influence

PART 4

tice

ıs

f
ıs,

group therapy, sensitivity training, team building, transactional analysis, and the Johari window are equated with group dynamics. Some of these techniques are covered in the next chapter and in Chapter 20, on organization development. A third view is the closest to Lewin's original conception. Group dynamics are viewed from the perspective of the internal nature of groups, how they form, their structure and processes, and how they function and affect individual members, other groups, and the organization. The following sections are devoted to this third view of group dynamics. A modern, comprehensive definition of a *group* that will be used as a point of departure for the rest of the chapter is the following: "A group is a collection of two or more interacting individuals with a stable pattern of relationships between them who share common goals and who perceive themselves as being a group."[1]

The Dynamics of Group Formation

Why do individuals form into groups? Before discussing some very practical reasons, it would be beneficial to examine briefly some of the classic theories of group formation or why people affiliate with one another. The most basic theory explaining affiliation is propinquity. This interesting word means simply that individuals affiliate with one another because of spatial or geographical proximity. The theory would predict that students sitting next to one another in class, for example, are more likely to form into a group than students sitting at opposite ends of the room. In an organization, employees who work in the same area of the plant or office or managers with offices close to one another would more probably form into groups than those who are not physically located together. There is some research evidence to support the propinquity theory, and on the surface it has a great deal of merit for explaining group formation. The drawback is that it is not analytical and does not begin to explain some of the complexities of group formation. Some theoretical and practical reasons need to be explored.

Theories of Group Formation. A more comprehensive theory of group formation than mere propinquity comes from the theory based on activities, interactions, and sentiments.[2] These three elements are directly related to one another. The more activities persons share, the more numerous will be their interactions and the stronger will be their sentiments (how much the other persons are liked or disliked); the more interactions among persons, the more will be their shared activities and sentiments; and the more sentiments persons have for one another, the more will be their shared activities and interactions. This theory lends a great deal to the understanding of group formation and process. The major element is *interaction*. Persons in a group interact with one another, not in just the physical propinquity sense, but also to accomplish many group goals such as cooperation and problem solving.

There are many other theories that attempt to explain group formation. Most often they are only partial theories, but they are generally additive in nature. One of the more comprehensive is a *balance theory* of group formation.[3] The theory states that persons are attracted to one another on the basis of similar attitudes

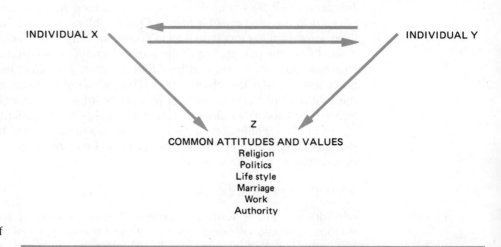

FIGURE 13.1 A balance theory of group formation.

toward commonly relevant objects and goals. Figure 13.1 shows this balance theory. Individual X will interact and form a relationship/group with individual Y because of common attitudes and values (Z). Once this relationship is formed, the participants strive to maintain a symmetrical balance between the attraction and the common attitudes. If an imbalance occurs, an attempt is made to restore the balance. If the balance cannot be restored, the relationship dissolves. Both propinquity and interaction play a role in balance theory.

Still another theoretical approach to group formation receiving considerable attention is *exchange theory*.[4] Similar to its functioning as a work-motivation theory, discussed in Chapter 9, exchange theory of groups is based upon reward-cost outcomes of interaction. A minimum positive level (rewards greater than costs) of an outcome must exist in order for attraction or affiliation to take place. Rewards from interactions gratify needs, while costs incur anxiety, frustration, embarrassment, or fatigue. Propinquity, interaction, and common attitudes all have roles in exchange theory.

Practicalities of Group Formation.   Besides the theoretical explanations for group formation, there are some very practical reasons for joining and/or forming a group. For instance, employees in an organization may form a group for economic, security, or social reasons. Economically, workers may form a group to work on a project that is paid for on a group-incentive plan or may form a union to demand higher wages. For security, joining a group provides the individual with a united front in combating indiscriminant, unilateral treatment. The adage that there is strength in numbers applies in this case. The most important practical reason why individuals join or form groups is, however, that groups tend to satisfy the very intense social needs of most people. Workers, in particular, generally have a very strong desire for affiliation. This need is met by belonging to a group. Research going as far back as the Hawthorne studies has found the affiliation motive to have a major impact on human behavior in organizations. Chapter 9 also discussed this motive.

Types of Groups

There are numerous types of groups. The theories of group formation that were just discussed are based partly upon the attraction between two persons—the simple dyad group. Of course, in the real world groups are usually much more complex than the dyad. There are small and large groups, primary and secondary groups, coalitions, membership and reference groups, in- and out-groups, and formal and informal groups. Each type has different characteristics and different effects on its members.

Primary Groups.

Often the terms *small group* and *primary group* are used interchangeably. Technically, there is a difference. A small group has to meet only the criterion of small size. Usually, no attempt is made to assign precise numbers, but the accepted criterion is that the group must be small enough for face-to-face interaction and communication to occur. In addition to being small, a primary group must have a feeling of comradeship, loyalty, and a common sense of values among its members. Thus, all primary groups are small groups, but not all small groups are primary groups.

Two examples of a primary group are the family and the peer group. Initially, the primary group was limited to a socializing group, but then a broader conception was given impetus by the results of the Hawthorne studies. Work groups definitely have primary group qualities. Research findings point out the tremendous impact that the primary group has on individual behavior, regardless of context or environmental conditions.

Coalitions.

In addition to primary groups, coalitions are very relevant to organizations. The concept of a coalition has been used in organizational analysis through the years. Although the concept is used in different ways by different theorists, a recent comprehensive review of the coalition literature suggests that the following characteristics of a coalition be included:

1. Interacting group of individuals
2. Deliberately constructed by the members for a specific purpose
3. Independent of the formal organization's structure
4. Lacking a formal internal structure
5. Mutual perception of membership
6. Issue-oriented to advance the purposes of the members
7. External forms
8. Concerted member action, act as a group[5]

Although the above have common characteristics with other types of groups, they are separate, usually very powerful entities in organizations.

Other Types of Groups.

Besides primary groups and coalitions, there are also other classifications of groups that are important to the study of organizational behavior. Two important distinctions are between membership and reference groups, and between in-groups and out-groups. These differences can be summarized by noting that membership groups are those to which the individual actually belongs. An example would be membership in a craft union. Reference groups are those to which an individual would like to belong—those he or she identifies with. An example would be a prestigious social group. In-groups are those who have or share the dominate values, and out-groups are those on the outside looking in. All these types of groups have relevance to the study of organizational behavior, but the formal and informal types are most directly applicable.

There are many formally designated groups and committees in the modern organization. The functional departments (finance, marketing, operations, and personnel) are examples, as are standing committees such as the finance committee, grievance committee, or executive committee. Committees as a type of formal group are given detailed attention later in the chapter. Self-managed work groups are also appearing in an increasing number of companies. For example, GM's Delco-Remy plant in Fitzgerald, Georgia, and its Cadillac engine plant in Livonia, Michigan, have been totally team-based for years. Tom Peters places them at the top of his list of prescriptions of how to make our companies competitive in the world today.[6] The accompanying Application Example spells out how this works and what the results are in an agribusiness firm. Systematic research on self-managed groups over time has also yielded some positive results.[7]

Application Example

Self-Managed Groups at A. E. Staley Company

A. E. Staley is an agriproducts corporation located in Lafayette, Indiana, that employs salaried technicians using computer-controlled machinery to convert corn into high-fructose syrup. Importantly from a group dynamics standpoint, the company consists of sixteen groups of about fifteen employees each organized around the traditional functions—production, maintenance, quality control—and shifts. Each group chooses two leaders from its ranks: one is charged with getting the job done and the other is in charge of training, discussion, and records. The groups make their own work assignments and have a voice in hiring, promotion, and discipline. The plant operates every day of the year, and the employees work there 12-hour days, have three days off, and then work three nights.

Although it took three years for this radical approach to justify itself, now it seems to be really taking hold and paying off handsomely. Operating costs are below those of other similar plants, absenteeism and turnover are under 1 percent, downtime is less than 1 percent in a 24-hour day, and production is at 115 percent of engineering specifications. The group solves problems and works as a team. For example, one day when something went wrong in the refinery process, the plant operations manager looked out at the refinery group and said, "It's like having fifteen foreman out there trying to solve the problem"—and they did.

Source: Adapted from Harry Bacas, "Who's in Charge Here?" *Nation's Business,* May 1985, pp. 57–58.

Informal groups form for political, friendship, or common interest reasons. For political purposes, the informal group may form to attempt to get its share of rewards and/or limited resources. Friendship groups may form on the job and carry on outside the workplace. Common interests in sports or ways to get back at management can also bind members into an informal group. The dynamics of these informal groups are examined in more detail in the last part of the chapter.

Implications from Research on Group Dynamics

Starting with the Hawthorne studies, there has been an abundance of significant research on groups that has implications for organizational behavior and management. Besides the Hawthorne studies, there are numerous research studies on group dynamics which indirectly contribute to the better understanding of organizational behavior. Table 13.1 summarizes the research findings on the functions that groups can serve for both the organization as a whole and the individual organizational participant.

In addition to the somewhat general conclusions shown in Table 13.1, there are a number of studies in social psychology which seem to have particular relevance to organizational behavior. The work of social psychologist Stanley Schachter seems especially important for the application of group dynamics research to human resources management.

The Schachter Study. In a classic study[8] Schachter and his associates tested the effect that group cohesiveness and induction (or influence) had on productivity under highly controlled conditions. Women college students were

TABLE 13.1 Summary of Research on the Impact That Groups Have on Organizational and Individual Effectiveness

The Impact of Groups on Organizational Effectiveness	The Impact of Groups on Individual Employee Effectiveness
1. Accomplishing tasks that could not be done by employees themselves	1. Aiding in learning about the organization and its environment
2. Bringing a number of skills and talents to bear on complex difficult tasks	2. Aiding in learning about oneself
3. Providing a vehicle for decision making that permits multiple and conflicting views to be aired and considered	3. Providing help in gaining new skills
4. Providing an efficient means for organizational control of employee behavior	4. Obtaining valued rewards that are not accessible by oneself
5. Facilitating changes in organizational policies or procedures	5. Satisfying important personal needs, especially needs for social acceptance and affiliation
6. Increasing organizational stability by transmitting shared beliefs and values to new employees	

Source: Adapted from David A. Nadler, J. Richard Hackman, and Edward E. Lawler, *Managing Organizational Behavior,* Little, Brown, Boston, 1979, p. 102.

used as subjects. *Cohesiveness* was defined as the average resultant force acting on members to remain in a group. The researchers assumed that by making the group appear attractive or not attractive, the subjects would correspondingly feel high or low cohesiveness. About half the subjects were told by the experimenter that they would be members of an extremely congenial group and that "there is every reason to expect that the other members of the group will like you and you will like them." The other half of the subjects were told by the experimenter that, because of scheduling difficulties, it was impossible to assemble a congenial group and that "there is no particular reason to think that you will like them or that they will care for you." In this manner, high and low cohesive groups were created by the experimenter.

All the subjects were told that their task was to make cardboard checkerboards. It was to be a three-person, assembly line operation consisting of cutting out pieces of cardboard, mounting and pasting them on heavier stock, and painting them through a stencil. For control purposes, all subjects were made cutters, but they thought they would pass on the cut boards to the other two members of their group (the paster and painter) in another room.

The subjects were informed that they could write notes to, and would receive notes from, their pasters and painters. Of course, the experimenter intercepted all the notes from the subjects and gave them prewritten notes. These notes were used to test the impact of positive and negative induction. In the first sixteen minutes of the experiment, each subject received five notes from her nonexistent paster and painter that made no attempt to influence productivity. In the remaining sixteen minutes of the experiment, half the subjects who believed they were members of high cohesive groups and half the subjects who thought they were members of low cohesive groups received six positive notes. These notes urged increased production, for example, "Time's running out, let's really make a spurt—Paster." The other half of the high and low cohesive subjects received negative notes urging them to slow down production. An example of a negative note was: "Let's try to set a record—let's be the slowest subjects they ever had—Painter."

Through the manipulations of cohesiveness and induction just described, the following experimental groups were created:

1. High cohesive, positive induction (Hi Co, + Ind)
2. Low cohesive, positive induction (Lo Co, + Ind)
3. High cohesive, negative induction (Hi Co, − Ind)
4. Low cohesive, negative induction (Lo Co, − Ind)

Thus, the independent variables in the experiment were cohesiveness and induction, and the dependent variable was productivity. Figure 13.2 summarizes the results. Although Schachter's experiment did not obtain a statistically significant difference in productivity between the high and low cohesive groups that were positively induced, a follow-up study which used a more difficult task did.[9]

Implications of the Schachter Study.   The results of Schachter's study contain some very interesting implications for the study of organizational behavior.

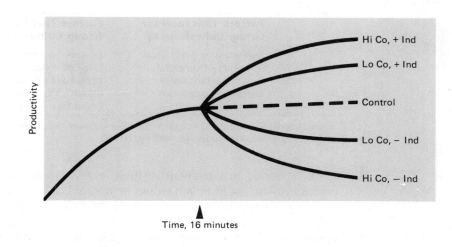

FIGURE 13.2 The "pitchfork" results from the Schachter study.

The "pitchfork" productivity curves in Figure 13.2 imply that highly cohesive groups have very powerful dynamics, both positive and negative, for human resources management. On the other hand, the low cohesive groups are not so powerful. However, of even more importance to human resources management is the variable of induction. Performance depends largely on how the high or low cohesive group is induced.

At least for illustrative purposes, leadership may be substituted for induction. If this is done, the key variable for the subjects' performance in the Schachter experiment becomes leadership. A highly cohesive group that is given positive leadership will have the highest possible productivity. On the other side of the coin, a highly cohesive group that is given poor leadership will have the lowest possible productivity. A highly cohesive group is analogous to a time bomb in the hands of management. The direction in which the highly cohesive group goes, breaking production records or severely restricting output, depends on how it is led. The low cohesive group is much safer in the hands of management. Leadership will not have a serious negative or positive impact on this group. However, the implication is that if management wishes to maximize productivity, it must build a cohesive group and give it proper leadership.

The above discussion does not imply that passing notes to college students cutting out checkerboards in a classroom laboratory setting can be made equivalent to managing human resources in the modern, complex organization. This, of course, cannot and should not be attempted. On the other hand, there are some interesting insights and points of departure for organizational behavior analysis that can come out of laboratory investigations such as Schachter's. For instance, the results of Schachter's study can be applied in retrospect to the work of Frederick W. Taylor or to the Hawthorne studies. Taylor accounted only for the Hi Co, − Ind productivity curve when he advocated "breaking up the group."

TABLE 13.2 Factors That Increase and Decrease Group Cohesiveness

Factors That Increase Group Cohesiveness	Factors That Decrease Group Cohesiveness
Agreement on group goals	Disagreement on goals
Frequency of interaction	Large group size
Personal attractiveness	Unpleasant experiences
Intergroup competition	Intragroup competition
Favorable evaluation	Domination by one or more members

Source: Adapted from Andrew D. Szilagyi, Jr., and Marc J. Wallace, Jr., *Organizational Behavior and Performance,* 4th ed., Scott, Foresman, Glenview, Ill., 1987, pp. 241–242.

If his scientific management methods could be considered + Ind, the best productivity he could obtain would be that of Lo Co, + Ind.

In other words, in light of the Schachter study, Taylor's methods could yield only second-best productivity. In the Hawthorne studies, both the relay room operatives and the bank wirers were highly cohesive work groups. As was brought out in Chapter 2, a possible explanation of why one highly cohesive work group (the relay room workers) produced at a very high level and the other highly cohesive group (the bank wirers) produced at a very low rate is the type of induction (supervision) that was applied. Both leadership and group dynamics factors, such as cohesiveness, can have an important impact on group performance in organizations. Chapter 16 is devoted to the leadership process, and Table 13.2 briefly summarizes some of the major factors that can increase and decrease group cohesiveness.

The Group's Contribution to Employee Satisfaction and Performance. Besides the work coming out of social psychology, more specific focus on the impact that groups have on employee behavior, especially the contribution to satisfaction and performance, has also received attention. A summary of the way to utilize groups to enhance satisfaction and performance would be the following:

1. Organizing work around intact groups
2. Having groups charged with selection, training, and rewarding of members
3. Using groups to enforce strong norms for behavior, with group involvement in off-the-job as well as on-the-job behavior
4. Distributing resources on a group rather than an individual basis
5. Allowing and perhaps even promoting intergroup rivalry so as to build within-group solidarity[10]

A recent review of the research literature also determined three factors that seem to play the major role in determining group effectiveness: (1) task interdependence (how closely group members work together); (2) outcome interdependence (whether, and how, group performance is rewarded); and (3) potency (members' belief that the group can be effective).[11]

Committee Organization

No discussion of group dynamics within the context of organizational behavior would be complete without a thorough analysis of the committee form of organization. The committee is the most important type of formally designated group found in today's organizations. Unfortunately, these committees are often described in the following manner:

> A camel is a horse designed by a committee.
> The best committee is a five-person committee with four members absent.
> In a committee, minutes are taken but hours are wasted.
> A committee is a collection of the unfit appointed by the unwilling to perform the unnecessary.

These remarks are jokes, but they represent the widespread negativism attached to the committee form of organization.

Despite the attacks, all indications are that the use and perceived value of committees in organizations are still increasing. Most committees seem to serve as a focal point for the exchange of different viewpoints and information, but some are making major decisions. There is considerable evidence that the use of committees is directly related to the size of the organization. With today's organizations becoming increasingly large and complex, the committee form of organization will undoubtedly become more important and more widely used in the future.

The Nature and Functions of Committees

There are many definitions of a *committee.* Most stress the idea that committees consist of groups that are formed to accomplish specific objectives. They can be conducted in either a formal manner (for example, the finance committee) or an informal manner (for example, the weekly staff meeting). Most often, committees have specified duties and authority. Some committees meet on an ad hoc basis to solve some specialized problem and then disband. Committees may be referred to as *teams, commissions, boards, groups,* or *task forces.*

Committees are found in all types of organizations. There is a myriad of committees in government, educational, religious, and business organizations. For example, the board of directors is a type of committee present in all corporate forms of organization. Other prevalent types in business are the finance, executive, operations, bonus, audit, and grievance committees. Although they are more frequent at the top of the pyramid, there is usually some type of formal committee on every level of the organization.

Committees perform many different functions. They may act in a service, advisory, coordinating, informational, or final decision-making capacity. In the decision-making function, a committee acts in a line capacity and is usually termed a *plural-executive committee.* Many companies are moving toward the plural-executive concept rather than a single executive head. Union Carbide is typical of this trend. The company's major policies evolve from the office of the president. This office is composed of the president and three executive vice presidents. This foursome serves as the central point of management authority in the company. This type of group management is becoming increasingly common.

Positive Attributes of Committees

Committee action has many advantages over individual action. Perhaps the greatest attribute of the committee group is the combined and integrated judgment which it can offer. The old adage says that two heads are better than one. To speak optimistically, committee members bring with them a wide range of experience, knowledge, ability, and personality characteristics. This agglomeration lends itself to the tremendous amount of diverse knowledge that is required to solve modern organizational problems. Today's organizations also need an averaging of personalities and a source of creative ideas. The committee form of organization can contribute a great deal to these requirements; as is pointed out in Chapter 18's presentation of the group decision-making techniques of Delphi and the Nominal Group Technique (NGT). The interacting group may also inhibit individual creativity, but at least at some point the interactive, group dynamics effects as found in a committee can be beneficial to group problem solving.

Committees can be a very effective organizational device to help reduce conflict and promote coordination between departments and specialized subunits. Through committee discussion, each member can empathize with the others' purposes and problems. In effect, committees foster horizontal communication. An example is the interdepartmental meeting at which each member receives information and insights about the others' departments. The production department is informed of delivery dates being promised by sales, and sales gets a firsthand look at the problems it may be creating for production scheduling and inventory. As Chapter 17 points out, the committee is about the only formalized vehicle for horizontal communication in most traditional forms of organization structure.

From a human standpoint, the biggest advantage of committees may be the increased motivation and commitment derived from participation. By being involved in the analysis and solution of committee problems, individual members will more readily accept and try to implement what has been decided. A committee can also be instrumental in human development and growth. Group members, especially the young and inexperienced, can take advantage of observing and learning from other members with much experience or with different viewpoints and knowledge. A committee provides the opportunity for personal development that individuals would never receive on their own.

Negative Attributes of Committees

The above discussion points out some definite advantages of committees, but the accompanying Application Example gives some of the problems that are inherent. Traditionally, management theorists have stressed the negative aspects. The classical theorist Luther Gulick wanted to limit the use of committees to

**Application
Example**

Committees May Not Be the Answer*

Most modern management theorists espouse the benefits of getting together in committees to make decisions. It allows individuals to give their input and increases motivation and commitment. However, committees may not be appropriate for all decision-making situations. For example, holding committee meetings may simply be a facade for managers' own insecurities. Afraid to take responsibility for a decision, a manager may call a meeting to make a decision. In doing so, the manager can use the committee as a scapegoat for poor decisions.

Norman Sigband, a management communications professor, uses an example of a meeting he observed at a small plastics manufacturing firm. A committee consisting of a division manager, six department heads, and the heads of three sections, was asked to discuss the replacement of an injured secretary. The group spent fifty minutes deciding whether a new person should be hired or a replacement acquired through a temporary service. As a result, the committee ran out of time to discuss the installation of a new fluorescent lighting system. This decision would have affected several departments and required an investment of $28,000. The secretarial decision, on the other hand, affected only one department and should have been made by the division manager. A side effect of such unnecessary meetings is a decline in committee attendance. When asked to address petty issues, members may become apathetic and skip meetings. Thus, when a really important issue needs to be addressed, relevant members may be absent. To overcome such problems, Sigband offers six suggestions for making committee meetings as productive as possible:

1. Only hold meetings for which there is a verifiable need.
2. Decide on an overall purpose and series of objectives each time.
3. Invite only people who can make a definite contribution.
4. Distribute an agenda and necessary handouts to each invitee prior to the session.
5. Make all mechanical arrangements ahead of time (room, projectors, seating, transparencies, etc.).
6. Begin and end every meeting on schedule.

*****Source:** Adapted from Norman B. Sigband, "The Uses of Meetings," *Nation's Business*, February 1987, p. 28.

abnormal situations because he thought they were too dilatory, irresponsible, and time-consuming for normal administration. The classical theorist Urwick was an even harsher critic. He listed no less than fourteen faults of committees, the main ones being that committees are often irresponsible, are apt to be bad employers, and are costly. Thus, the classicists tended to emphasize the negative, but in the more modern view, committees have both positive and negative attributes.

One very practical disadvantage is that committees are indeed time-consuming and costly. Anyone who has participated in committee meetings can appreciate the satirical definition, cited earlier, that a committee takes minutes but wastes hours. The nature of a committee is that everyone has an equal chance to speak out, but this takes a great deal of time, and time costs money. A $60,000-per-year manager costs about $30 per hour. Therefore, a five-person committee of this caliber costs the organization $150 per hour. Added to this figure may be transportation, lodging, and staff backup costs.

Most often, cost is discussed with regard to committee versus individual action. Taking another approach, it can be argued that committees are actually less expensive when compared with a series of repetitious conferences. In terms of work hours, a committee meeting at which a manager meets with five others for one hour represents six work hours. On the other hand, if the same executive meets for one hour with each of the five people individually, the expended time turns out to be ten work hours. Assume that the executive makes $60,000 ($30 per hour) per year and that the five others average $24,000 ($14 per hour). For the one-hour committee meeting the cost would be about $100, but for the five individual conferences the total cost would be about $220, over twice as much. The point of this elementary cost analysis is that one cannot automatically condemn all committees as being excessively expensive. The nature and purpose must be considered when assessing cost. Furthermore, it is difficult, if not impossible, to quantify for cost purposes the advantages of a committee in terms of member motivation and quality of decision or problem solution.

From an organizational standpoint, there are some potential problems inherent in committees. The most obvious is divided responsibility. This is saying that in a committee, there is group or corporate but no individual responsibility or accountability. Thus, critics argue, the committee in reality turns out to have no responsibility or accountability. In fact, individuals may use the committee as a shield to avoid personal responsibility for bad decisions or mistakes. One solution to this problem is to make all committee members responsible, and another is to hold the chairperson responsible. Both approaches have many obvious difficulties. For example, if the entire committee is held responsible for a wrong decision, what about the individual members who voted against the majority? Holding them accountable for the committee's decision could have disastrous effects on their morale, but holding only those who voted for a particular decision responsible would create an inhibiting effect that would destroy the value of committee action.

Besides being time-consuming and costly and having divided responsibility, committees may reach decisions that are products of excessive compromise, logrolling, and one-person or minority domination. The comment that the camel is a horse designed by a committee underscores this limitation. It represents the reverse of the advantages of integrated group judgment and the pooling of specialized knowledge. Where unanimity is either formally required or an informal group norm, the difficulties are compounded. The final decision may be so extremely watered down or "compromised to death" that the horse actually does turn out to be a camel. The strength of committee action comes through a synthesis and integration of divergent viewpoints, not through a compromise representing the least common denominator. One way to avoid the problem is to limit the committee to serving as a forum for the exchange of information and ideas. Another possibility is to let the chairperson have the final decision-making prerogative. Yet these solutions are not always satisfactory because when the committee is charged with making a decision, considerable social skill and a willingness to cooperate fully must exist if good-quality decisions are to evolve.

"Groupthink": A Major Problem with Committees and Groups

A dysfunction of highly cohesive groups and committees that has received a lot of attention recently has been called "groupthink" by Irving Janis. He defines it as "a deterioration of mental efficiency, reality testing, and moral judgment that results from in-group pressures."[12] Essentially, groupthink results from the pressures on individual members to conform and reach consensus. Committees that are suffering from groupthink are so bent on reaching consensus that there is no realistic appraisal of alternative courses of action in a decision, and deviant, minority, or unpopular views are suppressed.

Janis has concluded that a number of historic fiascos by government policy-making groups (for example, Britain's do-nothing policy toward Hitler prior to World War II, the unpreparedness of U.S. forces at Pearl Harbor, the Bay of Pigs invasion of Cuba, and the escalation of the Vietnam war) can be attributed to groupthink. The Watergate and, more recently, the Iran-*contra* affairs can be explained as a product of groupthink. For example, during the Senate hearing on Watergate, Herbert Porter, a member of Nixon's White House staff, answered in an interesting way the question, posed by then-Senator Howard Baker, as to how he became so involved in the dirty tricks of the campaign. Porter said that he "was not one to stand up in a meeting and say that this should be stopped. . . . I kind of drifted along." When Baker asked what, if any, reason Porter had for getting in such a predicament, Porter replied: "In all honesty, because of the fear of the group pressure that would ensue, of not being a team player. . . . I felt a deep sense of loyalty to him [President Nixon] or was appealed to on that basis."[13]

Although historically notorious news events can be used to dramatically point out the pitfalls of groupthink, it can commonly occur in committees in business firms or hospitals or any other type of organization. To date, there has been at least some partial support of the groupthink model when applied to areas such as leader behavior and decision making.[14] Table 13.3 summarizes some of the symptoms of groupthink that committees should recognize and then avoid if possible. For example, the first symptom leads to the so-called "risky shift phenomenon" of groups. Contrary to popular belief, research going back many years has shown that a group may make more risky decisions than the individual members would on their own.[15] This conclusion, of course, must be tempered by the values attached to the outcomes, but most of the research over the years finds that groups take more risks than individuals acting alone.

Such symptoms as this risky shift phenomenon and the others found in Table 13.3 should make groups take notice and be very careful that they do not slip into groupthink. To help overcome the potentially disastrous effects of groupthink, free expression of minority and unpopular viewpoints should be

TABLE 13.3 Symptoms of Groupthink

1. There is the illusion of *invulnerability*. There is excessive optimism and risk taking.
2. There are *rationalizations* by the members of the group to discount warnings.
3. There is an unquestioned belief in the group's *inherent morality*. The group ignores questionable ethical or moral issues or stances.
4. Those who oppose the group are *stereotyped* as evil, weak, or stupid.
5. There is *direct pressure* on any member who questions the stereotypes. Loyal members don't question the direction in which the group seems to be heading.
6. There is *self-censorship* of any deviation from the apparent group consensus.
7. There is the *illusion of unanimity*. Silence is interpreted as consent.
8. There are *self-appointed mindguards* who protect the group from adverse information.

Source: Adapted from Irving L. Janis, *Victims of Groupthink*, Houghton Mifflin, Boston, 1972, pp. 197–198.

encouraged and legitimatized, and the pros and cons of each proposed alternative course of action should be thoroughly examined.[16]

The Dynamics of Informal Groups

Informal groups play a significant role in the dynamics of organizational behavior. The major difference between formal and informal groups is that the formal group has officially prescribed goals and relationships, whereas the informal one does not. Despite this distinction, it is a mistake to think of formal and informal groups as two distinctly separate entities. The two types of groups coexist and are inseparable. Every formal organization has informal groups, and every informal organization eventually evolves some semblance of formal groups.

Norms and Roles in Informal Groups

With the exception of a single social act such as extending a hand upon meeting, the smallest units of analysis in group dynamics are norms and roles. Many behavioral scientists make a point of distinguishing between the two units, but conceptually they are very similar. *Norms* are the "oughts" of behavior. They are prescriptions for acceptable behavior determined by the group. Norms will be strongly enforced by work groups if they:

1. Ensure group success or survival
2. Reflect the preferences of supervisors or other powerful group members
3. Simplify, or make predictable, what behavior is expected of group members
4. Reinforce specific individual members' roles
5. Help the group avoid embarrassing interpersonal problems[17]

A role consists of a pattern of norms; the use of the term in organizations is directly related to its theatrical use. A role is a position that can be acted out by an individual. The content of a given role is prescribed by the prevailing norms. Probably *role* can best be defined as a position that has expectations evolving from established norms.

Informal Managerial Roles

Informal roles vary widely and are highly volatile. Table 13.4 summarizes some of the general informal roles that today's employees often assume. These role descriptions are not intended to be stereotypes or to imply that each organizational participant has only one role. The same person may have one role in one situation (a member of a middle management work group) and another role in another situation (the informal leader of the dissident group on a new project).

On the basis of observational studies of managerial work, Henry Mintzberg has proposed that managers perform the three types of roles shown in Figure 13.3. The *interpersonal roles* arise directly from formal authority and refer to the relationship between the manager and others. By virtue of the formal position, the manager has a *figurehead role* as a symbol of the organization. Most of the time spent as a figurehead is on ceremonial duties such as greeting a touring class of students or taking an important customer to lunch. The second interpersonal role is called the *leader role.* In this role the manager uses his or her influence to motivate and encourage subordinates to accomplish organizational objectives. In the third type of interpersonal role the manager undertakes a *liaison role.* This role recognizes that managers often spend more time interacting

TABLE 13.4 Informal Roles of Employees

Task-oriented employees: those who have the role of "getting the job done" and are known as those who "deliver the goods"

Technique-oriented employees: the masters of procedure and method

People-oriented employees: those who have the role of patron saint and good samaritan to people in need

Nay-sayers: those who counterbalance the "yes" persons and who have thick skins and can find fault with anything

Yes-sayers: those who counterbalance the nay-sayers; the "yes" persons who circumvent opposition

Rule enforcers: the "people of the book," those who are stereotype bureaucrats

Rule evaders: the "operators," those who know how to get the job done "irrespective"

Rule blinkers: the people who are not against the rules but don't take them seriously

Involved employees: those who are fully immersed in their work and the activities of the organization

Detached employees: slackers who either "go along for the ride" or "call it quits" at the end of regular hours

Regulars: those who are "in," who accept the values of the group and are accepted by the group

Deviants: those who depart from the values of the group—the "mavericks"

Isolates: the true "lone wolves," who are further from the group than the deviants

Newcomers: those who know little and must be taken care of by others; people who are "seen but not heard"

Old-timers: those who have been around a long time and "know the ropes"

Climbers: those who are expected to "get ahead," not necessarily on the basis of ability but on the basis of potential

Stickers: those who are expected to stay put, who are satisfied with life and their position in it

Cosmopolitans: those who see themselves as members of a broader professional, cultural, or political community

Locals: those who are rooted to the organization and local community

Source: Adapted from Bertram M. Gross, *Organizations and Their Managing,* Free Press, New York, 1968, pp. 242–248.

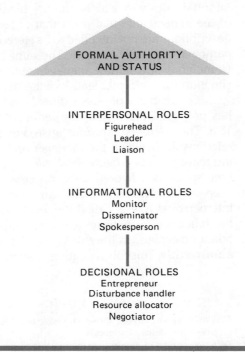

FIGURE 13.3
Mintzberg's managerial roles. (*Source:* Adapted from Henry Mintzberg, "The Manager's Job: Folklore and Fact," *Harvard Business Review,* July–August 1975, pp. 49–61.)

with others outside their unit (with peers in other units or those completely outside the organization) than they do working with their own superiors and subordinates.

Besides the interpersonal roles flowing from formal authority, Figure 13.3 shows that managers also have important *informational roles.* Most observational studies find that managers spend a great deal of time giving and receiving information. As *monitor,* the manager is continually scanning the environment and probing subordinates, bosses, and outside contacts for information; as *disseminator,* the manager distributes information to key internal people; and as *spokesperson,* the manager provides information to outsiders.

In the *decisional role,* the manager acts upon the information. In the *entrepreneurial role* in Mintzberg's scheme, the manager initiates the development of a project and assembles the necessary resources. The *disturbance handler,* on the other hand, instead of being proactive like the entrepreneur, is reactive to the problems and pressures of the situation. The disturbance handler has a crisis management type of role; for example, the employees are about to strike, or a major subcontractor is threatening to pull out. As *resource allocator* the manager decides who gets what in his or her department. Finally, the *negotiator* decisional role recognizes the time managers spend at all levels in the give-and-take of negotiating with subordinates, bosses, and outsiders. For example, a production manager may have to negotiate a grievance settlement with the union business agent, or a supervisor in a welfare department may have to negotiate certain benefit payments that one of the counselors wants to give a client.

These informal managerial roles suggested by Mintzberg get much closer to describing what managers really do than the formally described and prescribed functions of managers. Mintzberg's work has definitely shed some light on the nature of managerial work. More recent observational studies find these types of activities with some variations. One study of a small sample of general managers found networking and setting informal agendas to be important activities[18] and a large comprehensive observational study found traditional management (activities of decision making, planning, and controlling), communication, networking, and human resources management activities were what managers really do day-to-day.[19]

Informal Organization Structures

Besides the informal roles that managers perform, the overall informal organization structure has important dynamics for the study of organizational behavior. The classic Milo study conducted by Melville Dalton remains the best illustration of the power of the informal organization.[20] Figure 13.4a represents the formal organization at Milo. Through the use of intimates, interviews, diaries, observation, and socializing, Dalton was able to construct the informal organization chart shown in Figure 13.4b. This informal chart shows the actual power, as opposed to the formally designated power and influence, of the various managers at Milo.

Like the formal organization structures discussed in the next part of the book, the informal organization has both functions and dysfunctions. In contrast to formal organization analysis, the dysfunctional aspects of informal organization have received more attention than the functional ones. For example, conflicting objectives, restriction of output, conformity, blocking of ambition, inertia, and resistance to change are frequently mentioned dysfunctions of the informal organization.[21] More recently, however, organizational analysis has begun to recognize the functional aspects as well. For example, the following list suggests some practical benefits that can be derived from the informal organization:

1. Makes for a more effective total system.
2. Lightens the workload on management.
3. Fills in gaps in a manager's abilities.
4. Provides a safety valve for employee emotions.
5. Improves communication.[22]

Because of the inevitability and power of the informal organization, the functions should be exploited in the attainment of objectives rather than futilely combated by management. As a recent analysis of leadership points out, "informal social networks exert an immense influence which sometimes overrides the formal hierarchy. . . . Leadership goes beyond a person's formal position into realms of informal, hidden, or unauthorized influence."[23] This is especially true with regard to the informal communication system of an organization.

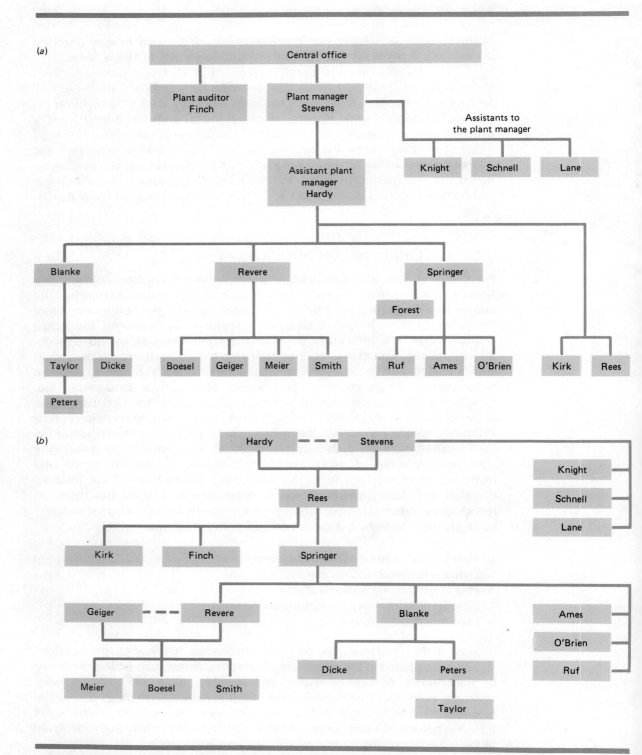

FIGURE 13.4 (*a*) A simplified formal organization chart of Milo; (*b*) an informal organization chart of Milo. (*Source:* Adapted from Melville Dalton, *Men Who Manage*, Wiley, New York, 1959, pp. 21–22.)

Informal Communication System

The term *grapevine* is commonly used to refer to the informal communication system in an organization. It can be traced back to the Civil War period, when telegraph lines were strung from tree to tree like grapevines. Messages sent over this haphazard system often became garbled, and any false information or rumor that came along was therefore ironically said to come from the grapevine.[24] The negative connotation of the grapevine, carried over to modern times, seems to have the following pattern: The informal communication system is equated with the grapevine; the grapevine is equated with rumor; and rumor is viewed as being bad for the organization. In management practice, the next step in the above sequence is to interpret the informal system of communication as being bad for the organization. Although admittedly the informal system is often misused and has potential dangers, most organization theorists now agree that it also has many positive functions.

Negative and Positive Aspects of the Grapevine. The informal system of communication can be used to spread false rumors and destructive information, or it can effectively supplement the formal channels of communication discussed in Chapter 17. It can quickly disseminate pertinent information that assists the formal systems to attain goals. However, whether the informal system has negative or positive functions for the organization depends largely on the goals of the person doing the communicating. Like any communication system, the entire informal system has a highly personal orientation, and, as has been pointed out earlier, personal goals may or may not be compatible with organizational goals. The degree of compatibility that does exist will have a major impact on the effect that the grapevine has on organizational goal attainment.

Some organization theorists are critical of the grapevine because its speed makes control of false rumors and information difficult to manage. By the same token, however, this speed factor may work to the advantage of the organization. Since the informal system is so personally based and directed, it tends to be much faster than the formal downward system of information flow. Important relevant information that requires quick responsive action by lower-level personnel may be more effectively handled by the informal system than by the formal system. As Chapter 17 will point out, the informal system is a major way that the necessary requirements for interactive and subordinate-initiated communication are accomplished. The formal horizontal and upward systems are often either inadequate or completely ineffective. The informal system is generally relied upon to coordinate the units horizontally on a given level and to provide valuable upward information about subordinate performance, ideas, and attitudes.

Types of Informal Communication. Since an informal organization structure will always coexist with a formal structure, there will be an informal communication system in every formal organization. Figure 13.5 shows four possible informal communication networks. The cluster type is the most prevalent form of informal communication. For example, "in one company when a quality-control problem occurred, 68 percent of the executives knew about it,

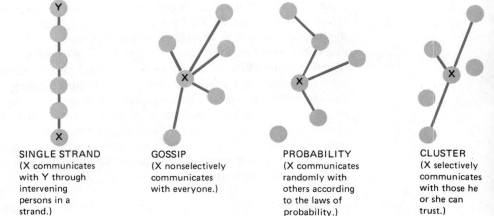

SINGLE STRAND
(X communicates
with Y through
intervening
persons in a
strand.)

GOSSIP
(X nonselectively
communicates
with everyone.)

PROBABILITY
(X communicates
randomly with
others according
to the laws of
probability.)

CLUSTER
(X selectively
communicates
with those he
or she can
trust.)

FIGURE 13.5
Informal
communication
networks in an
organization.

but only 20 percent of them spread the information. In another case, when a manager planned to resign, 81 percent of the executives knew about it, but only 11 percent passed the news on to others."[25]

Briefly, management must recognize that just as the informal organization is inevitable, so is the informal communication system. It should not be narrowly equated with false rumors. Rather, it should be recognized that the grapevine can be accurate and fast and can carry much information that is needed to supplement the formal systems of communication in an organization. Today's managers should attempt to manage and make use of the informal system to help them attain organization objectives.

Summary

Groups represent an important dynamic input into organizational behavior. Group formation, types, and processes and the dynamics of informal roles and organization are all of particular relevance to the study of organizational behavior. Group formation can be theoretically explained by propinquity; as a relationship between activities, interactions, and sentiments; as a symmetrical balance between attraction and common attitudes; and as a reward-cost exchange. Participants in an organization also form into groups for very practical economic, security, and social reasons. Many different types of formal and informal groups are found in modern organizations. Committees in particular are playing an increasingly important role in modern organizations. Although they can be time-consuming, costly, and conducive to divided responsibility, excessive compromise, and groupthink, they can lead to improved decisions through combined and integrated judgment, reduce conflict, facilitate coordination, and increase motivation and commitment through participation.

Informal roles are being found increasingly useful for describing the true nature of managerial work. Informal structure coexists with every formal structure. The informal structure is not formally designated, but rather is determined by the various group-status positions and roles. Traditionally, only the dysfunctional aspects of informal organization have been emphasized. More recently, the functional aspects have also been recognized. A good example is the informal communication system, which can either spread false rumors and cause destructive conflict or become an effective supplement to the formal systems of communication. Management in the future must be able to understand and, when possible, take advantage of group dynamics and informal roles and organization.

Questions for Discussion and Review

1. Briefly discuss the major theoretical explanations for group formation. Which explanation do you think is most relevant to the study of organizational behavior? Defend your choice.
2. What implications does the Schachter study have for the study of organizational behavior?
3. How can the disadvantages of committees be overcome?
4. What are some of the major symptoms of groupthink? Can you give an example from your own experience where this may have happened?
5. Summarize some of the informal managerial roles suggested by Mintzberg. Do you think that these roles are descriptive of what managers really do? Why or why not?
6. What are some functions of the informal organization? What are some of the dysfunctions?

References

1. Robert A. Baron, *Behavior in Organizations*, 2d ed., Allyn and Bacon, Boston, 1986, p. 240.
2. George C. Homans, *The Human Group*, Harcourt, Brace & World, New York, 1950, pp. 43–44.
3. Theodore M. Newcomb, *The Acquaintance Process*, Holt, New York, 1961.
4. John W. Thibaut and Harold H. Kelley, *The Social Psychology of Groups*, Wiley, New York, 1959.
5. William B. Stevenson, Jone L. Pearce, and Lyman Porter, "The Concept of 'Coalition' in Organization Theory and Research," *Academy of Management Review*, April 1985, pp. 261–262.
6. Tom Peters, *Thriving on Chaos: Handbook for a Management Revolution*, Knopf, New York, 1987, p. 297.
7. Toby D. Wall, Nigel J. Kemp, Paul R. Jackson, and Chris W. Clegg, "Outcomes of Autonomous Workgroups: A Long-Term Field Experiment," *Academy of Management Journal*, June 1986, pp. 280–304.

8. Stanley Schachter, Norris Ellertson, Dorothy McBride, and Doris Gregory, "An Experimental Study of Cohesiveness and Productivity," *Human Relations,* August 1951, pp. 229–239.
9. Leonard Berkowitz, "Group Standards, Cohesiveness, and Productivity," *Human Relations,* vol. 7, no. 4, 1954, pp. 509–519.
10. Barry M. Staw, "Organizational Psychology and the Pursuit of the Happy/Productive Worker," *California Management Review,* Summer 1986, p. 49.
11. Gregory P. Shea and Richard A. Guzzo, "Group Effectiveness: What Really Matters?" *Sloan Management Review,* Spring 1987, p. 25.
12. Irving L. Janis, *Victims of Groupthink,* Houghton Mifflin, Boston, 1972, p. 9.
13. *The Washington Post,* June 8, 1972, p. 20, as reported in Jerry B. Harvey, "The Abilene Paradox: The Management of Agreement," *Organizational Dynamics,* Summer 1974, p. 68, and also quoted in Stephen P. Robbins, *Organizational Behavior,* Prentice-Hall, Englewood Cliffs, N.J., 1979, pp. 208–209.
14. Carrie R. Leana, "A Partial Test of Janis' Groupthink Model: Effects of Group Cohesiveness and Leader Behavior on Defective Decision Making," *Journal of Management,* vol. 11, no. 1, 1985, pp. 5–17.
15. The original research on risky shift goes back to a master's thesis by J. A. F. Stoner, "A Comparison of Individual and Group Decisions Involving Risk," Massachusetts Institute of Technology, Sloan School of Industrial Management, Cambridge, Mass., 1961.
16. Clarence W. Von Bergen, Jr., and Raymond J. Kirk, "Groupthink: When Too Many Heads Spoil the Decision," *Management Review,* March 1978, pp. 44–49.
17. Daniel C. Feldman and Hugh J. Arnold, *Managing Individual and Group Behavior in Organizations,* McGraw-Hill, New York, 1983, pp. 447–448.
18. John Kotter, *General Managers,* Free Press, New York, 1982.
19. Fred Luthans, Richard M. Hodgetts, and Stuart A. Rosenkrantz, *Real Managers,* Ballinger, Cambridge, Mass., 1988.
20. Melville Dalton, *Men Who Manage,* Wiley, New York, 1959.
21. Ross Webber, *Management,* 2d ed., Irwin, Homewood, Ill., 1979, p. 118.
22. Keith Davis and John W. Newstrom, *Human Behavior at Work,* 7th ed., McGraw-Hill, New York, 1985, p. 311.
23. Louis B. Barnes and Mark P. Kriger, "The Hidden Side of Organizational Leadership," *Sloan Management Review,* Fall 1986, p. 15.
24. Davis and Newstrom, op. cit., pp. 314–315.
25. Ibid., p. 318.

REAL CASE: Female Managers: Tired of Fighting the Battle?*

Today, approximately 70 percent of all women between the ages of 25 and 54 are either employed or actively seeking employment. The number of two-income families is higher than ever. Despite the growing numbers, there are more and more well-educated female managers bailing out of business and choosing to become self-employed or stay at home and raise a family. Why? A large part of the answer appears to be based on the fact

***Source:** Adapted from Alex Taylor III, "Why Women Managers Are Bailing Out," *Fortune,* Aug. 18, 1986, pp. 16–23.

that female managers are tired of fighting the battle. They feel they are not getting an equal opportunity with men.

Fortune magazine recently analyzed the managerial career paths of men and women who received MBA degrees in 1976 from seventeen of the most prestigious business schools. The analysis revealed that 69 percent of both male and female graduates took jobs with large corporations or professional schools. In 1986, 44 percent of the men and 43 percent of the women were still working for large employers. However, there was a major difference between the rest of the people in these two groups. A large percentage of the women had dropped off the management track. *Fortune* found that 30 percent of the 1039 women from the class of 1976 were either self-employed or unemployed, compared with 21 percent of the men. A follow-up of these two respective groups that had dropped out of big companies uncovered another interesting fact. Most of the women indicated that they worked only part-time or not at all. The men, on the other hand, were almost all working; only 4 percent were found to be unemployed.

Why have so many women dropped out? A number of possibilities exist. One is that they feel they are not being given the important jobs. No matter how long women stay with a firm, men are being given the major promotions. A second is that many companies seem to feel that a woman's job is in one of the "three p's"—purchasing, personnel, or public relations. Thus, women have a difficult time getting into higher-paying, prestige line positions in marketing, operations, or finance. A third is that many women feel they are not paid as much as their male counterparts even though they do the same basic job, and the equal-pay-for-equal-work laws notwithstanding, the statistics indicate that the women are often right. A fourth is that for many women priorities change as they get older. The fact is that many married women still regard their marriage as more important than their career and if they cannot have both, they are likely to drop their career. This is particularly true for those who have children.

The bottom line for many companies is that they must recognize and begin to work hard to find ways of keeping their best women managers on the job. The attitudes and values of this disgruntled group of management talent is, to a large degree, not the same as that of male managers. One observer put it this way:

> So what is a company to do? Corporate management is by its nature a consultative process, difficult to pull off unless all the managers are present. But efficient companies should be able to afford women managers more flexibility in their hours, particularly at the beginning and end of the workday. Establishing a separate career track for women to permit extended leaves of absence may seem like perpetuation of their treatment as persons apart. But it may be the only way to keep them in the corporate fold. Companies will have to recognize, too, that nowadays their best future executives are often married to other promising managers. These busy people may not be willing to relocate or work a 70-hour week.

1. In what way can the balance theory of group formation help explain why female managers are leaving their organizations?
2. How can exchange theory help explain the reason(s) why female managers are not staying with large companies?
3. What can organizations do to reverse the situation described in this case? Apply the concept of exchange theory in your answer.

CASE: The Schoolboy Rookie

Kent Sikes is a junior at State University. He has taken a summer job in the biggest factory in his hometown. He was told to report to the warehouse supervisor the first day at work. The supervisor assigned him to a small group of men who were responsible for loading and unloading the boxcars that supplied the materials and carried away the finished goods of the factory.

After two weeks on the job, Kent was amazed at how little work the men in his crew accomplished. It seemed that they were forever standing around and talking or, in some cases, even going off to hide when there was work to be done. Kent often found himself alone unloading a boxcar while the other members of the crew were off messing around someplace else. When Kent complained to his coworkers, they made it very plain that if he did not like it, he could quit, but if he complained to the supervisor, he would be sorry. Although Kent has been deliberately excluded from any of the crew's activities such as taking breaks together or having a Friday afternoon beer after work at the tavern across the street, yesterday he went up to one of the older members of the crew and said, "What gives with you guys, anyway? I am just trying to do my job. The money is good and I just don't give a hang about this place. I will be leaving to go back to school in a few weeks, and I wish I could have gotten to know you all better, but frankly I am sure glad I'm not like you guys." The older worker replied, "Son, if you'd been here as long as I have, you would be just like us."

1. Using some of the theories, explain the possible reasons for the group formation of this work crew. What types of groups exist in this case?
2. Place this work group in the Schachter study. What role does the supervisor play in the performance of this group?
3. What are the major informal roles of the crew members and Kent? What status position does Kent have with the group? Why?
4. Why hasn't Kent been accepted by the group? Do you agree with the older worker's last statement in the case? Why or why not?

CASE: The Blue-Ribbon Committee

Mayor Sam Small is nearing completion of his first term in office. He feels his record has been pretty good, except for the controversial issue of housing. He has been able to avoid doing anything about housing so far and feels very strongly that this issue must not come to a head before the next election. The voters are too evenly divided on the issue, and he would lose a substantial number of votes no matter what stand he took. Yet with pressure increasing from both sides, he had to do something. After much distress and vacillation he has finally come upon what he thinks is an ideal solution to his dilemma. He has appointed a committee to study the problem and make some recommendations. To make sure that the committee's work will not be completed before the election comes up, it was important to pick the right people. Specifically, Sam has selected his "blue-ribbon" committee from a wide cross section of the community so that, in Sam's words, "all concerned parties will be represented." He has made the committee very large, and the members range from Ph.D's in urban planning to real estate agents to local ward committeepersons to minority group leaders. He has taken particular care in selecting people who have widely divergent, outspoken, public views on the housing issue.

1. Do you think Sam's strategy of using this committee to delay taking a stand on the housing issue until after the election will work? Why or why not?
2. What are some of the important dynamics of this committee? Do you think the committee will arrive at a good solution to the housing problems facing this city?
3. Do you think this committee will suffer from groupthink?
4. What types of informal roles is Sam exhibiting? Do you think he is an effective manager? Do you think he is an effective politician? Is there a difference?

⎡14⎤ Interactive Behavior and Conflict

Union-management disputes are an obvious example of intergroup conflict in organizations. A recent example has occurred between the United Steelworkers and the big steel company USX (formerly U.S. Steel). They clashed in the longest dispute of the company's history—twenty-three weeks.

Although conflict is recognized as inevitable and sometimes healthy for change, if union-management conflicts such as the one at USX are not settled, both sides begin to suffer. Workers, already strapped without wages, soon lose their unemployment benefits during a strike. In addition to the $100 million monthly losses incurred in the stoppage, USX also lost some of its business with the auto industry, its largest customer. Hostility was so high between the groups that communication became useless. As a result, an outside mediator was brought in. The mediator, Sylvester Garrett, attempted a win-win strategy to resolve the conflict. If such a strategy is effective, management wins wage-and-benefit concessions, putting the company on equal ground with its competitors. The union, on the other hand, wins limitations on USX's ability to contract out work to nonunion companies, thereby saving jobs for union members. However, it is questionable whether both sides will actually win or lose. Although a cut in wages gives USX an annual savings of $85 million, analysts estimate that the strike will bring net losses of up to $1 billion. The union also stands to lose. Because

*Source: Adapted from Matt Rothman and Gregory L. Miles, "It's a No-Win Situation for Both Sides at USX," *Business Week,* Jan. 19, 1987, p. 55–56.

of the glutted steel market, only the most efficient plants will survive. USX Chairman David M. Roderick believes that by 1990 steel may account for only 15 to 20 percent of USX's sales, compared with the current 45 to 50 percent. If Roderick is right, at least one-third of USX's capacity will be closed, which means job losses for union members. Thus, it is debatable whether the resolution at USX is a win-win or lose-lose outcome for either union or management.

Learning Objectives

- DISCUSS intraindividual conflict due to frustration, goals, and roles.
- ANALYZE interpersonal conflict.
- IDENTIFY the dimensions of transactional analysis and the Johari window.
- DEFINE the strategies of interpersonal conflict resolution.
- EXPLAIN intergroup behavior and conflict.
- RELATE the dimensions of organizational conflict.

Interactive behavior can occur at the individual, interpersonal, group, or organizational level. It often results in conflict at all these levels. Although such conflict, especially intraindividual conflict, is very closely related to stress (discussed in Chapter 8), conflict is given separate treatment here because of the emphasis on interactive behavior in this part of the book. Thus, this chapter first analyzes intraindividual conflict stemming from frustration, goals, and roles. Next, interpersonal dynamics and the resulting conflict are examined from the perspective of transactional analysis and the Johari window. The last two sections are concerned with intergroup behavior and conflict and organizational conflict. Potential strategies for conflict resolution at each of these levels of analysis of interactive behavior (that is, individual, interpersonal, group, and organizational) are presented.

Intraindividual Conflict

A smooth progression of the need-drive-goal motivational cycle (discussed in Chapter 9) and fulfillment of one's role expectations do not always occur in reality. Within every individual there are usually (1) a number of competing needs and roles, (2) a variety of different ways that drives and roles can be expressed, (3) many types of barriers which can occur between the drive and the goal, and (4) both positive and negative aspects attached to desired goals. These complicate the human adaptation process and often result in conflict. Intraindividual forms of conflict can be analyzed in terms of the frustration model, goals, and roles.

Conflict Due to Frustration

Frustration occurs when a motivated drive is blocked before a person reaches a desired goal. Figure 14.1 illustrates what happens. The barrier may be either overt (outward, or physical) or covert (inward, or mental-sociopsychological). An example of a frustrating situation might be that of a thirsty person who comes up against a stuck door and is prevented from reaching a water fountain. Figure 14.2 illustrates this simple frustrating situation. Frustration normally triggers defense mechanisms in the person. Traditionally, psychologists felt that frustration always leads to the defense mechanism of aggression. On becoming frustrated, it was thought that a person will react by physically or symbolically attacking the barrier. In the example in Figure 14.2, the person would react by kicking and/or cursing the jammed door.

More recently, aggression has come to be viewed as only one possible reaction. Frustration may lead to any of the defense mechanisms used by the human organism. Although there are many such mechanisms, they can be summarized into four broad categories: aggression, withdrawal, fixation, and compromise. In the illustration of Figure 14.2, backing away from the door and pouting would be an example of withdrawal; pretending the door is not jammed and continually trying to open it would be an example of fixation; and substituting a new goal (a cup of coffee already in the room) or a new direction (climbing out the window) would be an example of compromise.

Although the thirsty person frustrated by the stuck door is a very uncomplicated example, the same frustration model can be used to analyze more complex behavior. One example would be a black individual who comes from a disadvantaged educational and economic background but who still has intense needs for pride and dignity. A goal that may fulfill the individual's needs is

FIGURE 14.1 A simple model of frustration.

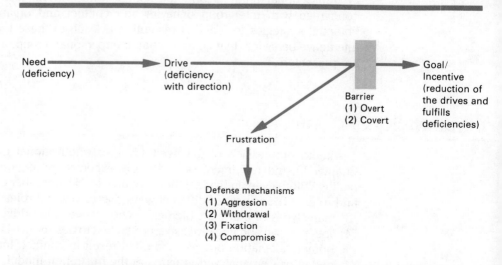

Need → Drive → Barrier → Goal/Incentive
(deficiency) (deficiency with direction) (1) Overt (2) Covert (reduction of the drives and fulfills deficiencies)

Frustration

Defense mechanisms
(1) Aggression
(2) Withdrawal
(3) Fixation
(4) Compromise

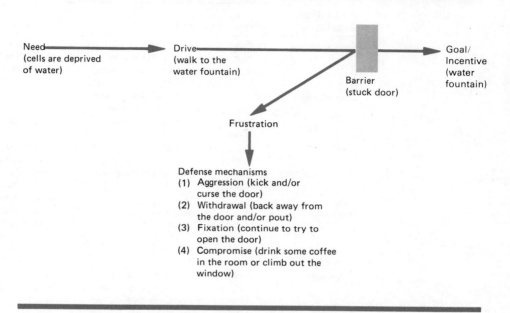

Need (cells are deprived of water) → Drive (walk to the water fountain) → Barrier (stuck door) → Goal/Incentive (water fountain)

Frustration

Defense mechanisms
(1) Aggression (kick and/or curse the door)
(2) Withdrawal (back away from the door and/or pout)
(3) Fixation (continue to try to open the door)
(4) Compromise (drink some coffee in the room or climb out the window)

FIGURE 14.2 A simple example of frustration.

meaningful employment. The drive set up to alleviate the need and accomplish the goal would be to search for a good job. The black person in this example who meets barriers (prejudice, discrimination, lack of education, and nonqualification) may become frustrated. Possible reactions to this frustration may be aggression (riot or hate), withdrawal (apathy and unemployment), fixation (pretending the barriers do not exist and continuing to search unsuccessfully for a good job), or compromise (finding expression of pride and dignity in something other than a good job, such as in a militant group).

The frustration model can be useful in the analysis not only of behavior in general but also of specific aspects of on-the-job behavior. Table 14.1 summarizes some behavioral reactions to frustration that may occur in the formal organization. These examples generally imply that there is a negative impact on the individual's performance and on the organization as a result of frustration. Some of this frustration may actually be translated into real costs to the organization. For example, a survey of forty-seven corporations found that one-third of the employees reported stealing company property and that nearly two-thirds reported taking long lunch breaks, misusing sick leave, or using alcohol or drugs while at work.[1] A recent congressional report estimated that lost productivity and health problems caused by drugs are costing U.S. business at least $70 billion a year, and the National Institute on Drug Abuse believes one in every ten workers uses drugs to the degree that it interferes with job performance.[2]

Although these problems may not all be the result of frustration, even stealing, which is costing American business an estimated $5 to $10 billion per year, can be considered a form of displaced aggression resulting from on-the-

TABLE 14.1. Examples of Reactions to Frustration

Adjustive Reactions	Psychological Process	Illustration
Compensation	Individual devotes himself to a pursuit with increased vigor to make up for some feeling of real or imagined inadequacy	Zealous, hard-working president of the Twenty-Five-Year Club who has never advanced very far in the company hierarchy
Displacement	Redirecting pent-up emotions toward persons, ideas, or objects other than the primary source of the emotion	Roughly rejecting a simple request from a subordinate after receiving a rebuff from the boss
Fantasy	Daydreaming or other forms of imaginative activity provide an escape from reality and imagined satisfactions	An employee' daydream of the day in the staff meeting when he corrects the boss's mistakes and is publicly acknowledged as the real leader of the industry
Negativism	Active or passive resistance, operating unconsciously	The manager who, having been unsuccessful in getting out of a committee assignment, picks apart every suggestion that anyone makes in the meetings
Projection	Individual protects himself from awareness of his own undesirable traits or unacceptable feelings by attributing them to others	Unsuccessful person who, deep down, would like to block the rise of others in the organization and who continually feels that others are out to "get him"
Rationalization	Justifying inconsistent or undesirable behavior, beliefs, statements, and motivations by providing acceptable explanations for them	Padding the expense account because "everybody does it"
Regression	Individual returns to an earlier and less mature level of adjustment in the face of frustration	A manager, having been blocked in some administrative pursuit, busies himself with clerical duties or technical details more appropriate for his subordinates
Resignation, apathy, and boredom	Breaking psychological contact with the environment, withholding any sense of emotional or personal involvement	Employee who, receiving no reward, praise, or encouragement, no longer cares whether or not he does a good job
Flight or withdrawal	Leaving the field in which frustration, anxiety, or conflict is experienced, either physically or psychologically	The salesman's big order falls through and he takes the rest of the day off; constant rebuff or rejection by superiors and colleagues pushes an older worker toward being a loner and ignoring what friendly gestures are made

Source: Adapted from Timothy W. Costello and Sheldon S. Zalkind, *Psychology in Administration: A Research Orientation,* Prentice-Hall, Englewood Cliffs, N.J., 1963, pp. 148–149.

job frustration. Thus, although the evidence indicates the dysfunctional nature of frustration, it should not be automatically assumed.

In some cases frustration may actually result in a positive impact on individual performance and organizational goals. An example is the worker or manager who has high needs for competence and achievement and who has a self-concept that includes confidence in being able to do a job well. A person of this type who is frustrated on the job may react in a traditional defensive manner, but the frustration may result in improved performance. The person may try harder to overcome the barrier or may overcompensate, or the new direction or goal sought may be more compatible with the organization's goals. In addition, it should be remembered that defense mechanisms per se are not bad for the individual. They play an important role in the psychological adjustment process and are "unhealthy" only when they dominate the individual's personality. Reactions to frustration are also influenced by external factors and the organizational, group, and individual stressors identified in Chapter 8. Also, as in the discussion of stress, it should be pointed out that in certain situations, frustration can lead to positive as well as negative organizational behavior. However, in general, a major goal of management should be to eliminate the barriers (imagined, real, or potential) that are or will be frustrating to employees.

Goal Conflict

Another common source of conflict for an individual is a goal which has both positive and negative features, or two or more competing goals. Whereas in frustration a single motive is blocked before the goal is reached, in goal conflict two or more motives block one another. For ease of analysis, three separate types of goal conflict are generally identified:

1. *Approach-approach* conflict, where the individual is motivated to approach two or more positive but mutually exclusive goals.
2. *Approach-avoidance* conflict, where the individual is motivated to approach a goal and at the same time is motivated to avoid it. The single goal contains both positive and negative characteristics for the individual.
3. *Avoidance-avoidance* conflict, where the individual is motivated to avoid two or more negative but mutually exclusive goals.

To varying degrees, each of these forms of goal conflict exists in the modern organization.

Approach-Approach Conflict.
This type of goal conflict probably has the least impact on organizational behavior. Although conflict may arise about making a choice between two positive goals, they are preferable to two negative goals or a goal with both negative and positive characteristics. For example, if both personal and organizational goals are attractive to organizational participants, they will usually make a choice rather quickly and thus eliminate their conflict. A more specific example would be the new college graduate who is faced with two excellent job opportunities or the executive who has the choice between

two very attractive offices in which to work. Such situations often cause the person some anxiety but are quickly resolved, and the person does not "starve between two haystacks."

Approach-approach conflict can be analyzed in terms of the well-known theory of cognitive dissonance.[3] In simple terms, dissonance is the state of psychological discomfort or conflict created in people when they are faced with two or more goals or alternatives to a decision. Although these alternatives occur together, they do not belong or fit together. The theory states that the person experiencing dissonance will be highly motivated to reduce or eliminate it and will actively avoid situations and information which would be likely to increase it. For example, the young person faced with two equally attractive job opportunities would experience dissonance. According to this theory, the young person would actively try to reduce the dissonance. The individual may cognitively rationalize that one job is really better than the other one and, once the choice is made, be sincerely convinced that it was the right choice and actively avoid any evidence or argument to the contrary.

Approach-Avoidance Conflict.   This type of goal conflict is most relevant to the analysis of organizational behavior. Normally, organizational goals have both positive and negative aspects for organizational participants. Accordingly, the organizational goal may arouse a great deal of conflict within a person and may actually cause the person to vacillate anxiously at the point where approach equals avoidance.

Figure 14.3 shows some possible gradients for approach and avoidance. X

FIGURE 14.3
Gradients of ap-
proach-avoidance
conflict.

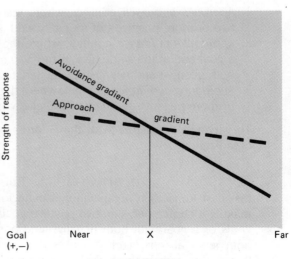

represents the point of maximum conflict, where the organism may come to a complete stop and vacillate. In order for the organism to progress beyond X, there must be a shift in the gradients so that there is a greater strength of response for approach than for avoidance. The slopes of the gradients shown in Figure 14.3 approximate those obtained from animals who are first trained to approach food at the end of a runway and are then shocked while feeding there. As shown, the pull or effort toward a positive goal is stronger the nearer the goal, but not as strong as the tendency to get away from a negative goal. The slope of the avoidance from the negative goal is steeper than the slope of the approach to reach the positive goal.

The approach-avoidance gradients for humans will not always resemble those found in Figure 14.3. The slopes may be different for different people and different goals. In general, however, it is safe to assume that the positive aspects of a given organizational goal are stronger and more salient at a distance (in time and/or space) than the negative aspects. On the other hand, as a person gets nearer to the goal, the negative aspects become more pronounced, and at some point the individual may hesitate or fail to progress any further. For example, managers engaged in long-range planning typically are very confident of a goal (plan) they have developed for the future. Yet, as the time gets near to commit resources and implement the plan, the negative consequences seem to appear much greater than they did in the developing stage. Managers in such a situation may reach the point where approach equals avoidance. The result is a great deal of internal conflict and stress, which may cause indecision, ulcers, or even neurosis. Such conflict and its aftermath are very common among decision makers and people in responsible positions in modern, complex organizations. On the other hand, the approach-avoidance type of conflict can often be resolved in the same manner as cognitive dissonance, or the gradients may be shifted by the individual so that either the positive or the negative aspects clearly predominate.

Avoidance-Avoidance Conflict. Analogous to approach-approach conflict, this type of conflict does not have a great deal of impact on organizational behavior. Avoidance-avoidance conflict is usually easily resolved. A person faced with two negative goals may not choose either of them and may simply leave the situation. If this can be done, the conflict is quickly resolved. In some situations, however, the person is unable to leave. This would be true of persons in nonvoluntary organizations, such as inmates in a prison, patients in a hospital, or members of the armed services. To a lesser extent, most personnel in modern organizations are also restricted from leaving, for example, workers who detest their supervisor and have too much pride to accept unemployment compensation. Such workers cannot easily resolve their avoidance-avoidance conflict in a time when jobs are very scarce.

Goal Conflict in Perspective. All three types of goal conflict might in certain instances benefit the organization. Approach-approach conflict can be mildly distressing for a person but represent the best of two worlds. Approach-avoidance conflict arising over organizational goals may force very careful planning and forecasting of exact positive and negative outcomes. Even avoidance-avoidance conflict may stimulate the person involved to examine and try to solve the problems causing the conflict. Yet, on balance, except for approach-approach conflicts, management should attempt to resolve goal conflicts. In particular, a major management effort should be devoted to building compatibility, not conflict, between personal and organizational goals.

Role Conflict and Ambiguity

Chapter 8 pointed out that role conflict and ambiguity is a major stressor. Closely related to the concept of norms (the "oughts" of behavior), *role* was defined as a position that has expectations evolving from established norms. Persons living in contemporary Western society assume a succession of roles throughout life. A typical sequence of social roles would be that of child, son or daughter, teenager, college student, boyfriend or girlfriend, spouse, parent, and grandparent. Each of these roles has recognized expectations which are acted out like a role in a play. As the accompanying International Application Example shows, sometimes these roles differ by culture and can result in conflict.

Besides progressing through a succession of roles such as those just mentioned, the adult in modern society fills numerous other roles at the same time. It is not uncommon for the adult middle-class male to be simultaneously playing the roles of husband, father, provider, son (to elderly parents), worker or manager, student (in a night program), coach of a Little League baseball team, church member, member of a social club, bridge partner, poker club member, officer of a community group, and weekend golfer. Although all the roles which individuals bring into the organization are relevant to their behavior, in the study of organizational behavior the organizational role is the most important. Roles such as assembly line worker, clerk, supervisor, salesperson, engineer, systems analyst, department head, vice president, and chairperson of the board often carry conflicting demands and expectations. The classic example of an organizational role in constant conflict and ambiguity is that of the first-line supervisor.

Role Conflict and Ambiguity in Supervisors.

The first-line supervisor is often described as the person in the middle. One set of expectations of this role is that the supervisor is part of the management team and should have the corresponding values and attitudes. A second set of expectations is that the supervisor came from, and is still part of, the workers' group and should have their values and attitudes. Still a third set of expectations is that supervisors are a separate link between management and the work force and should have their own unique set of values and attitudes. Conflict arises because supervisors themselves, like the workers and managers, do not know which set of expectations they should follow.

The first-line supervisor obviously represents the extreme case of organizational role conflict. Yet to varying degrees, depending on the individual and the situation, people in every other position in the modern organization also experience both intrarole and interrole conflict. Staff engineers are not sure of

**International
Application
Example**

> ### Cultural Conflict*
>
> As the Integrative Real Case for Part I "Working for Japan Inc." indicated, Japan's direct investment in the United States has increased dramatically in the last few years. This investment has not only brought new plants, technologies, and jobs to America but also has resulted in some conflict. The Japanese-run companies in the United States are an example of how cultural conflict can erupt. For instance, Japanese companies are known for their lifetime employment policies, which purportedly produce corporate loyalty. Employees often stay in a Japanese company throughout their entire career. American workers, on the other hand, may work for several companies in the course of their career. Asa Jonishi, senior director of Japan's Kyocera Corporation, says, "Most Americans are very, very individualistic—you could almost say egotistic; they are quite different from the way we would like our people to be." Two other important cultural differences are trade unions and assertive women. In U.S. industry, both are common. The Japanese, on the other hand, have had little experience with either. As a result, Japanese companies are becoming experienced with lawsuits. For example, former female employees of Sumitomo Corporation of America filed a sex-discrimination suit that alleged that Sumitomo restricted women to clerical positions. Sumitomo settled the suit by promising to increase the number of women in sales and management positions. In another case, the AFL-CIO won a dispute with Toyota and its Japanese contractor. To end the negative publicity of the unions' campaign, Toyota and its contractor agreed to hire union workers to build their new plant.
>
> It should be noted that some of the Japanese cultural values have been readily accepted in the American workplace. For instance, consensus management, which the Japanese are noted for, is being accepted in industries where autocratic leaders once existed. Pat Park, assistant general manager of Haseko, says, "There are many times when I'm the janitor here, picking up rubbish. But there are also many times the major decisions are made because I say so. There's more equity in Japanese companies." Thus, not all cultural differences lead to conflict. As all companies continue to transcend national borders, cultural differences may begin to narrow. However, culture still has a pervasive, but sometimes conflicting, influence on organizational behavior.
>
> ***Source:*** Adapted from Bill Powell, "Where the Jobs Are," *Newsweek,* Feb. 2, 1987, p. 42–46.

their real authority. The clerk in the front office does not know whether to respond to a union organizing drive. The examples are endless. The question is not whether role conflict and ambiguity exist—they do, and they seem inevitable. Rather, the key becomes a matter of determining how role conflict can be resolved or managed.

Interpersonal Conflict

Besides the intraindividual aspects of conflict, the interpersonal aspects of conflict are also an important dynamic of interactive behavior. The interrole conflict discussed in the last section certainly has interpersonal implications, and so do intergroup and organizational conflict, discussed in the next sections. But this section is specifically concerned with analyzing the conflict that can result when two or more persons are interacting with one another. Two popular ways to analyze this interpersonal conflict are through transactional analysis and the Johari window.

Transactional Analysis

Eric Berne is usually credited with having started the transactional analysis (TA) movement with his best-selling book *Games People Play;* Thomas Harris's book *I'm OK—You're OK* further popularized TA. TA is still popular today and has a wide appeal. In many respects it is a fad and is sometimes confused with the equally popular transcendental meditation (TM) movement. However, TA has been able to transcend the fad stage because it is based on a well-developed psychoanalytic theoretical base. A major reason for its popularity, and where Freud and other pioneering psychoanalytic theorists failed, is that it uses very understandable, everyday, relevant terminology. Everyone can readily relate to the concepts and practice of TA. The following sections give attention to the three major areas of transactional analysis: ego states, transactions, and strokes and games.

Ego States. The ego plays a central role in the Freudian psychoanalytic model. In the structure of the human personality, the ego represents reality, and it rationally attempts to keep the impulsive id and the conscience of the superego in check. The ego is a hypothetical construct because it is not observable; it is used to help explain the complex dynamics of the human personality. TA uses this psychoanalytic theory as a background for identifying three important ego states: child, adult, and parent. These three ego states are roughly equivalent to the Freudian concepts of id (child), ego (adult), and superego (parent). A more detailed look at the three ego states is necessary to understand TA:

1. *Child (C) ego state.* This is the state in which the person acts like an impulsive child. This "child" state could be characterized by being either submissive and conforming (the dutiful child) or insubordinate, emotional, joyful, or rebellious (the "little brat"). In either case the child state is characterized by very immature behavior. An example would be the employee who, when unfairly reprimanded by the boss, responds by saying, "You know best. Whatever you say." Another example would be the computer programmer who tells a coworker, "My boss makes me so mad sometimes I could scream" and then proceeds to burst into tears. Both examples illustrate immature, childlike behaviors.

2. *Adult (A) ego state.* In this state the person acts like a mature adult. In the adult state people attack problems in a "cool-headed," rational manner. They gather relevant information, carefully analyze it, generate alternatives, and make logical choices. In the adult state people do not act impulsively or in a domineering way. In dealings with other people, the adult state is characterized by fairness and objectivity. An example would be the sales manager who,

when presented with a relatively high expense account by a subordinate, replies, "Well, this appears high, but we will have to look at the reasons for it. It may be that our other salespersons' expenses are too low to do the kind of job that needs to be done."

3. *Parent (P) ego state.* In this state people act like domineering parents. Individuals can be either overly protective and loving or stern and critical. The parent state is also illustrated by those who establish standards and rules for others. They tend to talk down to people and to treat others like children. An example would be the supervisor who comes up to a group of workers and says, "Okay, you guys, stop fooling around and get to work. You have to earn your keep around here."

Transactions between Ego States. It should be pointed out that people generally exhibit all three ego states, but one state may dominate the other two. The strong implication is, of course, that the adult state is far superior to the child or parent state, at least for effective interpersonal relations. However, the TA authors generally stress that all three ego states are necessary to a healthy personality. More important than the ego state per se is how one ego state matches or conflicts with another ego state in interpersonal interaction. The transactions between ego states are at the heart of TA and can be classified into the following:

1. *Complementary transactions.* Figure 14.4 shows three possible complementary transactions. As shown, transactions are complementary if the message sent or the behavior exhibited by one person's ego state receives the appropriate and expected response from the other person's ego state. For example, suppose that the two people interacting in Figure 14.4 are a boss and an immediate subordinate. In Figure 14.4*a*, the boss says, "Joe, I want you to be

FIGURE 14.4
Complementary transactions.

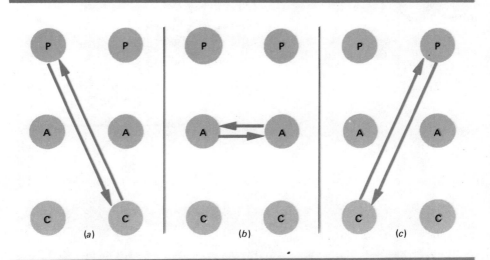

(a)   (b)   (c)

more careful in filling out a report on even the smallest accident. OSHA requirements are getting really tough, and we have to do better." The subordinate in Figure 14.4a replies, "Gee, boss, I really don't have time to fill out those dumb reports, but if you think I should, I will." In Figure 14.4b, the superior and subordinate both interact in an adult manner. For example, the boss says, "Joe, I would like your input on a report I am writing on how to improve the efficiency of the department." Joe responds by saying, "You bet, Jack. I have been gathering a lot of cost data over the past couple of months, and as soon as I analyze it, I would like to sit down with you and discuss it." In Figure 14.4c, the subordinate is in the parent state, and the boss is in the child state. Although rarer than the other two cases, an example might be the following dialogue:

Joe: Jack, I wish you would give more attention to maintenance around here. I can't do my job well unless you give me the proper support.

Boss: For heaven's sake! What do you want from me? You guys drive me up a wall. I can't take it anymore.

Once again it should be pointed out that although the adult-to-adult complementary transactions are probably most effective for organizational interpersonal relations, communication and understanding can also occur in the parent-child complementary transactions.

2. *Crossed transactions.* A crossed transaction occurs when the message sent or the behavior exhibited by one person's ego state is reacted to by an incompatible, unexpected ego state on the part of the other person. There are many more possible crossed transactions than there are complementary transactions. Figure 14.5 shows one crossed transaction that would typically occur in an organizational setting. As shown, the boss treats the subordinate

FIGURE 14.5
Crossed transactions.

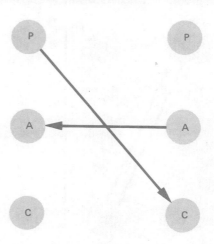

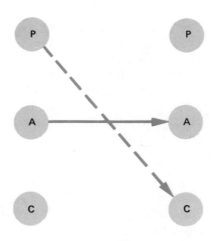

FIGURE 14.6
Ulterior transac-
tions.

like a child, but the subordinate attempts to respond on an adult basis. The dialogue in this example might be as follows:

Boss: I have told you over and over that I want those reports in on time. You are going to have to meet my deadlines or look for another job.

Subordinate: I did not realize that the timing of the reports was so critical. I will have to reorder my priorities.

Crossed transactions are the source of much interpersonal conflict in an organization. The result can be hurt feelings and frustrations on the part of the parties involved and possible dysfunctional consequences for the organization.

3. *Ulterior transactions.* The most complex are the ulterior transactions. These can be very subtle, but, like the crossed transactions, they are generally very damaging to interpersonal relations. As shown in Figure 14.6, the ulterior transactions always involve at least two ego states on the part of one person. The individual may say one thing (for example, project an adult state, as indicated in Figure 14.6) but mean quite another (for example, the parent state, as shown by the dashed line in Figure 14.6). Although there are many other possibilities besides the one shown in Figure 14.6, an example is this typical one in organizations, where the boss says, "My door is always open; come in so that we can air your problems and reach a rational solution together" (adult state), when what he or she really means is, "Don't come whining to me with your troubles. Find an answer yourself. That is what you're getting paid for" (parent state). Obviously, these ulterior transactions are the most difficult to identify and deal with in transactional analysis.

Strokes and Games in TA. The three ego states and the three types of transactions are the basic elements of TA. In addition, however, there are other concepts and dynamics inherent in the TA approach. Two of the more important are strokes and games:

1. *The concept of strokes.* TA experts feel that everyone has to have strokes. Using the common definition of the word, this means simply that beginning in infancy and continuing throughout their lives, people need cuddling, affection, recognition, and praise. Not everyone is turned on by the same strokes. (In the vernacular of TA this is stated as "different strokes for different folks.") But everyone needs them. It may be a simply "Good morning" or a pat on the back every once in a while. If people do not get such positive strokes, they will seek out negative strokes. The latter case may be the outgrowth of childhood experiences. People in this case tend to discount any attempts to give them positive strokes. Obviously, this TA concept of strokes is very closely related to the learning concept of reinforcement. For example, positive strokes could be thought of as social reinforcers.

2. *The games people play.* TA is also concerned with the ways that people structure their time. These games are a set or pattern of transactions that have surface logic but hidden meanings and attempt to draw in an unsuspecting participant. The outcome of games is almost always a win-lose proposition. Straightforward as well as devious people commonly play games. Games that are frequently played in organizations are summarized in Table 14.2. The games summarized in the table are only representative examples of the games people play in organizations. Anyone who has spent some time working can readily identify with many of these and other games that people play in organizational life. Most are dysfunctional for productive interpersonal relations and detract from organizational effectiveness. The goal should be to create an organizational climate that does not need or tolerate game playing. Chapter 20, on organization development, discusses some specific ways in which this may be accomplished.

The Johari Window

Besides transactional analysis, the other popular framework for analyzing the dynamics of interpersonal behavior is the Johari window. Developed by Joseph Luft and Harry Ingham (thus the name *Johari*), this model is particularly useful in analyzing interpersonal conflict. As Figure 14.7 shows, the model helps identify several interpersonal styles, shows the characteristics and results of these styles, and suggests ways of interpreting the conflicts that may develop between the self and others.

In simple terms, the self can be thought of as "me," and others can be thought of as "you" in a two-person interaction. There are certain things that the person knows about himself or herself and certain things that are not known. The same is true of others. There are certain things the person knows about the other and certain things that are not known. The following summarizes the four cells in the Johari window:

1. *Open self.* In this form of interaction the person knows about himself or herself and about the other. There would generally be openness and compatibility

TABLE 14.2 Games People Play in Organizations

Name of Game	Brief Description of Game
1. Now I've Got You, You S.O.B. (N.I.G.Y.Y.S.O.B.)	One employee gets back at another by luring her into what appears to be a natural work relationship. Actually the situation is rigged so that the other will fail. When the inevitable mistake is made, the game player pounces on the associate and publicly embarrasses her.
2. Poor Me	The person depicts himself to the boss as helpless. Criticisms for inadequate performance are avoided because the boss truly feels sorry for the individual, who may actually begin to feel sorry for himself.
3. Blemish	The boss appears to be objectively evaluating an employee's total performance. In reality, the boss is looking for some minor error. When the error is found, the employee is berated for the poor performance, the inference being that the whole project/task/report is inadequate.
4. Hero	The boss consistently sets up situations in which employees fail. At some point, the boss steps in to save the day miraculously.
5. King of the Hill	The boss sets up situations in which employees end up in direct competition with her. At the end, she steps in and demonstrates her competence and superiority while publicly embarrassing her employees.
6. Cops and Robbers	An employee continuously walks a fine line between acceptable and unacceptable behavior. The boss wastes unnecessary time desperately trying to catch the employee, while the employee stays one step ahead and laughs to himself through the day.
7. Prosecutor	The employee carefully carries around a copy of the union contract or organization regulations and investigates management practices. This employee dares the boss to act in an arbitrary manner. Once he does, the employee files a grievance and attempts to embarrass the boss.
8. If It Weren't for You. . . .	The employee discusses her problems openly but carefully works the conversation around so that she can rationalize her failure by blaming the boss for everything that goes wrong.
9. Yes, but. . . .	The boss responds with "Yes, but. . . ." to every good answer or idea that the subordinate may have. By doing this, the boss can maintain a superior position and keep subordinates in their place. It represents a form of pseudoparticipation; that is, the boss asks for participation but answers every suggestion with "Yes, but. . . ."

Source: Adapted from Fred Luthans and Mark J. Martinko, *The Practice of Supervision and Management*, McGraw-Hill, New York, 1979, pp. 386–387, which in turn is adapted from the literature on transactional analysis.

and little reason to be defensive. This type of interpersonal relationship would tend to lead to little, if any, interpersonal conflict.

2. *Hidden self.* In this situation the person understands himself or herself but does not know about the other person. The result is that the person remains hidden from the other because of the fear of how the other might react. The person may keep his or her true feelings or attitudes secret and will not open up to the other. There is potential interpersonal conflict in this situation.

3. *Blind self.* In this situation the person knows about the other but not about himself or herself. The person may be unintentionally irritating to the other.

FIGURE 14.7 The Johari window. (*Source:* Adapted from Joseph Luft, "The Johari Window," *Human Relations Training News,* vol. 5, no. 1, 1961, pp. 6–7.)

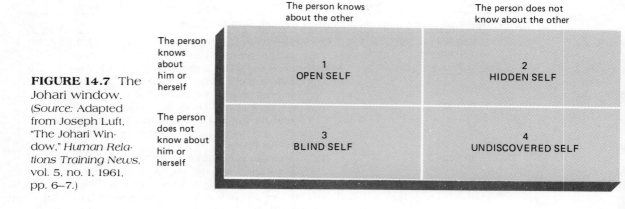

The person knows about the other | The person does not know about the other

The person knows about him or herself

1
OPEN SELF

2
HIDDEN SELF

The person does not know about him or herself

3
BLIND SELF

4
UNDISCOVERED SELF

The other could tell the person but may be fearful of hurting the person's feelings. As in the hidden self, there is potential interpersonal conflict in this situation.

4. *Undiscovered self.* This is potentially the most explosive situation. The person does not know about himself or herself and does not know about the other. In other words, there is much misunderstanding, and interpersonal conflict is almost sure to result.

The Johari window only points out possible interpersonal styles. It does not necessarily describe, but rather helps analyze, possible interpersonal conflict situations.

One way of decreasing the hidden self and increasing the open self is through the processes of self-disclosure. By becoming more trustful of others and disclosing information about themselves, people may reduce the potential for conflict. On the other hand, such self-disclosure is a risk for the individual, and the outcome must be worth the cost. To decrease the blind self and at the same time increase the open self, the other must give feedback, and the person must use it.

Strategies for Interpersonal Conflict Resolution

Besides the conflict resolution strategies inherent in the discussion of transactional analysis (for example, getting on an adult-to-adult level of transaction or quitting game playing), the Johari window (for example, moving to the open self or providing self-disclosure and feedback), and some simple ways of dealing with crises such as found in the accompanying Application Example, there are three other basic strategies that individuals can use in interpersonal conflict situations (for that matter, these could also be used in intergroup and organizational conflict resolution). These are the lose-lose, win-lose, and win-win approaches. The win-win strategy is the most effective, but since the other two types are so commonly used, they should also be understood.

**Application
Example**

> ### Dealing with Crises*
>
> A manager at a small cosmetics company learned that his firm had just been acquired by a large international conglomerate. His staff wanted to know how this would affect the firm's current plans for the new fiscal year. When he asked his boss, he was told, "Don't worry about anything. It's going to be business as usual." The manager had a difficult time accepting this. So did his staff, many of whom were convinced that their jobs were in jeopardy.
>
> This situation is common in industry these days, and the worst part for many managers is that they will not know for several months how everything is going to turn out. In the interim, they need a strategy for dealing with the resulting conflict. What can they do? Psychologists who have studied these situations have concluded that there are two phases to crisis management: (*a*) emotion and (*b*) reason and action. By mentally "walking through" these two phases, psychologists contend, it is possible to get oneself prepared for managing in a crisis. The emotional phase is typically characterized by negative responses. Some managers feel panic brought on by the dismay and confusion caused by the crisis. Most feel some degree of anger, which is then followed by feelings of guilt. However, these feelings are then typically replaced by a take-charge attitude. The manager begins looking for ways of straightening out the situation. This is when the second phase begins. The reason and action phase is characterized by an assessment of the facts, followed by effective decision making. This entails examining the situation and setting goals, assessing ways of straightening things out, rebuilding confidence among the subordinates, and developing effective two-way communication. At this point the situation is usually well under control.
>
> Whenever there is a setback or disaster, managers are likely to go through these two phases. The better that managers understand their emotional reactions to the crisis, the more effectively they tend to respond—and the more likely it is that they will succeed.
>
> *__Source:__ Adapted from Mortimer R. Feinberg and Bruce Serlen, "Crash Course in Crisis Management," *Working Woman,* January 1987, pp. 24, 26, 28.

Lose-Lose. In a lose-lose approach to conflict resolution, both parties lose. It has been pointed out that this approach can take several forms.[4] One of the more common approaches is to compromise or take the middle ground in a dispute. A second approach is to pay off one of the parties in the conflict. These payments often take the form of bribes. A third approach is to use an outside third party or arbitrator. A final type of lose-lose strategy appears when the parties in a conflict resort to bureaucratic rules or existing regulations to resolve the conflict. In all four of these approaches, both parties in the conflict lose. It is sometimes the only way that conflicts can be resolved, but it is generally less desirable than the win-lose or, especially, the win-win strategy.

Win-Lose. A win-lose strategy is a very common way of resolving conflict in American society. In a competitive type of culture, as is generally found in the United States, one party in a conflict situation attempts to marshal its forces to win, and the other party loses. The following list summarizes some of the characteristics of a win-lose situation:

1. There is a clear we-they distinction between the parties.
2. The parties direct their energies toward each other in an atmosphere of victory and defeat.
3. The parties see the issue from their own point of view.
4. The emphasis is on solutions rather than on the attainment of goals, values, or objectives.
5. Conflicts are personalized and judgmental.
6. There is no differentiation of conflict-resolving activities from other group processes, nor is there a planned sequence of those activities.
7. The parties take a short-run view of the issues.[5]

Examples of win-lose strategies can be found in superior-subordinate relationships, line-staff confrontations, union-management relations, and many other conflict situations found in today's organizations. The win-lose strategy can have both functional and dysfunctional consequences for the organization. It is functional in the sense of creating a competitive drive to win, and it can lead to cohesiveness and esprit de corps among the individuals or groups in the conflict situation. On the dysfunctional side, a win-lose strategy ignores other solutions such as a cooperative, mutually agreed-upon outcome; there are pressures to conform, which may stifle a questioning, creative atmosphere for conflict resolution; and highly structured power relationships tend to emerge rapidly. The biggest problem, however, with a win-lose strategy is that someone always loses. Those who suffer the loss may learn something in the process, but losers also tend to be bitter and vindictive. A much healthier strategy is to have both parties in a conflict situation win.

Win-Win.   A win-win strategy of conflict resolution is probably the most desirable from a human and organizational standpoint. Energies and creativity are aimed at solving the problems rather than beating the other party. It takes advantage of the functional aspects of win-lose and eliminates many of the dysfunctional aspects. The needs of both parties in the conflict situation are met, and both parties receive rewarding outcomes. A review of the relevant literature revealed that "win-win decision strategies are associated with better judgments, favorable organization experience, and more favorable bargains."[6] Although it is often difficult to accomplish a win-win outcome of an interpersonal conflict, this should be a major goal of the management of conflict.

Intergroup Behavior and Conflict

Conceptually similar to interpersonal behavior is intergroup behavior. The last chapter concentrated on *intra*group behavior and dynamics. There are also some interesting dynamics and resulting conflict that occur between groups. An understanding of the theoretical framework for intergroup behavior is a prerequisite for examining the conflict that often results.

Intergroup Behavior in Organizations

The chapters in Part 5 of the book deal specifically with organization process and design. One way to look at organizations, however, is in terms of interacting groups. Instead of depicting an organization as being made up of interacting individuals, one could think of it as consisting of interacting and overlapping role sets or groups joined by linking pins.

Interacting and Overlapping Role Sets.

Once again the role concept can be used in the understanding of intergroup behavior. In particular, all organizational participants would have certain expectations of others and of themselves concerning what would be involved in their roles. The organization could be thought of as a set of such roles, and when these roles are in interaction with one another, the organization could more realistically be pictured as a system of overlapping role sets; this often results in conflict.

Robert L. Kahn is most closely associated with the role-set theory of organization. In Kahn's view the organization is made up of overlapping and interlocking role sets. These role sets would normally transcend the boundaries of the classical conception of organizations. Figure 14.8 gives an example of the interacting role-set concept of organization. The figure shows only three possible role sets from a large manufacturing organization. The purchasing agent, executive vice president, and design engineer are called the *focal persons* of the sets shown. The supplier's and consultant's roles are vital in their respective sets but would not be included within traditional organizational boundaries. They are external to the classical organization. The design engineer is a member of the purchasing agent's role set but is also a focal person for another role set. The production manager is shown as a member of two role sets. The overlaps can result in role conflicts and ambiguities. Such dynamics become important in conflict analysis.

Linking Groups in Organizations.

Rensis Likert gave considerable attention to how groups are related in organizations. He felt that instead of the traditional individual-to-individual relationships in organizations, a more accurate depiction is a group-to-group relationship, with each individual serving as a linking pin. Figure 14.9 depicts the model. It is based on the concept that every individual functions as a linking pin for the groups above and below his or her own. Under this arrangement, every individual is a vital member of two groups. Each participant is the leader of the lower group and simply a group member of the upper one.

The linking-pin concept of intergroup relations has an upward orientation. Communication, supervisory influence, and goal attainment are all focused upward. This is in contrast to the classical views, which foster a downward orientation. In later work, Likert added horizontal (lateral) linkages to the model. Figure 14.10 recognizes the need for formalizing lateral linkages for communication, influence, motivation, and coordination purposes.

Likert was very careful to point out the important role that group processes play. All groups must be equally effective because the failure of any one group will have adverse consequences for the entire organization. In other words, the

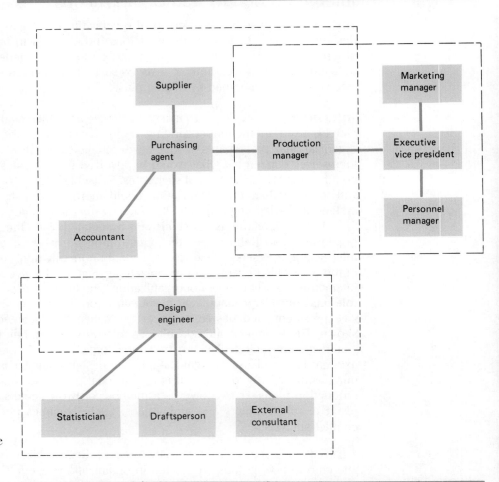

FIGURE 14.8 The organization as overlapping role sets.

linking-pin chain is only as strong as its weakest link. To protect the group chain from breaking, Likert recommended additional staff groups and ad hoc committees. These adjuncts provide multiple overlapping groups through which linking functions are performed and the organization is bound together. By the same token, interacting linking groups may generate dysfunctional conflict for organizational effectiveness.

The Impact of, and Strategies for, Intergroup Conflict

Presenting interacting groups in terms of the overlapping role set and linking-pin models provides a better understanding of the dynamics and resulting conflict that can occur. Groups in conflict have much different behavior from that of

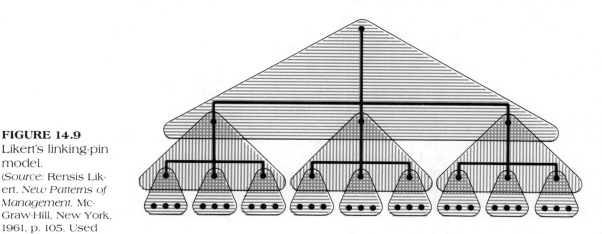

FIGURE 14.9
Likert's linking-pin model.
(*Source:* Rensis Likert, *New Patterns of Management*, McGraw-Hill, New York, 1961, p. 105. Used with permission.)

smoothly cooperating groups. There is evidence that groups in conflict change both internally and in relation to one another. "Unfortunately, these changes generally result in either a continuance or an escalation of the conflict."[7] In particular, after searching the relevant literature, Daft identified the following characteristics of groups in conflict:

1. There is a clear distinction and comparison between "we" (the in-group) and "they" (the out-group).
2. A group that feels it is in conflict with another group becomes more cohesive and pulls together to present a solid front to defeat the other group.

FIGURE 14.10
Vertical and horizontal linking pins.
(*Source:* Adapted from Rensis Likert, *The Human Organization*, McGraw-Hill, New York, 1967, pp. 168–169. Used with permission.)

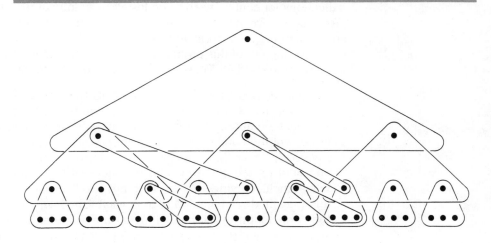

3. The positive feelings and cohesion within the in-group do not transfer to the members of the out-group. The members of the out-group are viewed as the enemy rather than as neutrals.

4. Threatened group members feel superior—they overestimate their strength and underestimate that of members of other groups.

5. The amount of communication between conflicting groups decreases. When there is communication, it is characterized by negative comments and hostility.

6. If a group is losing in a conflict, the members' cohesion decreases and they experience increased tension among themselves. They look for a scapegoat to blame their failure on.

7. The intergroup conflict and resulting hostility are not the result of neurotic tendencies on the part of individual members. These seem to be a product of group interaction, even when individuals in the group are normal and well adjusted.[8]

The above findings from research help describe and provide an understanding of the behavior of conflicting groups in organizations such as unions and management, production and sales, office personnel and operating personnel, nurses and doctors, and faculty and administrators. There is even some evidence that gender may affect intergroup behavior. Research indicates that although men and women are equally adept at helping groups solve conflict, women tend to seek changes in future behavior while men tend to push for more immediate results.[9]

There is also recent theoretical analysis indicating the importance that the origin of the group (for example, mandated versus voluntary) and the degree of externally imposed task structure (for example, high versus low) may have on the outcomes of intergroup interactions.[10] For example, mandated groups with high external task structure are predicted to have low member satisfaction and minimal quality of output while voluntary groups with low external task structure are predicted to have high member satisfaction and high quality of output. These indications, of course, need to be tested by empirical research, but if the model proves predictive, it could greatly help managers make better decisions in forming and structuring interacting groups.

Flowing out of this profile are a number of strategies that can be employed to reduce the conflict. These can be summarized into four major types:

1. *Avoidance.* This type of strategy attempts to keep the conflict from surfacing at all. Examples would be to simply ignore the conflict or impose a solution. This may be appropriate if the conflict is trivial or if quick action is needed to prevent the conflict from occurring.

2. *Defusion.* Under this strategy, an attempt is made to deactivate the conflict and cool off the emotions and hostilities of the groups involved. Examples would include trying to "smooth things over" by playing down the importance and magnitude of the conflict or of established superordinate goals that need the cooperation of the conflicting groups in order to be accomplished. This strategy is appropriate where a stopgap measure is needed or when the groups have a mutually important goal.

3. *Containment.* Under this strategy, some conflict is allowed to surface, but it is carefully contained by spelling out which issues are to be discussed and how they are to be resolved. To carry out this strategy, the problems and procedures may be structured, and representatives from the conflicting parties may be allowed to negotiate and bargain within the structure established. This is appropriate where open discussions have failed and the conflicting groups are of equal power.
4. *Confrontation.* Under this strategy, which is at the other end of the continuum from avoidance, all the issues are brought into the open, and the conflicting groups directly confront the issues and each other in an attempt to reach a mutually satisfactory solution. This may involve mutual problem solving or even formally redesigning jobs or responsibilities in order to resolve the conflict. This is most appropriate when there is a minimum level of trust, when time is not critical, and when the groups need to cooperate to get the job done effectively.[11]

There are many other strategies that could be used besides those described above. For example, the win-win perspective is important, and many of the organization development techniques presented in Chapter 20 are also applicable.

Organizational Conflict

So far, this chapter has focused, in turn, on intraindividual, interpersonal, and intergroup conflict. All these types of conflict take place within the organizational setting. However, now attention is directed at organizational conflict per se, but it must be remembered that intraindividual, interpersonal, and intergroup conflict are all inherent in organizational conflict.

Structural Conflict

Individuals in the organization have many conflicting organizational cross pressures operating on them. For example, in the classical organization there are four predominant types of structural conflict:

1. *Hierarchical conflict.* There may be conflict between the various levels of the organization. The board of directors may be in conflict with top management, middle management may be in conflict with supervisory personnel, or there may be general conflict between management and the workers.
2. *Functional conflict.* There may be conflict between the various functional departments of the organization. Conflict between the production and marketing departments in an industrial organization is a classic example.
3. *Line-staff conflict.* There may be conflict between line and staff. It often results from situations in which staff personnel do not formally possess authority over line personnel.
4. *Formal-informal conflict.* There may be conflict between the formal and informal organizations. For example, the informal organization's norms for

performance may be incompatible with the formal organization's norms for performance.

These forms of organizational conflict have been given attention in other chapters. However, the example of line-staff conflict is representative of organizational conflict. In particular, the classic research of Melville Dalton is a good example of an analysis of line-staff conflict.[12] Also covered in Chapter 13, his case study of Milo (a pseudonym), a factory of 8000 employees, has become a classic analysis of line-staff conflict. Through detailed observations, Dalton was able to record actual conflict that occurred between line and staff personnel at this plant. One of his major conclusions was that line managers often view staff advice as a threat. An example was the case of R. Jefferson, a staff engineer who devised a new plan for toolroom operations. At least two line supervisors admitted privately to Dalton that the plan had merit, but they nevertheless rejected it. One of them, H. Clause, explained why:

> Jefferson's idea was pretty good. But his . . . overbearing manner queered him with me. He came out here and tried to ram the scheme down our throats. He made me so . . . mad I couldn't see. The thing about him and the whole white-collar bunch that burns me up is the way they expect you to jump when they come around. . . . I been in this plant twenty-two years. I've worked in tool rooms, too. I've forgot more than most of these college punks'll ever know. I've worked with all kinds of schemes and all kinds of people. You see what I mean—I've been around, and I don't need a punk like Jefferson telling me where to head in. I wouldn't take that kind of stuff from my own kid—and he's an engineer too. No, his [Jefferson's] scheme may have some good points, but not good enough to have . . . him lording it over you. He acted like we had to use his scheme. . . . that noise! Him and the whole white-collar bunch—I don't mean any offense to you—can go to. . . . We've got too . . . many bosses already.[13]

In support of the classic conflict situation, Dalton documented that at Milo the staff personnel were substantially younger and had more formal education than the line supervisors. Combined with social factors, these personal characteristics were given as the major factors explaining the organizational conflicts which existed at Milo. However, in a later study, Dalton found some indication that the traditional line-staff conflict model may be changing, at least in some industries. His study of Transode Corporation, a fictitious name given to an electronics firm that employed a highly technical engineering staff that had no official hierarchy and a group of line officers who were formed into a strict hierarchy, provided insights into how conflict can be reduced. In this situation, friction was decreased by "assigning each individual a specific authority, by obscuring status symbols and by stressing symbols of science, quality, and service that allowed all officers to share the luster of association with a vital product."[14]

A very simple solution to help alleviate line-staff conflict and improve communications would be for all staff personnel to use the approach of "sell before tell" when dealing with line personnel. Taken philosophically and literally, this approach has great merit for improving line-staff relationships and thus resolving organizational conflict.

Besides the classic structural conflicts such as line-staff conflict, more contemporary organization designs (covered in Chapter 19) also contain potential conflict situations. The project and matrix organizations in particular have structurally created conflict. The project manager with responsibility but no authority and the manager in a matrix structure with a functional boss and a project boss present two prominent conflict situations. However, like other types of intraindividual, interpersonal, and intergroup conflict, conflict in modern organization designs can also be healthy. In some cases the modern designs may actually try to promote conflict to benefit the organization.

The Role of Conflict in Today's Organizations

Traditionally, the approach to organizational conflict was very simple and optimistic. It was based on the following assumptions:

1. Conflict is by definition avoidable.
2. Conflict is caused by troublemakers, boat rockers, and prima donnas.
3. Legalistic forms of authority such as "going through channels" or "sticking to the book" are emphasized.
4. Scapegoats are accepted as inevitable.[15]

Management traditionally relied on formal authority and classical organization restructuring to solve their "conflict problem." Individual managers often became hypocritical in order to avoid conflicts from above or below. They either tried to ignore conflict or rationalize it away with the position that there is nothing that can be done about it.

Starting with the wide acceptance of the Argyris thesis that there is a basic incongruence between the needs and characteristics of adult, mature employees and the requirements of the modern formal organization, the behavioral approach to management began to reexamine its assumptions and concerns about conflict. This development has, at least indirectly, been caused by the overall societal concern with conflict on national, organizational, group, and individual bases. The outcome has been a new set of assumptions about organizational conflict, which are almost the exact opposite of the traditional assumptions. Some of the new assumptions about conflict are the following:

1. Conflict is inevitable.
2. Conflict is determined by structural factors such as the physical shape of a building, the design of a career structure, or the nature of a class system.
3. Conflict is integral to the nature of change.
4. A minimal level of conflict is optimal.[16]

Summary

The dynamics of interactive behavior at individual, interpersonal, group, and organizational levels, and the resulting conflict, play an increasingly important role in the analysis and study of organizational behavior. Although conflict and stress are conceptually and practically similar, especially at the individual level, they are covered separately (Chapter 8 was devoted to stress). Conflict at the intraindividual level involves frustration, goal conflict, and role conflict and ambiguity. Frustration occurs when goal-directed behavior is blocked. Goal conflict can come about from approach-approach, approach-avoidance, or avoidance-avoidance situations. Role conflict and ambiguity result from a clash in the expectations of the various roles possessed by an individual. Interpersonal conflict was examined within the frameworks of transactional analysis and Johari window styles (open self, hidden self, blind self, and undiscovered self) and of the three major strategies of interpersonal conflict resolution (lose-lose, win-lose, and win-win). Next, intergroup conflict was examined from the perspective of overlapping role sets and linking pins and the strategies of avoidance, defusion, containment, and confrontation. The broader organizational perspective of conflict can be found in both the classical (hierarchical, functional, line-staff, and formal-informal) and modern (project and matrix) structures. Traditionally, the management of organizational conflict was based on simplistic assumptions. Formal authority and classical restructuring were used in attempts to eliminate it. The more modern approach is to assume the inevitability of conflict, recognize that it is not always bad for the organization, and try to manage it effectively rather than merely try to eliminate it.

Questions for Discussion and Review

1. What is frustration? What are some of its manifestations? How can the frustration model be used to analyze organizational behavior?
2. Explain approach-avoidance conflict. Give a realistic organizational example of where it may occur.
3. What are the three ego states in TA? Give an example of each of the three major transactions. What are strokes in TA? Give examples of some you have received in the last day or two. Can you describe any TA games you have been involved in lately?
4. Briefly summarize the four "selfs" in the Johari window. What implications does each have for interpersonal conflict?
5. How do groups in conflict behave? What are the four strategies that can be used to manage intergroup conflict effectively?
6. How do the traditional assumptions about organizational conflict differ from the modern assumptions? What implications do these new assumptions have for the management of organizational conflict?

References

1. "Survey: Third of Employees Stealing on Job," *Omaha World Herald*, June 11, 1983, p. 2.
2. "Workers' Drug Use Becomes a Drag on U.S. Productivity," *Lincoln Journal*, Mar. 3, 1986, p. 8.

3. Leon Festinger, *A Theory of Cognitive Dissonance,* Stanford University Press, Stanford, Calif., 1957.
4. Alan C. Filley, Robert J. House, and Steven Kerr, *Managerial Process and Organizational Behavior,* 2d ed., Scott, Foresman, Glenview, Ill., 1976, pp. 166–167.
5. Ibid., p. 167.
6. Ibid., p. 177.
7. James L. Gibson, John M. Ivancevich, and James H. Donnelly, Jr., *Organizations,* 6th ed., Business Publications, Plano, Tex., 1988, p. 314.
8. Richard L. Daft, *Organization Theory and Design,* West, St. Paul, Minn., 1983, pp. 424–425.
9. "Labor Letter," *The Wall Street Journal,* Jan. 10, 1987, p. 1.
10. Janice H. Schopler, "Interorganizational Groups: Origins, Structure, and Outcomes," *Academy of Management Review,* October 1987, pp. 702–713.
11. Daniel C. Feldman and Hugh J. Arnold, *Managing Individual and Group Behavior in Organizations,* McGraw-Hill, New York, 1986, pp. 223–225.
12. Melville Dalton, *Men Who Manage,* Wiley, New York, 1959; Melville Dalton, "Conflicts between Staff and Line Managerial Officers," *American Sociological Review,* June 1950, pp. 342–350; and Melville Dalton, "Changing Staff-Line Relationships," *Personnel Administration,* March–April 1966, pp. 3–5, 40–48.
13. Dalton, *Men Who Manage,* p. 75.
14. Dalton, "Changing Staff-Line Relationships," p. 45.
15. Joe Kelly, *Organizational Behaviour,* rev. ed., Dorsey-Irwin, Homewood, Ill., 1974, p. 555.
16. Ibid.

REAL CASE:
Good Morning,
You're Fired*

One of the major causes of conflict in today's organizations is being brought about by personnel cutbacks. For many years workers, especially in major corporations such as AT&T, IBM, General Electric, and Exxon, had come to expect lifetime employment. Anyone who did his or her job well would get to keep it. There were no firings or cutbacks. If the company had to pare down its work force in one area, it simply would transfer those people to another area. If the firm were moderately overstaffed, it would handle this problem through retirements and voluntary terminations. The personnel system was a type of closed loop that monitored itself. A few years ago, however, many of these firms began to conclude that they were overstaffed and needed to take immediate action to trim their ranks. This has taken a number of different forms. One is to encourage older workers to take early retirement through the use of enticements such as "5-5-4" packages. Under this arrangement, those willing to take early retirement can add five years to their age, five years to their time of service with the firm, and get four weeks of pay for every year that they have been employed. The latter is provided in the form of a lump-sum payment. Those too young to retire are given lump-sum payments and assistance in finding new jobs.

Source: Adapted from Bruce Nussbaum, "The End of Corporate Loyalty?" *Business Week,* Aug. 4, 1986, pp. 42–49.

The decision to trim the work force is having a dramatic effect on those people who are still with the company that is letting people go. Research shows that many of them are now less loyal than they were before and some believe that no matter how well they do their job they are likely to be dropped. A *Business Week*–Harris poll, which examined employee loyalty toward corporations, reported the following responses to select queries.

Do you think that as long as you do a good job, you can stay with your current employer for as long as you like?	Can stay . . . . .44% May not be able to . . . . .44 Not sure 12
In the layoffs . . . that have taken place, which group do you think gets the best treatment?	Top management . . . . 79% Middle management . . . . 5 Junior management . . . . 2 Clerical employees . . . . 3 About the same . . . . 5 Not sure 7
Compared with 10 years ago, do you feel that salaried employees are more loyal, less loyal, or about as loyal as they were back then?	More loyal. . . . . 5% Less loyal . . . . 65 About as loyal . . . . 29 Not sure 2

Discussed in the chapter on attitudes, this downsizing climate and the accompanying layoffs of loyal personnel obviously are having a big impact.

Most firms that have trimmed their ranks have defended their actions on economic grounds. However, it appears that in the process the companies may well have sacrificed the loyalty of the personnel. One of the biggest challenges that these firms must now face is that of dealing with the conflict caused by these staffing decisions. Only the future will tell how well the organizations manage to meet this challenge.

1. Why might employees in their late fifties face approach-avoidance conflict in their decision regarding early retirement?
2. In conveying a termination decision, how can transactional analysis be used to depict the situation?
3. In the conflict that can result from employee terminations, how can the organization promote a win-win situation? Give a specific example.

CASE:
Drinking Up
the
Paycheck

James Emery is the father of four children. He was raised in a hard-working immigrant family. His needs for achievement and power were developed while he was growing up. Now he finds himself in a low-paying, dead-end assembly line job with a large manufacturing firm. It is all he can do to get through the day, so he has started daydreaming on the job. On payday he often goes to the tavern across the street and generally spends a lot of money. The next day he is not only hung over but also very depressed because he knows that his wife cannot make ends meet and his children often go without the basic essentials.

Now he cannot take it any longer. At first he thought of going to his boss for some help and advice, but he really does not understand himself well enough, and he certainly does not know or trust his boss enough to openly discuss his problems with him. Instead he went to his union steward and told him about his financial problems and how much he hated his job. The steward told James exactly what he wanted to hear. "This darn company is the source of all your problems. The working conditions are not suited for a slave, let alone us. The pay also stinks. We are all going to have to stick together when our present contract runs out and get what we deserve—better working conditions and more money."

1. Explain James's behavior in terms of the frustration model.
2. Cite a specific example of role conflict in this case.
3. What type of transaction from TA and what style from the Johari window can explain James's relationship with his boss? With his union steward?
4. What type of conflict resolution strategy is the union steward suggesting? Do you think the real problems facing James are working conditions and pay? Why or why not?
5. What, if anything, can be done to help the James Emerys of the world? Keep your answer in terms of human resources management.

CASE:
Arresting
the
Neighbor's
Kid

Barney Kohl is a police officer assigned to the juvenile department of a large city. Part of the oath that Barney took was to uphold the law consistently for all people. The scope of his job includes investigation of youth drug traffic, alcoholism, and vandalism. Barney is also involved in the community outreach program, which works to build greater understanding and cooperation between the police department and the youth of the community.

Last night, Barney ran into one of the most difficult, if not the most dangerous, problems he has ever faced. While on patrol, he received a radio report to investigate some possible vandalism at a junior high school. Upon reaching the scene he found five youths, aged twelve to fifteen, engaged in malicious acts of vandalism. They were throwing rocks through the windows and had splashed paint against the walls. After calling backup units, he proceeded to run down and arrest the vandals. He was successfully holding the group at bay and was waiting for the backup unit to arrive when he noticed that one of the offenders was his neighbor's son. The city has a parents' responsibility law that makes parents financially liable for the damage caused by their children's actions. The damage looked as if it would be considerable, probably running into the thousands of dollars. Barney knows his neighbor can't afford the costs because he has a physical disability and out of work. He also knows this incident will lead to great problems in their family and, of course, would place a great strain on his own and his family's relationship with the neighbors.

1. What kind of conflict is this police officer experiencing? What should he do?
2. How do you explain the boys' behavior in terms of the frustration model?
3. If you were asked to conduct a training seminar for police officers on the management of conflict, what topics would you cover? What strategies would you suggest?

15 Power and Politics

Takeovers: A Climate Receptive to Power and Politics

Takeovers of one corporation by another have become common-place in American business. These takeovers often result in power plays and political manuvering. A case in point is when RJR took over F. Ross Johnson's Nabisco. In a strange turn of events, John-son seized control of a situation that was in limbo and became chief executive of the acquirer within a year. It was the second time Johnson had made such an almost unbelievable power play. He acquired his position at Nabisco the same way. Nabisco took over his Standard Brands, Inc., and he then took over the CEO position of Nabisco. How does he do it? The answer lies in Johnson's under-standing and use of power and political strategies. For example, when the board of directors became annoyed with the CEO of the acquiring company, Johnson seized the opportunity and informed directors that he did not intend to remain in the No. 2 position forever. He then was appointed by the board to head the acquiring company.

Corporate takeovers provide an excellent climate for power and politics. For example, there is much uncertainty regarding how resources will be allocated. There is also a lack of agreement on long-range strategic plans, and the newly merged organization's goals may be ambiguous. An assertive manager who knows how to use power and politics can use this uncertainty to his or her advantage.

Source: Adapted from Betsy Morris, "RJR Nabisco Is Jolted by a Boss Who Arrived through a Takeover," *The Wall Street Journal,* Jan. 20, 1987, p. 1.

As CEO, Johnson has exercised his power. He made some risky and often unpopular moves. For instance, he ousted RJR management and replaced them with his own team. He also managed to move company headquarters. Some speculate he may even go so far as to sell the tobacco business. However, Johnson is secretive about his plans. When he signed to buy Almaden wine, he turned around one week later and announced his intentions to sell RJR's entire wine, liquor, and beer business. And how does Johnson retain support from directors despite his controversial actions? It seems he has learned to develop his referent power in addition to his legitimate power. Friends describe him as a "charmer, a raconteur, a real knee-slapping kind of guy." Although he socializes with famous sports figures such as Don Meredith, Bobby Orr, and Frank Gifford, he still drives a jeep and eats peanut butter sandwiches. He is personally attractive to those both above and below him in the company.

Learning Objectives

- DEFINE power and its relationship to authority and influence.
- IDENTIFY the French and Raven classifications of reward, coercive, legitimate, referent, and expert power.
- DISCUSS the contingency approach to power.
- EXPLAIN a macro view of power.
- RELATE the political implications of power.
- PRESENT some political strategies for power acquisition in modern organizations.

Over the years, groups, informal organization, interactive behavior, conflict, and leadership have received considerable attention as important dynamics of organizational behavior; power and politics, however, have not. Yet it is becoming clear, and anyone who has spent any time in a formal organization can readily verify, that organizations are highly political and power is the name of the game. Power and politics must be brought "out of the closet" and recognized as an important dynamic in organizational behavior. For example, the dynamics of power—how to use it and how to abuse it—was recently discovered by Joseph O'Donnell, who was abruptly fired from his high-level executive position with JWT Group Inc. when he proposed stripping the CEO and chairman Don Johnston of his day-to-day operating duties. In other cases, however, such a grab for power has worked. The opening vignette is an example, and there are many others. Lewis Glucksman, for instance, pushed Peter Peterson from the head of Lehman Brothers a few years ago.[1]

　　　The first part of the chapter defines what is meant by power and politics and describes how the two concepts are related to each other. The next part concentrates on the various classifications of power. Particular attention is given to the French and Raven classification of the sources of power. After an examination of some of the research results on the French and Raven power types, attention is given to some contingency approaches (for example, the influenceability of the target and overall and managerial contingency models of power). Next, a more macro perspective of power is presented. Structured determinants of power are emphasized. The last part is concerned with organizational politics. Particular attention is given to a political perspective of power in today's organizations and to some specific political strategies for its acquisition.

The Meaning of Power

Although the concepts in the field of organizational behavior seldom have universally agreed upon definitions, *power* may have even more diverse definitions than most. Almost every author who writes about power defines it differently. Going way back, for example, the famous pioneering sociologist Max Weber defined power as "the probability that one actor within a social relationship will be in a position to carry out his own will despite resistance."[2] More recently, White and Bednar define power as "the ability or capacity to influence people or things, usually obtained through the control of important resources,"[3] and Robbins has supplied one of the most detailed, and perhaps most understandable, definitions: "Power refers to a capacity that A has to influence the behavior of B, so that B does something he or she would not otherwise do. This definition implies (1) a *potential* that need not be actualized to be effective, (2) a *dependence* relationship, and (3) that B has some *discretion* over his or her own behavior."[4]

Usually, definitions of power are intertwined with the concepts of authority and influence. For example, both definitions above use the word *influence* in describing power, the pioneering theorist Chester Barnard defined power in terms of "informal authority," and many modern organizational sociologists define authority as "legitimate power."[5] These distinctions between concepts need to be cleared up in order to understand power.

The Distinctions between Power, Authority, and Influence

In Chapter 9 the power motive was defined as the need to manipulate others and have superiority over them. Extrapolating from this definition of the need for power, "power" itself can be defined as *the ability to get an individual or group to do something—to get the person or group to change in some way.* The person who possesses power has the ability to manipulate or change others. Such a definition of power distinguishes it from authority and influence.

Authority legitimatizes and is a source of power. Authority is the right to manipulate or change others. Power need not be legitimate. In addition, the distinction must be made between top-down classical, bureaucratic authority and Barnard's concept of bottom-up authority based upon acceptance. In particular, Barnard defined *authority* as "the character of a communication (order) in a formal organization by virtue of which it is accepted by a contributor to or 'member' of the organization as governing the action he contributes."[6]

Such an acceptance theory of authority is easily differentiated from power. Grimes notes: "What legitimizes authority is the promotion or pursuit of collective goals that are associated with group consensus. The polar opposite, power, is the pursuit of individual or particularistic goals associated with group compliance."[7]

Influence is usually conceived of as being broader in scope than power. It involves the ability to alter other people in general ways, such as by changing their satisfaction and performance. Influence is more closely associated with leadership than power is, but both obviously are involved in the leadership process. Thus, authority is different from power because of its legitimacy and acceptance, and influence is broader than power, but it is so conceptually close that the two terms can be used interchangeably.

The above discussion points out that an operational definition of power is lacking, and this vagueness is a major reason why power has been largely ignored in the study of organizational behavior. Yet, especially when it is linked to the emerging concern for organizational politics, the study of power can greatly enhance the understanding of organizational behavior.

The French and Raven Classifications of Power

Any discussion of power usually begins and sometimes ends with the five categories of the sources of power identified by social psychologists John French and Bertram Raven.[8] Describing and analyzing these five classic types of power (reward, coercive, legitimate, referent, and expert) serves as a necessary foundation and point of departure for the entire chapter. Most of the examples and applications to organizational behavior come from these five types of power.

Reward Power.
This source of power depends on the person's having the ability and resources to reward others. In addition, the target of this power must value these rewards. In an organizational context, managers have many potential rewards such as pay increases, promotions, favorable work assignments, more responsibility, new equipment, praise, feedback, and recognition available to them. In operant terms, this means that the manager has the power to administer positive reinforcers. In expectancy terms, this means that the person has the power to provide positive valences and that the other person perceives this ability. To understand this source of power more completely, it must be remembered that the recipient holds the key. If managers offer subordinates what they think is a reward (for example, a promotion with increased responsibility), but subordinates do not value it (for example, they are insecure or have family obligations that are more important to them than a promotion), then managers do not really have reward power. By the same token, managers may not think they are giving a reward to subordinates (they calmly listen to chronic complainers), but if subordinates perceive this as rewarding (the managers are giving them attention by intently listening to their complaining), the managers never-

theless have reward power. Also, managers may not really have the rewards to dispense (they may say that they have considerable influence with top management to get their people promoted, but actually they don't), but as long as their people think they have it, they do indeed have reward power.

Coercive Power. This source of power depends on fear. The person with coercive power has the ability to inflict punishment or aversive consequences on the other person or, at least, to make threats that the other person believes will result in punishment or undesirable outcomes. This form of power has contributed greatly to the negative connotation that power has for most people. In an organizational context, managers frequently have coercive power in that they can fire or demote subordinates or dock their pay, although unions have certainly stripped some of this power away over the years. Management can also directly or indirectly threaten an employee with these punishing consequences. In operant terms, this means that the person has the power to administer punishers or negatively reinforce (terminate punishing consequences, which is a form of negative control). In expectancy terms, this means that power comes from the expectation on the part of the other persons that they will be punished if they do not conform to the powerful person's desires. For example, there is fear of punishment if they do not follow the rules, directives, or policies of the organization. It is probably this fear that gets most people to come to work on time and look busy when the boss walks through the area. In other words, much of organizational behavior may be explained in terms of coercive power rather than reward power.

Legitimate Power. This power source, identified by French and Raven, stems from the internalized values of the other persons which give the legitimate right to the agent to influence them. The others feel they have the obligation to accept this power. It is almost identical to what is usually called *authority* and is closely aligned with both reward and coercive power because the person with legitimacy is also in a position to reward and punish. However, legitimate power is unlike reward and coercive power in that it does not depend on the relationships with others but rather on the position or role that the person holds. For example, people obtain legitimacy because of their title (captain or doctor) or position (oldest in the family or officer of a corporation) rather than their personalities or how they affect others.

Legitimate power can come from three major sources. First, the prevailing cultural values of a society, organization, or group determine what is legitimate. For example, in some societies, the older people become, the more legitimate power they possess. The same may be true for certain physical attributes, sex, or vocation. In an organizational context, managers generally have legitimate power because employees believe in the value of private property laws and in the hierarchy where higher positions have been designated to have power over lower positions. The same holds true for certain functional positions in an organization. An example of the latter would be engineers who have legitimacy in the operations area of a company, while accountants have legitimacy in financial matters. The prevailing values within a group also determine legitimacy. For example, in a street gang the toughest member may have legitimacy, while in a work group the union steward may have legitimacy.

Second, people can obtain legitimate power from the accepted social structure. In some societies there is an accepted ruling class. But an organization or a family may also have an accepted social structure that gives legitimate power. For example, when blue-collar workers accept employment from a company, they are in effect accepting the hierarchical structure and granting legitimate power to their supervisors.

A third source of legitimate power can come from being designated as the agent or representative of a powerful person or group. Elected officials, a chairperson of a committee, and a member of the board of directors of a corporation or a union or management committee would be examples of this form of legitimate power.

Each of these forms of legitimate power creates an obligation to accept and be influenced. But, in actual practice, there are often problems, confusion, or disagreement about the range or scope of this power. Consider the following:

> An executive can rightfully expect a supervisor to work hard and diligently; may he also influence the supervisor to spy on rivals, spend weekends away from home, join an encounter group? A coach can rightfully expect [her] players to execute specific plays; may [she] also direct their life styles outside the sport? A combat officer can rightfully expect his men to attack on order; may he also direct them to execute civilians whom he claims are spies? A doctor can rightfully order a nurse to attend a patient or observe an autopsy; may [she] order [him or] her to assist in an abortion against [his or] her own will?[9]

These gray areas point to the real concern that many people in contemporary society have regarding the erosion of traditional legitimacy. These uncertainties also point to the complex nature of power.

Referent Power. This type of power comes from the desire on the part of the other persons to identify with the agent wielding power. They want to identify with the powerful person, regardless of the outcomes. The others grant the person power because he or she is attractive and has desirable resources or personal characteristics.

Advertisers take advantage of this type of power when they use celebrities, such as movie stars or sports figures, to do testimonial advertising. The buying public identifies with (finds attractive) certain famous people and grants them power to tell them what product to buy.

Timing is an interesting aspect of the testimonial advertising type of referent power. Only professional athletes who are in season (for example, baseball players in the summer and early fall, football players in the fall and early winter, and basketball players in the winter and early spring) are used in the advertisements, because then they are very visible, they are in the forefront of the public's awareness, and consequently they have referent power. Out of season the athlete is forgotten and has little referent power. Exceptions, of course, are the handful of superstars (for example, George Brett, Sugar Ray Leonard, Larry Bird, and

Magic Johnson) who transcend seasons and have referent power all year long, and even after they have retired.

In an organizational setting, referent power is much different from the other types of power discussed so far. For example, managers with referent power must be attractive to subordinates so that subordinates will want to identify with them, regardless of whether the managers later have the ability to reward or punish or whether they have legitimacy. In other words, the manager who depends on referent power must be personally attractive to subordinates.

Expert Power. The last source of power identified by French and Raven is based on the extent to which others attribute knowledge and expertise to the power seeker. Experts are perceived to have knowledge or understanding only in certain well-defined areas. All the sources of power depend on the target's perceptions, but expert power may be even more dependent on this than the others. In particular, the target must perceive the agent to be credible, trustworthy, and relevant before expert power is granted.

Credibility comes from having the right credentials; that is, the person must really know what he or she is talking about and be able to show tangible evidence of this knowledge. For example, if a highly successful football coach gives an aspiring young player some advice on how to do a new block, he will be closely listened to—he will be granted expert power. The coach has expert power in this case because he is so knowledgeable about football. His evidence for this credibility is the fact that he is a former star player and has coached championship teams. If this coach tried to give advice on how to play basketball or how to manage a corporation, he would have no credibility and thus would have no expert power. For avid football fans or players, however, this coach might have general referent power (that is, he is very attractive to them), and they would be influenced by what he has to say on any subject—basketball or corporate management.

Credibility is also important to expert power in areas such as foreign affairs and the conduct of a business. For example, the major reason Henry Kissinger had so much power in government several years ago and is still called upon in almost every international incident today is because of his expertise in foreign affairs. A former Harvard professor, he "wrote the book," so to speak, on international relations. Therefore, he was perceived by foreign and domestic government officials as being very knowledgeable and thus was granted considerable power by them.

In organizations, staff specialists have expert power in their functional areas, but not outside. For example, engineers are granted expert power in production matters but not in personnel or public relations problems. The same holds true for other staff experts such as computer experts or accountants. For example, the computer person in a small office may be the only one who really understands it and how to use it, and this knowledge gives him or her considerable power.

As already implied, however, expert power is highly selective, and, besides credibility, the agent must also have trustworthiness and relevance. By trustworthiness, it is meant that the person seeking expert power must have a reputation for being honest and straightforward. In the case of political figures, scandals such as the Iran-*contra* affair could undermine their expert power in the eyes of the American public. In addition to credibility and trustworthiness, a person must have relevance and usefulness to have expert power. Going back to the earlier example, if the football coach gave advice on world affairs or if Henry Kissinger gave advice on football, it would be neither relevant nor useful, and therefore neither of them would have expert power in these areas.

It is evident that expertise is the most tenuous type of power, but managers, and especially staff specialists, who seldom have the other sources of power available to them, often have to depend upon their expertise as their only source of power. As organizations become increasingly technologically complex and specialized, the expert power of organization members at all levels may become more and more important. This is formally recognized by some companies who deliberately include lower-level staff with expert power in top-level decision making. For example, the president of a high-tech firm stated: "In general, the faster the change in the know-how on which a business depends, the greater the divergence between knowledge and position power is likely to be. Since our business depends on what it knows to survive, we mix 'knowledge-power people' with 'position-power people' daily, so that together they make the decisions that will affect us for years to come."[10]

It must also be remembered that French and Raven did recognize that there may be other sources of power, but the ones they identified were considered to be the major ones. They also point out that the five sources are interrelated (for example, the use of coercive power by managers may reduce their referent power), and the same person may exercise different types of power under different circumstances and at different times. The latter point has recently led to some contingency models of power in organizations.

Contingency Approaches to the French and Raven Power Sources

As in other areas of organizational behavior and management, contingency approaches to power are beginning to emerge. Some authors have summarized the research literature into contingency statements such as the following:

1. The greater the professional orientation of group members, the greater relative strength referent power has in influencing them.
2. The less effort and interest high-ranking participants are willing to allocate to a task, the more likely lower-ranking participants are to obtain power relevant to this task.[11]

Besides these overall contingency observations, there is increasing recognition of the fact that power is a two-way street. The influence target is an important variable in the power relationship. The characteristics of influence targets (that is, their influenceability) have an important moderating impact on the types of power that can be successfully used. An examination of these characteristics of the target and some overall contingency models are presented next.

Influenceability of the Targets of Power. Most discussions of power imply a unilateral process of influence from the agent to the target. It is becoming increasingly clear, however, that power involves a reciprocal relationship between the agent and the target, which is in accordance with the overall social learning perspective taken in other chapters of the book. The power relationship can be better understood by examining some of the characteristics of the target. The following characteristics have been identified as being especially important to the influenceability of targets.[12]

1. *Dependency.* The greater the targets' dependency on their relationship to agents (for example, when a target cannot escape a relationship, perceives no alternatives, or values the agent's rewards as unique), the more targets are influenced.
2. *Uncertainty.* Experiments have shown that the more uncertain people are about the appropriateness or correctness of a behavior, the more likely they are to be influenced to change that behavior.
3. *Personality.* There have been a number of research studies showing the relationship between personality characteristics and influenceability. Some of these findings are obvious (for example, people who cannot tolerate ambiguity or who are highly anxious are more susceptible to influence, and those with high needs for affiliation are more susceptible to group influence), but some are not (for example, both positive and negative relationships have been found between self-esteem and influenceability).
4. *Intelligence.* There is no simple relationship between intelligence and influenceability. For example, highly intelligent people may be more willing to listen, but, because they also tend to be held in high esteem, they also may be more resistant to influence.
5. *Sex.* Although traditionally it was generally acknowledged that women were more likely to conform to influence attempts than men because of the way they were raised, there is now evidence that this is changing.[13] As women's and society's views of the role of women are changing, there is less of a distinction by sex of influenceability.
6. *Age.* Social psychologists have generally concluded that susceptibility to influence increases in young children up to about age eight or nine and then decreases with age until adolescence, when it levels off.
7. *Culture.* Obviously, the cultural values of a society have a tremendous impact on the influenceability of its people. For example, some cultures, such as Western cultures, emphasize individuality, dissent, and diversity, which would tend to decrease influenceability, while others, such as many Oriental cultures, emphasize cohesiveness, agreement, and uniformity, which would tend to promote influenceability. As the accompanying International Application Example, Taking as Long as It Takes, indicates, agenda and time in foreign cultures may be used to gain power and influenceability. These individual differences in targets greatly complicate the effective use of power and point up the need for contingency models.

An Overall Contingency Model for Power. Many other contingency variables in the power relationship besides the target could be inferred from the

International Application Example

> **Taking as Long as It Takes**
>
> In recent years many American firms doing business internationally have found, to their chagrin, that their overseas hosts have been using the agenda to gain power over visiting dignitaries. Here is a story related by a business lawyer who recently returned from Japan.
>
> "I went to Japan to negotiate a licensing agreement with a large company there. We had been in contact with these people for three months and during that time had hammered out a rough agreement regarding the specific terms of the contract. The president of the firm thought that it would be a good idea if I, the corporate attorney, went to Tokyo and negotiated some of the final points of the agreement before we signed. I arrived in Japan on a Sunday with the intention of leaving late Friday evening. When I got off the plane, my hosts were waiting for me. I was whisked through customs and comfortably ensconced in a plush limousine within 30 minutes.
>
> The next day began with my host asking me for my return air ticket so his secretary could take care of confirming the flight. I was delighted to comply. We then spent the next four days doing all sorts of things—sightseeing, playing golf, fishing, dining at some of the finest restaurants in the city. You name it, we did it. By Thursday I was getting worried. We had not yet gotten around to talking about the licensing agreement. Then on Friday morning we had a big meeting. Most of the time was spent discussing the changes my hosts would like to see made in the agreement. Before I had a chance to talk, it was time for lunch. We finished eating around 4 P.M. This left me only four hours before I had to leave for the airport. During this time I worked to get them to understand the changes we wanted made in the agreement. Before I knew it, it was time to head for the airport. Halfway there my host pulled out a new contract. 'Here are the changes we talked about,' he said. 'I have already signed for my company. All you have to do is sign for yours.' Not wanting to come home empty-handed, I signed. It turned out that the contract was much more favorable to them than to us. In the process, I learned a lesson. Time is an important source of power. When you know the other person's agenda, you have an idea of what the individual's game plan must be and can work it to your advantage. Since this time, I have all my reservations and confirmations handled stateside. When my guest asks me how long I will be staying, I have a stock answer, 'As long as it takes.'"

discussion of the various types of power, for example, credibility and surveillance. All these variables can be tied together and related to one another in an overall contingency model.

The classic work on influence processes, by social psychologist Herbert Kelman, can be used to structure an overall contingency model of power. Figure 15.1 shows such a model. It recognizes that there are several sources of power that input into three major processes of power.

According to the model, the target will *comply* in order to gain a favorable reaction or avoid a punishing one from the agent. This is the process that most supervisors in work organizations must rely upon. But in order for compliance to work, supervisors must be able to reward and punish (that is, have control

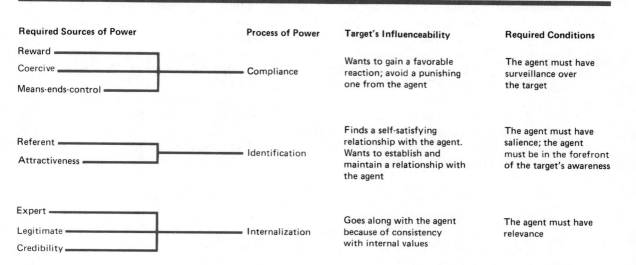

Required Sources of Power

Reward
Coercive ──────── Compliance
Means-ends-control

Referent
Attractiveness ──────── Identification

Expert
Legitimate ──────── Internalization
Credibility

Process of Power

Compliance

Identification

Internalization

Target's Influenceability

Wants to gain a favorable reaction; avoid a punishing one from the agent

Finds a self-satisfying relationship with the agent. Wants to establish and maintain a relationship with the agent

Goes along with the agent because of consistency with internal values

Required Conditions

The agent must have surveillance over the target

The agent must have salience; the agent must be in the forefront of the target's awareness

The agent must have relevance

FIGURE 15.1 An overall contingency model of power.
(*Source:* Adapted from Herbert C. Kelman, "Compliance, Identification, and Internalization: Three Processes of Attitude Change," *Journal of Conflict Resolution,* March 1958, pp. 51–60.)

over the means to their subordinates' ends) and keep an eye on their subordinates (that is, have surveillance over them).

People will *identify,* not in order to obtain a favorable reaction from the agent, as in compliance, but because it is self-satisfying to do so. But in order for the identification process to work, the agent must have referent power—be very attractive to the target—and be salient. For example, a research study by Kelman found that students were initially greatly influenced by a speech given by a very handsome star athlete; that is, they identified with him. However, when the students were checked six months after the speech, they were not influenced. The handsome athlete was no longer salient; that is, he was no longer in the forefront of their awareness, and his words carried no influence. As discussed earlier, except for the handful of superstars, athletes are soon forgotten and have no power over even their most avid fans. Once they have graduated or are out of season, they lose their salience and, thus, their power.

Finally, people will *internalize* because of compatibility with their own value structure. But, as Figure 15.1 shows, in order for people to internalize, the agent must have expert or legitimate power (credibility) and, in addition, be relevant. Obviously, this process of power is most effective. Kelman, for example, found that internalized power had a lasting impact on his subjects.

A Contingency Model of Managerial Power and Organizational Effectiveness. When directly applied in an organization and management context, the important variables for a contingency approach to power would include the manager, the subordinate, and the organization itself. In addition to the dynamics of the power sources of the manager, the influenceability of the subordinate, and the dynamics of the organizational environment, Shetty pinpoints several specific manager, subordinate, and organizational characteristics that he deems to be especially important to a contingency analysis of managerial power. Figure 15.2 summarizes this contingency model.

Shetty is careful to point out that the contingency factors identified in his model are not exhaustive but are intended to be representative of some of the more important research findings on managerial power. To take an example from each contingency factor, he cites relevant research findings and makes statements such as the following:

1. Authoritarian managers tend to emphasize legitimate power to achieve predictable behavior rather than to tolerate the ambiguity they perceive to be inherent in the use of expert and referent power.
2. Employees who are basically concerned with their physiological and security needs tend to be satisfied with legitimate and reward power.
3. In matrix organizations, where project managers lack position power, they must rely on personality, persuasive ability, and negotiation to influence functional team members.[14]

Other contingency statements can also be drawn from the identified characteristics in the model.

Regarding the effective use of power in today's organizations, Shetty draws two overall conclusions: "First, the successful manager is one who is aware of

FIGURE 15.2 A contingency model of the French and Raven power types.
(*Source:* Adapted from Y. K. Shetty, "Managerial Power and Organizational Effectiveness: A Contingency Analysis," *Journal of Management Studies,* May 1978, p. 184.)

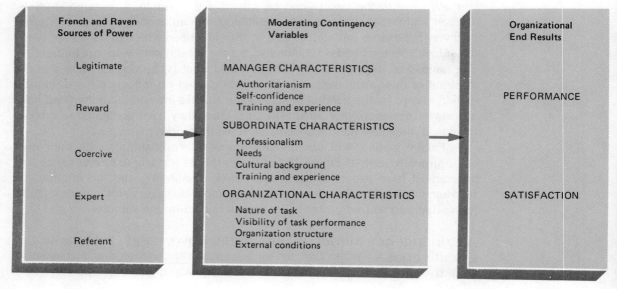

the existence of multiple sources of power in work situations. Second, the effectiveness of power types depends on the nature of managerial, subordinate, and organizational variables."[15]

McClelland's Two Faces of Power.

Whereas French and Raven's work has much relevance for the dynamics of organizational behavior, David McClelland has, as Chapter 9 pointed out, done considerable work on the impact of the motivational need for power (what he calls *n Pow*) on organizational power. He also is convinced that there are two major types of power, one negative and one positive.

Over the years, power has often had a negative connotation. The commonly used term *power-hungry* reflects this negative feeling about power. According to McClelland, power

> . . . is associated with heavy drinking, gambling, having more aggressive impulses, and collecting "prestige supplies" like a convertible or a Playboy Club Key. People with this personalized power concern are more apt to speed, have accidents, and get into physical fights. If . . . possessed by political officeholders, especially in the sphere of international relations, the consequences would be ominous.[16]

McClelland feels that this negative use of power is associated with *personal power*. He feels that it is primitive and does indeed have negative consequences.

The contrasting "other face" of power identified by McClelland is *social power*. It is characterized by a "concern for group goals, for finding those goals that will move people, for helping the group to formulate them, for taking some initiative in providing members of the group with the means of achieving such goals, and for giving group members the feeling of strength and competence they need to work hard for such goals."[17] Under this definition of social power, the manager may often be in a precarious position of walking a fine line between an exhibition of personal dominance and the more socializing use of power.

As the discussion of power and achievement motives in Chapter 9 indicated, McClelland is beginning to accumulate evidence that seems to indicate that managers who use social power may be the most effective. His data show that the successful manager has four discernible power-related characteristics:

> Firstly he believes in an authority system, that the institution is more important than the individuals in it. Secondly, he likes to work and he likes the discipline of work, which leads to orderly management. Thirdly, he is altruistic in that he will sacrifice his own self-interest for the welfare of the company and does this in some obvious way that everybody can see. And fourthly, he believes in justice above everything else, that people must have even-handed treatment.[18]

McClelland's position on the importance of power to successful management is in direct opposition to the more humanistic (McGregor's, Maslow's, or Likert's) positions, which emphasize the importance of democratic values and participative decision making. There is also recent empirical evidence that would counter McClelland's view. One study found that those with a high need for power may suppress the flow of information, especially information that contradicts their preferred course of action, and thus have a negative impact on effective managerial decision making.[19] But regardless of the controversy surrounding the definition and classification of power—be it by French and Raven or McClelland—it is clear that power is inevitable in today's organizations.

How power is used and what type of power is used will vitally affect human performance and organizational goals. In French and Raven's terms, the use of expert and referent power in organizations may be more effective than traditionally used legitimate and coercive power. In McClelland's terms, social power may be of greater value to the organization than traditionally used personal power. Research gives some indication that such conclusions are valid. But once again, the use of the various types of power depends on the situation. Thus, the contingency models of power seem to be a healthy development in the analysis and normative prescriptions of the use of power in today's organizations.

A More Macro View of Power

Although the discussion of power so far at least has organizational implications (especially the contingency models), there is a view from organization theory that structure actually determines power. For example, Pfeffer states:

> The design of an organization, its structure, is first and foremost the system of control and authority by which the organization is governed. . . . Thus, organizational structures create formal power and authority by designating certain persons to do certain tasks and make certain decisions and create informal power through the effect on information and communication structures within the organization.[20]

The position one occupies in the structure also is a determinant of power. For example, those at the top of the hierarchical structure (that is, upper-level management) have power sources such as formal position, resources, and control of decision premises, while lower-level managers may get their power from physical location or information flow.[21]

Besides the power implications of vertical structuring, there are also power differentials on each horizontal level of the structure. For example, even though the heads of the various functions of a business firm are on the same level, they do not possess the same power.

For example, which functional department head—production, marketing, or finance—has the most power will depend on the type of firm. In a manufacturing concern, production and engineering have the most power, but in a big oil company, marketing may have the most power. These horizontal power differentials, of course, will be contingent on a number of environmental factors such as the technology and the economy. In recent years, because of the economic and political climate, the financial and legal departments of many American organizations have become very powerful, but in Japan the operations, quality-control, and personnel functions are more powerful. In other words, like the more micro analysis of power, the macro analysis of power must also recognize the contingency approach. Some recently suggested contingency variables—to summarize what has just been discussed—include areas such as organizational environment, culture, structure, and process.[22]

Political Implications of Power

As the introductory part of the chapter pointed out, power and politics are very closely related concepts. A popular view of organizational politics is how one can pragmatically get ahead in an organization. The accompanying Application Example, It's Who You Know, provides such a view. Another view, however, deals with the acquisition of power. In this latter view, power and politics become especially closely intertwined. A recognition of the political realities of power acquisition in today's organizations and an examination of some specific political strategies for acquiring power are of particular interest for understanding the dynamics of organizational behavior.

**Application
Example**

It's Who You Know*

Harold Friedman is president of a union local of the International Brotherhood of Teamsters in Cleveland. So is C. Sam Theodus. Friedman's local has 6000 members; Theodus's has 5000 members. Friedman makes approximately $250,000 a year for presiding over his own union and two smaller ones that have been assigned to him by the top leaders of the Teamsters union. This salary allows him to keep quarter horses and have his own chauffeur. Theodus makes a little over $50,000 a year for presiding over his union. In recent years his salary has been slashed by 13 percent.

    Why does Friedman make so much more than Theodus? Some observers feel that the major reason may be that Friedman is highly supportive of the Teamster's top leadership. He is a team player. Theodus, on the other hand, has tried to have the president of the international union ousted. Result: Friedman has been given two additional unions to supervise and now carries the title of international vice president. All of this translates into extra money for Friedman. And he is not alone. Many local leaders are very supportive of the central union leadership because they know that if they cooperate with the union president and other top officials, they have a very good chance of being rewarded. If they try to fight them, they will be given nothing. Moreover, the Teamsters are one of the richest unions in the country. The president's annual salary is in excess of $500,000, and this still leaves plenty more to be distributed to team players.

    Doling out rewards on the basis of patronage or favoritism may seem unfair. But it is all legal because the president is empowered by the union's constitution to assign certain jobs and titles to top officials—and with this comes additional income. As one observer put it, "To get ahead in this union, what you know is not as important as who you know."

*__Source:__ Adapted from Jonathan Tasini and Dan Cook, "Union Leaders' Salaries: It's Not What You Know . . . ," *Business Week*, May 5, 1986, p. 82.

A Political Perspective of Power in Organizations

As Chapter 19 will discuss in detail, the classical organization theorists portrayed organizations as highly rational structures in which authority meticulously followed the chain of command and in which managers had legitimatized power. The discussion in Chapter 13 of informal managerial roles and organization portrayed another, more realistic view of organizations. It is in this more realistic view of organizations that the importance of the political aspects of power comes to the forefront.

Walter Nord has tried to dispel some of the dreams of ideal, rationally structured and humanistic organizations by pointing out some of the stark realities of political power. He suggests four postulates of power in organizations that help focus on the political realities:

1. Organizations are composed of coalitions which compete with one another for resources, energy, and influence.
2. Various coalitions will seek to protect their interests and positions of influence by moderating environmental pressures and their effects.
3. The unequal distribution of power itself has dehumanizing effects.
4. The exercise of power within organizations is one very crucial aspect of the exercise of power within the larger social system.[23]

In other words, the political power game is very real in today's organizations.

Some of today's large corporations have even formalized their political nature by creating political action committees (PACs) to support certain government positions. For example, the president of NBC, Robert Wright, recently created a stir when he proposed the network create a PAC and purportedly suggested that employees who don't contribute "should question their own dedication to the company and their expectations."[24] But like other aspects of organizational dynamics, politics is not a simple process; it can vary from organization to organization and even from one subunit of an organization to another. A recent comprehensive definition drawing from the literature is that "organizational politics consists of intentional acts of influence undertaken by individuals or groups to enhance or protect their self-interest when conflicting courses of action are possible."[25]

Research on organizational politics has identified several areas that are particularly relevant to the degree to which organizations are political rather than rational. These areas can be summarized as follows:

1. *Resources.* There is a direct relationship between the amount of politics and how critical and scarce the resources are. Also, politics will be encouraged when there is an infusion of new, "unclaimed" resources.
2. *Decisions.* Ambiguous decisions, decisions on which there is lack of agreement, and uncertain, long-range strategic decisions lead to more politics than routine decisions.
3. *Goals.* The more ambiguous and complex the goals become, the more politics there will be.
4. *Technology and external environment.* In general, the more complex the internal technology of the organization, the more politics there will be. The same is true of organizations operating in turbulent external environments.
5. *Change.* A reorganization or a planned organization development (OD) effort (see Chapter 20, on various OD techniques) or even an unplanned change brought about by external forces will encourage political maneuvering.[26]

The above implies that some organizations and subunits within the organization will be more political than others. By the same token, however, it is clear that most of today's organizations meet the above requirements for being highly political. That is, they have very limited resources; make ambiguous, uncertain decisions; have very unclear yet complex goals; have increasingly complex technology; and are undergoing drastic change. This existing situation facing organizations makes them more political, and the power game becomes increasingly important. Miles states: "In short, conditions that *threaten* the status of the powerful or *encourage* the efforts of those wishing to increase their power base will stimulate the intensity of organizational politics and increase the proportion of decision-making behaviors that can be classified as political as opposed to rational."[27] The next section presents some of these political strategies for power acquisition.

Specific Political Strategies for Power Acquisition

Once it is understood and accepted that contemporary organizations are in reality largely political systems, some very specific strategies can be identified to help organization members more effectively acquire power.

For over twenty years, various political strategies for gaining power in organizations have been suggested. Table 15.1 gives a representative summary of these strategies. Some modern organization theorists take more analytical approaches than most of the strategies suggested in Table 15.1, and they depend more on concepts such as uncertainty in their political strategies for power. For example, Pfeffer's strategies include managing uncertainty, controlling resources, and building alliances.[28] Others take a more pragmatic approach such as the

TABLE 15.1 Political Strategies for Attaining Power in Organizations

Taking counsel
Maintaining maneuverability
Promoting limited communication
Exhibiting confidence
Controlling access to information and persons
Making activities central and nonsubstitutable
Creating a sponsor-protegé relationship
Simulating competition among ambitious subordinates
Neutralizing potential opposition
Making strategic replacements
Committing the uncommitted
Forming a winning coalition
Developing expertise
Building personal stature
Employing trade-offs
Using research data to support one's own point of view
Restricting communication about real intentions
Withdrawing from petty disputes

Source: Adapted from Robert H. Miles, *Macro Organizational Behavior,* Goodyear, Santa Monica, Calif., 1980, pp. 174–175.

recent analysis that suggests that successful political behavior involves keeping people happy, cultivating contacts, and wheeling and dealing.[29]

One of the more comprehensive and relevant lists of strategies for modern managers comes from DuBrin.[30] A closer look at his suggested strategies provides important insights into power and politics in modern organizations.

Maintain Alliances with Powerful People. As has already been pointed out, the formation of coalitions (alliances) is critical to the acquisition of power in an organization. An obvious coalition would be with members of other important departments or with members of upper-level management. Not so obvious but equally important would be the formation of an alliance with the boss's secretary or staff assistant, that is, someone who is close to the powerful person.

Embrace or Demolish. Machiavellian principles can be applied as strategies in the power game in modern organizations. One management writer has applied these principles to modern corporate life. For example, for corporate takeovers, he draws on Machiavelli to give the following advice:

> The guiding principle is that senior men in taken-over firms should either be warmly welcomed and encouraged or sacked; because if they are sacked they are powerless, whereas if they are simply downgraded they will remain united and resentful and determined to get their own back.[31]

Divide and Rule. This widely known political and military strategy can also apply to the acquisition of power in a modern organization. The assumption, sometimes unwarranted, is that those who are divided will not form coalitions themselves. For example, in a business firm the head of finance may generate conflict between marketing and production in hopes of getting a bigger share of the limited budget from the president of the company.

Manipulate Classified Information. The observational studies of managerial work have clearly demonstrated the importance of obtaining and disseminating information.[32] The politically astute organization member carefully controls this information in order to gain power. For example, the purchasing agent may reveal some new pricing information to the design engineer before an important meeting. Now the purchasing agent has gained some power because the engineer owes the purchasing agent a favor.

Make a Quick Showing. This strategy involves looking good on some project or task right away in order to get the right people's attention. Once this positive attention is gained, power is acquired to do other, usually more difficult and long-range projects.

Collect and Use IOUs. This strategy says that the power seeker should do other people favors but should make it clear that they owe something in return and will be expected to pay up when asked. The "Godfather" in the famous book and movie of that name very effectively used this strategy to gain power.

Avoid Decisive Engagement (Fabianism).

This is a strategy of going slow and easy—an evolutionary rather than a revolutionary approach to change. By not "ruffling feathers" the power seeker can slowly but surely become entrenched and gain the cooperation and trust of others.

Progress One Step at a Time (Camel's Head in the Tent).

This strategy involves taking one step at a time instead of trying to push a whole major project or reorganization attempt. One small change can be a foothold that the power seeker can use as a basis to get other, more major things accomplished.

Wait for a Crisis (Things Must Get Worse before They Get Better).

This strategy uses the reverse of "no news is good news"; that is, bad news gets attention. For example, many deans in large universities can get the attention of central administration and the board of regents/trustees only when their college is in trouble, for instance, if their accreditation is threatened. Only under these crisis conditions can they get the necessary funding to move their college ahead.

Take Counsel with Caution.

Finally, this suggested political strategy is concerned more with how to keep power than with how to acquire it. Contrary to the traditional prescriptions concerning participative management, this suggests that at least some managers should avoid "opening up the gates" to their subordinates in terms of shared decision making. The idea here is that allowing subordinates to participate and to have this expectation may erode the power of the manager.

A Final Word on Power and Politics

Obviously, the strategies discussed above are only representative, not exhaustive, of the possible politically based strategies for acquiring power in organizations. Perhaps even more than in the case of many of the other topics covered in the book, there is little research backup for these ideas on power and, especially, politics. There is also a call for a framework and guidelines to evaluate the ethics of power and politics in today's organizations. This ethical concern goes beyond the notions of success or effectiveness. As one analysis pointed out, "when it comes to the ethics of organizational politics, respect for justice and human rights should prevail for its own sake."[33] Besides the possible ethical implications of power and politics carried to the extreme, there may be dysfunctional effects such as morale being weakened, victors and victims being created, and energy and time being spent on planning attacks and counterattacks instead of concentrating on getting the job done.[34] There is some empirical evidence that those managers who are observed to engage in more political activity are relatively more successful in terms of promotions, but are relatively less effective in terms of subordinate satisfaction and commitment and the performance of their unit.[35]

One thing about power and politics, however, is certain: Modern, complex organizations tend to create a climate that promotes power seeking and political maneuvering. It is a fact of modern organizational life, and it is hoped that future research will be forthcoming that will help managers better understand the dynamics, meaning, and successful application of power and politics.

Summary

This chapter has examined one of the most important and realistic dynamics of organizational behavior—power and politics. *Power* and *politics* have a number of different meanings. Power can be distinguished from authority and influence, but most definitions subsume all three concepts. Most of the attention given to power over the years has centered on the French and Raven classification of power types: reward, coercive, legitimate, referent, and expert. More recently, some contingency models for power have been developed which take into consideration the influenceability of the targets of power (that is, their dependency, uncertainty, personality, intelligence, age, and culture). Overall contingency models are also beginning to emerge. Closely related to the contingency models of the French and Raven power types is the view of power by McClelland. McClelland suggests that there are two faces of power: negative personal power and positive social power. Finally, a more macro view of power in organizations is needed for comprehensive understanding. Both vertical and horizontal structural arrangements have implications for power in organizations.

Politics is very closely related to power. This chapter gave particular attention to a political perspective of power in modern organizations, in terms of resources, decisions, goals, technology, external environment, and change, and to strategies for the acquisition of power. Some specific political strategies are to maintain alliances with powerful people, embrace or demolish, divide and rule, manipulate classified information, make a quick showing, collect and use IOUs, avoid decisive engagement, progress one step at a time, wait for a crisis, and take counsel with caution. Above all, it should be remembered that both power and politics represent the realities of modern organizational life. The study of these important dynamics can significantly improve the understanding of organizational behavior.

Questions for Discussion and Review

1. How would you define "power" in your own words? How does power differ from authority? From influence?
2. Identify, briefly summarize, and give some realistic examples of each of the French and Raven power types.
3. Using the contingency model of power, who would you use to advertise products in the fall, winter, spring and summer? Explain your choices.
4. In the chapter it is stated: "The political power game is very real in today's organizations." Explain this statement in terms of the discussion in the chapter and any firsthand experience you have had to verify it.

5. Identify three or four of the political strategies that are discussed in the chapter. Explain how these might actually help someone acquire power in a modern organization.

References

1. "Trying a Palace Coup Can Be Hazardous to an Executive's Career," *The Wall Street Journal,* Feb. 17, 1987, p. 1.
2. A. M. Henderson and Talcott Parsons (trans. and ed.), *Max Weber: The Theory of Social and Economic Organization,* Free Press, New York, 1947, p. 152.
3. Donald D. White and David A. Bednar, *Organizational Behavior,* Allyn and Bacon, Boston, 1986, p. 445.
4. Stephen P. Robbins, *Organizational Behavior,* 3d ed., Prentice-Hall, Englewood Cliffs, N.J., 1986, p. 269.
5. A. J. Grimes, "Authority, Power, Influence and Social Control: A Theoretical Synthesis," *Academy of Management Review,* October 1978, p. 725.
6. Chester I. Barnard, *The Functions of the Executive,* Harvard University Press, Cambridge, Mass., 1938, p. 163.
7. Grimes, op. cit., p. 726.
8. John R. P. French, Jr., and Bertram Raven, "The Bases of Social Power," in D. Cartwright (ed.), *Studies in Social Power,* University of Michigan, Institute for Social Research, Ann Arbor, 1959.
9. H. Joseph Reitz, *Behavior in Organizations,* 3d ed., Irwin, Homewood, Ill., 1987, p. 435.
10. Andrew S. Grove, "Breaking the Chains of Command," *Newsweek,* Oct. 3, 1983, p. 23.
11. Robbins, op. cit. (1st ed., 1979), p. 276.
12. Adapted from Reitz, op. cit., pp. 441–443.
13. Ibid., pp. 442–443.
14. Y. K. Shetty, "Managerial Power and Organizational Effectiveness: A Contingency Analysis," *Journal of Management Studies,* May 1978, pp. 181–184.
15. Ibid., p. 186.
16. David C. McClelland, "The Two Faces of Power," *Journal of International Affairs,* vol. 24, no. 1, 1970, p. 36.
17. Ibid., p. 41.
18. "McClelland: An Advocate of Power," *International Management,* July 1975, pp. 27–28.
19. Eugene M. Fodor and Terry Smith, "The Power Motive as an Influence on Group Decision Making," *Journal of Personality and Social Psychology,* January 1982, pp. 178–185.
20. Jeffrey Pfeffer, "The Micropolitics of Organizations," in Marshall W. Meyer et al. (eds.), *Environments and Organizations,* Jossey-Bass, San Francisco, 1978, pp. 29–50. Also see Jeffrey Pfeffer, *Power in Organizations,* Pitman, Marshfield, Mass., 1981.
21. Richard L. Daft, *Organization Theory and Design,* West, St. Paul, Minn., 1983, pp. 384–385, 389.
22. Anthony T. Cobb, "Political Diagnosis: Applications in Organizational Development," *Academy of Management Review,* July 1986, p. 490.
23. Walter Nord, "Dreams of Humanization and the Realities of Power," *Academy of Management Review,* July 1978, pp. 675–677.

24. "Labor Letter," *The Wall Street Journal,* Dec. 23, 1986, p. 1.
25. Barbara Gray and Sonny S. Ariss, "Politics and Strategic Change across Organizational Life Cycles," *Academy of Management Review,* October 1985, p. 707.
26. Robert H. Miles, *Macro Organizational Behavior,* Goodyear, Santa Monica, Calif., 1980, pp. 182–184.
27. Ibid., p. 182.
28. Jeffrey Pfeffer, "Power and Resource Allocation in Organizations," in Barry M. Staw and Gerald R. Salancik (eds.), *New Directions in Organizational Behavior,* St. Clair, Chicago, 1977, pp. 255–260.
29. Andrew Kakabadse, "Organizational Politics," *Management Decision,* vol. 25, no. 1, 1987, pp. 35–36.
30. These strategies are discussed fully in Andrew J. DuBrin, *Human Relations,* Reston, Reston, Va., 1978, pp. 113–122; DuBrin, in turn, abstracted them from the existing literature on power and politics.
31. Anthony Jay, *Management and Machiavelli,* Holt, New York, 1967, p. 6.
32. Fred Luthans, Richard M. Hodgetts, and Stuart A. Rosenkrantz, *Real Managers,* Ballinger, Cambridge, Mass., 1988.
33. Gerald F. Cavanagh, Dennis J. Moberg, and Manuel Velasquez, "The Ethics of Organizational Politics," *Academy of Management Review,* July 1981, p. 372.
34. Robert P. Vecchio, *Organizational Behavior,* Dryden, Chicago, 1988, p. 270.
35. Luthans, Hodgetts, and Rosenkrantz, op. cit.

**REAL CASE:
A Hollywood
Powerhouse***

Years ago the major movie studios used to be the most powerful group in Hollywood. Famous actors such as Clark Gable, Spencer Tracy, and Humphrey Bogart would have long-term contracts that bound them to a particular studio. When the studio sent over a script, these actors under contract would read it and then appear in the film. If they chose not to appear in the film or, worse yet, tried to hold out for more money, they might well find themselves fired and unable to ever work for anyone else in Hollywood. However, during the 1950s this stranglehold that the movie moguls had over the actors was broken. Today, the all-powerful studios have been replaced by another powerful group. Those following the Hollywood scene say that agents now have just as much power as the old studio bosses.

By some accounts, the most powerful agent in Hollywood these days is Michael Ovitz. President and cofounder of the Creative Artists Agency (CAA), Ovitz has a grip on a very large share of talent. For example, his CAA group represents, among others, Sylvester Stallone, Robert Redford, Jane Fonda, Sally Field, and Dustin Hoffman. With these celebrities in his corner, Ovitz has managed to put together some very lucrative film and TV deals. The strategy is fairly simple. CAA argues that such famous actors and actresses have a large following and, regardless of what role they play,

***Source:** Adapted from Michael Cieply, "An Agent Dominates Film and TV Studios with Package Deals," *The Wall Street Journal,* December 19, 1986, pp. 1; 19.

the public will flock to see them. This is true even if they appear in something that is less than first-rate. For example, when Robert Redford starred in *The Natural,* many reviewers said that the film would have lost money had anyone else been in the title role. Another Redford offering, *Legal Eagles,* received at best mixed reviews and did not break even at the box office. However, because of the actor's appeal, the film finally became profitable after being released on videocassette and cable. Despite such setbacks, Redford continues to remain a strong box office draw and is reported to make approximately $6 million per film. A large portion of this success is a result of Ovitz's clever packaging of film deals for his client. Another example of an actor who has profited from Ovitz's efforts is Sylvester Stallone. When he signed with Ovitz's agency, Stallone was coming off two box office losers. His first film under Ovitz's tutelage, *Rhinestone* with Dolly Parton, was another flop. However, he bounced back with his Rocky and Rambo films. As a result, today Stallone gets $15 million per picture and has five pictures under contract.

What does Ovitz bring to these movie deals besides the services of the actor? He also assembles the script. Working closely with the agents of popular writers such as Jackie Collins, Sidney Sheldon, Judith Krantz, and Danielle Steele, Ovitz is able to package the script and the actors before approaching movie or TV executives. The result is that success breeds success. Actors want him to represent them; literary agents are interested in his reviewing manuscripts of their authors. Ovitz is in an enviable position. People come to him to put together deals because they know he has the power to make things happen. In fact, his power is such that some people in the industry have questioned whether this development is good for the entertainment industry or whether it is simply good for Michael Ovitz.

1. Drawing upon French and Raven's classifications, what kind of power does Michael Ovitz have in the entertainment industry?
2. In terms of David McClelland's approach, what type(s) of power does Ovitz wield? Explain your answer.
3. What would have to happen in order for Ovitz to lose his present powerful position in the film industry?

CASE: Throwing Away a Golden Opportunity

Roger Allen was a man on the move. Everyone in the firm felt that someday he would be company president. To listen to his boss, Harry Walden, it was only a matter of time before Roger would be at the helm.

The current president of the firm was a marketing person. She had worked her way up from field salesperson to president by selling both the product and herself to customers and the company alike. In a manner of speaking, the marketing department was the "well-oiled" road to the top. Roger was the number 1 salesperson and, according to the grapevine, was due to get Harry Walden's job when the latter retired in two years. However, Roger was not sure that he wanted to be vice president of marketing. Another slot was opening up in foreign sales. Roger knew nothing about selling to Europe, but this was the firm's first venture outside the United States, and he thought he might like to give it a try. He talked to Harry about it, but the vice president tried to discourage him. In fact, Harry seemed to think that Roger was crazy to consider the job at all. "Kid," he said, "that's no place for you. Things are soft and cozy back here. You don't have to prove yourself to anyone. You're the number 1 boy around here. Just sit tight and you'll be president. Don't go out and make some end runs. Just keep barreling up the middle for 4 yards on each carry, and you'll score the big touchdown." Roger was not convinced. He thought perhaps it would be wise to discuss the matter with the president herself. This he did. The president was very interested in Roger's ideas about international marketing. "If you really think you'd like to head up this office for us, I'll recommend you for the job."

After thinking the matter over carefully, Roger decided that he would much rather go to Europe and try to help establish a foothold over there than sit back and wait for the stateside opening. He told his decision to Harry. "Harry, I've talked to the president, and she tells me that this new opening in foreign sales is really going to get a big push from the company. It's where the action is. I realize that I could sit back and take it easy for the next couple of years, but I think I'd rather have the international job." Harry again told Roger that he was making a mistake. "You're throwing away a golden opportunity. However, if you want it, I'll support you."

A week later, when the company selected someone else from sales to head the international division, Roger was crushed. The president explained the situation to him in this way: "I thought you wanted the job and I pushed for you. However, the other members of the selection committee voted against me. I can tell you that you certainly didn't sell Harry very strongly on your idea. He led the committee to believe that you were really undecided about the entire matter. In fact, I felt rather foolish telling them how excited you were about the whole thing, only to have Harry say he'd talked to you since that time and you weren't that sure at all. When Harry got done, the committee figured you had changed your mind after talking to me, and they went on to discuss other likely candidates."

1. Who had power in this organization? What type of power did Harry Walden have?
2. Do you think Roger played company politics well? If so, why didn't he get the international sales job?
3. At this point, what would you do if you were Roger? What political strategies could he use?

16 Leadership Processes and Styles

What is the profile of a successful leader? In the case of Ted Turner, most people agree that he is intelligent and possesses a high need for achievement. However, whether he has maturity or social skills is a matter of debate. When Turner first started out, most people regarded him as more of a brash loudmouth than a leader. Taking over a billboard business left to him in his father's will, Turner discovered that a deal to sell the small company had already been completed. Turner talked the buyers into abandoning the deal and letting him continue to run his father's business. Within a short period of time, he began expanding. He bought other billboard companies and then radio stations and, to the amazement of just about everyone, managed to avoid going broke while still carrying a large amount of debt.

Next in line was a rundown TV station, which he turned into a network by beaming its signal to cable systems nationwide via satellite. Today that station, WTBS, reaches over 36 million homes and is the most profitable advertiser-supported network in the country. In 1980 Turner took the cash flow from WTBS to create the Cable News Network (CNN), a 24-hour news network. Many people scoffed at this decision, but once again Turner proved to be right. He then spun off another news channel, called Headline News, which edits CNN's news footage into compact 30-minute segments.

Source: Adapted from Stratford P. Sherman, "Ted Turner: Back from the Brink." *Fortune,* July 7, 1986, pp. 25–31.

Today these two networks have an annual operating cash flow of $30 million.

In more recent years Turner paid $1.6 billion for Metro-Goldwyn-Mayer (MGM), which buried him under a mountain of debt. As always, his high-risk style got him through. Within ninety days of the purchase, Turner disposed of new MGM movies, video distribution, studio real estate, and the MGM film lab for $490 million to apply against the MGM purchase price. Does the large debt worry him? Not really, since Turner has often financially extended his operations to the point where he appeared about to go under and then somehow in the eleventh hour was able to get everything under control. Some industry analysts believe that the reason he has done so well is that he knows just how far to go—and then he ventures no further. "He knows just where the edge is, so he does not go over" is the way one close observer put it.

What does the future hold for "Terrible Ted"? In addition to managing his communications empire and paying off the large amount of debt he has accumulated, he is likely to launch yet another major acquisition. Is he really an effective leader with vision, or is he just lucky? There seems to be a diversity of answers to this question. One potential investor may have said it best when he explained, "(Turner's) not predictable. He's a fruitcake who's also brilliant." Simply put, Ted Turner is certainly a different type of leader.

Learning Objectives

- PRESENT the classic studies of leadership.
- DISCUSS the major theories of leadership including the trait, group and exchange, contingency, and path-goal approaches.
- IDENTIFY some other emerging theoretical frameworks for leadership such as social learning and substitutes for leadership.
- PRESENT the major styles of leadership, including Blake and Mouton's grid, Hersey and Blanchard's life cycle, Likert's four systems, and the Vroom and Yetton model.

This chapter is an appropriate conclusion to the interpersonal and organizational behavior dynamics part of the book. There is a close relationship—a dynamic relationship—between groups, interactive behavior and conflict, power and politics, and leadership. The first half of the chapter deals with the classical background and major theoretical perspectives of leadership. Particular attention is devoted to the contingency, path-goal, substitutes, and social learning theories of leadership. The second half of the chapter presents and analyzes various styles of leadership. Particular attention is given to the work of Blake and Mouton, Hersey and Blanchard, Likert, and Vroom and Yetton.

The Background of, and
Classic Studies on, Leadership

Leadership has probably been written about, formally researched, and informally discussed more than any other single topic. For example, it has recently been humorously proposed that leadership succession depends on birthdays. The discovery was made while developing a list of birth dates of famous people that the chairmen of large corporations often shared the same birthday as their successor. For instance, Edward G. Jefferson and his predecessor at Du Pont Corporation, Irving S. Shapiro, share a July 15 birthday. Although astrologers would suggest that companies need leaders with the same "sun signs" that influence their styles, the companies vigorously deny considering the calendar in making leadership appointments.[1]

Throughout history, it has been recognized that the difference between success and failure, whether in a war, a business, a protest movement, or a basketball game, can be attributed largely to leadership. The intensity of today's concern about leadership is pointed out by a *Fortune* magazine article:

> The exigencies of global competition, deregulation, and accelerating technological change have whipped that interest into an anxious search for new answers to old questions: Can leadership be taught? How do you spot potential leaders? And what, precisely, sets leaders apart from everyday managers?[2]

Yet, despite all the attention given to it and its recognized importance, leadership still remains pretty much of a "black box," or unexplainable concept. It is known to exist and to have a tremendous influence on human performance, but its inner workings and specific dimensions cannot be precisely spelled out. Despite these inherent difficulties, a review of some of the widely known classic studies on leadership can help set the stage for the analysis of modern theories and styles of leadership.[3]

The Iowa Leadership Studies

A series of pioneering leadership studies conducted in the late 1930s by Ronald Lippitt and Ralph K. White under the general direction of Kurt Lewin at the University of Iowa have had a lasting impact. Lewin is recognized as the father of group dynamics and as an important cognitive theorist. In the initial studies, hobby clubs for ten-year-old boys were formed. Each club was submitted to three different styles of leadership—authoritarian, democratic, and laissez faire. The authoritarian leader was very directive and allowed no participation. This leader tended to give individual attention when praising and criticizing but tried to be friendly or impersonal rather than openly hostile. The democratic leader encouraged group discussion and decision making. He tried to be "objective" in his praise or criticism and to be one of the group in spirit. The laissez faire leader gave complete freedom to the group; he essentially provided no leadership.

Under experimental conditions, the three leadership styles were manipulated to show their effects on variables such as satisfaction and frustration/aggression.

Some of the results were clear-cut and others were not. One definite finding was the boys' overwhelming preference for the democratic leader. In individual interviews, nineteen of the twenty boys stated they liked the democratic leader better than the authoritarian leader. The boys also chose the laissez faire leader over the autocratic one in seven out of ten cases. For most of the boys, even confusion and disorder were preferable to strictness and rigidity.

Unfortunately, the effects that styles of leadership had on productivity were not directly examined. The experiments were designed primarily to examine patterns of aggressive behavior. However, an important by-product was the insight that was gained into the productive behavior of a group. For example, the researchers found that the boys subjected to the autocratic leader reacted in one of two ways: either aggressively or apathetically. Both the aggressive and apathetic behaviors were deemed to be reactions to the frustration caused by the autocratic leader. The researchers also pointed out that the apathetic groups exhibited outbursts of aggression when the autocratic leader left the room or when a transition was made to a freer leadership atmosphere. The laissez faire leadership climate actually produced the greatest number of aggressive acts from the group. The democratically led group fell between the one extremely aggressive group and the four apathetic groups under the autocratic leaders.

Sweeping generalizations on the basis of the Lippitt and White studies are dangerous. Preadolescent boys making masks and carving soap are a long way from adults working in a complex, formal organization. Furthermore, from the viewpoint of modern behavioral science research methodology, many of the variables were not controlled. Nevertheless, these leadership studies have extremely important historical significance. They were the pioneering attempts to determine, experimentally, what effects styles of leadership have on a group. Like the Hawthorne studies, the Iowa studies are too often automatically discounted or at least deemphasized because they were experimentally crude. The values of the studies were that they were the first to analyze leadership from the standpoint of scientific methodology, and, more important, they showed that different styles of leadership can produce different, complex reactions from the same or similar groups.

The Ohio State Leadership Studies

In 1945, the Bureau of Business Research at Ohio State University initiated a series of studies on leadership. An interdisciplinary team of researchers from psychology, sociology, and economics developed and used the Leader Behavior Description Questionnaire (LBDQ) to analyze leadership in numerous types of groups and situations. Studies were made of Air Force commanders and members of bomber crews; officers, noncommissioned personnel, and civilian administrators in the Navy Department; manufacturing supervisors; executives of regional cooperatives; college administrators; teachers, principals, and school superintendents; and leaders of various student and civilian groups.

The Ohio State studies started with the premise that no satisfactory definition of leadership existed. They also recognized that previous work had too often assumed that *leadership* was synonymous with *good leadership*. The Ohio State group was determined to study leadership, regardless of definition or of whether it was effective or ineffective.

In the first step, the LBDQ was administered in a wide variety of situations. In order to examine how the leader was described, the answers to the questionnaire were then subjected to factor analysis. The outcome was amazingly consistent. The same two dimensions of leadership continually emerged from the questionnaire data. They were *consideration* and *initiating structure.* These two factors were found in a wide variety of studies encompassing many kinds of leadership positions and contexts. The researchers carefully emphasize that the studies show only *how* leaders carry out their leadership position. Initiating structure and consideration are very similar to the time-honored military commander's functions of mission and concern with the welfare of the troops. In simple terms, the Ohio State factors are task or goal orientation (initiating structure) and recognition of individual needs and relationships (consideration). The two dimensions are separate and distinct from each other.

The Ohio State studies certainly have value for the study of leadership. They were the first to point out and emphasize the importance of *both* task and human dimensions in assessing leadership. This two-dimensional approach lessened the gap between the strict task orientation of the scientific management movement and the human relations emphasis, which had been popular up to that time. However, on the other side of the coin, the rush for empirical data on leadership led to a great dependence on questionnaires in the Ohio State studies to generate data about leadership behaviors, and this may not have been justified. For example, Schriesheim and Kerr concluded after a review of the existing literature that "the Ohio State scales cannot be considered sufficiently valid to warrant their continued uncritical usage in leadership research."[4] In addition to the validity question is the almost unchallenged belief that these indirect questionnaire methods are in fact measuring leadership *behaviors* instead of simply measuring the questionnaire respondent's behavior and/or perceptions of, and attitudes toward, leadership. A multiple measures approach, especially observation techniques, seems needed for the future. The discussion later in the chapter will further explain this need for a behavioral emphasis in leadership studies and its accompanying observation measurement techniques.

The Early Michigan Leadership Studies

At about the same time that the Ohio State studies were being conducted, a group of researchers from the Survey Research Center at the University of Michigan began their studies of leadership. In the original study at the Prudential Insurance Company, twelve high-low productivity pairs were selected for examination. Each pair represented a high-producing section and a low-producing section, with other variables, such as type of work, conditions, and methods, being the same in each pair. Nondirective interviews were conducted with the 24 section supervisors and 419 clerical workers. Results showed that supervisors of high-producing sections were significantly more likely to be general rather than close in their supervisory styles and be employee-centered (have a genuine concern for their people). The low-producing section supervisors had essentially opposite characteristics and techniques. They were found to be close, production-centered supervisors. Another important, but sometimes overlooked, finding was that employee satisfaction was *not* directly related to productivity.

The general, employee-centered supervisor, described above, became the standard-bearer for the traditional human relations approach to leadership. The results of the Prudential studies were always cited when human relations advocates were challenged to prove their theories. The studies have been followed up with hundreds of similar studies in a wide variety of industrial, hospital, governmental, and other organizations. Thousands of employees, performing unskilled to highly professional and scientific tasks, have been analyzed. Rensis Likert, the one-time director of the Institute for Social Research of the University of Michigan, presented the results of the years of similar research in his books and became best known for his "System 4" leadership style, which is covered later in the chapter.

Theories of Leadership

The Iowa, Ohio State, and Michigan studies are three of the historically most important leadership studies for the study of organizational behavior. Unfortunately, they are still heavily depended upon, and leadership research has not surged ahead from this relatively auspicious beginning. Before analyzing the current status of leadership research, it is important to look at the theoretical development that has occurred through the years.

There are several distinct theoretical bases for leadership. At first, leaders were felt to be born, not made. This so-called "great man" theory of leadership implied that some individuals are born with certain traits that allow them to emerge out of any situation or period of history to become leaders. This evolved into what is now known as the *trait theory* of leadership. The trait approach is concerned mainly with identifying the personality traits of the leader. Dissatisfied with this approach, and stimulated by research such as the Ohio State studies, researchers switched their emphasis from the individual leader to the group being led. In the group approach, leadership is viewed more in terms of the leader's behavior and how such behavior affects and is affected by the group of followers.

Finally, in addition to the leader and the group, the situation began to receive increased attention in leadership theory. The situational approach was initially called *Zeitgeist* (a German word meaning "spirit of the times"); the leader is viewed as a product of the times and the situation. The person with the particular qualities or traits that a situation requires will emerge as the leader. Such a view has much historical support as a theoretical basis for leadership and serves as the basis for situational—and now, contingency—theories of leadership.

More recently, some of the expectancy concepts of motivation that were discussed in Chapter 9 began to be adapted to leadership. Called the *path-goal* theory of leadership, this modern approach is a step toward synthesizing motivational and leadership concepts. The leadership substitutes approach recognizes the limitations of existing theories and suggests that environmental factors may take the place of, or "substitute" for, leader traits, behaviors, or processes. Finally, analogous to developments throughout the field of organizational behavior, a behaviorally oriented social learning approach to leadership has been proposed. This comprehensive theory emphasizes the reciprocal determinism among the leader (including his or her cognitions), the environmental situation (including followers and macro variables), and the behavior itself. The following will examine in detail these major theoretical bases of leadership.

Trait Theories of Leadership

The scientific analysis of leadership started off by concentrating on leaders themselves. The vital question that this theoretical approach attempted to answer was, what characteristics or traits make a person a leader? The earliest trait theories, which can be traced back to the ancient Greeks and Romans, concluded that leaders are born, not made. The "great man" theory of leadership said that a person is born either with or without the necessary traits for leadership. Famous figures in history—for example, Napoleon—were said to have had the "natural" leadership abilities to rise out of any situation and become great leaders.

Eventually, the "great man" theory gave way to a more realistic trait approach to leadership. Under the influence of the behavioristic school of psychological thought, researchers accepted the fact that leadership traits are not completely inborn but can also be acquired through learning and experience. Attention turned to the search for universal traits possessed by leaders. The results of this voluminous research effort were generally very disappointing. Only intelligence seemed to hold up with any degree of consistency. When these findings are combined with those of studies on physical traits, the conclusion seems to be that leaders are bigger and brighter than those being led, but not too much so.

When the trait approach is applied to organizational leadership, the result is even cloudier. One of the biggest problems is that all managers think they know what the qualities of a successful leader are. Obviously, almost any adjective can be used to describe a successful leader. Recognizing these semantic limitations and realizing that there is no cause-and-effect relationship between observed traits and successful leadership, there is some evidence to suggest that empathy or interpersonal sensitivity and self-confidence are desirable leadership traits.[5]

In general, research findings do not agree on which traits are generally found in leaders or even on which ones are more important than others. Similar to the trait theories of personality, the trait approach to leadership has provided some descriptive insight but has little analytical or predictive value. The trait approach is still alive, but now the emphasis has shifted away from personality traits and toward job-related skills. Katz has identified the technical, conceptual, and human skills needed for effective management.[6] Yukl includes skills such as creativity, organization, persuasiveness, diplomacy and tactfulness, knowledge of the task, and the ability to speak well.[7] These skills are important and can be used both to select leaders and in training and development.

Group and Exchange Theories of Leadership

The group theories of leadership have their roots in social psychology. Classic exchange theory, in particular, serves as an important basis for this approach. Discussed in Chapters 9 and 13, this means simply that the leader provides more benefits/rewards than burdens/costs for followers. There must be a positive exchange between the leaders and followers in order for group goals to be accomplished. Chester Barnard applied such an analysis to managers and subordinates in an organizational setting more than a half-century ago. More recently, this social exchange view of leadership has been summarized as follows:

> The person in the role of leader who fulfills expectations and achieves group goals provides rewards for others which are reciprocated in the form of status, esteem, and heightened influence. Because leadership embodies a two-way influence relationship, recipients of influence assertions may respond by asserting influence in return. . . . The very sustenance of the relationship depends upon some yielding to influence on both sides.[8]

The above quotation emphasizes that leadership is an exchange process between the leader and followers and also involves the sociological concept of role expectations. Social psychological research can be used to support the exchange and role concepts applied to leadership. In addition, the original Ohio State studies and follow-up studies through the years, especially the dimension of giving consideration to followers, give support to the group perspective of leadership. A thorough review of research indicated that leaders who take into account and support their followers have a positive impact on attitudes, satisfaction, and performance.[9]

Followers' Impact on Leaders.   A few important research studies indicate that followers/subordinates may actually affect leaders as much as leaders affect followers/subordinates. For example, one study found that when subordinates were not performing very well, the leaders tended to emphasize initiating structure, but when subordinates were doing a good job, leaders increased their emphasis on consideration.[10] In a laboratory study it was found that group productivity had a greater impact on leadership style than leadership style had on group productivity,[11] and in another study it was found that in newly formed groups, leaders may adjust their supportive behavior in response to the level of group cohesion and arousal already present.[12] In other words, such studies seem to indicate that subordinates affect leaders and their behaviors as much as leaders and their behaviors affect subordinates. Some practicing managers, such as the vice president of Saga Corporation, feel that subordinates lack followership skills, and there is growing evidence that the newer generation of managers is increasingly reluctant to accept a followership role.[13] Moreover, it is probably not wise to ignore followership. Most managers feel that subordinates have an obligation to follow and support their leader. As the CEO of Commerce Union Corporation noted, "Part of a subordinate's responsibility is to make the boss look good."[14]

The Vertical Dyad Linkage Model.   Relevant to the exchange view of leadership is the vertical dyad linkage (VDL) approach,[15] sometimes called leader-member exchange (LMX).[16] The VDL theory says that leaders treat individual subordinates differently. In particular, leaders and subordinates develop dyadic (two-person) relationships which affect the behavior of both leaders and subordinates. For example, subordinates who are committed and who expend a lot of effort for the unit are rewarded with more of the leader's positional resources (for example, information, confidence, and concern) than those who do not display these behaviors.

Over time, the leader will develop an "in-group" of subordinates and an "out-group" of subordinates and treat them accordingly. Thus, for the same leader, research has shown that in-group subordinates report fewer difficulties in dealing with the leader and perceive the leader as being more responsive to their needs than out-group subordinates do.[17] Also, leaders spend more time "leading" members of the in-group (that is, they do not depend on formal authority to influence them), and they tend to "supervise" those in the out-group (that is, they depend on formal roles and authority to influence them).[18] Finally, there is evidence that subordinates in the in-group (those who report a high-quality relationship with their leader) assume greater job responsibility, contribute more to their units, and are rated as higher performers than those reporting a low-quality relationship.[19] This VDL theory has been around for some time now, and although it is not without criticism,[20] in general the research continues to be relatively supportive and seems to have considerable potential for predicting important dimensions of the leader-subordinate exchange.

Contingency Theories of Leadership

After the trait approach proved to fall short of being an adequate overall theory of leadership, attention turned to the situational aspects of leadership. Social psychologists began the search for situational variables that impact on leadership roles, skills, and behavior and on followers' performance and satisfaction. Numerous situational variables were identified, but no overall theory pulled it all together until Fred Fiedler proposed a widely recognized situation-based model for leadership effectiveness. A brief review of his research techniques and findings is necessary to fully understand his contingency theory of leadership effectiveness.

Least Preferred Coworker.

Fiedler developed a unique operational technique to measure leadership style. Measurement is obtained from scores that indicate the least preferred coworker (LPC). This LPC approach calculates the degree to which leaders favorably perceive their worst coworkers and relates to leadership style in the following manner:

1. The *human relations, or "lenient," style* is associated with the leader who gives a relatively favorable description of the least preferred coworker.
2. The *task-directed, or "hard-nosed," style* is associated with the leader who gives a very unfavorable description of the least preferred coworker.

Fiedler's Findings.

Through the years the performance of both laboratory groups and numerous real groups (basketball teams, fraternity members, surveying teams, bomber crews, infantry squads, open-hearth steel employees, and farm-supply service employees) was correlated with the leadership styles described above. The results were somewhat encouraging, but no simple relationships between leadership style as determined by the leaders' LPC score and group performance were developed. Eventually, Fiedler concluded that more attention would have to be given to situational variables. He became convinced that leadership style in *combination* with the situation determines group performance.

Fiedler's Contingency Model of Leadership Effectiveness

To test the hypothesis he had formulated from previous research findings, Fiedler developed what he called a *contingency model of leadership effectiveness*. This model contained the relationship between leadership style and the favorableness of the situation. Situational favorableness was described by Fiedler in terms of three empirically derived dimensions:

1. The *leader-member relationship,* which is the most critical variable in determining the situation's favorableness.
2. The *degree of task structure,* which is the second most important input into the favorableness of the situation.
3. The *leader's position power* obtained through formal authority, which is the third most critical dimension of the situation.[21]

Situations are favorable to the leader if all three of the above dimensions are high. In other words, if the leader is generally accepted by followers (high first dimension), if the task is very structured and everything is "spelled out" (high second dimension), and if a great deal of authority and power is formally attributed to the leader's position (high third dimension), the situation is very favorable. If the opposite exists (if the three dimensions are low), the situation will be very unfavorable for the leader. Fiedler was convinced that the favorableness of the situation in combination with the leadership style determines effectiveness.

Through the manipulation of research findings, Fiedler was able to discover that under very favorable *and* very unfavorable situations, the task-directed, or "hard-nosed," type of leader was most effective. However, when the situation was only moderately favorable or unfavorable (the intermediate range of favorableness), the human relations, or lenient, type of leader was most effective. Figure 16.1 summarizes this relationship between leadership style and the favorableness of the situation.

Why is the task-directed leader successful in very favorable situations? Fiedler offered the following explanation:

> In the very favorable conditions in which the leader has power, informal backing, and a relatively well-structured task, the group is ready to be directed, and the group expects to be told what to do. Consider the captain of an airliner in its final landing approach. We would hardly want him to turn to his crew for a discussion on how to land.[22]

As an example of why the task-oriented leader is successful in a highly unfavorable situation, Fiedler cited

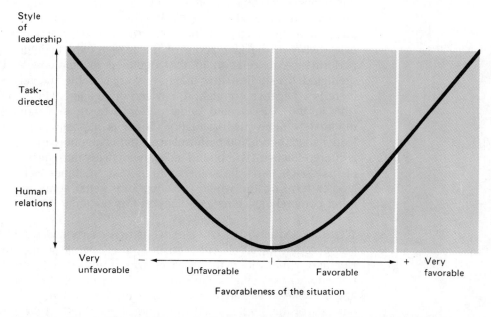

FIGURE 16.1
Fiedler's model of leadership.
(*Source:* Adapted from Fred E. Fiedler, *A Theory of Leadership Effectiveness*. McGraw-Hill, New York, 1967, pp. 142–148.)

... the disliked chairman of a volunteer committee which is asked to plan the office picnic on a beautiful Sunday. If the leader asks too many questions about what the group ought to do or how he should proceed, he is likely to be told that "we ought to go home."[23]

The leader who makes a wrong decision in this highly unfavorable type of situation is probably better off than the leader who makes no decision at all. Figure 16.1 shows that the human relations leader is effective in the intermediate range of favorableness. An example of such situations is the typical committee or a unit which is staffed by professionals. In these situations, the leader may not be wholly accepted by the other members of the group, the task may be generally vague and not completely structured, and little authority and power may be granted to the leader. Under such circumstances, the model predicts that a human relations, lenient type of leader will be most effective.

Research Support for the Contingency Model. As is true of any widely publicized theoretical development, Fiedler's model has stimulated a great deal of research. Not surprisingly, the results are mixed and a controversy has been generated. Fiedler and in particular his students have provided almost all the support for the model over the years. For example, to defend the validity of his theory, he cites thirty studies in a wide variety of teams and organizations, (Navy teams, chemical research teams, shop departments, supermarkets, heavy machinery plant departments, engineering groups, hospital wards, public health teams, and others) and concludes that "the theory is highly predictive and that the relations obtained in the validation studies are almost identical to those obtained in the original studies."[24] With one exception, which Fiedler explains away, he maintains that the model correctly predicted the correlations that should exist between the LPC score of the leader (which determines the style) and performance in relation to the identified favorableness of the situation. As predicted, his studies show that in very unfavorable and very favorable situations, there is a negative correlation between the leader's LPC score and performance (that is, the task-oriented leader performs best). In a moderately favorable and moderately unfavorable situation, there is a positive correlation between the leader's LPC score and performance (that is, the human relations-oriented leader is more effective). Although Fiedler recognizes that there is increasing criticism of his conclusions, he still maintains that "methodologically sound validation studies have on the whole provided substantial support for the theory,"[25] and other comprehensive reviews support this contention.[26]

Critical Analysis of the Contingency Model. Although there is probably not as much criticism of Fiedler's work as there is, for example, of Herzberg's motivation theory, a growing number of leadership researchers do not wholly agree with Fiedler's interpretations or conclusions. For example, Graen and his colleagues initially raised some criticisms of the procedures and statistical analysis of the studies used to support the validity of the model.[27] Schriesheim and his colleagues have been especially critical of the reliability and validity of the LPC instrument.[28] Fiedler[29] and his colleagues[30] have answered these criticisms of LPC to their satisfaction, but the fact remains that this questionnaire measure (and others such as those developed at Ohio State and Michigan) do have problems and may be a major reason why leadership understanding and predictability has not progressed as fast as it was once thought it would. As Korman took care to point out:

> The need for better measurement in leadership theory is a matter of prime necessity. Measurement and theory go hand-in-hand and the development of one without the other is a waste of time for all concerned. . . . The point is *not* that adequate measurement is "nice." It is *necessary, crucial, etc.* Without it, we have nothing.[31]

It may well be that there has been an overdependence on the LPC type of measure for leadership theory and research.

Applications of Fiedler's Work. In addition to the reliability and validity questions, there is also the criticism of Fiedler's extension of the model to the actual practice of human resources management. On the basis of the model, Fiedler suggests that management would be better off engineering positions so that the requirements fit the leader instead of using the more traditional technique of selecting and developing leaders to fit into existing jobs.[32] With this in mind, Fiedler and his colleagues then developed a self-programmed training manual (called *Leader Match*), which includes a series of questionnaires that identify the person's leadership style (LPC) and the situational dimensions of his or her job (task structure, leader-member relations, and position power).[33] Then the trainee is given a series of short problems with several alternative solutions.

Under Fiedler's leadership effectiveness training, the trainee is taught (on the basis of feedback compatible with the contingency model) ways to diagnose the situation so as to change it and optimize the leader style–leader situation match. Some of the suggested ways to modify leader-member relations include spending more (or less) informal time with subordinates and suggesting or effecting transfers of particular subordinates into or out of the unit. To decrease task structure, the leader may ask for new or unusual problems; to increase task structure, the leader may ask for more instructions and prepare a detailed plan. To raise position power, the leader could become an expert on the job, or to lower position power, the leader could call on subordinates to participate in planning and decision making.[34]

Most of the support for this Leader Match training has come from Fiedler and his students/colleagues. After a review of five studies conducted in civilian organizations and seven conducted in military settings, Fiedler concluded that all twelve studies yielded statistically significant results supporting Leader Match training.[35] He claims that these studies also support "the contested point that leaders are able to modify their leadership situations to a degree sufficient to increase their effectiveness."[36] Other, more recent research is critical of Leader Match as not being very consistent with what the contingency model should predict.[37]

Overall, there seems little question that Fiedler has provided one of the major breakthroughs for leadership theory and practice. Further research should put Fiedler's contingency approach on firmer ground, especially research leading to an understanding of what behavior is actually represented by the LPC response and specifying how the situational moderators will change as the leader exerts influence on subordinates.[38] Also, more research is needed on Leader Match training before it can effectively guide the future practice of human resources management, but as one recent analysis concluded: "Situational engineering and leadership match concepts are useful alternatives to the more traditional advice and training based on earlier leadership theories."[39] At the very least, Fiedler has done and continues to do considerable empirical research,[40] and he has set an important precedent for the development of empirically based contingency models. Fiedler's ideas certainly do not represent the ultimate in leadership theory, research, and practice, but he has made a lasting contribution to this field.

However, it should be remembered that there are a number of constraints and considerations besides those identified by Fiedler for a leader choosing or carrying out a particular style. A review of the literature reveals that factors such as the following must be taken into account: subordinate behavior; characteristics of subordinates; characteristics of the leader; the leader's superiors and peers; organizational policies, norms, and climate; and the nature of subordinates' tasks.[41]

Path-Goal Leadership Theory

The other widely recognized modern theoretical development for leadership studies, besides the contingency approach, is the path-goal theory derived from the expectancy framework of motivation theory. This is a healthy development because leadership is closely related to work motivation on the one hand (discussed in Chapter 9) and power on the other (discussed in the previous chapter). Any theory that attempts to synthesize the various concepts seems to be a step in the right direction.

Although Georgopoulos and his colleagues at the University of Michigan's Institute for Social Research used path-goal concepts and terminology many years ago in analyzing the impact of leadership on performance, the modern development is usually attributed to Martin Evans and Robert House, who wrote separate papers on the subject.[42] In essence, the path-goal theory attempts to explain the impact that leader behavior has on subordinate motivation, satisfaction, and performance. The House version of the theory incorporates four major types or styles of leadership.[43] Briefly summarized, these are:

1. *Directive leadership* This style is similar to that of the Lippitt and White authoritarian leader. Subordinates know exactly what is expected of them, and specific directions are given by the leader. There is no participation by subordinates.
2. *Supportive leadership* The leader is friendly and approachable and shows a genuine concern for subordinates.
3. *Participative leadership* The leader asks for and uses suggestions from subordinates but still makes the decisions.
4. *Achievement-oriented leadership* The leader sets challenging goals for subordinates and shows confidence that they will attain these goals and perform well.

This path-goal theory—and here is how it differs in one respect from Fiedler's contingency model—suggests that these various styles can be and actually are used by the same leader in different situations.[44] Two of the situational factors that have been identified so far are the personal characteristics of subordinates and the environmental pressures and demands facing subordinates. With respect to the first situational factor, the theory asserts:

> Leader behavior will be acceptable to subordinates to the extent that the subordinates see such behavior as either an immediate source of satisfaction or as instrumental to future satisfaction.[45]

And with respect to the second situational factor, the theory states:

> Leader behavior will be motivational (e.g., will increase subordinate effort) to the extent that (1) it makes satisfaction of subordinate needs contingent on effective performance, and (2) it complements the environment of subordinates by providing the coaching, guidance, support, and rewards which are necessary for effective performance and which may otherwise be lacking in subordinates or in their environment.[46]

Using one of the four styles contingent upon the situational factors as outlined above, the leader attempts to influence subordinates' perceptions and motivate them, which in turn leads to their role clarity, goal expectancies, satisfaction, and performance. This is specifically accomplished by the leader as follows:

1. Recognizing and/or arousing subordinates' needs for outcomes over which the leader has some control

2. Increasing personal payoffs to subordinates for work-goal attainment
3. Making the path to those payoffs easier to travel by coaching and direction
4. Helping subordinates clarify expectancies
5. Reducing frustrating barriers
6. Increasing the opportunities for personal satisfaction contingent on effective performance[47]

In other words, by doing the above the leader attempts to make the path to subordinates' goals as smooth as possible. But to accomplish this path-goal facilitation, the leader must use the appropriate style contingent on the situational variables present. Figure 16.2 summarizes this path-goal approach.

As is true of the expectancy theory of motivation, there has been a recent surge of research on the path-goal theory of leadership. So far, most of the research has concentrated on only parts of the theory rather than on the entire theory. For example, a sampling of the research findings indicates the following:

1. Studies of seven organizations have found that *leader directiveness* is (*a*) positively related to satisfactions and expectancies of subordinates engaged in ambiguous tasks and (*b*) negatively related to satisfactions and expectancies of subordinates engaged in clear tasks.
2. Studies involving ten different samples of employees found that *supportive leadership* will have its most positive effect on satisfaction for subordinates who work on stressful, frustrating, or dissatisfying tasks.
3. In a major study in an industrial manufacturing organization, it was found that in nonrepetitive ego-involving tasks, employees were more satisfied under *participative leaders* than under nonparticipative leaders.
4. In three separate organizations it was found that for subordinates performing ambiguous nonrepetitive tasks, the higher the *achievement orientation of the*

FIGURE 16.2 A summary of path-goal relationships.

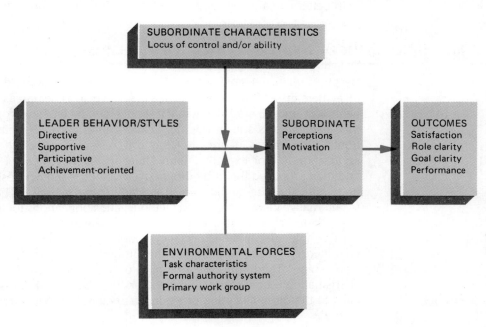

leader, the more subordinates were confident that their efforts would pay off in effective performance.[48]

The more recent reviews of the research on the path-goal theory are not as supportive as the above. For example, Schriesheim and DeNisi note that only a couple of hypotheses have really been drawn from the theory, which means that it may be incapable of generating meaningful predictions.[49] Another note of pessimism offered by these reviewers is that only one of the two hypotheses has received consistent empirical support. Research has generally substantiated the hypothesis that the higher the task structure (repetitiveness) of the jobs performed by subordinates, the higher the relationship between supportive leader behavior/ style and subordinate satisfaction. On the other hand, the second hypothesis— that the higher the task structure, the lower the correlation between instrumental (directive) leader behavior and subordinate satisfaction—has received, at best, mixed research support. Schriesheim and DeNisi then report results of their own research, which indicates that the path-goal theory is capable of producing meaningful and testable predictions beyond the two task structure hypotheses.[50] Also, a recent comprehensive review of forty-eight studies demonstrated that the mixed results of the individual studies, when cumulated, were transformed into support for continued testing of path-goal theory.[51]

Overall, the path-goal theory, like the other theories presented in this chapter and others, seems to need more research, but it certainly warrants further attention in the coming years. One recent analysis concluded that leaders will be perceived most favorably by their subordinates, and succeed in exerting most influence over them, when they behave in ways that closely match (1) the needs and values of subordinates and (2) the requirements of a specific work situation.[52] In other words, the path-goal theory, like the expectancy theory in work motivation, may help better explain the complexities of the leadership process.

Other Theoretical Frameworks for Leadership

Despite a relative degree of acceptance of the contingency and path-goal theories of leadership and the great (at least relative to other areas in organizational behavior) amount of research that has been conducted, few would disagree today that leadership is still in trouble. Leadership is currently being attacked on all fronts—in terms of theories relating to it, research methods for studying it, and applications.[53] For example, John Miner was very critical of leadership theory and then proposed that it be dropped altogether,[54] and Schriesheim and Kerr are quite critical of the methods used in leadership research.[55] The time seems ripe for alternative theories, research methods, and applications for leadership studies.

There are a number of modified and new approaches that have emerged. For example, just as the expectancy notions of motivation evolved into the path-goal theory of leadership, so has the attribution approach been used to analyze leadership.[56] There are also a number of new theoretical formulations such as charismatic and transformational leadership. Charismatic leadership is a throwback to the old conception of leaders as being those who "by the force of their personal abilities are capable of having profound and extraordinary effects on followers."[57] Although the charismatic concept or charisma goes as far back as the ancient Greeks and is cited in the Bible, its modern development is attributed to the work of Robert House.[58] This theoretical approach to leadership has only preliminary research findings and a recent behavioral framework contrasting noncharismatic and charismatic leaders.[59] Identifying charismatic characteristics of leaders can become very important as organizations transform traditional ways of being led to meet the challenge of dramatic change. It is this transformation process that has led to another new theoretical development of leadership.

Burns identified two types of political leadership: transactional and transformational.[60] The more traditional transactional leadership involves an exchange relationship between leaders and followers, but transformational leadership is based more on leaders' shifting the values, beliefs, and needs of their followers. Bass applied these ideas to managing modern organizations,[61] and there have been some recent theoretical development and analysis.[62]

On the basis of interviews with top executives of major companies, Tichy and Devanna stress that modern corporate leaders must use a transformational approach to cope with change and use innovation and entrepreneurship.[63] The effective transformational leaders share the following characteristics:

1. They identify themselves as change agents.
2. They are courageous.
3. They believe in people.
4. They are value-driven.
5. They are lifelong learners.
6. They have the ability to deal with complexity, ambiguity, and uncertainty.
7. They are visionaries.[64]

In addition to attributional, charismatic, and transformational theories, social learning and a substitutes approach have emerged to meet the challenge of understanding the complexities and alternatives to leadership.

A Social Learning Approach

Just as social learning theory was shown in Chapter 1 to provide the basis for an overall conceptual model for organizational behavior,[65] social learning theory can provide a model for the continuous, reciprocal interaction between the leader (including his or her cognitions), the environment (including subordinates/followers and macro variables), and the behavior itself.[66] These interactions are shown in Figure 16.3. This would seem to be a comprehensive and viable theoretical foundation for understanding leadership.[67]

Any of the other theoretical approaches, standing alone, seem too limiting. For example, the one-sided, cognitively based trait theories suggest that leaders are causal determinants that influence subordinates independent of subordinates' behaviors or the situation. The contingency theories are a step in the right direction, but even they for the most part have a unidirectional conception of interaction, in which leaders and situations somehow combine to determine

FIGURE 16.3 A social learning approach to leadership. [*Source:* Adapted from Albert Bandura, *Social Learning Theory,* Prentice-Hall, Englewood Cliffs, N.J., 1977; and Fred Luthans, "Leadership: A Proposal for a Social Learning Theory Base and Observational and Functional Analysis Techniques to Measure Leader Behavior," in James G. Hunt and Lars L. Larson (eds.), *Crosscurrents in Leadership,* Southern Illinois University Press, Carbondale, 1979, p. 205.]

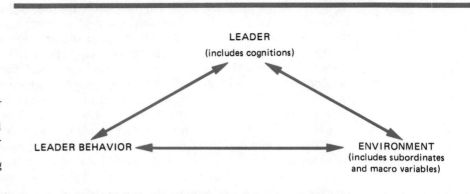

leadership behavior. Even those leadership theories which claim to take a bidirectional approach (either in the exchange sense between the leader and the subordinate/group or in the contingency sense between the leader and the situation) actually retain a unidirectional view of leadership behavior. In these theories, the causal input into the leader's behavior is the result of the interdependent exchange, but the behavior itself is ignored as a leadership determinant.

Obviously, the focus of a social learning approach, and what distinguishes it from the other approaches, is the role of leadership *behavior* and the *continuous, reciprocal interaction* between all the variables. With this as the focus of attention, the alternative research methods and application techniques for leadership naturally follow. As Kerlinger has noted, "observations must be used when the variables of research studies are interactive and interpersonal in nature."[68] Thus, there is a need for observational measures of leadership behaviors in naturalistic settings. The research foundation for a Leader Observation System (LOS) has been completed.[69] Now the LOS is being used to analyze various leadership situations and relevant variables.[70] This LOS approach may be an effective supplement, if not an alternative, to the more traditional questionnaire methods used in leadership research.

As far as leadership application for the social learning approach is concerned, the four-term contingency S-O-B-C (situation-organism-behavior-consequence) model introduced in Chapter 1 can be used by leaders to perform a functional analysis. Unlike the more limited A-B-C (antecedent-behavior-consequence) functional analysis used in O.B. Mod. (see Chapter 12), the variables in the S-O-B-C functional analysis can be either overt (observable), as in the operant view, or covert (unobservable), as recognized in the social learning view, and, of course, recognition is given to the role of cognitive mediating processes by the insertion of the O. The successful application of this S-O-B-C functional analysis to human resources management "depends upon the leader's ability to bring into awareness the overt or covert antecedent cues and contingent consequences that regulate the leader's and subordinate's performance behavior."[71] More specifically, in this leadership application, the subordinates are actively involved in the process, and together with the leader they concentrate on their own and one another's *behaviors,* the environmental contingencies (both antecedent and consequent), and their mediating cognitions. Some examples of this approach would be the following:

1. The leader becomes acquainted with the macro and micro variables that control his or her own behavior.
2. The leader works with the subordinate to discover the personalized set of behavioral contingencies that regulate the subordinate's behavior.
3. The leader and the subordinate jointly attempt to discover ways in which they can manage their individual behavior to produce more mutually reinforcing and organizationally productive outcomes.[72]

In such an approach, the leader and the subordinate have a negotiable, interactive relationship and are consciously aware of how they can modify (influence) each other's behavior by giving or holding back desired rewards.

Although work has been done on the theoretical development of a social learning approach to leadership, research and application are just getting under way.[73] Only time will tell whether it will hold up as a viable, researchable approach to leadership. However, because of its growing importance as a theoretical foundation for the fields of psychology and organizational behavior as a whole and because it recognizes the interactive nature of all the variables of previous theories, a social learning approach to leadership would seem to have potential for the future.

Substitutes for Leadership

Because of dissatisfaction with the progress of leadership theory and research in explaining and predicting the effects of leader behavior on performance outcomes, some of the basic assumptions about the importance of leadership per se are being challenged. In particular, Kerr and Jermier propose that there may be certain "substitutes" for leadership that make leader behavior unnecessary and redundant and "neutralizers" which prevent the leader from behaving in a certain way or which counteract the behavior.[74] These substitutes or neutralizers can be found in subordinate, task, and organization characteristics. Figure 16.4 gives specific examples of possible substitutes and neutralizers according to supportive/relationship leadership and instrumental/task leadership.

As shown, subordinate experience, ability, and training may substitute for instrumental/task leadership. For example, craftspersons or professionals such as accountants or engineers may have so much experience, ability, and training that they do not need instrumental/task leadership to perform well and be satisfied. Those subordinates who don't particularly care about organizational rewards (for example, professors or musicians) will neutralize both supportive/relationship and instrumental/task leadership attempts. Tasks that are highly structured and automatically provide feedback substitute for instrumental/task leadership, and those which are intrinsically satisfying (for example, teaching) do not need supportive/relationship leadership. There are also a number of organizational characteristics that substitute for or neutralize leadership.

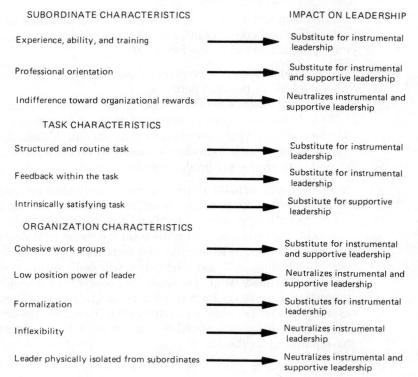

FIGURE 16.4
Substitutes and neutralizers for leadership.
(*Source:* Adapted from Steven Kerr and John M. Jermier, "Substitutes for Leadership: Their Meaning and Measurement," *Organizational Behavior and Human Performance,* December 1978, pp. 375–403.)

There has been further analysis of the leader substitutes concept,[75] and Kerr and Jermier have provided some empirical support from field studies of police officers.[76] They found that substitutes such as feedback from the task being performed had more impact on certain job-related activities than leader behaviors did. Other studies have also been interpreted (post hoc) to support organizational characteristics such as formalization as leader substitutes.[77] More recent direct tests have yielded mixed results. One study using hospital personnel with a wide variety of skills and backgrounds and in a wide variety of professions found several potential substitutes to predict subordinate satisfaction and commitment, but only one of the single substitutes (organizational formalization) rendered leadership impossible and/or unnecessary.[78] A follow-up study found that worker professionalism was an important moderator variable. It also found that professionals differed from nonprofessionals in that intrinsically satisfying work tasks and importance placed on organizational rewards were strong substitutes for leaders' support.[79]

Overall, the substitutes notion puts leadership back into proper perspective and may help explain the relatively poor track record of leadership research. In particular, the leadership situation (subordinate, task, or organization) may replace or counteract the leader's behavior in impacting on subordinate satisfaction and performance. It has recently been noted that "the idea of leadership substitutes and neutralizers helps to account for the largely mixed results of research on most leadership theories. Studies of leadership that ignore the effect of neutralizers and substitutes may fail to uncover hypothesized relationships because the particular leadership process is irrelevant, rather than because the theory is invalid."[80]

In other words, some things are beyond leaders' control; leaders do not have mystical powers over people. The situation does play a role. By the same token, leaders can have a considerable impact. The substitutes idea does not negate leadership; it just puts a more realistic boundary on what leadership is capable of achieving from subordinates. Some styles of leadership are more effective than others. The next section examines leadership styles.

Leadership Styles

The classic leadership studies discussed at the beginning of the chapter and the various leadership theories all have direct implications for what style the manager or supervisor uses in human resources management. The word "style" is roughly equivalent to the *way* in which the leader influences followers. The accompanying International Application Example indicates that this style may be influenced by culture, as seen in the differences between Japanese and Korean managers. The following discussion will first explore the implications for leadership style of the classic studies and the theories, and then it will present the most recent approaches that deal directly with style.

Style Implications of the Classic Studies and the Modern Theories

Chapter 2 discussed the major historical contributions to the study of organizational behavior. Most of this discussion had indirect or direct implications for leadership style. For example, the Hawthorne studies were interpreted in terms of their implications for supervisory style. Also relevant is the classic work done by Douglas McGregor, in which his Theory X represents the old, authoritarian style of leadership and his Theory Y represents the enlightened, humanistic style. The studies discussed at the beginning of this chapter are directly concerned with style. The Iowa studies analyzed the impact of autocratic, democratic, and laissez faire styles, and the studies conducted by the Michigan group found the employee-centered supervisor to be more effective than the production-centered supervisor. The Ohio State studies identified consideration (a supportive type of style) and initiating structure (a directive type of style) as being the major functions of leadership. The trait, group, and social learning theories have indirect implications for style, and the human relations and task-directed styles play an important role in Fiedler's contingency theory. The path-goal conceptualization depends heavily upon directive, supportive, participative, and achievement-oriented styles of leadership.

A rough approximation of the various styles derived from the studies and theories discussed so far can be incorporated into the continuum shown in Table

Japanese versus Korean Leadership Styles*

When America's productivity began to slide in comparison with Japan's, American management professors and practitioners looked toward Japanese management for answers. It was found that Japanese management gave extra attention to human resources management. Since then, American managers have adopted many of the Japanese practices. Quality circles and lifetime employment come quickly to mind. Recently, however, another success story is gaining America's attention. South Korea, not Japan, has been winning the competitive battle in many areas. Korean-run businesses such as Lucky-Goldstar, Samsung, Hyundai, and Daewoo are having tremendous success. They have posed a new threat to American business leadership. Thus, Americans are now looking toward Korean management for the answers.

In some ways the Koreans are similar to the Japanese. For instance, Korean managers espouse teamwork, employee participation, minimal hierarchies, and emphasis on the employee's personal needs. However, when the Koreans come to run their operations in the United States, they are more flexible than the Japanese. As a result, Koreans have adjusted better to American ways. For instance, although managers in Korea sit in open-air offices, Korean managers in America separate themselves with lightly tinted glass. Also, Americans are not asked to sing a company song or to take exercise breaks. Thomas G. Dimmick, a manager with the Korean firm Samsung, comments on the inflexibility of the Japanese: "The Japanese are from a homogeneous society, so they are less accepting of anything that is not Japanese. Korea is a land of division, so the people are willing to listen and not get their feet stuck in concrete."

The Korean-run plants in the United States have experienced considerable success. The average American worker at a Korean-run plant produced $94,000 in goods compared with $87,000 produced by American-owned companies. American workers at Japanese-run plants still produced the most: $155,000. However, management experts predict that the gap between Japanese and Korean plants will narrow. After all, Korean managers work 70 to 80 hours a week, Japanese managers work 60 to 70 hours, and Americans work around 50 hours. The diligence of the Koreans should pay off in the long run. If the Korean-run plants continue to succeed, Korean management may replace Japanese management as a model for managerial leadership.

*Source: Adapted from Laurie Baum, "Korea's Newest Export: Management Style," *Business Week*, Jan. 19, 1987, p. 66.

16.1. For ease of presentation, the styles listed may be substituted for the expressions "boss-centered" and "subordinate-centered" used by Tannenbaum and Schmidt in their classic leadership continuum shown in Figure 16.5. The verbal descriptions and the relationship between authority and freedom found in Figure 16.5 give a rough representation of the characteristics of the various styles of leadership. This depiction can serve as background for a more detailed examination of the specific application of styles to the practice of human resources management.

One thing is certain: leadership style can make a difference. For example, a recent survey found that senior executives view their companies' leadership

TABLE 16.1 Summary Continuum of Leadership Styles Drawn from the Classic Studies and Theories of Leadership

Boss-centered	Subordinate-centered
Theory X ⟷	Theory Y
Autocratic ⟷	Democratic
Production-centered ⟷	Employee-centered
Close ⟷	General
Initiating structure ⟷	Consideration
Task-directed ⟷	Human relations
Directive ⟷	Supportive
Directive ⟷	Participative

styles as pragmatic rather than conceptual and conservative rather than risk taking. Importantly, these same executives felt that to meet their current and future challenges, the styles should be the other way around.[81] The following section examines the basic leadership styles.

Managerial Grid Style

One very popular approach to identifying leadership styles of practicing managers is Robert R. Blake and Jane S. Mouton's managerial grid. Figure 16.6 shows that the two dimensions of the grid are concern for people along the vertical axis and concern for production along the horizontal axis. These two dimensions are of course equivalent to the consideration and initiating structure functions identified

FIGURE 16.5 A continuum of leadership behavior. (*Source:* Robert Tannenbaum and Warren H. Schmidt, "How to Choose a Leadership Pattern," *Harvard Business Review*, March–April 1958, p. 96. Used with permission.)

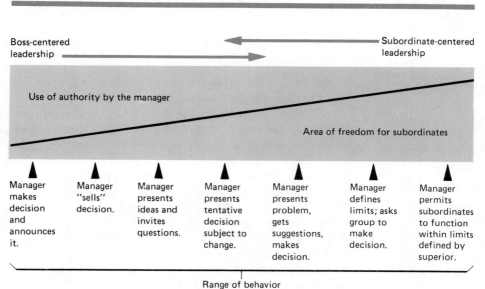

Boss-centered leadership — Subordinate-centered leadership

Use of authority by the manager

Area of freedom for subordinates

| Manager makes decision and announces it. | Manager "sells" decision. | Manager presents ideas and invites questions. | Manager presents tentative decision subject to change. | Manager presents problem, gets suggestions, makes decision. | Manager defines limits; asks group to make decision. | Manager permits subordinates to function within limits defined by superior. |

Range of behavior

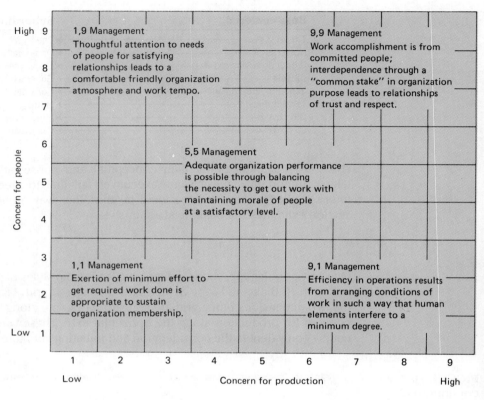

FIGURE 16.6 The managerial grid. (*Source:* Robert R. Blake and Jane S. Mouton, "Managerial Facades," *Advanced Management Journal,* July 1966, p. 31. Used with permission.)

by the Ohio State studies and the employee-centered and production-centered styles used in the Michigan studies.

The five basic styles identified in the grid represent varying combinations of concern for people and production. The 1,1 manager has minimum concern for people and production; this style is sometimes called the "impoverished" style. The opposite is the 9,9 manager. This individual has maximum concern for both people and production. The implication is that the 9,9 is the best style of leadership, and Blake and Mouton have stated in no uncertain terms: "There should be no question about which leadership style is the most effective. It's that of the manager whom we call, in the terminology of the Managerial Grid, a 9,9 team builder."[82] Blake and Mouton provided empirical evidence that their interactive notion of leadership style (that is, concern for people interacting with concern for production) has more predictive validity than additive situational approaches.[83] The 5,5 manager is the "middle-of-the-roader," and the other two styles represent the extreme concerns for people (1,9, "country club" manager) and production (9,1, "task" manager). A manager's position on the grid can be determined by a questionnaire developed by Blake and Mouton and can play an important role in organization development (OD). Chapter 20 will discuss this grid approach to OD and will analyze the research findings.

Hersey and Blanchard's Life-Cycle, or Situational, Approach

Another popular approach to management training and development is the *life-cycle* (later termed the *situational*) approach to leadership.[84] It is an extension of the managerial grid approach. Following the original Ohio State studies and the grid approach, Hersey and Blanchard's approach identifies two major styles:

1. *Task style* The leader organizes and defines roles for subordinates; the leader explains the tasks that each subordinate is to do and when, where, and how the subordinate is to do them.
2. *Relationship style* The leader has close, personal relationships with the members of the group, and there is open communication and psychological and emotional support.

Taking the lead from some of Fiedler's work on situational variables, Hersey and Blanchard incorporated the maturity of the followers into their model. The level of maturity is defined by three criteria:

1. Degree of achievement motivation
2. Willingness to take on responsibility
3. Amount of education and/or experience

Although they recognize that there may be other important situational variables, Hersey and Blanchard focus only on this maturity level of subordinates in their model.

Figure 16.7 summarizes the situational approach. The key for leadership effectiveness in this model is to match up the situation with the appropriate style. The following summarizes the four basic styles:

1. *Telling style* This is a high-task, low-relationship style and is effective when followers are at a very low level of maturity.
2. *Selling style* This is a high-task, high-relationship style and is effective when followers are on the low side of maturity.
3. *Participating style* This is a low-task, high-relationship style and is effective when followers are on the high side of maturity.
4. *Delegating style* This is a low-task, low-relationship style and is effective when followers are at a very high level of maturity.

Like the grid approach, Hersey and Blanchard's approach includes a questionnaire instrument which presents twelve situations that generally depict the various levels of maturity of the group; respondents answer how they would handle each situation. These responses follow the four styles. How closely respondents match the situation with the appropriate style will determine their effectiveness score.

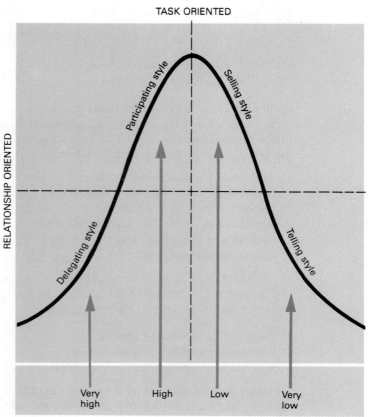

FIGURE 16.7
Hersey and Blanchard's situational leadership model. (*Source:* Adapted from Paul Hersey and Kenneth H. Blanchard, *Management of Organization Behavior: Utilizing Human Resources,* 3d ed., Prentice-Hall, Englewood Cliffs, N.J., 1977, p. 170.)

The theoretical rationale is generally criticized as being "weak, because Hersey and Blanchard have neglected to provide a coherent, explicit rationale for the hypothesized relationships."[85] They also, by their own admission, highly oversimplify the situation by giving only surface recognition to follower maturity. Also, as in the grid approach, there is a noted absence of any empirical tests of the model. One review of all facets of the approach was particularly critical of the instrument that Hersey and Blanchard used to measure leader effectiveness.[86] Overall, as is true of the other style approaches, this situational approach seems to be of some value in training and development work in that it can point out the need for flexibility and take into consideration the different variables affecting leaders, but until more supporting research is conducted, this type of approach has limited utility for identifying leadership effectiveness.

Likert's Four Systems of Management

The grid and situational approaches are both highly descriptive and at this time lack empirically validated research backup. In contrast, Rensis Likert proposes four basic systems or styles of organizational leadership that have evolved from the many years of research by the Michigan group. Table 16.2 summarizes these four styles, called *systems of management leadership.*

The manager who operates under a system 1 approach is very authoritarian and actually tries to exploit subordinates. The system 2 manager is also authoritarian but in a paternalistic manner. This benevolent autocrat keeps strict control and never delegates authority to subordinates, but he or she "pats them on the head" and "does it for their best interests." The system 3 manager uses a consultative style. This manager asks for and receives participative input from subordinates but maintains the right to make the final decision. The system 4 manager uses a democratic style. This manager gives some direction to subordinates but provides for total participation and decision by consensus and majority.

To give empirical research backup on which style is most effective, Likert and his colleagues asked thousands of managers to describe, on an expanded version of the format shown in Table 16.2, the highest- and lowest-producing departments with which they had had experience. Quite consistently, the high-producing units were described according to systems 3 and 4, and the low-producing units fell under systems 1 and 2. These responses were given irrespective of the manager's field of experience or of whether the manager was in a line or staff position.[87]

TABLE 16.2 Likert's Systems of Management Leadership

Leadership Variable	System 1 (Exploitive Autocratic)	System 2 (Benevolent Autocratic)	System 3 (Participative)	System 4 (Democratic)
Confidence and trust in subordinates	Manager has no confidence or trust in subordinates.	Manager has condescending confidence and trust, such as a master has in a servant.	Manager has substantial but not complete confidence and trust; still wishes to keep control of decisions.	Manager has complete confidence and trust in subordinates in all matters.
Subordinates' feeling of freedom	Subordinates do not feel at all free to discuss things about the job with their superior.	Subordinates do not feel very free to discuss things about the job with their superior.	Subordinates feel rather free to discuss things about the job with their superior.	Subordinates feel completely free to discuss things about the job with their superior.
Superiors seeking involvement with subordinates	Manager seldom gets ideas and opinions of subordinates in solving job problems.	Manager sometimes gets ideas and opinions of subordinates in solving job problems.	Manager usually gets ideas and opinions and usually tries to make constructive use of them.	Manager always asks subordinates for opinions and always tries to make constructive use of them.

Source: Adapted from Rensis Likert, *The Human Organization*, McGraw-Hill, New York, 1967, p. 4. Used with permission.

The Impact of Intervening Variables and Time. An important refinement of Likert's work is the recognition of three broad classes of variables that affect the relationship between leadership and performance in a complex organization.[88] Briefly summarized, these are:

1. *Causal variables* These are the independent variables that determine the course of developments and results of an organization. They include only those variables which are under the control of management; for example, economic conditions are *not* causal variables in this sense. Examples would include organization structure and management's policies and decisions and their leadership styles, skills, and behavior.
2. *Intervening variables* These reflect the internal climate of the organization. Performance goals, loyalties, attitudes, perceptions, and motivations are some important intervening variables. They affect interpersonal relations, communication, and decision making in the organization.
3. *End-result variables* These are the dependent variables, the outcomes of the organization. Examples would be productivity, service, costs, quality, and earnings.

Likert points out that there is not a direct cause-and-effect relationship between, for example, leadership style (a causal variable) and earnings (an end-result variable). The intervening variables must also be taken into consideration. For example, moving to a system 1 style of management may lead to an improvement in profits but a deterioration of the intervening variables (that is, attitudes, loyalty, and motivation decline). In time, these intervening variables may lead to a decrease in profits. Thus, although on the surface it appeared that system 1 was increasing profits, because of the impact on the intervening variables, in the long run system 1 may lead to a decrease in profits. The same can be said for the application of a system 4 style. In the short run, profits may dip, but because of the impact on intervening variables, there may be an increase in profit over time. Obviously, the time lag between intervention and the impact on end-result variables becomes extremely important to Likert's scheme. On the basis of some research evidence, Likert concludes: "Changes in the causal variables toward System 4 apparently require an appreciable period of time before the impact of the change is fully manifest in corresponding improvement in end-result variables."[89]

An Example of Time Lag. Likert's "time lag" helps explain the following relatively common sequence of events. A system 1 manager takes over an operation and immediately gets good performance results. In the meantime, however, the intervening variables are declining. Because of the good results, the system 1 manager is promoted. A system 4 manager now takes over the operation. Because of the time lag, the intervening variables, which were affected by the system 1 manager, now start to impact on performance. Under the system 4 manager, performance starts to decline, but the intervening variables start to improve. However, top management see that when the system 4 manager took over, performance started to decline. The system 4 manager is replaced by a system 1 manager to "tighten up" the operation. The intervening variables affected by the system 4 manager now start to affect performance, and the cycle repeats itself. Figure 16.8 depicts this situation. In other words, the cause-and-effect relationships that appear on the surface may be very misleading because of the time lag impact of the intervening variables. As in the example, top management evaluations often credit the wrong manager (the system 1 manager in this case) for improving performance and unjustly blame the wrong manager (the system 4 manager in the example) for poor performance. Some organizations may be guilty of this never-ending cycle of rewarding and punishing the wrong managers because of the time lag effect of intervening variables.

Analysis of Likert's Approach. One of the major criticisms of Likert's work concerns its overdependence on survey questionnaire measures for gathering data to develop the theory and application of system 4 management. Sole dependence on Likert scale (continuums of dimensions as shown in Table 16.2) questionnaire responses is not enough. As has been pointed out a number of times in this book, there is increasing criticism of data gathered only by questionnaires and interviews. Multiple measures of behaviorally oriented variables in organizations are needed. More use of archival information (existing records kept by every organization for other uses, for example, government reports, personnel records, and performance data) and data gathered through observation are needed.

Although ethical standards must always be maintained, subject awareness must be minimized to increase the reliability and validity of data that are gathered for research purposes. Both questionnaires and interviews have a great deal of subject awareness or intrusiveness. Archival analysis and some naturalistic

FIGURE 16.8 A hypothetical example depicting Likert's time lag impact of intervening variables on performance.

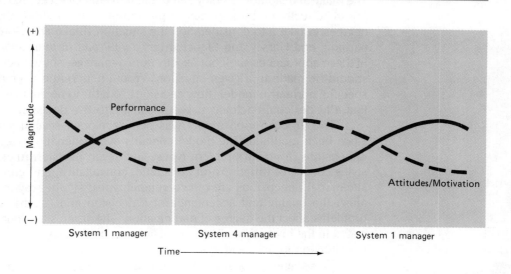

observational techniques minimize subject awareness and are called *unobtrusive measures.*[90] Not only Likert's work but also much of the other research reported in this book is based upon indirect questionnaire measures. What is needed is to supplement these measures with other measures such as observations and archival data. As Chapter 2 pointed out, the use of multiple measures increases tremendously the chance of getting better, more accurate, and more valid data.

Another problem inherent in Likert's scheme besides the real and potential measurement problems is the implication of the universality of the system 4 approach. Although Likert points out that "differences in the kind of work, in the traditions of the industry, and in the skills and values of the employees of a particular company will require quite different procedures and ways to apply appropriately the basic principles of system 4 management,"[91] he still implies that system 4 will *always* be more effective than system 1. Proponents of situational/contingency leadership theories and their research findings would, of course, counter this generalization.

Convincing arguments can be made for directive, rather than system 4, styles of leadership. This position was recently stated as follows:

> The inescapable fact is that many, many organizations who are less than "excellent" in the caliber of their people and support systems simply can't afford to have their managers be participative without a commensurate dose of direction. That is, in the vast majority of actual leadership situations democratic behaviors must be tempered with a measure of direction or follow-up to assure that organizational goals are accomplished efficiently and effectively.[92]

This position on leadership effectiveness was essentially ignored by Likert.

Normative Leadership Model

The Blake and Mouton, Hersey and Blanchard, and Likert approaches to leadership are all directly or by implication prescriptive. In addition, they try in varying degrees to take into consideration the situation (Blake and Mouton and Likert in passing, and Hersey and Blanchard as a vital part of their approach). But none of these approaches spell out exactly *how* a manager should act or what decision should be made in a given situation. Vroom and Yetton attempted to provide a specific, normative model (how decisions "ought" to be made in given situations) that a leader could actually use in making effective decisions.[93]

The Vroom-Yetton model was first developed several years ago and has since been modified. The model contains five leadership styles, seven situation dimensions, fourteen problem types, and seven decision rules. The leadership styles consist of variations on autocratic, consultative, and group styles, and the situational dimensions are of two general types: (1) the way in which problems affect the quality and acceptance of a decision and (2) the way in which the problems affect the degree of participation. The seven situational dimensions are stated in the form of "yes"-"no" questions, and the answers can quickly diagnose the situation for the leader.

Vroom and Yetton use a decision tree to relate the situation to the appropriate leadership style. Figure 16.9 shows the approach. The seven situational questions

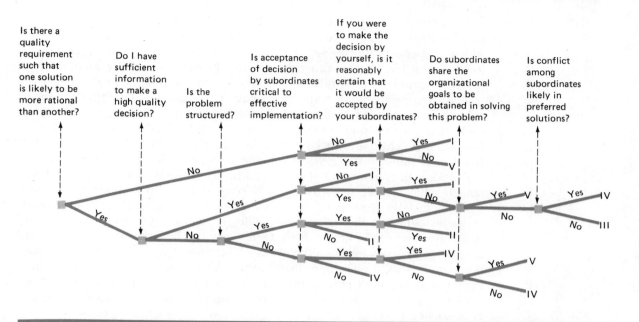

FIGURE 16.9 The Vroom-Yetton normative leadership model.
(*Source:* Adapted from Victor H. Vroom, "A New Look at Managerial Decision Making," *Organizational Dynamics,* Spring 1973, pp. 67, 70.)

are listed at the top. Starting at the left, the manager would answer each question above the box in the decision tree until it led to the appropriate style. In this way the manager could determine the appropriate style on the basis of the given situation. Vroom and Yetton also point out that the fourteen problem types (the combinations of the seven situational variables, listed as 1 through 14 in the decision tree) could actually have more than one acceptable leadership style. In order to be acceptable, the style must meet the criteria of seven decision rules that protect quality and acceptance. If more than one style remains after the test of both quality and acceptance (and many do), the third most important aspect of a decision—the amount of time—is used to determine the single style that ought to be used in the given situation. The styles shown at the ends of the various branches on the decision tree reflect the single best style that should be used in light of the way the situation was diagnosed by answers to the questions at the top.

The Vroom-Yetton model is a fitting conclusion to the discussion of leadership in this chapter. The progression has been from theory to styles to specific prescriptions. Several studies have tested this model.[94] Most of this research has been done by Vroom and his colleagues, and they do provide some evidence that the model is valid. However, more recent critiques that have closely examined the methodology used in these studies have led to questions about the validity of the model.[95]

Although the potential problem that support of the Vroom-Yetton model may be attributed to chance alone may be discounted,[96] there may be a problem with the dependence on the self-report data. For example, managers going through training and development programs are simply asked to recall a problem they have encountered and to indicate which of the five styles in the model they used to solve the problem. In addition, managers are given standardized problem cases and are asked which style from the model could best be used to solve each case. Such methods, of course, have a number of internal validity problems (experimenter effect and social desirability effect) and external validity problems (the use of standardized cases in a training situation may not generalize to the real world). In addition to the validity problems of the model, it may also have limited utility for two major reasons: "*First,* it is not as parsimonious as other models of leader decision process choice. *Second,* it deals with only one aspect of leader behavior, that of selecting different decision processes for different problem situations."[97] Vroom answers this criticism by reanalyzing his data and concludes that the relative complexity of his model is justified for predictive purposes.[98] Also, a revision of the model by Vroom and Jago that replaces the yes-no with five-point scales and adds new attributes dealing with time, information, and motivation contains recent research that indicates greater accuracy of prediction.[99]

Overall, the Vroom-Yetton model has much surface logic, and it does give precise answers to practicing managers. However, as in the case of the other approaches, more research is needed. On the positive side, its attempt to bridge the gap from theory to practice may be a step in the right direction, and it can serve as a prototype for the actual practice of contingency management.

Summary

This chapter presented and analyzed various theoretical and practical aspects of leadership. The classic research studies on leadership set the stage for the theoretical development of leadership. The trait theories concentrate on the leaders themselves but, with the possible exception of intelligence and empathy/ interpersonal sensitivity and self-confidence, really do not come up with any agreed-upon traits of leaders. In recent times the trait approach has surfaced in terms of managerial skills and abilities identified for selection and training/ development purposes.

The group and exchange theories emphasize the importance of followers, and although the vertical dyad linkage (VDL) model is still quite popular and is generating considerable research, the group/exchange theories in general are recognized to be only partial theories. Today, the widely recognized theories of leadership are situationally based. In particular, Fiedler's contingency model makes a significant contribution to leadership theory and potentially to the practice of human resources management. The path-goal approach is also an important contribution to leadership theory. It incorporates expectancy motivation concepts. Both the Fiedler and the path-goal approaches have generated a growing body of research on leadership dimensions, but there are still problems. A social learning approach that incorporates the leader, the situation, and the behavior itself is proposed as an alternative theory. This approach emphasizes the importance of behavior and the continuous, interacting nature of all the variables in leadership. Finally, it is now recognized that certain subordinate, task, and organizational characteristics may substitute for or neutralize the impact that leader behavior has on subordinate performance and satisfaction.

There are many style implications in both the classic leadership studies and the modern theories. Blake and Mouton's managerial grid, Hersey and Blanchard's situational model, and Likert's four systems focus attention directly on leadership styles. Each of these is of value in relation to the actual practice of human resources management. The grid is valuable mainly because it allows managers to describe their styles. Hersey and Blanchard's approach shows how well managers can match the appropriate style with the maturity level of the group being led, and Likert's work has implications for organizational effective-ness. Likert's recognition of intervening variables and their time lag effects has significant implications for practice. Finally, the Vroom-Yetton model attempts to prescribe exactly what style to use in a given situation. All these approaches to style need more and better research in order to make meaningful contributions to the actual practice of human resources management in the future.

Questions for Discussion And Review

1. Briefly summarize the findings of the three classical leadership studies.
2. How do the group theories differ from the trait theories of leadership?
3. What are the three critical situational variables identified by Fiedler? If these are very favorable, what is the most effective style to use?
4. In simple terms, what is the path-goal theory of leadership? What is the leader's function in this conceptualization?
5. What are the three variables in the social learning approach to leadership? How do they relate to one another? How can this approach be applied to the practice of human resources management?
6. What is meant by *substitutes* for, and *neutralizers* of, leadership? Give some subordinate, task, and organizational examples of these substitutes and neutralizers.
7. Briefly identify the major styles from Blake and Mouton's grid, from Hersey and Blanchard's situational model, and from Likert's four systems. Which are more effective or less effective?

References

1. Andrea Rothman, "Maybe Your Skills Aren't Holding You Back; Maybe It's a Birthday," *The Wall Street Journal*, Mar. 19, 1987, p. 35.

2. Jeremy Main, "Wanted: Leaders Who Can Make a Difference," *Fortune,* Sept. 28, 1987, pp. 92–93.
3. For a comprehensive historical review, see David D. Van Fleet and Gary Yukl, "A Century of Leadership Research," in Daniel Wren (ed.), *Papers Dedicated to the Development of Modern Management,* Academy of Management, 1986, pp. 12–23.
4. Chester A. Schriesheim and Steven Kerr, "Theories and Measures of Leadership: A Critical Appraisal of Current and Future Directions," in James G. Hunt and Lars L. Larson (eds.), *Leadership: The Cutting Edge,* Southern Illinois University Press, Carbondale, 1977, p. 22.
5. H. Joseph Reitz, *Behavior in Organizations,* 3d ed., Irwin, Homewood, Ill., 1987, p. 469.
6. Robert Katz, "Skills of an Effective Administrator," *Harvard Business Review,* September–October 1974, pp. 90–101.
7. Gary A. Yukl, *Leadership in Organizations,* Prentice-Hall, Englewood Cliffs, N.J., 1981, p. 70.
8. Edwin P. Hollander and James W. Julian, "Contemporary Trends in the Analysis of Leadership Processes," *Psychological Bulletin,* May 1969, pp. 387–397. [Reprinted in Richard M. Steers and Lyman W. Porter (eds.), *Motivation and Work Behavior,* McGraw-Hill, New York, 1975, p. 349.]
9. Alan C. Filley, Robert J. House, and Steven Kerr, *Managerial Process and Organizational Behavior,* 2d ed., Scott, Foresman, Glenview, Ill., 1976, pp. 219–222.
10. Charles N. Greene, "The Reciprocal Nature of Influence between Leader and Subordinate," *Journal of Applied Psychology,* vol. 60, 1975, pp. 187–193.
11. J. C. Barrow, "Worker Performance and Task Complexity as Causal Determinants of Leader Behavior Style and Flexibility," *Journal of Applied Psychology,* vol. 61, 1976, pp. 433–440.
12. Charles N. Greene and Chester A. Schriesheim, "Leader-Group Interactions: A Longitudinal Field Investigation," *Journal of Applied Psychology,* February 1980, pp. 50–59.
13. Keith Davis and John Newstrom, *Human Behavior at Work: Organizational Behavior,* 7th ed., McGraw-Hill, New York, 1985, pp. 160 and 182; Ann Howard and James A. Wilson, "Leadership in a Declining Work Ethic," *California Management Review,* Summer 1982, pp. 33–46.
14. Larry Reibstein, "Follow the Leader: Workers Face Dilemma When Boss Is Sinking," *The Wall Street Journal,* Mar. 10, 1987, p. 29.
15. F. Dansereau, Jr., G. Graen, and W. J. Haga, "A Vertical Dyad Linkage Approach to Leadership within Formal Organizations: A Longitudinal Investigation of the Role Making Process," *Organizational Behavior and Human Performance,* February 1975, pp. 46–78.
16. G. Graen, M. Novak, and P. Sommerkamp, "The Effects of Leader-Member Exchange and Job Design and Productivity and Satisfaction: Testing a Duel Attachment Model," *Organizational Behavior and Human Performance,* vol. 30, 1982, pp. 109–131.
17. Dansereau, Graen, and Haga, op. cit.
18. Fred Dansereau, Jr., Joseph A. Alutto, Steven E. Markham, and MacDonald Dumas, "Multi-plexed Supervision and Leadership: An Application of Within and Between Analysis," in James G. Hunt, Uma Sekaran, and Chester A. Schriesheim (eds.), *Leadership: Beyond Establishment Views,* Southern Illinois University Press, Carbondale, 1982, pp. 81–103.
19. Robert C. Liden and George Graen, "Generalizability of the Vertical Dyad Linkage Model of Leadership," *Academy of Management Journal,* September 1980, pp. 451–465.

Chapter 16: Leadership Processes and Styles **485**

20. Robert P. Vecchio, "A Further Test of Leadership Effects Due to Between-Group Variation and Within-Group Variation," *Journal of Applied Psychology*, April 1982, pp. 200–208; Richard M. Dienesch and Robert C. Linden, "Leader-Member Exchange Model of Leadership: A Critique and Further Development," *Academy of Management Review*, July 1986, pp. 618–634.
21. Fred E. Fiedler, *A Theory of Leadership Effectiveness*, McGraw-Hill, New York, 1967, pp. 13–144.
22. Ibid., p. 147.
23. Ibid.
24. Fred Fiedler and Martin M. Chemers, *Leadership and Effective Management*, Scott, Foresman, Glenview, Ill., 1974, p. 83.
25. Fred E. Fiedler and Linda Mahar, "The Effectiveness of Contingency Model Training: A Review of the Validation of Leader Match," *Personnel Psychology*, Spring 1979, p. 46.
26. Michael J. Strube and Joseph E. Garcia, "A Meta-Analytic Investigation of Fiedler's Contingency Model of Leadership Effectiveness," *Psychological Bulletin*, September 1981, pp. 307–321.
27. George Graen, D. Alvares, J. B. Orris, and J. A. Martella, "Contingency Model of Leadership Effectiveness: Antecedent and Evidential Results," *Psychological Bulletin*, October 1970, pp. 285–296; George Graen, James B. Orris, and Kenneth M. Alvares, "Contingency Model of Leadership Effectiveness: An Evaluation," *Organizational Behavior and Human Performance*, June 1973, pp. 339–355.
28. Schriesheim and Kerr, op. cit.; and Chester A. Schriesheim, Brendan D. Bannister, and William H. Money, "Psychometric Properties of the LPC Scale: An Extension of Rice's Review," *Academy of Management Review*, April 1979, pp. 287–290.
29. Fred E. Fiedler, "A Rejoinder to Schriesheim and Kerr's Premature Obituary of the Contingency Model," in Hunt and Larson, op. cit., pp. 45–51.
30. Robert W. Rice, "Reliability and Validity of the LPC Scale: A Reply," *Academy of Management Review*, April 1979, pp. 291–294.
31. Abraham K. Korman, "Contingency Approaches to Leadership: An Overview," in James G. Hunt and Lars L. Larson (eds.), *Contingency Approaches to Leadership*, Southern Illinois University Press, Carbondale, 1974, p. 194.
32. Fred E. Fiedler, "Engineer the Job to Fit the Manager," *Harvard Business Review*, September–October 1965, pp. 115–122.
33. Fred E. Fiedler, Martin M. Chemers, and Linda Mahar, *Improving Leadership Effectiveness: The Leader Match Concept*, Wiley, New York, 1976.
34. Ibid., pp. 154–158.
35. Fiedler and Mahar, op. cit.
36. Ibid., p. 61.
37. Arthur G. Jago and James W. Ragan, "The Trouble with Leader Match Is that It Doesn't Match Fiedler's Contingency Model," *Journal of Applied Psychology*, vol. 71, no. 4, 1986, pp. 555–559.
38. Filley, House, and Kerr, op. cit., p. 261.
39. John R. Schermerhorn, Jr., James G. Hunt, and Richard N. Osborn, *Managing Organizational Behavior*, Wiley, New York, 1982, p. 526.
40. Besides in the 1979 article on Leader Match (Fiedler and Mahar, op. cit.), Fiedler departs from his almost exclusive use of the LPC instrument by reporting data that suggest that leader experience and intelligence (that is, traits) may have differential effects on unit performance depending upon the amount of interpersonal stress (a new contingency variable) felt by the leader. See Fred E. Fiedler, "Organizational

Determinants of Managerial Incompetence," in James G. Hunt and Lars L. Larson (eds.), *Crosscurrents in Leadership,* Southern Illinois University Press, Carbondale, 1979, pp. 11–22.

41. Hugh J. Arnold and Daniel C. Feldman, *Organizational Behavior,* McGraw-Hill, New York, 1986, pp. 139–140.

42. Basil S. Georgopoulos, Gerald M. Mahoney, and Nyle W. Jones, "A Path-Goal Approach to Productivity," *Journal of Applied Psychology,* December 1957, pp. 345–353; Martin G. Evans, "The Effect of Supervisory Behavior on the Path-Goal Relationship," *Organizational Behavior and Human Performance,* May 1970, pp. 277–298; and Robert J. House, "A Path-Goal Theory of Leader Effectiveness," *Administrative Science Quarterly,* September 1971, pp. 321–338.

43. Robert J. House and Terence R. Mitchell, "Path-Goal Theory of Leadership," *Journal of Contemporary Business,* Autumn 1974, pp. 81–97.

44. Ibid.

45. Ibid., in Steers and Porter, op. cit., p. 386.

46. Filley, House, and Kerr, op. cit., p. 254.

47. House and Mitchell, op. cit., in Steers and Porter, op. cit., pp. 385–386.

48. Filley, House, and Kerr, op. cit., pp. 256–260.

49. Chester A. Schriesheim and Angelo DeNisi, "Task Dimensions as Moderators of the Effects of Instrumental Leadership: A Two Sample Applicated Test of Path-Goal Leadership Theory," *Journal of Applied Psychology,* October 1981, pp. 589–597. Also see Schriesheim and Kerr, op. cit.

50. Ibid., pp. 103–105.

51. Julie Indvik, "Path-Goal Theory of Leadership: A Meta-Analysis," *Academy of Management Best Papers Proceedings,* 1986, pp. 189–192.

52. Robert A. Baron, *Behavior in Organizations,* 2d ed., Allyn and Bacon, Boston, 1986, p. 292.

53. Representative of the critical analysis of modern leadership theory and research would be Korman, op. cit., pp. 189–195; Charles N. Greene, "Disenchantment with Leadership Research: Some Causes, Recommendations, and Alternative Directions," in Hunt and Larson (eds.), *Leadership: The Cutting Edge,* pp. 57–67; Schriesheim and Kerr, op. cit.; Barbara Karmel, "Leadership: A Challenge to Traditional Research Methods and Assumptions," *Academy of Management Review,* July 1978, pp. 475–482; and James S. Phillips and Robert G. Lord, "Notes on the Practical and Theoretical Consequences of Implicit Leadership Theories for the Future of Leadership Measurement," *Journal of Management,* vol. 12, no. 1, 1986, pp. 31–41.

54. John B. Miner, "The Uncertain Future of the Leadership Concept: An Overview," in James G. Hunt and Lars L. Larson (eds.), *Leadership Frontiers,* Kent State University, Comparative Administration Resources Institute, Kent, Ohio, 1975, pp. 197–208.

55. Schriesheim and Kerr, op. cit.

56. D. A. Gioia and H. P. Sims, Jr., "Cognitive-Behavior Connections: Attribution and Verbal Behavior in Leader-Subordinate Interactions," *Organizational Behavior and Human Decision Processes,* April 1986, pp. 197–229.

57. R. J. House and J. L. Baetz, "Leadership: Some Empirical Generalizations and New Research Directions," in B. M. Staw (ed.), *Research in Organizational Behavior,* vol. 1, JAI Press, Greenwich, Conn., 1979, p. 399.

58. Robert J. House, "A 1976 Theory of Charismatic Leadership," in Hunt and Larson (eds.), *Leadership: The Cutting Edge,* pp. 189–207.

59. Jay A. Conger and Rabindra N. Kanungo, "Toward a Behavioral Theory of Charismatic

Leadership in Organizational Settings," *Academy of Management Review*, October 1987, pp. 637–647.

60. J. M. Burns, *Leadership*, Harper & Row, New York, 1978.

61. B. M. Bass, *Leadership and Performance beyond Expectations*, Free Press, New York, 1985.

62. Karl W. Kuhnert and Philip Lewis, "Transactional and Transformational Leadership: A Constructive/Developmental Analysis," *Academy of Management Review*, October 1987, pp. 648–657.

63. Noel M. Tichy and Mary Anne Devanna, *The Transformational Leader*, Wiley, New York, 1986.

64. Noel M. Tichy and Mary Anne Devanna, "The Transformational Leader," *Training and Development Journal*, July 1986, pp. 30–32.

65. See Tim R. V. Davis and Fred Luthans, "A Social Learning Approach to Organizational Behavior," *Academy of Management Review*, April 1980, pp. 281–290.

66. See Fred Luthans, "Leadership: A Proposal for a Social Learning Theory Base and Observational and Functional Analysis Techniques to Measure Leader Behavior," in Hunt and Larson (eds.) *Crosscurrents in Leadership*, pp. 201–208; Fred Luthans and Tim R. V. Davis, "Operationalizing a Behavioral Approach to Leadership," *Proceedings of the Midwest Academy of Management*, 1979, pp. 144–155; and Tim R. V. Davis and Fred Luthans, "Leadership Reexamined: A Behavioral Approach," *Academy of Management Review*, April 1979, pp. 237–248.

67. See Luthans, op. cit., for an expanded discussion.

68. Fred N. Kerlinger, *Foundations of Behavioral Research*, Holt, New York, 1973, p. 554.

69. Fred Luthans and Diane L. Lockwood, "Toward an Observation System for Measuring Leader Behavior in Natural Settings," in J. G. Hunt, D. Hosking, C. A. Schriesheim, and R. Stewart (eds.) *Leaders and Managers: International Perspectives of Managerial Behavior and Leadership*, Pergamon, New York, 1984, pp. 117–141.

70. Fred Luthans, Stuart A. Rosenkrantz, and Harry W. Hennessey, "What Do Successful Managers Really Do? An Observation Study of Managerial Activities," *Journal of Applied Behavioral Science*, vol. 21, no. 3, 1985, pp. 255–270; Fred Luthans and Janet Larsen, "How Do Managers Really Communicate?" *Human Relations*, vol. 39, no. 2, 1986, pp. 161–178; Fred Luthans, Richard M. Hodgetts, and Stuart A. Rosenkrantz, *Real Managers*, Ballinger, Cambridge, Mass., 1988; and Fred Luthans, Dianne H. B. Welsh, and Lew Taylor, "A Descriptive Model of Managerial Effectiveness," *Group and Organization Studies*, June 1988.

71. Davis and Luthans, "Leadership Reexamined," p. 244.

72. Ibid., p. 245.

73. See Fred Luthans and Tim R. V. Davis, "Behavioral Self-Management: The Missing Link in Managerial Effectiveness," *Organizational Dynamics*, Summer 1979, pp. 42–60; and Tim R. V. Davis and Fred Luthans, "Defining and Researching Leadership as a Behavioral Construct: An Idiographic Approach," *Journal of Applied Behavioral Science*, vol. 20, no. 3, 1984, pp. 237–251. Also see the references in 70.

74. Steven Kerr and John M. Jermier, "Substitutes of Leadership: Their Meaning and Measurement," *Organizational Behavior and Human Performance*, December 1978, pp. 375–403. Also see Steven Kerr, "Substitutes for Leadership: Some Implications for Organization Design," *Organization and Administrative Sciences*, vol. 8, no. 1, 1977, p. 135; and Jon P. Howell, Peter Dorfman, and Steven Kerr, "Moderator Variables in Leadership Research," *Academy of Management Review*, vol. 11, no. 1, 1986, pp. 88–102.

75. J. Jermier and L. Berkes, "Leader Behavior in a Police Command Bureaucracy: A Closer Look at the Quasi-Military Model," *Administrative Science Quarterly,* March 1979, pp. 1–23; and S. Kerr and J. W. Slocum, Jr., "Controlling the Performances of People in Organizations," in P. C. Nystrom and W. H. Starbuck (eds.), *Handbook of Organizational Design,* Oxford, New York, 1981, pp. 116–134.
76. Kerr and Jermier, op. cit.
77. Robert H. Miles and M. M. Petty, "Leader Effectiveness in Small Bureaucracies," *Academy of Management Journal,* June 1977, pp. 238–250.
78. Jon P. Howell and Peter W. Dorfman, "Substitutes for Leadership: Test of a Construct," *Academy of Management Journal,* December 1981, pp. 714–728.
79. Jon P. Howell and Peter W. Dorfman, "Leadership and Substitutes for Leadership among Professionals and Nonprofessional Workers," *Journal of Applied Behavioral Science,* vol. 22, no. 1, 1986, pp. 29–46.
80. Robert P. Vecchio, *Organizational Behavior,* Dryden, Chicago, 1988, p. 309.
81. "Changing Perspectives," *The Wall Street Journal,* Nov. 25, 1986, p. 1.
82. Robert Blake and Jane S. Mouton, "Should You Teach There's Only One Best Way to Manage?" *Training HRD,* April 1978, p. 24.
83. Robert Blake and Jane S. Mouton, "Management by Grid Principles or Situationalism: Which?" *Group and Organization Studies,* December 1981, pp. 439–455.
84. Paul Hersey and Kenneth H. Blanchard, *Management of Organizational Behavior,* 4th ed., Prentice-Hall, Englewood Cliffs, N.J., 1982.
85. Gary A. Yukl, *Leadership in Organizations,* Prentice-Hall, Englewood Cliffs, N.J., 1981, pp. 143–144.
86. Claude L. Graeff, "The Situational Leadership Theory: A Critical View," *Academy of Management Review,* April 1983, pp. 285–291.
87. Rensis Likert, *The Human Organization,* McGraw-Hill, New York, 1967, pp. 3, 11.
88. Ibid., pp. 26, 29.
89. Ibid., pp. 80–81.
90. Eugene J. Webb, Donald T. Campbell, Richard D. Schwartz, and Lee Sechrest, *Unobtrusive Measures: Nonreactive Research in the Social Sciences,* Rand McNally, Chicago, 1966.
91. Likert, *The Human Organization,* p. 192.
92. Jan P. Muczyk and Bernard C. Reimann, "The Case for Directive Leadership," *The Academy of Management Executive,* November 1987, p. 309.
93. Victor H. Vroom and Philip W. Yetton, *Leadership and Decision-Making,* University of Pittsburgh Press, Pittsburgh, 1973, chap. 3.
94. For example, see Thomas E. Hill and Neal Schmitt, "Individual Differences in Leadership Decision Making," *Organizational Behavior and Human Performance,* August 1977, pp. 353–367; Victor Vroom and Arthur G. Jago, "A Test of Spuriousness in Descriptive Models of Participative Leader Behavior," *Journal of Applied Psychology,* April 1978, pp. 151–162; and Charles Margerison and Richard Glube, "Leadership Decision-Making: An Empirical Test of the Vroom-Yetton Model," *Journal of Management Studies,* February 1979, pp. 45–55.
95. R. H. George Field, "A Critique of the Vroom-Yetton Model of Leadership Behavior," *Academy of Management Review,* April 1979, pp. 249–257; and Larry E. Pate and D. C. Heiman, "A Test of the Vroom-Yetton Decision Model in Seven Field Settings," *Personnel Review,* vol. 16, no. 2, 1987, pp. 22–26.
96. William C. Wedley and R. H. George Field, "The Vroom-Yetton Model: Are Feasible Set Choices Due to Chance?" *Proceedings of the Academy of Management,* New York, 1982, pp. 146–150.

97. Field, op. cit., p. 256.
98. Arthur G. Jago and Victor H. Vroom, "An Evaluation of Two Alternatives to the Vroom-Yetton Normative Model," *Academy of Management Journal,* June 1980, pp. 347–355.
99. Arthur G. Jago, Jennifer T. Ettling, and Victor H. Vroom, "Validating a Revision to the Vroom/Yetton Model: First Evidence," *Proceedings of the Academy of Management,* 1985, pp. 220–223. For a complete discussion of the new model see V. H. Vroom and A. G. Jago, *The New Leadership: Managing Participation in Organizations,* Prentice-Hall, Englewood Cliffs, N.J., 1987.

REAL CASE: Presidential Leadership*

One of the most interesting looks at leadership can be found in presidential styles. Ronald Reagan, for example, was popular with some people and unpopular with others, but all agree on one basic fact: he had a leadership style that was interesting and in some ways unique. Close observers have concluded that some of the basic approaches that exemplified Reagan's style were the following:

1. He always put a great deal of emphasis on being able to communicate well. In fact, when his speech writers would hand him their material, the president would go over it and change some of their examples to ones he liked better and felt were more appropriate to his audience.
2. He always tried to convey an upbeat message. If things were not going well, his emphasis would be on how they could be improved.
3. He identified his major goals and continued moving toward them during his terms in office. He did not change his mind in midstream and begin shifting toward different major objectives. This consistency of behavior made it easier for him to keep his programs heading in a consistent direction.
4. He repeated his national goals over and over again so everyone knew what he wanted done. In particular, those who supported him were able to line up behind him. Having heard the message often enough, they became part of his cheering squad—something every effective leader needs.
5. He tried to compromise on those issues where he realized he would be unable to achieve all he was seeking. For example, if he wanted a $100 million for a program and could get only 70 percent of this, he would take it and then work on getting the other 30 percent the next fiscal year. He did not get himself caught up in an "all or nothing" strategy.
6. He focused on the major issues without getting bogged down in the day-to-day decision making. This was left for others who were more skilled than he at implementation.

***Source:** Adapted from Ann Reilly Dowd, "What Managers Can Learn from Manager Reagan," *Fortune,* Sept. 15, 1986, pp. 33–41.

7. During Cabinet meetings he encouraged people to speak their minds; if they disagreed with the majority, they should say so. In this way, Reagan was able to get input on both sides of the issue under discussion.

8. He believed that the most important thing a leader could do was surround himself with the best possible talent. Then he could delegate authority and let these people carry out the overall policy that had been agreed upon.

Over the next decade, a great deal of additional research is likely to be conducted regarding Ronald Reagan's leadership style. However, for the time being at least, most experts believe that his approach to leadership worked pretty well for him.

1. In terms of the managerial grid, what type of leader was President Reagan? Identify and describe his style in terms of the grid.
2. How can Fiedler's contingency model of leadership be used to explain the success of President Reagan's style?
3. How can the path-goal theory of leadership be used in explaining the President's approach? Cite an example in your answer.
4. Did any of the points about his style get him into trouble while in office?

CASE: If It Is Good Enough for Us, It Is Good Enough for Them

Jesse White is a training specialist for the personnel department of a large company. His boss, Rose O'Brien, called him in one day and said that she had just come back from an executive committee meeting. She had been given the charge of developing a leadership training program for all middle management personnel in the firm. She told Jesse that he would be in charge of the project. Jesse wanted to know what the objectives of the program were supposed to be. Rose replied that the top management of the company were concerned that the styles they were using now and had used in the past were not being used by the middle managers. For example, the executive vice president was concerned that the younger lower/middle managers were too idealistic about how to treat people. The others had all agreed with this observation. Then the vice president for finance added that it was their styles that had taken this company to the top of the industry, and if it was good enough for them, it should be good enough for the middle managers. Rose then said, "I have to follow orders, so what I would like you to do is first get a good understanding of the modern theoretical basis for leadership. Then find out what styles of leadership the president and the vice presidents are using in their present jobs. Based upon the theory and what you find out about their present styles, design a program that I can present to the executive committee for middle management leadership training."

1. Do you agree with the approach outlined by Rose to set up the training program? If you were Jesse, what would be some important theoretical considerations that would go into your program? What techniques would you use to determine the top managers' present styles?

2. On the basis of the comments of the executive vice president and the vice president for finance, what styles do you feel you would find for the top managers? For the middle managers? How would you be able to justify a program that was different from the styles of the top managers?
3. Using the Blake and Mouton, Hersey and Blanchard, or Likert approach to style, describe some of the details and implications of your leadership program.

CASE:
The Puppet

Rex Justice is a long-term employee of the Carfax Corporation, and for the last several years he has been a supervisor in the financial section of the firm. He is very loyal to Carfax and works hard to follow the company policies and procedures and the orders of the managers above him. In fact, upper-level management think very highly of him; they can always count on Rex to meet any sort of demand that the company places on him. He is valued and well liked by all the top managers. His employees in the financial section have the opposite opinion of Rex. They feel that he is too concerned with pleasing the upper-level brass and not nearly concerned enough with the needs and concerns of the employees in his department. For example, they feel that Rex never really pushes hard enough for a more substantial slice of the budget. Relative to other departments in the company, they feel they are underpaid and overworked. Also, whenever one of them goes to Rex with a new idea or suggestion for improvement he always seems to have five reasons why it can't be done. There is considerable dissatisfaction in the department, and everyone thinks that Rex is just a puppet for management. Performance has begun to suffer because of his style of leadership. Upper-level management seem to be oblivious to the situation in the finance section.

1. How would you explain Rex's leadership style in terms of one or more of the theories discussed in the chapter?
2. What advice would you give Rex to improve his leadership style?
3. Could a leadership training program be set up to help Rex? What would it consist of?

Integrative Real Case for Part 4

**Rakovica
Motor Works***

Beneath the saw-toothed roof of Rakovica Motor Works [in Yugoslavia] men build engines. They drive forklifts fast. They shape spinning blocks of steel on heavy lathes. They wear coveralls, and their fingernails are dirty.

Over in the executive wing, men make decisions. They sit around a glass-topped conference table in a carpeted meeting room at the end of a hall lined with potted ferns. They set pay and prices. They direct export deals. They approve annual reports. They wear coveralls, and their fingernails are dirty.

When six engine-builders cross the snow to sit at the big table and educate a guest in the factory's affairs, they don't bother inviting their managers. Managers have never counted for much at Rakovica Motor Works.

"We can dispose of them at any point," says a mechanic named Rados Karaklajic, proffering the gift of a company pin.

In the West and in the East, workers dream now and then of running the show. Some in West Germany have won a say. In Poland, many tried and pretty much failed. Now Mikhail Gorbachev talks about it: He wants Soviet workers to elect their bosses.

Big Revisions.   But he doesn't impress the Yugoslavs; here, the workers took charge ages ago. They have been in charge so long, as it happens, that some are tired of working for themselves. A movement has actually begun to hand some of the power back. Big revisions in the scope of worker control are under discussion with the government's active encouragement.

In some factories, including Rakovica, the changes are already under way. At Rakovica, the workers recently voted to scrap the basic building block of self-management. Mr. Gorbachev might do well to ponder that. Marshal Tito wouldn't believe it.

"The factories belonging to the workers!" Tito exulted when the idea was brought to him in 1949. After his rift with the Russians, giving workers sway was his way to out-Lenin Lenin. By Tito's fiat, Yugoslav workers still decide what to make and how to sell it. When profits come in, they decide how to divide them.

Yugoslavs call this "our socialist system of self-management." It is a source of national pride. Workers control every factory in the country. They control schools, hospitals, hotels, shoe stores, bus companies, ballet companies. The only thing workers don't control in Yugoslavia is the army.

Fat Raises.   And what do workers do when they run the show?

If the pride of Yugoslavia provides any pointers, the one thing they don't do is invest their profits. They do award themselves fat raises. Then they borrow. And when debt ruins the economy, inflation tops 85% and their buying power collapses—they strike.

At least that is what they have done lately. In the city of Maribor, the doctors

Source: Barry Newman, "Yugoslavia's Workers Find Self-Management Doesn't Make Paradise," *The Wall Street Journal,* Mar. 25, 1987, pp. 1, 16. Reprinted by permission of *The Wall Street Journal* © Down Jones & Company, Inc. (1987). All rights reserved.

went out last year; so did the vegetable vendors. In Split, on the Adriatic, 6,000 workers shut the shipyard and 140 bus drivers stranded 150,000 riders. Coal miners and mill hands and schoolteachers struck, too. So did the clerical staff of Croatia's Parliament. Close to 800 wildcat strikes hit Yugoslavia in 1986, twice 1984's number. Around 80,000 workers took part.

This month, things have suddenly become even worse. A wave of strikes has clobbered the country in response to the government's feeble efforts to impose some restraints on wages. In Croatia, walkouts reportedly forced 40 factories to close.

Head Scratching. In a Communist country where official documents don't even use the word "strike" (preferring euphemisms like "temporary cessation of labor"), this causes a certain amount of head scratching. "How come that in a state in which workers are in power these same workers go on strike?" wondered the newspaper Borba. "Against whom do they strike?"

Few Yugoslavs have a direct answer to that one, certainly not the state trade unions. "We are unprepared to deal with such issues," says Darko Marinkovic of the Serbian union council. He has an excuse: In Yugoslavia, raising doubts about the genius of worker control can land you in jail.

Yet everybody knows the economy has been wrecked, and everybody has somebody to blame. Workers and bureaucrats blame the Communist Party: The party doesn't have much to do when workers have all the power; it meddles, and politics pollute business. The party and the workers blame the bureaucrats: The bureaucrats swamp workers with information, hijack decisions with technocratic tricks and skim profits to pay paper shufflers.

Naturally, the bureaucrats and the party blame the workers. So do a number of academics, and sociologists, and foreigners.

"I want mine, Jack," is one Westerner's summary of the worker's mental set. Though many own small farms, they can't seem to believe society entrusts them with big factories. Apart from raising pay, hiring is the executive act workers relish most. They rarely fire anyone.

Asked how well self-management works, a British engineer on a Yugoslav joint venture replies: "Not hard."

There is one other view. It commits sacrilege and blames the system. Self-management, the argument goes, gives everyone the capacity to impede and no one the strength to implement.

"Self-management can't be exchanged for political democracy," says Radmila Nakarada, a Belgrade sociologist. "It has to be part of it." Voicing an opinion like that takes some guts here. But the country's political rulers already agree with Miss Nakarada's idea for a quick fix: more power to the executives.

"Even the workers want discipline," she says. "They're hungry for management."

They had a little of both until 1976, the year a new constitution carried decentralization to the outer limits. It diced the whole of Yugoslav society—offices, hospitals, colleges—into "basic organizations of labor." Each is a set of workers capable of making something salable. In other words, a department. A worker, the theory went, can make more waves in a small pond than in a big one.

Each department in each enterprise in the country became totally autonomous. Each now sets its own working conditions, holidays, benefits. Each has its own balance sheet and debts. Each hires its own manager. Under Yugoslavia's constitution (330 pages) and the related statute (419 pages), a factory isn't a company. It is a confederation.

Independent States. At Rakovica Motor Works, where the system is about to be turned on its ear, 5,000 workers have up to now inhabited 10 duchies in a set of buildings alongside the train tracks in suburban Belgrade. One duchy builds engines, another chassis, another transmissions. Maintenance has an independent state, as do the accountants and lawyers. So does the mountain resort run by the workers for their holidays.

"You see, this is rather complex," says Milorad Despotovic, a metalworker sketching out the organization chart on the glass-topped table in the meeting room. But things become a lot more complex when the factory's factions get down to building tractors.

For the moment, each elects a council and sends delegates to a central council. The general manager presents the central council with a budget. The council amends it and sends it to each of the other 10 councils. When all the councils have passed it, the budget goes to a vote of the entire work force. The process is only slightly more involved than amending the U.S. Constitution.

Any one of the 10 councils can veto the budget. Each can veto a project to build a new model or to buy new machinery. And for every variation of every product, each council negotiates a joint-venture deal with all the other councils. Rakovica has 78 of those. The meetings take up 18,000 man-hours a year, when they go smoothly. But they don't always go that way. That is why Rakovica workers strike about twice a year.

Like most strikes in Yugoslavia, the Rakovica walkouts begin when workers in one department find less than expected in their pay envelopes. They put down tools and demand redress. The self-defense committee goes on alert. But this isn't Poland, not yet, and the police usually don't appear. Strikes are neither legal nor illegal. Instead, management herds the strikers into the cafeteria and listens to their speeches. And then, nearly always, it does what they want.

"There is unhappiness with the accounts," Rados Karaklajic says from his seat at the conference table. When a missed delivery of parts cut [sic] engine production, the company cut his pay. He walked out. "It wasn't our fault," he says. "It was the purchasing department."

"Let's speak openly," says Zdrvko Petrovic, a lathe operator. "If there is even a tiny mistake in my pay, I revolt. In an economic crisis, workers lose patience."

They lose patience with the bureaucrats, in and out of Rakovica. The bureaucrats inside make up 45% of the work force, absurdly high by any standard, and take in an ever-fattening wad of blue-collar wages. Those outside, in the spirit of self-management, spend worker's taxes on more pay for themselves, not on more social services for Yugoslavia.

Mostly, though, workers lose patience with workers. They strike less over pay increases than over the way the factory's dwindling income is doled out among competing departments. Settling these fights according to the rules takes longer than workers can bear.

"If a department wants to be stubborn, it goes on forever," says Dragutin Zujovic from the far end of the table.

"Narrow interests become obstacles," Mr. Despotovic says. He used to head the factory's central council and belongs to the Serbian Parliament. He measures his words. "We will never exchange our system for another. But we have found that in a number of cases the system does not work."

And that is why Rakovica Motor Works recently became one of the first factories in Yugoslavia to decide that self-management's basic building block had to go. Soon, departments will be abolished and Rakovica will settle into a new style of self-management—with only one council and one general manager.

Constitutional Amendment. Doing that all over the country will require an amendment to the constitution. Yugoslavs are debating it. Meanwhile, Rakovica's manager intends to manage.

"Start with the fact that we must export," Strahinja Kostic says. "We have to fight our way into these markets. This is pure economics." Under self-management, he explains, a janitor can influence the organization of work. But under the proposed new system, he says, approvingly, "managers make decisions."

He wears a blue pin-stripe suit and a watch with an elegant gold band. The glass-topped conference table in his office accommodates far fewer people than the one in the workers' meeting room.

Says Mr. Kostic: "The crucial issue is this: Wherever the manager is, in Yugoslavia or America, it is up to him to determine all the elements of production strategy and to choose the best people to implement it. We should have done this 10 years ago."

The workers of Rakovica will soon have their productivity measured and the quality of their products monitored. On expensive machinery, they will work double shifts. They will spend drastically fewer hours in meetings. If they work slowly, Mr. Kostic will warn them. Even under the new system, he won't be able to fire them (and they will still be able to fire him), but if he finds that a part is made more cheaply someplace else, he will quit making it here.

Mr. Kovic stabs at a yellow pad with the sharp point of his pencil. "Managers are responsible for the production process," he says. "That is where the workers should not and cannot interfere. The workers' council has accepted this. Now I want results."

Questions

1. What implications does this case have for the topics of this part: (*a*) group dynamics, (*b*) interactive behavior and conflict, (*c*) power and politics, and (*d*) leadership? Give specific examples from the case.

2. One observation is that "self-management gives everyone the capacity to impede and no one the strength to implement." What is meant by this statement, and how could this problem be overcome?

3. Do you think the operation at Rakovica would be more effective under the American system? What techniques and approaches that you studied in this part of the book would be applicable at Rakovica?

Experiential Exercises for Part 4

EXERCISE: Groups and conflict resolution

Goals:
1. To compare individual versus group problem solving and decision making
2. To analyze the dynamics of groups
3. To demonstrate conflict and ways of resolving it

Implementation:
1. Divide any number of people into small groups of four or five.
2. Take about fifteen minutes for individual responses and thirty minutes for group consensus.
3. Each individual and group should have a worksheet. Pencils, a flip chart (newsprint or blackboard), marker pens, or chalk may also be helpful to the groups.

Process:
1. Each individual has fifteen minutes to read the story and answer the eleven questions about the story. Each person may refer to the story as often as needed but may not confer with anyone else. Each person should circle "T" if the answer is clearly true, "F" if the answer is clearly false, and "?" if it isn't clear from the story whether the answer is true or false.
2. After fifteen minutes each small group makes the same decisions using group consensus. No one should change his or her answers on the individual questions. The ground rules for group decisions are:
   a. Group decisions should be made by consensus. It is illegal to vote, trade, average, flip a coin, etc.
   b. No individual group member should give in only to reach agreement.
   c. No individual should argue for his or her own decision. Instead, each person should approach the task using logic and reason.
   d. Every group member should be aware that disagreements may be resolved by facts. Conflict can lead to understanding and creativity if it does not make group members feel threatened or defensive.
3. After thirty minutes of group work, the exercise leader should announce the correct answers. Scoring is based on the number of correct answers out of a possible total of eleven. Individuals are to score their own individual answers, and someone should score the group decision answers. The exercise leader should then call for:
   a. The group-decision score in each group
   b. The average individual score in each group
   c. The highest individual score in each group
4. Responses should be posted on the tally sheet. Note should be taken of those groups in which the group score was (1) higher than the average individual score or (2) higher than the best individual score. Groups should discuss the way in which individual members resolved disagreements and the effect of the ground rules on such behavior. They may consider the obstacles experienced in arriving at consensus agreements and the possible reasons for the difference between individual and group decisions

The story:
A businessman had just turned off the lights in the store when a man appeared and demanded money. The owner opened a cash register. The contents of the

cash register were scooped up, and the man sped away. A member of the police force was notified promptly.

Statements about the story:

1. A man appeared after the owner had turned off his store lights.	T	F	?
2. The robber was a man.	T	F	?
3. A man did not demand money.	T	F	?
4. The man who opened the cash register was the owner.	T	F	?
5. The store owner scooped up the contents of the cash register and ran away.	T	F	?
6. Someone opened a cash register.	T	F	?
7. After the man who demanded the money scooped up the contents of the cash register, he ran away.	T	F	?
8. While the cash register contained money, the story does *not* state *how much.*	T	F	?
9. The robber demanded money of the owner.	T	F	?
10. The story concerns a series of events in which only three persons are referred to: the owner of the store, a man who demanded money, and a member of the police force.	T	F	?
11. The following events in the story are true: someone demanded money, a cash register was opened, its contents were scooped up, and a man dashed out of the store.	T	F	?

Tally Sheet

GROUP NUMBER	GROUP SCORE	AVG. INDIVIDUAL SCORE	BEST INDIVIDUAL SCORE	GROUP SCORE BETTER THAN AVG. INDIV.?	GROUP SCORE BETTER THAN BEST INDIV.?

EXERCISE: Power and politics

Goals:
1. To gain some insights into your own power needs and political orientation
2. To examine some of the reasons people strive for power and what political strategies can be used to attain it

Implementation: *Directions:* Answer each question below with "mostly agree" or "mostly disagree," even if it is difficult for you to decide which alternative best describes your opinion.

	Mostly Agree	Mostly Disagree
1. Only a fool would correct a boss's mistakes.	_____	_____
2. If you have certain confidential information, release it to your advantage.	_____	_____
3. I would be careful not to hire a subordinate with more formal education than myself.	_____	_____
4. If you do a favor, remember to cash in on it.	_____	_____
5. Given the opportunity, I would cultivate friendships with powerful people.	_____	_____
6. I like the idea of saying nice things about a rival in order to get that person transferred from my department.	_____	_____
7. Why not take credit for someone else's work? They would do the same to you.	_____	_____
8. Given the chance, I would offer to help my boss build some shelves for his or her den.	_____	_____
9. I laugh heartily at my boss's jokes, even when they are not funny.	_____	_____
10. I would be sure to attend a company picnic even if I had the chance to do something I enjoyed more that day.	_____	_____
11. If I knew an executive in my company was stealing money, I would use that against him or her in asking for favors.	_____	_____
12. I would first find out my boss's political preferences before discussing politics with him or her.	_____	_____
13. I think using memos to zap somebody for his or her mistakes is a good idea (especially when you want to show that person up).	_____	_____
14. If I wanted something done by a coworker, I would be willing to say "If you don't get this done, our boss might be very unhappy."	_____	_____
15. I would invite my boss to a party at my house, even if I didn't like him or her.	_____	_____
16. When I'm in a position to, I would have lunch with the "right people" at least twice a week.	_____	_____
17. Richard M. Nixon's alleged bugging of the Democratic head-quarters would have been a clever idea if he hadn't been caught.	_____	_____
18. Power for its own sake is one of life's most precious commodities.	_____	_____
19. Having a high school named after you would be an incredible thrill.	_____	_____
20. Reading about job politics is as much fun as reading an adventure story.	_____	_____

Interpretation of scores:

Each statement you check "mostly agree" is worth one point toward your power and political orientation score. If you score 16 or over, it suggests that you have a strong inclination toward playing politics: A high score of this nature would also suggest that you have strong needs for power. Scores of 5 or less would suggest that you are not inclined toward political maneuvering and that you are not strongly power driven.

The customary caution is again in order. This questionnaire is designed primarily to encourage you to introspect about the topic of power and politics. It lacks the scientific validity of a legitimate, controlled test.

Exercise: Leadership questionnaire

Goal: To evaluate oneself in terms of the leadership dimensions of task orientation and people orientation

Implementation:
1. Without prior discussion, fill out the Leadership Questionnaire below. Do *not* read the rest of this until you have completed the test.
2. In order to locate yourself on the Leadership Style Profile Sheet, you will score your own questionnaire on the dimensions of task orientation (T) and people orientation (P).
3. The scoring is as follows:
   a. Circle the item number for items 8, 12, 17, 18, 19, 30, 34, and 35.
   b. Write the number 1 in front of a *circled item number* if you responded S (seldom) or N (never) to that item.
   c. Also write a number 1 in front of *item numbers not circled* if you responded A (always) or F (frequently).
   d. Circle the number 1's which you have written in front of the following items: 3, 5, 8, 10, 15, 18, 19, 22, 24, 26, 28, 30, 32, 34, and 35.
   e. *Count the circled number 1's.* This is your score for the level of your concern for people. Record the score in the blank following the letter P at the end of the questionnaire.
   f. *Count the uncircled number 1's.* This is your score for your concern for the task. Record this number in the blank following the letter T.
4. Next look at the Leadership Style Profile Sheet on p. 502 and follow the directions.

Variations:
1. Participants can predict how they will appear on the profile prior to scoring the questionnaire.
2. Paired participants already acquainted can predict each other's scores. If they are not acquainted, they can discuss their reactions to the questionnaire items to find some bases for this prediction.
3. The leadership styles represented on the profile sheet can be illustrated through role playing. A relevant situation can be set up, and the "leaders" can be coached to demonstrate the styles being studied.
4. Subgroups can be formed of participants similarly situated on the shared leadership scale. These groups can be assigned identical tasks to perform. The work generated can be processed in terms of morale and productivity.

Leadership Questionnaire

Name _____ Group _____

Directions: The following items describe aspects of leadership behavior. Respond to each item according to the way you would most likely act if you were the leader of a work group. Circle whether you would most likely behave in the described way: always (A), frequently (F), occasionally (O), seldom (S), or never (N). Once the test is completed, go back to numbers 2 and 3 under implementation.

A	F	O	S	N	1. I would most likely act as the spokesperson of the group.
A	F	O	S	N	2. I would encourage overtime work.
A	F	O	S	N	3. I would allow members complete freedom in their work.
A	F	O	S	N	4. I would encourage the use of uniform procedures.
A	F	O	S	N	5. I would permit the members to use their own judgment in solving problems.
A	F	O	S	N	6. I would stress being ahead of competing groups.
A	F	O	S	N	7. I would speak as a representative of the group.
A	F	O	S	N	8. I would needle members for greater effort.
A	F	O	S	N	9. I would try out my ideas in the group.
A	F	O	S	N	10. I would let the members do their work the way they think best.
A	F	O	S	N	11. I would be working hard for a promotion.
A	F	O	S	N	12. I would tolerate postponement and uncertainty.
A	F	O	S	N	13. I would speak for the group if there were visitors present.
A	F	O	S	N	14. I would keep the work moving at a rapid pace.
A	F	O	S	N	15. I would turn the members loose on a job and let them go to it.
A	F	O	S	N	16. I would settle conflicts when they occur in the group.
A	F	O	S	N	17. I would get swamped by details.
A	F	O	S	N	18. I would represent the group at outside meetings.
A	F	O	S	N	19. I would be reluctant to allow the members any freedom of action.
A	F	O	S	N	20. I would decide what should be done and how it should be done.
A	F	O	S	N	21. I would push for increased production.
A	F	O	S	N	22. I would let some members have authority which I could keep.
A	F	O	S	N	23. Things would usually turn out as I had predicted.
A	F	O	S	N	24. I would allow the group a high degree of initiative.
A	F	O	S	N	25. I would assign group members to particular tasks.
A	F	O	S	N	26. I would be willing to make changes.
A	F	O	S	N	27. I would ask the members to work harder.
A	F	O	S	N	28. I would trust the group members to exercise good judgment.
A	F	O	S	N	29. I would schedule the work to be done.
A	F	O	S	N	30. I would refuse to explain my actions.
A	F	O	S	N	31. I would persuade others that my ideas are to their advantage.
A	F	O	S	N	32. I would permit the group to set its own pace.
A	F	O	S	N	33. I would urge the group to beat its previous record.
A	F	O	S	N	34. I would act without consulting the group.
A	F	O	S	N	35. I would ask that group members follow standard rules and regulations.

T _____ P _____

T-P Leadership Style Profile Sheet

Name _____   Group _____

Directions: To determine your style of leadership, mark your score on the concern for task dimension (T) on the left-hand arrow below. Next, move to the right-hand arrow and mark your score on the concern for people dimension (P). Draw a straight line that intersects the P and T scores. The point at which that line crosses the shared leadership arrow indicates your score on that dimension.

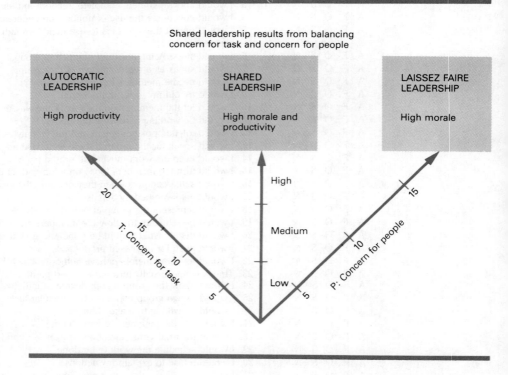

Shared leadership results from balancing concern for task and concern for people

AUTOCRATIC
LEADERSHIP

High productivity

SHARED
LEADERSHIP

High morale and
productivity

LAISSEZ FAIRE
LEADERSHIP

High morale

High

Medium

Low

20

15

10

5

T: Concern for task

15

10

5

P: Concern for people

The Processes and Structure of Organizational Behavior

17 Communication

The space shuttle *Challenger* tragedy (in which a schoolteacher and six astronauts were killed) was an unfortunate example of a breakdown in organizational communication. Head NASA administrators, who made the final decision to launch the shuttle, were not fully informed of the engineers' serious reservations regarding the safety of the shuttle. This lack of upward communication resulted in a national tragedy.

The major obstacle in the communication flow seemed to be at the Marshall Center, one of NASA's organizational units. The communication system itself provided for upward communication. Top administrators were plugged into a communication network that allowed everyone at a console to listen to discussions during the 48-hour countdown. However, the Marshall Center did not pass on the discussion regarding the shuttle's safety because managers felt the decision could be handled appropriately at their level. This is an example of how intermediate organization levels often determine what is actually heard at the top. NASA insiders agree that the safety debate was unprecedented in its intensity and should have been conveyed upward.

The communication breakdown that led to the fatal launch decision was indicative of the problems that besieged the entire space shuttle program. For instance, the shuttle schedule did not include

*Source: Adapted from Michael Brody, "NASA's Challenge: Ending Isolation at the Top," *Fortune*, May 12, 1986, pp. 26–32.

reporting arrangements that would have allowed top administrators to review lower-level decisions. In addition, there was a lack of horizontal communication between the organizational units. Although the Marshall, Kennedy, and Johnson space centers are supposed to work closely together, they operate as virtually independent units.

Several suggestions have been made for improving organizational communication at NASA. Jerome F. Lederer, a former NASA executive, suggests that NASA's safety oversight team should report directly to James C. Fletcher, the new NASA administrator. At present the safety team reports to the headquarters engineering office. Since the safety team oversees decisions made by the engineering office, there is a conflict of interest within this reporting relationship. Former NASA general counsel S. Neil Hosenball suggests that engineers from contractors be present at headquarters so their ideas do not become lost in the bureaucratic channels. NASA budget analyst Richard Cook promotes the development of a computer system that tracks the flow of engineering and production problems.

The communication problems facing NASA are typical of those found in many large organizations, both government and business. The people at the top are often isolated from what is actually going on in the organization. Upward communication channels need to be improved so that top managers receive all the available information for making decisions. It is unfortunate that at NASA the breakdown cost lives instead of profits.

Learning Objectives

- DEFINE the perspective, historical background, and meaning of communication in organizations.
- EXPLAIN the nature of management information systems.
- IDENTIFY the dimensions of nonverbal communication.
- ANALYZE interpersonal communication.
- DISCUSS the downward (supervisor-subordinate), upward (subordinate-initiated), and horizontal (interactive) organizational communication systems.

Communication is one of the most frequently discussed dynamics in the entire field of organizational behavior, but it is seldom clearly understood. In practice, effective communication is a basic prerequisite for the attainment of organizational goals, but it has remained one of the biggest problems facing modern management. Communication is an extremely broad topic and of course is not restricted to the organizational behavior field. Some estimates of the extent of its use go up to about three-fourths of an active human being's life, and even higher proportions of a typical manager's time. A recently completed study that directly observed a wide cross-section of what were called "real managers" in their day-to-day behaviors found that they devote about a third of their activity to routine communication—exchanging routine information and processing paperwork.[1] Importantly, however, the communication activity made the biggest relative contribution to effective managers. Figure 17.1 summarizes these findings.

FIGURE 17.1
Results of the study of real managers.
(*Source:* Fred Luthans, Richard M. Hodgetts, and Stuart A. Rosenkrantz, *Real Managers*, Ballinger, Cambridge, Mass., 1988, pp. 27, 68. Reprinted with permission, copyright 1988, Ballinger Publishing Company.)

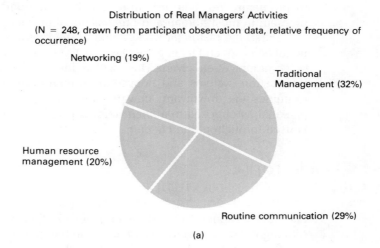

Distribution of Real Managers' Activities

(N = 248, drawn from participant observation data, relative frequency of occurrence)

Networking (19%)

Traditional Management (32%)

Human resource management (20%)

Routine communication (29%)

(a)

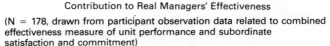

Contribution to Real Managers' Effectiveness

(N = 178, drawn from participant observation data related to combined effectiveness measure of unit performance and subordinate satisfaction and commitment)

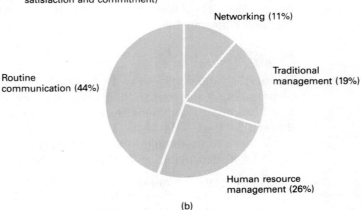

Networking (11%)

Routine communication (44%)

Traditional management (19%)

Human resource management (26%)

(b)

There seems little doubt that communication plays an important role in managerial and organizational effectiveness. Yet, on the other side of the same coin, communication is commonly cited as being at the root of practically all the problems of the world. It is given as the explanation for lovers' quarrels, ethnic prejudice, war between nations, the generation gap, industrial disputes, and organizational conflict. These are only representative of the numerous problems attributed to ineffective communication. Obviously, this thinking can go too far: communication can become a convenient scapegoat or crutch. Not all organization and interpersonal difficulties are the result of communication breakdown. Other matters discussed in this book—motivation, decision making and control, stress, organization structure, to name but a few—can also contribute to problems. Yet it is also true that the communication process is a central problem in most human and organizational activities.

First, the historical background of the role of communication in organizational behavior and management will be briefly discussed, and a precise definition of communication given. Then will come a brief discussion of management information systems and nonverbal communication. The heart of the chapter examines the downward, upward, and interactive communication systems. A personal as opposed to a *linear* information-flow perspective of communication is used throughout the chapter.

Historical Background of the Role of Communication

Early discussions of management gave very little emphasis to communication. Although communication was implicit in the management function of command and the structural principle of hierarchy, the early theorists never fully developed or integrated it into management theory. At the same time, they did generally recognize the role of informal communication in relation to the problem of supplementing the formal, hierarchical channels. But the pioneering management theorist Henri Fayol was about the only one who gave a detailed analysis of, and supplied a meaningful solution to, the problem of communication.

Fayol's Contribution

Figure 17.2 shows how Fayol presented a simplified version of the formal organization. If the formal channels in this organization were strictly followed and F wanted to communicate with P, the communication would have to go through E—D—C—B—A—L—M—N—O—P and back again. In other words, F would have to go through a total of twenty positions. On the other hand, if F could lay a "gangplank" to P, it would, in the words of Fayol,

> . . . allow the two employees F and P to deal at one sitting, and in a few hours, with some question or other which via the scalar chain would pass through twenty transmissions, inconvenience many people, involve masses of paper, lose weeks or months to get to a conclusion less satisfactory generally than the one which could have been obtained via direct contact as between F and P.[2]

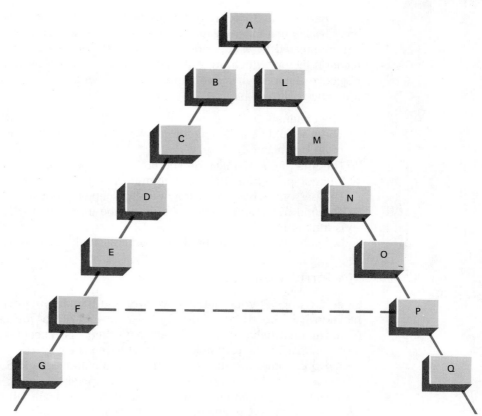

FIGURE 17.2
Fayol's gangplank
concept.
(*Source:* Henri Fayol,
*General and Indus-
trial Management,*
trans. by Constance
Storrs, Pitman, Lon-
don, 1949, p. 34.)

This gangplank concept has direct implications for horizontal communication systems in modern formal organizations. Unfortunately, such classical insights were few and far between.

Barnard's Contribution

It largely was Chester Barnard in the late 1930s who meaningfully developed communication as a vital dynamic of organizational behavior. He was convinced that communication is the major shaping force in the organization. He ranked it with common purpose and willingness to serve as one of the three primary elements of the organization. To him, communication both makes the organization cooperative system dynamic and links the organization purpose to the human participants. Communication techniques, which he considered to be written and oral language, were deemed not only to be necessary to attain organization purpose but also to be a potential problem area for the organization. In Barnard's words, "The absence of a suitable technique of communication would eliminate the possibility of adopting some purposes as a basis of organization. Communication technique shapes the form and the internal economy of organization."[3]

Barnard also interwove communication into his concept of authority. He emphasized that meaning and understanding must occur before authority can be communicated from superior to subordinate. He listed seven specific communication factors which are especially important in establishing and maintaining objective authority in an organization. He believed them to be, in brief, the following:

1. The channels of communication should be definitely known.
2. There should be a definite formal channel of communication to every member of an organization.
3. The line of communication should be as direct and short as possible.
4. The complete formal line of communication should normally be used.
5. The persons serving as communication centers should be competent.
6. The line of communication should not be interrupted while the organization is functioning.
7. Every communication should be authenticated.[4]

Modern Perspective

Since the original contributions by Fayol and Barnard, the dynamics of communication have been one of the central concerns, if not *the* central concern, of organizational behavior and management theorists. Except in the principles of those management textbooks which still rely heavily on a classical process framework, communication is given major attention. In addition, there has been a deluge of books and articles which deal specifically with interpersonal and organizational communication. Unfortunately, practically all this vast literature gives only a surface treatment of the subject and is seldom based upon systematic research findings. For example, there have been complaints about an uncritical acceptance of the effectiveness of open communication, when a contingency perspective would be more in line with the evidence.[5]

One recent exception was the Real Managers study, which combined direct observation of managers in their natural setting with self-report measures to try to determine how they communicated.[6] The model shown in Figure 17.3 gives the results. The first dimension of the managerial communication model represents a continuum ranging from the Humanistic Interactor (who frequently interacts both up and down the organization hierarchy and exhibits human-oriented activities) to the Mechanistic Isolate (who communicates very little, except on a formal basis). The other dimension describes a continuum from the Informal Developer (who communicates spontaneously in all directions and exhibits activities related to developing his or her people) to Formal Controller (who uses formally scheduled communication interaction and exhibits monitoring/controlling activities).[7] This empirically derived model describes two major dimensions of managerial communication. It provides a framework for *how* managers communicate on a day-to-day basis and can be used as a point of departure for formally defining communication and the processes and systems of communication in today's organizations.

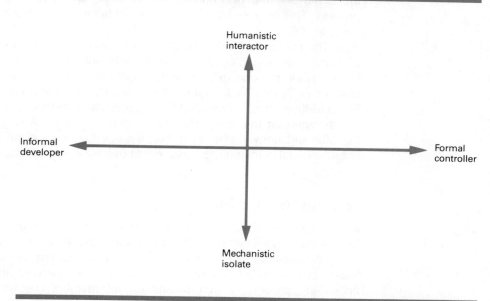

FIGURE 17.3
Managerial communication model: How real managers communicate. (*Source:* Adapted from Fred Luthans and Janet K. Larsen, "How Managers Really Communicate," *Human Relations,* vol. 39, no. 2, 1986, p. 175.)

The Definition of Communication

The term *communication* is freely used by everyone in modern society, including members of the general public, organizational behavior scholars, and management practitioners. In addition, as noted earlier, the term is employed to explain a multitude of sins both in the society as a whole and in work organizations. Despite this widespread usage, very few members of the general public and not a great many more management people can precisely define the term. Part of the problem is that communication experts have not agreed upon a definition themselves.

Most definitions of "communication" used in organizational behavior literature stress the use of symbols to transfer the meaning of information. Seemingly of more importance, however, is the fact that communication is a personal process that involves the exchange of behaviors. The personal aspects have been noted in no uncertain terms by most organizational behavior scholars. For example, Ivancevich and Matteson recently noted that "communication among people does not depend on technology, but rather on forces in people and their surroundings. It is a 'process' that occurs 'within' people."[8]

In addition to its being a personal process, a communication expert emphasizes the *behavioral* implications of communication by pointing out that "the only means by which one person can influence another is by the behaviors he performs—that is, the communicative exchanges between people provide the sole method by which influence or effects can be achieved."[9] In other words, the behaviors that occur in an organization are vital to the communication process. This personal and behavioral exchange view of communication takes many forms.

The continuum in Figure 17.4 can be used to identify the major categories of communication that are especially relevant to the study of organizational behavior. On the one extreme is the computer-based management information systems (MIS) approach, and on the other extreme is nonverbal communication. The middle ground is occupied by organizational and interpersonal approaches, which represent the perspective taken in this chapter. A very brief overview of the MIS and nonverbal approaches is necessary to put the discussion of the organizational and interpersonal communication approaches into proper perspective.

Management Information Systems

Management information systems, or MIS, are becoming increasingly important in modern organizations. Although information systems do not have to be computerized, normally they are. With the common use of personal computers today, almost all information processing is done by computers. MIS involves generating, processing, and transmitting information. The system itself involves not only computer hardware and software but also data and people—both MIS personnel and users.

Although MIS is usually associated with integrated networks of information that support management decision making,[10] MIS can also be used for strategic planning (for example, American Hospital Supply used MIS to change the perspective and direction of the company) and for communication per se. The next chapter, on decision making, will devote attention to how computerized systems, especially artificial intelligence and expert systems, can support decision making, but for now it can be said that MIS can be used as part of the interpersonal and organizational communication systems. For example, managers can get on the system to ask others for information about solving problems or can use the system to monitor the literature on particular technological developments. Because of the information explosion now occurring in all organizations, the systematic management of this information is becoming increasingly vital to effective communication.

Nonverbal Communication

The opposite end of the computer-based management information systems approach to communication is nonverbal communication. Although verbal communication has long been recognized as being important, nonverbal com-

FIGURE 17.4 The continuum of communication in organizational behavior.

| Management information systems (MIS) | The organizational communication process | Interpersonal communication | Nonverbal communication |

munication has only recently been given attention in the study of communication. Sometimes called the "silent language," *nonverbal communication* can be defined as "nonword human responses (such as gestures, facial expressions) *and* the perceived characteristics of the environment through which the human verbal and nonverbal messages are transmitted."[11] Thus, whether a person says something or, equally important, does *not* say anything, communication still can take place.

There are many forms of nonverbal communication. Probably the most widely recognized is body language. Body movements convey meanings and messages. This includes facial expressions and what people do with their eyes, feet, hands, and posture. For example, good salespeople, advertisers, and even poker players capitalize on their knowledge of people's eyes. As explained by Preston:

> . . . when an individual is excited or aroused, the pupils of the eyes will dilate. When haggling over a price, a buyer will unconsciously signal an alert seller that a particular price is acceptable. . . . Some colors or shapes cause more excitement than others, and the reaction registers in the shopper's eyes. With this research information, marketing people redesign their products to better appeal to buyers in a competitive environment. Good poker players watch the eyes of their fellow players as new cards are dealt. The pupil dilation very often will show if the card being dealt improves the player's hand.[12]

Besides the obvious meanings attached to things such as a firm handshake or touching the other person when making an important point, at least one communication expert believes that what the person does with the lower limbs is the key to body language. He explains:

> That is where the tension and anxiety show. The person may claim to be relaxed, yet the legs are crossed tightly, and one foot thrusts so rigidly in the air that it appears to be on the verge of breaking off. *Insight:* People concentrate on hiding their tension from the waist up. Their real state is revealed in their legs and feet.[13]

Even a person's clothing can become important in body language. For example, in his best-selling book *Dress for Success,* John Molloy points out: "The most authoritative pattern is the pinstripe, followed in descending order by the solid, the chalk stripe and the plaid. If you need to be more authoritative, stick with dark pinstripes."[14] In addition to dress, physical appearance in general seems important. From her research with clients, one consultant concluded that physical attractiveness is "the single most important quality in determining your success at every stage in your life. People who are attractive are judged to be nicer people, more intelligent, more capable, more desirable mates and better employees."[15]

Besides the truly silent dimensions of nonverbal communication such as body language, time (for example, being late or early), or space (for example, how close one gets during a conversation or seating arrangements in a committee meeting), there are also *ways* in which people verbalize that are an important dimension of nonverbal communication. Sometimes called *paralanguage,* these include things such as voice quality, volume, speech rate, pitch, nonfluencies (saying "ah," "um," or "uh"), laughing, and yawning.[16] Also, *who* says a word (for example, whether the boss or a coworker asks for "volunteers") and in what *environmental context* it is said (for example, in the boss's office or out on the golf course) make a difference.

Cultural differences can also play an important role. The following are a few guidelines affecting communication in foreign cultures: expect more physical closeness in Latin American; the use of "thumbs up" is fine almost anywhere except Australia; and take your hands out of your pockets when meeting a Japanese person. The accompanying International Application Example gives

International Application Example

Nonverbal and Verbal Communication

One of the best ways of coping with foreign cultures and customs is to be careful in the use of both verbal and nonverbal communication. This means saying and doing the right things and, perhaps even more important, not saying or doing wrong things. Here are some guidelines that American managers are finding useful in treading their way through the intercultural maze of foreign countries.

1. In Europe, act as if you are calling on a rich old aunt. Dress well, do not chew gum, do not smoke without first seeking permission, do not use first names unless invited to do so by the other party, be punctual to meetings, and, if you are unsure of the proper dress, err on the side of conservatism.
2. When in France, speak English to your hosts. They know how to speak English and typically are appalled at the performance of foreigners trying to communicate in their tongue. Stick to the language you know best. Also, be on time for all engagements. The French are sticklers for promptness.
3. Remember that the Germans differ from the French in a number of ways. One of these is that they are even bigger sticklers for promptness. Also, remember that gentlemen walk and sit to the left of all ladies and men of senior business rank. Do not get on the wrong side.
4. In Britain, social events are not used for discussing business. This is left at the office. Also, remember that the British religiously keep engagement calendars, so if you are inviting some people to lunch or dinner, send your invitation well in advance or you are likely to find that date already filled in your prospective guest's calendar. If you are attending a formal dinner, it is common to toast Her Majesty's health after the main course. This is the signal that you may now smoke. Do not light up prior to this time. Also, remember that while promptness is valued, if you are invited to dinner at 8 P.M., you may show up five or ten minutes late, but it is not good manners to show up early.
5. In Italy, it is common to shake hands with everyone. However, do not expect them to remember your name. No one does on the first introduction. Also, get in the habit of calling people by their title. For example, university graduates often prefer to be addressed as such, and there are different titles depending on the individual's field of study.
6. In Spain, punctuality is taken seriously only when attending a bullfight. Most offices and shops close for siesta from 1:30 P.M. to 4:30 P.M., and restaurants do not usually reopen until after 9 P.M. or get into full swing before 11 P.M.. An early dinner in Spain often ends around midnight; a late dinner goes into the wee hours of the morning. If you are invited to dinner and are unaccustomed to late hours, take an afternoon nap. You are going to need it if you hope to last through dessert.

some further guidelines for both nonverbal and verbal communication in foreign cultures. Overall, nonverbal dimensions are extremely important to interpersonal and organizational communication and must be given as much recognition as the more technical transmissions from information systems.

Organizational and Interpersonal Communication

The organizational and interpersonal approaches to communication represent the middle ground between management information systems on the one extreme and nonverbal communication on the other. Traditionally, the organization structure was viewed as a network over which there were linear information flows. Especially in classical organization structures, communication consisted simply of the following:

1. Instructions and commands to do or not to do something are always communicated down the chain of command, and only from one person to others directly below that person in the hierarchy.
2. Reports, inquiries, and requests are always communicated up the chain of command, and only to the one person directly above the communicator in the hierarchy.
3. Subgroups do not communicate directly with other subgroups at their level on the chart, but instead communicate up the chain of command until the message arrives at an office where both subgroups share a supervisor, and then down the chain of command to the recipient subgroup.
4. The staff plays the role of communication gadfly; that is, it is given free rein to collect and disseminate nonauthoritative information in its role as an extension of the boss.[17]

Interpersonal Communication

In interpersonal communication, the major emphasis is on transferring information from one person to another. Communication is looked upon as a basic method of effecting behavioral change, and it incorporates the psychological processes (perception, learning, and motivation), on the one hand, and language, on the other. Listening sensitivity and nonverbal communications are also closely associated with this approach. For example, Bill Marriott, Jr., the CEO of the hotel chain, spends nearly half his time listening and talking to front-line employees. Importantly, he listens and then talks to his people.[18]

The Importance of Feedback

The often posed philosophical question that asks, "Is there a noise in the forest if a tree crashes to the ground but no one is there to hear it?" demonstrates some of the important aspects of interpersonal communication.[19] From a communications perspective, the answer is "no." There are sound waves but no noise because no one perceives it. There must be both a sender and a receiver in order for interpersonal communication to take place. The sender is obviously

TABLE 17.1 Characteristics of Feedback for Effective and Ineffective Interpersonal Communication in Human Resources Management

Effective Feedback	Ineffective Feedback
1. Intended to help the employee	1. Intended to belittle the employee
2. Specific	2. General
3. Descriptive	3. Evaluative
4. Useful	4. Inappropriate
5. Timely	5. Untimely
6. Employee readiness for feedback	6. Makes the employee defensive
7. Clear	7. Not understandable
8. Valid	8. Inaccurate

Source: Fred Luthans and Mark J. Martinko, *The Practice of Supervision and Management,* McGraw-Hill, New York, 1979, p. 183.

important to communication, but so is the neglected receiver who gives feedback to the sender.

The importance of feedback cannot be overemphasized because effective interpersonal communication is highly dependent on it. Proper follow-up and feedback requires establishing an informal and formal mechanism by which the sender can check on how the message was actually interpreted. Feedback makes communication a two-way process.[20]

Table 17.1 summarizes some characteristics of effective and ineffective feedback for employee performance. The following list explains these characteristics in more detail:

1. *Intention.* Effective feedback is directed toward improving job performance and making the employee a more valuable asset. It is not a personal attack and should not compromise the individual's feeling of self-worth or image. Rather, effective feedback is directed toward aspects of the job.
2. *Specificity.* Effective feedback is designed to provide recipients with specific information so that they know what must be done to correct the situation. Ineffective feedback is general and leaves questions in the recipients' minds. For example, telling an employee that he or she is doing a poor job is too general and will leave the recipient frustrated in seeking ways to correct the problem.
3. *Description.* Effective feedback can also be characterized as descriptive rather than evaluative. It tells the employee what he or she has done in objective terms, rather than presenting a value judgment.
4. *Usefulness.* Effective feedback is information that an employee can use to improve performance. It serves no purpose to berate employees for their lack of skill if they do not have the ability or training to perform properly. Thus, the guideline is that if it is not something the employee can correct, it is not worth mentioning.
5. *Timeliness.* There are also considerations in timing feedback properly. As a rule, the more immediate the feedback, the better. This way the employee has a better chance of knowing what the supervisor is talking about and can take corrective action.

6. *Readiness.* In order for feedback to be effective, employees must be ready to receive it. When feedback is imposed or forced upon employees, it is much less effective.
7. *Clarity.* Effective feedback must be clearly understood by the recipient. A good way of checking this is to ask the recipient to restate the major points of the discussion. Also, supervisors can observe nonverbal facial expressions as indicators of understanding and acceptance.
8. *Validity.* In order for feedback to be effective, it must be reliable and valid. Of course, when the information is incorrect, the employee will feel that the supervisor is unnecessarily biased, or the employee may take corrective action which is inappropriate and only compounds the problem.[21]

Other Important Variables in Interpersonal Communication

Besides feedback, other variables, such as trust, expectations, values, status, and compatibility, greatly influence the interpersonal aspects of communication. If the subordinate does not trust the boss, there will be ineffective communication. The same is true of the other variables mentioned. People perceive only what they expect to perceive; the unexpected may not be perceived at all. The growing generation gap can play havoc with interpersonal communication; so can status differentials and incompatibilities of any sort. Giving attention to, and doing something about, these interpersonal variables can spell the difference between effective and ineffective communication.

Interpersonal communication plays a central role in the organizational communication process and is directly relevant to the study of organizational behavior. It is given further attention in this chapter in terms of upward and downward communication and interactive communication.

Superior-Subordinate Communication

Traditionally, one of the dominant themes of organizational communication has been the so-called "downward" system. However, when a personal perspective replaces a linear information flow perspective, the downward system is more accurately portrayed as superior-subordinate communication. There are interpersonal linkages, not just information flows, in the downward system.

The Purposes and Methods of Downward Communication

Katz and Kahn have identified five general purposes of superior-subordinate communication in an organization:

1. To give specific task directives about job instructions
2. To give information about organizational procedures and practices
3. To provide information about the rationale of the job
4. To tell subordinates about their performance
5. To provide ideological information to facilitate the indoctrination of goals[22]

In the past, most organizations have concentrated on and accomplished only the first two of these purposes; to a large extent, this is still the case today. In general, superior-subordinate communication on job performance and the rationale-ideological aspects of jobs have been neglected.

A communication system that gives only specific directives about job instructions and procedures and fails to provide information about job performance or rationale-ideological information about the job has a negative organizational impact. This type of downward orientation promotes an authoritative atmosphere which tends to inhibit the effectiveness of the upward and horizontal systems of communication. Communicating the rationale for the job, the ideological relation of the job to the goals of the organization, and information about job performance to employees can, if properly handled, greatly benefit the organization. As Katz and Kahn point out: "If people know the reasons for their assignment, this will often insure their carrying out the job more effectively; and if they have an understanding of what their job is about in relation to their subsystem, they are more likely to identify with organizational goals."[23] This does not imply that management should tell assembly line workers that their jobs are extremely important to the success of the company—that the company would fold unless they put on a bolt right or welded a fender properly. Obviously, this type of communication can backfire. The workers would justifiably reason: "Who are they trying to kid? My job isn't *that* important. It is just another hypocritical con job by management." What is meant is that providing *full* information about the job, its ramifications for the rest of the organization, and the quality of the employee's performance in it should be an important function of superior-subordinate communication.

Media Used for Downward Communication

Traditional downward communication systems rely on many types of media to disseminate information. Some examples of written media are organizational handbooks, manuals, magazines, newspapers, and letters sent to the home or distributed on the job; bulletin-board items, posters, and information displays; and standard reports, descriptions of procedures, and memos. For example, United Airlines has a daily *Employee Newsline* and a monthly employee newspaper. Of particular interest, however, is its biweekly *Supervisors' Hotlines*, which both informs supervisors and encourages them to communicate accurate information in the *Hotline* to those who report to them.[24]

Examples of oral media utilized in the system include direct verbal orders or instructions from superiors, speeches, meetings, closed-circuit television sets, public address systems, and telephones. Arthur Morrissette, president and founder of Interstate Van Lines in Springfield, Virginia, has key managers address their employees every morning and every couple of weeks; he even has a sing-along where employees belt out the lyrics to the company anthem.[25] In addition, of course, computerized information systems have become the major contributor to the downward flow of communication in most organizations.

The numerous types of media give an indication of the avalanche of information that is descending on personnel from the downward system. An example would be the manager of a metal-fabricating division of a large firm:

> He received six hundred pages of computer printout each day detailing the output of each production line, the location of various materials, and other indexes of the operation. He said that it would take him approximately three full days to simplify the information into usable form. Instead, he found an empty storage room, stacked the printouts there, and subcontracted with a trash removal firm to remove the printouts, untouched, once a month.[26]

Unfortunately, this is not an extreme example. The author observed that in the basement of one large organization, the trash bin used for miscellaneous throwaway items was always neatly stacked and never full. However, next to it was a bin marked for discarded computer printout paper that was always overflowing into the aisle and was stacked dangerously high, literally threatening to become a dangerous avalanche at any time.

Ways to Improve Downward Communication

Quality of information has often been sacrificed for quantity. Some organizations have tried to solve their downward communication problems by the management information systems discussed earlier. For example, the New York Transit Authority has an information system whereby if one of its buses breaks down, six months of service records are immediately available on a computer monitor at the service depot.[27] This new MIS approach helps solve some of the information overload problem of the downward system. In addition, a research study found that although decision makers who perceive information overload may be more satisfied than those who perceive information underload, they may not perform as well.[28]

To improve the effectiveness of superior-subordinate communication, more attention must be given to the receiver and to the use of multimedia techniques. Most studies show that combined oral and written methods are most effective and that oral methods only are better than written methods only.

Even written communication can be much improved. The accompanying Application Example indicates that this problem of written communication extends to the popular business literature as well.

The biggest problem, however, is ignoring the importance of the receiver. This problem, of course, is symptomatic of taking a linear (in this case, downward) information flow perspective, as opposed to a personal perspective. After an extensive review of the literature, one communications researcher concluded that the downward flow of information can affect receivers in the following ways:

1. People's interpretations of communications follow the path of least resistance.
2. People are more open to messages which are consonant with their existing image, their beliefs, and their values.
3. Messages which are incongruent with values tend to engender more resistance than messages which are incongruent with rational logic.
4. To the extent that people positively value need fulfillment, messages which

Application Example

Communicating with the *HBR* Readers*

The *Harvard Business Review* (*HBR*) is widely read by business managers. Current circulation is around 200,000, and the magazine can often be found on the desk or the coffee table in executive suites across the country. Unfortunately, in recent years the *HBR* has been facing declining circulation, and some businesspeople are beginning to feel that the journal is not really worth their time.

What has caused this problem? The answer may be that the *HBR* fails to communicate relevant information and ideas to today's managers. Specifically, the *HBR* is regarded by some managers as lacking in practicality and too difficult to read. One manager, when asked how the journal could be improved, replied, "Get rid of the calculus." Upon searching through back issues of the magazine, the editor found that there had been no mathematical equations of any kind in articles over the past six years. Quite obviously the critic meant that the magazine was too difficult to read, not that it had too much math.

In an effort to maintain a strong link with the business community and to bolster its flagship publication, the Harvard Business School has been making some major changes in the journal. One has been to reduce the number of articles by academics and to start bringing in well-known business and political contributors. The journal even managed to get Mikhail Gorbachev to agree to submit an article on U.S.-Soviet trade. Another development has been the addition of brief story summaries so that busy executives do not have to read the entire article to get the gist of the message. A third is a reduction of approximately 25 percent in the length of the average article, thus making it easier to read. A fourth is the use of cartoons.

Will these changes make the *HBR* more interesting reading? Theodore Levitt, the new editor, certainly thinks so, and he plans still other changes to liven up the magazine and increase its relevancy to the business community. The jury of practicing managers is still out, but one thing is certain. In this era of information overload, managers do not have time to wade through volumes of material in an effort to find useful information. Journals have to make their data easily available if they hope to maintain readership. For years the Harvard Business School has taught the importance of communication. The success of the *HBR* will show how well the institution understands its own message.

*****Source:** Adapted from Alex Beam, "Dusting Off the *Harvard Business Review*," *Business Week*, Dec. 15, 1986, p. 58.

facilitate need fulfillment are more easily accepted than messages which do not.
5. As people see the environment changing, they are more open to incoming messages.
6. The total situation affects communication; a message interpreted as congruent in one situation may be interpreted as incongruent in another.[29]

If managers understand these impacts of communication on subordinates and do something about them, communication can become more effective. There is a series of studies indicating that if subordinates do get needed information (that is, if superior-subordinate communication is effective), they perform better as individuals and in groups.[30]

Telecommunication Technology

Paralleling the development of computerized MIS has been that of telecommunications, which has had a tremendous impact on downward communication. The major new techniques to assist downward communication include electronic mail, voice messaging, and electronic bulletin boards.

Cheaper then long-distance telephoning and faster than a regular letter or memo, electronic mail uses electronic circuitry to transmit written messages via computer terminals instantaneously to other people within the organization or to other organizations around the world.[31] In voice messaging, the computer acts as a sophisticated answering machine. The computer answers the phone, relays memos, gives out information, and takes messages.[32] Electronic bulletin boards also use computers to communicate routine information or can be used to reduce paperwork and filing by storing policy manuals, job descriptions, telephone directory listings, and other documents to which managers and employees can gain access.[33] For example, at Ford Motor Credit Company, employees can use the computer terminals at their desks to catch up on job postings and bulletin board announcements.[34]

Subordinate-Initiated Communication

Just as the downward system becomes superior-subordinate communication from a dynamic, interpersonal perspective, the upward system becomes subordinate-initiated communication in the personal view. In the traditional view, the classical organization structure formally provided for vertical information flows, downward and upward. However, in practice, except for feedback controls, the downward system completely dominated the upward system. Whereas the downward system is highly directive—giving orders, instructions, information, and procedures—the upward system is characteristically nondirective in nature. While bureaucratic authority facilitates a directive atmosphere, a free, participative supervisory approach is necessary for subordinate-initiated communication. Traditionally, bureaucratic authority has prevailed over the more participative styles, with the result that subordinate-initiated communication has often been outwardly stifled, badly misused, or conveniently ignored by management.

Methods of Improving the Effectiveness of Upward Communication

The hierarchical structure is about the only formal method that the classical approach used to communicate upward, and, as has been pointed out, in practice this has not worked out well. Other techniques and channels for subordinate-initiated communication are necessary. The following are some possible ways to promote more effective subordinate-superior communications:

1. *The grievance procedure.* Provided for in most collective bargaining agreements, the grievance procedure allows employees to make an appeal upward beyond their immediate superior. It protects individuals from arbitrary action

by their direct superior and encourages communication about complaints. A growing number of companies, such as Federal Express, General Electric, and Borg-Warner, have been instituting peer-review boards to resolve grievances.[35] These boards mostly consist of three peers (those on the same level or below) and two management representatives, and their decisions are binding on both parties.

2. *The open-door policy.* Taken literally, this means that the superior's door is always open to subordinates. It is a continuous invitation for subordinates to come in and talk about anything that is troubling them. Unfortunately, in practice the open-door policy is more fiction than fact. The boss may slap the subordinate on the back and say, "My door is always open to you," but in many cases both the subordinate and the boss know the door is really closed. It is a case where the adage "actions speak louder than words" applies.

3. *Counseling, attitude questionnaires, and exit interviews.* The personnel department can greatly facilitate subordinate-initiated communication by conducting nondirective, confidential counseling sessions; periodically administering attitude questionnaires; and holding meaningful exit interviews for those who leave the organization. Much valuable information can be gained from these forms of communication.

4. *Participative techniques.* Participative decision techniques can generate a great deal of communication. This may be accomplished by either informal involvement of subordinates or formal participation programs such as the use of junior boards, union-management committees, suggestion boxes, and quality circles. There is also empirical research evidence indicating that participants in communication networks are generally more satisfied with their jobs, are more committed to their organizations, and are better performers than those who are not involved in the communication process.[36]

5. *The ombudsperson.* A largely untried but potentially significant technique to enable management to obtain more subordinate-initiated communication is the use of an ombudsperson. The concept has been used primarily in Scandinavia to provide an outlet for persons who have been treated unfairly or in a depersonalized manner by large, bureaucratic government. It has more recently gained popularity in American state governments, military posts, and universities. Although it is just being introduced in a few business organizations, if set up and handled properly, it may work where the open-door policy has failed. As business organizations become larger and more depersonalized, the ombudsperson may fill an important void that exists under these conditions.

Perhaps the best and simplest way to improve upward communication is for managers to develop good listening habits and systems for listening. For example, the top managers of a Canadian forest products company felt they were great communicators until an employee survey revealed differently. Here is what they did to solve the problem:

> The two owners undertook a series of thirty dinners in the course of the next year. Ten employees and their spouses, eventually including everyone at the mill, went to dinner with their bosses. After the meal, there was a sociable and often long and intense question-and-answer session. "We all wanted to be listened to," says the

president. "By the end of the evening, I'd often see a remarkable change in attitude on the part of even the crustiest of the union guys."[37]

Types of Information for Upward Communication

Overall, subordinates can supply basically two types of information: (1) personal information about ideas, attitudes, and performance and (2) more technical feedback information about performance, a vital factor for the control of any organization. The personal information is generally derived from what subordinates tell their superiors. Some examples of such information are:

1. What the persons have done
2. What those under them have done
3. What their peers have done
4. What they think needs to be done
5. What their problems are
6. What the problems of the unit are
7. What matters of organizational practice and policy need to be reviewed[38]

The other type of upward information, feedback for control purposes, is necessary if the organization is to survive. As has been pointed out, "Decision centers utilize information feedback to appraise the results of the organization's performance and to make any adjustments to insure the accomplishment of the purposes of the organization.[39] The role that feedback communication plays has already been stressed earlier in the chapter. Its role in the control process is covered in Chapter 18.

Interactive Communication in Organizations

The classical hierarchical organization structure gives formal recognition only to vertical communication. Nevertheless, most of the classical theorists saw the need to supplement the vertical with some form of horizontal system, as Fayol did with his gangplank concept. Horizontal communication is required to make a coordinated effort in achieving organizational goals. The horizontal requirement becomes more apparent as the organization becomes larger, more complex, and more subject to dramatic change. The modern organization designs that will be discussed in Chapter 19, the project and matrix, recognize this need by formally incorporating horizontal flows into the structure. However, as with vertical (downward and upward) flows in the organization structure, the real key to horizontal communication is found in people and behaviors. Because of the dynamic, interpersonal aspects of communication, the *interactive* form seems more appropriate than the *horizontal* form. The horizontal flows of information (even in a matrix structure) are only part of the communication process that takes place across an organization.

The Extent and Implications of Interactive Communication

Most management writers today stress the important but overlooked role that interactive communication plays in organizations. In most cases the vertical communication process overshadows the horizontal. For example, the recent study of "real managers" reported at the beginning of the chapter found that approximately 100 interactions per week reportedly occurred between managers and their subordinates (both to them and from them). "While there was far more communication downward (between managers and their subordinates) than upward (between managers and their superiors), there were no specific differences determined by initiation of interaction."[40] The horizontal communication in this study was mainly represented by the networking activity (socializing/politicking and interacting with outsiders) that was shown to be related to successful managers (those promoted relatively fast) more than any other activity.[41] Other studies have also found a relationship, although complex, between communication activities and leadership.[42]

Just as in other aspects of organizational communication, there are many behavioral implications contained in the interactive process. Communication with peers, that is, with persons of relatively equal status on the same level of an organization, provides needed social support for an individual. People can more comfortably turn to a peer for social support than they can to those above or below them. The result can be good or bad for the organization. If the support is couched in terms of task coordination to achieve overall goals, interactive communication can be good for the organization. On the other hand, "if there are no problems of task coordination left to a group of peers, the content of their communication can take forms which are irrelevant to or destructive of organizational functioning."[43] In addition, interactive communication among peers may be at the sacrifice of vertical communication. Persons at each level, giving social support to one another, may freely communicate among themselves but fail to communicate upward or downward. In fact, in the study of "real managers," Figure 17.1 showed that networking had the least relative relationship with effective managers (those with satisfied and committed subordinates and high-performing units), but routine communication activities (exchanging information and processing paperwork) had the highest.[44]

The Purposes and Methods of Interactive Communication

Just as there are several purposes of vertical communication in an organization, there are also various reasons for the need for interactive communication. Basing his inquiry on several research studies, a communications scholar has summarized four of the most important purposes of interactive communication:

1. *Task coordination.* The department heads may meet monthly to discuss how each department is contributing to the system's goals.
2. *Problem solving.* The members of a department may assemble to discuss how

they will handle a threatened budget cut; they may employ brainstorming techniques.

3. *Information sharing.* The members of one department may meet with the members of another department to give them some new data.

4. *Conflict resolution.* The members of one department may meet to discuss a conflict inherent in the department or between departments.[45]

The examples for each of the major purposes of interactive communication are mainly departmental or interdepartmental meetings. Such meetings and the system of committees that exist in most organizations have been the major methods of interactive communication. In addition, most organizations' procedures require written reports to be distributed across departments. The quantity, quality, and human implications discussed in relation to the vertical communication process are also inherent in the traditional methods of interactive communication.

Also like downward communication, telecommunication technology via computers and television has had a recent impact on interactive communication in organizations. Via their computer terminals, members of an organization at the same location or dispersed throughout the world can communicate with one another. For example, to stimulate sharing ideas and technological developments among its engineers, Hewlett-Packard has about sixty computer conferences running simultaneously.[46] Live television hookups can also be used to hold meetings with participants at various geographical locations. This is less costly and time-consuming than bringing everyone into one location and, because it is face-to-face, improves communication over traditional telephone conferencing.

Because of the failure of the classical structures to meet the needs of interactive communication, the informal organization and groups have filled the void. Informal contacts with others on the same level are a primary means of interactive communication. Chapter 13 explored some of the dynamics of informal group communication.

Summary

At every level of modern society, communication is a problem. One of the problems when applied to organizations has been the failure to recognize that communications involves more than just linear information flows; it is a dynamic, interpersonal process that involves behavior exchanges. Knowledge of both management information systems and nonverbal approaches is a necessary background for understanding interpersonal and organizational communication.

The contemporary view is that communication is a dynamic, personal process. The three major dimensions of communication from this perspective are superior-subordinate, subordinate-initiated, and interactive processes. Each has varied purposes and methods. The downward system is generally adequate in the superior-subordinate process, but better techniques are needed to improve the upward and horizontal systems. All three processes in organizations can greatly benefit from increased attention given to the dynamic, interpersonal aspects of communication.

Questions for Discussion and Review

1. Explain Fayol's "gangplank" concept. What are some of its advantages and disadvantages?
2. Compare and contrast the management information systems and the nonverbal approaches to communication.
3. Why is feedback so important to communication? What are some guidelines for the effective use of feedback?
4. What are some of the major purposes and methods of supervisor-subordinate communication?
5. What are some techniques for improving subordinate-initiated communication?
6. What are the major purposes and methods of interactive communication?

References

1. Fred Luthans, Richard M. Hodgetts, and Stuart A. Rosenkrantz, *Real Managers*, Ballinger, Cambridge, Mass., 1988, p. 27 and chap. 6.
2. Henri Fayol, *General and Industrial Management* (trans. by Constance Storrs), Pitman, London, 1949, p. 35.
3. Chester I. Barnard, *The Functions of the Executive*, Harvard University Press, Cambridge, Mass., 1938, p. 90.
4. Ibid., pp. 175–181.
5. Eric M. Eisenberg and Marsha G. Witten, "Reconsidering Openness in Organizational Communication," *Academy of Management Review*, July 1987, pp. 418–426.
6. Fred Luthans and Janet K. Larsen, "How Managers Really Communicate," *Human Relations*, vol. 39, no. 2, 1986, pp. 161–178.
7. Ibid.
8. John M. Ivancevich and Michael T. Matteson, *Organizational Behavior and Management*, Business Publications, Plano, Tex., 1987, p. 631.
9. Aubrey Fisher, *Small Group Decision Making*, McGraw-Hill, New York, 1974, p. 23.
10. David H. Holt, *Management*, Prentice-Hall, Englewood Cliffs, N.J., 1987, p. 55.
11. Don Hellriegel, John W. Slocum, Jr., and Richard W. Woodman, *Organizational Behavior*, 4th ed., West, St. Paul, Minn., 1986, p. 221.
12. Paul Preston, *Communication for Managers*, Prentice-Hall, Englewood Cliffs, N.J., 1979, p. 161.
13. Martin G. Groder, "Incongruous Behavior: How to Read the Signals," *Bottom Line*, Mar. 30, 1983, p. 13.
14. John T. Molloy, *Dress for Success*, Warner Books, New York, 1975, p. 46.
15. V. Hale Starr, quoted in "Expert: Non-Verbal Body Language Counts," *Omaha World Herald*, Dec. 20, 1982, p. 2.
16. Dalmor Fisher, *Communication in Organizations*, West, St. Paul, Minn., 1981.
17. Eugene Walton, *A Magnetic Theory of Organizational Communication*, U.S. Naval Ordnance Test Station, China Lake, Calif., 1962.
18. James L. Heskett, *Managing in the Service Economy*, Harvard Business School Press, Boston, 1986, p. 127.
19. Peter F. Drucker, *Management*, Harper & Row, New York, 1974, p. 483.
20. Andrew D. Szilagyi, Jr., and Marc J. Wallace, Jr., *Organizational Behavior and Performance*, Scott, Foresman, Glenview, Ill., 1987, p. 410.

21. Fred Luthans and Mark J. Martinko, *The Practice of Supervision and Management,* McGraw-Hill, New York, 1979, pp. 180–182.
22. Daniel Katz and Robert Kahn, *The Social Psychology of Organizations,* 2d ed., Wiley, New York, 1978, p. 440.
23. Ibid., p. 443.
24. Heskett, op. cit., p. 127.
25. Nelson W. Aldrich, Jr., "Lines of Communication," *Inc.,* June 1986, p. 142.
26. Szilagyi and Wallace, op. cit., p. 408.
27. "Manager's On-Line Design Keeps New Yorkers Rolling," *Computerworld,* Dec. 10, 1984, p. 8.
28. Charles A. O'Reilly, "Individuals and Information Overload in Organizations," *Academy of Management Journal,* December 1980, pp. 684–696.
29. Donald F. Roberts, "The Nature of Communication Effects," in Wilbur Schramm and Donald F. Roberts (eds.), *The Process and Effects of Mass Communication,* rev. ed., University of Illinois Press, Chicago, 1971, pp. 368–371.
30. Charles A. O'Reilly, "Supervisors and Peers as Information Sources, Group Supportiveness, and Individual Performance," *Journal of Applied Psychology,* October 1977, pp. 632–635; and Charles A. O'Reilly and Karlene H. Roberts, "Task Group Structure, Communication, and Effectiveness in Three Organizations," *Journal of Applied Psychology,* December 1977, pp. 674–681.
31. Richard L. Daft, *Management,* Dryden, Chicago, 1988, p. 605. The information on telecommunication is largely drawn from this source.
32. "Let a Computer Do the Walking (and the Talking)," *Working Woman,* April 1986, p. 104.
33. Daft, op. cit.
34. Melinda Grenier Guiles, "Bulletin Boards Go High-Tech at More Firms," *The Wall Street Journal,* Apr. 9, 1986, p. 29.
35. Larry Reibstein, "More Firms Use Peer Review Panel to Resolve Employees' Grievances," *The Wall Street Journal,* Dec. 3, 1986, p. 25.
36. Karlene H. Roberts and Charles A. O'Reilly, "Some Correlations of Communication Roles in Organizations," *Academy of Management Journal,* March 1979, pp. 42–57.
37. Tom Peters, *Thriving on Chaos: Handbook for a Management Revolution,* Knopf, New York, 1987, p. 305.
38. Katz and Kahn, op. cit., p. 446.
39. William G. Scott and Terence R. Mitchell, *Organization Theory,* rev. ed., Irwin, Homewood, Ill., 1972, p. 147.
40. Luthans and Larsen, op. cit., p. 168.
41. Fred Luthans, Stuart A. Rosenkrantz, and Harry W. Hennessey, "What Do Successful Managers Really Do? An Observational Study of Managerial Activities," *Journal of Applied Behavioral Science,* vol. 21, no. 3, 1985, pp. 255–270.
42. J. Fulk and E. R. Wendler, "Dimensionality of Leader-Subordinate Interactions: A Path-Goal Investigation," *Organizational Behavior and Human Performance,* vol. 30, 1982, pp. 241–264; and Larry E. Penley and Brian Hawkins, "Studying Interpersonal Communication in Organizations: A Leadership Application," *Academy of Management Journal,* June 1985, pp. 309–326.
43. Katz and Kahn, op. cit., p. 445.
44. Luthans, Hodgetts, and Rosenkrantz, op. cit., chap. 4.
45. Gerald M. Goldhaber, *Organizational Communication,* Wm. C. Brown, Dubuque, Ia., 1974, p. 121.
46. Henry C. Mishkoff, "The Network Nation Emerges," *Management Review,* August 1986, pp. 29–31.

REAL CASE:
A Failure to
Communicate*

While union membership has been on the decline in recent years, there are other pressing problems currently facing labor leaders these days. In many cases the leadership of national unions is having difficulty keeping the rank and file in line. For example, more and more union members are refusing to ratify the contracts that have been painstakingly hammered out by their union officials. Here are some examples that have occurred over the last few years:

Union (Employer)	Members' Reaction and the Result
Auto Workers (General Motors)	4400 members of Local 645 delayed for three years new work-rule changes that were proposed by General Motors and United Auto Worker leaders
Food & Commercial Workers (Kroger)	Kroger sold 45 stores after 2800 members of Local 23 turned down wage and work-rule concessions that had been agreed to by the union leadership
Electronic Workers (General Electric)	The 8500 members of Local 201, unhappy with the concessions that were proposed in their national contract, voted the local's executive board out of office
Teamsters (Richard A. Shaw, Inc.)	Local 912's 1700 members resisted wage concessions and went on strike in defiance of their local's leaders
Food & Commercial Workers (Hormel)	The 1500 members of Local P-9 rejected wage cuts in defiance of the international union leadership
State, County & Municipal Employees (City of Detroit)	7000 members of Michigan Council 25 rejected a wage deal accepted by their leaders, thus forcing a continuation of a strike

Why are the rank and file so angry at their union leadership? One reason is that they believe their officials are buckling under to management and not fighting hard enough for better wages and working conditions. In particular, many union members are upset over the concessions that were made to management during the early 1980s when the economy was in poor shape. They want to see their lowered wages and benefits given back through vigorous bargaining. This is especially true among union members in companies such as those in the auto industry that have clearly bounced back and are now making large profits.

Another cause of rank-and-file anger is the breakdown of pattern bargaining. For decades unions had been able to hammer out labor agreements in which companies in the same industry paid the same rates. However, because of such factors as deregulation, increased competition, and foreign imports, such pattern bargaining has been weakened. As a result, union workers in firms that compete with one another in the same

Source: Adapted from Jonathon Tasini, "Unions Divided: The Revolt of the Rank and File," *Business Week,* Aug. 11, 1986, pp. 72–73.

industry sometimes have different pay rates. The rank and file wants everyone to be moved up to the highest rates.

Some union members have gone on strike and, in spite of demands by their leadership that they return, have stayed out. Moreover, other locals around the country have begun to assist these rebellious units by sending them money and other forms of support.

The bottom line in this latest development in the labor movement is that the leadership appears to be out of step with the membership. As one individual put it, "what we have here is a failure to communicate." This communication failure appears to be mostly a result of the leadership's failure to get feedback from the members regarding the direction in which they would like to see the union move. As a result, some labor relations experts are wondering how effective unions can hope to be over the next few years if the members are moving in one direction and the leadership is moving in another.

1. Why does there appear to be a breakdown in communication between the rank and file and the leadership? After all, aren't the elected leaders supposed to be representing their members?
2. Is this breakdown a result of poor upward communication or poor downward communication? Explain.
3. How can the problem discussed in this case be resolved? What steps need to be taken? Explain.

CASE: Doing My Own Thing

Rita Lowe has worked for the same boss for eleven years. Over coffee one day, her friend Sara asked her, "What is it like to work for old Charlie?" Rita replied, "Oh, I guess it's okay. He pretty much leaves me alone. I more or less do my own thing." Then Sara said, "Well, you've been at that same job for eleven years. How are you doing in it? Does it look like you will ever be promoted? If you don't mind me saying so, I can't for the life of me see that what you do has anything to do with the operation." Rita replied, "Well, first of all, I really don't have any idea of how I am doing. Charlie never tells me, but I've always taken the attitude that no news is good news. As for what I do and how it contributes to the operation around here, Charlie mumbled something when I started the job about being important to the operation, but that was it. We really don't communicate very well."

1. Analyze Rita's last statement: "We really don't communicate very well." What is the status of superior-subordinate communication in this work relationship? Katz and Kahn identified five purposes of the superior-subordinate communication process. Which ones are being badly neglected in this case?
2. It was said in this chapter that communication is a dynamic, personal process. Does the situation described verify this contention? Be specific in your answer.

3. Are there any implications in this situation for subordinate-initiated communication and for interactive communication? How could feedback be used more effectively?

CASE: Bad Brakes

Michelle Adams is the maintenance supervisor of a large taxicab company. She had been very concerned because the cabdrivers were not reporting potential mechanical problems. Several months ago she implemented a preventive maintenance program. This program depended upon the drivers' filling out a detailed report when they suspected any problem. But this was not happening. On a number of occasions a cab left the garage with major problems that the previous driver was aware of but had not reported. Calling out the field repair teams to fix the breakdown was not only costing the company much time and trouble but also was very unsafe in some cases and created a high degree of customer ill will. The drivers themselves suffered from a loss of fares and tips, and in some cases their lives were endangered by these mechanical failures. After many verbal and written threats and admonishments, Michelle decided to try a new approach. She would respond directly to each report of a potential mechanical problem sent in by a driver with a return memo indicating what the maintenance crew had found wrong with the cab and what had been done to take care of the problem. In addition, the personal memo thanked the driver for reporting the problem and encouraged reporting any further problems with the cabs. In less than a month the number of field repair calls had decreased by half, and the number of turned-in potential problem reports had tripled.

1. In communications terms, how do you explain the success of Michelle's follow-up memos to the drivers?
2. Explain and give examples of the three communications systems in this company (that is, superior-subordinate, subordinate-initiated, and interactive).

18 Decision Making and Control

Avon's Calling: But No One Answered in Terms of Decision Making and Control*

Decision making and control are two important processes for organizational effectiveness. Managers who make good decisions and maintain control can contribute to goals and performance; those who do not perform these processes effectively can create dire consequences for the organization. Take the case of Avon Products Inc. When Hicks Waldron took over the beauty products firm in 1983, he had his work cut out for him. Earnings had been falling since 1979, and the stock had tumbled from a high of $140 in 1973 to a meager $25 a share. Eager to turn the company around, Waldron made some decisions without first gathering the necessary information or considering other possible alternatives. For example, Waldron decided to reward sales representatives who generated the bigger orders. Unfortunately, Waldron ignored the fact that a significant amount of Avon's sales were from small-order customers and a lot of this business was lost.

With troubles brewing at Avon's core business of beauty products, Waldron decided to diversify. In 1984 he bought Foster Medical Care, a medical equipment rental company. This decision proved fruitful. Foster showed 100 percent annual growth for the next two years. But now this subsidiary is in trouble because Waldron did not implement proper control mechanisms. Although he followed the delegation principle in his newly diversified operation, he

*Source: Adapted from Gretchen Morgenson, "Anyhow, It Was Nice While It Lasted," *Forbes*, Jan. 12, 1987, pp. 50–52.

531

failed to maintain control. In particular, in his struggle to reverse the decline of the beauty products line, he delegated all authority to Foster Medical Care to run their end of the company. Foster, however, did not use this authority well. Since oxygen therapy accounts for 22 percent of Foster's total revenues, Foster's management should have been aware of their environment, especially government guidelines for Medicare reimbursements. In October 1985, the government announced it would not reimburse oxygen treatments unless patients were certified by their physicians. The government gave oxygen therapy concerns such as Foster one year to get their patients recertified. However, at the year's end, Foster had not completed the necessary paperwork. As a result, they lost $10 to $11 million in Medicare revenues. Such a lack of control was unexcusable for Foster management and Waldron, the head of the parent company. Needless to say, Waldron discovered that delegating without control can have disastrous consequences.

Learning Objectives

- DEFINE the phases in the decision-making process.
- IDENTIFY the models of decision-making behavior.
- PRESENT the behaviorally oriented decision-making techniques.
- DISCUSS artificial intelligence and expert systems.
- EXPLAIN the control process.

In this chapter the important processes of decision making and control are given attention. A process is any action which is performed by management to achieve organizational objectives. Thus, decision making and control are organizational processes because they transcend the individual and have an effect on organizational goals. These two processes are a vital part of the organization system and have extremely important behavioral implications. First, the overall nature of the decision-making process is explored. This is followed by a discussion of behavioral models and of the implications of decision making and some behavioral and computer-based decision techniques. The last half of the chapter is devoted to control. After some misconceptions about control are cleared up, the process is carefully defined, and its basic elements are emphasized. The last part of the chapter gives specific attention to the behavioral implications of control.

The Nature of Decision Making

Decision making is almost universally defined as *choosing between alternatives.* It is closely related to all the traditional management functions. For example, when a manager plans, organizes, and controls, he or she is making decisions. The classical theorists, however, did not generally present decision making this way. Fayol and Urwick were concerned with the decision-making process only to the extent that it affects delegation and authority, while Frederick W. Taylor alluded to the scientific method only as an ideal approach to making decisions. Like most other aspects of modern organization theory, the beginning of a meaningful analysis of the decision-making process can be traced to Chester Barnard. In *The Functions of the Executive,* Barnard gave a comprehensive analytical treatment of decision making and noted: "The processes of decision . . . are largely techniques for narrowing choice."[1]

Phases in the Decision-Making Process

Most discussions of the decision-making process break it down into a series of steps. For the most part, the logic can be traced to the ideas developed by Herbert A. Simon, the well-known Nobel Prize–winning organization and decision theorist, who conceptualizes three major phases in the decision-making process:

1. *Intelligence activity.* Borrowing from the military meaning of *intelligence,* Simon describes this initial phase as consisting of searching the environment for conditions calling for decision making.
2. *Design activity.* During the second phase, inventing, developing, and analyzing possible courses of action take place.
3. *Choice activity.* The third and final phase is the actual choice—selecting a particular course of action from among those available.[2]

Closely related to these phases, but with a more empirical basis (that is, tracing actual decisions in organizations), are the stages of decision making of Mintzberg and his colleagues:

1. *The identification phase,* during which *recognition* of a problem or opportunity arises and a *diagnosis* is made. It was found that severe, immediate problems did not have a very systematic, extensive diagnosis but that mild problems did.
2. *The development phase,* during which there may be a *search* for existing standard procedures or solutions already in place or the *design* of a new, tailormade solution. It was found that the design process was a groping, trial-and-error process in which the decision makers had only a vague idea of the ideal solution.
3. *The selection phase,* during which the choice of a solution is made. There are three ways of making this selection: by the *judgment* of the decision maker, on the basis of experience or intuition rather than logical analysis; by *analysis* of the alternatives on a logical, systematic basis; and by *bargaining* when the selection involves a group of decision makers and all the political maneuvering that this entails. Once the decision is formally accepted, an *authorization* is made.[3]

Figure 18.1 summarizes these phases of decision making based on Mintzberg's research.

Whether expressed in Simon's or Mintzberg's phases, there seem to be identifiable, preliminary steps leading to the choice activity in decision making.

FIGURE 18.1
Mintzberg's empirically based phases of decision making in organizations.
(*Source:* Adapted from Henry Mintzberg, Duru Raisin-ghani, and André Theoret, "The Structure of 'Unstructured' Decision Processes," *Administrative Science Quarterly,* June 1976, pp. 246–275.)

Also, it should be noted that decision making is a dynamic process, and there are many feedback loops in each of the phases. "Feedback loops can be caused by problems of timing, politics, disagreement among managers, inability to identify an appropriate alternative or to implement the solution, turnover of managers, or the sudden appearance of a new alternative."[4] The essential point is that decision making is a dynamic process.

Behavioral Implications of Decision Making

Why does a decision maker choose one alternative over another? The answer to this question involves decision rationality and behavioral decision models. These are given attention in the following sections.

Decision Rationality

The most often used definition of *rationality* in decision making is that it is a means to an end. If appropriate means are chosen to reach desired ends, the decision is said to be rational. However, there are many complications to this simple test of rationality. To begin with, it is very difficult to separate means from ends because an apparent end may be only a means for some future end. This idea is commonly referred to as the *means-ends chain* or *hierarchy*. Simon points out that "the means-end hierarchy is seldom an integrated, completely connected chain. Often the connection between organization activities and ultimate objectives is obscure, or these ultimate objectives are incompletely formulated, or there are internal conflicts and contradictions among the ultimate objectives, or among the means selected to attain them."[5]

Besides the complications associated with the means-ends chain, it may even be that the concept is obsolete. Decision making relevant to the national economy supports this position. Decision makers who seek to make seemingly rational adjustments in the economic system may in fact produce undesirable, or at least unanticipated, end results. Simon also warns that a simple means-ends analysis may have inaccurate conclusions. The following three points should help in avoiding the inherent problems of means-ends analysis:

First, the ends to be attained by the choice of a particular behavior alternative are often incompletely or incorrectly stated through failure to consider the alternative ends that could be reached by selection of another behavior.

Second, in actual situations a complete separation of means from ends is usually impossible.

Third, the means-end terminology tends to obscure the role of the time element in decision making.[6]

One way to clarify means-ends rationality is to attach appropriate qualifying adverbs to the various types of rationality. Thus, *objective* rationality can be applied to decisions that maximize given values in a given situation. *Subjective* rationality might be used if the decision maximizes attainment relative to knowledge of the given subject. *Conscious* rationality might be applied to decisions in which adjustment of means to ends is a conscious process. A decision is *deliberately* rational to the degree that the adjustment of means to ends has been deliberately sought by the individual or the organization; a decision is *organizationally* rational to the extent that it is aimed at the organization's goals; and a decision is *personally* rational if it is directed toward the individual's goals.[7]

Models of Decision-Making Behavior

There are many descriptive models of rationality-of-choice behavior. In effect, these have become models for much of management decision-making behavior. The models attempt to describe theoretically and realistically how practicing managers make decisions. In particular, the models strive to determine to what degree management decision makers are rational. The models range from complete rationality, as in the case of the *economic* or *econologic* model, to complete irrationality, as in the case of the *social* model. Figure 18.2 summarizes on a continuum the two major extremes and the in-between models of Simon's bounded rationality and the Peters-Waterman model coming out of their analysis of well-managed companies. These models deal specifically with management decision-making behavior, whereas the discussion in Chapter 1 was more concerned with the overall nature of human behavior.

The Econologic Model. This model comes from the classical economic model, in which the decision maker is perfectly and completely rational in every way. Regarding decision-making activities, the following conditions are assumed:

1. The decision will be completely rational in the means-ends sense.

FIGURE 18.2 The continuum of decision-making behavior.

| Econologic model | Simon's bounded rationality model | Peters' and Waterman's "well-managed" model | Social model |

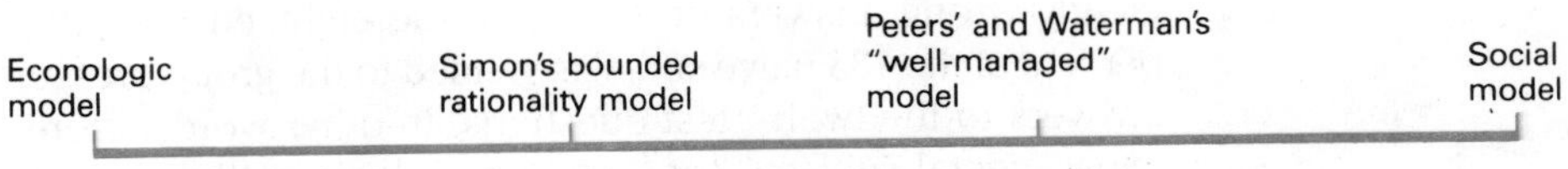

2. There is a complete and consistent system of preferences which allow a choice among the alternatives.
3. There is complete awareness of all the possible alternatives.
4. There are no limits to the complexity of computations that can be performed to determine the best alternatives.
5. Probability calculations are neither frightening nor mysterious.[8]

With this almost infallible ability, the decision maker always strives to maximize outcomes in the business firm, and decisions will be directed to the point of maximum profit where marginal cost equals marginal revenue (MC = MR).

Most economists and quantitative decision theorists do not claim that this depiction is a realistic descriptive model of modern decision-making behavior. But because this rational model and its accompanying quantitative methods have been embraced by the business schools, most of today's managers equate "good" management decision making with this approach. This may be dangerous and may be a leading cause of many of today's problems. As Peters and Waterman observed: "The numerative, rationalist approach to management dominates the business schools. It seeks detached, analytical justification for all decisions. It is right enough to be dangerously wrong, and it has arguably led us seriously astray."[9] Obviously, Peters and Waterman are not saying "throw the rascal out," nor are other critics of the rational model. It has made and will continue to make a significant contribution to effective decision making. For example, the most successful consumer marketers, such as Procter & Gamble, Chesebrough-Pond's, and Ore-Ida, are known for their rational approach and accompanying quantitative backup. The point that Peters and Waterman are making is that the rational model is not the be-all and end-all of effective decision making and that, if carried to the extreme, it can actually be harmful to the decision-making process.

The Social Model. At the opposite extreme from the econologic model is the social model of psychology. Sigmund Freud presented humans as bundles of feelings, emotions, and instincts, with their behavior guided largely by their unconscious desires. Obviously, if this were an accurate description, people would not be capable of making effective decisions.

Although most contemporary psychologists would take issue with the Freudian description of humans, almost all would agree that social influences have a significant impact on decision-making behavior. Furthermore, social pressures and influences may cause managers to make irrational decisions. The well-known conformity experiment by Solomon Asch demonstrates human irrationality.[10] His study utilized several groups of seven to nine subjects each. They were told that their task was to compare the lengths of lines. All except one of the "subjects" in each group had prearranged with the experimenter to give clearly wrong answers on twelve of the eighteen line-judgment trials. About 37 percent of the 123 naive subjects yielded to the group pressures and gave incorrect answers to the twelve test questions. In other words, more than one-third of the experimental subjects conformed to a decision they knew was wrong.

If over one-third of Asch's subjects conformed under "right and wrong," "black and white" conditions of comparing the lengths of lines, a logical conclusion would be that the real, "gray" world is full of irrational conformists. It takes little imagination to equate Asch's lines with the alternatives of a management decision. There seems to be little doubt of the importance of social influences in decision-making behavior.

There is still much to be learned about the impact of social pressures on decision-making behavior. This even applies to how one makes decisions in the international arena. Knowing the correct social protocol can be very important to U.S. managers in an international assignment. The accompanying International Application Example gives some of these basic rules.

International Application Example

Some Basic Rules of Protocol

There are many rules of protocol that Americans serving in foreign assignments should recognize. Some are confusing; most are not. In any event, it is important to know these guidelines in order to be as effective as possible. Here are the most useful rules:

1. In many countries of the world, a person's name denotes social rank or family status. A mistake can be an outright insult. So American managers who are going to be meeting some important nationals should find out who they are beforehand and write their names out and memorize them for correct pronunciation.
2. Keep in mind that there are different rules of protocol in different cultures. For example, in Latin America people's names are a combination of the father's and the mother's, but only the father's name is used in conversation. In Spanish-speaking countries, the father's name comes first. For example, Carolos Migoya-Gutierrez is called Mr. Migoya. However, in Portuguese-speaking countries, it is the other way around, i.e., Mr. Gutierrez. To make it even more confusing, in the Orient the rules often vary by country. For example, in Korea which of a man's names to use is determined by whether he is the first son or the second son. In Japan, people should be addressed by their surname, while in Thailand you should call people by their given name, i.e., Mr. Ho Chin would be called Mr. Ho. How can an American manager be sure of not making a mistake? The one best way is: ask your host.
3. In the United States it is acceptable to bypass food you do not like. When overseas, however, you should take whatever is put on your plate and make a valiant effort to eat it regardless of taste. If it's something you have never had before, do not ask what it is. You may be unpleasantly surprised.
4. Before getting to the destination, find out the types of clothes that people wear. Remember that color is as important as fashion. If the American male manager is in doubt, a conservative business suit will usually be acceptable, although in the Philippines a barong (a loose, frilly, usually white or cream-colored shirt with tails out) is proper dress, and in Latin countries a guayabera (similar to a barong) will get him through. For women there would be different rules.
5. Despite what is commonly heard about locals in other countries wanting Americans to speak their language, English is still the primary tongue in the international arena. Most educated people understand this language, and many speak it fluently. Unless American managers are absolutely sure of what they are going to say in a foreign tongue, they should stick with English.

Certainly, the completely irrational person depicted by Freud is too extreme a case to be useful. On the other hand, as the chapters in this book have pointed out, there is little question of the important role that human behavior can and does play in management decision making. Some management behavior is irrational but still very realistic. For example, the author and a colleague conducted two studies that showed that subjects in both laboratory and field settings who did not have computer experience were more influenced in their choice activities by information presented on computer printout paper than they were by information presented on regular stenographic paper.[11] On the other hand, for those subjects with computer experience, the reverse was true. In other words, decision makers are influenced in their choice activities even by the type of format in which information is presented to them. Managers without computer experience may be in awe of the computer and place more value on computer-generated information than is justified, while those with computer experience may be highly skeptical and may underrate the importance of computer-generated information.

Simon's Bounded Rationality Model. To present a more realistic alternative to the econologic model, Herbert Simon proposed what he called "administrative man." He felt that management decision-making behavior could best be described as follows:

1. In choosing between alternatives, managers attempt to satisfice, or look for the one which is satisfactory or "good enough." Examples of satisficing criteria would be adequate profit or share of the market and fair price.
2. They recognize that the world they perceive is a drastically simplified model of the real world. They are content with this simplification because they believe the real world is mostly empty anyway.
3. Because they satisfice rather than maximize, they can make their choices without first determining all possible behavior alternatives and without ascertaining that these are in fact all the alternatives.
4. Because they treat the world as rather empty, they are able to make decisions with relatively simple rules of thumb or tricks of the trade or from force of habit. These techniques do not make impossible demands upon their capacity for thought.[12]

In contrast to the econologic model, Simon's model is rational and maximizing, but it is bounded. Decision makers end up satisficing because they do not have the ability to maximize. The case against maximizing behavior has been summed up by noting that objectives are dynamic rather than static; information is seldom perfect; there are obvious time and cost constraints; alternatives seldom lend themselves to quantified preference ordering; and the effect of environmental forces cannot be disregarded.[13] Simon's model recognizes these limitations. The econologic model's assumptions are viewed as unrealistic. But in the final analysis, the difference between the econologic model and Simon's model is one of relative degree because, under some conditions, satisficing approaches maximizing, whereas in other conditions satisficing and maximizing are very far apart.

There are many economic, social, and organizational variables which influence the degree to which satisficing becomes maximizing. An example of an economic variable is market structure. The more competitive the market, the more satisficing may approach maximizing. In an agricultural products market situation, satisficing will by necessity become maximizing. Economists generally recognize that in a purely competitive environment, profit maximization lends itself to the very survival of the firm. Thus, the decision maker must make maximizing decisions. In an oligopolistic market situation (for example, the automobile and steel industries), satisficing is quite different from maximizing. Oligopolistic firms can still survive on the basis of adequate profit or share of the market. They do not have to operate at the point where marginal cost equals marginal revenue, and, in fact, they may be unavoidably prevented from maximizing.

Besides the economic market constraints, there are many socially based obstacles which prevent maximization in practice. Some of these social barriers are not consciously recognized by the management decision maker. Examples are resistance to change, desire for status, concern for image, organizational politics, and just plain stupidity. On the other hand, the decision maker may in some cases consciously avoid maximizing. Examples of the latter behavior include decisions which discourage competitive entry or antitrust investigation, restrain union demands, or maintain consumer goodwill.

Peters and Waterman's "Well-Managed" Model. In their analysis of well-managed companies, Peters and Waterman found that the decision-making process in these firms did not always follow the rational model. In particular, they found that the rational model, and its accompanying emphasis on quantitative analysis, had the following dysfunctional effects on the companies they studied.[14]

1. The rational approach has a built-in conservative bias that causes cost reduction to take priority over revenue enhancement. For example, the rational model would not be able to justify on a cost basis Frito-Lay's 99.5 percent service level, Caterpillar's or Maytag's overcommitment to reliability, or the fetish for cleanliness that characterizes McDonald's and Disney. Yet these are the things that generate revenue and make these companies successful.
2. If allowed to go too far, the rational model can lead to an abstract, heartless philosophy. The obsession with "body counts" in the Vietnam war would be an example here.
3. An overly narrow rational approach is often negative. This problem was brought out by the chief executive of Mobil, who explained why his company did not get involved in some offshore oil tracks. "The financial people in this company did a disservice to the exploration people—the poor people in exploration were adversely impacted by the people who know nothing about oil and gas."[15]
4. Some versions of rationality do not value experimentation and crack down on those who make a mistake or fail. One company following the rational model may spend years and years developing and avoiding all mistakes on a single "home-run" product, while well-managed companies such as "Digital, 3M,

HP, and Wang, amid a hot bed of experimentation, have proceeded 'irrationally' and chaotically, and introduced ten more new products each during the same period."[16]

5. A climate of antiexperimentation fostered by the rational model leads to overcomplexity and inflexibility. This may be a problem with the defense system. As one Pentagon official explained: "Our strategy of pursuing ever-increasing technical complexity and sophistication has made high-technology solutions and combat readiness mutually exclusive."[17] Peters and Waterman interpret this as meaning that the more money the country spends on defense, the less able it is to fight because more money has produced fewer, but more complex, planes and communication systems, which do not work much of the time and which are unlikely to survive during a war.

In addition, Peters and Waterman point out that there are other problems with the rational model, such as stressing the formal rather than the informal, deemphasizing the importance of corporate values, and stifling internal competition.

Peters and Waterman discovered that to counter these problems, well-managed companies have their own brand of rationality with the following characteristics and strategies:

1. *Fluidity.* The successful companies studied tend to be very fluid—their managers are very informal and get about "among the troops" to see what is going on.
2. *Chunking.* The managers try to do only one thing at a time. They use small groups, not formally designated, to accomplish a limited set of objectives.
3. *Experimenting.* The successful companies are action-oriented and are always trying things. There is no fear-of-failure syndrome, and in most of these companies it is risky not to take a risk.
4. *Speed and numbers.* Doing things now—and the more things done, the better—is a strategy in the successful companies. Successful oil exploration companies simply drill more wells. But, to quote a line from the famous Kenny Rogers song about the gambler, "you have to know when to hold 'em and know when to fold 'em." In other words, the successful companies know when to pull out, but, importantly, they are not afraid to get in the next game.
5. *Invisible and leaky systems.* As systems become increasingly formalized and complex, "bootlegging" (as it is called at General Electric) or "scrounging" (as it is called at 3M) becomes necessary for innovation and for moving the organization ahead. At successful companies such as GE and IBM, the important breakthroughs have come not from the formal systems but from leaks in the system where innovative individuals bootleg and scrounge for funds and people to make a significant contribution.[18]

This newest model of decision making is placed toward the nonrational end of the continuum. Unlike the others, it is based on empirical support of how successful companies are being run. Although recent analysis questions this empirical support and suggests that Peters and Waterman's work may be based more on advocacy than science,[19] it does at least deal with examples and problems from real organizations. In the final analysis, all the models presented are appropriate under certain conditions and are used in combination with one another. This last one, however, has been largely ignored up to very recent times. Obviously, it has to be taken into consideration for effective decision making in today's organizations. Besides the strategies and techniques coming out of the "well-managed" model, the behavioral techniques discussed next can also be helpful for effective decision making.

Behaviorally Oriented Decision-Making Techniques

Most of the behavioral techniques, at least traditionally, have revolved around the concept of participation. Used as a technique, participation involves individuals or groups in the decision-making process. It can be formal or informal, and it entails intellectual and emotional as well as physical involvement. The actual amount of participation in making decisions ranges from one extreme of no participation, wherein the superior makes the decision and asks for no help or ideas from anyone, to the other extreme of full participation, where everyone connected with, or affected by, the decision is completely involved. In practice, the degree of participation will be determined by factors such as the experience of the person or group and the nature of the task. The more experience and the more open and unstructured the task, the more participation there will tend to be.

In today's organizations there is an awakened interest in participation. Faced with declining productivity and foreign competition, especially from the Japanese, who have received much publicity concerning participation techniques such as quality circles, many companies are now taking a hard look at the use of participation techniques. They have been talked about ever since the early human relations movement, and now some organizations and individual managers are actually trying them.

Individual, Group, and Program Participation Techniques

Participation techniques can be applied informally on an individual or a group basis or formally on a program basis. Individual participation techniques are those in which a subordinate somehow affects the decision making of a superior. Group participation utilizes consultative and democratic techniques. Under consultative participation, the superiors ask for and receive involvement from subordinates, but they maintain the right to make the decision. In the democratic form, there is total participation, and the group, not the individual head, makes the final decision by consensus or majority vote. Although participation has long been discussed and advocated, only recently has there been research support that it enhances employee performance.[20]

Examples of formal programs of participation include the autonomous work groups in the sociotechnical projects described in Chapter 10 and also junior boards of executives, collective bargaining between union and management, union-management cooperation committees, Scanlon Plan committees, suggestion plans, and quality circles. The junior board, first used at McCormick & Company, enables junior executives to participate in top management decision making. Normally, the junior executives are limited to an advisory role. Collective bargaining, defined as the negotiation and administration of an agreement between labor and management over wages, hours, and employment conditions, is generally not associated with participation techniques of decision making. Yet, technically, if the union is a legally elected bargaining agent for the employees, the union participates through collective bargaining in the decisions affecting the employees. Union-management cooperation committees are formally established to encourage participation of union members in practically all areas of management decision making. Such a committee is usually set up as a last resort to save an organization from closing down.

The Scanlon Plan is a special form of labor-management cooperation. The plan, originated by Joseph Scanlon (who was at first with the steelworkers' union and later MIT) nearly fifty years ago, consists of a system of committees which encourage labor to participate in management decisions. The unique feature of the Scanlon Plan is that the rewards for an individual's successful suggestion are equally divided among all members of the group. A comprehensive analysis of the Scanlon Plan tested several hypotheses that were derived out of the extensive literature on the plan during the preceding thirty years. By examining twenty-three firms that had the Scanlon Plan in operation, it was concluded that success was positively related to (1) the average level of participation in decision making reported by employees, (2) the number of years the company had been using the plan, and (3) management's—especially the chief executive officer's—attitudes toward, and expectations of, the plan.[21]

Commonly used suggestion plans or boxes are also a formal type of participation program. At A&P grocery stores, the company cut back wages but gives bonuses for suggestions and inputs to its participation program. In the Philadelphia area alone, A&P has paid out $10 million in bonuses in a five-year period.[22] If employee responses are properly handled and adequately rewarded, the suggestion box can be a very effective method of obtaining participation in the decision-making process from anyone in the organization.

Quality Circles

Introduced in Chapter 13, quality circles really started in this country but were developed and are widely used in Japan. Recently they have been imported back to this country. A group participation process, quality circles "typically are small groups of volunteers from the same work areas who meet regularly to identify, analyze, and solve quality and related problems in their area of responsibility. Members of a group choose a particular problem to study, gather data, and use such methods as brainstorming, Pareto analysis, histograms, and control charts to form a recommendation that can be presented to management."[23] Now groups are trained in communication and problem-solving skills and in quality/measurement strategies and techniques.

Participation Techniques in Perspective

There are many positive and negative attributes of the participation techniques of decision making. Balancing these off in evaluating the effectiveness of participative decision making is difficult because of moderating factors such as leadership style or personality of the parties involved and situational, environmental, and contextual factors.[24] Also a recent extensive review of research found that the different forms of participative techniques had markedly different outcomes. For example, informal participation was found to have a positive effect on employee productivity and satisfaction; representative participation had a positive impact on satisfaction, but not productivity; and short-term participation was ineffective by both criteria.[25]

One problem is the tendency toward pseudoparticipation. Many managers ask for participation, but whenever subordinates take them up on it by making a suggestion or trying to give some input into a decision, they are put down or never receive any feedback. In some cases managers try to get their subordinates involved in the task but not in the decision-making process. This can lead to a boomerang effect regarding employee satisfaction. If the superior claims to want participation from subordinates but never lets them become intellectually and emotionally involved and never utilizes their suggestions, the results may be disastrous. Also, participation can be very time-consuming, and it has the same general disadvantages of committees. From a behavioral standpoint, however, the advantages far outweigh the disadvantages. Most of the benefits are touched upon throughout this book. Perhaps the biggest advantage is that the participation techniques recognize that each person can make a meaningful contribution to the attainment of organizational objectives.

Group Decision-Making Techniques

Practically all the advances that have been made in decision-making techniques over the past several years have been quantitative in nature. Only the participative behavioral techniques discussed so far have been available to managers, and there have been only scattered attempts to develop new techniques for helping make more creative and problem-solving types of decisions. Yet it is the latter decisions which are the major challenge facing modern management.

New, creative ideas are scarce and do not seem to be coming out of students educated in business schools. For example, General Foods held a competition in which student teams from prestigious business schools were given the charge to develop a new marketing plan that would stem the plunging sales of Sugar-Free Kool-Aid. Although they used models and the right terminology, they offered very few original ideas that the company could or would be able to use. The marketing manager concluded, "There were a couple of ideas that were of interest, but nothing we haven't looked at before."[26] Fortunately, Delphi and nominal grouping have emerged to offer some help in making creative and problem-solving decisions.

The Delphi Technique

Although Delphi was first developed by N. C. Dalkey and his associates in 1950 at the Rand Corporation's Think Tank, it has only recently become popularized as a decision-making technique, for example, for long-range forecasting. Today, numerous organizations in business, education, government, health, and the military are using Delphi. No decision technique will ever be able to predict the future completely, but the Delphi technique seems to be as good a crystal ball as is currently available.

The technique, named after the oracle at Delphi in ancient Greece, has many variations, but generally it works as follows:

1. A panel (usually of experts, but in some cases nonexperts may be deliberately used) is formed, but, importantly, the members are not in face-to-face interaction with one another. Thus, the expenses of bringing a group together are eliminated.
2. Each member is asked to make anonymous predictions or input into the problem/decision the panel is charged with.
3. Each panel member then receives composite feedback from what the others have inputted. In some variations the reasons are listed (anonymously), but mostly just a composite figure is used.
4. On the basis of the feedback, another round of anonymous inputs is made. These iterations take place for a predetermined number of times or until the composite feedback remains the same, which means everyone is sticking with his or her position.

A major key to the success of the technique lies in its anonymity. Keeping the responses of panel members anonymous eliminates the problem of "saving face" and encourages the panel experts to be more flexible and thus to benefit from the estimates of others. In the traditional interacting group decision-making technique, the experts may be more concerned with defending their vested positions than they are with making a good decision.

Many organizations testify to the success they have had so far with the Delphi technique. McDonnell Douglas Aircraft uses the technique to forecast the future uncertainties of commercial air transportation. Weyerhaeuser, a building supply company, uses it to predict what will happen in the construction business, and Smith, Kline, and French, a drug manufacturer, uses it to study the uncertainties of medicine. TRW, a highly diversified, technically oriented company, has fourteen Delphi panels averaging seventeen members each. The panels suggest products and services which have future marketing potential and predict technological developments and significant political, economic, social, and cultural events. Besides business applications, the technique has been used successfully on various problems in government, education, health, and the military. In other words, Delphi can be applied to a wide variety of program planning and decision problems in any type of organization.

The major criticisms of the Delphi technique center on its time consumption, cost, and Ouija-board effect. The third criticism implies that, similar to the parlor game of that name, Delphi can claim no scientific basis or support. To counter this criticism, Rand has attempted to validate Delphi through controlled experimentation. The corporation set up panels of nonexperts who use the Delphi technique to answer questions such as, "How many popular votes were cast for Lincoln when he first ran for President?" and "What was the average price a farmer received for a bushel of apples in 1940?" These particular questions were used because the average person does not know the exact answers but knows something about the subjects. The result of these studies showed that the original estimates by the panel of nonexperts were reasonably close to being correct, but with the Delphi technique of anonymous feedback, the estimates greatly improved.

The Nominal Group Technique

Closely related to Delphi is the nominal group approach to group decision making. The nominal group has been used by social psychologists in their research for almost three decades. A nominal group is simply a "paper group." It is a group in name only because no verbal exchange is allowed between members. In group dynamics research, social psychologists would pit a fully interacting group against a nominal group (a group of individuals added together on paper but not verbally interacting). In terms of number of ideas, uniqueness of ideas, and quality of ideas, research has found nominal groups to be superior to real groups. The general conclusion is that interacting groups inhibit creativity. This, of course, applies only to idea generation because the interactive effect of group members is known to have a significant effect on other variables. The latter type of effect was given attention in Chapter 13, on group dynamics.

When the nominal group approach is used as a specific technique for decision making in organizations, it is labeled the *nominal group technique* (NGT) and consists of the following steps:

1. Silent generation of ideas in writing
2. Round-robin feedback from group members, who record each idea in a terse phrase on a flip chart
3. Discussion of each recorded idea for clarification and evaluation
4. Individual voting on priority ideas, with the group decision being mathematically derived through rank ordering or rating[27]

The difference between this approach and Delphi is that the NGT members are usually acquainted with one another, have face-to-face contact, and communicate directly. Although more research is needed, there is some evidence that NGT-led groups come up with many more ideas than traditional interacting groups and may do as well as, or slightly better than, groups using Delphi.[28] A study also found that NGT-led groups performed at a level of accuracy that was equivalent to that of the most proficient member.[29] However, another study found that NGT-led groups did not perform as well as interacting groups whose participants were pervasively aware of the problem given the group and when there were no dominant persons who inhibited others from communicating ideas.[30] Thus, as is true of most of the techniques discussed in this book, there are moderating effects. A review of the existing research literature on Delphi and NGT concluded:

In general, the research on both Delphi and nominal group techniques suggests that they can help improve the quality of group decisions because they mitigate the problems of interacting groups—individual dominance and groupthink. A skillful chairperson, therefore, may adapt these techniques to particular decision-making situations.[31]

Artificial Intelligence and Expert Systems

Computers, of course, have literally revolutionized management approaches to decision making. For example, there is growing evidence that with the use of personal computers and portables, many managers are even making decisions at home. For example, Digital Equipment Corporation reports that thousands of its employees use computers at home after hours, and Blue Cross and Blue Shield of Massachusetts advocate the use of computers at home to do company business.[32] In the future, computers may also have a significant impact on the more creative, problem-solving decisions. This possibility lies in the development of artificial intelligence (AI).

The newest generation of computers emphasizes both hardware and software. Supercomputers today, such as NASA's Numerical Aerodynamic Simulation system, are currently capable of 250 million computations per second and in a decade will be capable of a mind-boggling 10 billion computations per second.[33] Personal computers today have powerful microprocessor chips and vast amounts of memory. In terms of computer software, the technology for hearing and speech are already available and will become more dependable and usable in the near future. As one computer expert noted, "in terms of possibilities, we're at infinity."[34]

Artificial intelligence is the use of computers to mimic human intellectual activity. IBM executive Herbert Schorr notes that AI represents the second generation of the information revolution. The first involved the automation of routine data processing. Now, in the second, AI will improve productivity through the automation of decision making.[35] When applied to actual diagnosis and decision making in organizations, this technology has become known as *expert systems*. More specifically, expert systems use a new way of organizing information in computers that uses symbols rather than just numbers as in conventional software. These systems are capable of handling complex reasoning related to real-world facts. "In the typical expert system, these facts are organized into a vast, tree-like diagram that depicts all their interrelationships. Interpreting the facts is left to a separate web of logic—comprising rule-of-thumb premises based on input by human experts—that reasons through every known circumstance."[36]

Almost all large firms today in a variety of industries are using expert systems. Some representative examples include the following:

- Westinghouse has spent more than $20 million to date in developing several sophisticated expert systems that do things such as detect power failure of turbines and plan and schedule manufacturing operations.

- American Express has an expert system called "Laurel's Brain" because it is based on the decision-making talents of Laurel Miller, a credit authorization manager. With Laurel's expertise fed into the system, the system screens out bad credit risks among the company's 23 million card holders. Amex has experienced big productivity and financial gains from this expert system, and Laurel says, "There's no question it can do as good a job as I can."[37]
- Digital Equipment developed one of the world's largest expert systems to figure out what combinations of computers, disk drives, terminals, and communication cables a given customer requires.[38]

The use of expert systems and artificial intelligence in general has had and will continue to have a tremendous impact on decision making. In the final analysis, however, human beings, not machines, must make the decisions that guide organizations into the future and make them effective. One important set of human decisions revolves about how, when, and where to implement expert systems.[39]

The Control Process

So far the processes of communication (last chapter) and decision making (this chapter) have been examined. Closely related is the control process.

The first step in the analysis of the control process is to clear up some of the common misconceptions about it. Some of the misconceptions stem from the negativism attached to the common usage of the term. The American cultural value of individual freedom is supposedly threatened by any form of control. Highly simplified, the argument goes that freedom is good and control is bad. Despite this widely held value, the daily life of every American is highly controlled, from waking to the sound of the alarm clock in the morning to watching the ten- or eleven-o'clock news at night. Inside as well as outside the organization, today's employees have many rules to follow—where to park, when to punch the time clock or report to the office, how to comply with safety regulations, and what to wear are just a few examples. In addition, there is the controlling atmosphere inherent in the superior-subordinate authority relationship, which exists in every formal organization.

More specific behavioral implications of control are given later, but for now it can be said that control per se is not categorically "bad" for the individual. In addition, as the accompanying Application Example indicates, there are some new control techniques that seem to be more compatible, even in areas such as cost controls, for the people involved.

Although they do not readily admit it, most people probably prefer some degree of control over their lives because it gives them some stability and contributes to their general welfare and safety. Nevertheless, the negative connotation of control still exists and is amplified by the ways in which controls have been traditionally set, implemented, and used in formal organizations.

**New Cost Control Strategies as Alternatives
to Simple Budget Cuts***

In recent years cost-cutting controls have become a way of life for many organizations. Years ago this process used to be handled through simple budget cuts. However, today it is becoming increasingly apparent that such approaches are only partially successful. There is a lot more to cost controls than the one-time budget reduction. Companies are beginning to realize that redesigning products, plants, and even organization structures are also important.

Consider the case of Brunswick Corporation. A maker of industrial and recreational products, the firm found itself facing large expenses associated with fending off a takeover by another corporation. In order to pay these expenses the company began selling off part of its product line. It then trimmed its corporate structure to fit with the reduced scale of operations.

Xerox is another interesting example. While Xerox long dominated the market for copying machines, in the early 1980s Kodak began to gain the upper end of this market while Canon began nibbling away at the lower end. Xerox countered by using a cost-analysis control technique known as benchmarking. This involves the purchase of competitive products for the purpose of stripping them down, examining how they are built and then using this information in order to build similar products that are cheaper and/or of higher quality. Attention is also given to the way the products are packaged and marketed. The end result in Xerox's case was a more competitive product that allowed it to win back some of its market share.

The Celanese Corporation provides yet another example of new control strategies that help keep down costs. The firm has reduced the number of financial reports that corporate-level management gets from operating managers. This allows the company to monitor operations at reduced cost. Another step taken by Celanese is the "cost of quality" measure. This involves a determination of how much it costs to do things a second time. Once these data are made available to operating personnel, steps are then taken to prevent the initial mistakes. In particular, the company focuses on preventing those errors that are most costly.

One overall result of all these cost control strategies is that operations are more efficient without losing the goodwill and support of the people involved. At the same time the company using these approaches can become more competitive in the marketplace. A recent survey of *Fortune* 500 firms revealed that cost control was at the top of their list of things to do. In the past, simple budget cuts were very negative and sometimes had a devastating effect on the people involved. Now there seem to be some ways to cut costs without negatively affecting the people.

*Source: Adapted from Maggie McComas, "Cutting Costs without Killing the Business," *Fortune,* Oct. 13, 1986, pp. 70–76.

The Meaning of Control

Despite the many misconceptions about the nature of control, there is, surprisingly, general agreement about its formal definition. Fayol's definition, which he gave in 1916, set a precedent that has been followed through the years and is commonly accepted today. In the very last section of his pioneering book, he states: "In an undertaking, control consists in verifying whether everything occurs in conformity with the plan adopted, the instructions issued and principles established. It has for its object to point out weaknesses and errors in order to rectify them and prevent recurrence. It operates on everything, things, people, actions."[40]

Most management experts follow the Fayol definition, but more recently, control has taken on more of a computerized information systems perspective. The cybernetic system concept in particular is an important conceptual basis for the organizational control process. Automatic feedback control mechanisms play a significant role in steering the modern organization. The general systems approach emphasizes feedback, which is an inherent part of any control process. Control decisions are traditionally based upon the feedback that is obtained from accounting information in the upward system of an organization.

The new emphasis is also on the *feedforward* aspects of control. This feedforward approach recognizes that the feedback process alone is not enough for effective control. The input variables of a system are controlled in a feedforward system. It has been pointed out that "feedforward control would take place if management identified and nipped grievances in the bud to prevent a strike from occurring in the first place. Just as a cardiovascular fitness program is more efficient and less costly than open heart surgery, preventive feedforward control is far and away the preferable option for effective management."[41]

The very existence of the control process implies that the other processes are not perfect. The tremendous complexity of the modern organization, combined with certain psychological dependencies of personnel on order and stability, makes the control process a necessity. For example, because of an organization's size and complexity, planning decisions do not always work out in practice. Moreover, the organizational communication process can easily break down. A control process is required to anticipate and point out these types of difficulties and to try to get them corrected. In addition, many of the problems at which the control process is aimed are human in nature.

Although controls can become inhibiting and inflexible for employees, the absence of any organizational controls would probably lead to anarchy and psychological problems because people have learned to depend on various controls in their daily lives. The argument in the behavioral approach to management is not whether controls are to exist but rather how they are to be set and used in the modern organization. The control process per se is necessary for the attainment of objectives and ultimately for the very survival of the organization.

Basic Elements of Control

Inherent in the definition of control are three basic elements. First, control sets the standards and objectives which serve as the guidelines for performance. Second, control measures and evaluates inputs and performance according to the standards and objectives. Third, control takes corrective action in the form of a control decision. Sometimes control is mistakenly equated with only one of the three elements. The control process includes all three elements and is very broad in scope.

Objectives and Standards.

The objectives-and-standards phase of the control process is linked to planning and the goal-setting process discussed in Chapter 10. Control standards and objectives are set for each organizational unit and range from a small work group at the bottom to the governing board at the top.

Traditionally, control units were structurally defined and assigned as a budget area. Recently, because of behavioral influence, the trend has been toward identifying control units by area of responsibility. The responsibility units are often expressed as profit centers. This type of "responsibility accounting" can be traced back to Sloan's profit-centered concept of decentralization, which he installed in General Motors in the 1920s. The philosophy and practice of responsibility-centered control are now beginning to be implemented in most modern organizations. The controllable variables are distinguished from the uncontrollable ones when standards are being set for performance. For example, overhead items (heat, light, water, and depreciation) and union wage rates cannot generally be controlled by middle- or lower-level unit managers. Therefore, these uncontrollable variables would be excluded from their standards for performance.

Measurement and Evaluation.

Once standards have been set, the next phase of the control process is to measure and evaluate inputs and performance. Measurement of inputs and outcomes may take the form of either personal observation or sophisticated managerial accounting procedures. Personal observation is the most widely used method of measuring in the control process. It is relied upon especially when controlling human performance. One systematic strategy for controlling by personal observation is what Tom Peters calls MBWA (management by walking around). He describes how Andy Pearson, when CEO of PepsiCo, did it:

> Much of [his] time was spent visiting subsidiaries. When he did so, the routine was standard. He ignored the executive suite at first, and headed for the office of the most recently hired member of the brand management staff. "What's up? What've you got going in the test market? How're they reacting to the new umpty-ump flavor?" And so on. Implicit (pretty explicit, come to think of it) was the message that something had better be going on.[42]

Although PepsiCo, Hewlett-Packard, GE, and many other "excellent" companies have successfully used observational data by their managers through MBWA, not all managers are capable of obtaining and using observation to measure performance effectively. What the visual sense picks up, the perceptual interpretation, and the reality may be three completely different things, as was discussed in detail in Chapter 6. The complex psychological process of perception greatly influences the use of personal observation as a measuring technique. In addition, the other psychological processes of learning and motivation strongly affect observation. Besides having a complicating psychological impact, personal observation is very time-consuming. Despite these real and potential problems, most management experts maintain that personal observation is one of the best ways to control people.

Traditionally, accounting theory and practice concentrated on providing information for external users. In recent years, the emphasis in accounting has shifted to internal or management usage. Managerial accounting and computerized information systems generate considerable objective financial and operating data, and have become a major method of measurement in the control process.

Corrective Control Decisions. The third and final element of the control process is corrective action taken in the form of a control decision. Merely setting standards and measuring and evaluating inputs and performance do not achieve control. A control decision must be made in order for the control process to be complete. The third phase occurs in the same place as the first phase—the decision-making center. For example, suppose that a deviation from standards is detected by the measuring devices. An evaluation may lead to one of the following conclusions: The standards were set wrong; there is a need to "tighten up" and obtain conformance between standards and inputs or performance; new motivational techniques are needed to gain compliance with standards; or maintenance of the current deviation should be attempted. Each of these possible conclusions requires a corresponding control decision. If the first conclusion is adopted, the decision will be to reexamine present standards and/or make new ones. With the second conclusion, the decision may be to reprimand or fire the personnel involved and put on more pressure. The third conclusion may lead to a decision that installs a new wage-incentive plan or supervisory style. For the fourth conclusion, the decision would be to maintain the status quo and continue to do things as they have been done in the past.

In effect, the manager who is trying to control is like the captain of a ship. The captain receives information on the location and bearing of the ship and then adjusts the course in order to arrive at the planned destination. In a similar manner, the manager receives feedforward or feedback information about the inputs or performance of the unit and then makes a control decision that will accomplish the unit's objectives.

Behavioral Implications of Control

The behavioral approach to management has probably caused more concern about control than about any of the other processes. Much of this concern is a carryover from the assumption that any form of control restricts individual freedom. The introductory discussion attempted to modify this totally negative attitude toward control. Some forms and degrees of control are essential and are even desired by most people. On the other hand, organizational controls, when put into practice, often create a situation in which personnel attempt to work against, rather than with, the control system. In a typical control process, personnel frequently try to reap the rewards of good results for themselves but shift the blame for poor results to someone else. The NIH factor (not invented here) seems to go into effect whenever anything goes wrong. Some of the specific behavioral opposition to control can be found at each step of the process—disagreement with the objectives and standards, how performance is measured and evaluated, and, in some cases, the corrective decisions that are made.

Although there is undoubtedly justifiable criticism of the design, implementation, and use of control, there seems to be no legitimate argument against the need for control itself. Controls can create more predictability in a person's own behavior and in the behavior of other relevant persons in the situation. The individual tends to equate predictability with freedom.

There is nothing behaviorally wrong with the control process per se. The key to organizational effectiveness is to obtain an optimum mix composed of freedom *and* control. Both are necessary, and too much of either may have a detrimental effect on organizational performance. What the exact mix turns out to be depends upon many variables. Fortunately, there are some behaviorally oriented techniques that can help today's managers control their operations more effectively.

Until recent years, many organizations had suffered from what could be called the "vicious-cycle syndrome." This simply means that in many organizations controls had become ends in themselves: there were controls to control the controls. Behaviorally oriented techniques have emerged to combat this vicious cycle. Included would be participative budgeting and goal setting.

Although the techniques of control are becoming more behaviorally oriented and although there is a movement toward techniques such as participative budgeting and goal setting, if the control process is to be fully compatible with the human being, a sense of self-control must ultimately be developed. The background and specific strategies of self-control were covered in Chapter 12.

Summary

This chapter has been devoted to two of the most important organizational processes: decision making and control. *Decision making* is defined as choosing between two or more alternatives. However, viewed as a process, the actual choice activity is preceded by gathering information and developing alternatives. The relevant behavioral models for analyzing decision-making rationality include the completely rational econologic model on one extreme, Herbert Simon's bounded rationality model and the Peters-Waterman "well-managed" model in the middle range, and the irrationally based social models of psychology on the other extreme. Each of these models gives insights into decision-making rationality, but the findings of Peters and Waterman are currently having the biggest impact on actual decision-making practice.

The techniques for decision making have been dominated mainly by quantitative models. The participation techniques do not begin to approach the sophistication of the quantitative models. Yet it is the creative, problem-solving management decisions which are crucial for organizational success. Group techniques such as Delphi and NGT and computer-assisted techniques such as artificial intelligence and expert systems offer some hope for the future.

The management control process consists of three basic elements; (1) standards and objectives, (2) measurement and evaluation, and (3) corrective action. The first phase is closely associated with planning and goal setting. The standards and objectives that are set reflect the performance levels and criteria for management plans. Management can measure and evaluate inputs and performance against standards and objectives in several ways. Measurement depends largely on personal observation through MBWA and managerial accounting and computerized information systems. The last phase of the control process occurs when a corrective control decision is made.

All three elements of control have a significant impact on human behavior in organizations. The behavioral theorists have aimed a great deal of criticism at the ways in which management has traditionally controlled. The problem is not with control per se but rather with how controls have been set and used in practice. Recently, there has been a definite trend toward making controls more behaviorally compatible through such techniques as participative budgeting and goal setting. The ultimate goal is to create self-control among organizational participants.

Questions for Discussion and Review

1. What are the three steps in Simon's decision-making process? Relate these steps to an actual decision.
2. Compare and contrast the econologic model and the social model.
3. Describe the major characteristics of Simon's bounded rationality model. Do you think this model is descriptive of practicing executives? How does this compare with what Peters and Waterman found in the well-managed companies?
4. Explain a hypothetical situation in which Delphi and/or NGT could be used.
5. What role do you feel artificial intelligence and expert systems will play in the future of managerial decision making?
6. Explain the statement, "The existence of the control process implies that the decision-making and communication processes are not perfect."
7. What is the difference between feedforward and feedback control? Give an example of feedforward control.
8. What are the three basic elements of the control process? Briefly describe the major facets of each element.
9. What are some behavioral implications of control?

References

1. Chester I. Barnard, *The Functions of the Executive,* Harvard University Press, Cambridge, Mass., 1938, p. 14.
2. Herbert A. Simon, *The New Science of Management Decision,* Harper, New York, 1960, p. 2.
3. Henry Mintzberg, Duru Raisinghani, and André Theoret, "The Structure of 'Unstructured' Decision Processes," *Administrative Science Quarterly,* June 1976, pp. 246–275.

4. Richard L. Daft, *Organization Theory and Design,* West, St. Paul, Minn., 1983, pp. 357–358.
5. Herbert A. Simon, *Administrative Behavior,* 2d ed., Macmillan, New York, 1957, p. 64.
6. Ibid., p. 65.
7. Ibid., pp. 76–77.
8. Ibid., p. xxiii.
9. Thomas J. Peters and Robert H. Waterman, Jr., *In Search of Excellence: Lessons from America's Best-Run Companies,* Harper & Row, New York, 1982, p. 29.
10. Solomon E. Asch, "Opinions and Social Pressure," *Scientific American,* November 1955, pp. 31–35.
11. Fred Luthans and Robert Koester, "The Impact of Computer-Generated Information on the Choice Activity of Decision Makers," *Academy of Management Journal,* June 1976, pp. 328–332; and Robert Koester and Fred Luthans, "The Impact of the Computer on the Choice Activity of Decision Makers: A Replication with Actual Users of Computerized MIS," *Academy of Management Journal,* June 1979, pp. 416–422.
12. Simon, *Administrative Behavior,* pp. xxv–xxvi.
13. E. Frank Harrison, *The Managerial Decision-Making Process,* Houghton Mifflin, Boston, 1975, p. 69.
14. Peters and Waterman, op. cit., pp. 44–52.
15. Ibid., p. 47.
16. Ibid., p. 48.
17. Ibid., p. 49.
18. Thomas J. Peters and Robert H. Waterman, Jr., "In Pursuit of Excellence," *Continental,* March 1983, pp. 70, 88–93, 96.
19. Michael A. Hitt and R. Duane Ireland, "Peters and Waterman Revisited: The Unended Quest for Excellence," *Academy of Management Executive,* May 1987, pp. 91–98.
20. Miriam Erez, P. Christopher Earley, and Charles L. Hulin, "The Impact of Participation on Goal Acceptance and Performance: A Two-Step Model," *Academy of Management Journal,* March 1985, pp. 50–66.
21. J. Kenneth White, "The Scanlon Plan: Causes and Correlates of Success," *Academy of Management Journal,* June 1979, pp. 292–312.
22. "Worker Participation at A&P Stores Gives the Chain a Boost," *The Wall Street Journal,* Jan. 6, 1987, p. 1.
23. George Munchus, "Employer-Employee Based Quality Circles in Japan: Human Resource Policy Implications for American Firms," *Academy of Management Review,* April 1983, p. 255.
24. David M. Schweiger and Carrie R. Lena, "Participation in Decision Making," in Edwin A. Locke (ed.), *Generalizing from Laboratory to Field Settings,* Lexington Books, Lexington, Mass., 1986, p. 148.
25. John L. Cotton, David A. Vollrath, Kirk L. Froggatt, Mark L. Lengnick-Hall, and Kenneth R. Jennings, "Employee Participation: Diverse Forms and Different Outcomes," *Academy of Management Review,* January 1988, pp. 8–22.
26. Trish Hall, "When Budding MBAs Try to Save Kool-Aid, Original Ideas Are Scarce," *The Wall Street Journal,* Nov. 25, 1986, p. 31.
27. Andre L. Delbecq, Andrew H. Van deVen, and David H. Gustafson, *Group Techniques for Program Planning,* Scott, Foresman, Glenview, Ill., 1975, p. 8.
28. A. H. Van deVen, *Group Decision-Making Effectiveness,* Kent State University Center for Business and Economic Research Press, Kent, Ohio, 1974.
29. John Rohrbaugh, "Improving the Quality of Group Judgment: Social Judgment Analysis and the Nominal Group Technique," *Organizational Behavior and Human Performance,* October 1981, pp. 272–288.

30. Thad B. Green, "An Empirical Analysis of Nominal and Interacting Groups," *Academy of Management Journal,* March 1975, pp. 63–73.

31. David R. Hampton, Charles E. Summer, and Ross A. Webber, *Organizational Behavior and the Practice of Management,* 5th ed., Scott, Foresman, Glenview, Ill., 1987, p. 274.

32. "Home Computing for After-Hours Work Gains in Popularity," *The Wall Street Journal,* Jan. 6, 1987, p. 1.

33. "NASA Unveils Supercomputer," *Lincoln Journal,* Mar. 9, 1987, p. 12. Also see: Philip Elmer-Dewitt, "Fast and Smart," *Time,* March 28, 1988, pp. 54–58.

34. "The Next Computers," *Newsweek,* Apr. 6, 1987, p. 60.

35. Thomas P. Kehler, "AI, or 'Knowledge Processing,' Will Be a Boon to MIS," *Information Week,* Jan. 26, 1987, p. 46. Also see: Eugene Linden, "Putting Knowledge to Work," *Time,* March 28, 1988, pp. 60–63.

36. Fred V. Guterl, "Computers Think for Business," *Dun's Business Month,* October 1986, p. 34.

37. Ibid., p. 32.

38. William M. Bulkeley, "Expert Systems Are Entering into Mainstream of Computers," *The Wall Street Journal,* Dec. 5, 1986, p. 35.

39. For example, see Dorothy Leonard-Barton, "The Case for Integrative Innovation: An Expert System at Digital," *Sloan Management Review,* Fall 1987, p. 7.

40. Henri Fayol, *General and Industrial Management* (trans. by Constance Storrs), Pitman, London, 1949, p. 107.

41. Fred Luthans and Robert Kreitner, *Organizational Behavior Modification and Beyond,* Scott, Foresman, Glenview, Ill., 1985, p. 94.

42. Tom Peters and Nancy Austin, *A Passion for Excellence,* Random House, New York, 1985, p. 23.

**REAL CASE:
Getting
Additional
Information***

In recent years managers have begun to realize one important fact about decision making and control: the more information they can gather on a particular area or problem, the more likely it is that they can make a good decision and have effective control. The result has been the mushrooming of the information processing business.

As early as the 1970s many entrepreneurs with a close eye on what was needed in management decision making and control were forecasting an "information market" boom. They believed that both business firms and consumers would be willing to pay to have information provided to them. For example, General Motors might want to know the most recent articles or news releases on cars with front-wheel drive. One way to get this information would be to have someone in the public relations department cut and clip every piece of information found in all the newspapers and journals that the company purchased. An easier way, however, would be to subscribe to a news retrieval service that would provide all this same information for the asking. All subscribers have to do is use the computer to the tell the retrieval service the types of information they want. The

Source: Adapted from Anne R. Field and Catherine L. Harris, "The Information Business," *Business Week,* Aug. 25, 1986, pp. 82–90.

computer will then search its files and print out everything related to the topic areas requested by the customer.

Today, a number of firms are providing information services to clients. Examples include the following:

- Dow Jones News/Retrieval accumulates information collected by the company's news organization, divides it into categories such as financial data, stock prices, and international news, and sells each separately to subscribers.
- Reuters, the news agency, sells software that allows currency and commodities traders to spot opportunities based on their own strategies. The data used by the software are obtained from Reuters's database.
- The Institute for Scientific Information scans approximately 7000 scientific and medical journals and indexes them for 300,000 customers.
- Telerate sells financial information on such things as money market and foreign currency rates.

In addition to the examples above, a number of other new information services are springing up. One is that of Strategic Intelligence Systems (SIS) Inc., which has built databases on eighteen separate industries. These data include economic trends, product development, and other information useful for strategy formulation and implementation. By interviewing its clients and finding out the kinds of information they need, SIS helps client managers make better decisions and control operations more effectively. Another service is CompuServe Inc., which provides its subscribers everything from airline schedules to stock reports to electronic shopping services to games. As management finds itself needing more and more timely information for decision making and control, computerized information services are likely to become increasingly important.

1. When managers use the services to provide themselves with information, what phase of the decision-making process and the control process are they focusing on?
2. Of what value are information services to today's decision makers? Do these services allow the manager to make decisions along the line of the econological model?
3. Are we likely to see greater use of these information services in the future? Why or why not?

**CASE:
Harry Smart
or Is He?**

Harry Smart, a very bright and ambitious young executive, was born and raised in Boston and graduated from a small New England college. He met his future wife, who was also from Boston, in college. They were married the day after they both graduated cum laude. Harry then went on to Harvard, where he received an MBA. He is now in his seventh year with Brand Corporation, which is located in Boston.

As part of an expansion program, the board of directors of Brand has decided to build a new branch plant. The president personally selected Harry to be the manager of the new plant and informed him that a job well done would guarantee him a vice presidency in the corporation. Harry was appointed chairperson, with final decision-making privileges, of an ad hoc committee to determine the location of the new plant. At the initial meeting, Harry explained the ideal requirements for the new plant. The members of the committee were experts in transportation, marketing, distribution, labor economics, and public relations. He gave them one month to come up with three choice locations for the new plant.

A month passed and the committee reconvened. After weighing all the variables, the experts recommended the following cities in order of preference: Kansas City, Los Angeles, and New York. Harry could easily see that the committee members had put a great deal of time and effort into their report and recommendations. A spokesperson for the group emphasized that there was a definite consensus Kansas City was the best location for the new plant. Harry thanked them for their fine job and told them he would like to study the report in more depth before he made his final decision.

After dinner that evening he asked his wife, "Honey, how would you like to move to Kansas City?" Her answer was quick and sharp. "Heavens, no!" she said. "I've lived in the East all my life, and I'm not about to move out into the hinterlands. I've heard the biggest attraction in Kansas City is the stockyards. That kind of life is not for me." Harry weakly protested, "But, honey, my committee strongly recommends Kansas City as the best location for my plant. Their second choice was Los Angeles and the third was New York. What am I going to do?" His wife thought a moment and then replied, "Well, I would consider moving to New York, but if you insist on Kansas City, you'll have to go by yourself!"

The next day Harry called his committee together and said, "Gentlemen, you should all be commended for doing an excellent job on this report. However, after detailed study, I am convinced that New York will meet the needs of our new plant better than Kansas City or Los Angeles. Therefore, the decision will be to locate the new plant in New York. Thank you all once again for a job well done."

1. Did Harry make a rational decision?
2. What model of decision rationality does this incident support?
3. What decision techniques that were discussed in the chapter could be used by the committee to select the new plant site?

CASE: Lake Industries

Lake Industries is a small textile mill in northern Wisconsin that manufactures woolen clothing. For many years Lake has had a reputation for high-quality, long-lasting sportswear. Most of the employees were hired right after World War II. Most had fought in the war, returned home, and gone to work for Lake, the biggest employer in the small town. In recent years, these employees have begun to retire and are being replaced by young men and women from Milwaukee, the largest city in the state, which is 100 miles south. The labor pool in town dried up many years ago, and Milwaukee people who cannot find jobs at home migrate north to fill the openings at Lake Industries.

In recent years the quality of the clothing has badly deteriorated. The materials are still the best that money can buy, but the workmanship on the clothes is very sloppy and getting worse. Customers in the immediate region are beginning to cut back on their purchases of Lake Industries apparel, and the company's hard-earned reputation is beginning to crumble. The chief operating executive has held several meetings with his staff, and the problem seems to be that the production controls are breaking down. The older production supervisors complain that the new, younger workers refuse to be controlled, and spot checks with rank-and-file employees (old and young) indicate that the existing quality control has seemed to become an end in itself. Many of the old-timers mention that self-controls have been replaced by tight, bureaucratic controls in recent years. The chief executive is determined to turn the situation around. He feels that the company will have to reexamine the whole concept of control and institute some new control techniques to improve the quality of its clothes.

1. What do you think are some of the problems contributing to the quality deterioration of this company's products?
2. Analyze the finding that the "older production supervisors complain that the new, younger workers refuse to be controlled." What does this have to say about the control process at Lake? What about the statement that "self-controls have been replaced by tight bureaucratic controls"?
3. What would be involved in the reexamination of the whole concept of control at Lake? What would be involved in each of the three phases of control?

⑲ Organization Theory and Design

Is Bureaucracy on the Decline?*

Most predictions are that organizations will continue to downsize—eliminate middle layers of management—in the 1990s. Such downsizing has transformed the structure of modern organizations—and will continue to do. Observers feel there are three major factors behind the decline of middle management:

1. Because of increased competition, companies can no longer afford to retain "number-crunching and report-writing" middle managers.
2. Advances in computer and communications technology make it possible for machines to perform traditional middle-management duties more cheaply and accurately.
3. The growth of the service sector has created a demand for middle managers from the traditional goods-producing industries.

The managers who survive downsizing will see a change in some of their duties and functions. One change will be a shift away from simply providing staff backup and overseeing the work of others to that of directly contributing to the company's bottom line. These "new" managers will be required to add value to the products or the organization itself and are therefore referred to as "value-added managers." Mark Buler, senior vice president of human resources at Bankers Trust, comments: "Managing used to mean getting things

*Source: Adapted from Peter Nulty, "The Economy of the 1990s: How Managers Will Manage," Fortune, Feb. 22, 1987, pp. 47–50.

done through others. Now it means getting value added, and that's a revolution." While such changes make the manager's job more demanding, it also makes his or her job much more meaningful. Instead of performing bureaucratic tasks such as writing reports and filling out forms, the new manager will be practicing the craft (e.g., sales or engineering) he or she started with.

Downsizing also marks a move away from the classical bureaucratic organization. As the middle-management layer is eliminated, the pyramidal shape characteristic of bureaucracies is flattened. Some organizations have replaced the classic bureaucratic structure with a matrix design. For instance, General Electric, which has cut 90,000 from its ranks in the last five years, has centralized its functions and adopted a matrix system. As a result, a product manager is now responsible for working with one or two specialists from each division (designing, engineering, production, marketing) rather than being accountable for all the people in each fuction. Thus, in this type of structure, rather than the traditional vertical structure of communication and authority, a manager must know how to exchange information and manage horizontally. If these predictions ring true, the 1990s will see major changes in organization structure. Bureaucracy may indeed finally be on its way out.

Learning Objectives

- DEFINE the bureaucratic model.
- ANALYZE the dysfunctions of bureaucracy.
- DISCUSS the modifications of bureaucracy, including centralization/ decentralization, flat/tall, departmentation, and staff dimensions.
- EXPLAIN the modern organization theories of open systems, information processing, and contingency.
- PRESENT the modern project and matrix designs of organization.

In this chapter, the inductive conceptual framework moves to the extreme macro level of analysis for organizational behavior. This chapter is concerned with organization theory and design. Organization structure represents the skeletal framework for organizational behavior. As the discussion of the conceptual model in Chapter 1 pointed out, the organization structure is the dominant environmental factor that interacts with the person and the behavior. This chapter presents the organization from the viewpoint of classical and modern theory and design. The bureaucratic model of organization dominates the classical approach. After presenting and discussing this model, the chapter gives an overview and analysis of some of the extensions and modifications represented by the concepts of centralization and decentralization, flat and tall structures, departmentation, and line and staff.

Although the classical approach is still much in evidence today, as the introductory vignette pointed out, organizations are in the process of dramatic change. Traditional ways of structuring are no longer always relevant to the modern situation. New theories and structural designs are emerging to meet new demands of growth, complexity, and change. In general, the modern approach to organization assumes more complexity and is more comprehensive in nature. For example, one modern organization theorist has noted: "Organization structure is more than boxes on a chart; it is a pattern of interactions and coordination that links the technology, tasks, and human components of the organization to ensure that the organization accomplishes its purposes."[1] The chapter reflects this more comprehensive theoretical understanding of organizations and presents some specific, newer structural designs. After a brief look at the roots of modern organization theory, the chapter discusses the systems, information processing, and contingency theories of organization. This is followed by a description and an analysis of project and matrix designs.

The Bureaucratic Model

A logical starting piont in the analysis of any theory is the ideal. Max Weber, one of the pioneers of modern sociology, presented what he thought was an ideal organization structure called a *bureaucracy*. His concern for the ideal was a natural extension of his interest in the development and change of Western society. He believed that rationalization is the most persistant cultural value of Western society. On an organizational level, the bureaucracy represented a completely rational form.

The Characteristics of Bureaucracy

Weber specified several characteristics of an ideal organization structure. The four major ones are the following:

1. *Specifications and division of labor.* Weber's bureaucracy contained "A specified sphere of competence. This involves (a) a sphere of obligations to perform functions which has been marked off as part of a systematic division of labor (b) The provision of the incumbent with the necessary authority . . . (c) That the necessary means of compulsion are clearly defined and their use is subject to definite conditions."[2] This statement implies that Weber recognized the importance of having the authority and power to carry out assigned duties. In addition, the bureaucrats must know the precise limits of their sphere of competence so as not to infringe upon that of others.

2. *Positions arranged in a hierarchy.* Weber stated: "The organization of offices follows the principle of hierarchy; that is, each lower office is under the control and supervision of a higher one."[3] This bureaucratic characteristic forces control over every member in the structure. Some organization theorists, such as Herbert Simon, have pointed out that hierarchy is in the natural order of things. An example lies in the biological subsystems, such as the digestive and circulatory systems; these are composed of organs, the organs are composed of tissues, and the tissues are composed of cells. Each cell is in turn hierarchically organized into a nucleus, cell wall, and cytoplasm. The

same is true of physical phenomena such as molecules, which are composed of electrons, neutrons, and protons.[4] In a manner analogous to the biological and physical structures, hierarchy is a basic characteristic of complex organization structures.

3. *A system of abstract rules.* Weber felt a need for "a continuous organization of official functions bound by rules."[5] A rational approach to organization requires a set of formal rules to ensure uniformity and coordination of effort. A well-understood system of regulations also provides the continuity and stability that Weber thought were so important. Rules persist, whereas personnel may frequently change. They may range from no smoking in certain areas to the need for board approval for multithousand-dollar capital expenditures.

4. *Impersonal relationships.* It was Weber's belief that the ideal official should be dominated by "a spirit of formalistic impersonality, without hatred or passion, and hence without affection or enthusiasm."[6] Once again, Weber was speaking from the viewpoint of ideal rationality and not of realistic implementation. He felt that in order for bureaucrats to make completely rational decisions, they must avoid emotional attachment to subordinates and clients/customers.

The four characteristics just described are not the only ones recognized and discussed by Weber. Another important aspect of the ideal bureaucracy is that employment is based on technical qualifications. The bureaucrat is protected against arbitrary dismissal, and promotions are made according to seniority and/ or achievement. In total, it must be remembered that Weber's bureaucracy was intended to be an ideal construct: no real-world organization exactly follows the Weber model. The widely recognized modern organization theorist Peter M. Blau summarizes Weber's thinking as follows:

> Weber dealt with bureaucracy as what he termed an ideal type. This methodological concept does not represent an average of the attributes of all existing bureaucracies (or other social structures), but a pure type, derived by abstracting the most characteristic aspects of all known organizations.[7]

It has been pointed out that the classical, rational approach to structure is of value to managers of formal work organizations that have no conflict or whose subordinates have no power,[8] but, of course, this is the ideal, not reality. The ideal is only the starting point, not the end, of organizational analysis.

Bureaucratic Dysfunctions

With the exception of Weber, sociologists and philosopers have been very critical of bureaucracies. For example, Karl Marx believed that bureaucracies are used by the dominant capitalist class to control the other, lower social classes. According to Marx, bureaucracies are characterized by strict hierarchy and discipline, veneration of authority, incompetent officials, lack of initiative and imagination, fear of responsibility and a process of self-aggrandizement.[9] This interpretation of bureaucracy is basically a list of functions opposite to what Weber proposed. The Weber model can serve equally well in analyzing either the functional or the dysfunctional ramifications of classical organization structure.

The Dysfunctions of Specialization.

The Weber bureaucratic model emphasizes that specialization serves efficiency. The model ignores, but can be used to point out, the dysfunctional qualities of specialization. Empirical investigation has uncovered both functional and dysfunctional consequences. In other words, specialization has been shown to lead to increased productivity and efficiency but also to create conflict between specialized units, to the detriment of the overall goals of the organization. For example, specialization may impede communication between units. The management team of a highly specialized unit has its own terminology and similar interest, attitudes, and personal goals. Because "outsiders are different," the specialized unit tends to withdraw into itself and not fully communicate with units above, below, or horizontal to it.

The Dysfunctions of Hierarchy.

What was said of specialization also holds true for the other characteristics of a bureaucracy. The functional attributes of a hierarchy are that it maintains unity of command, coordinates activities and personnel, reinforces authority, and serves as the formal system of communication. In theory, the hierarchy has both a downward and an upward orientation, but in practice, it has often turned out to have only a downward emphasis. Thus, individual initiative and participation are often blocked, upward communication is impeded, and there is no formal recognition of horizontal communication. Personnel who follow only the formal hierarchy may waste a great deal of time and energy.

The Dysfunctions of Rules.

Bureaucratic rules probably have the most obvious dysfunctional qualities. Contributing to the bureaucratic image of red tape, rules often become the ends for more effective goal attainment. The famous management consultant Peter Drucker cites the following common misuses of rules that require reports and procedures:

First is the mistaken belief that procedural rules are instruments of morality. They should not determine what is right or wrong conduct.

Second, procedural rules are sometimes mistakenly substituted for judgment. Bureaucrats should not be mesmerized by printed forms; forms should be used only in cases where judgment is not required.

The third and most common misuse of procedural rules is as a punitive control device from above. Bureaucrats are often required to comply with rules that have nothing to do with their jobs—for example, plant managers who have to accurately fill out numerous forms for staff personnel and corporate management which they cannot use in obtaining their own objectives.[10]

Drucker would like to see every procedural rule put on trial for its life at least every five years. He cites the case of an organization in which all reports and forms were totally done away with for two months. At the end of suspension, three-fourths of the reports and forms were deemed unnecessary and were eliminated.[11]

Dysfunctions of the Impersonal Characteristics.

The impersonal quality of the bureaucracy has even more dysfunctional consequences than specialization, hierarchy, and rules. Behaviorally oriented organization theorists and researchers have given a great deal of attention to the behavioral dysfunctions of bureaucratic structures. Much discussion in this book is critical of the impersonal characteristic of bureaucracies. The same is true of today's consumers and employees. Everyone has horror stories and everyday irritations dealing with impersonal bureaucracies.

The Modern View of Bureaucracies

The acknowledged bureaucratic dysfunctions have led most people to readily accept Parkinson's popular "laws" (for example, bureaucratic staffs increase in inverse proportion to the amount of work done[12]) and the popular "Peter principle" (managers rise to their level of incompetence in bureaucracies[13]). These "laws" and "principles" have received wide public acceptance because everyone has observed and experienced what Parkinson and Peter wrote about. But as one organizational scholar has noted:

> These two writers have primarily capitalized on the frustrations toward government and business administration felt by the general public, which is not familiar with the processes necessitated by large-scale organization. Parkinson and Peter made a profit on their best sellers; they added little to the scientific study of organizations.[14]

In addition to the popularized criticisms of bureaucracy, a more academic analysis also uncovers many deficiencies. Bennis summarized some of them as follows:

1. Bureaucracy does not adequately allow for personal growth and the development of mature personalities.
2. It develops conformity and "groupthink."
3. It does not take into account the "informal organization" and the emergent and unanticipated problems.
4. Its systems of control and authority are hopelessly outdated.
5. It has no juridical process.
6. It does not possess adequate means for resolving differences and conflicts between ranks and, most particularly, between functional groups.
7. Communication and innovative ideas are thwarted or distorted as a result of hierarchical divisions.
8. The full human resources of bureaucracy are not being utilized because of mistrust, fear of reprisals, etc.
9. It cannot assimilate the influx of new technology or scientists entering the organization.
10. It modifies personality structure in such a way that the person in a bureaucracy becomes the dull, gray, conditioned "organization man."[15]

Parkinson, Peter, and Bennis represent the extreme critics of bureaucratic organization. Nevertheless, during the past few years popular writers, scholars, practitioners, and the general public have felt increasing dissatisfaction and frustration with classical bureaucratic structures. This was reflected in the election of Ronald Reagan, whose major campaign platform was that he was going to reduce the size of the federal bureaucracy and make it more efficient; the consumerism movement, which is largely a grass-roots reaction to the impersonality of large bureaucracies in the private sector; and the tremendous appeal of best-selling books such as *In Search of Excellence: Lessons from America's Best-Run Companies*[16] and *The One Minute Manager*,[17] whose basic theme is that organizations should be made more fluid and less bureaucratic and that it should be realized that there are effective alternatives to the rational model of organizations.

In Tom Peters's latest book, he colorfully describes how he would like manangers to engage in bureaucracy bashing:

> Rant and rave. Tear up papers. Refuse to read them. Don't attend meetings. . . . Be outrageous. Get rid of all your file cabinets. . . . Put big cardboard boxes around your desk, and throw all the junk you receive into them—unread. Put a big red label on the boxes: "This week's unread paperwork."[18]

He recognizes that such drastic actions may jeopardize one's career, but feels that unless it is done, organizations depending on bureaucratic structuring, especially those which use vertical processing of information, will not be competitive or even, in the long run, survive.

Taken in perspective, the argument is not necessarily that the classical bureaucratic model is completely wrong but, rather, that the times have rendered many of those concepts and principles irrelevant. Bureaucratic organization is thought to be too inflexible to adapt readily to the dynamic nature and purpose of many of today's organizations and public needs. Flexibility and adaptability are necessary requirements for modern organization structures. The increasing size of organizations (as a result of both mergers and internal growth), computerization and the tremendous strides made in all types of technology, and the huge social and economic upheavals in recent years are but a few of the things which have contributed to a new organizational environment. As the opening vignette of the chapter indicated, many of today's organizations are reorganizing just to survive.

Well over half of the 1000 largest firms in America have undergone significant reorganization in the 1980s. Examples include Gulf & Western, which spun off sixty-five diverse subsidiaries worth more than $4 billion; IBM, which closed three domestic plants and cut back its work force 7 percent; AT&T, which cut back 32,000 employees, including 11,600 managers; and United Airlines, which cut back more than a quarter of its Chicago headquarters staff.[19] Much of this restructuring is the result of external forces—a slumping economy, foreign competition, and merger and acquisition activity. The traditional bureaucratic organization structure has not been able to deal with these dramatic changes. Something else is needed. The rest of this chapter discusses this "something else" besides bureaucratic principles that can and is being used to structure today's organizations.

Modifications of Bureaucratic Structuring

The classical bureaucratic model has served as a point of departure for modified vertical and horizontal structural arrangements in recent years. Vertical analysis concentrates on centralization versus decentralization and on flat versus tall structuring. These represent modifications of the classical principles of delegation of authority and limited span of control. Decentralization expands the principle of delegation to the point of an overall philosophy of organization and management. A *tall* organization structure means a series of narrow spans of control, and a *flat* structure incorporates wide spans. The bureaucratic principle of hierarchy is also closely related to the vertical concept.

Horizontal structural analysis is concerned with organizing one level of the hierarchy. The concepts of departmentation and of line and staff represent this approach. They are derived chiefly from the bureaucratic doctrine of specialization. Departmentation concentrates on organizing each level to attain optimum benefit from high degrees of specialization. The staff concept attempts to resolve the vertical and horizontal conflicts that appeared in the classical scheme. In general, the concepts discussed in the rest of this chapter carry the classical concepts one step further. They give greater weight to the human element and recognize that simple, mechanistic structural arrangements are not satisfactory for complex organizations.

Centralization and Decentralization

The terms *centralization* and *decentralization* are freely tossed about in the management and organization theory literature and in actual management and organization design. Most often, both the scholar and the practitioner neglect to define what they mean by the concept. There are three basic types of centralization and decentralization.

The first type is *geographic*, or *territorial,* concentration (centralization) or dispersion (decentralization) of operations. For example, the term *centralized* can be used to refer to an organization that has all its operations under one roof or in one geographic region. On the other hand, the dispersion of an organization's operations throughout the country or the world is a form of decentralization. The word "geographic" is often not stated, which adds to the confusion.

The second type is *functional* centralization and decentralization. A good example is the personnel function of an organization. A separate personnel department that performs personnel functions for the other departments is said to be centralized. However, if the various functional departments (for example, marketing, production, and finance) handle their own personnel functions, then personnel is considered to be decentralized. Both *geographic centralization* and *functional centralization* and *decentralization* are descriptive terms rather than analytical terms.

The third type is the only analytical use of the concept. This is where the terms *centralization* and *decentralization* refer to the retention or delegation of decision-making prerogatives or command. From an organization theory and analysis standpoint, this third type is the most relevant use of the concepts of centralization and decentralization. They are relative concepts because every organization structure contains both features, and the concepts differ only in degree.

Contrary to common belief, it is not possible to determine whether an organization is centralized or decentralized merely by looking at the organization chart. The determining factor is how much of the decision making is retained at the top and how much is delegated to the lower levels. This amount of retention or delegation is not reflected on the organization chart.

Optimum Degree of Decentralization.

Traditionally, the implication has been that decentralization is somehow better than centralization. In truth, neither concept is an ideal or intrinsically good or bad. Generally speaking, decentralization is much more compatible with the behavioral aspects of management. This relevancy is due in part to the lower-level participation in decision making that results from decentralization. Increased motivation is an extremely important by-product. Besides the behavioral benefits, more effective decisions are possible beca'ise of the speed and firsthand knowledge that decentralization provides. Decentralization also affords invaluable experience in decision making for lower-level executives. Finally, it allows more time for top management to concentrate on policymaking and creative innovation.

Many organizations are still experiencing success in moving from centralization to decentralization. For example, under the leadership of General W. L. (Bill) Creech, the Tactical Air Command (TAC) moved from a highly centralized to a highly decentralized structure. By making subunits more autonomous and creating pride of ownership, he was able to turn the Air Force's worst command into its best.[20] As a result of his success the Pentagon now gives commanders new authority to abolish regulations, streamline procedures, and do whatever is necessary to get the job done.

In business, Johnson & Johnson, the highly successful and largest U.S. pharmaceutical firm, has 165 units worldwide. Each has considerable autonomy. Although corporate headquarters in New Jersey sets overall corporate policies on financial and certain administrative matters, the unit presidents, many in their late thirties and early forties have full responsibility for their unit's research and development, manufacturing, marketing, and sales. For example, Johnson & Johnson sent thirty-eight-year-old Carl Spalding to head up its consumer products unit in South Africa. He not only independently ran the business but also had to hire, train, and promote black employees, even build housing for them, often in violation of local apartheid laws.[21] This is decentralization in action.

Behavioral Implications of Decentralization.

Although delegation was probably the most behaviorally oriented classical principle, decentralization represents an even more concerted attempt to incorporate behavorial ideas into organization structure. Decentralization recognizes and actually capitalizes on the importance of the human element. Most important, decentralization provides an opportunity for individual responsibility and initiative at the lower levels. Because of the popularity of decentralization, many organizations have been stimulated to incorporate the accompanying behavioral ideas. Yet, as has been pointed out, decentralization may be more fiction than fact in actual practice. Moreover, as mentioned earlier, there are indications tl it recentralization is occurring. Such a turn of events may wipe out the behaviorally oriented advances in organization that have been stimulated by decentralization.

From another viewpoint, there is a convincing argument that decentralization, as practiced, never did have a behavioral impact. Nobel Prize–winning organization theorist Herbert Simon gives two reasons for this view:

> *First,* we should observe that the principle of decentralized profit-and-loss account-
> ing has never been carried much below the level of product-group departments
> and cannot, in fact, be applied successfully to fragmented segments of highly
> interdependent activities. *Second,* we may question whether the conditions under
> which middle managment has in the past exercised its decision-making prerogatives
> were actually good conditions from a motivational standpoint.[22]

It is fair to say that, overall, decentralization has supported, and in some cases has stimulated, the behavioral approach to management. At the same time, there is little doubt that a wide discrepancy exists between the theory of decentralization and its practice. Yet, because of its wide acceptance, decentralization has had a definite impact on developing a managerial attitude favoring the implementation of behavioral concepts in organizations. However, in the future this may all change because of the movement toward recentralization.

Flat and Tall Structures

In organizational analysis, the terms *flat* and *tall* are used to describe the total pattern of spans of control and levels of management. Whereas the classical principle of span of control is concerned with the number of subordinates one superior can effectively manage, the concept of flat and tall is more concerned with the vertical structural arrangements for the entire organization. The nature and scope are analogous to the relationship between delegation and decentralization. In other words, span of control is to flat and tall structures as delegation is to decentralization.

The tall structure has very small or narrow spans of control, whereas the flat structure has large or wide spans. In tall structures, the small number of subordinates assigned to each superior allows for tight controls and strict discipline. Classical bureaucratic structures are typically very tall.

Advantages and Disadvantages.
Tall structures assume a role in assessing the value of flat structures similar to that of centralization in assessing the relative merits of decentralization. Tall structures are often negatively viewed in modern organizational analysis. More accurately, there are advantages and disadvantages to both flat and tall structures. Furthermore, flat and tall are only relative concepts; there are no ideal absolutes.

Both flat and tall structures could have the same number of personnel. However, the tall structure could have four levels of management, and the flat one only two levels. The tall structure has the definite advantage of facilitating closer control over subordinates. Notice that the term *closer* and not *better* control was used. The classicists, of course, equated *closer* with *better;* the more behaviorally oriented theorists do not. The very nature of flat structures implies that superiors cannot possibly keep close control over many subordinates. Therefore, they are almost forced to delegate a certain amount of the work. Thus, wide spans structurally encourage decentralization. The behavioral theorists would say that this opens up the opportunities for individual initiative and self-control.

From a behavioral viewpoint, self-control is much more effective than control imposed from above. This behavioral advantage of flat organization hinges on the assumption that there are capable people who can produce under conditions of relative independence. In other words, the analysis of flat and tall structures depends a great deal on what approach is taken to the human side of organizations. For discussion purposes, Douglas McGregor's famous Theories X and Y assumptions may be used to assess the merits of flat versus tall structures.

Relationship to Theories X and Y. McGregor's widely recognized traditional Theory X sees humans as innately lazy and in need of close control. In this view, the individual prefers to be told what to do and shuns responsibility. If this is correct, tall structures which encourage close controls would be the most appropriate form of structure. Theory Y takes an essentially opposite view of people, holding that they are not inherently productive. People's behavior depends on how they have been treated. If they have been under close controls and given no responsibilities, they will react by being stubborn and uncooperative. On the other side of the coin, if they are not given close controls but are assigned responsibility, according to Theory Y they will react by being highly motivated and self-controlled, and they will seek more responsibility. If in fact Theory Y depicts the nature of humans, a flat structure—which has build-in loose controls or, more appropriately, ends-oriented controls in which a great deal of responsibility is given to subordinates—will be more effective than a tall structure.

As to which view is correct, there are no ready answers. There is no doubt, however, that a simple Theory X or Theory Y interpretation of human behavior is much too abstract and limiting. The preceding chapters in this book have given a more comprehensive and meaningful analysis of human behavior than Theories X and Y. In general, however, the assumptions of Theory Y are probably more compatible with what is now known about human behavior than those of Theory X. But it should be remembered that the nature of organizational behavior is much more complex and varied than is implied by McGregor's theories.

Behavioral Implications of Flat versus Tall Structures. One behavioral implication that is often overlooked in analyzing flat versus tall structures is the opportunity that tall structures offer for more personal contact between superiors and subordinates. This contact is generally assumed to be negative and conflicting, but it need not be. In a tall structure, the superior may create a positive rapport with his or her subordinates that may not be possible in a flat structure.

Another consideration besides personal contact is the levels of communication in the two structures. In the flat structure there are few levels, which means that both downward and upward communication are simplified. There should be less distortion and inaccuracy. The red tape and endless communication channels associated with a bureacratic tall structure are not present in a flat structure. On the other hand, the increased equality that exists between subordinates in a flat structure may lead to communication problems. If no status or authority differentials are structurally created, a heavy burden is placed upon horizontal communications. As Chapter 17 brought out, the horizontal communication system is notably deficient in most organizations. The problem may be compounded in flat organizations, where more dependence is placed on this type of communication, but it is not structurally facilitated. Also, coordination may be seriously impaired by a flat structure for the same reason.

Overall, the flat structure, at least from a behavioral standpoint, is generally preferable to the tall structure. It can take advantage of the positive attributes of decentralization and personal satisfaction and growth. Although managers who have wide spans will have to give a great deal of attention to selecting and training subordinates, a flat structure has the advantage of providing a wealth of experience in decision making.

Together with these advantages, however, it must be remembered that flat structures only encourage decentralization and individual responsibility and initiative. The supervisor of a small span does not always keep close control and may occasionally decentralize, and the supervisor of a large span does not always create an atmosphere of self-control and decentralization. The degree of centralization or its reverse depends on the overall management and organization philosophy and policies and on individual leadership style and personality. All a flat or a tall arrangement does is structurally promote, not determine, centralization or decentralization and the approach taken toward the behavioral aspects of managing.

Departmentation

Departmentation is concerned with horizontal organization on any one level of the hierarchy, and it is closely related to the classical bureaucratic principle of specialization. There are several types of departmentation. Traditionally, purpose, process, persons or things, and place were the recognized bases for departmentation.[23] In more recent terminology, *product* is substituted for *purpose, functional* has replaced *process,* and *territorial* or *geographic* is used instead of *place.* In addition, time, service, customer, equipment, and alphanumeric have also become recognized types of departmentation. Each of these latter types of departmentation is fairly self-explanatory. Examples of each are as follows:

1. *Time* may be divided into first shift, second shift, and third shift.
2. *Service* may reflect first class, second class, and tourist class on a passenger ship.
3. *Customer organization* may exist in a large commercial loan department that lends to farmers, small businesses, and large industries.
4. *Equipment* may be broken down in a production unit into drill-press, punch-press, and polishing departments.

5. *Alphanumeric* departmentation may be utilized in telephone servicing where numbers 0000 to 5000 are placed in one department and numbers 5001 to 9999 are placed in another.

Because organizations of any size will contain more than one hierarchical level, there will always be different types of departmentation represented. A typical large industrial corporation may be territorially organized on the first major horizontal level, and each succeeding level may be organized by product, function, time, and equipment. Confusion is often created when a given organization is identified as having one type of departmentation; for example, General Motors has traditionally been known as a product-departmentalized structure. The confusion can be cleared up if it is remembered that an organization is identified as having one particular type of departmentation because at the primary level (that is, the first major organizational breakdown) it is organized and identified in this way. General Motors has been known as a product-departmentalized company because the primary level was organized into automotive and nonautomotive product divisions. However, it must be noted that many other types of departmentation are found in the lower levels of GM or any other organization that is designated by only one particular type of departmentation.

Functional Departmentation.

By far the most widely used and recognized type of departmentation is functional in nature and may be found in all types of organization. For example, in a manufacturing organization the major functions usually are production, marketing, and finance—the vital functions that enable a manufacturing concern to operate and survive. On the other hand, in a railroad organization the major functions may be operations, traffic, and finance, and in a general hospital they may be medical service, housekeeping, dietetics, and business. Although the titles are different, the railroad and hospital functions are nevertheless analogous to the manufacturing functions in terms of importance and purpose. The titles of various functional departments may differ among industries and even in organizations within the same industry. All businesses, hospitals, universities, government agencies, and religious organizations, as well as the military, contain vital functions and can be functionally departmentalized.

The greatest single advantage of functional departmentation is that it incorporates the positive aspects of specialization. Theoretically, functionalism should lead to the greatest efficiency and the most economical utilization of employees. In practice, however, certain dysfunctions that were discussed with regard to specialization may also negate the advantages of functional departmentation. For example, functional empires may be created that conflict to the point of detracting from overall goal attainment.

A typical case is that of the salesperson who is guided by the sales department goal of maximizing the number of units sold. In order to sell 2000 units to a customer, this salesperson may have to promise delivery by the end of the week and require no money down. The production department, on the other hand, has a goal of keeping costs as low as possible and therefore does not carry a very large inventory. It cannot possibly supply the customer with 2000 units by the end of the week. Finance has still another goal. It must keep bad-debt expense at a minimum and therefore must require substantial down payments and thorough credit checks on every customer. In this situation, the sales department is in conflict with production and finance. If the salesperson goes ahead and makes the sale under the conditions in the example, the customer may not receive the order on time, and if and when it is received, the customer may not be able to pay the bill. In either outcome, the company goals of customer goodwill and minimization of bad-debt expense will suffer because of the salesperson's action.

It is easy to place the blame in the above example on the individual salesperson or on the lack of management coordination and communication. They are both definitely contributing factors. However, an equal, if not overriding, difficulty is the subgoal loyalties that are fostered by functionalization. A true story told by Peter Drucker provides an example of this mentality:

> A railroad company reported a $20,000 per year cost item for broken glass doors in their passenger stations. Upon investigation it was found that a young accountant had 'saved" the company $200 by limiting each station to one key for the rest room. Naturally, the key was always lost and the replacement cost only 20 cents. The catch, however, was that the key cost was set up by financial control to be a capital expenditure which required approval from the home office. This home office approval accompanied by the appropriate paperwork took months to accomplish. On the other hand, emergency repairs could be paid immediately out of the station's cash account. What bigger emergency than not being able to get into the bathroom? Each station had an axe and the result was $20,000 for broken bathroom glass doors.[24]

The presentation of such examples does not imply that conflict is always bad for the organization. In fact, as Chapter 14 pointed out, many modern organization theorists think that conflict has a good effect on the organization that, in fact, outweighs the bad. Yet, as in the cases cited above, where functionalization creates conflict that hinders overall goal attainment, conflict is detrimental.

Product Departmentation. At the primary level, many organizations have chosen to organize along product or unit rather than along functional lines. The product form of departmentation is particularly adaptable to the tremendously large and complex modern organizations. It goes hand in hand with profit-centered decentralization. It allows the giant corporations, such as General Motors, General Electric, and Du Pont, to be broken down into groups of self-contained, smaller product organizations. Thus, the advantages of both large and small size can occur in one large organization. As companies such as Kodak, described in the accompanying Application Example, begin to diversify their product lines, product departmentation will take on even more importance.

The classical principle of specialization was earlier said to be the greatest benefit derived from functional departmentation. Although often ignored, specialization can also be applied to product departmentation. This was brought out as follows: "The executive who heads a battery manufacturing department

Application Example

Product Diversification Forces Restructuring at Kodak*

Executives at Kodak used to point out that few firms could achieve the high profit margins that their company received from its photography business. In fact, photography was just about the only business that Kodak was in. Today all of this has changed. The photo industry has become very competitive, costs have risen, and profits have plummeted for many firms. In responding to these developments, Kodak has now become a multiproduct firm with a host of autonomous units in its organization structure.

In an effort to expand quickly, Kodak has begun acquiring firms. For example, it recently purchased Texas-based Fox Photo for $96 million, now making it the nation's largest wholesale photofinisher. At the same time Kodak is introducing a host of new products into the marketplace, including printers, optical memory systems, a medical imaging device, and a 35-millimeter "point-and-shoot" camera. The company is also slashing its work force by 13,000 people, thereby reducing its overhead. The old days of being a single-product company are gone. Kodak is now positioned to be a multiproduct line firm that is better able to respond to its external environment. These developments at Kodak have required considerable restructuring of its organization. Only time will tell if this will pay off.

*****Source:** Adapted from Leslie Helm and James Hurlock, "Kicking the Single-Product Habit at Kodak," *Business Week*, Dec. 1, 1986, pp. 36–37.

generally knows more about production than other functional executives, but he also knows more about batteries than other production executives."[25] However, a greater advantage of organization on a product basis is the matter of control. Because of their self-contained nature, product departments are very adaptable to accounting-control techniques and management appraisal. Product department performance, measured according to several different criteria, can usually be objectively determined. Another advantage is that product departments can be readily added or dropped with a minimum of disruption to the rest of the organization.

As a structural form, product departmentation is very compatible with the behavioral approach. Many of the conflicts that exist in the upper level under functional departmentation are generally resolved by product departmentation. Under product organization, however, the functional conflicts may disappear at the upper levels but reappear in the lower levels that are functionalized. Yet, from the standpoint of overall organizational goals, functional conflict at lower levels may be preferable. Besides reducing the potential for conflict, product division can provide many of the same behavioral advantages offered by decentralization and flat structures. These include more opportunity for personal development, growth, and self-control. Once again, this is not a universal truth, because the advantages still depend on many other personal and organizational variables. All in all, however, product or unit organization, because of its self-contained characteristics, is potentially more structurally adaptable to the behavioral aspects of organization than functional departmentation is.

The Staff Concept of Organization

Staff organization goes way back in history. The military is given credit for its development. As early as the seventeenth century, Gustavus Adolphus of Sweden used a military general staff. The Prussians, with some influence from the French, refined the theory and practice of this concept. At the beginning of the twentieth century, the European version of military staff was installed in the U.S. armed forces. However, it was not until after the Great Depression that the staff concept was widely adapted to American business and industry.

Staff is not a clear-cut organizational concept. It often creates confusion and problems for the organization. Many of the problems stem from conflicting definitions regarding line and staff and the hybrid forms of staff used by many organizations. The military has escaped some of these problems because it has precisely defined and successfully implemented a pure staff system. Under the "pure" military approach, line carries command or decision-making responsibilities, whereas staff gives advice.

The Modified Staff Concept.

Almost every type of modern American organization has attempted to adopt to some degree the military staff concept. In contrast to the military, however, business, hospital, educational, and government organizations have not given proper attention to defining operationally the difference between line and staff. In the military, there definitely exists an informal, implied staff authority, but everyone understands the system and realizes that conflicts can be resolved by reverting to pure line-staff relationships. Unfortunately, this is generally not the case in other types of organizations. What usually develops is a lack of understanding of the line-staff roles and relationships, which often results in a breakdown of communication and open conflict. A typical example is the business corporation which has a myriad of line-staff roles and relationships. It is not unusual to find many lower and middle managers who do not really know whether and when they are line or staff. One reason is that they generally wear more than one hat. Normally, managers are line within their own departments and become line or staff when dealing with outside departments. The manager's functional authority is often not spelled out in the policies of the organization. As a result, personal conflicts and dual-authority situations are rampant. Chapter 14 gave specific attention to the problems of role ambiguity and conflict that can result from such line-staff relationships.

Although these weaknesses exist in a hybrid staff concept, benefits have also been derived. The larger, more technologically complex organizations depended a great deal on staff specialization during the 1960s and 1970s. However, there is evidence that in recent years many of these companies have gone "overboard" by adding too many staff personnel. This "staff proliferation" exists especially at corporate levels, and some management analysts feel that it has been a major reason for the problems many companies have had in recent years. Peters and Waterman noted that their "excellently managed" companies had comparatively few corporate staff personnel. For example, Emerson Electric has 54,000 employees, but fewer than 100 in its corporate headquarters; Dana has 35,000 employees, but decreased it corporate staff from about 500 in 1970 to around 100 today; and Schlumberger, a $6 billion diversified oil service company, runs its worldwide empire with a corporate staff of 90.[26] Because of the success of these companies with small staffs and the need to cut back on personnel costs as a result of the poor economy, all companies today are taking a hard look at their need for corporate staff personnel, and many are drastically reducing them.[27] They are beginning to look at more radical alternatives, rather than just modifications of classical structures. The next section presents these alternative ways of theorizing and structuring organizations.

The Roots of Modern Organization Theory

There are some recent aruguments that Weber's view of the classical bureaucratic model was mistranslated and that he really did not intend for it to be an ideal type of structure. Instead, he was merely using bureaucracy as an example of the structural form taken by the political strategy of rational-legal domination.[28] In other words, some of the orginal theories of classical structure may contain underpinnings for modern organization theory.

The real break with classical thinking on organizational structure is generally recognized to be the work of Chester Barnard. In his significant book *The Functions of the Executive,* he defined a *formal organization* as a system of consciously coordinated activities of two or more persons.[29] It is interesting to note that in this often cited definition, the words "system" and "persons" are given major emphasis. People, not boxes on an organization chart, make up a formal organization. Barnard was critical of the existing classical organization theory because it was too descriptive and superficial.[30] He was especially dissatisfied with the classical bureaucratic view that authority should come from the top down. Barnard, utilizing a more analytical approach, took an opposite viewpoint. As Chapter 15 pointed out, he maintained that authority really came from the bottom up.

Besides authority, Barnard stressed the cooperative aspects of organizations. This concern reflects the importance that he attached to the human element in organization structure and analysis. It was Barnard's contention that the existence of a cooperative system is contingent upon the human participants' ability to communicate and their willingness to serve and strive toward a common purpose.[31] Under such a premise, the human being plays the most important role in the creation and perpetuation of formal organizations.

From this auspicious beginning, modern organization theory has evolved in three major directions. The first major development in organization theory was to view the organization as a system made up of interacting parts. Especially the open-systems concept, which stresses the input of the external environment, has had a tremendous impact on modern organization theory. This was followed by an analysis of organizations in terms of their ability to process information in order to reduce the uncertainty in managerial decision making. Finally, the most recent development in organization theory has been the contingency approach. The premise of the contingency approach is that there is no single best way to

Example Executive Epigrams by Country*

An epigram typically is a poem or line of verse that is witty and/or satirical. Some international business managers have taken this idea one step further and created what today are called executive epigrams. These are charts that humorously depict the organization structure by country in which they operate. The following figure shows some of them along with the logic behind the specific structure.

In the United States everyone in the organization is convinced that he or she has a direct pipeline to the top person.

American

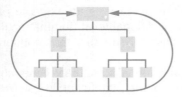

Italian organization have terrible lateral communication.

Italian

In Albania the second in command is typically bypassed by the boss who goes further down the line in his direct communications.

Albanian

Arab countries have no communication between the personnel.

Arabian

British organizations have excellent lateral communication but very little upward communication

British

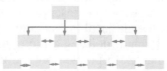

In Ireland, the bosses report to the workers — or so it seems.

Irish

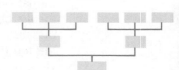

Norwegian

In Norway, no one in the hierarchy tells the lower-line workers anything. Their information is provided by subordinates who represent them on the board of directors.

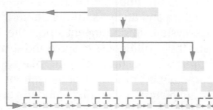

Source: Adapted from Simcha Ronen, *Comparative and Multinational Management*, Wiley, New York, 1986, pp. 318–319. The epigrams in turn were derived from a variety of sources, including Robert M. Worcester of the UK-based Market and Opinion Research International (MORI), Ole Jacob Raad of Norway's PM Systems, and anonymous managers.

organize. The organizational design must be fitted to the existing environmental conditions. The cultural environment even plays a role in organization structure. The accompanying International Application Example humorously depicts this cultural impact in its hypothetical structures by country.

Obviously, the three approaches are very closely related, and the contingency approach in particular tries to integrate them all. They serve as the foundation for the actual design of practicing organizations, which is covered at the end of this chapter.

The Organization as an Open System

Both the closed- and open-systems approaches are utilized in modern organization theory and practice. However, in today's dramatically changing environment an open-systems approach is becoming much more relevant and meaningful. The key for viewing organizations as open systems is the recognition of the external environment as a source of significant input. In systems terminology, the boundaries of the organization are permeable to the external environment (social, legal, technical, economic, and political).

The simplest open system consists of an input, a transformation process, and an output. This is depicted thus:

Input $\longrightarrow$ Transformation process $\longrightarrow$ Output

A system cannot survive without continuous input, the transformation process, and output.

There are many types of inputs, transformation processes, and outputs. For example, one kind of input actually enters the open system in the "closed" sense. In other words, this type of input has a direct effect on the internal system rather than an outside effect—in systems jargon, it loads the system. Another type of input affects the system in an "open" sense. Generally, this input would consist of the entire environmental influence on the system. Still another kind of input takes the form of replacement or recycling. When a component of the system is ejected or leaves, the replacement becomes an input. This recycling process perpetuates the system. Specific examples of inputs into a business organization include monetary, material, and human resources.

At the heart of the open system are the processes, operations, or channels which transform the inputs into outputs. Here is where the internal organization design plays an important role. The transformation process consists of a logical network of subsystems which lead to the output. The subsystems are translated into a complex systems network that transforms the inputs into the desired outputs.

The third and final major component of any simple open system is the output. This is represented by the product, result, outcome, or accomplishment of the system. Specific examples of the outputs of a business organization system that correspond to the inputs of monetary, material, and human resources are profit or loss, product sales, and role behaviors.

The simple open-systems concept has universal applicability. Any biological, human, social, economic, or technical phenomenon can be conceptualized in open-systems terms. As has been shown, an economic institution receives inputs of people, raw materials, money, laws, and values. The system then transforms these inputs via complex organizational subsystems into outputs, such as products, services, taxes, dividends, and pollution. From an organization structure standpoint, the critical factor is the design of the transformation process. Oddly, this transformation design involves a closed-systems analysis. In other words, the closed system is a subsystem of the open system. The closed-systems aspects of the transforamtion process are concerned with the interrelated and interdependent organizational subsystems of structure, processes, and technology. These subsystems must be organized in such a way that they will lead to maximum goal attainment or output.

Although the approach has decreased in popularity in recent years, it has been pointed out that, to date, very little research on organizations has been guided by open-systems thinking.[32] It is not that the open-systems approach has proved to be wrong or lacking in some way but rather that "in order to most fruitfully utilize the systems paradigm of organizations, scholars in the field must re-examine their beliefs about the paradigm and, perhaps, re-educate themselves about how they should think about and study organizations as systems."[33]

Information Processing View of Organizations

The recent view of organizations as information processing systems facing uncertainty serves as a transition between systems theory, which has just been discussed, and contingency theory, which is discussed next. The information processing view makes three major assumptions about organizations.[34] First, organizations are open systems that face external, environmental uncertainty (for example, technology or the economy) and internal, work-related task uncertainty. Jay Galbraith defines task uncertainty as "the difference between the amount of information required to perform the task and the amount of information already possessed by the organization."[35] The organization must have mechanisms and be structured in order to diagnose and cope with this environmental and task uncertainty. In particular, the organization must be able to gather, interpret, and use the appropriate information to reduce the uncertainty. Thus, the second assumption is as follows: "Given the various sources of uncertainty, a basic function of the organization's structure is to create the most appropriate configuration of work units (as well as the linkages between these units) to facilitate the effective collection, processing, and distribution of information."[36] In other words, organizations are information processing systems.

The final major assumption of this view deals with the importance of the subunits or various departments of an organization. Because the subunits have different degrees of differentiation (that is, they have different time perspectives, goals, technology, and so on) the important question is not what the overall organization design should be but, rather, "(a) What are the optimal structures for the different subunits within the organization (e.g., R&D, sales, manufacturing); (b) What structural mechanisms will facilitate effective coordination among differentiated yet interdependent subunits?"[37]

Taking the answers to these questions as a point of departure, Tushman and Nadler draw on the extensive relevant research to formulate the following propositions about an information processing theory of organizations:

1. The tasks of organization subunits vary in their degree of uncertainty.
2. As work-related uncertainty increases, so does the need for increased amount of information, and thus the need for increased information processing capacity.
3. Different organizational structures have different capacities for effective information processing.
4. An organization will be more effective when there is a match between the information processing requirements facing the organization and the information processing capacity of the organization's structure.
5. If organizations (or subuits) face different conditions over time, more effective units will adapt their structures to meet the changed information processing requirements.[38]

The above propositions summarize the current state of knowledge concerning the information processing view of organizations. "The key concept is information, and the key idea is that organizations must effectively receive, process, and act on information to achieve performance."[39] Although the focal point of this approach is the interface between environmental uncertainty—both external and internal—and information processing, it is very closely related to systems and contingency theories, and some organization theorists would argue that it could even be subsumed under either one.

Contingency Organization Theory

Analogous to the development of management as a whole has been the recent emphasis given to contingency views of organization theory and design. Open-system theory and information processing recognize environmental input, but the contingency approach goes one step further and relates this environment to specific organization structures. The starting point for contingency organization theory is generally recognized to be some significant research conducted at England's Tavistock Institute[40] by Joan Woodward[41] and by Burns and Stalker.[42] These pioneering efforts have since been refined by James Thompson[43] and Lawrence and Lorsch,[44] and more recently by the Aston group[45] (a group of researchers from the University of Aston in England), Charles Perrow[46] and others.[47] While it is not within the scope of this chapter to review all this research in detail, the pioneering work of Woodward and of Lawrence and Lorsch is still the most significant and is representative of contingency organization research.[48] Each of the others has a somewhat different emphasis, but the key is that all contingency theorists relate the environment to organization structure.

Modern Organization Designs

Along with organization theorists, many practicing managers are becoming disenchanted with traditional ways of designing their organizations. Up until a few years ago, most managers attempted only timid modifications of classical structures and balked at daring experimentation and innovation. However, many of today's managers have finally overcome this resistance to making drastic organizational changes. They realize that the simple solutions offered by the classical theories are no longer adequate for many of their complex problems. In particular, the needs for flexibility, adaptability to change, and overcoming environmental uncertainty are among the biggest challenges facing a growing number of modern organizations.

For example, Miles and Snow recently identified a new organizational form that they call the *dynamic network*. This involves a unique combination of strategy, structure, and management processes. They also suggest that in the future, new insights and terminology, such as vertical desegregation, internal and external brokering, and full-disclosure information systems, will become commonplace.[49] For now, however, the more widely recognized project and matrix structures will be discussed.

Project Designs

From a rather restricted beginning in the aerospace industry and in those firms having contracts with the Department of Defense, the use of project designs has increased in all organizations that require a great deal of planning, research, and coordination. In addition to the aerospace industry, project designs are becoming widely used in other industrial corporations and also in financial institutions, health care facilities, government agencies, and educational institutions. For example, project design has been credited with successfully downsizing General Motors automobiles in response to the gasoline shortage. Normally, such a major undertaking would be very cumbersome and complex and would take a very long time. But by creating project teams for the various divisions, GM was able to accomplish this major effort successfully in less than two years.[50]

Projects of various degrees of importance and magnitude are always under way in an organization. The project structure is created when management decide to focus a great amount of talent and resources for a given period on a specific project goal.

There are different ways in which the project approach can be designed. Figure 19.1*a* shows that the project managers under this design have no activities or personnel reporting directly to them. The project manager, along with the heads of quality control, research and development, contract administration, and scheduling, acts in a staff capacity to the general manager. The project manager must rely on influence and persuasion in performing a monitoring role, with direct line authority exercised only by the general manager.

Another type is shown in Figure 19.1*b*. Here, project managers have all the personnel necessary for the project. They have staff and functional line personnel reporting directly to them. Figure 19.1*b* shows that the project managers under the aggregate design have full authority over the entire project. In reality, the aggregate project organization is very similar to the traditional product or unit form of departmentation, which was presented earlier in the chapter.

There are other possible variations besides the two shown in Figure 19.1, and the project organization almost always coexists with the more traditional functional structure. But project experts stress that even though there are many similarities between project and functional organizations, project managers must take a new approach to their jobs:

1. They must become reoriented away from the purely functional approach to the management of human and nonhuman resources.
2. They must understand that purposeful conflict may very well be a necessary way of life as they manage their project across many vertical organizational lines.
3. They must recognize that project management is a dynamic activity in which major changes are almost the order of the day.[51]

These three statements make it clear that the project concept is a philosophy of management as well as a form of structural organization. The project viewpoint is quite different from the functional one.

Matrix Designs

When a project structure is superimposed on a functional structure, the result is a matrix. Sometimes the matrix organization is considered to be a form of project

FIGURE 19.1 *(a)* Types of project designs.

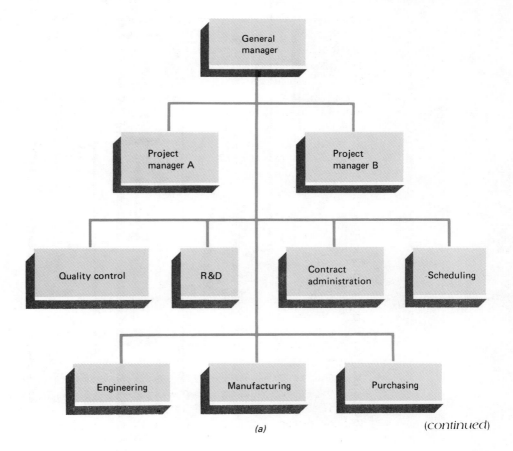

(a)

(continued)

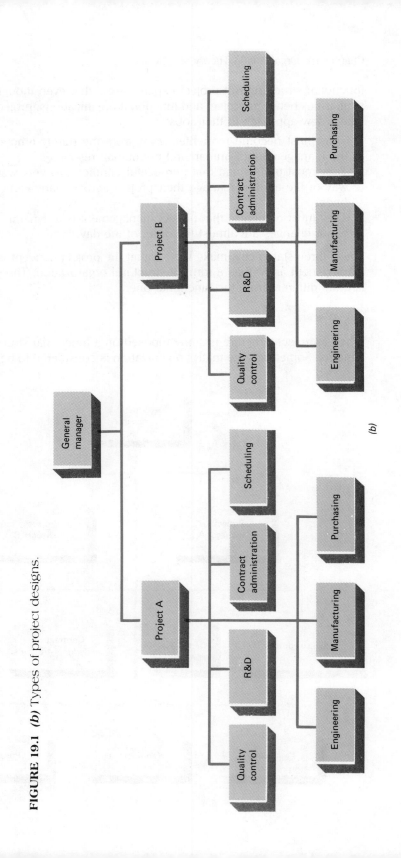

FIGURE 19.1 (*b*) Types of project designs.

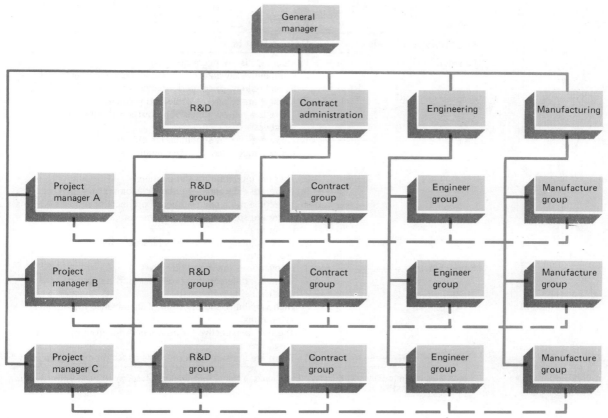

FIGURE 19.2 An example of a matrix design.

organization, and the terms are used interchangeably. However, a more accurate portrayal would show that the matrix organization is a project organization *plus* a functional organization. Figure 19.2 shows a very simplified matrix organization. Here, the functional department heads have line authority over the specialists in their departments (vertical structure). The functional specialists are then assigned to given projects (horizontal structure). These assignments are usually made at the beginning of each project by a collaboration between the appropriate functional and project managers.

It has been argued that the matrix structure evolves as shown in Table 19.1. Once the company has reached the matrix stage, there are also stages or degrees of this form of organization. The first stage of the matrix is usually just a temporary task force; this is followed by the creation of permanent teams or committees organized around specific needs or problems. The last stage occurs when a manager is appointed and held responsible for coordinating the activities and inputs of the teams or committees.[52] Similar to a project manager, the matrix manager needs negotiation skills and a high tolerance for ambiguous power relationships.[53] There is also recent support for the use of matrix designs as

TABLE 19.1 Determinants of the Evolutionary Stages of Matrix Designs

Organization Design	Determinants
Functional ⟶	1. Efficiency is the major objective.
	2. Competitive advantage is along a single parameter such as technology, price, performance, or delivery.
	3. Markets are relatively stable and predictable.
	4. There is a narrow range of products with long-term perspectives.
Project ⟶	1. There are several simultaneous objectives (for example, performance, cost, price, schedule, technology, and efficiency).
	2. There is moderate market change.
	3. There are differentiated clients/customers and markets.
	4. There is a moderate number of products or projects.
	5. There are specified time horizons for each client/customer or project.
	6. There is interconnectedness between outside and local organizations.
Product/matrix ⟶	1. Innovation is the major objective.
	2. There are differentiated products, markets, and customers/clients.
	3. High variability and uncertainty characterize the product-market mix.
	4. The time perspective for products varies from medium to long.
Matrix ⟶	1. There are the same determinants as for product/matrix.

Source: Adapted from Harvey F. Kolodny, "Evolution to a Matrix Organization," *Academy of Management Review,* October 1979, p. 551.

being appropriate and responsive to the strategies of diversified multinational corporations.[54]

Direct Violation of Classical Principles. Matrix designs violate the classical organizational principles. The hierarchy principle and the principle of unity of command are flagrantly violated. Furthermore, the matrix concept does not coincide with the usual line-staff arrangements discussed earlier in the chapter. Obviously, a great deal of conflict is generated in matrix organizations. An organizational specialist with IBM has observed that besides fostering conflict, the matrix structure discourages informal groups and the nurturing of supervisor-subordinate relations. After ten years of experience with the transition from traditional hierarchical to matrix organizations, he concluded that the matrix structure "has seemingly reduced participant motivation for all but the most aggressive personalities and has reduced corporate loyalty and identification with the organization."[55] An extensive empirical investigation of the engineering division of an aircraft manufacturing firm found that the matrix structure led to a decrease in the quality of communication and negative effects on relevant role perceptions, work attitudes and coordination.[56] These disadvantages are balanced by many positive aspects of the matrix organization.

Advantages of Matrix Designs. The matrix organization attempts to combine the best of both worlds. In an eclectic manner, it includes the positive aspects of both the functional and the project designs. These advantages can be summarized as follows:

1. The project is emphasized by designating one individual as the focal point for all matters pertaining to it.
2. Utilization of personnel can be flexible because a reservoir of specialists is maintained in functional organizations.
3. Specialized knowledge is available to all programs on an equal basis; knowledge and experience can be transferred from one project to another.
4. Project people have a functional home when they are no longer needed on a given project.
5. Responsiveness to project needs and customer desires is generally faster because lines of communication are established and decision points are centralized.
6. Management consistency between projects can be maintained through the deliberate conflict operating in the project-functional environment.
7. A better balance between time, cost, and performance can be obtained through the built-in checks and balances (the deliberate conflict) and the continuous negotiations carried on between the project and the functional organizations.[57]

Theorists who advocate a matrix structure maintain that these advantages outweigh the inherent disadvantages. Many contemporary organizations which are facing tremendous structural and technical complexity have no choice but to move to such an arrangement. The critical need for coordination and functional interrelationships can be met by adding a horizontal dimension to the functional structure.

Summary

Bureaucracy dominates classical organization theory and structure. Weber's bureaucratic model consists of specialization, hierarchy, rules, and impersonal relationships. Weber believed that this model was an ideal organization structure that would lead to maximum efficiency. Unfortunately, it does not always turn out this way in practice. In fact, there are probably as many dysfunctions as there are functions of bureaucracy. Specialization or hierarchy can lead to organizational efficiencies, but either can provoke detrimental conflict and impede the communication process. Rules often become ends in themselves rather than means toward goal attainment, and everyone can attest to the dysfunctional consequences of the impersonal characteristic of bureaucracies. Because of these and a number of other dysfunctions, many of today's theorists are predicting the decline and fall of the classical bureaucratic form of organization. Decentralization, flat structures, departmentation, and staff organization have developed to extend and modify the pure bureaucratic classical principles of organization. In general, the behavioral approach is more compatible with the modified structural concepts, but the dramatic changes that have occurred in recent years have led to the search for new, alternative ways to organize.

Modern organization theory was presented from the perspective of systems, information process, and contingency approaches. Systems theory emphasizes the impact of the external environment. The information processing approach views the importance of information flows in an organization to cope with internal differentiation and external environmental uncertainty. Contingency theory gives specific attention to the environment by relating it to organization structure and design.

The new organizational models that have recently come on the scene have been designed by practitioners primarily to meet their dramatically changing needs. The project and matrix structures represent a significant departure from the classical, bureaucratic model. The new structures flagrantly violate classical principles such as unity of command and equal authority and responsibility. Nevertheless, organizations with technologies that require flexibility and adaptability to change are willing to sacrifice the classical concepts. Only time will tell whether the new structural forms are suitable replacements for the classical structure. On the other hand, there seems little doubt that the new designs in general and the systems, information processing, and contingency concepts in particular have already proved themselves valuable enough to become a significant part of organization theory and practice.

Questions for Discussion and Reveiw

1. What are the major characteristics of Weber's bureaucratic model? Discuss the functions and dysfunctions of each.
2. Do you agree or disagree with those who are predicting the fall of bureaucracy? Defend your answer.
3. What are the various kinds of centralization and decentralization? Which one is most relevant to organizational analysis? Why?
4. Defend centralization as an important organizational concept. Do the same for decentralization.
5. Critically analyze functional versus product (unit) departmentation.
6. Why are many companies today cutting back on their corporate staff? What will happen to the specialized functions they performed for line managers?
7. What was Chester Barnard's contribution to organization theory?
8. How does the open-systems theory differ from the information processing and contingency approaches? How does the open-systems concept apply to organizations? How does the information processing concept apply to organizations? How does the contingency concept apply to organizations?
9. What are two different types of project structures? How does the project manager differ from the traditional functional manager?
10. The matrix design of organization is variously said to rest on classical, behavioral, systems, information processing, and contingency bases. Explain how each of these approaches could serve as the basis for the matrix design.

References

1. Robert Duncan, "What's the Right Organization Structure?" *Organizational Dynamics,* Winter 1979, p. 59.
2. A. M. Henderson and Talcott Parsons (trans. and ed.), *Max Weber: The Theory of Social and Economic Organization,* Free Press, New York, 1947, p. 330.
3. Ibid., p. 331.
4. Herbert A. Simon, *The New Science of Management Decision,* Harper, New York, 1960, pp. 40–41.
5. Henderson and Parsons, op. cit.
6. Ibid., p. 340.
7. Peter M. Blau, *Bureaucracy in Modern Society,* Random House, New York, 1956, p. 34.
8. Gregory K. Dow, "Configuration and Coactivational View of Organization Structure," *Academy of Management Review,* January 1988, p. 61.
9. Rolf E. Rogers, *Organizational Theory,* Allyn and Bacon, Boston, 1975, p. 4.
10. Peter Drucker, *The Practice of Management,* Harper, New York, 1954, pp. 133–134.
11. Ibid., p. 135.
12. C. Northcote Parkinson, *Parkinson's Law and Other Studies in Administration,* Houghton Mifflin, Boston, 1957.
13. Laurence J. Peter, *The Peter Principle,* Morrow, New York, 1969.
14. Rogers, op. cit., p. 4.
15. Warren Bennis, "Beyond Bureaucracy," *Trans-Action,* July–August 1965, p. 33.
16. Thomas J. Peters and Robert H. Waterman, Jr., *In Search of Excellence: Leasons from America's Best-Run Companies,*, Harper & Row, New York, 1982.
17. Kenneth Blanchard and Spencer Johnson, *The One Minute Manager,* Morrow, New York, 1982.
18. Tom Peters, *Thriving on Chaos: Handbook for a Management Revolution,* Knopf, New York, 1987, p. 459.
19. George Russell, "Rebuilding to Survive," *Time,* Feb. 16, 1987, p. 44.
20. Jay Finegan, "Four-Star Management," *Inc.,* January 1987, pp. 48, 51.
21. Jeremy Main, "Wanted: Leaders Who Can Make a Difference," *Fortune,* Sept. 28, 1987, p. 94.
22. Simon, op. cit., pp. 46–47.
23. Luther Gulick, "Notes on the Theory of Organization," in Luther Gulick and Lyndall Urwick (eds.), *Papers on the Science of Administration,* Institute of Public Administration, New York, 1937, p. 15.
24. Drucker, op. cit., p. 125.
25. Henry H. Albers, *Principles of Management,* 4th ed., Wiley, New York, 1974, p. 95.
26. Peters and Waterman, op. cit., p. 311.
27. "A New Era for Management," *Business Week,* Apr. 25, 1983, pp. 50–86. Also see Thomas Moore, "Goodbye, Corporate Staff," *Fortune,* Dec. 21, 1987, p. 65.
28. Richard M. Weiss, "Weber on Bureaucracy: Management Consultant or Political Theorist?" *Academy of Management Review,* April 1983, pp. 242–248.
29. Chester I. Barnard, *The Functions of the Executive,* Harvard, Cambridge, Mass., 1938, p. 73.
30. Ibid., p. vii.
31. Ibid., p. 82.
32. Donde P. Ashmos and George P. Huber, "The Systems Paradigm in Organization Theory: Correcting the Record and Suggesting the Future," *Academy of Management Review,* October 1987, pp. 607–621.

33. Ibid., p. 618.
34. These assumptions are identified in Michael L. Tushman and David A. Nadler, "Information Processing as an Integrating Concept in Organization Design," *Academy of Management Review,* July 1978, pp. 614–615.
35. Jay Galbraith, *Designing Complex Organizations,* Addison-Wesley, Reading, Mass., 1973, p. 5.
36. Tushman and Nadler, op. cit., p. 614.
37. Ibid., p. 615.
38. Ibid.
39. James L. Gibson, John M. Ivancevich, and James H. Donnelly, Jr., *Organizations,* 6th ed., Business Publications, Plano, Tex., 1988, p. 513.
40. The most famous Tavistock study is E. L. Trist and K. W. Bamforth, "Some Social and Psychological Consequences of the Longwall Method of Coal-Getting," *Human Relations,* February 1951, pp. 3–38.
41. Joan Woodward, *Industrial Organization,* Oxford, London, 1965.
42. Tom Burns and G. M. Stalker, *The Management of Innovation,* Tavistock, London, 1961.
43. James Thompson, *Organization in Action,* McGraw-Hill, New York, 1967.
44. Paul R. Lawrence and Jay W. Lorsch, *Organization and Environment,* Harvard Business School, Division of Research, Boston, 1967.
45. Examples of the Aston group's research would be D. S. Pugh, D. J. Hickson, S. Hinings, and C. Turner, "The Context of Organization Structure," *Administrative Science Quarterly,* March 1969, pp. 91–114; and D. J. Hickson, D. S. Pugh, and D. C. Pheysey, "Operations Technology and Organizational Structure," *Administrative Science Quarterly,* September 1969, pp. 378-397.
46. Charles Perrow, *Organizational Analysis,* Wadsworth, Belmont, Calif., 1970.
47. Paul D. Collins and Frank Hull, "Technology and Span of Control: Woodward Revisited," *Journal of Management Studies,* March 1986, pp. 143–164.
48. See Robert A. Baron, *Behavior in Organizations,* Allyn and Bacon, Boston, 1986, chap. 14, for a review of this literature.
49. Raymond E. Miles and Charles C. Snow, "Organizations: New Concepts for New Forms," *California Management Review,* Spring 1986, p. 62.
50. Charles G. Burck, "How GM Turned Itself Around," *Fortune,* Jan. 16, 1978, pp. 92–96.
51. David I. Cleland and William R. King, *Systems Analysis and Project Management,* McGraw-Hill, New York, 1968, p. 152.
52. Don Hellriegel, John W. Slocum, Jr., and Richard W. Woodman, *Organizational Behavior,* West, St. Paul, Minn., 1986, p. 417.
53. H. F. Kolodny, "Managing in a Matrix," *Business Horizons,* March–April 1981, pp. 17–35.
54. Jay R. Galbraith and Robert K. Kazanjian, "Organizing to Implement Strategies of Diversity and Globalization: The Role of Matrix Designs," *Human Resource Management,* Spring 1986, pp. 37–54.
55. Michael V. Fiore, "Out of the Frying Pan into the Matrix," *Personnel Administration,* July–August 1979, p. 6.
56. William F. Joyce, "Matrix Organization: A Social Experiment," *Academy of Management Journal,* September 1986, pp. 536–561.
57. Cleland and King, op. cit., p. 172.

REAL CASE:
Leaner
and Meaner*

During the 1970s General Motors was so large and so successful that it was afraid the government might try to break it up. By the early 1980s this was no longer a problem. The automotive giant was reeling under competition from Ford, Chrysler, and the foreign imports. Its market share was down 5 percent, and GM found it had to run just to keep up.

One of GM's biggest problems has been its bureaucratic structure. For decades the huge automaker has trained its managers to do things by the book. By the 1980s, when GM finally realized that greater autonomy and decision making had to be given to the middle- and lower-level managers, the company had a major problem on its hands. Many managers were unaccustomed to making decisions and doing things on their own. Moreover, the bureaucracy was so large that to get anything done took a long time. One past president noted that the Chevy division had become such a monster that if you twist its tail "nothing happens on the other end for months and months."

GM is now in the process of reducing its bureaucracy and becoming leaner and meaner. Some of the steps it has already taken include:

1. The five auto divisions have been reorganized into two profit centers: BOC (Buick, Oldsmobile, and Cadillac group) and CPC (Chevrolet, Pontiac, and GM of Canada).
2. Rather than having their own engineering, design, personnel, and other staff, the five car lines now share these tasks at the group level.
3. The General Motors Assembly Division, which managed most of the assembly plants, and Fisher Body, which built the auto bodies, have both been eliminated.
4. Workers in some assembly line operations have been organized into groups of ten to twelve and given authority for decisions in their own areas. As a result, work productivity has increased dramatically.

The company is also in the process of cutting layers of bureaucratic management. It estimates that between 1986 and 1990 it will reduce its managerial work force by 25 percent. Bureaucracy helped GM build a major auto empire. To the extent that it can reduce the inefficiencies of the monster it created, the company will continue to remain viable in a very competitive environment.

1. How did the bureaucratic form of organization help GM increase its size and become the largest firm in the industry?
2. Why is GM having to modify its bureaucracy? What is going wrong with it?
3. What benefits does a less bureaucratic structure offer to the firm?

***Source:** Adapted from Anne B. Fisher, "GM Is Tougher than You Think," *Fortune*, Nov. 10, 1986, pp. 56–64.

CASE: The Grass Is Greener— or Is It?

Alice Jenkins had been a supervisor of caseworkers in the county welfare department for nine years. The bureaucratic procedures and regulations became so frustrating that she finally decided to look for a job in private industry. She had an excellent education and employment record and soon landed a supervisory position in the production end of a large insurance firm. After a few weeks on her new job she was having coffee with one of the supervisors of another department. She said, "I just can't win for losing. I quit my job at county welfare because I was being strangled by red tape. I thought I could escape that by coming to work in private industry. Now I find out that it is even worse. I was under the illusion that private industry did not have the bureaucratic problems that we had in welfare. Where can I go to escape these insane rules and impersonal treatment?"

1. Is Alice just a chronic complainer, or do you think her former job was as intolerable as her present job, as she indicates? Do you think Alice is typical of most employees in similar types of positions?
2. How would you answer Alice's last question? Can you give an example of a large organization that you are familiar with that is not highly bureaucratized? Does the county welfare department or the insurance company have to be bureaucratized?
3. Can the concepts of decentralization, flat structures, departmentation, and staff be used in a welfare department or in the clerical area of a large insurance company? Give some examples if possible.

CASE: The Outdated Structure

Jake Harvey has a position on the corporate planning staff of a large company in a high-technology industry. Although he has spent most of his time on long-range, strategic planning for the company, he has been appointed to a task force to reorganize the company. The president and board of directors are concerned that they are losing their competitive position in the industry because of an outdated organization structure. Being a planning expert, Jake convinced the task force that they should proceed by first determining exactly what type of structure they have now, then determining what type of environment the company faces now and in the future, and then designing the organization structure accordingly. In the first phase they discovered that the organization is currently structured along classical bureaucratic lines. In the second phase they found that they are competing in a highly dynamic, rapidly growing, and uncertain environment that requires a great deal of flexibility and response to change.

1. What type or types of organization design do you feel this task force should recommend in the third and final phase of the approach to their assignment?
2. Explain how the systems, information processing, and contingency theories of organization can each contribute to the analysis of this case.
3. Do you think Jake was correct in his suggestion of how the task force should proceed? What types of problems might develop as by-products of the recommendation you make in question 1?

20 Organization Change, Development, and the Future

Well-known author and consultant Tom Peters recently declared that the United States was coming off 150 years of making big things that didn't work very well and if business didn't change, we could turn into a nation of shopkeepers and assemblers. Although most would not state the situation as dramatically as Peters, few businesspeople or members of the general public would disagree. American organizations need to change to be competitive in the global marketplace and in many cases even to survive.

One way of getting new ideas and ways of doing things to change today's organizations is through what author Gifford Pinchot calls intrapreneurship. A takeoff of old entrepreneurship, intrapreneurs are risk takers and innovators. But unlike old entrepreneurs, intrapreneurs work to change existing organizations rather than concentrate on starting up new ventures. Intrapreneurs have two dominant characteristics in their approach to the job. They have vision— they are looking for new ways to do things, they are full of new ideas; and, secondly, they are action-oriented—they want to move on things, take risks, get things done.

In the past, organizations have failed to identify and nourish intrapreneurs within their own ranks. In fact, intrapreneurs were often stifled and punished for not being "yes men" and for taking too many risks. Today, as organizations try to meet their challenging situations, many are trying to identify who their intrapreneurs are

*__Source:__ The examples of intrapreneuring are found in John Naisbitt and Patricia Aburdene, __Reinventing the Corporation,__ Warner Books, New York, 1985, pp. 64–67.

and giving them the necessary freedom and resources to make changes and get the job done. Some are even attempting to create a climate that will breed and develop intrapreneurs.

Many companies have alrady created such an intrapreneurial climate. For example, 3M requires that managers not only contribute to profits but also introduce at least 25 percent of new products every five years. Terra Tek, a small Salt Lake City high-tech firm, awards innovation grants to its people. And in Sweden, a shift worker at a paper mill built a large greenhouse heated by the company's excess heat and produces 125 tons annually of commercial grade tomatoes; and a draftsman at a steel mill started up an eel farm (yielding 100 tons annually) in an abandoned section of the plant.

Learning Objectives

- ANALYZE the competitive, economic and international forces of change impacting on today's and tomorrow's organizations.
- DISCUSS the background and process of organization development (OD).
- EXPLAIN the major techniques used in organization development (OD).
- IDENTIFY the trends that will affect the study and application of organizational behavior in the future.

Whereas the other chapters in this part were concerned with processes and structure of organizations, this chapter is aimed at the change and development of organizations. The term *organization development,* or simply OD, is used to represent an applied, macro-level approach to planned change and development of complex organizations. Many of the concepts and techniques (for example, job enrichment, MBO, and O.B. Mod.) discussed in previous chapters could be considered part of OD. However, this chapter is directly concerned with the general issue of the management of change and with widely recognized human and structural OD techniques.

After a general discussion of the impact of change, the overall characteristics of OD will be explored. Then the traditional and more modern OD techniques will be presented and analyzed. The overall track record of OD will be examined. The chapter will conclude with a brief look into the future of organizations and organizational behavior.

The Impact of Change

Most managers today recognize the inevitability of change, that the only constant is change itself. Take the case of General Radio. For more than thirty years this company dominated the market for electronic test equipment.[1] However, while competitors took advantage of changes in technology (computers and production system) and ways to deal with people (both customer service and human resources management), General Radio stayed with approaches they knew best, stayed with what had worked in the past. Then the company hit the skids—market share and profits declined. Only when the company made a complete transformation through new management did things turn around. Today, all organizations are facing such change, and they must be able to manage it, or not survive.

A wide variety of forces bombarding the modern organization make change inevitable. These forces can be summarized into broad areas of competitiveness, the economy, and internationalization.

Competitiveness as a Force for Change

While competition exists in every industry, and had traditionally been the "American Way," the 1980s have seen a dramatic increase in the competitive nature of many industries. One reason is the current social and political climate leading to decreased governmental regulation. The following examines this competitiveness in three representative industries.

The Case of the Airlines.   The airline industry used to be heavily regulated. Beginning in the 1980s, however, the government started relaxing its controls, and the competitive environment dramatically changed for the industry. At first the major airlines believed that the elimination of petty government controls would result in increased efficiency and greater bottom-line results. This was not to be.

As barriers for entry into the industry were lowered, capital investment became a much more important factor for success. Any firm that could raise sufficient capital was in a position to buy aircraft and get into the industry. Moreover, it was no longer necessary to receive governmental permission before flying a particular route. The more lucrative routes such as New York–Miami and the Northeast corridor (Washington–New York–Boston) became the focal point of intense competition. The result was that the daily number of available passenger seats increased and the competitors soon began engaging in vigorous price wars.

The combination of rising costs and decreased ticket prices drove many airlines to a breakeven point of around 60 percent of aircraft capacity. Unfortunately, for many of the companies, the vigorous competition kept their occupancy rate well below this percentage. At first passengers got low-priced fares and most of the airlines suffered drastic losses. Now, there have been many mergers and passenger service has suffered.

The Case of Personal Computers.   The mass market for personal computers, or PCs, was opened up by Apple Computer in the late 1970s. By the early 1980s, IBM, realizing that there was a potentially very large market among households, small businesses and large firms that could benefit from desktop models, entered this market. Apple's market share began to erode while Big Blues' rose toward 30 percent. By the mid-1980s, however, increased competition from "clones" was taking its toll. Foreign-manufactured IBM look-alikes were flooding the market at much lower prices than that charged by the computer giant. At the same time other companies were attempting to segment smaller shares of the market for themselves. Digital Equipment and Hewlett-Packard developed lap models that weighed less than 10 pounds, and Toshiba introduced a competitive product with a plasma screen.

As consumers became more knowledgeable about the product line, price became an important factor. Aware of what these machines could do and knowledgeable about how to use them, customers were now better able to compare the features of each. Result: only those personal computers which offered the most for the money were able to make the grade. IBM's PC Jr. was scrapped, and the firm begain slashing the prices of its other PC, AT, and XT models. Apple countered by offering large academic discounts and attempting to firm up its position in elementary schools and high schools. As everyone settled in for an extended battle, it was becoming clear that the profitability of the PC market was going to be much smaller than was thought a few years before.

The Case of Automobiles. In the early 1980s, Chrysler was able to bounce back from the "grim reaper" of bankruptcy. However, even Iacocca realized that Detroit's heyday was over. The Japanese had entrenched themselves so firmly in the American auto market that all of the Big Three American car producers entered into joint ventures with them. At the same time, European automakers were also doing quite well in the United States. For example, by the mid-1980s, Jaguar had come back strong and Porsche was holding a larger share of the market than ever.

As these foreign competitors began to carve out niches for themselves, the dominance of the American auto firms in the United States suffered serious erosions. In fact, Detroit has basically acknowledged that over the next twenty-five years its share of the American auto market will decline. Initially, General Motors hoped to solve its competitiveness problem with its small-car Saturn project. When the project was announced a few years ago, GM's chairman Roger Smith hailed it as "the key to GM's long-term competitivenesss, survival, and success as a domestic producer."[2] But this optimism soon dampened. GM halved Saturn's start-up budget and did not expect it to get fully off the ground until 1992. As a result, GM and the other auto firms cast about for additional business in which to invest for the future. An example is provided by General Motors' purchase of Hughes.

Because of the weakening dollar and productivity increases, auto production costs have recently lowered and the American companies have bounced back as a competitive force in world markets. For example, at the late 1980s exchange rate, the famous $2500 gap between cars made in Detroit and in Toyota City in Japan had disappeared, and costs were 5 to 10 percent lower than in Europe. This development has prompted Japanese and even Korean carmakers to set up factories in America. By 1990 Japan will have ten such plants (either on their own or in joint ventures with U.S. companies) and produce 2.5 million cars—the equivalent of another Chrysler.[3]

The airline, computer, and auto industries are highly visible, but not the only segments of the economy currently undergoing drastic change. Virtually all of today's organizations, in both the public and private sectors, are facing similar competitive pressures.

The Economic Force for Change

The state of the economy has always been a major, if not *the* major, force for change in a free enterprise economy. In good economic times, organizations, especially in the private sector but also to a large degree in the public sector, can "bury" their mistakes; they look good no matter what they do. But in bad economic times, no matter how good they are, it may not make a difference.

In the last decade there have been two recessions, the last one being the deepest and most severe since the Great Depression. These economic downturns brought about a large number of bankruptcies. In fact, toward the end of the 1980s savings and loan association failures were running at their highest annual rate since the 1930s. Many of these institutions had been lending money at 10 to 11 percent, and when the inflation of the early 1980s pushed interest rates beyond 14 percent, some S&Ls were no longer able to survive. It was costing them more to borrow money than they were receiving from their loans. Seeing difficult years ahead, many financial institutions such as Bright Banc Savings Association, a big Texas S&L, reacted by keeping a lid on hiring.[4]

Small businesses were also caught up in the inflationary squeeze. When interest rates got above the 12 to 13 percent ranges, the profitability of many small enterprises dried up. Many large companies were caught in the same squeeze. As operations drained cash and expected large sales revenues failed to materialize, the large companies turned to short-term borrowing to shore themselves up. But the high interest rates on these loans were prohibitive—and with the stock market depressed, companies were unable to float equity offerings with which to pay down their debt. As a result, they found earnings lower than they had been in decades, and the operating focus, in many cases, switched from long-range to short-range. Projects that did not pay for themselves were dropped; product lines that provided only marginal returns were sold to competitors or investors; research and development and training programs for all levels of personnel were cut back; and new product lines were curtailed. Some firms have dealt with the need to cut back their personnel in innovative and humane ways, and, unfortunately, some have not. The accompanying Application Example, More than Just a Gold Watch, gives examples of companies that are dealing with early retirements in ways that can greatly benefit the individuals affected.

Even the turnaround of the mid-1980s did not solve all of these problems. While the stock market boomed, the general economy remained sluggish. Inflation slowed to a crawl, but government economic data revealed that many families are not better off today than they were fifteen years ago. In fact, for many, their real purchasing power has declined.

Growth was restricted to selected sectors of the economy, and many industries found themselves facing a decline in real growth. For example, steel, agriculture, and the airlines were hard hit across the board. Retailing, computer

**Application
Example**

More Than Just a Gold Watch*

When a manager retired years ago, the individual could look forward to a gold watch and a small retirement pension. Today, all of this has changed. The gold watch is gone, but the retirement package more than makes up the difference. This is particularly true among managers who are being enticed into taking early retirement.

AT&T, Exxon, Kodak, and IBM, to name but four, have all been trying to pare their management staffs by getting some of their personnel to retire early. Many people resist. After all, early retirement typically means a much smaller monthly stipend. Aware of this, companies are now putting together very attractive packages. Exxon, for example, offers its people a "3 & 3 & ½ plan." Under this arrangement, managers can add three years to their age and to their length of service and retire at half pay. So a manager retiring at fifty-five after thirty years of service and making $60,000 can now get out as a fifty-eight-year-old manager with thirty-three years of service at $30,000 annually (minus a small deduction for retiring before sixty). IBM offers a similar plan but gives its people an extra five years on both their age and their length of service.

In addition, there are a number of other benefits being offered, including cash separation payments, standard retirement benefits, a continuation of health insurance, career counseling, and assistance in job searches. Cash separation payments often equal four weeks for every year of service. So the manager making $60,000 after thirty-three years with the firm would receive $79,200 ($60,000 × 1.32). In some cases, companies are supplementing the package with a "Social Security bridge." Under this arrangement, the firm pays the manager a specific sum of money annually (such as $3,000) until the individual can start collecting Social Security benefits.

These retirement packages are so lucrative that some individuals have been able to retire before age sixty and never have to work again. In most cases, however, the managers are taking the money and moving to other firms that are hiring experienced executives. If the manager can get ten years of service at this new company, the individual usually qualifies for an additional retirement program. So for some managers, early retirement is proving to be an opportunity for them to start a second career.

Source: Adapted from Bruce Nussbaum, "Bracing Yourself for the Golden Boot," *Business Week*, Nov. 3, 1986, pp. 152–153.

software, and autos had mixed results. Some of the large conglomerates were hurrying to purchase other firms (e.g., General Electric bought RCA, Philip Morris purchased General Foods, R. J. Reynolds bought Nabisco, and U.S. Steel acquired Texas Oil & Gas). At the same time, a number of other firms were selling divisions that had not worked out for them. Gulf & Western got rid of Wickes, Simmons, and Kaiser Roth, to name but three; and ITT was going through an even more radical paring down by selling so many of its holdings that overall revenues actually declined.

Then the stock market crashed. On Black Monday, October 19, 1987, the Dow Jones Industrial Average plunged 508 points. This was the biggest one-day drop ever and even the 1929 Crash that signaled the start of the Great Depression paled by comparison. The severity of the drop was attributed to computer programs that triggered sell orders when the stock prices began to go down. Nevertheless, the state of the economy in general, and especially the huge debt and trade deficit (imports exceeding exports), led to a lack of confidence in the American economy. Although a total meltdown of the stock market came close to happening[5] but didn't, the economic outlook facing today's organizations is very uncertain.

In short, for many firms, the uncertain economy has created a whole new ball game. Rather than ride out industry downturns or stagnation, corporations began switching their holdings by dropping losers or marginal lines and/or seeking to buy companies that held, or promised to hold, more potential. There were also many shifts in management personnel. For example, in 1986, sixty-five chief executives from the 500 largest companies switched jobs (or were pushed from their jobs).[6]

Internationalization

As Chapter 4 brought out, organizations today are operating in a shrinking world. This is as true in Hastings, Nebraska, as it is in Detroit, Michigan. The pace of internationalization has dramatically increased. In some cases, this internationalization has caused problems for the way American managers have conducted themselves. For example, guidelines for how American businesswomen are supposed to conduct themselves seems like a step backward in time (see the International Application Example: After-Hours Etiquette).

International Application Example

After-Hours Etiquette

In the United States, women have much greater freedom than they have in many other parts of the world. So when businesswomen are working overseas, it is important that they understand that things may be different. Some interesting, if distasetul, suggested guidelines are the following:

1. Do not eat or drink alone in a restaurant that the locals or business travelers use to pick up women. This usually includes most European-style restaurants and hotel dining rooms. As an alternative, use room service or invite female or male acquaintances to join you for dinner (on your expense account, of course).
2. Unless you have been given a gift from the home office and asked to pass it along to a male colleague, do not give any gifts except the most perfunctory. The only exception is a gift that is clearly earmarked for the home or for children.
3. If you are (or were) married, use a Mrs. title even if you do not do so back home.
4. If you are married and/or have children, make it a point to mention them to your male counterparts. Also, ask about their families, and, if the question of dinner arises, invite the families as well.
5. When you are introduced to the family, stop talking business at that point and focus on striking up a rapport with the others.
6. Most importantly, if you meet someone with whom you are there to do business, do not date the individual no matter how great the temptation. Wait until he comes to the United States.

American firms that used to dominate the *Fortune* list of largest multinational corporations (MNCs) now account for less than half of this number. The latest ranking by sales shows that only 42 percent of these firms are American-based. On the other hand, it should be remembered that American MNCs still represent the most formidable force in the international arena. For example, the ten largest account for over $40 billion in international sales, and the fifty largest account for over $70 billion.

In terms of internationalization affecting the management of change, probably the biggest impact comes from foreign-based corporations doing business in the United States. Not only have the Germans and British made strong inroads in the auto market, but of course the Japanese, and now the Koreans, and soon the Chinese, are making vigorous headway in cars, computers, and electronic goods. Moreover, and surprising perhaps, even the U.S. agricultural industry has felt foreign competition. Today, even though there is still a surplus in many agricultural products, America, overall, buys more farm produce from abroad than it sells.

Fortunately, the internationalization movement does not have to wreak havoc on American organizations. Many American MNCs have been quite successful in selling overseas. For all its problems, General Motors still manages to do almost $9 billion a year in the international market; Ford Motor garners around $6.5 billion annually; Boeing is just under $6 billion; GE does over $4 billion; and IBM reported overseas sales of almost $3.5 billion. Nonindustrials also do extremely well. Coca-Cola, McDonald's, Kellogg's, Warner-Lambert, and Avon are some visible examples. So are a number of smaller firms. For example, American Family Life Assurance of Columbus, Georgia, does more business in Japan than in the United States, and the cleaning firm Service Master has fifteen major hospital contracts in Japan.[7] As Chapter 4 pointed out, there are many challenges stemming from internationalization, but the recognition and then the strategic management of this and the other forces for change can and must be done if American organizations are to remain dominant leaders in the world.

Americans often rightly accuse the Japanese of copying our technology and productive processes, but it may be time to turn the tables and copy some of the ways in which the Japanese have become successful in international markets such as China. The Japanese and the Chinese have been bitter enemies throughout history, but Japanese goods and services constitute the lion's share of Chinese imports. The United States is way behind. A summary of the reasons for the Japanese success, and the lessons American firms should learn, follows:

1. A presence of many firms in many locations and the establishment of a strong infrastructure, even if it is initially unprofitable.
2. A willingness to learn the language (for example, Citicorp has three offices in China but only one Chinese-speaking American) and accept long assignments with close-to-the-people living arrangements.
3. Operating informally, creating personal bonds and trust, rather than insisting on reams of paperwork and the involvement of lawyers.[8]

These guidelines will not guarantee success for American organizations going international, but they suggest how we differ from the way the Japanese operate in China where they are, to date, gaining a much stronger foothold in the market of tomorrow.

OD: The Modern Approach to The Management of Change

The modern approach to the management of change and the development of human resources is called *organization development.* Although there is still not a universally agreed-upon definition, one recent applications view stated that "organization development programs" lead to improved organization performance through an improved decision-making climate. OD practitioners (internal or external consultants) may counsel decision makers on an individual basis; work to improve working relationships among the members of a work group or team (often including the top-management team); work to improve relationships among interacting and interdependent organizational groups; and gather attitudinal data throughout the organization and feed this data back to selected individuals and groups, who use this information as a basis for planning and making needed improvements.[9]

More traditionally, French and Bell offered this comprehensive definition:

> Organization development is a long-range effort to improve an organization's problem-solving and renewal processes, particularly through a more effective and collaborative management of organization culture—with special emphasis on the culture of formal work teams—with the assistance of a change agent, or catalyst, and the use of the theory and technology of applied behavior science, including action research.[10]

Burke has a simple definition:

> Organization development is a planned process of change in an organization's culture through the utilization of behavioral science technology, research, and theory.[11]

Using definitions like these as a point of departure and summarizing what the leaders in the OD movement emphasize, Filley, House, and Kerr suggest that several elements make up the modern OD approach to the management of change.[12] The following are the major characteristics of OD:

1. *Planned change.* This was one of the first emphases in OD, the need for systematic, planned change. This "planned" emphasis separates OD efforts from other kinds of more haphazard changes that frequently occur in modern organizations.
2. *Comprehensive change.* Most OD experts emphasize that OD efforts generally involve a "total system." The entire organization or an identifiable unit within it is the unit of analysis.
3. *Emphasis upon work groups.* Although some OD efforts are aimed at individual and organizational change, most are oriented toward groups. There is a sociological flavor to much of OD.

4. *Long-range change.* OD experts emphasize that the process takes months or, in some cases, years to implement. Although there is pressure for quick results, the OD process is not intended to be a stopgap measure.
5. *Participation of a change agent.* Most OD experts stress the need for an outside, third-party "change agent" or catalyst. "Do-it-yourself" programs are discouraged.
6. *Emphasis upon intervention and action research.* The OD approach results in an active intervention in the ongoing activities of the organization. Action research attacks practical problems but differs from applied research in that the researcher (change agent) is involved in the actual change process in OD.

The desired organizational outcomes of OD efforts include increased effectiveness, problem solving, and adaptability. For human resources development, OD attempts to provide opportunities to be "human" and to increase awareness, participation, and influence. An overriding goal is to integrate individual and organizational objectives.[13]

The Historical Development of OD

As with other behavioral approaches, it is difficult to pinpoint the precise beginning of OD. French and Bell, who have done the most work on the historical development of OD, feel that "organization development has emerged from applied behavioral science and social psychology and from subsequent efforts to apply laboratory training and survey-feedback insights into total systems."[14] Thus, the two major historical stems for OD are laboratory training and survey feedback. The work of the pioneering social psychologist Kurt Lewin was instrumental in both approaches. Today, almost every organization of any size is pursuing some form of organization development.

OD Techniques

Although the beginnings of OD can be traced to laboratory or training group techniques—sometimes called sensitivity training or "T" (for training) groups—the most popular techniques over the years have been grid training, survey feedback, team building, and transactional analysis.

Grid Training.
Grid training as used in OD is an outgrowth of the managerial grid approach to leadership discussed in Chapter 16. A 9,9 position on Blake and Mouton's leadership grid, shown in Chapter 16, indicating a maximum concern for both people and production, is an implied goal of grid training. A more comprehensive step-by-step approach is taken when grid training is used in OD.

Summarized, the six phases of grid training for OD are the following:

1. *Laboratory-seminar training.* The purpose of this first phase is to introduce the participants to the overall concepts and materials used in grid training. The seminars that are held are not like therapeutic sensitivity training. There

is more structure and more concentration on leadership styles than on developing self-insights and group insights.

2. *Team development.* This is an extension of the first phase. Members of the same department are brought together to chart how they are going to attain a 9,9 position on the grid. In this stage, what was learned in the orientation stage is applied to the actual organizational situation.

3. *Intergroup development.* Whereas the first two phases are aimed at managerial development, this phase marks the beginning of overall organization development. There is a shift from the micro level of individual and group development to a macro level of group-to-group organization development. Conflict situations between groups are identified and analyzed.

4. *Organizational goal setting.* In the manner of management by objectives, in this phase the participants contribute to, and agree upon, the important goals for the organization. A sense of commitment and self-control is instilled in the participants.

5. *Goal attainment.* In this phase the participants attempt to accomplish the goals which they set in the fourth phase. As in the first phase, the participants get together, but this time they discuss major organizational issues, and the stakes are real.

6. *Stabilization.* In this final phase, support is marshaled for changes suggested earlier, and an evaluation of the overall program is conducted.[15]

These six phases of grid training may take from three to five years to implement, but in some cases they may be compressed into a shorter period of time.

Most of the support for grid training has come from its founders, Robert R. Blake and Jane S. Mouton. They and their colleagues have maintained over the years that "managerial and team effectiveness *can* be taught by managers with outside assistance. Furthermore, it appears that this type of educational strategy can help to make significant contributions to organizational effectiveness."[16]

In a later work, *The New Managerial Grid,* Blake and Mouton continue to suggest that research indicates that grid training is very effective.[17] A review of the research on OD gives some support to their claims. Although it was found to have the least rigorous research (along with survey feedback), the four studies reviewed found grid training to have a 43 percent substantial positive impact on process variables, and three studies found a 68 percent positive impact on outcome variables.[18] The impact of grid training on outcome variables was higher than that of any of the other OD techniques, but, again, this finding was based on only three studies. Conclusions are still tentative at this point because more and better research is needed in the future before any firm conclusions can be drawn; nevertheless, the use of grid training does seem to be justified. One thing is certain: It has been very widely used.

Survey Feedback. Besides grid training, another popular OD technique has been survey research and feedback of the data. Once again Kurt Lewin had the original influence, but over the years the survey-feedback approach has been most closely associated with the University of Michigan's Institute for Social Research (ISR).

As the terminology indicates, this approach to OD surveys the unit of analysis (for example, a work group, a department, or a whole organization) by means of questionnaires and feeds back the data to those who generated them. The data are used in the action research sense of diagnosing problems and developing specific action plans to solve the problems. Either the questionnaire can be tailor-made for each situation, or, as has been more common in recent years, a standardized version is researched and developed by the ISR. A number of revisions have been made through the years, but the typical ISR questionnaire provides data in the areas of leadership, organizational climate, and employee satisfaction.

Normally an external consultant will accumulate, present, and interpret the data for the group. The consultant will then, usually in a process-consultation or team-building approach (covered in the next section), help the group diagnose and solve its problems.

In terms of its effectiveness, one review of three rigorous studies on survey feedback indicated it had a 53 percent substantial positive change on outcome variables,[19] and a later review found that three studies yielded an overall 50 percent positive change in productivity. However, the latter analysis found no impact on work-force measures such as turnover, absenteeism, and grievances, and compared with structured laboratory training and team building, survey feedback had the least impact.[20] Used in combination with team building, it had a more positive impact.

Team Building.   Both grid training and survey feedback are fairly specialized and associated with a leading advocate (Blake and Mouton in the case of the grid and the Michigan group in the case of survey feedback). Of wider appeal and application is team building. Whereas oldtime sensitivity training "scared off" many managers because of the controversy surrounding it and the potentially harmful psychological implications inherent in it, team building is seen as accomplishing some of the same goals as sensitivity training but tends to be more task-oriented. Table 20.1 shows that team-building activities can be applied to either "family" groups or special groups (for example, task forces, committees, or interdepartmental groups) within the organization.

In general it can be said that team building is an organization development effort aimed at improving overall performance. Perhaps with the exception of widely marketed, commercially based grid training, there is little question that team building has become the most popular OD technique in recent years. French and Bell go as far as to say that "probably the most important single group of interventions in OD are the team-building activities the goals of which are the improvement and increased effectiveness of various teams within the organization."[21]

As an OD process, team building generally follows the classic change procedure originally formulated by Kurt Lewin:

1. *Unfreezing.* The first task is to make the team aware of the need for change. A climate of openness and trust is developed so that the group is ready for change.

TABLE 20.1 Various Approaches to Team Building

Family Groups (Members from the Same Organizational Unit)	Special Groups (Start-Up Teams, Task Forces, Committees, and Interdepartmental Groups)
1. Task accomplishment (for example, problem solving, decision making, role clarification, and goal setting)	1. Task accomplishment (special problems, role and goal clarification, resource utilization, etc.)
2. Building and maintaining effective interpersonal relationships (for example, boss-subordinate relationships and peer relationships)	2. Relationships (for example, interpersonal or interunit conflict and underutilization of each other as resources)
3. Understanding and managing group processes and culture	3. Processes (for example, communications, decision making, and task allocations)
4. Role analysis technique for role clarification and definition	4. Role analysis technique for role clarification and definition
5. Role negotiation techniques	5. Role negotiation

Source: Adapted from Wendell L. French and Cecil H. Bell, *Organization Development,* 2d ed., Prentice-Hall, Englewood Cliffs, N.J., 1978, p. 119.

2. *Moving.* Basically using a survey-feedback technique, the team makes a diagnosis of where it is and develops action plans to get to where it wants to go.
3. *Refreezing.* Once the plans have been carried out and an evaluation has been made, the team starts to stabilize into more effective performance.

The above, of course represents only a very general idea of what team building is all about and can also apply to the other OD techniques.

A more specific team-building program actually used in a large industrial plant is described as follows:

1. *Team skills workshop.* The production team in this plant first went through a two-day workshop that consisted mainly of a series of experience-based exercises. The purpose of this first phase was essentially to unfreeze the various teams and get them ready to accept change.
2. *Data collection.* In a questionnaire survey, data were collected on organizational climate, supervisory behavior, and job content from all first-line supervisors in the program.
3. *Data confrontation.* The consultants presented the teams with the data gathered in step 2. The teams, with the consultant present, openly discussed problem areas, established priorities, and made some preliminary recommendations for change.
4. *Action planning.* On the basis of what went on in step 3, the teams developed specific plans for the changes to be actually carried out on the job.
5. *Team building.* The first four phases were preliminary to the actual team building. In this phase, each team met as a whole to identify barriers to effectiveness, developed ways of eliminating the barriers, and agreed upon plans to accomplish the desired changes.
6. *Intergroup building.* In this final phase there were two-day meetings held between various teams that were interdependent in accomplishing goals. The

purpose of this phase was to establish collaboration on shared goals and problems and to generalize the OD effort to the total organization.[22]

This program took over a year to complete. The outside consultant in a team-building OD approach such as the above plays an important facilitative role but is not as central to the approach as in process consultation or third-party peacemaking.

The advantages of team building are all those which are attributed to old-fashioned teamwork. The process can create a team effort in an open, participatory climate. There can be improved communication and problem solving, and individual team members can experience psychological growth and improve their interpersonal skills. For example, one research study found that four trained teams reported significantly higher levels of group effectiveness, mutual influence, and personal involvement and participation than the eight control groups.[23] Evaluation of the six-step program described above also found that the program produced a positive impact on organizational performance (quality of output and profit but not quantity of output) and favorably affected the attitudes and perceptions of the members of the teams studied.[24]

As the above studies indicate, there is relatively more and better research on team building than on any of the other OD techniques. Porras and Berg found far more acceptable research studies (40 percent of the thirty-five studies which met their minimum criteria) on team-building studies that examined process variables, 45 percent had a substantial positive change, and of the three studies that analyzed the impact on outcome variables, 53 percent were deemed to have a substantial positive change.[25] The later Nicholas review looked at four team-building studies and found that there was a 50 percent overall positive impact on work-force, monetary, and productivity hard measures of performance.[26] It came out better than survey feedback, but was behind structured laboratory training. However, one of the latest studies conducted with hard-rock miners produced inconclusive results.[27] So, although there is considerable evidence that team building can be beneficial, it is still open to question *how* and, in some cases, *if* team building works.

Besides having demonstrated that it can have a positive impact on its own as an OD intervention strategy, team building has the strength of being able to be effectively used in combination with other OD techniques. For example, as mentioned earlier, Nicholas found that if it was used in combination with survey feedback, there was a much more positive effect on hard performance measures than if survey feedback was used by itself.[28] Also, there have recently been calls for combining team building with O.B. Mod. approaches. One suggestion along this line was to use a task hierarchy to reinforce the team as it progresses up a behavior skills hierarchy (for example, listening, communicating, monitoring, and feedback skills).[29] There also seem to be successful applications for a team-building approach internationally, but the intervention must be carried out in a culturally sensitive manner.[30] Team building seems to have a bright future.

Transactional Analysis. The background and a detailed discussion of the facets of transactional analysis (TA) were given in Chapter 14. Most OD experts do not feel that TA is a full-fledged intervention strategy; rather, they treat it as a useful tool to help people better understand themselves and their effect on others. The application of TA is not limited to OD efforts. Similar to sensitivity training, TA has diverse applications in counseling and is widely used to analyze group dynamics and interpersonal communication. It has been pointed out that as an OD tool, the purpose of TA is to "help the people involved better understand their own ego states and those of others, to understand the principles behind transactions and games, and to interact in more meaningful ways with one another."[31]

Despite the fact that TA is not a mainline OD technique like the others discussed so far, it is becoming increasingly popular with management practitioners. Many companies in a wide variety of industries have sponsored TA programs for their managerial personnel and people in certain key positions, such as customer service representatives. Questionnaire instruments that identify people's dominant ego states (parent, child, or adult) and exercises that help people understand and analyze their transactions with others (complementary, crossed, or ulterior) have been developed.

When used as an OD approach, TA has attempted to develop more adult states in people and complementary transactions with others. TA is also used in certain phases of the interpersonal OD techniques such as team building. There is some recent evidence that its use as an OD technique is having increased acceptance. After a comprehensive analysis of TA as an OD technique, Bowen and Nath offered the following guidelines for successful application:

1. If TA is to be employed in OD, it will be more effective if introduced early in the diagnostic phase.
2. The planning, action, and stabilization phases should be designed to encourage continued application of the TA framework.
3. The application of TA in OD should be undertaken only within a broader framework of a systems model of OD.
4. Where TA is employed as an unfreezing mechanism, it is probably most effective to employ the general pattern of experimental activity followed by cognitive input and analysis of the activity, rather than beginning with the cognitive element.
5. TA will tend to be of greatest value in OD designs emphasizing interpersonal relationships and process consultation.
6. Employing a TA approach to change does not reduce the demands for interpersonal competence on the part of the consultant.[32]

Such guidelines are certainly helpful, but the actual effectiveness of TA approaches to OD is largely unknown.

To date, only a few studies have attempted to evaluate the impact that a TA intervention has had on the attitudes or behaviors of employees in organizations and these have had mixed results. For example, one study in the customer service department of a large utility found that those employees trained in TA reacted very favorably and learned the concepts, and found evidence of significant improvements in employees' perceptions of customer satisfaction at the beginning and end of transactions. However, even though customers' ratings of employee behavior were significantly more favorable during and after the TA intervention, as compared with before the intervention, and although selected areas of departmental performance improved, when compared with a control group who did not receive the TA intervention, there were no significant differences.[33]

Besides this very sparse research, about the only evidence of the value of TA as an OD technique is the testimony of TA consultants and the results of a few questionnaire studies that asked participants how well they liked the TA program and whether they thought it did them any good back on the job. All the TA consultants, of course, gave glowing testimony as to the effectiveness of TA.[34] The same was true of the questionnaire studies. The participants were generally very positive about the TA program and felt that it had done them some good back on the job.[35] However, as Huse notes, "Since the results of most of these programs are given in anecdotal or questionnaire-response form, the true value of TA and its long-term influence on employees, groups, or the larger social system have yet to be determined."[36] In other words—and the reader is probably getting tired of seeing this at the end of each section, but it is nevertheless true—more research is needed on the relatively new and exciting applications of TA to the field of organization development.

OD in Perspective

OD has matured. On the one hand, it is now clear that OD is not going to be a panacea for all management's problems. On the other hand, it is also clear that OD can definitely help management meet the challenges that change and complexity present to modern organizations and their effectiveness. The review articles by Porras and Berg and by Nicholas, which were cited in the discussion of the various OD techniques, shed some important new light on the impact of OD. Although overall they found relatively little systematic research evidence on OD, their conclusions do counter some of the traditional assumptions that OD makes people happier or more satisfied, and, also contrary to common belief, they found that OD had at least as great an impact on outcome variables (for example, openness, self-awareness, goal emphasis, decision making, motivation, and influence).

For those interested in the "bottom-line" impacts of intervention strategies, OD may possess a heretofore overlooked advantage. However, before becoming too optimistic about the value of OD and overturning all the negative assumptions about it, it is well to remember, as Porras and Berg point out, that "the data support the belief that OD does not have an important impact on overall organizational processes but instead impacts primarily on the individual."[37] Nicholas concludes that "the single most apparent finding of this research is that no one change technique or class of techniques works well in all situations."[38]

Another caution is the rigor of the research that has been employed in OD studies. Although there is a clear trend toward more rigorous methods and designs,[39] there are still problems. For example, one analysis of OD research found an inverse relationship between the degree of methodological rigor and the reported outcome success of OD,[40] but a later study did not verify this.[41]

Another recent observation is the role that self-fulfilling expectations may have on OD interventions. Although pointing out that it should not be thought of as detrimental, Dov Eden hypothesizes that an OD intervention's effectiveness is in direct proportion to the expectations for improved performance it arouses.[42]

Thus, the value of OD as a group-wide and/or organization-wide approach to the management of change is not yet totally supported by the research to date. This conclusion is also consistent with the conclusions of others who have observed OD and argued that it rarely diffuses throughout the entire organization and that it is too limited.[43] There is also the problem that OD has been faddish. The accompanying Application Example, What's In and What's Out, points to this problem: the humorous definitions indicate that some people do not take some of the techniques too seriously.

**Application
Example**

What's In and What's Out*

According to a recent cover story in *Business Week*, a number of fads have been proposed over the years to help manage change and develop organizations. Here is a partial list of their humerous views of what is currently "in" and "out" and what each really means:

What's Out	What's In
• CENTRALIZATION (Father knows best.)	• CORPORATE CULTURE (Get everybody singing the same song and hope they're in key.)
• DECENTRALIZATION (Then again, maybe Father doesn't know best.)	• INTRAPRENEURSHIP (Discovering the entrepreneurs in your own ranks. That may be easier than keeping the bureaucracy at bay once you do.)
• FACTORY OF THE FUTURE (Robot heaven. Not yet available on earth.)	
• QUANTITATIVE MANAGEMENT (The numbers tell it all. Except what to do next.)	• PAY FOR PERFORMANCE (It used to be known as piecework.)
• T-GROUPS (Building team spirit. "I am he . . . as you are me and we are all together." Oh well, at least the Beatles made millions.)	• TOUCHY-FEELY MANAGERS (The boss is a really nice guy. He's also still the boss.)
	• WELLNESS (Part of the health craze. You'll know it's arrived when they stop serving lemon meringue pie in the company cafeteria.)

Source: Adapted from Stuart Jackson, "Management Lingo: How to Read between the Lines," *Business Week*, Jan. 20, 1986, p. 58.

A recent comprehensive survey of 1618 American Management Association member companies found that organizations of all sizes in both the public and private sector are actually using alternatives to traditional ways of getting work done.[44] These new alternatives are not just fads. Table 20.2 shows the most and least popular work alternatives. A simple list of things that experience says to avoid in major system changes can also be helpful:

1. Do not promise that all employees undergoing a change effort will be winners.
2. Do not blame those who lose out for their negative attitudes.

TABLE 20.2 Work Alternatives from a Large Sample of Diverse Organizations:

The Most Popular	Percentage Using
Cross training	44.6%
Quality circles	36.3
Flextime	34.8
Permanent part-time jobs	34.1
Project teams	27.6

The Least Popular	Percentage Using
Internal venture funds	6.9%
Parallel structures	8.5
Pay-for-capability/skills	10.0
Work-at-home arrangements	10.2
Job sharing	10.9

Source: Adapted from Rosabeth Moss Kanter, David V. Summers, and Barry Stein, "The Future of Work," *Management Review*, July 1986, p. 33. Reprinted by permission of the publisher © 1986 American Management Association, New York. All rights reserved.

3. Do not focus only on the new and forget the old.
4. Avoid symbolic or pseudoparticipation in the change effort.
5. Avoid destroying the old culture without building a new one.
6. Do not launch human resource management programs in the context of a major change without the necessary time and resources to support them.[45]

These practical guidelines are not meant to dampen the excitement and enthusiasm for change efforts but to put realistic expectations into the process.

Future Trends

The introductory discussion of changes affecting organizations will carry over into the future. More specifically, Naisbitt (author of the best selling *Megatrends*) and Aburdene have identified ten considerations for the future of organizational behavior and human resources management.

1. The best and brightest will be drawn to organizations that foster personal growth.
2. The new role of managers is that of coach, teacher, and mentor.
3. The best and brightest want ownership (both psychic and actual) in their organization.
4. Organizations will increasingly turn to outside contractors for their people, shifting from hired labor to contract labor.
5. An authoritarian management style will give way to a networking, people-oriented style.
6. Intrapreneurship is creating new products and new markets and revitalizing organizations inside out.
7. Quality will be the dominant thrust of organizations.
8. Intuition and creativity are challenging the quantitative ("it's all in the numbers") business-school approach.

9. Large organizations are learning from and copying the positive and productive qualities of small organizations.
10. The coming of the information economy has fostered a massive shift from infrastructure to quality of life.[46]

These identified trends are all compatible and relevant to the perspective and specialized discussions of this book. The key to Naisbitt and Aburdene's trends is that they were derived and supported by real-world organizations. Here are some actual examples of companies whose actions reflect each of the trends suggested by Naisbitt and Aburdene:

- Successful companies such as Hewlett-Packard, 3M, and W. L. Gore have a commitment to and actual programs for personal growth (trend #1).
- Apple Computer is only interested in the new type of manager. As one Apple spokesperson noted, "we are looking for people who are coaches and team builders and expanders, not controllers of people" (trend #2).
- 3M awards 11 percent of company stock below the officer level, and Cummins Engine's 14,000 employees receive a payment based on productivity (trend #3).
- Vicks and Squibb plants in Greensboro, North Carolina, lease about 20 percent of their assembly line workers from Norrell Temporary Services (trend #4).
- Big advertising agencies such as BBD&O and J. Walter Thompson operate after-hours membership clubs available to everyone from the CEO to the mail clerk (trend #5).
- IBM permits technical managers to allot 15 percent of their budget to pet interests or what are called "off-the-record" projects, and Aluminum Company of America and AT&T fund research on how to foster intrapreneurship (trend #6).
- At Campbell Soup they teach their people to focus on quality first, cost second (trend #7).
- The former chairman of Norton Simon Company credits his intuition, or what he calls his "judgment," in helping make his most difficult business decisions (trend #8).
- Huge IBM watched smaller Digital Equipment take the market lead in minicomputers and Apple in personal computers (trend #9).
- IBM opened research offices in Boca Raton, San Jose, Austin, and Boulder—cities with ambience and a quality of life attractive to creative people (trend #10).[47]

Well-known management consultant and writer Peter Drucker sees the coming of a new type of organization. He sees business organizations of the future resembling hospitals, universities, and even symphony orchestras more than yesterday's or today's manufacturing firms. The new organizations will have fewer than half the levels of management of their counterparts today, and no more than a third of the managers. He sees the new organizations as mainly containing specialists who direct and discipline their own performance through organized feedback from colleagues, customers, and headquarters. For this reason, he calls them information-based organizations.[48]

The Future of Organizational Behavior

The above emerging trends signal what lies ahead for the field of organizational behavior. First, it can be said that organizational behavior has truly arrived as an identifiable field of academic study, with definite implications for the effective management of human resources in modern, complex organizations. This recognition of organizational behavior as a legitimate academic and applied field should become even greater in the future. More attention will be given to the field as a result of the changes brought about by competitiveness, the economy, and internationalization discussed at the beginning of the chapter. Other, more specific concerns, such as those recently expressed by Robert Guest, will also focus more attention on the field:

1. We are not making full use of the skills and motivational potential of our human resources—from top to bottom.
2. Our organizational structures and communication system for managing our human resources are becoming obsolete.
3. We are not adequately managing change—changes in technology, changes in the external environment, and changes in the aspirations and value systems held by those who are expected to be the workers and managers in tomorrow's organizations.[49]

Second, there is now a clear distinction between organizational behavior and other areas such as general management and personnel administration. For example, organizational behavior is concerned with human behavior in organizations, while personnel management is recognized as a function of the organization and is concerned mainly with topics such as wage and salary administration and labor relations. The field of organizational behavior is recognized to be very broad, and as one theorist recently emphasized, "It is the people behaving in them that make organizations what they are."[50] In addition, the micro-macro split in the topics and conceptual framework for organizational behavior, which was at first thought to be getting wider (even in the last editions of this text), now seems to be lessening. Recognition is given to the important role of macro structural variables and the environment in the social learning theoretical framework. Macro variables play a major role, although still not as proportionately as great a role as micro variables, in this edition and in the field in general.

Third, the topical coverage of the field of organizational behavior will continue to move away from the traditional general topics in behavioral science (for example, perception, personality, and group dynamics) and toward topics more specifically identified with organizational behavior per se (organizational culture, job stress, job design, goal setting, job satisfaction, organizational behavior modification, behavioral self-management, job conflict, organizational power and politics, informal organization, managerial roles, interpersonal communication, managerial leadership, organization development, and managerial and work-group decision making and control). The exceptions here are the mainstays of experimental psychology—attitudes, motivation, and learning. These topics continue to be very important areas in organizational behavior. But whereas in the past, motivation played a much greater role in the study of organizational behavior, in the future, learning may have an equal, if not even a more important, role to play in terms of both theory and practice. This is true not only of operant learning theory but also of the more recent social learning theory.

Finally—and this, of course, most students and practitioners will be happy to hear—the trend toward making the organizational behavior approach more understandable and applications-oriented should continue. Although there is a definite trend away from simple answers to complex organizational behavior problems at all levels of analysis—individual, group, and organizational—in order to be considered useful it must be both understandable and applicable to the real world.[51] The successive editions of this text have given evidence of this trend. The organizational behavior approach is clearly aimed at the more effective management of human resources. With emphasis on areas such as coping with organizational culture, international management, job stress, job design, goal setting, organizational behavior modification, behavioral self-management, political strategies, leadership styles, organization development, and decision-making and control techniques, this aim at applications should become clearer and be more likely to hit the target of more effective human resources management in the years to come.

The future of the field of organizational behavior looks very bright and exciting. Although there will be some shifting emphasis in conceptual framework and topical coverage, the "bottom-line" is that the study and application of the areas covered in this book will help make better, more effective managers of the most important and underutilized resource in any organization: *people*. The effective management of people (both others and oneself) is really what organizational behavior is all about.

Summary

Organizations today are faced with tremendous forces for change, mainly stemming from competitiveness, the economy, and internationalization. A systematic, planned way of managing this change is through the process of organization development. The major techniques of OD are grid training, survey feedback, team building, and transactional analysis. However, like the other techniques and approaches, more rigorous research and contingency applications need to be forthcoming. Yet there is little question that OD has a fairly bright future in helping solve some of the tremendous challenges facing today's organizations. The last section of the book looked into the crystal ball of the future and identified some recent trends and challenges facing the field of organizational behavior and the management of human resources.

Questions for Discussion and Review

1. What are some of the major forces for change that are confronting today's organizations?
2. What are some of the major characteristics of organization development?

3. In your own words, briefly describe three approaches to OD. Discuss some of their major advantages and limitations.

4. Identify the major emerging trends that are relevant to organizational behavior. Do you agree that these are important? Can you propose any others that should be included? Which one or two do you think are more important and will have a bigger impact than the rest of the identified trends?

5. Do you agree with the view that the future of organizational behavior is bright and exciting? Do you have anything to add to this view?

References

1. This example is found in Michael Tushman and David Nadler, "Organizing for Innovation," *California Management Review,* Spring 1986, p. 74.
2. Dale D. Buss, "GM Slows Big Drive for Saturn to Produce Small Car in Five Years," *The Wall Street Journal,* Oct. 30, 1986, p. 1.
3. Sylvia Nasar, "America's Competitive Revival," *Fortune,* Jan. 4, 1988, p. 48.
4. "Labor Letter," *The Wall Street Journal,* Nov. 11, 1986, p. 1.
5. James B. Stewart and Daniel Hertzberg, "How the Stock Market Died and Rose Again a Day after the Crash," *The Wall Street Journal,* Nov. 20, 1987, p. 1.
6. "Labor Letter," *The Wall Street Journal,* Feb. 17, 1987, p. 1.
7. Tom Peters, *Thriving on Chaos: Handbook for a Management Revolution,* Knopf, New York, 1987, p. 125.
8. Ibid.
9. Gerald D. Klein, "Employee-Centered Productivity and QWL Programs: Findings from an Area Study," *National Productivity Review,* Autumn 1986, p. 350.
10. Wendell L. French and Cecil H. Bell, Jr., *Organization Development,* 2d ed., Prentice-Hall, Englewood Cliffs, N.J., 1978, p. 14.
11. W. Warner Burke, *Organization Development,* Little, Brown, Boston, 1982, p. 10.
12. Alan C. Filley, Robert J. House, and Steven Kerr, *Managerial Process and Organizational Behavior,* 2d ed., Scott, Foresman, Glenview, Ill., 1976, p. 488.
13. Ibid., pp. 489–490.
14. French and Bell, op. cit., p. 27.
15. Robert R. Blake, Jane S. Mouton, Louis B. Barnes, and Larry E. Greiner, "Breakthrough in Organization Development," *Harvard Business Review,* November–December 1964, pp. 137–138.
16. Ibid., p. 155.
17. Robert R. Blake and Jane S. Mouton, *The New Managerial Grid,* Gulf, Houston, 1978.
18. Jerry I. Porras and P. O. Berg, "The Impact of Organization Development," *Academy of Management Review,* April 1978, pp. 259–260.
19. Porras and Berg, op. cit.
20. John M. Nicholas, "The Comparative Impact of Organization Development Intervention on Hard Criteria Measures," *Academy of Management Review,* October 1982, p. 536.
21. French and Bell, op. cit., p. 119.
22. Warren R. Nielsen and John R. Kimberly, "The Impact of Organizational Development on the Quality of Organizational Output," *Academy of Management Proceedings,* 1973, pp. 528–529.
23. Frank Friedlander, "The Impact of Organizational Training Laboratories upon Effectiveness and Intervention of Ongoing Work Groups," *Personnel Psychology,* Autumn 1967, pp. 289–308.

24. John R. Kimberly and Warren R. Nielsen, "Organizational Development and Change in Organizational Performance," *Administrative Science Quarterly*, June 1975, pp. 191–206.

25. Porras and Berg, op. cit.

26. Nicholas, op. cit.

27. Paul F. Buller and Cecil H. Bell, Jr., "Effects of Team Building and Goal Setting on Productivity: A Field Experiment," *Academy of Management Journal*, June 1986, pp. 305–328.

28. Nicholas, op. cit.

29. Ray V. Rassmussen, "Team Training: A Behavior Modification Approach," *Group and Organization Studies*, March 1982, pp. 51–66.

30. Richard B. Polley, "Intervention and Cultural Context: Mediation in the U.S. and Norway," in Frank Hoy (ed.), *Academy of Management Best Papers Proceedings*, 1987, pp. 236–240; and Alfred M. Jaeger, "Organization Development and National Culture: Where's the Fit?" *Academy of Management Review*, January 1986, pp. 178–190.

31. Edgar Huse, *Organization Development and Change*, West, St. Paul, Minn., 1975, p. 290.

32. Donald D. Bowen and Raghu Nath, "Transactional Analysis in OD: Applications within the NTL Model," *Academy of Management Review*, January 1978, pp. 86–87.

33. Mark J. Martinko and Fred Luthans, "An Experimental Analysis of the Effectiveness of a Transactional Analysis Program in Industry," *Transactional Analysis Journal*, July 1981, pp. 229–235. For a couple of other systematic evaluations of TA in a work setting, see D. D. Ely and J. T. Morse, "TA Reinforcement Theory," *Personnel*, March–April 1974, pp. 38–41; and N. Nykodym, "Transactional Analysis: A Strategy for the Improvement of Supervisory Behavior," *Proceedings of the Midwest Academy of Management*, 1977, pp. 346–357.

34. For example, see Dorothy Jongeward and contributors, *Everybody Wins: Transactional Analysis Applied to Organizations*, Addison-Wesley, Reading, Mass., 1973.

35. Ibid., in particular, pp. 99–101.

36. Huse, op. cit., p. 291.

37. Porras and Berg, op. cit., p. 264.

38. Nicholas, op. cit., p. 540.

39. John M. Nicholas and Marsha Katz, "Research Methods and Reporting Practices in Organization Development: A Review and Some Guidelines," *Academy of Management Review*, October 1985, pp. 737–749.

40. David Terpstra, "Relationship between Methodological Rigor and Reported Outcomes in Organizational Development Evaluation Research, *Journal of Applied Psychology*, October 1981, pp. 541–542.

41. Richard W. Woodman and Sandy J. Wayne, "An Investigation of Positive-Findings Bias in Evaluation of Organization Development Interventions," *Academy of Management Journal*, December 1985, pp. 889–913.

42. Dov Eden, "OD and Self-Fulfilling Prophecy: Boosting Productivity by Raising Expectations," *The Journal of Applied Behavioral Science*, vol. 22, no. 1, 1986, pp. 1–13.

43. Richard Walton, "The Diffusion of New Work Structures: Explaining Why Success Didn't Take," *Organizational Dynamics*, Winter 1975, pp. 3–22; and George Strauss, "Organizational Development: Credits and Debits," *Organizational Dynamics*, Winter 1973, pp. 2–19.

44. Rosabeth Moss Kanter, David V. Summers, and Barry Stein, "The Future of Work," *Management Review*, July 1986, p. 30.

45. Jeffrey K. Liker, David B. Roitman, and Ethel Roskies, "Changing Everything All at Once: Work Life and Technological Change," *Sloan Management Review*, Summer 1987, pp. 43–44.

46. John Naisbitt and Patricia Aburdene, *Reinventing the Corporation*, Warner Books, New York, 1985, pp. 45–46.
47. These examples are drawn from ibid., pp. 46–77.
48. Peter F. Drucker, "The Coming of the New Organization," *Harvard Business Review*, January–February 1988, p. 45.
49. Robert H. Guest, "Management Imperatives for the Year 2000," *California Management Review*, Summer 1986, p. 62.
50. Benjamin Schneider, "The People Make the Place," *Personnel Psychology*, vol. 40, 1987, p. 438.
51. James L. Gibson, John M. Ivancevich, and James H. Donnelly, Jr., *Organizations*, 6th ed., Business Publications, Plano, Tex., 1988, pp. 755–756.

**REAL CASE:
Going On
Indefinitely***

For years, organizations had mandatory retirement programs. When employees reached sixty-five years of age, they retired. Legislation then pushed this up to seventy years of age. However, recent action by Congress prevents most employers from forcing their personnel to retire at any age.

This dramatic change reduces an organization's ability to shape its work force. The law also makes it more difficult to fire older workers because this can be viewed as age discrimination—a sign that the firm is trying to get rid of older employees to make room for younger (and lower paid) employees. Prior to the latest federal legislation, there were thirteen states, including California, Florida, New Jersey, and New York, that had already outlawed mandatory retirement. Beginning in 1987, all U.S. firms were required to do the same.

What effect will this change have on organizations? For one thing, it will mean that the average age of employees is likely to increase since it will be more beneficial for older workers to stay on the job rather than take retirement. This is true for two reasons. First, annual pay is greater than retirement pay, so the longer the person postpones retirement, the more annual income the individual will earn. Second, retired people typically receive a percentage of their annual pay, and the longer a person works the greater this percentage. So, at least from a monetary standpoint, it pays to delay retirement.

Many companies disagree with the new legislation. They argue that older workers often have more sick days and that the expenses associated with their medical benefits push up the rates on group insurance policies. They also contend that older workers tend to be slower and make more mistakes. A third argument is that if they had mandatory retirement, companies could really help older workers in the long run. The logic is that under mandatory retirement, those older workers whose productivity or interest in the job has waned could still be kept on the payroll until 65. Without mandatory retirement the firm has no choice but to terminate the

Source: Some of the information in this case can be found in Vicky Cahan, "Mandatory Retirement Gets Put Out to Pasture," *Business Week*, Nov. 3, 1986, pp. 31–32.

ineffective older workers and, in the process, let everyone else know that they are unfit for the job. A fourth argument is that mandatory retirement ensures that there will be job openings up the line and provides career opportunities for younger workers. If this door of opportunity is closed, it will become difficult for companies to keep younger managers. Nevertheless, like it or not, companies are going to have to learn to live with voluntary retirement.

1. What are some of the potential benefits of keeping older people on the job?
2. Can organizational development techniques be used to manage this change in the composition of the work force of most organizatons?
3. What types of organizational behavior challenges are voluntary retirements likely to create for businesses?
4. Is the law against mandatory retirement a good or bad idea? Explain.

CASE: The High-Priced OD Consultant

The middle managers of a large firm were told by the corporate personnel office that a group of consultants would be calling on them later in the week. The purpose of the consultants' visit would be to analyze intergroup relations throughout the firm. The consultants had been very effective in using an OD intervention called *team building*. Their particular approach used six steps. When their approach was explained to the managers, a great deal of tension was relieved. They had initially thought that team building was a lot of hocus-pocus, like sensitivity training, where people attack each other and let out their aggressions by heaping abuse on those they dislike. By the same token, these managers generally felt that perhaps the consultants were not needed. One of them put it this way: "Now that we understand what is involved in team building, we can go ahead and conduct the sessions ourselves. All we have to do is to choose a manager who is liked by everyone and put him in the role of the change agent/consultant. After all, you really don't need a high-priced consultant to do this team-building stuff. You just have to have a good feel for human nature." The other managers generally agreed. However, the corporate personnel director turned their suggestion down. He hired the OD consultants to do the team building.

1. What is a team-building approach to organization development? Do you think the managers had an accurate view of the technique?
2. Do you think the managers had an accurate view of the role of the external consultant? Do you agree or disagree with the corporate personnel director's decision to turn down their suggestions? Why?

Integrative Real Case for Part 5

Global Competition: The United States Takes On the World*

Should an economic power as large as the U.S. get excited about the sale of a few thousand autos or tons of steel to a foreign country? Yes, indeed. For America in the 1980s, a modest export can represent a major industrial breakthrough. Cases in point: Chrysler Chairman Lee Iacocca announced in September that for the first time in nearly ten years, the automaker would begin selling U.S.-made autos in six West European countries—and at prices lower than those of competitive models. Earlier this year the largest U.S. steelmaker, USX, sold 20,000 tons of hotrolled bands to an Osaka tube company at a price some 12% below what Japanese producers were offering.

Some successes might have been unthinkable only a few years ago, when the world tended to view many American products as singularly unattractive in quality and price. In retrospect it was no wonder, since U.S. industries were saddled with an overvalued dollar, vast payrolls, clanky factories and an overstuffed management. Yet in a relatively short span, the attitude and substance of much of American industry have changed. Competitiveness has become a top economic priority, and an overworked buzzword, from Main Street to Capitol Hill. American companies have slimmed down and smartened up, while at the same time the 35% fall in the value of the dollar during the past two years has made U.S. products more affordable overseas.

In the nick of time too, because a bruising global battle has really just begun. As more countries become industrial powerhouses and their companies seek larger marketplaces, the U.S. will meet more and stronger competitors. Japan, the most potent of them all, is pushing into such American strongholds as biotechnology and supercomputers. Western Europe is coming up fast in aeronautics and office equipment. The newly industrialized countries are staking out their turf as low-cost producers of everything from steel to TV sets. And the U.S. may face a fresh competitive breeze from Canada as a result of the free-trade agreement the two countries reached on Oct. 4.

U.S. export performance in the 1980s has been discouraging. Its share of world exports slipped from 12% in 1980 to 11% last year, while most other industrial countries made gains. The share held by the least developed countries fell sharply, generally because of plunging world prices of commodities ranging from oil to rubber to tin.

America's leadership in some industries is probably gone for good. The U.S. may never be able to make a significant comeback in mass-manufactured commodities, among them textiles, shoes, consumer electronics and machine tools. But the more complex the product, the more likely America can hold its edge. The U.S. is still strong in such products as semiconductors (world market share: 40%), personal computers (68%) and jet engines (90%). Moreover, the U.S. remains the leading force in health care, entertainment and financial services.

As a barometer of America's competitive position, the U.S. trade deficit has become the era's most closely watched economic statistic. And that gap, which

*Source: Stephen Koepp, "Taking On the World," Time, Oct. 19, 1987, pp. 46–47. Copyright 1987, Time, Inc. All rights reserved. Reprinted by permission from TIME.

reached $156 billion last year, is starting to show subtle signs of improvement. The weaker dollar has fostered an export surge, starting with such price-sensitive goods as paper, lumber and chemicals. During the first half of the year, U.S. exports of manufactured products rose 17% over the same period in 1986. But on the other half of the trade equation, the flood of imports to the U.S. remains strong. Though the volume of goods coming in has declined, the reduced buying power of the dollar has increased their total cost.

Besides help from a cheaper dollar, corporate America is enjoying lower costs, thanks to its drive to restructure and streamline. "For the first time in 30 years," declares USX Chairman David Roderick, "we have lower costs of producing steel for our customers in the U.S. than the Japanese industry has in providing steel to their customers in Japan." At Xerox, management chopped manufacturing costs 20% during the period from 1982 through 1986, even though overall inflation totaled 16.6% during those five years.

Of course, competitiveness comes at a price for U.S. workers. Some 2 million manufacturing jobs have been slashed during the 1980s out of a total industrial work force of 20.3 million. Fortunately, a robust economy helped ease this transition by creating 13.4 million new U.S. jobs in that period. One company alone, Exxon, has cut 48,000 workers, or nearly one-third of its employees. Such vast layoffs have enabled management to negotiate more flexible work rules and smaller raises. For many Americans, the downward pull of low foreign wages will result in a stagnating or even declining standard of living.

Companies are boosting efficiency by scrapping their oldest plants and equipment. In one sweeping program, General Electric shut down 30 aged plants and opened 20 new ones between 1981 and 1986. As a result, a prime yardstick of U.S. competitiveness, manufacturing productivity (output per worker hour), increased by 3.5% last year. That figure, the best since the 1960s, is better than the improvement in Japan (2.8%) and West Germany (1.9%). But some economists fear that the benefits of America's corporate streamlining are a one-time deal. "To what degree is this improved productivity record sustainable? If it is due to closures of old plants, it can only go on for so long," says Robert Lawrence, a senior fellow at the Brookings Institution.

As old companies are shaping up, many newer firms have flourished that feature both minimum manpower and ultramodern processes. One such firm is Nucor, a steel company (1986 sales $755 million) based in Charlotte, N.C., that employs a headquarters staff of just 17. Called a minimill because it makes steel products from molten scrap metal rather than smelting the raw material from iron ore, Nucor manages to undercut the prices of both foreign and domestic steel companies. Result: Nucor's profits have quadrupled during the past decade, reaching $46.4 million last year.

Just as important as efficiency for American industry is quality. The most obvious improvement has been in Detroit, where automakers were shamed in the 1970s by their products' poor performance. Today in the Hewlett Packard parking lot in California's Silicon Valley, where not long ago a U.S.-made car was a rare find, the sun shimmers off the sleek bodies of hundreds of Ford Taurus sedans. The electronics company was so impressed with the style and solidness of the autos that it bought a fleet of 8,000 for staffers to drive.

As countries with extremely low wage rates and local costs take over the production of simple commodities, U.S. manufacturers are increasingly turning to market niches in which products are more complex and specialized. This is especially true in the semiconductor industry, where Japanese companies have taken over the market for mass-produced memory chips. Thus Silicon Valley chipmakers like Cypress Semiconductor (1986 sales: $51 million) thrive on diversity. Cypress makes 80 different types of chips in a factory that can accommodate several tooling changes every day. Says T. J. Rodgers, the company president: "You can be very competitive with the Japanese if you understand what they're good at and don't bash into them head on."

Despite many inspiring advances, however, corporate America still suffers from handicaps that will impair its ability, to keep up with the rapid evolution of products. An oft cited complaint is the lengthy lead times between the moment an idea is conceived and the time it finally rolls off an assembly line. In U.S. auto plants, that process takes as long as five years, twice as long as in Japan.

Another structural flaw that tends to undermine competitiveness is the U.S. Government's heavy borrowing. Though Congress has finally put the federal deficit on a downward path, from a record $221 billion in fiscal 1986 to an estimated $157 billion this year, the shortfall is still large enough to keep U.S. interest rates high in comparison with those of other industrial countries. The steep cost of loans, in turn, tends to discourage corporations from borrowing to make long-term improvements in plants and equipment.

Lately, business leaders have been warning about an even more deep-seated problem: a lack of basic skills among workers. While America's colleges and universities are second to none, its high schools are failing to give students the verbal and math basics they need for increasingly technical jobs. When New York Telephone recently administered a test of fundamental skills to 22,880 job applicants, 84% failed. Better job-training programs are key parts of major competitiveness-boosting trade bills now being considered in Congress.

Business leaders are bullish on their competitive ability. According to a poll conducted this year for the Coopers & Lybrand accounting firms, 88% of the 300 top manufacturing executives surveyed said they thought the U.S. could regain its edge in the auto industry, while 71% felt that way about the steel business. But what alarmed the accounting firm's top manufacturing expert, Henry Johansson, was that the majority of the U.S. executives (55%) still see their main competition as domestic rather than foreign. Too many business leaders fail to recognize the global marketplace. For those Americans, said one electronics executive, "it's wake-up time."

Questions

1. How have U.S. companies revamped their processes and structures, as discussed in this part of the text, to meet global competition?
2. Do you agree with the large majority of business executives who believe the United States can regain its competitive edge in many basic industries? What specific decision-making, control, and structural changes will be needed?

Experiential Exercises for Part 5

EXERCISE: Organizations

Goals:
1. To identify some of the important organizations in your life
2. To determine relevant, specific characteristics of organizations
3. To describe some of the important functions of management in organizations

Implementation: Read the "Overview" and "Procedure" sections. Complete the "Profile of Organizations" form, which follows those sections.

Overview: Undoubtedly, you have had recent experiences with numerous organizations. Ten to fifteen minutes of reflective thinking should result in a fairly large list of organizations. Don't be misled by thinking that only large organizations, such as your college or General Motors, are relevant for consideration. How about the clinic, with the doctors, nurses, and secretary/bookkeeper? Or the corner garage or service station? The local tavern, McDonald's, and the neighborhood theater are all organizations. You should have no difficulty listing several organizations with which you have had recent contact.

The second part of the exercise, however, is tougher. Describe several of the key characteristics of the organizations that you have listed. One of the major issues in studying and describing organizations is deciding *what* characteristics or factors are important. Some of the more common characteristics considered in the analysis of organizations are:

1. Size (small to very large)
2. Degree of formality (informal to highly structured)
3. Degree of complexity (simple to complex)
4. Nature of goals (what the organization is trying to accomplish)
5. Major activities (what tasks are performed)
6. Types of people involved (age, skills, educational background, etc.)
7. Location of activities (number of units and their geographic location)

You should be able to develop a list of characteristics that you think are relevant for each of your organizations.

Now to the third, final, and most difficult task. Think about what is involved in the management of these organizations. For example, what kinds of functions do their managers perform? How does one learn the skills necessary to be an effective manager? Would you want to be a manager in any of these organizations?

In effect, in this exercise you are being asked to think specifically about organizations you have been associated with recently, develop your own conceptual model for looking at their characteristics, and think more specifically about the managerial functions in each of these organizations. You probably already know a great deal more about organizations and their management than you think. This exercise should be useful in getting your thoughts together.

Procedure: *Step 1.* Prior to class, list up to ten organizations (for example, work, living group, club) in which you have been involved or with which you have had recent contact.

Step 2. Enter five organizations from your list on the following form.

1. List the organization.
2. Briefly outline the characteristics that you consider most significant.
3. Describe the managerial functions in each of these organizations.

Step 3. During the class period, meet in groups of five or six to discuss your list of organizations, the characteristics you consider important, and your descriptions of their management. Look for significant similarities and differences across organizations.

Step 4. Basing your selections on this group discussion, develop a list entitled "What we would like to know about organizations and their management." Be prepared to write this list on the blackboard or on newsprint and to share your list with other groups in the class.

Profile of Organizations

Organization	Key characteristics	Managerial functions
1. _____	_____	_____
2. _____	_____	_____
3. _____	_____	_____
4. _____	_____	_____
5. _____	_____	_____

EXERCISE: Paper Plane Corporation

Goals:
1. To work on an actual organizational task
2. To experience the managerial functions of organizing, decision making, and control

Implementation: Unlimited groups of six participants each are used in this exercise. These groups may be directed simultaneously in the same room. Approximately a full class period is needed to complete the exercise. Each person should have assembly instructions and a summary sheet, which are shown on the following pages, and ample stacks of paper (8½ by 11 inches). The physical setting should be a room large enough so that the individual groups of six can work without interference from the other groups. A working space should be provided for each group.

1. The participants are doing an exercise in production methodology.
2. Each group must work independently of the other groups.
3. Each group will choose a manager and an inspector, and the remaining participants will be employees.

INSTRUCTIONS FOR AIRCRAFT ASSEMBLY

STEP 1: Take a sheet of paper and fold it in half, then open it back up.

STEP 2: Fold upper corners to the middle.

STEP 3: Fold the corners to the middle again.

STEP 4: Fold in half.

STEP 5: Fold both wings down.

STEP 6: Fold tail fins up.

COMPLETED AIRCRAFT

4. The objective is to make paper airplanes in the most profitable manner possible.
5. The facilitator will give the signal to start. This is a ten-minute, timed event utilizing competition among the groups.
6. After the first round, everyone should report his or her production and profits to the entire group. Each person also should note the effect, if any, of the manager in terms of the performance of the group.
7. This same procedure is followed for as many rounds as there is time.

Paper Plane Corporation: Data Sheet

Your group is the complete work force for Paper Plane Corporation. Established in 1943, Paper Plane has led the market in paper plane production. Presently under new management, the company is contracting to make aircraft for the U.S. Air Force. You must establish an efficient production plant to produce these aircraft. You must make your contract with the Air Force under the following conditions:

1. The Air Force will pay $20,000 per airplane.
2. The aircraft must pass a strict inspection made by the facilitator.
3. A penalty of $25,000 per airplane will be subtracted for failure to meet the production requirements.
4. Labor and other overhead will be computed at $300,000.
5. Cost of materials will be $3000 per bid plane. If you bid for ten but make only eight, you must pay the cost of materials for those which you failed to make or which did not pass inspection.

Summary sheet

Round 1:

Bid: _____ Aircraft @ $20,000 per aircraft = _____
Results: _____ Aircraft @ $20,000 per aircraft = _____
Less: $300,000 overhead
_____ × $3000 cost of raw materials
_____ × $25,000 penalty
Profit: _____

Round 2:

Bid: _____ Aircraft @ $20,000 per aircraft = _____
Results: _____ Aircraft @ $20,000 per aircraft = _____
Less: $300,000 overhead
_____ × $3000 cost of raw materials
_____ × $25,000 penalty
Profit: _____

Round 3:

Bid: _____ Aircraft @ $20,000 per aircraft = _____
Results: _____ Aircraft @ $20,000 per aircraft = _____
Less: $300,000 overhead
_____ × $3000 cost of raw materials
_____ × $25,000 penalty
Profit: _____

EXERCISE: Organization Development at J. P. Hunt

Goals: To experience an OD technique—in this case the use of survey feedback—to diagnose strengths and weaknesses and develop an action plan.

Implementation: Set up groups of four to eight members for the one-hour exercise. The groups should be separated from each other and asked to converse only with members of their own group. Each person should read the following:

J. P. Hunt department stores is a large retail merchandising outlet located in Boston. The company sells an entire range of retail goods (e.g., appliances, fashions, furniture, and so on) and has a large downtown store plus six branch stores in various suburban areas.

Similar to most retail stores in the area, employee turnover is high (i.e., 40 to 45 percent annually). In the credit and accounts receivable department, located in the downtown store, turnover is particularly high at both the supervisor and

Survey Results for J. P. Hunt Department Store: Credit and Accounts Receivable Department

Variable	Survey Results*			Industry Norms*		
	Managers	Supervisors	Non-supervisors	Managers	Supervisors	Non-supervisors
Satisfaction and rewards						
Pay	3.30	1.73	2.48	3.31	2.97	2.89
Supervision	3.70	2.42	3.05	3.64	3.58	3.21
Promotion	3.40	2.28	2.76	3.38	3.25	3.23
Coworkers	3.92	3.90	3.72	3.95	3.76	3.43
Work	3.98	2.81	3.15	3.93	3.68	3.52
Performance-to-intrinsic rewards	4.07	3.15	3.20	4.15	3.85	3.81
Performance-to-extrinsic rewards	3.67	2.71	2.70	3.87	3.81	3.76
Supervisory behavior						
Initiating structure	3.42	3.97	3.90	3.40	3.51	3.48
Consideration	3.63	3.09	3.18	3.77	3.72	3.68
Positive rewards	3.99	2.93	3.02	4.24	3.95	3.91
Punitive rewards	3.01	3.61	3.50	2.81	2.91	3.08
Job characteristics						
Autonomy	4.13	4.22	3.80	4.20	4.00	3.87
Feedback	3.88	3.81	3.68	3.87	3.70	3.70
Variety	3.67	3.35	3.22	3.62	3.21	2.62
Challenge	4.13	4.03	3.03	4.10	3.64	3.58
Organizational practices						
Role ambiguity	2.70	2.91	3.34	2.60	2.40	2.20
Role conflict	2.87	3.69	2.94	2.83	3.12	3.02
Job pressure	3.14	4.04	3.23	2.66	2.68	2.72
Performance evaluation process	3.77	3.35	3.19	3.92	3.70	3.62
Worker cooperation	3.67	3.94	3.87	3.65	3.62	3.35
Work-flow planning	3.88	2.62	2.95	4.20	3.80	3.76

*The values are scored from 1, very low, to 5, very high.

subordinate levels, approaching 75 percent annually. The department employs approximately 150 people, 70 percent of whom are female.

Due to rising hiring and training costs brought on by the high turnover, top department management began a turnover analysis and reduction program. As a first step, a local management consulting firm was contracted to conduct a survey of department employees. Using primarily questionnaires, the consulting firm collected survey data from over 95 percent of the department's employees. The results are shown in the exhibit, by organizational level, along with industry norms developed by the consulting firm in comparative retail organizations.

Instructions for the exercise:

1. Individually, each group member should analyze the data in the exhibit and attempt to identify and diagnose departmental strengths and problem areas.
2. As a group, the members should repeat step 1 above. In addition, suggestions for resolving the problems and an action plan for feedback to the department should be developed.

Name Index

Subject Index